CHILD SEXUAL ABUSE AND THE CATHOLIC CHURCH

Child Sexual Abuse and the Catholic Church

GENDER, POWER, AND ORGANIZATIONAL CULTURE

Marie Keenan

OXFORD
UNIVERSITY PRESS

OXFORD
UNIVERSITY PRESS

Oxford University Press, Inc., publishes works that further
Oxford University's objective of excellence
in research, scholarship, and education.

Oxford   New York
Auckland   Cape Town   Dar es Salaam   Hong Kong   Karachi
Kuala Lumpur   Madrid   Melbourne   Mexico City   Nairobi
New Delhi   Shanghai   Taipei   Toronto

With offices in
Argentina   Austria   Brazil   Chile   Czech Republic   France   Greece
Guatemala   Hungary   Italy   Japan   Poland   Portugal   Singapore
South Korea   Switzerland   Thailand   Turkey   Ukraine   Vietnam

Copyright © 2012 by Oxford University Press, Inc.

Published by Oxford University Press, Inc.
198 Madison Avenue, New York, New York 10016
www.oup.com

Oxford is a registered trademark of Oxford University Press

Library of Congress Cataloging-in-Publication Data

Keenan, Marie.
Child sexual abuse and the Catholic Church : gender, power,
and organizational culture / Marie Keenan.
    p. cm.
Includes bibliographical references and index.
ISBN 978-0-19-989567-0 (hardcover)   1. Child sexual abuse by clergy.
2. Child sexual abuse by clergy—Case studies. 3. Catholic Church—Clergy—Sexual behavior.
4. Catholic Church—Clergy—Sexual behavior—Case studies. 5. Catholic Church—Discipline.
6. Child sexual abuse—Religious aspects—Catholic Church. I. Title.
BX1912.9.K44 2011
261.8'3272088282—dc23   2011026902

1 3 5 7 9 8 6 4 2

Printed in the United States of America
on acid-free paper

For your love and inspiration: Imelda McCarthy, Nollaig Byrne, and Julia Maloney, my mother.

Contents

Acknowledgments

The experience of writing this book was enhanced by the support I received from my many colleagues at home and abroad, and I would like to pay tribute to them for their generosity and encouragement Nollaig Byrne, Sean L'Estrange, Nick Gould, Karl Hanson, Martin Kafka, Bryan Fanning, Brendan Geary, Patricia Kennedy, John Allan Loftus, Bill Marshall, Imelda McCarthy, Ian O'Donnell, Friedemann Pfäfflin, Stephen Rossetti, Tony Robinson, Fainche Ryan, Richard Sipe, Gerardine Taylor, Karen Terry, and Tony Ward. In the clinical sphere, I wish to thank my colleagues in Ireland who joined hands with me in trying to make a difference for children and adults caught up in the web of sexual trauma and abuse.

I would like to thank Carmel Flaskas and the staff of the School of Social Sciences and International Studies, University of New South Wales, Sydney, Australia, for their kindness, hospitality, and for the many inspiring conversations during my stay there as a visiting fellow in 2010, when I worked on the final stages of this project. Thanks to Tony Fahey, the then Head of School at the School of Applied Social Science, University College Dublin for making this time abroad possible.

Working with my editor, Maura Roessner, Senior Editor at Oxford University Press (OUP), has been a joy from start to finish, and I wish to thank Maura for seeing the potential in the project and for believing in it from the beginning. I also wish to thank Nicholas Liu, Assistant Editor at OUP, for his ongoing support; Karen Kwak, the OUP production editor; and Smitha Raj, this book's project manager, for their expertise and especially for their patience. I also want to acknowledge the helpful comments from Henry Kaufman.

I cannot begin to stress my gratitude to the anonymous reviewers of the earlier drafts of this manuscript for their time, generosity, and expertise. The work of these anonymous reviewers has, without doubt, strengthened the text and shaped the book into what it has finally become. Of course what is finally presented is totally my own and for which I take complete responsibility.

The many men and women who were clients of my therapeutic practice for a period spanning more than 25 years with a variety of life issues and concerns have influenced my life, my research interests, and my therapeutic practice in the most profound of ways. I wish to thank my unnamed teachers for the important lessons they patiently allowed me learn, especially regarding the complexity of life, love, trauma, and abuse.

The many conversations I had with several bishops, priests, and religious brothers helped me understand the internal workings of the Catholic Church in ways that were invaluable, and I would like to acknowledge the importance of these men's contributions and for sharing their invaluable inside knowledge and wisdom with me.

Having tried and failed to secure funding from external academic and business sources for my earlier research with Catholic clergy who had sexually offended against minors (part of which is included in this book), I wish to acknowledge the contributions made by the Irish Bishops' Conference and two religious orders who responded to my request for funding with no conditions attached. This funding allowed me buy myself out of teaching for a semester to write and enabled me to employ modest research assistance.

This book could not have been written without the men who participated in my study, who agreed to share their life stories with me, and gave so much of themselves in their attempts to give something back to their victims, their Church, and their society. In gratitude to them, and in honor of all children and adults who experienced sexual abuse, and the families of both victims and perpetrators, I commit myself anew to working for a world in which all can be held in a spirit of safety, social justice, and reconciliation. I also wish to acknowledge the generosity of the four clerics and former clerics who filled in questionnaires and replied to my questions, as I attempted to deepen my understanding of the life of the Roman Catholic priest from as many perspectives as possible.

A big thank you to friends, colleagues in University College Dublin, and in particular to my brother Joe, my sisters Lillian, Paula, and Linda, and their partners Ann, Sean, and Paul, for providing the much-needed relief from the intensity of my writing and research. My mother's enduring love and my father's faith in me (both of whom are now deceased), kept me warm and hopeful, especially on the cold and dark days.

I want finally to thank my children, Kate and Colm Keenan, who have endured their mother's obsession with social justice through all of their conscious lives, as yet again they were asked to create a space for this special project on child sexual abuse. As young Irish citizens, who watched the situation of sexual abuse unfold in the Catholic Church in Ireland and across the world, they kept their mother firmly grounded with their questions, comments, and provocations. Writing on a complex topic of public importance with all that it entailed, I came to realize how much my children are my champions, and how much I am theirs. As the fullness of my thoughts are now unveiled after many years of research and writing, I hope I have honored childhood and displayed a compassion for all human beings with an understanding of a complex topic of which they can be proud.

Introduction

ONE CAN FIND many examples in literature, classical and modern, in which sexuality and cruelty are dealt with in a complex way, yet described on a human scale and with a human vision that makes social action and in particular sexuality intelligible. This is most unlike the discussions that seem to prevail in much of the public sphere nowadays, particularly when the issues of sexuality, cruelty, and religion (or a combination of all three) are at stake. Two modern examples of such writing craft stem from the pen of Robert Musil, the émigré Austrian writer who had to flee from the Nazis.

One is a poignantly and timely crafted novella, *The Young Törless*, and the other is a masterful novel called *The Man Without Qualities*. *Törless* is set in a boarding school somewhere in the Austro-Hungarian empire. It relates to the mental and psychological makeup of those who would later fight, get injured, or die in the First World War. It tells the story of a young boy who witnesses a comrade's sexual abuse by two school peers. The narrator reveals his own ambivalence and silence, until the entire story comes to a sudden halt in a kind of strange anticlimax. All participants suffer, there is no hero in the story, and there is no perceivable positive end or obvious lesson to be learned. The reader can only anticipate that one bad event (sexual abuse) is followed by another (the massive destruction and killings of World War I).

The Man Without Qualities also tackles the problem of sexuality, control, and latent violence, but links it more to the politics of wishful state- and empire-building than does the short novella. Musil sets *The Man Without Qualities* in Kakania, a country steering into the catastrophe of the First World War. While the novel's content and timing hints at World War I, it was actually written in the context of emerging European fascism, and therefore rather gives an inkling of the mental map of the latter's rise than the catastrophe of the First World War. At one point Musil introduces the perverse killer and sexual predator Moosbrugger. While other themes, such as the incestuous attraction that Ulrich (the hero and main character of the novel, a kind of intellectual advisor to the government) holds for his sister Agathe, that are described in great detail, Musil reserves his most detailed and somewhat illustrative and illuminative descriptions for the murderer and sexual predator Moosbrugger. This is not the place to narrate and recall the entire novel; suffice to say that Musil is interested in the psychological makeup of his generation and his country.

Despite the Continental connotations of both novella and novel there is a universal and humanist theme at work here. What stands out in Musil's work is his distinct treatment of sexuality, sexual perversion, and cruelty. What distinguishes his sensibility when compared to the discourses and comments we get today from either the press or TV or religious commentary is the description of the full human dimension—or better, the revelation of the full scale or continuum of possible human action with which the writer treats his main characters. What Musil seems to say is that nothing is more human than to fail in the most human of human affairs, that of sexual relations, as radically one-sided as they often appear and sometimes are. At the same time, it is always clear where Musil stands morally. All his other publications, such as his numerous essays and a good number of short stories and plays, make clear that Musil is probably the most enigmatic and sophisticated of all anti-totalitarian writers between the two world wars. His work is clearly directed against cruelty and against institutional and personal hypocrisy, but in his fiction, and particularly in the two works mentioned, nothing is ever off the human scale, not even in the case of the most perverse of all murderers. In Musil we have an example of somebody for whom to understand all never means to forgive it all. However, one of the hallmarks of our present age is an increasingly strong belief in the collective capacity to right past wrongs and provide effective redress through the medium of the law (O'Malley, 2009, p. 95). However, the growth of public apologies internationally, individual, collective and political, and of restorative and transformative justice, suggests the limitations of the law in healing the wounds of the past and the need for additional processes. In my study I will try to live up to Musil's writing, if not in literary skill than at least in how I try to engage with the complexity of our most human of our human problems.

My reference to Musil gives me a chance to warn against a possible misreading of my study. The very fact that my research draws on and tells the story of clerical perpetrators should not be mistaken as meaning that my attempts to understand these men and their lives epitomizes a call to forgiveness. Forgiveness and reconciliation require another project. My project represents the perpetrators' stories and my interpretation of them, which when taken all together, invites a paradigm shift from victim to perpetrator as part of the attempt to understand and prevent sexual violence, maybe not unlike the paradigm shift that has occurred in other difficult terrains and fields of study, such as the history of the Holocaust.

However, we should also be careful not to make wrong comparisons. Despite all the horrific accounts of abuse that have emerged in relation to the Catholic Church, none has suggested intentional persecution. I am not aware of any Catholic order that has demanded or asked individuals to abuse children. For all their failings, I am not aware of any claim that the pope or any of the bishops ever gave an order to abuse and to maltreat children. Without intention and widespread policies to inflict harm I find the Holocaust a limiting comparison in the context of sexual abuse by clergy. At the same time however, it is perhaps understandable that some victims have drawn on the analogy of the Holocaust to try to convey the depth of their suffering.

In the case of sexual abuse and how to deal with it, it might be more appropriate to argue both sociologically and functionally that once abuse remains unpunished and becomes widespread, as suggested in some reports into institutional abuse in Ireland (Report of the Commission to Inquire into Child Abuse, 2009), and that individuals and institutions learn that there are no limits to these behaviors and bystanders won't protest, the abuse and violence becomes "normal practice," which is what it appears to have become. Bearing such a more functional and contextual explanation in mind, as citizens and as bystanders we are all in the "political responsibility dock" for allowing such individual and institutional hypocrisy to produce such cruelty and for it to last for such a long time.

MOTIVATIONS AND METHODOLOGY

My interest in the subject matter of this book arose from my clinical experience as a systemic psychotherapist and as a social worker who has worked for many years both with victims of sexual abuse and with perpetrators of sexual violence. More specifically, my interest in Roman Catholic clergy who had perpetrated child sexual abuse developed when I, along with two colleagues, set up a community-based treatment program for child sexual offenders in Ireland in 1996. From its inception the treatment facility attracted a number of Roman Catholic priests and religious for the treatment of sexually abusive behavior. Apart from offering treatment, I became interested in a number of issues. First, I wanted to understand how priests and religious brothers who were attending the treatment center made sense of their own lives, as they looked back with hindsight. I was also interested in discovering how these men understood those aspects of their lives that had given way to their sexual offenses. Although appearing somewhat irrational to outsiders, deviance is known to have its own internal logic, and I was interested to understand that "logic." Usually, people join the ranks of Catholic clergy for a number of reasons, and while there is no evidence that the main reason for joining is the betterment of the human race, my experience of working with clergy in Ireland for over two decades led me to believe that the motivation for many was to be of service and to help others. I therefore wanted to know what had gone so wrong.

Despite occasional mutterings in the public press and the rare suggestion in the empirical literature, there is no evidence to suggest that Catholic clergy enter clerical and religious life with the purpose of gaining access to children to abuse them. In fact, the most comprehensive research ever carried out on sexual abuse by Catholic clergy, conducted by researchers in the United States (John Jay Study, 2004, 2006, 2011), reports that whatever else formed the priests' motivation for joining, there is no evidence to suggest that gaining access to children to abuse is part of it. My own experience confirms this. The more I met with the clerical men, who had abused, the more intrigued I became. Put simply, I was not in the presence of "monsters," nor was I in the presence of individuals who had an "illness." I began to think there must be more to this problem, situational and institutional dimensions beyond the well-documented mishandling of abuse complaints in Ireland, England, the United States, Canada, Australia, and now other parts of Europe.

From the early days of my involvement with clerical men who had sexually abused minors I realized that as well as their offending there was another dimension to the abuse problem: the handling of abuse complaints by the Catholic hierarchy. This has become apparent in almost every country in the world in which sexual abuse by clergy has come to light.

While seen by some as two separate and distinct problems, it was clear to me from the outset that the two problems were interlinked. It is my thesis that some of the factors that contributed to a climate in which clerical men could sexually offend also contributed to the conditions that made it possible for the Church hierarchy to act as they did in handling the abuse complaints. In essence, they were both part of the same institutional culture. However, within this culture not all priests were abusive, and so it was important to determine the particular dynamic circumstances that gave way to sexual offending on the part of some clerical men, without forgetting the larger cultural landscape within which this abuse took place. That is part of my project.

The main aim of this book is to understand and analyze child sexual abuse by Catholic clergy in its individual and systemic dimensions, and to offer a perspective that combines both. It is based on over a decade of research. The book draws on empirical and qualitative data that are used to illustrate possible interpretations of the problem and to suggest possible ways forward. A number of sources are used for this analytical and theoretical work: research involving the first-person narratives of nine Roman Catholic priests and religious brothers who were willing to discuss their lives and experiences, having admitted to sexually abusing minors (the interested reader is referred to the Appendix for further information); research involving four non-abusive Catholic clergy and former clergy who were willing to share their experiences with me; a wide-ranging analysis of the key literature in the area; my extensive clinical experience with victims and perpetrators of sexual crime, both outside and inside the Church; and my experience of working with Catholic clergy in general. As part of the methodology of the book I also visited treatment centers for abusive clergy in Canada, the United States, the United Kingdom, and Australia and had conversations and communication with colleagues throughout the world. The general results are of course also conditioned by my training and experience as a systemic family therapist who worked over many decades with victims and perpetrators of sexual abuse and their families, who in different ways and for different reasons felt themselves to be marginal and marginalized. As Byrne and McCarthy (1998) have argued in *Marginal Illuminations,* the margins can often illuminate the center—if we allow them.

However, this is not a book-length description of an empirical project with clerical perpetrators, and it is not structured like one. Rather, the book is an analysis of sexual abuse within the Catholic Church and the responses to it, drawing from policy, theory, and empirical studies and data. Although the interviews with the offending clergy are an important source of information, as are the questionnaires and interviews conducted with the non-offending clergy, the ideas presented in this book are also strongly influenced by my reading of a number of reports and commissions into the handling of abuse complaints and by my direct contact with many of the key players involved.

Another important aim of this work is to try to understand the "logic" of the Church hierarchy in their responses to abuse complaints, and to set this understanding in its systemic context. For this I draw primarily on secondary sources, which is itself a serious limitation, and on my clinical experience. My primary sources for this work are three government-commissioned reports into the handling of sexual abuse by the Church hierarchy in Ireland (Report of the Commission into Child Abuse in Ireland, 2009; Report of the Commission of Investigation into the Archdiocese of Dublin, 2009; The Inquiry into the Diocese of Ferns, 2005), and seven official reports in the United States (Office of the Attorney

General, Commonwealth of Massachusetts, 2003; Office of the Attorney General, New Hampshire, 2003; Office of the Attorney General, State of Maine, 2004; Office of the Grand Jury, Philadelphia, 2005, 2010; Suffolk County Supreme Court Special Grand Jury, 2002; Westchester County Grand Jury, 2002), as well as other documentary sources and literature. This is an area of work that would benefit enormously from further research with the Catholic hierarchy.

In weaving together my own "thick description" (C. Geertz) based on these rich and varied sources and experiences, my overall aim is that the book will provide a model of performance that helps to conceptualize and understand, but never justify, the perplexing phenomenon of child sexual abuse by Roman Catholic clergy. It provides a new way of thinking about the clerical sexual offender as someone whose clerical masculine identity and way of "doing" priesthood or religious brotherhood is built on a life that is impossible to live. It addresses the question of how the problem of child sexual abuse within the Catholic Church can best be understood—namely by combining the clerical perpetrators, the Church hierarchy, and other subject positions in what I refer to as the multilevel relational and contextual framework for understanding child sexual abuse by Roman Catholic clergy. This framework emerges from an analysis of the problem that combines institutional, organizational, and cognitive dimensions. By understanding the meaning of the problem and its developmental and systemic pathways, it may be possible to go some way towards preventing future offending by Catholic clergy. My hope is that the book will make a contribution towards improved safety for children and adults, will lead to a better understanding of clerical perpetrators, and will suggest a more considered and informed way for the future.

DECIPHERING MEANING OR "JUST THE FACTS, MADAM": INTERPRETIVE VS. "SCIENTIFIC" APPROACHES

Before discussing some of my findings, I should draw the reader's attention to the fact I am not approaching the topic of sexual abuse by clergy by means of an exact science, nor do I think it suffices to employ what are thought to be "scientific" methods to simply gather ever more data in an attempt to give my study a more "objective" touch. *Au contraire*, I continue to have serious doubts about how the attribute "scientific" is awarded when it comes to studying and understanding complex social phenomena. I share the critique of the notion that there is only one thing called "science," and that this has a clear and obvious nature to which all must conform, especially in the social sciences. From the earlier debates on the philosophy of science from the 1960s (Kuhn, 1962 Popper, 1959, for example) up until today, there has been over 50 years of (scientific) work on science that has led to tendencies within the field of social scientific research that are less about specific theories or disciplinary methods than about the conception of enquiry and the implicit underpinning "philosophies" of science (see Sismondo, 2009, for a review). This field of study suggests there are multiple disciplines and multiple forms of enquiry and practices of research, all of which have an important place in the social "sciences." These multiple forms of research do not have to follow the same rules (such as representative sampling) to gain the title "empirical," nor is there a singular essence that can serve as the norm to chastise all "deviants." I have been influenced by notions of interpretive social science, first conceived by Max Weber (1978) and later refined by other scholars such as Clifford Geertz (1973), Jürgen Habermas (1971), and

Jeffrey C. Alexander (2003), to name just a few. An interpretive social science perspective underpins my work.

Weber pointed out that the subject matter of social research differs considerably from that of the natural sciences. He argued that in the context of social science research we are always dealing with human beings (in the case of social action at least two) who give meanings to their actions. In contrast, when it comes to research in the hard or natural sciences the subject matter of study does not give meaning to anything. For example, trees, plants, cells, kidneys, water, or iron never talk back, and it does not make sense to think of them as giving meaning to their existence, never mind attempting to make sense of or have doubts about it. If this basic assumption holds true we begin to think of social science research in different terms to research in the natural sciences. However, many social scientists disagree with this perspective and attempt to emulate the natural sciences in method and approach, seeking out "reality" or "truth" through "objective" methodologies. In contrast, interpretive social science perspectives aim to understand humans' actions first (from their perspective) (an operation called *verstehen*) as part of the attempt to explain (*erklären*) the action or behavior. The role of interpretation in this process gives rise to the label "interpretive" social science.

The problem with an interpretive approach is of course the fact that it is hard to think of it as a progressive enterprise—a clear disadvantage when compared to the facts that the natural sciences seem to produce in a systematic and cumulative fashion. Having said that, since Thomas Kuhn's groundbreaking study of how scientific paradigms have developed historically, are maintained, and are occasionally revolutionized by nonscientific circumstances in *The Structure of Scientific Revolutions* (1962) or Robert Merton's study of serendipity patterns in the history of science (Merton & Barber, 2004), we also have learned that progress in the natural and social sciences is less obvious or self-evident than often perceived.

We also witness in social scientific scholarship all kind of attempts by those social scientists (*sic*!) who maintain that what they do is "objective" in their attempts to claim the title "scientific". The restless attempts to appear more serious, less biased, more "objective," and more "empirical" becomes a constant effort to produce "facts" by resorting to the number game. The history of the "the impossible science" (sociology and the social sciences) is full of such attempts. As Wolf Lepenies, one of the great internationally renowned historians of the social sciences noted, sociology emerged first as a third culture situated between literature and science (Lepenies, 1988). Famously, Lepenies concluded that to pretend otherwise or to ignore this fact would be to sell sociology, and consequently the social sciences, short and seriously undermine the complex nature of their enterprise to a reductionist model.

Since Weber first established the interpretive paradigm and since it has been fine-tuned by other, perhaps more "watertight" accounts, the basic circumstances he referred to have not changed. While we continue to exist, we are meaning-producing social animals who try (and often fail) to understand and make sense of each other's actions. It often appears messy, to say the least, and often so do interpretive social science accounts. However, despite what might appear as rather unsystematic and not very "scientific," there is also a great opportunity in such approaches. First of all, we come to an understanding of human action that other approaches are simply unable (and often simply unwilling) to understand, such as irrational or a-rational behavior. Second, there is an element of open-endedness, contingency, and "possibilism" in human action, which some of the more reductionist social science perspectives haven't even started to think about much less capture. It might be helpful, as Lepenies has argued, to realize that *savoir* (to know) and *savoir vivre* (to know how to live) are related to each other (Lepenies, 1997, p. 47). Third, moral and ethical questions and concerns, which are never far away when talking about sexual abuse, are also more likely to be addressed by an interpretive approach. As Alan Wolfe (1989) has suggested, social science and moral obligation should not be treated as two totally different entities or enterprises. Deep moral questions penetrate our work. At the same time Wolfe realizes that "no abstract and formal rules exist specifying that we owe to others and others owe us. Instead, moral obligation ought to be viewed as a socially constructed practice, as something we learn through the actual experience of trying to live together with other people" (p. 20). Herein lies indeed a great chance for the social "sciences" to remain relevant, a chance that should not be missed. Since I am engaging with normative and deviant positions (which I hold lightly in order to leave open the possibility for deeper understanding and explanation as knowledge evolves), I hope that my work can contribute to what has been called retributive and transformative justice as well as to hope and repair. This is something that a mere "scientific" approach (based on notions of here's the researcher, there are the research "subjects," here are my "objective" methods and my "findings,") will simply not do.

I do not want to use up all the space in this introduction to go into the finer details of interpretive approaches, nor is this the place to go into extensive epistemological debates. Suffice to say that that interpretive approaches to research have clearly identifiable advantages, and my hope is that this will become even clearer in the course of my argument. Be that as it may, I should stress that following an interpretive approach does of course not imply that I reject or that I am in neglect of the usefulness of collecting simple data and making use of statistics or other empirical findings (as the reader will see, I actually do so, sometimes even extensively). My point here is that there are constellations in social life, particularly when it comes to micro-sociological environments, for which interpretive approaches are better suited, than, let's say, massive data collections or employing strictly "scientific" notions or methodologies. Of course one cannot ever fully exclude the possibility that, for example, sexual abusers have a different biological, physical, or even psychological makeup. However, just a cursory reading of the situation will immediately show that employing "scientific" explanations for complex historical, religious, cultural, and sexual notions will not serve us well when such interrelated circumstance really cry out for social understanding and explanation.

I would like to turn briefly now to the question of what kind of conclusions I can realistically draw from my own research with clerical perpetrators and my analysis of the reports and inquiries into the handling of abuse complaints by the Church hierarchy, both of which form the core of this book, particularly since what the reader has before him or her is best seen as a case study stemming from observations from a particular environment (i.e., Ireland and within that area a small cohort of Catholic priests who have sexually abused and two Catholic dioceses that were investigated). As any conscious reader will realize, by definition one cannot extrapolate too much from a small sample. On the other side, however, case studies can often produce insights that other macro-based studies and investigations seem to miss. As Howard Becker has argued (in Ragin & Becker, 1992), case studies are helpful because the researcher begins to know more about fewer people. Also, story-telling (and listening to the stories of the clerical perpetrators) is based on a different logic when compared to large data sampling. We arrive at questions such as: "What kind of an organization could accommodate a part like this? What would the rest of the organization have to be like for this part to be what it is? What would the whole story have to be for this step to occur as we have seen it occur?" (p. 213).

I will say more about my own case study in the course of this book (particularly in what I consider to be the core of my argument in Chapters 6 to 10). What I would just like to point out to the potential skeptics among my readers is that case studies, when properly contextualized, can actually produce quite surprising insights and results. (One of the founding fathers of empirical research, Paul Lazarsfeld, was well aware of this when he invented the focus group—as we all know, to great success.) Although my own small and unique research environment cannot be regarded as resembling anything close to Lazarsfeld's focus groups (it was never intended as such; its original motivations and concerns were totally different), in a surprising way its results fulfill a similar function. My work links detailed knowledge of the Church administration and the institution of the Catholic Church to the personal narratives of some offenders, and in fact each reflects back on the other. When the results of my own micro-research are interpreted in the larger context, it becomes obvious that there are noticeable links between what happens on the grand scale of things and on the local level, and that the individual, the organization, and the institutional dimensions are actually influencing each other and bound together in particular dynamic relations. Such observations might reveal that the classic micro/macro distinction is a rather artificial construction. As Clifford Geertz has pointed out, it makes sense to see social interpretation as "a continuous dialectical tracking between the most local of detail and the most global of global structure in such a way as to bring both into view simultaneously ... Hopping back and forth between the whole conceived through the parts that actualize it, and the parts conceived through the whole which motivates them, we seek to turn them, by a sort of intellectual perpetual motion, into explications of one another" (Geertz, 1979, p. 239).

Whether it is possible to achieve a full interpretive understanding through a process of grasping an actor's intent is widely debated. Having said that, on this issue I sympathize very much with Geertz (1979, p. 225), who argues that genuine understanding comes from the act of looking over the shoulders of the actor and trying to figure out, both by observation and conversation, what it is that he or she means. The idea of trying to grasp the clerical men's understanding of their offending was certainly one of my central epistemological interests. While I am also interested in trying to grasp the Church leaders' understanding of their responses to abuse complaints, the dearth of data on their perspectives makes such a prospect a little illusive for the moment. Those studies that have undertaken such first-person research are of course consulted (Balboni, 1998; Goode et al., 2003).

THE CONTEXT

The project of this book began in a treatment program in Ireland for sexually offending men and for victims of sexual abuse, and by way of setting the scene I will describe a little of that early setting. Needless to say, the contours of influence for what was to become the final endeavor spread far and wide, taking me a long way from that treatment center into many libraries and conversations in the United States, Canada, Australia, South Africa, and the

United Kingdom. I have also corresponded and spoken with colleagues in Europe more recently, something I will continue into the future.

The treatment program in which the research began was primarily of a narrative nature; however, we also drew on cognitive-behavioral approaches to help the men in therapy for sexual offending find ways of reorienting their lives so that it totally avoided abuse of minors. The therapeutic aim of the work was to put all children beyond risk and to help the men to live non-abusive lives. We also wanted to offer a systemic ear to individuals who came to the center so that the experiences of all could be held and honored in the interest of healing, collective restoration, and transformation. The therapy involved individual, group, and family therapy modalities, as well as accountability meetings, workshops on specific topics, and self-help groups for families. For the men who had perpetrated sexual abuse, weekly group therapy sessions of five hours, supplemented by weekly or fortnightly individual counseling sessions, formed the core of the treatment program. Accountability meetings involved the offender, significant people in his social and professional network, and key treatment staff, and took place at regular intervals. In the case of the Catholic clergy who attended for therapy, these meetings involved the cleric's bishop or his immediate superior and other Church personnel. Members of the cleric's family of origin were also offered help and support. The family support group for the families of all of the men attending the treatment center met on a monthly basis and consisted of family members, mainly women, who had played an important role in clients' lives.

The initial three practitioners involved in setting up the program came from differing professional backgrounds and had different clinical orientations. The director was a registered psychologist who practiced primarily in the tradition of humanistic/integrative psychology. The consultant therapist, who was a registered psychiatric nurse and psychoanalyst, practiced in the tradition of psychoanalytic psychotherapy. As a consultant psychotherapist and the coordinator of the treatment program, I had trained as a social worker and systemic therapist and practiced in the tradition of systemic and narrative therapy. Within this environment, cognitive-behavioral approaches (Abel et al., 1984; Knapp, 1984; Marshall, Anderson & Fernandez, 2000) and relapse prevention ideas (George & Marlette, 1989; Pitchers, 1990), which dominate much of the outcome studies on successful sexual offender treatment, were reinterpreted through a narrative frame (Keenan, 1998).

The research aim of the treatment center was primarily to extend the understanding of the problem of sexual abuse beyond the context of deviance and psychological damage. In particular, we wanted to understand the wider relational and personal experiences of the offender. It was clear from a review of the literature that the predominant focus on child sexual offenders was a medico-forensic-legal one and dealt mainly with deviance, criminality, and psychological dysfunction. In general, clerical offenders were largely seen as sexual deviants or moral degenerates or suffering from psychological dysfunctions. Much of the literature on victims focused on psychological pathology and the symptoms that accompany or result from the trauma. Victims were seen as psychologically damaged (by the trauma), and little attention appeared to focus on the individual's resistance, with some exceptions (Todd & Wade, 2003; Wade, 1997; White, 2000, 2004b). We were interested in the idea that the clients' symptoms or problems might be first honored as a form of resistance to the practices of power that were impoverishing their lives.

The focus of many therapy programs for sexual offenders is on gaining detailed accounts of the offending act, with the implied contingent risk of further offending (Eldridge & Wyre, 1998, p. 86; Loftus & Cameron, 1993, p. 300; Wyre, 1996). Professional and legal discourses caution against "believing" the offenders' accounts (Eldridge & Wyre, 1998, p. 82; Wyre, 1996) because of the assumed denial, minimizations, and rationalizations that are thought to be hidden in their stories. Working with such a conceptual framework inevitably silences and marginalizes first-person accounts. As a result the voices of men who had abused were absent from public debate. The perpetrators' silence in response to exposure was interpreted in public discourses as evidence of further deviance and pathology. Such an interpretation troubled me. By undertaking research with clerical perpetrators my aim was to create the space for more personal and context-specific narratives to emerge.

However, in undertaking research with individuals based on their narratives, it is important to contemplate the possibility that these narratives are shaped and guided by the available social explanations and the forms of professional discourse that are available to them. It could be argued that the clergymen who participated in my research were influenced by the societal discourses of child sexual abuse and by the professional discourses in which they were embedded. Their narratives could thus be seen as "re-presenting" a number of storylines influenced by such perspectives, with the narratives acting as a powerful describer of society or of therapy. One problem in using clients or patients in research is therefore the possibility that they might tell you what they have learned in therapy.

In modern society sex acts with children are illegal because of the likelihood of harm to children. However, there is evidence to show that children are not universally harmed by sexual abuse (Clancy, 2010), although some are. For some individuals it is a relatively unimportant event in their lives, or even a challenge from which they have gained strength. Clancy argues that survivors of childhood sexual abuse are victimized not only by their abusers (whose acts often leave them both confused, due to incomprehension, and sometimes frightened), but also and inadvertently by well-intentioned health professionals, whose interpretations of abusive experiences are often more traumatic than actual events and effects themselves. Here Clancy is drawing attention to the social discourse in which the problem is embedded. Drawing on case studies, statistics, and technical data, Clancy opposes the view that abusive acts destabilize the neurobiology of the victim, as in other traumas. Positing that the trauma model damages victims with inaccurate predictions and ineffective treatments, she suggests that what hurts most victims is not always the experience itself but the meaning of the experience and how victims make sense of what happened, in line with the available societal and therapeutic discourses, and how these understandings make them feel about themselves and others. It would be quite possible to make sex with children illegal on grounds other than harm to the victim, such as an affront to public morals, which in turn would influence the way the problem is described and languaged. This would in turn influence the narratives of child sex offenders.[1]

In my research with the clerical perpetrators, as an attempt to counteract some of these problems, I distinguished the men's *explanations* for how they came to act as they did from their *descriptions* of their lives and their abuse of children. Their narratives contain both. Their explanations tended to portray storylines strongly influenced by societal or therapeutic discourses of "distorted thinking," "minimizations," and "justifications" that appeared to be filtered through legal, psychological, and medical rationality that were in turn "owned" by the men. In contrast, their descriptions of their lived experiences portrayed fewer societal and therapeutic judgments and overtones. This is an observation also reported in other fields of "lay" narrative research (Shaw, 2002, p. 289). De Swaan (1990, pp. 100–101) observed that laypeople redefine their troubles in line with the basic concepts of the particular profession with which they are in close contact. This reflects the fact that the discourse surrounding particular problems is dominated by professional rationality (Shaw, 2002, p. 293). In the case of sexual offending it is predominantly medico-legal and psychological discourses of pathology and deficit that prevail.

This book is therefore the result of a research process that began in a treatment center. However, the research continued with the clerical perpetrators long after they had left treatment and had been released from prison and/or had finally settled into what appeared indeed to be very unsettled lives. But it is also a book that focuses on the institutional dimensions of sexual abuse within the Catholic Church and on the response of the Church hierarchy to the problem.

FINDING A PLACE TO STAND

Confronting sexual abuse of minors goes to the very heart of what most adults appear to abhor, and in writing on this subject I had a number of concerns. Whose truth matters and whose account can claim to be final? Whose story is to be privileged and whose is to be marginalized? Can a space be created in which all voices are held and honored, and in which no one is disqualified? What position or observation point should an author take when it comes to criminal acts that have been committed? What about "us" and "them" distinctions? Are perpetrators of abuse part of humanity too, or must they be cast out along with their abusive behavior? Should perpetrators tell their story or should they be listened to only through the lens of lawful and clinical assessment and through legal judgment and punishment? While I was always clear about the powerlessness of the child victim in situations of sexual abuse, I wondered about other dimensions of victimhood and perpetrator-hood and who defines and reifies these crucial distinctions. While registering differences in scale, in different situations and different contexts, I wondered whether we have all been victims in some contexts while taking on the perpetrator role in others. Furthermore, are there contexts in which we have all been bystanders, particularly in situations that involved sexual violence? In contemplating the personal violence involved in sexual abuse of minors, I wondered about social violence and how it too goes unaddressed. I also wondered if our reactions to the violence and the continued trauma could be transformed into compassionate witnessing for all, with the potential for addressing and finding healing from the pain (Weingarten, 2003, p. 7).

It is always challenging to try to locate oneself in the place of another person. To do this with men who have sexually abused minors is even more difficult. To do so with the bishops who were seen as covering up the defilement of children is no less easy. This is so because it is not easy to acknowledge or accept one's own potential for inflicting pain on another person, or to contemplate for a moment that I could be like "him." The psychological threat of identification with the "otherness" of people who abuse children, which is always challenging, is even more difficult when one is in the midst of a problem of truly global proportions, and involving seemingly privileged men who have broken the most sacred of sacred trusts. Discourses of guilt, shame, blame, sorrow, rage, and disqualification are omnipresent in such a constellation. Many people are directly and personally affected by child sexual abuse, primarily the immediate victims, but we also know that the effects extend way beyond the immediate and identifiable victims—to their families, the perpetrators' families, their colleagues and friends, the perpetrators themselves, Church leaders, and those who work with them. However, the social-psychological processes necessary to live through such extreme emotions and the life trajectories and stories that underpin them are not usually part of the public conversation. Almost no public debate focuses on the psychological process involved in living through such public/personal trauma for the victims, public humiliation and vilification for the perpetrators, and the pain of their families and those who love them. Little public debate focuses on how difficult it must be for aged and sometimes unwell bishops to be the focus of intense public anger on a daily basis. The debate is usually limited to typical themes such as deviance, pathology, and betrayal by perpetrators, trauma and damage to victims and their families, and "cover-up" and betrayal by the Church leaders. Understandable as this might be at one level, it also leaves a psychosocial void.

The shock that we experience as a result of the revelations of sexual violence against minors and adolescents has no useful place to go either. No appropriate language is easily available that allows for compassionate witness; all healing language seems to be eclipsed by the language of blame. This is the general context in which I set out to write this book, and to find a place to stand in which I could do so. I wanted to embrace all stories and silence no one. However, if sides had to be taken I knew where I stood. I had found that place many years ago in working with victims and perpetrators of trauma and violence, as I walked and talked and sat in witness. I am taking a stand on the side of all human beings who are trying to find a way through life in the best and only way possible, while taking a radical stand against cruelty, violence, injustice, and institutional and personal hypocrisy in all its many manifestations.

In undertaking the research for this book I was also particularly challenged by the complexities involved in being both an insider and an outsider. Having worked therapeutically with victims and perpetrators of sexual crime and with clergy in general, I now wanted to research their lives and I wanted to get close to the thinking that might have propelled the Church leaders to act as they did. I know that some commentators will be critical of or dismiss my work because I might be seen as being too close either to the victims or too close to the perpetrators, or even too close to the "inside" of the Catholic Church in Ireland, since I have chaired some sessions of the bishops' conference on child sexual abuse and acted on independent advisory groups for some religious orders. For others, the fact that I have never been a priest or a religious or a victim of sexual abuse (or a man for that matter) might mean I could never fully understand those perspectives. At the same time, I know that for others still, my unique access to victims and to clerical perpetrators and to the systems involved with them would provide good reason to take my work seriously. In any case, the challenges involved with being an insider and an outsider had to be addressed, and I did so by relying on colleagues who acted as a kind of group of "critical friends" and by adopting a suitable methodology. In the case of the primary research with the clerical perpetrators I adopted a grounded theory methodology in which the research participants were consulted and re-consulted on numerous occasions throughout the research, until the final interpretations were formulated. This approach was taken to ensure that I would get as close as possible to what the men were trying to convey and to accurately represent their perspective. For the purposes of this introduction I maintain that what is presented in the final version of this book meets both the rigors of academic standards and the compassion that the subject warrants.

TOTALIZING "PERPETRATOR" AND "VICTIM"

Beyond serving the important function of providing a language for legal proceedings and of giving emphasis to the criminal aspects of the behavior of sexual abuse and violence that has hitherto gone in the main unrecognized, the language of perpetrator and victim is actually a limiting one, acting as a constraint and barrier in any endeavor to understand the complex issues involved, and to find a way forward. When does one stop being cast as a perpetrator: 1 year, 10 years, 40 years after the offense? When can one stop being cast as a victim, or is this always the description that accompanies one through life? When is the attribution of these descriptions something personal and when is it a public process?

Modern popular culture appears to accept that there are unjust limitations imposed on individuals who have experienced abuse when their identities are totalized as victims, and in response to calls from victims themselves, society accepts some of the other descriptions of such individuals, such as "survivor" or "thriver." However, these labels do not always do justice to the complexities and richness of the lives and the skills and knowledge that many individuals who have experienced sexual abuse in childhood give testimony to. In the public domain we all too often focus on the negative effects of trauma. This is of course important and must be highlighted time and time again. However, we usually do so without ever considering the importance of the individual's "response" to trauma and what this shows about the wisdom and bravery of abuse survivors. We know from the trauma literature that wherever there is a story of oppression, there is a parallel story of resistance, and it is in these small, maybe even ordinary or neglected stories of resistance that we see the bravery and "agency" of even the smallest child, who took on the offender in the most skilful of ways (Wade, 1997; White, 2000, 2004b). In neglecting to focus on human responses to trauma and the enormous steps that individuals, including children, take to prevent abuse and to resist its aftereffects, we are disqualifying or rendering invisible huge reserves in the human spirit. I have long been persuaded by the work of Michael White, an Australian psychotherapist, who tells us that the ways in which people respond to trauma are based on what they give value to, or what they hold precious (White, 2004b, p. 48). What is often really striking in trauma work is how individuals continue to privilege certain values in life and to preserve what is precious to them, such as love or justice, despite everything they have been through. So what is required is actually a double listening: listening for the effects of trauma and being open to the responses to trauma, too (p. 48). By having an open ear for both, we are listening not just for disempowerment, but for personal agency, in the magnificent and incredible ways all victims of trauma try to resist, prevent, or modify its effects. Sometimes the language of "victim" neglects or omits to capture such vital skills, wisdom, and bravery.

Whatever the problems are with the broad acceptance of the limited view that identifies and totalizes victims of abuse as "victims," popular culture is even less prepared to even think about its own black spots when it comes to defining "perpetrators." By totalizing the identity of men who have perpetrated sexual abuse as solely "perpetrators" we are rendering invisible aspects of the men's lives that either stand in contrast to the abuse or that bear testimony to an otherwise blameless life of good works. The public discourse on sexual offenders presents the offenders as "embodied evil," and research is often unfairly cited to confirm a view that sex offenders are fundamentally different from the rest of mankind (Keenan, 2009). Despite the best of intentions of therapists and do-gooders, so the argument goes, no help in the world can change these men. The common belief and perception of clerical perpetrators is that they are fundamentally flawed and fundamentally bad; they just managed to hide that fact for a long time. Public belief rests on the premise that "once a child sexual offender; always a child sexual offender." The idea of "flawed nature" dominates reports and public debate. In the paradigm of criminal essentialism (Lofland, 1969; Maruna, 2001, p. 5), the sexual offender is bad and cannot ever be good. In the somewhat popular paradigm of pedophilia, the sexual offender is simply regarded as sick and cannot ever recover from his condition. Reductionist models of explanation and intervention are *en vogue*. In the rush to condemn, some things get noticed but even more gets missed. The stage is set for extremes of hate. In the world of good versus evil, the good are allowed the occasional mistake, but "the essentially evil" deserve no consideration whatsoever. In the current climate, Catholic clergy who have perpetrated sexual abuse against minors are largely seen and treated as a cast of unreformable men. They have almost become "untouchables," total outcasts. The hierarchy who are accused of "cover-up" are also seen as beyond redemption.

With my discussion I want to draw attention to the unhelpful dichotomies and dangers that arise from identifying and totalizing the identity of any individual. Against the prevailing popular perception, I maintain that victims of abuse constitute a heterogeneous group, and so do abuse perpetrators. Rather than enforcing what Tocqueville has called the tyranny of the majority, we might do better by remembering that what really matters is the subjective experience. If the latter assumption holds true, this means also that there must be room for all in their different manifestations and experiences. By casting "victims" and "perpetrators" as homogenized groups, each with identifiable symptoms and absolute and unchangeable identities, further social injustices are likely to occur, this time couched in the language of social justice.

AN ORGANIZATIONAL PERSPECTIVE

Child sexual abuse is not limited to any one church or to any one profession, and its occurrence in relation to Catholic clergy is reported in both predominantly secular countries where mass adherence to religious practices is weak, such as Germany (Schneider, 2010), just as in predominantly Catholic countries where religion is very much part of daily life, such as Ireland. It is difficult to get a clear comparative picture of the international situation because of the dearth of empirical data. Nonetheless, in Chapter 1 I discuss what we know in this regard. However, some important factors distinguish sexual abuse within the Catholic Church from that occurring among other professionals and among leaders and ministers of other churches. Roman Catholic clergy are all male, similarly educated, subject to one authority, professing one belief, and vowing obedience to one supreme head, currently Pope Benedict XVI. They also represent a group of men pledged to celibacy and service to others, and the occurrence of sexual activity, especially of an abusive kind, contradicts everything that the institution publicly stands for, such as chastity and protecting the young and vulnerable. The fact that an unusually consistent pattern has emerged in the handling of abuse complaints by Catholic Church leaders across jurisdictions and continents appears to have compounded the problem, adding another dimension to a complex problem that needs to be seen in its global context as well as in its national dimensions and varieties. Finally, what is perceived as mysterious and secretive in the workings of the Vatican's papal bureaucracy, the Roman *Curia*, particularly in relation to sexual abuse, gives the whole crisis an additional touch of intrigue, something that doesn't particularly bear well when it comes to a topic that is already poorly understood.

Apart from the military, which now includes women, and which has never subjected its recruits to pledges of celibacy, there is no suitable comparative organization. As the Australian bishops advocated in their pastoral letter to the Catholic people of Australia on April 24, 1996, a study is required "of any factors peculiar to the Catholic Church which might lead to sexual abuse by priests, religious or other Church workers" (point 7). This eminently sensible suggestion recognizes the fact that while valuable insights can be gained from studies involving child sexual offenders in general, and from other organizations and faith communities who have experienced these problems, the distinctive aspects of the Catholic Church's pattern of ministry, governance, and sexuality distinguishes it from other organizations, requiring its own in-depth analysis. Any organization that has been plagued by enduring abuses of power, including multiple incidents of sexual and other violations of children and of workers, must investigate the specific organizational factors that may be contributing to the problem. Such an in-depth analysis is also important in trying to work towards physical and psychological safety and health for all.

It is also reported that sexual exploitation and boundary-breaking is more likely to occur in closed organizations where individuals are trying to meet their personal, professional, social, and sexual needs inside the boundary of the one organization (White, 1995, p. 190). White found in such organizations that the intensity and duration of abuse incidents tended to be greater and more debilitating for victims than in more open systems (p. 191). The potential for abuses of power in closed systems and the intensity of abuses in such organizations are magnified by the poor general working conditions, such as a poor work/life balance for workers, the loss of outside sources of replenishment (for both workers and the organization), the depletion of staff's energy and health, and, last but not least, the distortion of the organizational values resulting from lack of feedback that limits its sense of reality. In essence, a closed organization that does not actively engage with or listen to those it purports to serve is likely to be at high risk in terms of sexual and other physical or mental exploitation. The risk is even higher if and when the leadership is centralized and not accountable, and when there are insufficient checks and balances. In these organizations, exploitation by workers and exploitation of workers are likely to emerge out of the same abuses of power (p. 191). The German example, where victims of sexual abuse have also been coming forward from Protestant institutions, from secular boarding schools, from elite academies, and from children's homes, makes clear that abuse has often taken place in closed institutions where male educators have charge of male children (Schneider, 2010). These findings and insights also apply to the large organization that is the Catholic Church.

In some very important work on what she refers to as "the dark side of organizations," Vaughan helps us think sociologically about how things go wrong in socially organized settings (Vaughan, 1997, 1999). She is interested in organizational pathologies that adversely affect the public and in how mistakes, misconduct, and disasters are produced in and by organizations (Vaughan, 1999, p. 272). The distinctions between these three concepts are also at the core of her work, one differing from the other in the normative standards violated (internal rules, legal mandates, social expectations), the categories of the public harmed, the extent of the harmful consequences, the social group whose expectations are violated, and the response of the public to the incident (p. 273). Vaughan argues that in popular explanations of organizational failure, the full set of socially organized circumstances that give rise to these harmful outcomes, such as the tensions and affinities that have been behind the scene, often remain obscure. When we apply rational choice assumptions about means-ends–oriented social action, as does the paradigm underpinning the accusation of "cover-up" against individuals in the Catholic hierarchy, we neglect to consider the socially patterned forms of institutional and organizational action that may more usefully explain such organizational failings.

Vaughan (1999, p. 274) argues that much organizational deviance is a routine byproduct of the characteristics of the system itself. Drawing on Merton (1936, 1940), she suggests that in certain instances, organizational deviance is the product of "routine" nonconformity rather than specific nonconformity, and in fact routine nonconformity may become routine conformity, which is just as likely to lead to organizational deviance, depending on the institutional norms that are being adapted. Organizational deviance refers to "an event, activity or circumstance, occurring in and/or produced by a formal organization that deviates from both formal design goals and normative standards or expectations" (Vaughan, 1999, p. 273). The broad social and institutional environment, the specific organizational characteristics (structure, processes, and tasks), and the cognitive practices of individuals are all thought to contribute to organizational deviance (p. 274).

Vaughan's (1997) work is very helpful in offering concepts and insights that help shed light on the organizational practices of the Catholic Church. It is eminently feasible that those bishops and Church leaders who have been accused of errors or nonconformity in their handling of abuse complaints may in fact have been conforming fully to the institutional norms. Vaughan's work is also important because it shows not only that poor and undesirable outcomes are a routine aspect of social life in organizations, but when they occur they are socially organized phenomena that are produced by the connections between the institutional environment (which also includes the social context, including political, technological, economic, demographic, legal, cultural, and ecological aspects), the particular organizational characteristics, and individual cognition. This lens allows us look at organizational failings in a comprehensive manner. I take up more of these ideas in discussing the Church's handling of abuse complaints in Chapter 9.

IRELAND

According to the 2006 Census, the population of Ireland stands at 4.23 million. This figure tells an important story, a story of stagnation from the 1920s to the 1940s, depression during the 1950s, recovery during the 1970s, a slight dip again during the 1980s due to another period of high unemployment and high emigration, and a strong upward movement that returned in the 1990s, especially towards the middle of the decade (Fahey, 2007, p. 14). The total population, which stood at 3.53 million in 1991, rose to 3.92 million by 2002 and to 4.23

million by 2006. This growth rate, at 2% per year, is the highest population growth rate on record for Ireland.

Compared to other countries in Europe, where population numbers are static or falling, Irish total population numbers are rising. The Irish population also has a strong proportion of active-age adults, as distinct from the pattern of rapid population aging that can be seen in other European countries (Fahey, 2007, p. 13). This rise in population is explained both by a modest natural increase in the existing population and by net migration, which has soared. Due to an unprecedented rapid economic boom during the 1990s, Irish levels of immigration broke global records in their rapidity in proportion to the indigenous population (Nic Ghiolla Phádraig, 2009). Immigrants officially accounted for 10% of the Irish population by 2006 (Statistical Yearbook of Ireland, 2008, p. 5). The growth of immigration provides a new sense of diversity in religious as well as other cultural matters.

Until the final decade of the 20th century, religious patterns in Ireland were exceptional in Western Europe. High levels of religious practice were reported through the 1970s and 1980s (Nic Ghiolla Phádraig, 1976, 1988) which were at the time explained as a form of assertion of Irish identity in the face of British imperialism. However, much has changed in the hearts and minds of Irish Catholics since that time, which can be linked to broader social and cultural changes in Irish society. In 2008, data available from the International Social Survey Programme (see Nic Ghiolla Phádraig, 2009) reported that Irish respondents who were raised as Catholics (93%) still claim this affiliation. However, the influence of Catholicism has declined in many aspects of their lives, as the influence of Catholicism has declined in other respects in Irish life during the same period (Inglis, 2007; Nic Ghiolla Phádraig, 2009). As the numbers of clergy and other religious communities decrease, it means that their earlier strong presence in the social institutions and fabric of the country, such as family, education, health, and social welfare, has virtually vanished. In the past, the Church was able to influence business, politics, and the media through its monopoly over the socialization of each new generation, ensuring that the Irish thought and acted from a Catholic moral viewpoint (Inglis, 2007b, p. 67). Today such a monopoly position within culture and civil society is no longer possible.

In 2010 the Catholic perspective must take its place alongside multiple competing influences and points of view. This change is reflected in Church–State relations, as the strong relationship that existed between Church and State since the foundation of the State in 1922 has been reconfigured. While the new Irish State was marked out in the West by its uniquely Catholic "mind" and what in effect became a Catholic civil society (L'Estrange, 2005), since the second half of the 20th century the modern Irish State responds to an increasingly multicultural and modernizing agenda, bringing forth legislative changes in the area of family law, sexuality, human reproduction, and civil partnership (Inglis, 2007b, p. 68; Nic Ghiolla Phádraig, 2009).

Although the Irish still regard themselves as Catholic (93%) and still go to Mass on Sunday (79% of individuals over 65 years; 19% of those aged 18 to 24 years), the latest data show a decline in religious practice since the 1960s (Nic Ghiolla Phádraig, 2009). While 90% of Irish Catholics attended a religious service at least once a week in 1973, this figure was 62% in 1988 and 43% in 2008 (Nic Ghiolla Phádraig, 2009). In 1994 Davie (1994) argued that religion had been "privatized" in Ireland, and that as attendance at public Church services fell, private religious practices such as private prayer increased. However, the recent ISSP data show a marked decline in the frequency of personal prayer by Irish people, indicating a trend towards withdrawal from all formal religious behavior, not just from public practice (Nic Ghiolla Phádraig, 2009). Inglis (2007b, p. 68) suggests that Irish Catholics have become emotionally detached from the institutional Church, in an Ireland that has become increasingly secularized. He also argues that in becoming more detached from the institutional Church, and in developing their own relationship with God, Irish Catholics are in terms of their religiosity becoming more like Protestants (Hervieu-Léger, 2003; Inglis, 2007b). Inglis sees this as the individualization of Catholic Ireland. However, Nic Ghiolla Phádraig demonstrates that alongside a withdrawal from all religious behavior, Irish Catholics also report a decline in belief in God, particularly since 1998 (Nic Ghiolla Phádraig, 2009), a time when Ireland was rocked by sexual abuse scandals. However, other beliefs have remained constant and widespread, such as a belief in life after death (82%), heaven (87%), hell (58%), and religious miracles (71%).

What is interesting about modern Irish Catholicism is the percentage of self-declared Catholics who are atheist or agnostic or do not believe in a personal God (Nic Ghiolla Phádraig, 2009). One in six Catholics "belong but do not believe" (Nic Ghiolla Phádraig, 2009). Inglis refers to these Catholics as "cultural Catholics," Catholics who identify less with the institutional Church but strongly with their Catholic heritage and tradition. They do not see the Church as a spiritual or moral force in their lives, but "they have strong links to the chain of collective memory" (Hervieu-Léger, 2000; Inglis, 2007b, p. 81). Although levels of religious adherence and affiliation are still high in Ireland by international standards, material, legal, and cultural changes have ushered in a more secular society. Churches and religious organizations evoke less confidence than heretofore, and their scope and influence have diminished (Inglis, 2007b; Nic Ghiolla Phádraig, 2009). Despite this, there are areas of continuity, with beliefs regarding the afterlife and fidelity in marriage showing little change (Nic Ghiolla Phádraig, 2009). Inglis (2007b, p. 82) wonders if what is happening in Ireland can be explained as religion becoming less institutionalized, but that this does not mean that Irish Catholics are becoming less religious. Rather, they are finding alternative, more personal paths to meaning and transcendental experience than those provided by the institutional Church. For many Irish Catholics, being religious may not even involve a belief in God or the supernatural, as they find new ways and new rituals that can over time become sacred (Inglis, 2007b).

Because of Irish patterns of emigration, particularly since the time of the Famine (1845–1848), it was not unusual for Irish people to settle in the United States, Canada, and Australia. Irish Catholics are well represented in these countries. It did not go unnoticed, therefore, when revelations of child sexual abuse by clergy came to public attention in the United States, Canada, and Australia, that the Irish Christian Brothers were at the center of some of the abuse allegations, and many of the abusive clergy had Irish surnames (Sipe, 1998, p. 144). Sipe investigated the ethnic structure of the Catholic Church in the United States in the period 1960 to 1970, during which time most of the abuse by clergy had occurred, and discovered that while Irish Americans represented 17% of the population of the United States, 54% of priests were Irish American or Irish and 85% of the archbishops and 75% of the bishops were Irish American (p. 146). A number of questions on Irish Catholicism and abuse by Catholic clergy worldwide were beginning to be raised: (1) What actually is the rate of sexual abuse and sexual activity by priests in Ireland versus priests in the United States, Canada, and Australia? (2) How many sexually abusive priests in the United States, Canada, Australia, and elsewhere were born or educated in Ireland? (3) Is the proportion of known sexually abusive Irish-born or Irish-educated priests greater or less than their representation in the indigenous clergy pool in the United States, Canada, and Australia? (p. 147). These questions are important, and although Rigert (2008) has attempted to investigate the issues a little further, for the moment the dearth of international comparative studies on sexual abuse by Catholic clergy confines these questions to the realm of interesting speculation.

In conducting a study on Irish Catholic clergy who have sexually abused minors (which is reported in Chapters 7 and 8) and in reporting on the handling of abuse complaints by the Irish hierarchy (which is reported in Chapter 9) and in linking the two, my work offers the Irish situation as a possible exemplar of the situation involving sexual abuse within the Catholic Church worldwide, which puts flesh on the bones of certain aspects of the literature analysis. While the analysis of the Irish situation is important in its own right, and certain local conditions apply, the Irish situation may have particular resonances for other local Churches worldwide and indeed for other closed organizations. My work is therefore both local and international, in that local conditions are set against the background of an international perspective.

THE OUTLINE OF THE BOOK

The book is laid out in 10 chapters and a conclusion. The first three chapters deal mainly with "who and what" questions (Who are the main actors? What exactly is happening?). In Chapter 1 I introduce the reader to child sexual abuse and the Catholic Church and the scope or spread of the problem, including data relating to the extent of the problem and what we know about sexual abuse in other organizations. Chapter 2 focuses on the Roman Catholic Church as institution and reviews those institutional conditions that are presumed to have made sexual abuse by the Catholic Church and the response of the Catholic hierarchy possible. Chapter 3 describes what is considered to be "normal" clergy, based on the empirical literature, and it also critically reviews some of the empirical literature on clerical sexual offenders. The chapter proposes that sexual abuse of minors by Catholic clergy cannot be considered outside of the context of their lives as ministers of the Roman Catholic Church.

The next three chapters offer the reader a broad theoretical picture of how sexual offending can be accounted for in its individual, social, and gendered dimensions. Readers who may not have a background in the research on sexual offending and sexual socialization might find in these chapters some important concepts with which we can think about sexual abuse and sexual offending. Chapter 4 offers a critical examination of the key themes emerging from the psychological and psychiatric literature. It examines what happens when the individual is the focus of analysis. Chapter 5 considers the social constitution of social problems, including language and discourse, identity formation, and the problematic role of labeling and shame. This chapter also discusses the changing understanding of childhood and child sexual abuse. Chapter 6 offers a gendered perspective and raises some questions about how power is conceptualized in discussions relating to child sexual abuse.

Chapters 7 to 10 attempt to provide answers to "why" questions (why exactly is this happening? is there a meaning that we need to decipher?). In many ways these chapters form the core of my argument. Chapter 7 offers the first part of the thematic analysis of the accounts of clerical men who have sexually abused minors as they consider some of the factors that gave rise to their sexual violations. This chapter examines, in particular, the sexual dimensions of the men's offending. Chapter 8 explores the social, emotional, and institutional context of the men's offending, paying particular attention to rules, obedience, loneliness, power, and opportunity. Chapter 9 reviews the Church's handling of sexual abuse complaints. The issues are explored on a comparative basis. Ireland and the United States provide the primary context here, although for the purpose of comparison other jurisdictions, such as Canada, Australia, and some Continental European countries, will be considered, too. Chapter 10 provides a new way of conceptualizing the clerical offender and synthesizes the data from the previous chapters, developing a model for understanding sexual abuse in the Catholic Church and how it came to be. I first discuss issues that are pertinent to the clerical offenders and then extend the analysis to include the broader organizational and institutional perspective. In an attempt to understand the clerical offenders I focus on the paradoxes of clerical masculinity and explore why some clergy turn to children to satisfy their sexual and emotional needs, while other clerics who appear to have similar training and life conditions do not. The chapter draws upon a model for "doing" priesthood and clerical masculinity that emerges from the men's accounts, which is conceptualized as Perfect Celibate Clerical Masculinity. I see this version of clerical masculinity as a significant factor in sexual abuse and boundary violations by Catholic clergy. In an attempt to explain sexual abuse within the Catholic Church more broadly I develop a model that I call the multilevel relational and contextual framework; it comprises cognitive, organizational, and institutional features and involves a number of subject positions: the clerical perpetrator, the Church hierarchy, the institutional leadership, and the Catholic laity. According to this framework we are all in the responsibility and accountability dock for the individual and institutional hypocrisy that has allowed such cruel abuse of children to occur and to endure for so long.

The conclusion is an attempt to make sense of what has been discussed so far and contains the book's final theoretical reflections. In this chapter I also discuss the various prospects, visions, and agendas and the implications that my findings have in shaping future discussions and debates. The book finishes with some thoughts on the role of hope and repair.

PART ONE

Sexual Abuse, the Catholic Church, Clerical Men

A CRITICAL REVIEW

1

Child Sexual Abuse by Roman Catholic Clergy

THE SCALE AND HISTORY OF THE PROBLEM

MUCH HAS BEEN written on child sexual abuse by Roman Catholic clergy, and perhaps this is not surprising. The Catholic Church is one of the largest religious organizations in the world, representing approximately 20% of the six billion individuals on the planet (World Religious Statistics, 2006). Because of its size, age, and history, it is an influential force in many societies and in particular in the lives of its many believers. It is a powerful institution, with global reach and a 2,000-year history of some depth and complexity. The leadership of the Catholic Church comprises ordained men who have pledged themselves to celibate living. Women cannot be ordained to priesthood or to the leadership of this religious organization. It is therefore not surprising that disclosures of sexual abuse of children and young people by Roman Catholic clergy have sent shock waves through many communities, and that sexual abuse of minors by Roman Catholic clergy has become a significant international problem, receiving worldwide attention, particularly in the Anglophone world but by no means limited to it. While sexual abuse by Catholic clergy has been reported in many countries on all five continents, the countries that have received most attention include the United States, Canada, Australia, the United Kingdom, Ireland, and, most recently, Germany, Belgium, Austria, the Netherlands, France, Malta, Italy and Switzerland. If current patterns persist, disclosures of sexual abuse are likely to continue and to be the focus of international concern for some time to come.

While sexual abuse by Catholic clergy is clearly a significant problem for the Catholic Church, other churches and religions as well as other professional groups have also recorded similar problems, although not to the same extent. Church leaders in several churches and religions (Baptist, Episcopal, Jewish, Lutheran, Presbyterian, Mormons, Jehovah's Witnesses, Buddhist, Hare Krishna) have been accused or convicted of child sexual abuse (Francis & Turner, 1995, p. 218; Jenkins, 2003, p. 142; John Jay College, 2011, pp. 20-22; Plante, 2004, p. xx), and so have professionals in other front-line caring professions (Calvert, 1993; Gonsiorek, 1995; Hare-Mustin, 1993; John Jay College, 2011, pp. 16-19; White, 1993).

There is much anecdotal information concerning child sexual abuse by Catholic clergy, and it is a topic on which many people, not only Catholics, appear to have strong views, particularly in those countries where the problem is the focus of intense debate, such as Ireland and the United States. This is where I wish to begin. In this chapter I analyze the available data on what is known about the problem of sexual abuse within the Catholic Church. I also consider how the available data compare with data from other churches and religious groups, as well as with what we know about child sexual abuse by other "caring" professionals. While these issues are explored on a comparative basis, Ireland and the United States are used as the primary contexts, since most of the available quantitative data on sexual abuse by Catholic clergy emanate from these two countries. Other jurisdictions, such as Canada, Australia, the United Kingdom, and several in Europe, are referred to for comparative purposes.

INTERNATIONAL PREVALENCE OF CHILD SEXUAL ABUSE

It is difficult to estimate the extent of sexual abuse in a community and the extent of sexual offending in the general population, and it is equally difficult to estimate the extent of sexual offending by Roman Catholic clergy. There are many reasons for these problems. Some scholars work with incidence data, whereas others rely on prevalence, making comparisons difficult. (*Incidence* refers to the number of new cases of a particular event or behavior occurring over a particular period of time, usually 1 year, whereas *prevalence* refers to the proportion of a population that has experienced the event or behavior). Most estimates of sexual offenders are derived from forensic sources, and some studies acknowledge that those arrested or convicted represent only a fraction of all men, and the smaller number of women, who commit these abuses (Abel, Becker, Mittelman, Cunningham-Rathner, Rouleau, & Murphy, 1987, p. 89; Department of Justice, 1993, p. 11; O'Mahony, 1996, p. 210). There is not universal agreement on what constitutes a sexual offense in law, and each jurisdiction defines sexual offenses in diverse ways. This is dependent on having a sufficiently developed legal framework in which to conceive of the problem in legal and criminal terms in the first instance. The level of reporting can also be viewed as reflecting not only a community's awareness of the problem but also its willingness to accept the criminal and legal parameters of the issues involved. Information about incidents of abuse also varies in different jurisdictions, as cases proceed in distinct ways through the criminal and juvenile justice systems, social services, child and family services, and other such organizations. In addition, much sexual abuse isn't reported at all and some is reported beyond the statute of limitations and hence is not included in any assessment of incidence.

For all of these reasons it is difficult to provide reliable data on sexual offending in a given community or on the prevalence of the problem worldwide. However, some researchers have attempted to estimate the extent of sexual offending in the general adult male population, taking into account all of the above limitations (Hanson, 2010; Marshall, 1997). Rooting his analysis on the actual number of convicted sex offenders in the United States and the United Kingdom as a percentage of the adult males, which is 1% in California (Hanson) and 1% to 2% in the United Kingdom (Marshall), Hanson adjusted the figures based on the information already known about conviction rates per victim for child sexual offenders, (which is between 1 in 5 and 1 in 10), to suggest that the real rate of child sexual abuse perpetrated by the general adult male population is about 6%. Although this figure is helpful, it must be cautiously interpreted and may be useful as a guide rather than as yet verifiable fact.

Sometimes the extent of sexual offending in a community is deduced from the numbers of victims, but again this is difficult to estimate because sexual abuse of children is believed to be significantly underreported (McGee, 2002; O'Mahony, 1996; Russell, 1983). In addition the number of perpetrators can only be surmised from the available victim data, as some perpetrators have many victims and many perpetrators are never reported. Differences in values, customs, definitions, and methodologies also make it difficult to compare international and comparative studies (Finkelhor, 1994). However, a meta-analysis of a number of studies on victim prevalence in the United States is currently accepted as offering a good overall view of the available international data (Bolen & Scannapieco, 1999). The Bolen and Scannapieco study reports that the overall prevalence of boys who are sexually abused is 13% (approximately 1 in 7 boys) and the prevalence of girls who are sexually abused is 30% to 40% (1 out of 3 girls) (p. 281). In the Irish situation, McGee et al. (2002, p. xxxii) found that 1 in 5 women (20.4%) reported experiencing contact sexual abuse in childhood, with a further 1 in 10 (10%) reporting non-contact sexual abuse. One in 6 men (16.2%) reported experiencing contact sexual abuse in childhood, with a further 1 in 14 (7.4%) reporting non-contact sexual abuse (p. xxxiii). Overall, almost one third of women (30.3%) and a quarter of Irish men (23.6%) reported some level of sexual abuse in childhood in Ireland. Attempted or actual penetrative sex was experienced by 7.6% of girls and 4.2% of boys. The prevalence rate of sexual abuse for boys in Ireland is higher than for many other countries. Overall, the prevalence of sexual abuse in Ireland is staggering. These statistics also mask the extent of human suffering involved. While the data give clues to current trends, it remains the case that it is difficult to assess both the extent of the problem of child sexual abuse and the actual number of sexual offenders.

PREVALENCE OF CHILD SEXUAL ABUSE BY CATHOLIC CLERGY

Estimating the extent of the problem of sexual abuse by Roman Catholic clergy also raises particular difficulties, as information on perpetrators is not always available in general crime statistics, research reports, and service uptake figures, and the Catholic Church has traditionally been slow to release the relevant data (Berry, 1992, p. xi). It is not altogether clear how much or what data the Roman Catholic Church compiles on sexual offenses by clergy, and it is difficult to access data from that source. The Report by the Commission of Investigation into the Catholic Archdiocese of Dublin (hereafter referred to as the Murphy Report) (2009, p. 64) reported that in May 2001 the Vatican issued an instruction, entitled *Sacramentorum Sanctitatis Tutela,* which provided that all allegations of child sexual abuse against clergy that had reached the threshold of "a semblance of truth" were to be referred directly to the Congregation for the Doctrine of the Faith in Rome. Although the Murphy Report suggests that the policy was adopted "in order to ensure a co-ordinated and uniform response to allegations of child sexual abuse against clergy throughout the entire Roman Catholic Church" (p. 64), it would also have had the effect of gathering data on allegations of abuse from that time hence, had the policy endured. In the event, the Chancellor of the Archdiocese of Dublin informed the Dublin Commission that the policy was subsequently modified because "Rome was unable to deal with the vast number of referrals" (p. 64). The current policy, he told the Commission, was that all cases brought to the attention of the Archdiocese before April 2001, and which were outside prescription,[1] would not be dealt with by the Congregation for the Doctrine of the Faith; bishops would deal with these cases themselves. What this suggests in terms of data accumulation is that data gathered by the Congregation for the Doctrine of the Faith may be a significant underestimation.

In a remarkable departure from Vatican policy, on March 13, 2010, the Promoter of Justice for the Tribunal of the Congregation for the Doctrine of the Faith, Monsignor Charles J. Scicluna, published data from the Vatican on sexual abuse by clergy in the journal *Avvenire* (Thavis, 2010; The Tablet, March 20, 2010). He said that in a nine year period (2001–2010) the Congregation for the Doctrine of the Faith had discussed allegations concerning cases of about 3,000 diocesan and religious priests for crimes committed in the previous 50 years. He also revealed the breakdown of the cases handled. Roughly "60% of cases are acts of ephebophilia (that is, due to sexual attraction to adolescents of the same sex), in another 30%, heterosexual sex, and 10% of acts of paedophilia true and proper, that is, determined by the sexual attraction to prepubescent children," he said. In the case of pedophilia, that amounts to about 300 in 9 years, according to Monsignor Scicluna's figures. Of the 3,000 accused, 20% of cases had been subject to a criminal or administrative process; 60% had not been subject to a legal canonical process, mainly due to the advanced age of the accused, but administrative and disciplinary rules were applied, such as the obligation not to celebrate Mass, not to hear confession, and to lead a retired life of prayer.

At a consultation by a group of psychologists and psychiatrists at the Vatican in 2003, the results of which were published in a book (Hanson et al., 2004), Hanson encouraged the Congregation for the Doctrine of the Faith to gather data on every case of abuse by Catholic clergy worldwide, and to develop a suitable methodology for doing so, in order to enable more thorough research in the future. However, a reliable conclusion is that the data on child sexual abuse by Catholic clergy currently held within the Congregation for the Doctrine of the Faith or the Roman *Curia* (the papal bureaucracy of the Roman Catholic Church), is likely to be incomplete to date. It is not clear if the Conference of Bishops[2] in any country has yet developed a centralized databases on this topic either, as the structure of the Catholic Church is one in which each bishop has complete jurisdiction over his own diocese and is accountable only to Rome. However, in an important development the American Bishops' Conference commissioned a number of studies on the extent and scope of clergy abuse in the United States and on the causes and context of the problem and this research, although not without its acknowledged limitations, makes an important contribution (John Jay College, 2004, 2006, 2011). Returning to the global situation briefly, my conclusion is that the data on which to estimate the extent of sexual abuse by Catholic clergy are simply not available, and short of going to every diocese and religious order in the world for the relevant data, and they being willing to release their figures, the extent of the problem continues to be elusive. The need for rigorous quantitative studies cannot be made often enough, but this also applies to other faith communities and also to other caring professional groupings.

In the absence of official figures (apart from in the United States), the prevalence of sexual abuse within the Catholic Church has been estimated by social scientists in various jurisdictions (Fones et al., 1999; Greeley, 1993; Loftus & Camargo, 1993; McGee et al., 2002;

Sipe, 1995), by investigative journalists (*Boston Globe*, 2002; Goodstein, 2003; Quinn, 2005), by government-appointed committees (for example, Ferns Report, 2005; Office of the Attorney General, Commonwealth of Massachusetts, 2003; Report by the Commission of Investigation into the Catholic Archdiocese of Dublin, 2009; Report of the Commission to Inquire into Child Abuse, 2009), and by some victim websites that were established to keep track of abuse by Catholic clergy.[3] The results of these findings however should be cautiously interpreted, since small sample sizes make some of the studies hardly generalizable (Fones et al., 1999; Greeley, 1993) some studies are critiqued because they are based on clinical experience and not quantitative research methodologies (Sipe, 1995) and the websites track individual cases and may miss some of the emerging data. Nonetheless, for all their limitations and cautions, the overall numbers emerging from these varied and various sources begin to shed some light upon the evolving situation.

By far the most comprehensive study to date on the problem of child sexual abuse by Catholic clergy is the study commissioned by the U.S. Conference of Catholic Bishops (John Jay College, 2004) on the nature and scope of the problem of sexual abuse by Catholic clergy in the United States. When put together with the supplementary study, which analyzed some of the descriptive data (John Jay College, 2006), and the follow up study on the causes and context of the problem, which was released in 2011 (John Jay College, 2011), a wealth of information has been produced regarding sexual abuse by Catholic clergy and the responses of the Church hierarchy in the United States. However, while the studies of 2004 and 2006 make a significant contribution to our understanding of the extent of the problem in the United States, the methodological limitations suggest an underestimation, as 2% of diocesan priests and a large group of religious priests were not included, and the survey was based on records contained in files, which in some instances were incomplete. However, the John Jay studies provides the best data available to date.

Based on survey responses from 97% of Catholic dioceses (amounting to 195 dioceses in total) and 64% of religious communities (representing 83% of religious priests across the country), John Jay College (2004, p. 6–11) reported that allegations of child sexual abuse were made against 4% of the 109,694 priests in active ministry during the period 1950–2002. This amounted to 4,392 men. Allegations were made against approximately 4.3% of secular priests and 2.7% of priests of religious orders. However since the study was completed, many more Catholic priests or bishops in the United States have been named in relation to child sexual abuse allegations for the relevant period. Other studies and reports have estimated that between 2% and 8% of Catholic clergy in the United States have been involved in sexual abuse of minors (Goodstein, 2003; Greeley, 1993; Sipe, 1995).

Moving to Canada, a treatment center produced the second most comprehensive set of data on clerical sexual abuse (Camargo, 1997; Camargo & Loftus, 1992: Loftus & Camargo, 1993), and although these studies are old they are still referred to, as few other data exist on the Canadian situation. In a longitudinal study of clinical files from every male resident (n = 1,322) attending the treatment center for clergy from March 1966 to Feb. 28, 1991, 2.7% admitted to having sexual contact with children under the age of 13 and 8.4% of clergy attending this center admitted to some explicit genital activity with a person under the age of 19 years (Loftus & Camargo, 1993, p. 292). This study used 19 years as the age for victims, making accurate comparison difficult with most other studies which used 18 years as the cut off. In a follow-up study at the same treatment facility, but with a more expansive case-file review, 8.9% of the population was reported as having sexual contact with or having sexually abused people under the age of 19 years; 2.7% admitted to the sexual abuse of a child under the age of 13 years.

In Australia there has been no published statistical information similar to the John Jay study in the United States, and although I was told in 2007 that two studies were under way, one to develop a national database of Catholic clergy who have sexually abused minors and the second to compare abuse by Catholic clergy with similar groups of ministers within the Protestant tradition, I have been advised by the Secretary to the Australian Bishops' Conference that no study has been published. It is not clear whether the study was conducted in private and is not in the public domain or whether no studies have in fact been done. While the child protection offices for the Australian bishops publish the reports of sexual abuse against clergy and lay staff on an annual basis, it is nonetheless difficult to get the overall picture. Broken Rites Australia (2009), a support organization for victims of sexual abuse by clergy, reports 112 known cases where Catholic priests and religious have been sentenced in Australian courts for child sexual offenses.

It is also difficult in the African, European and Latin American context to get a comprehensive picture of the extent of the problem. Stories of sexual abuse by Catholic clergy continue to be reported, some in parishes, some in schools, and also through crime reports, but such singular cases or even groups of cases in schools or parishes do not amount to a clear or exact picture. Nonetheless, child sexual abuse by Catholic clergy has been reported in Argentina, Austria, Belgium, Brazil, Chile, China, Columbia, Czechoslovakia, France, Germany, Hong Kong, Ireland, Italy, Jamaica, Malawi, Malta, Mexico, the Netherlands, Nigeria, the Philippines, Poland, Scotland, South Africa, Spain, Switzerland, Tanzania and the United Kingdom, as well as Australia, New Zealand, Canada and the United States, (Associated Press, 2010, April 8, 2010; Frawley-O'Dea, 2007, pp. 165, 249–251; *New York Times*, March 24, 2010). In 2010 the Dutch bishops ordered an independent inquiry into more than 200 allegations of sexual abuse by Catholic priests and inquiries have also begun in Germany, Switzerland and Austria.

In Ireland, the Sexual Abuse and Violence in Ireland study (SAVI) (McGee et al., 2002, p. 88) estimated that of those who are now adults, and who had been abused as children, Roman Catholic clergy were the perpetrators in 3.9% of cases (5.8% of all male victims and 1.4% of all female victims). Data collated by an Irish journalist from a number of Catholic dioceses (Quinn, 2005, pp. 26, 27) estimated that 4% of all priests and religious in Ireland have been accused of abusing minors over a period of 50 years. The Ryan Report (2009), which studied all forms of abuse and neglect in Ireland's industrial and reformatory schools over a period of 40 years, named 800 abusers (religious and lay people) in 26 institutions. The Ferns Report (2005, p. 246) investigated over 100 complaints of child sexual abuse against 21 priests operating under the aegis of the Diocese of Ferns prior to April 2002. Ninety people alleging abuse attended oral hearings and a further 57 submitted written statements. The Murphy Report (2009, p. 2) received information about complaints, suspicions, or knowledge of child sexual abuse in respect to 172 named priests (and 11 unnamed priests, who may of course have been included in the 172 named priests) between 1975 and 2004. In the 46 of these cases that the Murphy Commission selected for more in-depth analysis, 320 children were reported as having been abused by these men.

In data available from the Dublin Archdiocese itself in March 2010 regarding sexual abuse complaints against clergy serving in the diocese from 1940 to 2009, the Archdiocese has on record allegations of abuse against 84 priests of the diocese, suspicions were raised concerning 9 priests of the diocese, allegations were made against 60 religious priests or priests from other dioceses who held an appointment in Dublin, allegations were made against 9 religious priests or priests from other dioceses who worked temporarily in Dublin, and suspicions were raised concerning 4 religious priests who held appointments in the diocese. These statistics date over a period of 69 years. Since 1940 over 1,350 diocesan priests served in Dublin and around 1,450 priests from religious congregations held appointments there. The number of priests who may have worked temporarily or what is sometimes known as doing supply work in Dublin in this period is unquantifiable but significant. The statistics constitute a record of allegations made and suspicions raised irrespective of the eventual outcome. They include allegations that have been substantiated, those that have not, and allegations that are false or mistaken. A conservative estimate suggests that 450 people are known or suspected to have suffered abuse by priests of the diocese. While these data are in themselves interesting, their complexity give some sense of the difficulties involved in gathering accurate data on the extent of the problem worldwide. However, a quantitative study of the extent of the problem nationally and internationally would significantly enhance scholarly work on the subject.

From the above analysis of the available international data it is evident that the full extent of the problem of sexual abuse of minors in general and by Roman Catholic clergy specifically is unknown, and further prevalence studies are required. The incomplete data that result from media investigations, victim accounts, social science studies, and victim websites are effectively all that are currently available. Nonetheless, these data give us a sense of the emerging picture, although the numbers are likely to reflect a serious underestimation of the problem.

CHILD SEXUAL ABUSE BY OTHER PROFESSIONALS

Questions are often raised as to whether the incidence of sexual abuse of minors is higher for Catholic clergy is than it is for leaders of other churches and faith communities and for other caring professionals, such as doctors, psychologists, social workers, childcare workers, and psychotherapists. While these are important questions, giving rise to many speculative answers, scholars are of the view that the paucity of empirical studies on these topics and on the various groups involved, means it is not possible to reliably and fully answer these questions.[4] The global reach and structure of the Catholic Church, with its centralized features, makes collating data in this organizational context much more possible than in other churches and faith communities, and in other professions. While the Congregation for the Doctrine of the Faith of the Catholic Church has the opportunity to gather data on abuse by Catholic clergy worldwide, no comparable centralized institution exists for other churches and faith traditions, or for other professional groups, making comparative work almost impossible. While sexual abuse of children has been reported against ministers of many churches and religions, and the Anglican Church in Australia has carried out an important study into child sexual abuse (Parkinson, Oates, & Jayakody, 2009; henceforth referred to as the Australia Study), researchers are mostly left wandering in the wilderness, trying to make meaning from the meager data that are available.

The study into sexual abuse by Anglican ministers and church volunteers and workers in Australia analyzed 191 alleged cases of child sexual abuse involving 135 accused persons (133 men and 2 women) in 17 dioceses across Australia between 1990 and 2008, representing not all but a significant number of abuse complaints against Anglican ministers in the relevant period[5] (Parkinson, Oates, & Jayakody, 2009, p. 16). Anglican clergy represented two thirds of the accused, with other church workers and volunteers representing the remaining group. One third of complaints on the files were not studied because they referred to sexual violations against adults over the age of 18 years.

In a discussion of sexual abuse in the Episcopalian Church, Richards (2007, p. 171), who served as a member of the senior staff of the Episcopalian Bishop of New York from 1995 until 2001, and who had responsibility for responding to clergy misconduct, reported that during her time in office, no case of child sexual abuse was reported to her, although she dealt with many complaints of sexual violations by priests against adults. Richards notes, however, that while she dealt with no case involving sexual abuse of a child, "there were numerous such cases in the Church at large during that time" (p. 171). Richards' experience leads her to suggest that there are fewer reported cases of child sexual abuse by priests in the Episcopalian Church than in the Catholic Church, although she says she cannot provide statistical evidence for this. Smith (2007, p. 196), a rector of an Episcopalian parish, reports that she has been involved in parishes where sexual misconduct occurred by two different female priests, but both cases involved sexual relationships with adult female parishioners. While these two cases are important, they clearly do not relate to sexual abuse of minors.

Ferguson (2007, p. 190), a Presbyterian pastor, suggests that "[c]ontrary to myth, Protestants also struggle with the trauma of clergy sexual abuse." In his 22 years in his presbytery, which covers several counties in New York State, Ferguson had been asked to serve on six subcommittees that have investigated six pastors accused of sexual violations against minors in his local Presbyterian jurisdiction. He had not been asked to serve on all investigative committees, so a full extent of the allegations is unclear. Reformation.com, a national movement for support of abuse survivors, catalogs newspaper articles about Protestant ministers alleged to have sexually abused children. As of July 2010, 838 ministers were listed on the website (Reformation.com, 2010).

In the United States, reports of sexual abuse within the Jewish community are also surfacing with increasing regularity and two survivors' organizations have been established (see The Awareness Center, Survivors for Justice and the Jewish Week, 2010). The Awareness Center lists 107 rabbis accused of sexual misconduct, 279 other trusted members of the Jewish community similarly accused as well as 85 unnamed perpetrators[6].

While psychologists, psychiatrists, social workers, childcare workers, teachers, voluntary workers with youth, sports coaches and psychotherapists have been accused of sexually violating children[7] and these issues are debated by their professional organizations, none of these bodies has as international a reach as the Catholic Church, and as such, direct comparisons are again difficult. In Germany, for instance, the health system is a matter of the individual 17 states of the country, and there is no national register on abuse by professionals. If a psychotherapist is accused of sexual abuse by a client, it is dealt with individually by the court. Usually it is not discussed as a matter of "all" psychotherapists, comparable to "the" Church, but as an individual failing of one person. The same is true for nurses in institutions for the handicapped, for sports teachers, and for men conducting groups with youths or adolescents.[8] There are no comparative data available on the extent to which sexual abuse of minors is perpetrated by Catholic clergy when compared to professionals in other organizations or leaders of other churches or faith communities and scholars[9] caution restraint in over interpreting the data that do exist.

After studying the available data, my sense of the emerging patterns is that sexual abuse of minors is more often reported against Catholic clergy than against other caring frontline professionals or against leaders and ministers of other churches and religions (but this must be regarded as a very tentative view). It also appears to me that sexual violations against adults, sometimes referred to as sexual misconduct or professional boundary violations, are reported against Catholic clergy, just as they are against other professionals and leaders of other churches and faith communities. It is not possible to offer a comparative analysis of sexual violations against adults by Catholic clergy or other professionals as again the dearth of data hinders such an analysis. For the moment, sexual abuse of minors appears to be the predominant focus of international concern and of current scholarship.

Although priests are a highly selected, often highly educated, highly trained group of men, there is in fact no evidence that child sexual abuse is less prevalent in the educated or highly educated male population. In fact, some might argue that highly educated men might be more able to hide abuses, and that it may even be more prevalent in this group of men. Some might even argue that the available data on child sexual abuse provide good support for the argument that the extent of sexual abuse of minors by Roman Catholic clergy is no greater than in the general male population. Hanson (2010), one of the leading researchers on sexual offending in the world, summarizes these rates as being as "in the same range," taking into account that detection rates for abuse by Catholic clergy would be higher (certainly in recent years) than the conviction rate but lower than the real rate, since priests, in the United States and Ireland, may still not have been reported and many have not been convicted (for a variety of reasons, including the statute of limitation in the United States). This of course is also true for non-clerical perpetrators, many of whom as we know, are not reported. Based on this evidence, one might be inclined to argue there is no special case to be answered, or even understood, in relation to sexual abuse by Catholic clergy.

Although these are important considerations, my contention is that sexual abuse by Catholic clergy is a subject that requires further research and understanding because Catholic clergy are distinguished from other men in a number of aspects. Roman Catholic clergy form a homogeneous group, which is restricted to males who are similarly educated, subjected to one authority, professing one belief, vowing obedience to one supreme head, and professing perfect and perpetual celibacy. As moral leaders and official representatives of Jesus Christ, Catholic clergy hold particular power in the lives of the Catholic faithful. It is therefore incumbent on any organization especially a highly gendered one, that has been plagued by enduring abuses of power and sexual exploitation to review itself and analyze its culture in order to understand the specific features of its own institution and culture that may be contributing to the abuse problem. This is particularly so for an organization that purports to work for and on behalf of "an all-loving God." All experts acknowledge that sexual activity with minors is common in all countries, cultures, and social strata; however, the unique features of Catholic clergy and the Catholic Church make it a significant group and organization to study in order to observe the dynamic occurrence of this problem.

FEATURES OF CHILD SEXUAL ABUSE BY ROMAN CATHOLIC CLERGY

Back in the United States, the John Jay study (2004, pp. 6–11) found that 81% of the victims of Catholic clergy were male and 19% were female. Male victims tended to be older than females. Over 40% of all victims were males between the ages of 11 and 14. Approximately 78% of the victims (male and females) were between the age of 11 and 17, 16% were between 8 and 10, and 6% were younger than 7. However, an important finding is that some men abused both males and females, although there were more male than female victims in all offender categories (those with one, two or three, four to nine, and over ten victims). Other studies and reports on sexual abuse by Catholic clergy also report this significant trend that the majority of cases involving child sexual abuse by Catholic clergy usually concerns post-pubertal males (*Boston Globe*, 2002, p. 167; Haywood, Kravitz, Grossman, Wasyliw, & Hardy, 1996, p. 530; Murphy Report, 2009, p. 3; Rossetti & Lothstein, 1990, p. 14). In relation to the Archdiocese of Dublin, the Murphy Report (2009) recorded a ratio of two or three boys to one girl who experienced sexual abuse by Catholic clergy. In my own study, which is discussed in Chapters 7 to 10 (with data pertinent to the participants given in the Appendix), eight of the nine participants sexually abused postpubertal males, while one man sexually abused younger boys ages 10 to 14. There was one allegation of abuse of a postpubertal female against one of the nine men. Unlike the patterns of abuse in the general population, this trend was also noted in the Australian Study (Parkinson, Oates, & Jayakody, 2009, p. 5). Of the 191 alleged cases that were reported to the 17 Anglican dioceses throughout Australia, three quarters of the complainants were male and most were 10 to 15 years old at the time of the abuse.

Cozzens (2000, pp. 72–80) points to the age aspect of the choice of victim and believes it indicates a level of psychosexual immaturity on the part of the clerical perpetrators, who are thought to feel more comfortable sexually and emotionally with adolescent males. Other scholars link it to priestly celibacy and to a pattern of arrested psychosexual development of young men who are on their way towards a celibate vocation (Frawley-O'Dea, 2004; Sipe, 1995). Frawley-O'Dea (2004, pp. 129–130) thinks that several aspects of priestly formation combine "to infantilize many priests and to keep them eternal boys intellectually, sexually and relationally." Lothstein (2004) suggests there are different patterns of abuse by Catholic clergy, and he links it to different personality types. Berlin and Krout (1986) see biogenetic factors as significant and suggest a theory that the object of sexual attraction is genetically determined.

Some scholars focus on the gender aspect of victim selection, and again there are a number of suggestions as to why Catholic clergy predominantly abuse boys. Based on their clinical and research experience with clerical perpetrators, Rossetti and Lothstein (1990, p. 12) suggest that some priests believe that having sexual relations with teenage boys does not amount to a breach of their celibate vocation, and this understanding is related to how celibacy is perceived by them. They also found that priests who have abused children admitted to growing up believing that they must stay away from girls, and that sexual desire concerning women was perceived as wrong and sinful (p. 13). For the clerical offender, sex with women was perceived as the ultimate sin and a fundamental threat to a celibate vocation. Such priests were said to believe that sex with a woman could challenge the entire vocation and priestly existence. Priests who sexually abused adolescent males were not thought to believe the same negative messages about sex with boys, although adult-to-adult male sexual activity was also seen as problematic. Although sex with a boy was wrong and sinful it was seen as the lesser sin and in the past at least, the priest did not feel it would threaten his entire vocation and priestly existence. For Rossetti and Lothstein (1990, p. 12), while this rationalization is an example of how clerical perpetrators may defend themselves against a painful truth, it also suggests a kind of thinking that was fostered from an early age. Terry (2008) suggests that victim selection is a question of access. She argues that Catholic clergy have the most unrestricted access to males. In the past, at least, the opportunities for Catholic clergy to be alone with younger boys were frequent, through their work with altar-servers, in Catholic schools, and through their sacramental ministries. However, while opportunity is clearly important, on its own it is unable to explain why some clergy abuse minors and others do not.

The pattern of victim selection often raises questions in relation to sexual orientation of Catholic clergy. Is the sexual abuse of minors by Catholic clergy the result of the ordination of men of a homosexual orientation? Is homosexuality *per se* responsible for the sexual abuse of minors by Roman Catholic clergy? At once this is a simple and a complex issue. There is no evidence that sexual identity and sexually abusive behavior have the same origins. When Tallon and Terry (2008, p. 615) closely examined the data gathered on clergy offenders in the United States, they found that where priests had multiple victims, fewer than half of them had abused victims of the same gender and age. The majority of the 4,392 priests with allegations of sexual abuse had one allegation made against them (56%) (n = 2,411) (John Jay College, 2004). However, of those with multiple victims for which the files contained full details of the victims' ages and gender (n = 1,548), 693 men had abused minors of the same age and/or gender and 855 had abused minors of a different gender and/or age (Tallon & Terry, 2008, p. 615). This pattern is further reported in the John Jay College Study (2011, pp. 54-74). In my own study, the one priest who had abused an adolescent girl as well as adolescent boys was clearer than many of the other men that his sexual orientation was homosexual. Thus, while the majority of priests and religious have abused adolescent boys, the picture is not a simple linear construction. In one large sample of men who had sexually abused adolescents in the United States (n = 505) a significant number also acknowledged sexually abusing prepubertal boys or girls (Abel, 2000, cited in Kafka, 2004, p. 53). Thus, the combination of data that are now emerging clearly points to the fact that that sexual orientation has little or no bearing on sexual abuse of children or on victim selection.

There is no evidence to suggest that sexual orientation is involved in the sexual abuse of minors—heterosexuality, homosexuality, or what is regarded as pedophilia or ephebophilia. Sexual abuse of minors has in fact little to do with sexual orientation. Adult heterosexuality is still the predominant sexual orientation of men who sexually abuse prepubescent boys and girls (Jenny, Roesler, & Poyer, 1994; Langevin, 2000, p. 537), and adult men who sexually abuse adolescent boys are more likely to be men of a homosexual orientation. However, to conclude that men who sexually abuse boys do so because of their homosexual orientation is to obscure the facts, in the same way that it is meaningless to suggest that heterosexual men abuse girls because they are heterosexual in orientation.

Other data that are significant in relation to sexual abuse of minors by Catholic clergy suggest that the largest number of priests (40%) began abusing when they were between the ages of 30 and 39 years, on average after 11 years in ministry (John Jay College, 2011, p. 9; Terry, 2008, p. 560). The age of the perpetrators ranged from mid 20s to 90 at the time they first abused. The men in my study began abusing when they were somewhat younger, but towards their late 20s, and usually within the first 5 to 10 years of ministry. The emerging profile from both studies is therefore not one of pedophilia, a paraphilia that is thought to develop earlier than in the middle to late 20s (see Chapter 4 for a fuller discussion of pedophilia). The John Jay College team (John Jay, 2004, 2006, 2011) worked hard to discern the evidence of paraphilia in the data they studied and concluded that most of the priests who had allegations of abuse made against them were not pedophiles. Tallon and Terry (2008, p. 625) suggest that because the clerical perpetrators did not abuse until their late 20s or 30s, and many of them did not abuse a child for a long time after they had unrestricted access to children, and because many of them did not target only one age group or gender of victim, whatever else is happening, it is not likely that most clerical abuse of children is driven by sexually arousing fantasies about prepubescent children or adolescents. Something other than pedophilia is propelling sexual abuse by clergy. Even those men who initiated sexual abuse soon after ordination and whose abusive pattern spanned a long duration did not meet the classification of pedophilia. The John Jay College team (2004, 2011) concluded that the data did not support the finding that most of these acts of child sexual abuse were predicated by pathology or paraphilic behavior such as pedophilia (Smith et al., 2008, p. 580; Tallon & Terry, 2008, p. 625; Terry, 2008, p. 567). This finding concurs with my research and clinical experience. In my research one man sexually abused or attempted to abuse male seminarians as well as adolescent boys, and three men admitted to engaging in "consenting" sexual relationships with adult men during the course of their priesthoods.

Just as homosexuality is not "the" cause of sexual abuse by Catholic clergy, neither is pedophilia. A problem occurs only if and when the power differential between a child and an adult person are exploited by the adult, regardless of sexual orientation. We know that some adults who abuse children are heterosexual in orientation, some are homosexual in orientation, and others would fit the definition of pedophilic. There is no evidence to suggest that those who are pedophilic in orientation are more likely to abuse children than other men, but there is evidence to suggest that men of a heterosexual orientation are the most likely to sexually abuse children.

The majority of accused priests in the United States (55.7%) had one formal allegation of abuse made against them, 26.4% had two or three allegations, 17.8% had four to nine allegations, and 3.5% had ten or more allegations. "Allegations" in this instance refers to individual victims, and there were in many cases several offenses perpetrated against the same victim. Men with one allegation made against them were more likely than those with further allegations to have abused a girl rather than a boy, and to have a victim in the 15- to 17-year-old age range (Terry, 2008, p. 560). The men in my research had on average 15 to 20 victims. In the Australian Study of abuse within the Anglican Church (2009, p. 21) 80% of the accused had one complaint made against them. The remaining 20% were accused of 43% of all complaints made. Interestingly, it may be the case that case files underestimate the number of victims, as they clearly record only those victims who make complaints, whereas the men in my research on qualitative interviews admitted to abusing a higher number of children or young people. It could also be the case, of course, that men who ended up in treatment programs were more likely to have had the highest number of victims and the longest period of abusing minors.

In the John Jay study (2004) the duration of abusive behavior was calculated by using the date of the first incident of abuse and the date of the most recent reported incident. Although these figures did not necessarily represent continuous abusive activity, the data calculated in this manner suggested that 31% of priests abused minors for less than 1 year overall (Terry, 2008, p. 562). These data were reasonably stable during the period of more than 50 years (1950–2004) (Terry, 2008, p. 562). Eight of the nine men in my research admitted to abusing minors for a period that spanned up to 20 years. Three of these men were in long-term abusive "relationships" with the boys they abused, in which the abuse occurred over a period of up to 3 years. However, these patterns were not uniform. In some cases the pattern of abuse was opportunistic in nature; in others it was more planned and occurred on a number of occasions. In the Australian Study (2009, pp. 24, 25) of Anglican priests accused of sexual abuse, complaints of long-term abusive relationships were not uncommon. Almost 35% of men accused of abuse were accused of being in an abusive "relationship" with the complainant for 3 to 5 years, and 5% were in abusive "relationships" for more than 5 years. However, overall, church workers were accused of abuse of minors to whom they had immediate and convenient access.

In the John Jay study (2004, pp. 6–11) priests ordained in the early 1970s were more likely to have been accused of sexual abuse of a minor than priests ordained in any other period. Approximately 10% of priests ordained from 1970 to 1975 had allegations of abuse made against them, with a significant decline thereafter (p. 565). With the exception of one man, all of the participants in my research were ordained in the late 1960s or early 1970s. Overall the John Jay data show a steady rise in the incidence of abuse between the 1950s and the 1980s in the United States and a sharp decline by 1990. Nearly 40% of the accused priests participated in some form of psychological treatment, broadly in line with that offered to Anglican priests accused of abuse in Australia (Parkinson, Oates, & Jayakody, 2009).

While the data presented in this chapter are included to provide a context for the central thesis of this book, that child sexual abuse by Catholic clergy must be considered in the context of the overall context of the organization of the Catholic Church and not as a problem of "flawed individuals," these statistics are recognized as incomplete by the authors, and for this reason they must be cautiously interpreted (John Jay College, 2004, 2006; Parkinson, Oates, & Jayakody, 2009). Statistics tell only part of a story, and it can happen that inferences are drawn, based on very weak data, to present neat answers to very complex problems. This is certainly not my intention. At the same time, statistics of the kind presented above represent the best that are available in current times, and as such, used in the spirit of caution, they suggest some tentative shape to the problem of sexual abuse by clergy within the Catholic Church.

STUDY INTO THE CAUSES AND CONTEXT OF CLERICAL SEXUAL ABUSE OF MINORS IN THE UNITED STATES

As well as seeking to understand the extent of the problem, researchers from the John Jay College of Criminal Justice were commissioned by the U.S. Conference of Catholic Bishops to undertake research on the causes and context of the sexual abuse crisis in the Catholic Church in the United States to supplement the original research undertaken by the John Jay College (2004, 2006) on the nature and scope of the problem (U.S. Conference of Catholic Bishops, 2007). The American bishops called for this Causes and Context study as part of their response to the sexual abuse crisis when they adopted the *Charter for the Protection of Children and Young People* in 2002. The causes and context research attempts to explain the rise in incidence of sexual abuse by Catholic priests in the late 1960s and 1970s in the United States and its subsequent decline after 1985. The study sets the incidence data on sexual abuse of minors by Catholic priests in the United States from the 1960s through to 2002 within an overall sociological framework of social change.

The study involved gathering and analyzing archival research and collecting data from priests, psychologists, sociologists, and the U.S. bishops, including data from seminaries, dioceses, and treatment centers (John Jay College, 2011). The final report was launched in May 2011. Overall, the study found that data on cases of abuse reported after 2002 showed the same pattern of incidence as that found nationally in the earlier works: the data indicated a rise in sexual abuse by Catholic clergy in the 1960s in the United States and a decline in the 1980s that has continued until today. There is no evidence to suggest that unreported cases will be brought forward that change the overall timeframe or pattern of the problem. Other findings suggest there is no single cause of the sexual abuse "crisis", that individual level characteristics of priests do not predict subsequent abuse, that priest abusers do not differ psychologically from non abusive clergy, but that they have experienced higher levels of childhood sexual abuse themselves. The study confirms the earlier work that most priests who had allegations of abuse are not pedophiles and that homosexuality is not the cause of sexual abuse by priests. The John Jay College team rather thought that situational factors and opportunity to abuse played a more significant role in the onset and continuation of abusive acts. A significant finding of the Causes and Context study is the fact that clergy who as seminarians had explicit human formation preparation during their years of training for priesthood seem to have been less likely to abuse than those without such preparation. This is a finding that has implications for the Catholic Church and that is in line with my qualitative research analysis and clinical experience, both of which will be discussed later.

The Causes and Context study (John Jay College, 2011) also suggests that the pattern of deviant sexual behavior by Catholic clergy is consistent with several other behavioral changes in American society between the 1960s and the 1990s, including the use of drugs and an increase in divorce and criminal behavior. This is a finding that has already proven to be quite controversial. Finally, the John Jay researchers report that the diocesan responses to charges of sexual abuse by Catholic clerics have changed substantially over a 50-year period, with a decrease in reinstatement and more administrative leave being given to clerical offenders in recent years. The response of the Church hierarchy to the handling of abuse complaints over the relevant period, which was to privilege the priest over the victim, is seen as having contributed significantly to the problems.

While welcomed as an important study, the Causes and Context research (John Jay College, 2011) has also met with criticism since its release. The principle criticisms refers to the lack of knowledge on the part of the research team of the internal workings of the Church hierarchy or of the dynamics of the Catholic Church and the report's failure to include the substance and conclusions of Grand Jury reports and to take account of the structure, pattern and practice of Church response revealed in criminal and civil cases (Fox, 2011). The conclusion that priests' behavior was influenced by and reflected turmoil in American culture during the 1960s and 1970s is also called into question, or at least qualified given the revelations of similar widespread scandals in the United Kingdom and several European countries (Roberts, 2011). Dominican Fr. Thomas Doyle, who has long advocated for victims of clergy abuse and currently consults with plaintiffs' attorneys internationally, said he thinks the report is missing important data about the increased number of cases of abuse that are said to have occurred before the 1960s. (Doyle cited in Roberts, 2011). Despite its limitations this study is important because it outlines many of the Catholic church's problems with human sexuality as they impact its clergy and it points to areas where further research needs to be undertaken.

THE WAVE OF REVELATIONS OF SEXUAL ABUSE BY ROMAN CATHOLIC CLERGY IN THE UNITED STATES, CANADA, AUSTRALIA, AND EUROPE

The recent wave of sexual abuse complaints against clergy can be seen as beginning in Louisiana with the case of Father Gilbert Gauthe (*Boston Globe*, 2002, p. 37). Gauthe was suspected of molesting up to 100 boys in four parishes in which he worked over a period of 20 years, especially during his years of ministry in Louisiana (1978–1983). During 1984, several parents brought civil charges against the diocese over Gauthe's activities, and later in the same year criminal charges were filed (*Boston Globe*, 2002, p. 39). Gauthe was sentenced to 20 years in prison, and the family of one of his victims, who refused to settle out of court, was awarded damages of $1.25 million. The case received publicity across the United States and resulted in a book concerning the affair (Berry, 1992). The floodgates opened in the English-speaking Catholic world, and in the avalanche that followed the publicity surrounding the Gauthe affair, child sexual abuse by clergy came onto the public agenda. Revelations of sexual abuse by priests came primarily from adults who had been sexually abused as children and who now sought civil claims and criminal charges against their offenders. Some adults in various jurisdictions who had been sexually abused as children also wrote books on the subject, revealing the accounts of their suffering (Doyle, 2002; Fahy, 1999; Madden, 2003, O'Gorman, 2010). Revelations of sexual abuse by clergy also came from investigative reporting by national and international reporters (Berry, 1992; *Boston Globe*, 2002; Moore, 1995), resulting in numerous articles and news reports on the subject of child sexual abuse by Roman Catholic clergy in the past 20 years.

The extent of the revelations of sexual abuse by clergy evoked deep concern in some Catholic observers in the United States, and in 1985 a confidential report entitled *The Problem of Sexual Molestation by Roman Catholic Clergy: Meeting the Problem in a Comprehensive and Responsible Manner* (Mouton, Doyle, & Peterson, 1985) was submitted to the American Catholic hierarchy. The authors were Gauthe's solicitor, F. R. Mouton, and two priests: T. P. Doyle, a canon lawyer attached to the Apostolic Nuncio in Washington D.C., and M. Peterson, the founder of St. Luke's Institute, Maryland, an institute that offered a therapy program for sexually troubled priests. The authors urged Catholic leaders to take strong and effective action to deal with the impending crisis, in view of the escalating scandal and the multimillion-dollar legal actions to which these problems could give rise. Each bishop received a copy of the report, and the U.S. National Conference of Catholic

Bishops discussed the issue in secret sessions at one of its gatherings (Balboni, 1998). However, after these private discussions, the bishops limited themselves to a commitment to combat child abuse on an individual basis wherever it arose (Balboni, 1998). In essence, any suggestion of a national response by the American bishops, or wider, a worldwide Church investigation and response to the child abuse problem, ran against the essential structure of the Catholic Church, in which each bishop is autonomous in his diocese and responsible only to the pope in Rome.

Doyle spoke publicly at a meeting of the Canon Law Society of America in 1986, about the grave prognosis that he and his colleagues predicted suggesting that child sexual abuse by clergy was the most serious issue that the Catholic Church had faced in centuries (Coldrey, 2000, p. 7). In Coldrey's (2000, p. 7) opinion, Doyle's public pronouncements offended many bishops. Doyle's career at the Vatican diplomatic mission came to an end. Following some time working as a U.S. Air Force chaplain in Germany, Doyle became an advocate for victims of clergy abuse and has given expert testimony in numerous cases involving sexual abuse by clergy ever since (Doyle, Sipe, & Wall, 2006).

The Canadian story of sexual abuse by clergy broke first in Newfoundland in 1988, with criminal prosecutions for repeated abuses on minors perpetrated by two parish priests (Allen, 1989, p. 66). Over time, other priests were implicated in the sexual abuse of minors until almost 10% of diocesan clergy had allegations made against them; some of them were arrested, tried, and convicted. In 1989 attention shifted to the Irish Christian Brothers Congregation in Mount Cashel boys' home in St. John's. This time the allegations concerned physical and sexual abuse against teenage boys who had been in their care (Bartlett, 1989, p. 46; Harris, 1990).

The sexual abuse crisis in Australia was influenced by events in the United States but commenced with the controversy over child migration and the claims of widespread abuses committed against children housed in Western Australian Catholic orphanages after World War II (Coldrey, 2000, p. 12). The focus was on Catholic institutions managed by religious brothers. This time the object of attention was St. Joseph's Farm School in Bindoon, Western Australia. However, it was only in 1989 that the issue of sexual abuse by clergy really came to the focus of the Australian public, with the showing of a television documentary based on Bean and Melville's 1989 book *Lost Children of the Empire* (Coldrey, 2000, p. 13). Similar to the situation in the United States, the United Kingdom, and Ireland, television documentaries were to contribute to the growing awareness of the problem in Australia. Further books were released on the subject of child migration and the Australian orphanage history, which added to the growing public concern (Coldrey, 2000, p. 13). The consistent allegations of widespread physical and sexual abuse by some staff at respected Church and charitable institutions raised the hitherto dormant issue before the public and made further allegations likely from other areas of the Church's ministry, which is exactly what happened (Coldrey, 2000, p. 13).

It is notable in the literature on child sexual abuse by clergy that much of the information about abuse comes from industrialized countries, where legal remedies are more readily available and where the concept of the child has developed to one that includes the idea of vulnerability and the need for child protection (Corby, 2000, p. 12). In non-industrialized societies, where child welfare and child protection policies are not so defined, child sexual abuse is not on the public agenda. To date, child sexual abuse by Catholic clergy has emerged almost exclusively in First World nations, and yet it is highly likely that the both the abuse itself and the same response of the Church hierarchy have occurred in developing countries too. In situations where there is disparity of power between the clergy and the laity, with more economic dependence of the laity on Church officials, less active journalism, and less well-established law enforcement and legal frameworks, as is the case in some developing countries, it is reasonable to speculate that we do not know what is happening in relation to sexual abuse by anybody, including Catholic clergy.

REVELATIONS OF SEXUAL ABUSE BY CLERGY IN IRELAND

While the Irish public was aware of serious individual child sexual abuse cases during the early 1990s, such as the X[10] case (Coughlan, 1992, p. 1; Cusack, 1992, p. 2), the Kilkenny incest case (McGuinness, 1993; O'Halloran, 1994, p. 6; O'Moráin, 1994, p. 12), and the West of Ireland Farmer case in 1995, widespread public awareness of child sexual abuse by clergy in Ireland began only with the media coverage of the case of Father Brendan Smyth in 1994, in particular with the airing of the television documentary *Suffer Little Children* (Agnew, 1994, p. 3; Ferguson, 1994, p. 12; Moore, 1995; O'Toole, 1994, p. 5; Pollak, 1994, p. 11). While many of the earlier cases demonstrated that child sexual abuse takes place within the family, it was not until the Smyth case that Irish society was awakened to the phenomenon of sexual abuse by third parties who are in a position of trust and authority over them. In 1994, Smyth pleaded guilty to 74 charges of indecent and sexual assault and was sentenced to 12 years in prison. This case became especially significant when it emerged that the State had failed to extradite Smyth from the Republic of Ireland to answer similar sex abuse charges in Northern Ireland. This resulted in the resignation of the then Taoiseach, the leader of the Irish Parliament, Albert Reynolds, and the President of the High Court, Harry Whelehan, who had been attorney general at the time (McGarry, 1994, p. 2; Moore, 1995). These events concluded with the collapse of the Irish Government. The case helped to focus attention on various aspects of child abuse, and it also drew attention to the relationship between the Catholic Church and the Irish State. It was argued that the Catholic Church was afforded protection by the State when one of the Church representatives was accused of serious crime (Agnew, 1994, p. 3; O' Toole, 1994a, p. 5; Pollak, 1994, p. 11). This case opened the floodgates: case after case of abusing priests who had held positions in orphanages, parishes, and educational establishments began to emerge. Cases of abuses by third parties in other organizations followed too, mainly in sporting organizations that dealt with young people. After a number of allegations were received by authorities regarding the behavior of two swimming coaches in the Leinster region, an inquiry headed by a senior barrister, now a High Court judge, was conducted into how these allegations were handled by the swimming authorities. The Roderick Murphy Inquiry (1998) is the only other inquiry in Ireland that dealt with the issues of child sexual abuse outside of the family or outside of the Church context.

The case of Father Brendan Smyth came at a time when the Irish Catholic priesthood was already beginning to be seriously questioned, particularly after a string of revelations of sexual impropriety on the part of clergy. First, in the early 1990s it emerged that Bishop Eamonn Casey, Bishop of Galway, was the father of a 19-year-old boy, living in the United States with his mother, Annie Murphy (Carroll, 1992, p. 3; Kennedy, 1992, p. 1). The news was followed by more headlines reporting the death of a priest of the Dublin Diocese in a gay sauna in Dublin (O'Toole, 1994b, p. 6; Toibín, 1995, p. 45). Then came the revelation that Father Cleary, a media personality and a radio talk show host, was alleged to have lived as a couple with his housekeeper and to have fathered a child with her (MacCartaigh, 1995, p. 7; Smyth, 1995). This led to a situation where clerical celibacy and the power of the Roman Catholic Church in Ireland were being continuously discussed in public (Brown, 1995, p. 14; Sheridan, 1995, p. 7).

A series of television documentaries (*Dear Daughter*, 1996; *States of Fear*, 1999; *Suing the Pope*, 2002; *Cardinal Secrets*, 2002) drew further attention to abuse of children by Catholic clergy and to the abuse of children in institutions run by religious orders on behalf of the State and added to the growing public concern. Just as in the United States, Australia, and the United Kingdom, television documentaries played a large part in "breaking the silence" (Inglis, 1998, p. 92). Alongside these television documentaries, accounts of abuse by clergy, written by journalists and as already mentioned by adult victims, began to appear in print, and the Church's handling of abuse disclosures came in for critique and analysis (*Boston Globe*, 2002; Fahy, 1999; Madden, 2003; Moore, 1995; Raftery & O'Sullivan, 1999). The Irish Government responded to the series of television documentaries by offering a public apology to those who had experienced abuse in the institutions run by religious orders on behalf of the State and made funds available for a national counseling service. It also established a number of initiatives: the Commission to Inquire into Child Abuse under the *Commission to Inquire into Child Abuse Act* (2000) and the *Commission to Inquire into Child Abuse (Amendment) Act* (2005) to investigate the complaints and listen to personal testimonies of those abused; the Residential Institutions Redress Board under the *Residential Institutions Redress Act* (2002) to offer monetary compensation to people who had suffered abuse in the residential institutions for children; an inquiry into the management of clergy sexual abuse cases in the Ferns Diocese (Ferns Report, 2005); the Commission of Investigation into the handling of abuse complaints in the Archdiocese of Dublin (2006) under the new *Commissions of Investigation Act* (2004); and the Commission of Investigation into the handling of abuse complaints in the Diocese of Cloyne. I will return to these initiatives in Chapter 9 when I discuss the Church's responses to sexual abuse by Catholic clergy.

Taken together (the revelations in the television documentaries and the subsequent reporting of the issue of sexual abuse by clergy), an image was created of the Roman Catholic Church as punitive and the State as opting out of the welfare and protection of children (Ferguson, 2000, p. 27). Clerical celibacy and the power of the Catholic Church in Ireland would now be on the public agenda and the relationship between the Roman Catholic Church and the Irish State would undergo significant review (Inglis, 1998, p. 204). Sipe (1998, p. 144) regards the clergy abuse situation in Ireland as unique because of the dominant power position of the Roman Catholic Church in Ireland. The close relationship between the Irish Church and State, which had a long history connected to the country's emancipation from Britain, meant that the bishops and church hierarchy had considerable influence on the Irish political process (Whyte, 1980). As a monocultural society rendering Ireland "the most Catholic country in the world" (Blanchard, 1954, p. 17), the Roman Catholic Church was considered the ultimate arbiter of morality in Ireland (Inglis, 1998). At the same time the relationship between Church and State was not a simple one of domination by the Catholic Church, nor can it be said that all the problems of Irish sexuality should be laid at the door of the Catholic Church (Ferriter, 2009). These relationships are much more complex than an initial reading might suggest. Nonetheless, the clergy abuse situation in Ireland has had profound implications for Irish society, which is partly why Ireland acts as a useful case study for an in-depth analysis of sexual abuse within the Catholic Church.

THE ROMAN CATHOLIC CHURCH AND CHILD SEXUAL ABUSE, NEW PROBLEM OR OLD

Some contemporary writers (Burkett & Bruni, 1993, p. 8) argue that early Church history shows a persistent fear on the part of the Church authorities of sexual contact between men and boys. The growth of Christianity led to the condemnation of pederasty in ancient Rome, and the condemnation of pederasty, incest, bestiality, and homosexual practices was to be a common feature of the regulative documents of the early medieval Church (Payer, 1982, p. 10). The earliest Church council for which there are records (Elvira in 309 AD) has 81 canons, of which 38 deal with sex (Laeuchli, 1972, p. 47). Among those who were threatened with irrevocable exclusion were "Bishops, presbyters and deacons committing a sexual sin" (Canon 18) and "those who sexually abuse boys" (Canon 71) (Laeuchli, 1972, p. 47). According to Payer (1982, p. 11), historians also recognize that during the 10th and 11th centuries, "clerical sexual immorality" became a central problem. Boswell (1990, p. 362) interpreted the writings of St. Basil, a Benedictine monk, to suggest that the writings of St. Basil showed great concern for the sexual attraction of the adult monks towards their young pupils, and he imposed strict penalties on the monks for any bad treatment of children in the monasteries.

According to Boswell (1990, p. 428), in the early Middle Ages, when abandonment of children was one of the methods used throughout Europe by poor families to control family size, the monasteries provided havens for unwanted children by means of the practice of oblation. This practice meant that boys between the ages of 5 and 7 lived secluded in monastic life until they reached the age of profession, when turning 15 years old (Boswell, 1990, p. 428). Throughout this time, the Benedictines set out and revised a number of rules regarding sexual behavior between monks and the boys (Payer, 1982, p. 10). Sexual relations between monks and boys were considered "particularly undesirable and offensive" (Payer, 1982, p. 10). In cases where sexual "relations" were known to have existed, the adult monk and the young oblate were given a penance. A typical penance involved fasting or whipping; both the young boy and the adult were seen as being equally responsible and therefore equally punishable (Payer, 1982, p. 10).

Sipe (1995, p. 10) argues that the Council of Trent (1545–1563) revealed how disconnected the doctrine was from the actual behavior of its clergy. The Council that upheld the celibacy laws was presided over for the second session of the Reform Council (1552–1554) by Pope Julius III, who himself had entered into a sexual liaison with a 15-year-old boy whom he had picked up on the streets of Parma. The Pope even appointed the young man as a cardinal before his death. Doyle (2003, p. 197) sourced Church documents on canon law in relation to clergy sexual abuse to suggest that the official documentation shows that the Roman Catholic Church has repeatedly attempted to deal effectively with the problem of sexual abuse of minors by clergy. The documentation indicates that clergy sexual abuse has indeed been a serious problem from the earliest years of the Roman Catholic Church (Doyle, 2003, p. 197). While the extent of the problem is not clear from the documentation, according to Doyle (2003, p. 197) the very fact of the existence of the official notification is an indicator of the existence of a problem. However, Jenkins (1996, p. 19) sounds a note of caution regarding much of this analysis, stating that much of the contemporary writing on the history of clergy sexual abuse represents a flawed analysis of the historical documents, which are difficult to trace in the first instance.

While the history of child sexual abuse within the Roman Catholic Church may be a contested affair, documents regarding recent occurrences of child sexual abuse within the Church can be less subject to dispute (*Boston Globe*, 2002; Ferns Report, 2005; Murphy Report, 2009; Office of the Attorney General, Commonwealth of Massachusetts, 2003; Raftery & O'Sullivan, 1999; Ryan Report, 2009). Although authorities in the Catholic Church responded during the 1980s and 1990s to revelations of sexual abuse of minors by clergy with shock and surprise, suggesting that this phenomenon was only relatively new, ecclesiastical records seem to suggest a different reading (*Boston Globe*, 2002, p. 43; Doyle, Sipe, & Wall, 2006, p. 3; Ferns Report, 2005; Murphy Report, 2009; Raftery & O'Sullivan, 1999, p. 256). Ample evidence exists that child sexual abuse by clergy had come to the attention of Church and State in the 1960s in Ireland and in the United States (*Boston Globe*, 2002, p. 44; Raftery & O'Sullivan, 1999, p. 256). Chopko and Stinski (1992, p. 23) demonstrated that the Catholic Church in the United States had been visited by such legal scandals in 1914, for example, when the Supreme Court of Massachusetts heard a civil case brought by a young woman who was raped by a Catholic priest on Church grounds when she was 17 years old. The *Boston Globe* (2002) uncovered evidence that the U.S. bishops had been dealing with the problem of clergy sexual abuse "behind closed doors" since the 1960s. In a study carried out on behalf of the Church hierarchy in Ireland (Goode, McGee, & O'Boyle, 2003, p. 174–178) some bishops acknowledged that they had become aware of child sexual abuse by clergy much earlier than the 1990s. The Murphy (2009) and Ryan (2009) reports confirm this. The revelation that the bishops in Ireland set up the Stewardship Fund in the 1980s, partly funded by an insurance company, to cover the cost of litigation and compensation and other expenses resulting from child sexual abuse by clergy, is also an indicator of such early awareness (Murphy Report, 2009, p. 142; Raftery & O'Sullivan, 1999, p. 256).

While this early awareness of the problem of sexual abuse by Catholic clergy and the Church hierarchy's reaction has been used to suggest a cover-up, this is a subject that requires further analysis. Although it is humanly attractive to have someone to blame, it may be that neat linguistic solutions appear to be found to significantly complex problems, prematurely punctuating the understanding of what had occurred, and laying blame at the feet of individuals. Just as was found in many child abuse inquiries in the United Kingdom during the 1980s and 1990s, blame and criticism of individuals seems almost irresistible in these situations (Reader et al., 1993, p. 1). By blaming "them" "we" feel better, and while the collective "we" can broadly acknowledge our part in the saga, at the same time "we" escape without consequences. While passing judgment and focusing on degrees of blameworthiness might be important and even understandable, learning constructively from what went wrong in the past, including what were the emotional and context factors within the professional and religious networks that allowed the relevant Church leaders and clerical perpetrators to be dislodged from making good judgments, appears to me to be very important too. So too is preventing further abuses. At its core are paradigms of responsibility and accountability.

CONCLUDING COMMENTS

There is now sufficient literature available on the subject of abuse by Catholic clergy to suggest that despite their protestations to the contrary, the Catholic Church hierarchy in Ireland and the United States had knowledge of sexual abuse by clergy from the 1960s onwards (Balboni, 1998; *Boston Globe*, 2002; Doyle, Sipe, & Wall, 2006; Ferns Report, 2005; Goode, McGee, & O'Boyle, 2003; Murphy Report, 2009; Office of the Attorney General, Commonwealth of Massachusetts, 2003; Raftery & O'Sullivan, 1999). Further, the historical documents suggest that throughout periods of its history, the Catholic Church hierarchy had some concerns about the occurrence of sexual relationships between its ministers and boys and, in fact, had taken steps to impose penalties on those who had failed (Doyle, Sipe, & Wall, 2006; Raftery & O'Sullivan, 1999). It is interesting, therefore, that the Church hierarchy was not forthcoming when the problems of sexual abuse by clergy began to be reported by the media in the 1980s and 1990s, particularly in Ireland, the United Kingdom, the United States, Canada, and Australia (*Boston Globe,* 2002, p. 31; Raftery & O'Sullivan, 1999, p. 256). A review of the Church's handling of the abuse complaints, and of the explanations for the actions taken by Church leaders, will throw more light on this subject (see Chapter 9).

What can be ascertained, though, is the failure of the Catholic Church to learn from its own history. It is interesting how some important historical facts and teachings come down through generations and how others get lost along the way. Understanding how and why this occurs may teach us much about the societies in which we live. Such an analysis is beyond the scope of this particular study, but what can be said is that the Catholic Church's failure to teach its priests the history of its own sexuality and abuses within its organization turns out to be a significant failing on its part. It is little wonder that priests and theologians like Dorr (2009) make the plea for reform without amnesia. It might, of course, also be noted that the Catholic Church is not the only institution in the world that has failed to learn the lessons of history.

2

Organized Irresponsibility (I)

THE ORGANIZATIONAL AND INSTITUTIONAL

CULTURE OF THE CATHOLIC CHURCH

SINCE THE BEGINNING of the public coverage of sexual child abuse cases involving Catholic clergy, it has become clearer that there are actually two dimensions to the abuse problem: the sexual abuse itself and the responses of the Church hierarchy to the abuse complaints. Since the early revelations it has been clear that we are dealing not only with cases of abusive clerics but with the fairly consistent response patterns of individual bishops, not just across individual countries but across entire continents. Whenever documents are released or legal authorities conduct investigations into abuse by Catholic clergy, what emerges is that the depth and scale of the problem is greater than previously acknowledged by Church authorities. While not every publication carries a similar weight, a careful and considered reading of this literature suggests some important patterns. I devote Chapter 9 to the Church's handling of abuse complaints, as the issues that are becoming apparent are complex and require detailed commentary.

While some commentators view the two dimensions of the abuse problem as quite separate and see them as emanating from very different sources, my own take is that they are very much interlinked. I further maintain that we are dealing here with features that are directly linked to the cultural and organizational structure of the Roman Catholic Church. This chapter focuses on the broad institutional features of the Roman Catholic Church that some scholars and many commentators believe have contributed to a climate in which child sexual abuse by Catholic clergy became possible and in which Church leaders responded to the problem the way they did. Later, I will also address some of the more specific issues that relate particularly to the clerical perpetrators (Chapters 7 and 8) and, separately, to the Church leaders (Chapter 9).

To understand clerical perpetrators and the bishops who responded to abuse complaints, the unique context of their lives and work as Roman Catholic ministers within the Roman Catholic Church must be understood. Catholic clergy who sexually abused minors and bishops who responded to abuse complaints did so within the context of their lives as celibate men who pledged their lives in service to God. Therefore, sexual abuse by Catholic clergy cannot be separated from all other relevant aspects of clergy life, and the bishops' handling of abuse complaints cannot be separated from all relevant aspects of their lives as leaders of the Roman Catholic Church. My argument is that the problem must be seen within its unique Catholic context, and the reasons for opting for this perspective will be developed throughout this chapter. Child sexual abuse by Roman Catholic clergy represents a complex network of personal, relational, social, theological, and moral interconnections: some parts relate to other parts, but the whole is greater than the sum of its parts. Dokecki (2004, p. 1) argues further that beyond matters of personal responsibility, sexual desire, and criminal or civil accountability, child sexual abuse by clergy takes place in an "overlapping set of historically influenced contexts and social structures and processes involving actors both inside and outside the church."

A number of broad areas dominate the literature on institutional aspects. The Roman Catholic Church is regarded as having created the conditions in which some clergy offended and in which some bishops acted as they did in responding to abuse complaints. Some commentators even suggest that certain aspects of the institution of the Catholic Church, which are in turn influenced by its traditions and teachings, have rendered sexual abuse by clergy and the subsequent responses of the Catholic hierarchy almost inevitable (Berry, 1992; Celenza, 2004; Cozzens, 2004; Dokecki, 2004; Doyle, 2003, 2004; Frawley-O'Dea, 2004; Gordon, 2004; Küng, 2003; Oakley & Russett, 2004; Papesh, 2004; Ranson, 2002a, 2002b; Sipe, 1995). What is important here is the interrelationship between several factors, including the forces of gender and sexuality, power relations, and clerical culture, and their enabling and constraining powers and potentialities on the lives of those men who were to become the clerical perpetrators, those who were to become the Church hierarchy, and those who were to become what are hereafter referred to as "normal" clergy. How these three subject positions are threaded together in concert with others to give shape to the current problem will be examined in Chapter 10. For the moment, I will limit myself to analyzing the institutional dimensions of the problem by trying to specify some of the mechanisms through which each variable contributes to sexual abuse within the Catholic Church.

CATHOLIC MORAL TEACHING

One element that is often questioned as constituting the core of the systemic genesis of sexual abuse among Catholic clergy is the Church's position on sexuality (Celenza, 2004; Cozzens, 2004; Frawley-O'Dea, 2004; Gordon, 2004; Kennedy, 2001; Papesh, 2004; Ranson, 2002a; Sipe, 1999). Catholic teaching on sexual morality can best be considered within the context of its teaching on marriage, because according to Church teaching, it is only within marriage that human beings and human sexual expression can adequately be realized and respected (Lawler, Boyle, & May, 1998, p. 21). According to the moral teaching of the Catholic Church, every sexual thought, word, desire, and action outside of marriage is a mortal sin (Catechism of the Catholic Church, 1994, pp. 2331–2364). Sexual acts within marriage that are not open to conception are also regarded as sinful. Sexual misbehavior constitutes mortal sin in every instance. Hence, chastity is the norm that forms the basis of official Catholic thinking on sexuality. According to this moral norm, every unmarried person is held to the same level of chaste behavior as a vowed religious or an ordained cleric.

Catholic Sexual Ethics

From apostolic times right up to the present day, Catholic scholars, saints, and Church leaders have sought to understand the meaning of human sexuality and the norms of sexual morality in the light of the word of God. During this long time errors have undoubtedly been made (Lawler et al., 1998, p. 46) as varying interpretations of scripture and of Biblical teaching on sex have been proffered. Fagan, a theologian (2009, p. 19), suggests that the origin of the Church's teaching on sexuality can be traced back to the concept of original sin. What original sin teaches is that babies are born with original sin, which is linked to Adam's transgressions, and to the genitalia. Because of this, babies require baptism to exorcise them of the sin, and until recent times their mothers needed to be "churched" to purify them after childbirth. Until a few years ago the Church also taught that unborn babies, or babies who died at birth, had to go to Limbo to be purified before they would eventually be released into the Heavenly experience. According to Fagan, such thinking "crucified" generations of devout Catholic mothers who worried, some until today, about the fate of their unborn children. Only recently has the Church's theological approach to Limbo changed.

Within the Catholic Church, the teaching of St. Augustine of Hippo (354–430) on marriage and sexuality has been accepted as the bedrock of official teaching down to the present day (Fagan, 2009, p. 19; Lawler et al., 1998, p. 50). Fagan (2009, p. 19) reads Augustine as believing there was nothing good in the act of sexual intercourse and of seeing the human body's response to passion, particularly the male erection, as beyond the control of the will, leading Augustine to declare that "the inability to control the genital organs becomes a punishment for sin inscribed in the body" (Fagan, 2009, p. 20). For Augustine, carnal desire, not motivated by the desire for procreation, was never acceptable, even in marriage, although it could be forgiven as something that arose as a result of concupiscence (Lawler et al., 1998, p. 51). Augustine held that concupiscence, which he saw as a source of "restless burning" that distorts all natural desires, while not exactly the same as original sin, is caused by it and inclines individuals to sin (p. 51). Fagan suggests (2009, p. 21) that Augustine's version of the theology of marriage and sexuality is totally incompatible with the Christian mystics, or with the tradition of Judaism. Fagan suggests that Augustine's views were influenced by the culture of his time, but his ideas have in fact taken on a status as theological absolutes that have in many ways endured in Catholic sexual ethics until today.

Between the death of Augustine in 430 and the development of university-based scholarship in the 12th and 13th centuries, communities of monks took on the task of instructing the Catholic faithful in the Christian way of life. The penitential books that they wrote are the main sources for studying the attitudes of the early Christian churches towards sexuality (Bieler, 1963, p. 10; Spear, 1979, p. 42). The *Penitentials* illuminated every possible variation on the theme of sex and estimated the relative seriousness of all sexual sin by devising penances and penalties for each offence. The *Penitentials* taught that there were three processes through which private bodily mortification began to define guilt and conscience for the modern Christian (Inglis, 1998, p. 129). They introduced (a) a scaled system of penance, which became the basis of a legalistic mentality that was later to dominate Western moral practice (Spear, 1979, p. 42), (b) a shift from public confession and penance to a private relationship between confessor and penitent that increased the power of the priest and inculcated individual shame and guilt (Inglis, 1998, p. 129), and (c) an emphasis on celibacy and virginity that separated married people and those who did not have this higher-order calling from the clergy (Spear, 1979, p. 36). Irish monks are said to have been the primary authors of the *Penitentials,* which much later, in the 19th century, were to play a major role in the shaping of Irish Catholicism (Inglis, 1998, p. 128).

For some scholars, the *Penitentials* represented an attempt to regulate sexual activity among laypeople and to eliminate it from the lives of clerics, monks, and nuns (Condren, 2002; Inglis, 1998; Spears, 1979). Chastity was seen as a means of controlling "animal passion" and proclaiming a superior character for oneself. Scholars suggest that the people accepted the *Penitentials* as a means of achieving this aim (Spears, 1979, p. 425). "It was through a systematic classification and analysis of bodily, especially sexual functions and activities, as well as traditional penitential practices such as praying, kneeling and fasting, that sexual instincts were controlled and regulated" (Inglis, 1998, p. 130). Condren (2002, p. 87) and others (Inglis, 1998, p. 129; Ranke-Heinemann, 1990, p. 87) argue that the regulation of sexuality was central to the Church's governance and central to developing and maintaining its power. Exercising power over the body and sexuality made it easy to "gain a foothold in men's minds" (Condren, 2002, p. 87). For the ecclesiastically consecrated character, however, chastity was recognized as a pathway to perfection and as a way to win favor with God (James, 1997, p. 249). Through chastity man sacrificed his body, one of his most precious gifts, to God.

Condren (2002), following Foucault (1998), suggests that early Celtic monks, through the *Penitentials,* created a situation whereby sexuality was split apart into thought, word, intention, involuntary urges, and actual deeds, that eventually would underpin and inform a science of sexuality. By teaching that virginity and continence were superior to marriage and by preferring this way of living for everyone who was able to do so, in effect sexuality and physical sexual expression were supremely elevated in importance. At the same time, natural urges were to be feared. To be sure, such dualistic framing of human life as body/spirit actually existed before the *Penitentials* (and can be traced to the Gnostics[1]) (Lawler, Boyle, & May, 1998, p. 47). However, the *Penitentials* reiterated and strengthened the dualism, a position that bedeviled the Christian churches in the past and still persists to the present day. Written in the fifth and sixth centuries, the *Penitentials* could have been written by all of the priests and religious who participated in my research, so much influenced were they by this thinking.

How the *Penitentials* of the fifth and sixth centuries could influence the Irish Catholic psyche of the 20th century is of course subject to debate. While sociologists and historians agree that there may be cultural residues lying deep within a culture that carry forward into practices of a later generation (Connolly, 1982, p. 113; Inglis, 1998, p. 275;), it is doubtful whether these residues were carried from the fifth and sixth centuries. Connolly argues that Irish clergy were particularly receptive to rigorist[2] and legalist[3] influences from England or the Continent because of the Penitential tradition. This perspective forms the basis of an ongoing debate and discussion among historians and sociologists of religion.

Other theologians took up Augustine's ideas, particularly his emphasis on the sinfulness of man and the innate corruption of human nature (Fagan, 2009, p. 22), and for centuries these ideas were developed and refined. When combined with an image of God as an auto-cratic and all-punishing figure, the views of sexuality, propagated by the Church's most dis-tinguished scholars through the centuries, sowed the seeds for fear, anxiety, and scrupulosity in how Catholics lived their lives (p. 23). The combination also gave rise to Jansenism, a movement that began in France in the 17th and 18th centuries and was also strong in Spain. It was brought back to Ireland by priests who had studied in France. Jansenism emphasized the darker side of human nature, which was viewed as distorted because of original sin, and required harsh measures to control. Jansenism also contained a theory of grace, premised on a special appreciation of the liturgy and a reverential awe of the holy (p. 23). While the rela-tive influence of Augustinianism and Jansenism is much debated in the scholarly literature, particularly regarding their influence on Irish Catholicism and Irish sexuality (Connolly, 1982, pp. 45, 47, 113, 185), Fagan is of the view that when combined with the Irish Church's own traditions, Jansenism gave rise to a combination of idealized perfectionism with harsh asceticism, two features that were to become the hallmark of Irish Catholicism for centuries to come (Fagan, 2009, p. 23).

The Catholic Church doesn't have a good record in trying to overcome the split between "matter" and "spirit." Flannery (1999, p. 51) has observed that many clergy are called upon to reject the body and to believe that not only can they compensate for such a loss spiritually, but that such spiritual exercise is actually a good thing too. Beattie (2009) suggests that the loathing for the sexual body, which underlies much of the Church's teaching, constitutes a dysfunctional dimension of the Catholic tradition that has a potentially catastrophic impact on those in positions of care for the vulnerable, who are trapped in dark fantasies of sexual self-hatred and repressed desire. Many commentators argue that current Roman Catholic teaching on sexuality is inadequate for the present time (Flannery, 1999, p. 51; Loftus, 2004, p. 92; Ranson, 2002a, p. 390; Sipe, 2004, p. 64) and that it also ignores all that is most obvi-ous about human development and human sexuality (Dominion, 2007; Green, 1997). It is a theology that is devoid of the influence of modern knowledge that comes to us through the disciplines of biology, sociology, and psychology. It also denies all forms of sexual expression as lacking authenticity, outside of procreative heterosexual couples, which alienates many Catholics from the human family, such as individuals who are sexual without the desire to procreate, individuals in second unions, individuals of a homosexual orientation. The pro-creative heterosexual couple is at the heart of Catholic sexual ethics.

According to O'Hanlon (2010, p. 13), one event that crystallized the crisis of sexuality in the Catholic Church and linked it with a crisis of power was the promulgation of *Humanae Vitae* in 1968. The papal commission leading up to this promulgation included laymen and laywomen and married couples, as well as medical and other experts. This commission was originally established to advise the pope on issues of population control in response to devel-opments in the United Nations. In the initial stages it simply accepted without question the traditional Church teaching on contraception (p. 13). However, it found, much to its own surprise, that it could not establish the intrinsic evil of contraception on the basis of natural law or reasoning. Four theologians (from a commission variously estimated as comprising 58 to 70 persons) dissented from this finding. Pope Paul VI in his encyclical took the side of the four dissenting voices and effectively decided the issue by papal authority and power. A large majority of practicing Catholics have not accepted the teachings of *Humanae Vitae* because they do not find it meaningful (O'Hanlon, 2010, p. 13). Theologians have pointed to an overly physicalist notion of natural law underpinning Church teaching on contraception, as well as an overly static notion of what tradition entails. These tendencies continue with regard to many other areas of the Church's sexual teaching, such as premarital sex, remarriage, homosexuality, the role of women in ministry, and mandatory clerical celibacy.

If we probe a little deeper into Catholic moral thought, what becomes evident is an inconsistency in the methods of theological reflection used in official Church documents, depending on whether they are referring to social teaching or sexual ethics (Curran, 1988, 1991, 2002; O'Hanlon, 2010). Curran (1988, 1991, 2002), for example, argues that two different methodologies are apparent here. In social teaching documents produced during the 1960s and 1970s, a theological method that is informed by historical consciousness is identified, one that avoids absolutism or universalism in favor of a contextual approach to social institutions and social values. This is particularly apparent in the call to "read the signs of the times" in formulating theological arguments and propositions. Although Pope John Paul II was cautious of this approach, Curran argues that in fact he strengthened and even developed the shift to "personalism," which had been emerging gradually during the 20th century and which emphasized freedom, equality, and participation over the more authoritarian approaches of earlier papal writings. For Curran, this represents a shift to a relational-responsibility ethical model in more recent papal social teaching, in which ethical reflection is shaped less by abstract top-down rules and regulations and more by the person's multiple relationships with God, neighbor, world, and self, and the call to live responsibly in the midst of these relationships.

By contrast, official Catholic teaching with regard to sexual morality is informed by deductive methods of reasoning that privilege law and "nature" over the human person, leading to absolutist distinctions between right and wrong, with no room for gray areas (Beattie, 2009; Curran, 1988, 1991, 2002; O'Hanlon, 2010). Several theologians suggest that official Church teaching in the area of human sexuality is guilty of physicalism, which in effect essentializes sexuality as something fixed and unchanging. This approach to sexuality insists that human beings cannot interfere with what they regard as the physical, biological structure of the sexual faculty. Thus, while many aspects of Catholic social teaching are somewhat flexible in that they react to constantly changing political, economic, and social circumstances, the teaching in relation to sexual matters appears to be rather static, fixed in time. O'Hanlon (2010, p. 13) points to the absolutist nature of Church teaching on sexuality in the recent encyclical on human development in charity and truth, *Caritas in Veritate* (2009), in contrast to its more tentative stance on disputed economic and political matters. Is it not curious, he says, that the Church can claim such certainty on a matter as complex as human sexuality, while being more modest about truth-claims in other spheres, and even admitting that natural law is not something that we know fully but rather something about which we grow in knowledge (O' Hanlon, 2010, drawing on the *Catholic Teaching Compendium of the Social Doctrine of the Church*, 2005, p. 384)?

Sexuality, Priesthood, Religious Life

Several commentators, themselves priests or former priests, argue that the inadequate theology of sexuality serves to make sexuality into something dark, secretive, and troublesome for many clerical men (Flannery, 1999, p. 51; Loftus, 2004, p. 92; Ranson, 2002a, p. 390;

Sipe, 2004, p. 64). In these circumstances sexuality becomes split from other aspects of the priest's life. Clergy try to ignore the fact that they are sexual as well as spiritual beings. Clerical celibacy and the inadequacy of the seminary training in the practices involved in celibate living are often seen as contributing to this scenario.

The most frequently cited reason for the practice of celibacy itself is asceticism—self-sacrifice for the love of God, the imitation of Christ, and freedom for the service of others (Sipe, 2004, p. 66). For Sipe, this rationale is valid. It reaches back to ancient times, not in terms of priesthood of course but as a separate vocation of isolation and spiritual concentration (p. 66). Many Church personnel value celibacy on these terms, seeing it as a sacrifice, as a mode of mortification that man offers to God. For the deeply religious, celibacy has a spiritual purpose and value. There is good evidence that celibacy is part of the archetype of the religiously inspired, as it is found in committed practitioners of diverse religions and is institutionalized in many (e.g., Buddhist monks and Hindu *sadhus*). Sipe (2004) does an excellent job of describing celibacy as valid and as a valuable part of spiritual life, while at the same time being very critical of forced celibacy as a policy.[4] In essence, Sipe believes that celibacy is the natural state of certain individuals with saint-like qualities and is not to be expected among most mere mortals.

When celibacy came to be legislated in canon law, in the 11th century, however, asceticism was not the primary rationale behind it. Three other elements were also present: paternity, property, and power. According to Sipe (2004), bishops and priests were not allowed to father children, in the interest of social, political, and institutional simplicity. Control of the clergy could be ensured when they did not have partners or families and when they were dependent on and accountable to a single superior. In this scenario, Church property would remain in the hands of the Church and its ownership would be unquestioned by spouse or children (Sipe, 2004). Furthermore, power over a person's sexuality confers significant individual and institutional power. Power over Catholic clergy is consolidated by legislated celibacy (Condren, 2002; Sipe, 2004, p. 66).

In the context of a prohibition on all forms of sexual activity for its ordained priesthood, many argue that a conspiracy of secrecy surrounds the subject of clerical sexuality (Kennedy, 2001, p. 93; Sipe, 2004, p. 69). It is an area where there are few official statements on priests' sexuality and very little leadership. Until recently, papal statements on Catholic sexuality were usually directed at laypeople and many texts on Catholic sexual ethics hardly mention priesthood or ordained celibacy. A notable recent exception is the papal encyclical on homosexuality in the priesthood (Congregation for the Catholic Education, 2005; Gallagher, 2006; Hannon, 2006). Since any and all sex is forbidden for Catholic clergy, and hence there is no discussion of criteria for moral responsibility in sexual behavior, one might reasonably ask if abuses and boundary violations are not almost inevitable.

According to Sipe (1999, p. 123), one of the basic problems underlying sexual abuse by Catholic clergy is the problem that the theology of sexuality is inadequate for modern conditions. The modern priest faces a conundrum as he tries to live and minister within the parameters of the Church's sexual teachings, in a secularized world that values sexual freedom and sexual expression and views the vow of celibacy with some suspicion. When combined with an inadequate formation, the modern priest is left floundering, trying to make sense of his life and his ministry, largely alone. As he listens to the complexities of individuals' lives and he experiences the gaps and tensions between his religious education and the practical realities of his daily experiences, what is the modern-day priest to do? How is he to develop the wisdom and integrity to help the people who come to him for guidance as he refrains from intimate relationships himself? How is he to respond to the people who seek his help with relationships and sexuality concerns, while at the same time he tries to refine his celibate dedication without adequate institutional support or guidance?

Hoge (2002, p. 96) reports that 10% to 15% of American priests who had been ordained 5 years or less years had resigned from active ministry. The major reasons given by these young priests for their resignation were isolation and loneliness. Celibacy was the reason given by about one sixth of priests for leaving the priesthood (p. 96). However, for Hoge, celibacy will not lead a priest to resign from the priesthood unless at the same time he feels lonely or unappreciated. Greeley (2004, p. 60) argues that priests leave the priesthood primarily because they are unhappy in the work, and a desire to marry comes from that unhappiness. In data that will be further explored in Chapter 3, 10% of priests are approached sexually during the time of their theological studies (Sipe, 1995, p. ix) and up to 50% of clergy are reported to be sexually active at any one time (p. 69), giving evidence for what Coldrey (2000, p. 50) describes as the "sexual underworld" of clergy. According to Coldrey (2000, p. 58), the clerical sexual underworld creates an environment that covertly gives permission for priests and religious to be sexually active while maintaining a celibate aura.

Within the current rules of celibacy and the seminary formation that accompanies it, there are a number of options for the priest or seminarian as he responds to his own sexual/ celibate development. He can discard the Church's teaching on celibacy as impossible; he can decide that the Church's teaching on celibacy is impossible for him, yet hold others to a standard he does not himself live; he can impose his own sexual needs on the vulnerable whom he is supposed to serve; or he might become one of those men who manage to keep the vow of celibacy with integrity (Sipe, 1999, p. 122). One wonders how a seminary can effectively teach celibacy to its seminarians when Church teaching on celibacy and sexuality is in need of such reform (Ranson, 2008). In the past the *structure* of seminary life, including prayer, theological reflection, and celibate community life, was meant to *be* the seminarian's instruction in celibacy, but it is clear that this method has often failed.

Clerical celibacy is today under attack, and questions regarding the role of celibacy in sexual abuse by Catholic clergy are continuously raised in public debate. For Sipe (2004, p. 66), celibacy is under attack not because it lacks idealism, but because it lacks sufficient reality to make it convincing, apart from those individuals with saint-like qualities. Celibacy suffers because of lack of attention to modern conditions and to recent developments in knowledge of human growth and sexual development, sexual identity, sexual behavior, and sexual love.

It is clear that the literature on celibacy is difficult to decipher, in part because of impartiality and vested interests on all sides. Many of the writers on clerical celibacy were or are priests themselves and have varying personal experiences with the celibate commitment, which may color their perspective. However, this should not detract us from considering their work, in particular that of Sipe (1995, 1999; 2004), Greeley (2004) and Ranson (1999, 2000, 2002a, 2002b, 2008). While Greeley (2004) argues that celibacy *per se* is not a problem for many priests, Sipe rejects such a notion and sees the mandatory elements of celibacy as problematic. Defenders of celibacy do not accept that mandatory celibacy may have devastating consequences for many clerical men who remain within the priesthood or religious life by living a double life, living in a clerical sexual underworld and developing an almost dual existence. Ranson (2002a, p. 3) argues that a "celibate heart" is a necessary precondition for priestly or religious ministry, but the Catholic Church is continuing to ordain and profess men who have never discerned whether or not they have "a celibate heart." He sees this as an inadequacy in the formation process. While much can be done to improve such discernment, my experience tells me that even when a man enters a seminary at 18 years old with "a celibate heart," he might discover at age 30 that life or love has changed all that.

Whatever the complexities inherent in the practices of clerical celibacy, it is clear that the Catholic Church does not maintain a theology of sexuality that provides guidance for priests in trying to balance the numerous roles and dual relationships that they experience in ministering in the modern world. There is still little if any training offered in seminaries in the management of appropriate boundaries. Mentors and older clerics are remarkably secretive about their own sexuality. There are few official statements and very little leadership beyond preaching blanket abstinence and spiritualizing the issue. Church leaders appear in the main to be unwilling to engage with the problem of sexuality and celibacy for Catholic priests and religious; when they do, they are censured from Rome. In 1995, in a decade in which the Irish Catholic Church was humiliated with the outpouring of allegations of sexual abuse by clergy, the then Bishop of Ferns, Brendan Comiskey, suggested that the celibacy requirement for priests should be relaxed. He was admonished and summoned to Rome to explain himself (Ferriter, 2009, p. 533). Three years later he again called for a debate on the subject, arguing there were already married priests in the Catholic Church and using the example of those Anglican men who had converted to Catholicism. What is interesting here is how little support Bishop Comiskey received, publicly at least, from his fellow bishops in Ireland, although another bishop, Willie Walsh, also raised the issue on a number of occasions. In more recent times, as the sexual abuse crisis gathered momentum in Europe, celibacy as a requirement for priesthood is an issue that is being raised by some bishops in Europe as a topic and a practice that requires debate.

Sipe (1995, p. 4,) points out that the current situation of sexual abuse within the Catholic Church, although real and significant in itself, is primarily a symptom of "an essentially flawed celibate/sexual system of ecclesiastical power." He suggests that it is ultimately part of a theoretical system of unaddressed questions and a product of the religious system itself. He comments critically that "to address the problem of sexual trauma in the Church in any narrower a context runs the risk of self-deception and certain failure, similar to applying a bandage to a cancerous lesion" (Sipe, 1995, p. 5, 1999, 2003, 2004). Berry (1992/2000, p. xii), like Sipe (1999), suggests that the crisis in the Catholic Church lies not with the fraction of priests who have sexually abused minors but in an ecclesiastical power structure that conceals sexual behavior patterns among its clerics.

While the role of celibacy in relation to sexual abuse by Catholic clergy is a complex matter (and one that I discuss in Chapter 7 with clerical men who have sexually abused minors), at the very least it is becoming clear that the involuntary nature of celibacy is problematic for many priests and religious (Flannery, 1999, p. 75). Küng (2003, p. 211) makes the case for voluntary rather than compulsory celibacy. He believes that the law of celibacy is having a catastrophic effect on recruitment to the priesthood, as many men are rejecting priesthood because of the celibate commitment and others are attracted to priestly and religious life to avoid sexuality altogether. For these reasons Küng is concerned about the psychological makeup of men entering priestly and religious life.

It is hard to see how sexual violations by Catholic clergy can be contained, especially if sexual acting out is seen as an isolated phenomenon, unrelated to the problems of mandatory clerical celibacy, formation for celibate commitment and support in living the live and to questions of the Church's sexual teaching. While the incidence of sexual abuse of minors by Catholic clergy may be dropping, if the data contained in the John Jay Report (2004, 2006) hold firm, we do not know the full extent of other sexual violations by Catholic clergy, as these stories are only beginning to be told. The history suggests that an approach to the problem of sexual violations that sees it as one of individual failing alone is essentially part of the problem. Opposition by the current Church leadership to discussing the broader issues of Catholic moral thought and in this context the issue of mandatory celibacy appears to rest more on theological ideology and political controversy than on rational argument. Leaving fundamental issues such as these unaddressed, particularly in the current whirlwind of revealed sexual abuse cases by Catholic clergy, appears highly problematic and maybe even irresponsible (Kennedy, 2001; Loftus, 1999, 2004; Sipe, 1999).

An opposing view suggests that while celibacy might be in need of review, it is not responsible for the ills it is currently accused of, such as child sexual abuse and the exodus from the priesthood (Greeley, 2004, p. 61; Plante, 1999, p. 173). Plante (1999, p. 173) argues that blaming celibacy for child sexual abuse by clergy is "illogical, unreasonable and unproductive," given the fact that non-celibate clergy also sexually abuse minors. Nonetheless, he suggests that the way in which celibacy is conceptualized, practiced, and administered within the Roman Catholic Church, and not the discipline of celibacy itself, may create an environment for problematic sexual acting out by some priests.

It can be argued that taboos against speaking of priestly sexuality leave priests without enlightenment for their pastoral duties and for their own growth and development. Similarly, efforts to conceal the sexual behavior of the clergy breed a culture lacking in sincerity, sexual honesty, truthfulness, openness, accountability, and transparency (Flannery, 1999, p. 74; Sipe, 2004, p. 64). These features have also been directly linked to providing a context for child sexual abuse. The greatest challenge to the authority of the Catholic hierarchy has come about as a result of sexual abuse in the Catholic Church. Child sexual abuse by clergy could in time turn out to be the greatest catalyst for change in the celibate sexual system of the Catholic Church.

But Catholic moral teaching should not change with the times, so the argument goes, because it is based on absolute truths and fundamental teachings, which cannot be subject to change just because popular culture says so. Does not this subscribe to the very charge of relativism, to which the current pope seems to object so much? Linden (1997, p. 6) suggests there are two types of theologian: one who acknowledges the political and social contextualization of theological utterances and the other who views theology as essentially apolitical. The latter, suggests Linden (p. 6), "is itself a political position providing cover support for the *status quo*". Cardinal Ratzinger (now Pope Benedict XVI) belongs within this latter category (Corkery, 2009b, p. 184). Liberation theologians make a distinction between praxis-based theology and orthodoxy-based theology to distinguish different approaches to theological reflection (Corkery, 2009b, p. 184; Linden, 1997, p. 6). Praxis-based theology suggests that through political activity we participate in the transformation of unjust social structures and thereby do God's work on earth. Orthodoxy-based theology, on the other hand, is based on the acceptance of inherited rules and regulations. Some liberation theologians even talk about the need to privilege "orthopraxy," meaning right practice, over orthodoxy.

THE ECCLESIASTICAL STRUCTURE OF GOVERNANCE, POWER RELATIONS, AND HIERARCHICAL AUTHORITY

A second feature of the Roman Catholic Church that is often seen as central to the systemic genesis of the abuse crisis is the ecclesiastical structure of Church governance. The Church's governmental system is strictly hierarchical. Furthermore, all power resides in individuals and not in collective bodies. The Vatican is the administrative center of the Catholic Church, and the Roman *Curia* is the decision-making hub; both are governed by the pope. Councils, synods, and the Episcopal conferences have largely a consultative role, serving mainly to advise the pope. Any deliberate power is given to these bodies by canon law itself (which, in turn, is totally subject to the approval of the pope), or by the pope or diocesan bishop, which is in turn responsible to that authority. Decrees of the Ecumenical Council, the highest collective body in the Catholic Church, are also subject to the approval of the pope (Canon Law Society, 1983, Canon 338). The pope is the supreme authority for the Universal Church, and the Catholic Church teaches that this supreme power and the hierarchical structure are of divine origin (Canon Law Socity, 1983, Canons 330, 331, 333). According to Papesh (2004, p. 127), "[t]he Vatican is a secretive organization of mazelike operation that as vigorously protects its rights as it exercises its responsibilities."

Priests have to obey their bishop, and bishops must take an oath of fidelity to the Holy Apostolic Roman Church and to the pope (Murphy Report, 2009, p. 49). At his ordination a priest is required to answer a question from his bishop in the affirmative: "Do you promise respect and obedience to me and my successors?" Professed religious (men and women) take a vow of chastity, poverty, and obedience. The secular life of the 21st century does not hold such presumed virtues in high esteem; instead it privileges individual choice and free will, and individuals are encouraged to make their own decisions, choose their own actions, and reap the benefits or suffer the consequences accordingly (James, 1997, p. 249). In contrast, subjecting one's will to that of another is one of the current spiritual hallmarks of the life of the ordained and professed members of the Catholic Church, and for many the practice of obedience is of spiritual significance. Obedience appears to spring from the general religious phenomenon of self-surrender and giving oneself over to a higher power. In effect, it becomes an ascetic sacrifice that the ordained or religious members of the Catholic Church offer to God (p. 250). At a more functional level the system of authority and governance of the Catholic Church is fundamentally linked to the workings of obedience.

As an administrative unit, the Catholic Church is divided into dioceses, which are administered by bishops. On the local or diocesan level the bishop enjoys almost total power, but critically he is subject to the pope as his immediate superior. This is hugely significant, and in my view the full extent of such dependencies have not been recognized in current discussion of the bishops' handling of sexual abuse complaints and the issues involving accountability and responsibility. I will come back to this point again in Chapter 9. However, in his diocese, each bishop holds full judicial, legislative, and executive powers (Canon Law Society, 1983, Canon 391).

Over the centuries there have been different methods of choosing and appointing bishops. Increasingly the appointments are seen as political. While the bishops and the priests of a region have a right to submit names and express their views and preferences, their views can easily be ignored. Ultimately, all power for the appointment of bishops belongs to the Congregation for Bishops in Rome and to the pope (Robinson, 2007, p. 280). Coinciding with what is seen as the rise in papal power, particularly during the reign of John Paul II, the pope is seen to more and more reserve the right both to choose and appoint them. The Holy Spirit is believed to guide the pope in this task (Canon Law Society, 1983, Canon 375). It has been argued that the centralization of Episcopal appointments into the hands of the Vatican has made the bishops less accountable to the people they are appointed to serve (Küng, 2003, p. 211). Controlling the appointment of bishops is obviously a powerful means of controlling the Church (Robinson, 2007, p. 280).

Some commentators argue that the bishops and Episcopal conferences have become extremely dependent on and controlled by the Roman *Curia*. The latter are accused of being more likely to be "yes-men" for the pope (Küng, 2003 p. 211; Papesh, 2004, p. 131). Furthermore, bishops have no free forum in which to discuss burning issues of the day, openly and honestly. Loyalty to the Roman line comes first, and according to some commentators (Küng, 2003, p. 211) as long as a bishop toes the party line he has nothing to fear. Critics argue that even when Roman policy is a fiasco, bishops will, in the main, adopt the Roman line (Küng, 2003). Transparency by the Roman *Curia* has been raised as a source of concern by Church critics and supporters alike. This lack of transparency is the soil in which many problems, including sexual abuse, can thrive.

According to Robinson (2007, p. 125), a former Auxiliary Bishop of Sydney, Australia, the College of Bishops does not play the role in the Church today that it should. In his 25 years of working as an active bishop he can remember very few occasions when the pope consulted the body of bishops, and none when the pope asked the bishops to vote on an issue. They were not asked to vote before the publication of the document on the ordination of women, not even when the Cardinal Prefect of the Congregation for the Doctrine of the Faith spoke of this teaching as "infallible," with the pope doing nothing to contradict him. No explanation was given as to why the bishops were not consulted. In Robinson's opinion it may have been that people close to the pope were afraid that the bishops would not give the teaching their endorsement. It is also interesting that the bishops didn't object to the use of the word "infallible" in speaking of this proposal, as Robinson is of the view that "the majority would have been opposed to the idea of attaching the work 'infallible' to any teaching on the subject" (p. 125).

In trying to address some of the governmental issues that the Church was facing, the Second Vatican Council (1961–1965) reached many compromises; one was in relation to the power of the bishops in Church governance. While bishops are powerful in the running of their diocese, the same cannot be said of their level of influence in the running of the Universal Church. For Robinson (2007, p. 137), placing the power of the pope and the power of the College of Bishops side by side as being equally supreme was one of the compromises of Vatican II. It is difficult to have two bodies holding the same supreme power within the same organization, and it is almost inevitable that eventually one will in practice dominate the other. That is exactly what happened. "In the time since the Council, it has been evident that, in fact and in practice, the Pope has possessed supreme power, while the

College of Bishops has not" (Robinson, 2007, p. 137). The pope's claim to infallibility on certain matters has strengthened his position. It was during the reign of Pope John Paul II that power became even more centralized in the papacy, with the result that the authority of the National Conferences of Bishops to develop policies uniquely suited to their country's need became diminished (Reese, 1996, p. 33).

The Synod of Bishops meets every 3 years, and many people perceive this as a powerful body, but according to some bishops, including Robinson (2007, p. 125), this is in fact also very carefully and thoroughly controlled: "It is the Pope alone who determines what a Synod finally says, so the Bishops can do no more than offer advice, and even the advice is carefully filtered" (p. 125). Reese (1996, p. 42–65) reports that the Synod of Bishops, which is theoretically an opportunity for bishops worldwide to advise their pope, became a forum whereby bishops tried to impress the pope with their knowledge of his documents and writings under John Paul II, and so prove their personal loyalty to him. Robinson (2007, p. 125) reports on at least two occasions the bishops have been told they may not even discuss certain matters. At the Synod on the Laity they were told that they may not discuss the question of the ordination of women, and at the Synod on the Priesthood they were told that they may not discuss celibacy (p. 135). Rather disturbingly, Robinson reports that at the Synod for Oceania in 1998 he was told by the Cardinal Secretary of the Synod that the meeting worked by consensus, not by majority, and that a vote of 90% constituted a consensus. However, the Vatican officials who were appointed to that synod made up more than 10%, effectively meaning that it required every other participant attending the Synod to vote together to even have a chance of arriving at the required 90% consensus for a decision to be carried. In effect, the Vatican officials who attended the synod had the power to block even a near-unanimous vote of all of the other bishops put together. The late Cardinal Bernardin of Chicago is reported as having once complained that the pope treated his bishops like altar boys (Cornwell, 2001, p. 259)!

The Roman *Curia* forms a central administrative unit of the Catholic Church (in a sense a public service akin to a civil service for a government), an administrative unit that perhaps the Church or the pope could not function without. The Catholic Church exists in almost every country in the world, and the *Curia* has a formidable task trying to preserve unity in the midst of such cultural and historical diversity. According to Robinson (2007, p. 127), while the College of Bishops and the faith of the whole Church provide few restrictions on the exercise of the power by the pope, the Roman *Curia* does provide significant restrictions. The *Curia* prevents any pope from being willful or arbitrary or from indulging in the excesses of popes in past centuries. At the same time "the members of the *Curia* protect Papal power, and they make no secret of the fact that this is the task above all others that they are specifically employed to do" (p. 126). Robinson's experience (which I will discuss in more detail in Chapter 9) teaches him that the *Curia* has been a major force in using modern telecommunication technology in order to control, but not consult, the bishops and the Catholic clergy. Such one-sided application keeps both the College of Bishops and the whole Church under strict control.

According to Robinson (2007, p. 128), the most usual complaint one hears of the *Curia* by bishops is that the *Curia* exercises tight control on the affairs of the Church; it can be "high-handed" and there is a pervasive atmosphere of secrecy surrounding its workings. For Robinson, the problem does not lie with individual members of the *Curia* but rather with the system: "Papal power has gone too far and there are quite inadequate limits on its exercise ... The Roman *Curia* has been heavily involved in this process and it is committed to supporting unrestricted Papal power" (p. 128). Robinson argues that no change in personnel within the *Curia* will resolve the problem. Like most aspects of the system of governance within the Catholic Church, only serious changes to the papal system and the *Curia* are likely to bring true resolution. What sets Robinson apart from other bishops is his frankness in discussing these matters, which has not come without a personal price—a matter to which I will return in Chapter 9.

The Silencing of Issues

The silencing of issues and the lack of debate are two of the features of the hierarchal system of power and control that are at the heart of the governance of the Roman Catholic Church. If the pope or his delegates make it clear that certain topics are not open for discussion, then important questions and concerns will not be addressed. In turn, the spirit and morale of priests, religious, and the laity are undermined (Cozzens, 2004, p. 14). Cozzens argues that the bishops' interpretation of loyalty to and responsibility for the institution of the Catholic Church comes into play in this scenario. In declining or neglecting to engage in discussion of important issues, perhaps the bishops are propelled by a fear that they would be seen as anything other than in complete harmony with the current discipline and practice of the Church. Cozzens believes the bishops interpret their responsibilities as Church leaders as requiring them to respond defensively to any calls for change within the structure of the institution (p. 17). By failing to engage in open and effective communication with the lower-ranking clergy and the Catholic laity, the bishops in effect contribute to their own alienation and to frustration on the part of Church members, even if they do keep in good standing with Rome. The accusation that the Catholic Church belongs to the bishops, who are interested only in power, position, and prestige, grows out of this fortress-like situation (Cozzens, 2004). The preservation of the institution, with its doctrine and dogma, is seen to be constantly privileged over more open and transparent debate and dialogue.

Papal infallibility was declared in 1870, not long after the communication technology introduced by the Industrial Revolution had begun to make its presence felt in the world. Robinson (2007, p. 117) sees the official upgrading of papal authority through the declaration of infallibility and a practical increase in papal power through modern means of communication as having occurred together. The new constellation resulted in a subtle but significant[5] shift in papal power. Citing an example from the middle of the 19th century, Robinson tells the story of the Australian bishops who sought advice from Rome on a problem. They had to wait 2 years for the response, in part due to the route the letter had to take to get from Australia to Rome and back again. In 1999, when an Australian bishop made a decision of which some did not approve, within 2 days his action had been reported to Rome and a facsimile reply had returned from a Roman cardinal ordering him to stop. Robinson notes critically that the development "has enabled a detailed control of every aspect of the Church in every part of the world in a manner that Popes of earlier centuries, even one as recent as Pius IX, could not have dreamed of" (Robinson, 2007, p. 117). Robinson adds, rather sadly I detect, that the technology used to gain greater papal control over the Church could equally have been used to listen to the views of the whole Church when the sexual abuse issue began to come to light, but "it must be said that this has not happened" (p. 117). In Chapter 9 I will return to the issue of papal power and to why the bishops didn't rebel against the Vatican line and speak out in relation to sexual abuse by Catholic clergy, even when it became clear that Rome had been slow in reacting to some earlier revelations (Ferns Report, 2005; Murphy Report, 2009; Robinson, 2007).

The term "official truth" is often used to prevent discussion of certain topics and to suggest that many items of Catholicism are not and cannot be changed (Cozzens, 2004, p. 21). While it is true that some official dogma cannot be changed, it is also true that "official truth" also contains teachings, traditions, practices, disciplines, and customs that fall outside of the rubric of divine revelation and that are in effect non-dogmatic "truths." These are factors that give form to Catholic culture. Cozzens argues that when human experience, supported by theological and pastoral reflection, no longer supports these non-dogmatic "truths," then serious review and discussion is required. These non-dogmatic "truths" ought to thus remain valid only insofar as they reflect the authentic human experience. Without such a possibility, silence descends and the reality of the lived experience is denied, eventually ending in organizational and individual dishonesty. When personal experiences and convictions are not in harmony with the institutional culture and when there is no route to open, honest dialogue, it is inevitable that such differences and behaviors will be carefully guarded and covered over until they are discovered in a surprise moment. The signals that individuals are trying to communicate to the organization are weak or mixed, and weak and mixed signals and the responses to them make for organizational mistakes, misconduct, and disasters (Vaughan, 1997, pp. 250–251, 413–415). Cozzens (2004, p. 29) believes the game becomes one of "selected blindness" and secrecy, individually, collectively, and systemically. Vaughan's (1997) work on organizations tends to attribute less mal-intent to individuals. She is rather more inclined to highlight the complex relationships between individual, organizational and institutional processes. Within organizational cultures in which there are structural barriers to talk and in which there are organizational norms, rules, and procedures governing who can speak and on what topic, it is likely that the well of secrets and secret-keeping will flourish.

During the pontificate of John Paul II (1978–2005), theologians, teachers, priests, brothers, and women religious, identified by the Vatican to be in dissent, were silenced and censured by the Congregation for the Doctrine of the Faith, headed by Cardinal Ratzinger, now Pope Benedict XVI. According to Corkery (2009b, p. 83), Ratzinger had a strong tendency to view Catholics, especially theologians who dissented from non-infallible teachings of the Church, as misconceiving the nature of the Church and the workings of the Magisterium (the teaching office of the Church). Many theologians already saw the Church's teaching office as authoritarian and antidemocratic, but Ratzinger was so reluctant to engage with any form of theological dissent from any kind of Church teaching that "theologians began to wonder what space if any remained for them to pursue any kind of critical work" (Corkery, 2009b, p. 84). Dissent in regard to sexual morality and liberation theology appeared to be of particular concern to Pope John Paul II and to Cardinal Ratzinger. Many of those theologians who were censured during the reign of John Paul II describe the processes as humiliating (Cornwell, 2001, pp. 210–214). Bernard Häring, the German moral theologian, for example, who was persecuted by the Nazis as a young man, said after having been investigated and ultimately censured by the Catholic Church, "I would prefer Hitler's courts to another papal interrogation. Hitler's trials were more dangerous, but they were not an offence to my honour" (cited in Cornwell, p. 210). Häring was presumably not the only theologian who experienced such humiliation.

Accountability

In a hierarchical system that still has some elements of a monarchy, accountability poses real problems (Doyle, 2004, p. 31; Inglis, 1998, p. 45). Accountability is expected to function in a bottom-up fashion. The laity and lower-ranking clergy are accountable to the hierarchical leadership and the bishops are accountable to the pope, but there is no accountability the other way round. Conway (2004, p. 75) argues that the theology of priesthood underpinning the top-down accountability structure of the Catholic Church, one that originated with the Council of Trent, emphasizes the distinctions between the ordained and the non-ordained, the priest and the laity, in such a way that the priest is set apart and set above the laity. The priest is seen as *repraesentatio Christi*. In contrast, an understanding of priesthood in which the ordained is seen as *repraesentatio ecclesiae,* in which the priest is more in communion with and in service of the laity, following Vatican II, demands an alternative structure in terms of accountability. Conway argues that responsive engagement with the findings of the reports into the handling of child sexual abuse by Catholic clergy across the Universal Catholic Church requires consideration of the culture of management and leadership of the institution and the theology that underpins it.

Rigidly hierarchical models of accountability that are accompanied by rigid hierarchies of power foster by their very nature mechanisms of denial and structural secrecy (Berry, 2000, p. xxii; *Boston Globe*, 2002, p. 31; Wills, 2000, p. 13). To gain approval and remain in good standing, inferiors on the hierarchical ladder will strive to exemplify the institution's values and deny or repress their own realities when they are in conflict with institutional values. In subtle ways "deviance" begins to occur, usually with lasting and devastating institutional effect. Superiors may feel little obligation to seek "advice" from inferiors and are unlikely to admit to personal or professional failure for fear that admitting wrongdoing may undermine their authority to govern. Equally, they will want to remain in good standing with the "top." Taken-for-granted scripts become normalized and turn into invisible rules for behavior. Individual action is pushed into certain directions, in the long run leading to informal organizational practices that everybody knows about but nobody talks about openly (Vaughan, 1997, p. 37). Such an organizational culture is prone to errors, mistakes, misconduct, and disasters (pp. 409–422).

Wills (2000, p. 13) argues that many institutions, even those claiming to be guardians of "truth" with a special relationship to God, can display an institutional instinct that makes their first priority the enhancement of the organization and the reinforcement of the organization's authority. Systems of accountability with appropriate checks and balances, while still prone to the dynamics of structural secrecy, may diminish the likelihood of system failure (Cozzens, 2004, p. 30). In contrast to prime ministers or chancellors who are accountable to their parliaments, with the judiciary acting as a check on the executive power of government, and in contrast to institutions such as the military and the police forces who are ultimately accountable to a higher authority, power and control within the Catholic Church resides ultimately with the pope who is effectively accountable to no one but God.

Arthurs, Ferguson, and Grace (1995, p. 462) argue that secrecy within the Roman Catholic Church is one of the impediments to growth for its clergy, creating an environment in which it is impossible for clergy to be open and honest. Within this environment there is the potential for abuse of power flowing from a lack of honest engagement, the reluctance of the institution to allow debate and dialogue as the caste of priests become keepers of secrets. According to Arthurs, Ferguson, and Grace (1995, p. 464), the response to such a constraining environment for some male clerics is to leave the priesthood or brotherhood altogether; for others it becomes a pathway to illicit relationships.

The canons try to promote accountability within the Catholic Church by distinguishing between the external and the internal forum. The external forum represents the Church's public forum for judicial acts. In the external forum all due-process procedures are recorded and preserved. In contrast, conversations that take place in the internal forum, which is the forum of conscience, in which private conversations of conscience take place, are generally regarded as having the status of the sacramental confession, with the seal of privacy and confidentiality. Doyle (2004, p. 32) argues that the misuse of the internal forum by the bishops for matters of sexual abuse by clergy has led to some bishops claiming that their records were privileged and confidential, when in fact canon law dictates that the records belong to an external forum. He argues that the bishops either misused canon law or were not sufficiently knowledgeable of how to apply it. (This is a point to which I will return in chapter 9.) Inglis (1998, p. 46), in contrast, argues that the existence of the external forum and the internal forum has been one of the organizational strengths of the Catholic Church. In practice, it means that the pope and the bishops may say one thing and the priests may state and do the opposite. Some priests argue that the existence of the external and internal forums provide a means for managing moral dilemmas, particularly regarding the pastoral issues involved in advising Church members on Church law pertaining to contraception, as determined by *Humanae Vitae* (1963). However, the current structure equally facilitates priests in being dishonest. In effect, clergy can pay lip service to one thing in public, but in the privacy of the confessional they can give alternative advice to the laity who seek their help. As the sexual abuse cases demonstrate, the gray area between the internal and external forum needs further exploration.

Canon Law

I am mentioning Canon law at this point to illustrate that Canon law is a core feature of the apparatus of governance of the Catholic Church. However, a fuller treatise of Canon law in relation to the sexual abuse crisis will be deferred until Chapter 9. The Catholic Church has its own legal system known as canon law. Canon law is the oldest continuously functioning legal system in the world. Its roots go back to the fourth century, when gatherings of bishops enacted rules to deal with problems facing the infant Church (Doyle, 2004, p. 25). Change was also noted in the 12th century, when a systematic compilation of the scattered Church laws that incorporated some of the discoveries from Roman law was promulgated.

Canon law as we know it today is a codified law system, and the basis of what is regarded as canon law today was promulgated in 1917. The second code was promulgated in 1983, when reforms of the Second Vatican Council (1965) necessitated changes (Coriden, Green, & Heintschel, 1985). The years between 1965 and 1983 were marked by debate in canonical scholarship regarding, among other topics, the scope of canon law and the role of bishops in penal matters involving clergy (Congregation for the Doctrine of the Faith, 2010).

Canon law features significantly in discussions of child sexual abuse by Catholic clergy, mainly in relation to the handling of abuse complaints by the Church hierarchy. Canon law is sometimes regarded as having played a maintenance role in the sexual abuse, as the law is understood to have provided the legal means of allowing clerical perpetrators to remain in ministries, even long after their abuses had come to the attention of the Church authorities. Varying interpretations of the code that resulted in varying practices are now seen as having contributed to the overall problem. Canon law also provides the key infrastructure for removing abusive clergy from pastoral ministries and in many instances removing them from the clerical state altogether. We need to understand the conflicting perspectives and complex contextual circumstance in which canon law has come to be debated in relation to sexual abuse by Catholic clergy. This discussion will be undertaken in Chapter 9, when I discuss the bishops' handling of abuse complaints.

CLERICAL CULTURE

Clerical culture must be seen as a third broad feature of the Roman Catholic Church that has helped to create an environment conducive to child sexual abuse (Cozzens, 2000, 2002; Dokecki, 2004; Doyle 2003; Flannery, 1999; Frawley-O'Dea, 2004; Gordon, 2004; Greeley, 2004; Papesh, 2004; Ranson, 2002a). Increasingly, a number of bishops themselves have been drawing attention to the role of clerical culture in creating the conditions in which child sexual abuse in the Catholic Church came to be (Coleridge, 2010). Cozzens (2002, p. 151) identifies the clerical world as "a medieval clerical culture, a closed, male society of privilege, exemption and deference" (p.151). Papesh (2004, p. 47) defines clerical culture as "the trajectory of material reality, relationship structures and universe of ideas that, across the centuries, have come to characterize the world of the ordained in the Latin Rite of the Western Dispensation of the Roman Catholic Church." Greeley (2004, p. 104) believes that clerical culture imposes an iron law of denial and silence on priests that contributes to many of the problems in the priesthood today.

It is clear from the literature that members of the clergy are introduced to the closed world of clerical culture in seminaries (Cozzens, 2004; Greeley, 2004; Papesh, 2004; Ranson, 2002a). According to Greeley (2004, p. 107), generations of priests and religious have been encouraged in seminaries to socialize on holidays only with other priests and to believe that priesthood and the religious life represent a great fraternity of men who will always support each other. However, to remain in good standing, a priest must not publicly express unusual ideas or criticize accepted practice, nor must he appear to be too successful (p. 107). Indirect negative commentary and undermining someone who is not conforming is often very effective (Greeley, 2004, p. 106). Within such an environment the group becomes effective in policing itself in relation to the performative aspects of priesthood, such as how priests talk, walk, dress, and speak. At the same time the more private and in many ways more important aspects of his life remain hidden or are denied. Within such a clerical culture human frailty is concealed and the lived reality of many priests and religious is ignored or obliterated (Greeley, 2004, p. 107; Ranson, 2002a, p. 394). The result can be disappointment, isolation, and loneliness.

Of itself, a clerical culture in which the closest and most intimate confidants of priests are priests and where loyalty exists by priests to priests is not problematic. Clerical culture becomes problematic only when the priest's only friends are other priests, when the values of fellow clergy create the only perspective on the world, when gossip about other priests is the principal subject of small talk, and when the priest is isolating himself from other people (Greeley, 2004, p. 106). In a situation where the main social network of clergy is clergy, the priest can easily become a prisoner in a hermetical world from which it seems impossible to escape. Papesh (2004, p. 98) suggests that trying to maintain appropriate professional boundaries is a constant source of concern for priests, especially as many of them live their lives always and constantly in the priestly role. They also minister in a climate where they are, or more likely were, regarded as holy and mysterious, possessing special wisdom about life and the spiritual world. For Papesh, the celibate status of priesthood bestows additional power, such as when one is regarded as "sexually safe". At the same time this can also cause problems for clergy if in some cultures it is thought to mean being "available." Papesh suggests that the logical conclusion for clergy is that the only true friends they should have are family, old friends, and fellow clergy. No matter how a priest meets new friends, the potential charge could always be made that the "relationship" involves a breach of boundaries. The challenges for priesthood in the 21st century are indeed immense, and for these and other reasons, alternative paradigms of priesthood and models of Church ought to be considered.

Clericalism

The word *clericalism* is used to describe the situation where priests live in a hermetical world, set apart from and set above the non-ordained members of the Catholic Church. The word is often used to describe the attitude that the clerical state is of divine origin and that it represents a higher calling than that of the lay state. It is a word often associated with a presumption of superiority.

Clerics are presumed, by clergy and laity alike, to form an elite group within the Roman Catholic Church; they are superior to the laity because of their ordained status and their celibate commitment. They are also seen as closer to God because of their powers as sacramental ministers (Doyle, 2003, p. 209; Inglis 1998, p. 2). According to Inglis, the current model of Catholic Church constructs the sacramental system in such a way that the sacraments, the traditional means of salvation for Roman Catholics, are ministered by clerics who control access to them.

Doyle (2004, p. 33) argues that clericalism has its roots in the privileged place claimed and nurtured by the clerical establishment itself. This exalted status for clerics is supported by the canon law tradition of the Roman Catholic Church (Canon Law Society, 1983, Canons 273–289). Official Church teaching has always supported two classes of people: clerics and lay. Part of the problem lies in the idea that on ordination a man is "ontologically changed" and that the character received at ordination is never lost. If a man is dismissed from or leaves active ministry he does not cease to be a priest, although this theological absolute is currently under review in relation to clerical perpetrators with the advent of recent Vatican policy regarding such men. Being a member of the clerical state, however, is a matter of Church law. As a member of the lay state, a former priest is forbidden from exercising any of the functions of priesthood. The official canonical terminology for the change in status is *reduction* to the lay state, an expression that supports the thesis that despite the aspirations of the Second Vatican Council that the Church would be a Church of the People of God, the official institution still holds on to the notion that ordination represents the "higher" state. Church history shows that as the rank of priest becomes more significant, the role or office also subsumes the man (*Catechism of the Catholic Church*, 1994, p. 393).

Flannery (1999, p. 28) points out that one of the greatest traps for a priest is when he identifies totally with the role and draws personal security from it. The trap is in thinking of oneself as belonging to an elite group of particularly "good-living" people. For Flannery, this form of Catholicism and priesthood is repugnant. Flannery wryly writes, "I don't want to live in a paradise from which the bulk of the human race is excluded" (p. 30). Ranson (2000, 2002a) argues that within an all-male culture of superiority, participants develop a competitive energy, with a growing incapacity for genuine internal reflection, an inability to relate with intimacy, dependence on role and work for self-identification, and the loss of humanizing tenderness. Such a scenario breeds isolation and discontent. It is important to recognize that Ranson, Greeley, Cozzens, Doyle, and Flannery are all Catholic priests, committed to and working for the Catholic Church and whose experiences in priesthood represent three continents—Ranson (Australia); Greeley and Cozzens (United States); Doyle (United States and Europe); and Flannery (Europe).

Doyle (2003, p. 211) explored some of the reasons for the development of clericalism, and he suggests that most clerics progressed from early adolescence to adulthood within an ecclesiastical milieu and came from families who possessed a high reverence for the Church and the clergy. Although a somewhat different situation exists today, with the closure of many secondary or high-school-type seminaries, in the past many men entered the seminary system at the secondary school level and progressed right through until they reached ordination. Seminaries at all levels were isolated; some had high walls around them, literally and metaphorically; and academic instruction and personal formation took place within an all-male environment where future priests had minimal contact with the secular world. The Church was the clerical world, and this was *their* world (Doyle, 2003, p. 211). This all-male unmarried clerical subculture unofficially defined itself as "the Church."

The effects of clericalism are found in clerics and laity alike. One symptom commonly seen in the past in the laity was an attitude that it was sinful to make any unkind accusation against a priest. There was also a belief that the priests and bishops could and would not do wrong. The effect of clericalism on clergy was the belief that they were not only set apart and set above the laypeople, but they were also thought to be above the civil or criminal law. Doyle (2004, p. 35) argues that the entire multifaceted phenomenon of sexual abuse by clergy has been propelled by clericalism, in part because clericalism is directly related to why victims remained silent about the abuse until many years afterwards. Doyle may be overstating the case here in relation to why victims do not report their abuse, as there are often other psychological and social factors influencing the timing of the decision to disclose. Nonetheless, the power differential between the priest and the laity, the ordained and the non-ordained, and the revered position of the ordained relative to the laity have in the past been significant in the disclosure patterns of victims of clerical sexual abuse. Clericalism may also help to explain why the institutional Church reacted to reports of abuse in the way that it did and why some secular institutions deferred to the institutional Church when dealing with sex abuse cases (Murphy Report, 2009; Ryan Report, 2009).

The Theology of "Church"

Despite the changes in the Catholic Church since Vatican II, it is still difficult for many clerics and laity to move away from definitions of "Church" as belonging to the clergy to a notion of the Church that is much less defined by traditional political structures. Even the language of *clergy* and *laity* is problematic, as it keeps the basic distinctions between the ordained and the non-ordained as foundational. Increasingly, using words such as *lay* and *laity* as part of the ordinary vocabulary of the Catholic Church is proving to be problematic. The child sexual abuse crisis seems to be propelling a move towards consideration of alternative Church models in which these distinctions are no longer defended, particularly in countries where the awareness of the problem has undermined the moral authority of the Church leadership and forced a juxtaposition of faith and belief versus organizational structure and political system onto the public agenda.

The history of how we got where we are, in terms of the institutional arrangements of Church, is most interesting. Sanks (1997, p. 43) tells us that the symbols employed by the early followers of Jesus to understand Him and themselves were taken from the symbolic deposit of Jewish scriptures and traditions. Early Christians gradually took to themselves titles that had previously referred to Israel: "a chosen race, a royal priesthood, a holy nation, God's own people." To make sense of Jesus, they adopted and adapted symbols such as the Messiah, Son of Man, and Son of God, symbols that also belonged to the Judaism of the first century. Distinguishing themselves from their Jewish heritage was a process that took time, as the religious institutions of Israel came to be regarded as finished (at least for Christians) and Christianity began to appear as the new religion to be followed (Brown, Fitzmyer, & Murphy, 1990, par. 24, p. 1344). The New Testament and the earliest writings of the first Christians contain many references to such a newly perceived community (Sanks, 1997, p. 43).

Biblical scholars teach that the New Testament is not a homogeneous book but rather a collection of writings of various genres, written at different times and places (Browne, 1990; Jay, 1980; Sanks, 1997). As Sanks (1997, p. 44) observes, it should come as no surprise that it contains a plurality of communal self-understandings and images to denote the Christian community, depending on the concerns of the concrete communities from which the writings emerged or to which they were directed.[6] Some of the more popular images and symbols used to refer to "the community" in the New Testament are the Body of Christ, the People of God, the Temple of the Holy Spirit, the New Creation, and the Community of Saints (Sanks, 1997, p. 44). *Ekklēsia* (Church) was one of the earliest terms used by the first Christians to refer to community. There are many uses of the term *ekklēsia* in the writings of the New Testament, and these refer to "gatherings of Christians in particular places such as houses, gatherings in particular cities or regions and to the whole Church dispersed geographically" (Sanks, 1997, p. 44). *Ekklēsia* is a term that has multiple meanings. Every image and symbol used to refer to "the community" or "the Church" in the New Testament brings forth a different theology of the Church and what it is to constitute a faith community.

The image of the Church as the Body of Christ calls on Christians to be members of one body, with Christ as its head (Colossians 1:18, 24; Ephesians 1:22–23, 5:23). The image of the body also denotes the interdependence of its members and the vitality of a living organism (Sanks, 1997, p. 46). The image of the Church as the Household of God (1 Timothy 3:15) furnishes a picture of a more institutionalized and ordered Church (Wild, 1990, pp. 892–893). This theology of the Church appeals to those who favor a model of the Church as an institution (Sanks, 1997, p. 47). For Luke it is the presence of the Spirit at Pentecost that marks the real birth of the Church community, with a sense of mission to preach the resurrection and the coming of the Kingdom (Sanks, 1997, p. 47). According to Sanks, the portrait of a community guided by the Spirit in Luke's writings has influenced the Church's trust that the Spirit continues to guide it throughout history (p. 48). Matthew's Gospel sees the Church as the new People of God and Jesus as the teaching authority (Matthew 21:43). For Matthew the term *ekklēsia* means the Church as a visible structure, "having authoritative officials and authoritative functions" (Brown & Meier, 1983, p. 65). However, a second use of *ekklēsia* in Matthew's Gospel shows a local community disciplining a sinner (Matthew 18:17). According to Sanks (1997, p. 49), such a reading of Matthew's Church says that it is not one leader who makes the decision but the Church who decides as a group. Although Matthew's ecclesiology sees Peter the Apostle as the chief teacher for the Church, Matthew also issued warnings to Church leaders against using distinctive clothing or seeking places of honor (Sanks, 1997, p. 49).

Somewhat in contrast is John's Gospel, which shows little interest in Church offices or structures. This Gospel emphasizes the "the relationship of the individual believer to Jesus and the dwelling of the Paraclete-Spirit in the believer" (Brown, 1984, p. 85). It invokes the image of vine and shepherd to depict the relation of Jesus to individual Christians. The core of this ecclesiology is "a personal, ongoing relation to the life-giver come down from God" (Brown, 1984, p. 85). There is, in other words, "a pervasive egalitarianism" in John's gospel (Sanks, 1997, p. 49). Apostles are not mentioned and the emphasis is on discipleship (p. 49). The egalitarianism also extends to women in this Gospel, in a distinctive manner from other Gospels (p. 50).

What emerges from a reading of the different Gospels and traditions of the New Testament is the variety and diversity of community self-understanding, ecclesiological paradigms and possible models and of Church. This is important because "too often the Church is presumed to be a homogeneous and monolithic organization from the moment after Pentecost" (Sanks, 1997, p. 50). However, as well as demonstrating a plurality of images and self-understandings of early Christians, which gave rise to varying theologies of the Church, the New Testament also shows some remarkable continuities. Put differently, unity and pluralism in ecclesiology could be encountered even then (Sanks, 1997, p. 51).

Ryan (2009, p. 588) argues that the rich significance of the Church's theology of the Church has yet to be realized. While the post-Vatican II Church emphasized the theology of the Church as the Church of the People of God, with all Church members sharing in the ministry of Christ, for Ryan there are problems in matching this theology with the lived experience of "Church" (p. 590). Part of the difficulty lies in the very teachings of Vatican II itself, particularly the ecclesiological dualism that it contains (pp. 588–589). While emphasizing the equality of all of God's people, often the activity of the People of God is severely constrained by specific interpretations of the theology of Vatican II, which retain a "sense of the Church as a *societas inequalis,* a hierarchically structured 'perfect' society with its God-given authority and chain of command" (Ryan, 2009, p. 589; *Lumen Gentium,* pp. 18, 28). While pastors are reminded that "they were not ordained by Christ to take upon themselves alone the entire salvific mission of the Church to the world" and therefore are asked to recognize the ministries and charism of the laity (*Lumen Gentium,* p. 30), according to Ryan (2009, p. 589) this ministry is deemed to pertain predominantly to the secular world and not to the central sacramental ministries. While certain men and women can take on certain ecclesiastical functions that are given to them by the hierarchy, functions that are to be per-formed for a spiritual purpose (*Lumen Gentium,* p. 30), these functions are assumed not by virtue of their baptismal vocation but rather by decision of the hierarchy (Ryan, 2009, p. 589). The dichotomy regarding what it means to be an equal member of the Catholic Church is not only a problem of language or terminology ("lay" vs. "clergy"); it also relates to power.

While the theology of Vatican II renders the baptized community theoretically empowered, it does so in very impractical ways (Ryan 2009, p. 593). While the baptized are affirmed as full participants in the Church, the organizational structures of the Church clearly favor the ordained. Power relations within the institutional structures of the Catholic Church even overshadow the real central authority: all power comes from God and through baptism all Christians are empowered by the Holy Spirit (p. 593). Through Vatican II, "powerlessness and service seem to be the lot of the non-ordained while those who enjoy Episcopal ordination are to exercise decisive effective authority in the commu-nity of Christians" (Ryan, 2009, p. 593; *Lumen Gentium,* pp. 21, 22, 36, 37). The distinction between service and authority seems to be crucial here. Stressing authority without paying attention to service opens itself to abuses of power. (At the same time, emphasizing service at the expense of self-care can lead to a multitude of problems, including abuses, as Chapters 7 and 8 demonstrate.)

While it is in a certain sense inevitable, the tension in the Church's ecclesiology is possibly stifling growth. While there is a need for a diversity of functions and the maintenance of order in any institution, within the Catholic Church this endeavor should not overshadow the essential equality of all of its members (Ryan, 2009, pp. 590, 591). While all human insti-tutions require structure and leadership, part of the current problems in the organization of the Catholic Church is the identification of the structural and public aspects of the Church with the ordained. A second problem is the centralization of all power in the papacy, with-out adequate checks and balances. Thus, one of the greatest challenge facing the Catholic Church as it attempts to recover and learn from the sexual abuse crisis is the lack of trust in the current model of "the Church," including the theology that underpins it. A new theol-ogy of the Church in which all members are equal, in which distinctions between the ordained and non-ordained no longer hold firm, and in which new ways of ministering to its members needs attention. Such a theology of the Church will be less about control and laws and regulations and more about shared beliefs and communal ministry. To realize such a vision, careful consultation, deep discernment, and, more often than not, simply humble elegance are required.

Although the post-Vatican II era has witnessed a multitude of growth-producing changes in the Catholic Church and a significant reduction in the distance between the clergy and the laity, there remain many elements of clericalism that are at the root of some of the Church's problems. The clerical world is still shrouded in secrecy; there is no room for mis-takes; the idea that Church authority is intertwined with divine will lingers; the dominant model of the Church renders its members unequal rather than equal by fostering a distinc-tion between the clergy and the laity; there are inadequate checks and balances in the exer-cise of papal power; there is an absence of real dialogue between bishops and priests; and there is a demand for "blind" loyalty at all levels of the ecclesiastical power structure. It is Doyle's view (2003, p. 221) that within such a situation, abuses are still likely to occur.

Theologians such as O'Hanlon (2010a, 2010b) who argue for a more collegial Church in the spirit of Vatican II, with an active lay participation in which the power of the papacy is balanced with the influence of local churches, don't seem to go far enough in arguing for a new model of the Church, particularly since some of the current suggestions appear to keep in place the problematic inequalities that are reliant on the existing distinction between the ordained and the non-ordained. Many religious (men and women), as well as the laity, know this only too well. In my view a new model of the Church, a new ecclesiology, is what is required.

Why reforms in the structure of the Catholic Church are not forthcoming may be in part due to what theologian Nicholas Lash (2008) and retired bishop Geoff Robinson (2007) have identified as the success of the Roman *Curia* in resisting reform and effectively ensuring that collegiality has yielded to a more entrenched centralization. The ecclesiological dualism contained in the documents of Vatican II (Ryan, 2009) as well as the conflicting interpretations of some of its teachings may also be part of the problem. The reluctant attitude towards reform may also relate to power. Ultimately the question as to what model of the Church is most relevant for modern conditions must be considered. However, as the Archbishop of Dublin recently pointed out (Martin, 2010), "the Church" must not just become a place where individuals gather to celebrate human experiences without a deep reference to God. Otherwise, this "civil" religion ends up being empty and unresponsive to the search for God. Whatever its organizational structure—and this is central to current debate—Catholicism demands that "the Church" is a place where Christ addresses the believers and invites them to meet Him and be challenged by His love. Any organizational structure must reflect such commitments. The Archbishop of Dublin cautions that "there is a danger that when some say that the Church is the 'People of God,' they really want to say that it is up to the people to determine who God is and how God is useful. But, whoever encounters only their own God does not encounter the God revealed in Jesus Christ" (Martin, 2010).

SEMINARIES AND FORMATION

The literature on sexual abuse by Catholic clergy also points to the formation or training programs for clergy, as contributing both in content and in structure to the complex web of factors that facilitate child sexual abuse within the Catholic Church. Formation programs have been accused of providing an inadequate training for the clerical apprentices (Bennett et al., 2004; Cozzens, 2004; Greeley, 2004; Loftus, 1999; Papesh, 2004; Ranson, 2002a, 2002b; Sipe, 1995). There are many common features in the training of clergy internationally, and the absence of an environment in which the realities of clerical life can be honestly discussed appears to be a recurring feature.

Prior to 1992, the formation curriculum for clergy focused on the spiritual and intellectual aspects of the students' lives. Mostly the training consisted of 7 years, typically taken up with philosophical and theological studies. Under canon law (Canon Law Society, 1983, Canon 241), the bishop had the final say in who was admitted to the seminary. In all cases the applicant filled out an application form, supported by a letter of recommendation from his parish priest. Directors of vocations appointed by the bishop had responsibility for seeing the candidate through the application process. This often involved further contact with the parish priest to establish the candidate's good character and general suitability. Medical examinations and interviews with a member of the college staff were also fairly routine.

In the mid-1970s psychological assessments were introduced for candidates entering the priesthood in Ireland; this practice was also happening in other jurisdictions (John Jay College, 2011), although it was not mandated by Rome. Presumably, the tests were designed to enable the authorities select only the most suitable candidates. Once admitted to the college, all candidates were required to have a spiritual director, who was the student's choice but was subject to ratification by college staff. The spiritual director functioned as a spiritual mentor and at times as a confessor. During their formation students were evaluated on an ongoing basis, although in Ireland, going back over the records of men trained for the Archdiocese of Dublin, the Murphy Commission could not find any records of such evaluations having been carried out on any of the men in their sample (Murphy Report, 2009, p. 156). While subject to variability across jurisdictions, these procedures broadly constituted the entry process to priestly formation in practice.

In the mid-1990s the curriculum for the training of clergy expanded on direction of the pope. This initiative was designed to add human and pastoral development to the already existing two elements of philosophical and theological study (*Pastores Dabo Vobis,* 1992). *Pastores Dabo Vobis* (1992) makes for interesting reading and it makes a good case for including these subjects in the formation curriculum. However, as Ranson (2002a, p. 394) observed in practice, the rhetoric did not measure up to reality. In effect, what happened in many seminaries and houses of formation in the 1990s was that the new subjects of human and pastoral development were attached to an already overcrowded academic schedule, and the subjects were not given due attention. In Ranson's opinion—and he ought to know as a retreat director of several of the Catholic seminaries in Australia—the integration of human and pastoral formation was largely dependent on the sensibilities and abilities of the formation staff, many of whom were themselves formed in a different era and therefore lacked the skill or vision necessary to develop new programs. As several commentators have suggested, the culture of the seminaries is predominantly one of education to orthodoxy and not education of the whole person (Papesh, 2004; Ranson, 2002a, p. 394). Research that I undertook not only with older clergy who had abused minors but also with other clerics and former clerics of a newer generation confirms this view (and will be further discussed in Chapters 7 and 8). Ranson's observations are very much in line with my clinical observations of the Irish situation.

The formation of candidates to the priesthood is primarily the responsibility of the bishop, who in his role as Shepherd calls the candidate to Orders and the service of the People of God. In some countries bishops collaborate in this part of their mission and agree on the use of one seminary or several for the education of the clergy. In other situations individual bishops adopt their own approach. As in all aspects of the Catholic Church, bishops disagree on how to train the clergy. In these situations tensions are evident. There are now examples of individual bishops and religious leaders drawing on the resources and expertise within and outside of their own diocese or religious order as they undertake the process of priestly formation in ways that fit with their own orientation and vision of the Church. The training comprises human, spiritual, intellectual, and pastoral formation, in line with *Pastores Dabo Vobis* (1992), but sometimes in a living environment that suits the conditions of modern life and ministry. I have reviewed two such programs, one in an Australian diocese and one in a religious order in Ireland. These programs support and challenge the seminarians to be of service in the name of God while also supporting them to take care of themselves, physically, emotionally, and spiritually. Most importantly, the senior leadership engages with the new recruits in the most human and honest of ways, offering a mentoring experience that is based on the lived experience of complexity. In my view these formation programs offer seminarians the best theological, philosophical, pastoral, and human formation that is available, in an appropriate community setting. Unfortunately, these models are more the exception than the rule.

The Commissions of Investigation into the handling of sexual abuse by Catholic clergy in Ireland also inquired into seminary formation. Both the Murphy Report (2009) and the Ferns Report (2005) found that in many regards training for clergy in Ireland is improving. The Murphy Report indicates that students in formation for priesthood now have courses and talks on sexuality, with an extra emphasis placed on understanding celibacy in the final years leading up to ordination. The seminars are provided by personnel who are trained counselors with expertise in the psychosexual area. To ensure that candidates possess the psychosexual and social maturity necessary for priesthood, the main diocesan seminary in Ireland, St. Patrick's College Maynooth, assured both Commissions of Inquiry that it has been providing more resources for students today than ever before. The Ferns Committee was assured that "celibacy formation is integrated into the entire seminary programme through conferences, formal lectures and advice from formation personnel, spiritual direction and the full-time availability of professional counselling" (Ferns Report, 2005, p. 35). There has also been much greater emphasis placed on screening the clergy on entry (Ferns Report, 2005, p. 35). However, as one seminary educator indicated to the Murphy Commission, a student's sexuality and issues related to celibacy were matters to be dealt with privately in conjunction with a spiritual advisor (Murphy Report, 2009, p. 158). This approach to formation for celibate living is in fact part of the problem for the Catholic Church. While a celibate commitment clearly involves individual and personal dimensions, the institutional dimensions need open and honest discussion. It is also conceivable that older clerics could mentor younger clergy by honestly sharing their successes and challenges in this domain of life with them.

In acknowledging that there have been improvements in some aspects of seminary formation since the Second Vatican Council (1961–1965), many commentators on priesthood and clinicians working with clergy, as well as clergy themselves, are not as convinced as the Commissions in Ireland that everything is well in seminary education for Catholic clergy, be it in Ireland or elsewhere (Bennett et al., 2004; Cosgrave, 2001, p. 129; Flannery, 1999, p. 12; Ranson, 2002a, p. 394). However, in the United States the John Jay College (2011, p. 46) found that seminary education changed significantly over the period of the study (1950s to 2010) and the development of a human formation curriculum is correlated with low incidence of reported sexual abuse. In contrast, those men who were to become the majority of the abuse perpetrators were formed in an era in which they had little human preparation for the life and ministries they were undertaking.

Apart from the seminary content, the inadequacy of the structure of seminary life as the place to educate men into the priesthood is raised by a number of commentators who are themselves priests (Cosgrave, 2001, p. 129; Flannery, 1999, p. 12; Ranson, 2002a, p. 394). An all-male clerical environment is considered to be a constraining environment for the education of men wishing to become priests or religious (Frawley-O'Dea, 2004, p. 129; Greeley, 2004, p. 107; Ranson, 2002a, p. 394). Institutional life is said to breed dependency and a type of illusory security, which does not prepare the students for the reality that is the priestly life (Cosgrave, 2001, p. 129; Flannery, 1999, p. 12; Ranson, 2002a, p. 394). At a time when young adults ought to be developing their own identity and sense of personal autonomy, the seminary structure demands that they develop a collective identity and a "corporate" voice, *uno voce* (Cosgrave, 2001, p. 129). In such conditions, individual expression of difference is discouraged, giving rise to a rather covert competitiveness between the individual and "the system." This can result in alienation of the individual, often infused with anger. The impersonal caliber of the institution and the exclusively male environment is also known to lead to loneliness and emotional isolation (Ranson, 2002a, p. 394). In such an impersonal and covertly conflictual environment intimacy can be met only in a covert fashion (Cosgrave, 2001, p. 129). As Marshall (1993, p. 109; 1989, p. 491) has argued, when aggression and intimacy needs combine, sexual acting out becomes a distinct possibility.

Seminaries as Total Institutions

The sociologist Erving Goffman (1961/1975, p. 11) has described a total institution as "a place of residence and work where a large number of like-situated individuals, cut off from the wider society for an appreciable period of time, together lead an enclosed, formally administered round of life." While individuals in modern society tend to sleep, play, and work in different places, "with different co-participants, under different authorities and without an over-all rational plan," the arrangements are different in total institutions (Goffman, 1961/1975, p. 17). As I began to work with Catholic clergy and heard accounts of their lives and training, Goffman's total institutions came to mind immediately.

In the course of the seminary training for Catholic clergy with whom I worked, (1) most aspects of their lives were conducted in the same place and under the same single authority; (2) each part of the individual's activities was carried out in the immediate company of a group of others, all of whom were treated alike and required to do the same thing together; (3) all phases of the day's activities were fairly tightly scheduled and the whole sequence of activities were imposed from above by a system of explicit format rulings; and (4) various enforced activities were brought together into a single plan, purportedly designed to fulfill the official aims of the institution—ordination (Goffman, 1961/1975, p. 17).

For Goffman (1961/1975, p. 22), total institutions are "forcing houses for changing persons," each carefully designed to change the self. While it is true that all institutions capture something of the time and interest of its members and therefore have encompassing tendencies, total institutions are even more encompassing. Their encompassing nature is symbolized by the prevention of having social intercourse with the outside world and by a heavy reliance on rules and regulations. Within such a system of total institutional control and power the total institution sets about its work of changing the individual to fit the institutional agenda (p. 24). In Goffman's (1961/1975, p. 24) view, the self is "systematically, if unintentionally, mortified" and the individual begins to show signs of a radical shift in terms of his moral career.

The first curtailment of self arises as the individual is dispossessed of familiar roles, his clothes, and sometimes his name. Institutionally approved substitutes are provided. As will be shown later in the narratives of clerical perpetrators, as they adopted to the role of seminarian, priest, or religious brother, their new identities began to supersede older identities that the men had been accustomed to, such as brother, son, or friend. They were simply cut off from what would have been important sources of "outside" support. Many of the men had already partially withdrawn from their connection with home. However, as they began to prepare for a life of priesthood and celibate living, this withdrawal happened mostly at a time when many of them were making the transition from boyhood to manhood.

As in other total institutions, the process of entrance to seminary life meant saying good-bye to what one was accustomed to. In the new environment of seminary, compliance and deference, rather than autonomy and honesty, were valued. Often strategies of fear and shame were used to this end. As Cozzens (2004, p. 151) observed, within the environment of seminary, lessons in deference and compliance are accompanied by lessons in silence and secrecy. What emerges is an unquestioning loyalty towards the institutional Church. Conflict is avoided, and fear of the consequences of speaking out prevailed. If and when individuals showed defiance they received immediate visible punishment. None of the men who participated in my research was overtly defiant during his seminary years. In fact, most of them could be described as exceptional rule keepers, adopting a submissive way of living for the most part. However, while the features of their socialization would later become part of my understanding and explanation of why sexual offenses occurred, it would be a mistake to think that this was the only pathway to offending.

My main argument for conceptualizing seminaries as total institutions in the context of sexual abuse of minors by Roman Catholic clergy is to throw light on the process of how seminaries create a template for clerical culture, clerical masculinity and clerical living that was problematic for many. Drawing on Goffman's work (1961/1975) to illustrate a point, I suggest that such total institutions set the tone for clerical life which included silence and denial, an atmosphere of deference and submission, and an environment in which conflict and emotion were permitted to find expression only in covert ways. My research suggests that this way of living provided the structure in which sexual abuse of minors by Roman Catholic clergy became possible. All clergy, including those men who would later become the abuse perpetrators, "normal" clergy, or the Church hierarchy, were socialized in these clerical norms, providing the institutional thread that binds them in the current crisis. In Chapter 10 I return to Goffman's work as I attempt to understand the factors that distinguish clergy members who abused minors from those who did not, based on my understanding of how individuals adapt to or resist, the effect of total and totalizing institutions. While sexual abuse by Catholic clergy and the response by the Catholic hierarchy are systematically produced by the interconnection of social environment, organizational conditions, and individual features; no single factor can adequately explain this phenomenon.

CONCLUDING COMMENTS

It is difficult to "prove" or "demonstrate" how exactly an institutional culture or context can contribute to a problem that is perpetrated by individuals, especially when some individuals who were socialized in the very same culture did not commit any offense or crime. For those who have an interest in preserving the institution as it is, it is easy to dismiss cultural and contextual factors in favor of individual failing. In a world that increasingly privileges individual moral responsibility over social or relational responsibility, looking to the institutional dimensions of a problem can also be seen to be providing perpetrators with excuses. However, we know that life takes place in a social context and that human action is influenced by the lived experience, ranging from the earliest relationships to more complex identities in the realms of culture, race, gender, ability, sexuality, and class. We are shaped and formed in interaction with our environment; individual agency always interacts with structural and institutional conditions to produce social action.

Within all cultures, particular meanings are accorded to certain events and physical entities, and behaviors and ways of seeing and understanding the world evolve. This also applies to clerical culture and to the culture of the Catholic Church. Individuals learn to interact and communicate through observing and relating to the group they belong to, or are placed in. This process of socialization is easy to understand in children but is no less significant in adults. It is particularly important in closed organizations, particularly an organization like the Catholic Church, where the sense of security, predictability, and order stems from the experience of belonging. This in turn is affected by adopting institutional norms and the means through which an individual can express them. In short, while individual agency is important in explaining how individuals act as they do, institutional context and structure, including socialization, cannot be ignored.

By throwing the spotlight on the institutional aspects of the problem of abuse by Catholic clergy, my intention is not to provide abuse perpetrators or the Church hierarchy with excuses for their behavior, but rather to open all aspects of the problem for analysis and discussion. Through the available qualitative and the quantitative data and by drawing on the reports of insiders as well as outsiders, my view is that a theory of sexual abuse by Catholic clergy that links the individual with the institutional dimensions holds the best promise for making sense of sexual abuse by clergy. Such a work makes the link between current understandings, individual responsibility, and systemic accountability. In this chapter I focused on those aspects of the organization of the Catholic Church that are theorized as giving rise to a climate in which the problem of sexual abuse by Catholic clergy can and does arise.

It is notable that there is an explanatory process operative within the Catholic Church that limits responsibility for the offending solely to the individual perpetrator. Over and over again one hears the institutional disclaimer of responsibility for the abuse, even if in more recent times there is some acknowledgement of the mishandling of abuse complaints. This disclaimer reinforces the assumption that abusiveness comes entirely from outside the ecclesiastical system and that better screening will prevent the "dysfunctional" people from getting in. The argument presumes that priests who abuse minors have invaded the Church and penetrated its history of good works and the body of honest priests. It also presumes that the "erring" bishops who are guilty of mistakes, misconduct, poor judgment, or the popular notion of "cover-up" are in fact guilty of nonconformity with the right protocols or practices or the relevant aspects of canon law. This, I believe, is an inaccurate analysis of the situation. It is conformity, rather than non-conformity, with the cultural contours of the organization that is at the heart of the problem. Such conformity includes institutional, organizational, and individual dimensions.

According to Sipe (1998, p. 138), the Catholic Church has tried hard to separate individual clergy abuse from the possible systemic dimensions. Its almost-2,000-year history is littered with examples of its tendency to sacrifice individuals in favor of its own preservation. Rarely does the senior leadership see the necessity for a root-and-branch review of the manmade aspects of the very institution itself. It has been long established by social scientists and theologians that reviews of the Church's governance structures, power relation, and sexual ethics are long overdue. In light of the sexual abuse crisis, change is now even more pertinent. Despite the various wakeup calls, the current line from Rome makes clear that these topics must remain untouched. To the extent that a full analysis of the factors that gave rise to the current crisis is not forthcoming, and the systemic dimensions of the problem are not understood or addressed, the problem will continue to be crisis-managed but not really confronted. This is regrettable. The need for more comprehensive research on the causes of and the solutions to the many dimensions of the abuse problem cannot be emphasized enough.

The logic goes like this. If clergy sexual abuse has been caused by the intrusion of "deviants," then true prevention through a reinforced and revitalized screening of candidates would have sorted out the problem. As we know, in the past screening alone has not prevented sexual abuse problems from arising. Even with better screening measures, my own view is that such pursuits will have little effect. Let there be more screening by all means, but real solutions must be found elsewhere. Similarly, if the problem in the Church's response to abuse complaints is merely a problem of nonconforming bishops, it is likely that the problem would have been sorted out by the policy of appointing only "yes-men" to the ranks of the Episcopate. As an explanation, nonconformity on the part of the erring bishops does not make sense. One of the central theses of this book is that just as clerical men who sexually abused minors were not in the main psychological or moral "deviants" who infiltrated the system, neither were the bishops who "erred" nonconforming deviants who did not obey the institution's rules. On the contrary, my argument is that both were rule-keepers in an organization whose very institutional condition gave shape to the contours of the problem.

Few studies have compared a priest's qualities before he enters the seminary and after he completes his training; fewer still have followed priests 5 or 10 years after their ordination. This research is most important. In terms of trying to understand the problem of abuse, most promising to me seems to be a systemic perspective that seeks explanations for sexual abuse by Catholic clergy in the complex interaction of many variables, including social environment, specific organizational conditions, individual cognition, and of course choice. This seems to be more realistic than following the route of pathologizing the individual perpetrator or looking for nonconformist bishops. This is not to say that individuals are not to be held accountable for their actions and inactions.

While differences in theological paradigms may partly explain why the current Vatican line is so unrepentant when it comes to matters relating to sexuality, it is also important to acknowledge that it is not just the content of Catholic sexual ethics that is in need of reform. The problematic nexus of issues around sexuality, power, relationship, male domination, and the distinctions between the ordained and the non-ordained, all of which are implicated in the current crisis of sexual abuse within the Catholic Church, could benefit from further scholarly analysis. What matters here are the power dynamics that are at work in a human institution that will not allow itself to be comprehensively examined, even when the calls from such an examination come increasingly from within. Ironically, it may be the case that it is precisely the child sexual abuse by Catholic clergy that finally puts the need for institutional examination onto the Church agenda.

3

The View from the Ground

CLERICAL MEN

MUCH OF THE LITERATURE on Roman Catholic clergy comes from a number of sources, scholarly books and essays, empirical research studies, newspaper reports and some relevant websites. Although not exclusively so, much of the scholarly work on clergy is written by current priests and religious (male and female) who have a professional and/or personal interest in the subject (Balboni, 1998; Cozzens, 2004; Greeley, 1972a, 1972b, 1993, 2004; McGlone, 2001; Papesh, 2004; Ranson, 2002a, 2002b, Rossetti, 1994) or former priests or religious (Kennedy, 1971, 2001; Nines, 2006; Noyes, 1997; Robinson, 1994; Sipe, 1995; 1999, 2003). There are advantages and disadvantages to clergy engaging in this type of research. On the one hand they have an intimate knowledge of seminary and clerical life and the inner workings and dynamics of the Church hierarchy and the institution of the Roman Catholic Church, a knowledge that is invaluable. On the other hand, the risk of bias may be inflated. In this chapter I draw on this literature and other sources to outline the state of the field in relation to Catholic clergy. I first discuss the literature on "normal" clergy, followed by a review of the literature on clerical men who have sexually abused minors, and then I briefly compare both. I conclude the chapter by arguing for an expansive lens through which to understand sexual abuse by Catholic clergy. In my search for understanding, there is no attempt to condone the men's abusive behavior. On the contrary, it is one of the central theses of this book that by understanding the internal "logic" of the apparently illogical action, we learn more about the phenomenon and are in a position to take more decisive and informed action to prevent its occurrence in the future.

NORMAL CLERGY

In the United States during the 1960s and 1970s, priests became the subject of sociological surveys (Greeley, 1972) and empirical psychological research, mainly because of the great exodus of priests during the 1960s and the need of the American Church hierarchy to understand why they left (Balboni, 1998). In the early 1970s, Kennedy (Kennedy and Heckler, 1971), a psychologist based at Loyola University in Chicago was commissioned by the American National Conference of Catholic bishops to study American Catholic clergy. Kennedy was the lead investigator on the project that involved a team of other researchers. In reporting their findings, Kennedy and Heckler (1971, p. 7) described 66% of American clergy as psychologically "underdeveloped", 8% as "maldeveloped", 18% as "developing", and 7% as "developed". They drew attention in particular to personal immaturity, intimacy deficits, poor psychosexual integration, poor self-awareness, and the protective function of the priestly role for the men who were classified as "underdeveloped" (pp. 7-12). According to Kennedy's analysis, the "underdeveloped" men were good at covering up their underdevelopment; they lacked adult relationships and had few close friends. Kennedy reported that "uncertainty about their sexuality affects their sense of personal identity and makes it difficult for them to accept and deal with the challenges of intimacy" (Kennedy and Heckler, pp.11-12). Kennedy wondered why, given that priests are carefully selected and supervised during a long period of training, nobody in authority had noticed the level of psychological underdevelopment among the clergy before or had taken steps to remedy the situation.

In 1972, in another study commissioned by the American National Conference of Catholic bishops, Greeley (1972b, p. 311) reported, that while priests were no more or less emotionally immature than any other group of men, they did report dissatisfaction with work life and with the ecclesiastical structures of decision-making, and they were lonely. Recommendations were made for the American church hierarchy to address the authority concerns and feelings of loneliness among the American clergy. Fichter (1974, p. 9) also studied clergy and argues "clergy represent a kind of marginal man. They cannot be of service to men if they remain strangers to the life and conditions of men." He saw the need for the institutional Church to take better care of its priests, particularly in relation to their personal and professional development. When Kennedy did a follow-up study by telephone and e-mail in 1997 and 1998, he found that little had changed: this time, 57% were said to be "underdeveloped", 29% were "developing", 8% were "maldeveloped", and only 6% were "emotionally and psychosexually developed" (Kennedy, 1998, cited in Balboni, 1998).

In 1998, Balboni undertook research with the American bishops in which she wanted to find out more about their handling of allegations of sexual abuse against Catholic clergy. In the course of this research Balboni (1998) discovered that the American bishops had not taken action on Kennedy's (1971) findings. She found that the signs of a crisis with Catholic clergy, of distress, immaturity, and unmet human and spiritual needs, that had been identified since the early 1970s were ignored consistently by the Church hierarchy in the United States. Even after they had commissioned several studies and received data on priests' "underdevelopment," Balboni could find no evidence that the American National Conference of Bishops had initiated discussions on the findings or made any attempt to follow through on the suggestions made or to respond to the needs of the struggling priests. No effort appears to have been made to address the questions raised in Kennedy and Heckler's (1971) research. In Balboni's opinion, the crisis with sexual abuse by Catholic clergy might have been averted, in the United States at least, had the Church hierarchy intervened in the early 1970s to help the struggling clergy, who happened to be the majority.

In Ireland, Lane (1997) reported findings suggesting high levels of dissatisfaction and unhappiness in the Catholic clergy and also made recommendations, none of which have been significantly addressed by the Church hierarchy in Ireland either. If anything, reports suggest that Catholic clergy in Ireland are suffering even lower levels of morale and deflation than they were in 1997, particularly in those dioceses where there have been disclosures of a significant amount of abuse by their colleagues (Duffy, 2009; Hoban, 2010). There are also reports of tensions and rifts between some of the bishops and the priests of their dioceses (Duffy, 2009, p. 116). In my view, bishops ignore these relational break-downs at their peril, if lessons are to be learned from the U.S. situation.

Since the 1970s a number of other smaller studies on normal Roman Catholic clergy have examined various aspects of clerical life, especially in the United States (Benyei, 1998; Connors, 1994; Hoge, 2002 Keddy, Erdberg, & Sammon, 1990; Lane, 1997; Loftus, 1999, 2004; Madden, 1990; Plante & Boccaccini, 1997; Plante, Manuel, & Tandez, 1996), but there remains a dearth of in-depth studies in particular on the sexual lives and experiences of Catholic clergy (Kennedy, 1971, 2001; McGlone, 2001; Nines, 2006; Sipe, 1990, 1995, 1999, 2003, 2004). Of the studies that are available, most emanate from the United States. In addition, the limitations of the studies, such as small sample sizes and non-matched controls, indicate the need for caution in interpreting many of the findings. What is perhaps more useful is to consider some of the themes that emerge in the empirical literature on those men who are described as the "normal" clergy and on what they have to say about their lives.

Plante, Manuel, and Tandez (1996, p. 30) tested 21 applicants for the Roman Catholic priesthood in the United States and made a number of observations about successful candidates for the priesthood. They tended to maintain a defensive and especially repressive style of relating with a high degree of concern for controlling hostile impulses. Successful candidates for the priesthood demonstrated elevated scores on the Masculinity-Femininity and Feminine Gender Role scales on the MMPI-2, indicating traditional feminine interests. They scored high on Responsibility scales, indicating a higher sense of social responsibility than the general population. On the 16 Personality Factor test the group produced results suggestive of a high degree of imaginativeness, sensitivity, and trust.

In a study of 143 Roman Catholic priests in the United States, Madden (1990, p. 80) found that the priests reported job demands that exceeded their personal and professional resources, but they were unable to acknowledge their need for support. The intense demands of the job and the absence of sufficient support were also reported in a survey of priests in Ireland (Lane, 1997, p. 62). In the Lane (1997, p. 40) study, priests felt less support from Church leaders than from family and friends; they also reported that the Mass, preaching, and their spiritual ministries generally helped sustain and support them. Dunn (1990, p.133) reviewed the professional literature concerning MMPI investigations with Catholic priests and found that priests tend to be more perfectionist, worrisome, and introverted and, in more extreme cases, more isolated and withdrawn than other men. Hoge (2002, p. 11) argued that the overextension of priests in their ministries has implications not only for the quality of the work done, but also for the men's spiritual lives and for their happiness. A study by Plante and Boccaccini (1997, p. 112) involving a group of Roman Catholic priests and 100 college students found that the college students viewed the priests as more introverted and less sociable than the priests viewed themselves. Benyei (1998, p. 37) in the United States reported that a high percentage of clergy came from family experiences that resulted in tendencies towards low self-esteem, reluctance to trust others, and reluctance to admit to personal neediness, pain, or the need for help. Such clergy were likely to be other-directed and overly dependent on the perceptions of others. In a more recent study of 80 clergy in the United States, McGlone (2001, p. 119) reported an interesting finding: 59% of the participants said they had received some form of psychological treatment or counseling at some time in their priesthood, mainly relating to depression, sexual orientation, sexual identity, and alcoholism. This finding may signal a shift in the attitudes of "normal" clergy towards seeking psychological help for their problems, but further research is required to assess this issue more comprehensively.

Few studies have researched clergy attitudes towards sexuality, partly because of the secrecy surrounding the topic and the difficulty in persuading clergy to participate in such research (McGlone, 2001, p. 6; Nines, 2006, p. 16). The issue is compounded by the reluctance of the Catholic hierarchy to support such research. In Nines' (2006) study of the sexuality of "normal" clergy and in McGlone's (2001) comparative study of clergy who had abused with those who had not, Church leaders in the United States actively intervened to prevent clergy from participating in the studies (McGlone, 2001, p. 60; Nines, 2006, p. 132). Thus, while it is the case that no one knows very much within the bounds of empirical fact about clergy attitudes towards sexuality, a small number of studies throw some light on certain aspects of the topic.

Keddy, Erdberg, and Sammon (1990, p. 155) found in a small study of 36 Roman Catholic clergy in the United States that 44% of the study participants experienced significant sexual concerns, particularly in relation to celibacy and sexual orientation. In relation to celibacy and sexual activity, a number of other small studies also give an overview of trends in relation to the sexuality issues for priests in the United States. In his study of 80 clergy, McGlone (2001, p. 108) reported that 53% of the clergy participants were sexually active at the time—28% with a female, 22% with a male, and 3% with both a male and a female. Forty-three percent of those participants who were sexually active had been in a sexual relationship for 1 year or more. According to McGlone (2001, p. 114) heterosexual priests and homosexual priests were sexually active in equal measures, contrary to the myth that it is only homosexual clergy who are sexually active. A clear majority of McGlone's subjects (92% of them) reported that even though they knew of Church doctrine on celibacy and chastity, they engaged in sexual activity because they saw this as a necessary part of their humanity (p. 114). They did not agree with the Church's discipline of mandatory celibacy for all priests. The priests who reported being sexually active said that they chose not to accept the Church's doctrine on celibacy and chastity. They were in direct but silent conflict with Church rule and discipline while still exercising ministry within the Church. While sexuality posed challenges for all priests, those priests who described themselves as being of a homosexual orientation expressed considerable internal struggle, especially with regard to exposure of their sexual orientation (p. 114). Based on their analysis of a range of data, the John Jay College (2011: 74) reported, that priests who were in seminaries in the 1960s and earlier, had some level of psychosexual vulnerability. The clinical data confirm that many priests, ordained between 1930 and 1970 had difficulty sustaining a celibate life. The data also confirm that 80% of those who had received psychological treatment for a range of emotional and psychological issues had been sexually active after ordination, primarily with adults.

Sipe (2003, p. 89) conducted an ethnographic study of celibacy in the priesthood that spanned 40 years and included data on 2,776 active and resigned priests. He estimated that at any one time 50% of clergy are practicing celibacy, and it is their intention to become

celibate even if they experience occasional lapses along the way; 28% are involved in heterosexual relationships, associations, experimentation, or patterns of behavior; 11% are involved
in homosexual relationships, associations, experimentation, or patterns of behavior; 5% are
involved with problematic sexual behaviors; and the remaining 6% are sexually active with
minors (pp. 50–51). According to Sipe (2003, p. 51), two thirds of those clergy who are heterosexually active are involved in a more or less stable sexual relationship with a woman or
with a sequence of women in an identifiable pattern. The remainder is at a stage of heterosexual exploration. According to Sipe (2003, p. 51), half of the Catholic clergy who are of a
homosexual orientation are sexually active and more than half of them are in a stable homosexual relationship. Like McGlone (2001, p. 114), Sipe (2003, p. 51) also reported that both
heterosexually active and homosexually active clergy in the United States experience little
guilt about their breach of celibacy. However, some homosexual clergy experience guilt
about their sexual orientation and the sexual acts they participate in; they use sacramental
confession or some means of spiritual direction to deal with these feelings (Sipe, 2003,
p. 52).

Not everyone agrees with Sipe's figures, most notably Andrew Greeley. Greeley's figures
(2004, pp. 34–40), from about 2,000 active priests, suggest that 82% of priests honor their
promise of celibacy. Hoge and Wenger (2003) also found in a survey of over 1,200 priests
that a relatively small number, 11%, cited celibacy as a serious problem. There was a difference between active and resigned priests in another survey conducted by Hoge (2002),
which found that priests who had resigned expressed much less satisfaction with celibate
living than men who remained priests.

In an in-depth analysis of a survey of 176 active priests and 27 former priests (also in the
United States), Nines (2006, p. 110) found that taken together, 28% of the respondents were
of a homosexual or bisexual orientation. However, when Nines (2006, p. 116) analyzed the
data further he found that of those men who were still active in the priesthood, 42.8% were
of a homosexual orientation, and the majority of men who had resigned from the priesthood
identified themselves as heterosexual. Sipe (1995, p. 136) estimated that 30% of all Roman
Catholic clergy in the United States are of a homosexual orientation, while Cozzens (2000,
p. 97) suggests a figure of 45% to 50%. McGlone (2001, p. 106) reports that 40% of the clergy
participants in his study in the United States were either homosexual or bisexual in orientation (homosexuality 31%, bisexuality 9%). Nines (2006, p. 118) found that the priests
who described themselves as homosexual pledged fidelity to Church teaching publicly,
and said that public support for the position of the Church was important to them.
However, privately these men were strained and feared that their sexual orientation would
be discovered.

What is at issue here is the fact that significant numbers of Catholic clergy are sexually
active, a situation that is either denied or ignored as the Catholic Church continues to pro-
claim celibate living by its clergy. While loving, consenting relationships between Catholic
clergy and adult women or men can and do exist, and may even be helpful to the cleric in
avoiding loneliness and becoming more effective in his work, these relationships are embedded in secrecy and dishonesty and are in effect supporting a myth. The myth needs to be
confronted for the health of all—the men, the women, and future generations of clergy.
Otherwise the very commitment to celibacy itself is becoming a means of compromising
a man's integrity. As well as this, in circumstances where priests are involved in sexual

relationships with partners, not only might there be a power differential inherent in the relationship, depending on the circumstances of the meeting, but there may also be an ethical violation of the priest's fiduciary obligations (as well as a breach of celibacy). These relationships are also fraught with difficulty when they end, with many former partners of clergy feeling used and abused. These are often the circumstances in which many people get hurt, even those who were or are "consenting."

Homosexuality within the clergy is an issue that is also raised in relation to "normal" clergy and it is an area one must discuss with care, given the level of misunderstanding that can arise in a society that is predominantly heterosexual and in which homosexual men and lesbian women suffer continuous discrimination. The unfortunate and inaccurate link that is sometimes made between homosexuality and child sexual abuse by Catholic clergy makes the topic even more sensitive and one which must be treated sensitively and rigorously.

From the early 1960s and maybe even before, seminaries attempted to deal with homosexuality by a prohibition on "particular friendships" as they were called. The men were trained in communal and highly regulated regimes in which there were clear codes governing prayer-life, study and social interaction. In some seminaries, seminarians were directed to wear bathing suits in the shower (Frawley-O'Dea, 2007, p. 118). However, since the 2002 sexual abuse crisis in the United States, Frawley-O'Dea argues that some seminaries have been cast as "pink palaces" in which "seminarians and their staffs openly tolerate gay sex whilst sometimes discriminating against straight seminarians by excluding them, usually subtly, from the social world of the seminary" (p. 119). I have no way of checking the veracity of this claim except to say that it does not appear to match the Irish experience, as far as I can determine. Frawley-O'Dea draws on numerous case examples and anecdotal material to support her thesis that some seminaries in the United States have a gay subculture. Hoge and Wenger (2003, p. 102) found that 41% of priests felt there was probably a homosexual subculture in the seminary they attended. However, this perception was matched with age. Among diocesan priests over 66 years of age, only 3% held this view. That number increased to 11% for priests between 56 and 65, 38% for men between 36 and 45, and 47% for clergy age 35 and under. It may well be that the number of gay seminarians has increased as society has become more accepting of homosexuality and as the rules against "particular friendships" were relaxed in the United States gay seminarians in the United States felt more comfortable seeking out each other's company. However, anecdotal evidence suggests that the situation is still highly policed in Irish seminaries, although the President of the National Seminary says this is not so (Murphy Report, 2009, p. 163). He draws a distinction between homosexual orientation and homosexual behavior, the latter forming the formal grounds for dismissal of a clerical student from the college.

Other studies also report clergy sexual activity in a number of other contexts. There are reports of abuse of adult women, under the guise of "consent" (Fortune, 1992, 1994; Kennedy, 2003), there are reports of sexual abuse of religious sisters by priests and bishops when they were serving in Africa (France, 2004, p. 391; Smith, 2003) and there are reports of abuse of seminarians by faculty-members (Sipe, 1995). Smith (2003) suggests there is evidence for abuse of religious sisters by priests and bishops in 23 countries worldwide, including the United States. Sipe (1995, p. 40) reports that 10% of clergy in the United States report having been sexually abused during their studies for ordination. He argues that sexual abuse within seminaries by faculty-member priests is a significant problem for the

Catholic Church. One of the nine men who participated in my research was sexually abused in a seminary, and in the course of my clinical work I have worked with several men who were sexually abused by priests in Irish seminaries. Overall, there are many sexuality concerns for "normal" clergy that call out for serious institutional understanding and attention.

The Need for Better Formation

Several studies advocate the need for better education and formation for priests and semi-narians, in the area of sexuality and celibacy and in clerical and religious life in general (Cozzens, 2004, p. 38; Hoge, 2002, p. 98; Loftus, 2004, p. 92; Papesh, 2004, p. 70; Sipe, 2003, p. 277). According to Hoge (2002, p. 96) priests complained that seminary formation did not prepare them adequately to deal with the laity. Both resigned and active priests rec-ommended the need for more openness about sexuality in seminaries. They also recom-mended more realistic seminary training for the life of the priest (Hoge, 2002, p. 96; Nines, 2006, p. 120). For Hoge there is a litany of explicitly sexual issues for clerics and seminarians that cry out for more openness and research (p. 103). In 1995, Father Colm Kilcoyne, an Irish religious affairs columnist with the Irish newspaper the *Sunday Press* wrote: "In seven years in Maynooth I never had a minute's advice on how to live in celibacy and still stay normal and warm. In thirty-five years as a priest I have never been at a local conference in our Diocese when we talked openly and honestly about celibacy" (cited in Hegarty, 1996). How the sem-inarians and priests of the future can be better educated and prepared for a life of priestly ministry and celibate living is raised time and again in the literature on "normal" clergy. Many individuals who have worked with clergy for decades continually make the plea for better formation for clergy (Hoge, 2002, p. 98; Loftus, 2004, p. 92; Sipe, 2003, p. 277). A number of clinicians also show concern that priests have an understanding of their celi-bate commitment that seems overly intellectualized (Connors, 1994; Loftus, 1999, 2004; Sipe, 1990, 1995).

Working Conditions

The literature on normal Catholic clergy is best summarized as presenting a scenario where the conditions or expectations under which clergy function can create enormous stress, par-ticularly for people who discount their personal needs and who take too much responsibility for the well-being of others, over whose lives they have little control (Brenneis, 2001; Cozzens, 2000; Lane, 1997). If the priest takes a defensive and repressive stance towards his inner life especially with the material that poses an emotional threat, such as loneliness, feel-ings of isolation, and hostile, aggressive, and sexual feelings, the stress is significantly ampli-fied, and ways of coping may include abuse of alcohol or other substances and sexual acting out (Brenneis, 2001, p. 23). Perfectionist attitudes towards the self, a defensive approach to self-awareness and personal disclosure, a reluctance to identify vulnerability and ask for help, and an emotionally demanding profession in which interpersonal boundaries are often not clear all combine to present significant challenges for the modern cleric. The fact that the laity maintain high expectations of clergy (although child sexual abuse by clergy has lowered such expectations), along with the fact that many of the activities of priests are directed towards the spiritual and emotional needs of others, means that the social environment may not be conducive for clerics to discuss their human concerns in an open and honest manner.

Close friendships need to be fostered, but this too creates dilemmas. Be that as it may there is strong supporting evidence for the view that if priests don't find a space in which to speak honestly and in which to resolve their innermost conflicts, these unresolved conflicts can lead to all kinds of acting out, including alcohol abuse and various sexual behaviors (Brenneis, 2001, p. 24). In reviewing the literature on "normal" clergy, one is struck by the question of why more priests are not in crisis, rather than why some are.

In many regards, the above literature points to a conclusion that priests live in an environment that is beset with contradictions, such as a promise to celibacy but little preparation for living it; a need for intimacy but inability to ask for it; problems with sexuality and sexual orientation but a need to conceal it. Considerable skill is required for living the life of the clergyman, and one would imagine that the training for clergy would be hugely important in this regard. It is interesting, therefore, to note that the literature on "normal" clergy shows consistently that clergy do not feel well prepared in the seminaries and houses of formation for their lives and ministries (Hoge, 2002, p. 98; Loftus, 2004, p. 92; Papesh, 2004, p. 70; Sipe, 2003, p. 277), nor do they feel adequately supported by Church hierarchies in living that life (Lane, 1997, p. 62). This is a theme that also arises in my research and that will be examined again later.

One can also conclude from the above literature that the spaces for clergy in which to speak are few, leading some of them towards the protective environments of spiritual direction, personal psychotherapy, and confession (McGlone, 2001, p. 119; Ranson, 2002b, p. 220). However, overall the picture is one of clergy keeping their personal, sexual, and emotional selves as private, and not shared honestly with other clergy. Cozzens (2004, p. 112) argues that clerical culture supports such nondisclosure of emotion or emotional distress. In my research, the confessional emerges as the most important site for disclosure of personal distress for the clerical participants, including sexual offending, and the confessional also emerges as the most important site from which the participants seek emotional support. Few of the men in my research used spiritual direction for this or any other purpose. This theme is more fully explored later.

A most striking feature of the above examination of the literature on "normal" clergy is the finding that up to 50% of Roman Catholic clergy (in the studies that have been conducted in the United States) are sexually active at any one time, despite adopting a vow of chastity and a commitment to celibate living. Several studies (McGlone, 2001; Nines, 2006; Sipe, 2003, John Jay College, 2011) report this trend. This is an important finding because it indicates that sexual abuse of minors by Catholic clergy may be part of a bigger problem of celibate sexuality for the Roman Catholic Church.

Clergy engaging in consensual sexual relationships is merely a disciplinary matter for the Roman Catholic Church and of itself is not of civil or criminal concern, nor can its effects be compared with the sexual abuse of children. However, the widespread lack of celibate practice in the Roman Catholic Church *is* relevant to the central issue of the sexual abuse of minors by Catholic clergy because an organization that publicly proclaims the sexual abstinence of its members while at the same time tolerating or denying the very existence of their sexual activity is already in trouble. Celibacy—the state of non-marriage and the practice of perfect chastity—is a requirement for ordination to the Catholic priesthood in the Latin Rite (Canon Law Society, 1983, Canon 227). The Catholic bishop is mandated to supervise and ensure compliance with this requirement. Celibacy is an ongoing requirement for the active priesthood, an image that the Church hierarchy, including bishops, religious superiors, and the Vatican, has diligently fostered. The fact that "consensual" sexual activities take place by clergy in secret and within the institutional rhetoric of an all-male celibate clergy suggests systemic denial and failure to address the problems that celibacy poses, thus creating an unhealthy organizational culture (Cozzens, 2004; Ranson, 2002a, 2002b). Even if celibacy is not a direct cause of a problem as complex as sexual abuse by Catholic clergy, an unhealthy organizational culture in which the problems of sexuality are ignored, may be part of the context in which this problem becomes possible.

SEXUALLY OFFENDING CATHOLIC CLERGY: EMPIRICAL STUDIES

Much more research has been undertaken with non-clerical men who have sexually abused minors than with clergy offenders, and that research will be analyzed in Chapter 4. However, some important data are emerging on clerical perpetrators that give clues to what might be some of the constituent elements in their sexual-offending trajectories. The key findings of the empirical literature on clerical perpetrators will now be summarized.

Haywood, Kravitz, Wasyliw, Goldberg, and Cavanaugh (1996, p. 1241) and Loftus and Camargo (1993, p. 292) found that clergy who abuse minors are more likely to do so as the result of psychosexual adjustment and development issues than as a result of a psychiatric disorder or antisocial personality traits. Clergy who sexually abuse minors are generally not suffering from psychiatric conditions. In a study of 111 sexually abusive clergy at a treatment program in Canada, loneliness emerged as a significant finding in the men's histories (Loftus & Camargo, 1993, p. 292). This finding is also noted in the work of several clinicians with extensive experience of involvement with sexually offending clerics (Kennedy, 2001; Loftus, 1999; Sipe, 1995). Other scholars (Plante, Manuel, & Bryant, 1996, p. 135; Robinson, 1994, p. 365) report that clerical perpetrators have considerable difficulty in expressing emotional concerns and there are some findings to indicate levels of depression (prior to the abuse as well as afterwards). Robinson (1994, p. 365) compared non-offending and offending clergy in the United States and found that sexually abusing clergy were more depressed than the comparison group. The offending clergy also had more difficulty in identifying and disclosing emotions than their non-offending colleagues.

In relation to seeking help for psychological distress, while McGlone (2001, p. 88) found that 59% of "normal" clergy identified themselves as having received some form of psychological treatment or counseling in the previous years (mainly relating to depression, sexual orientation, sexual identity issues, and alcoholism), Flakenhain et al. (1999, p. 330) found that only 1.8% to 2.5% of sexually offending clergy ever sought psychological help prior to treatment for their sexual offending. Clergy who were identified as child sexual offenders simply did not seek help for their sexual and emotional problems. In my research, clergy who had sexually abused minors did not disclose emotional distress to others and did not seek help for their problems prior to disclosure of their abuse of minors and their subsequent referral for sexual offender treatment. In contrast, the "normal" clergy I interviewed had sought help for their life problems.

Plante, Manuel, and Bryant (1996, p. 135) compared 80 sexually abusive Roman Catholic priests with 80 controls, also Roman Catholic priests, and found that over-controlled hostility was the only item that differentiated the offending group from the control group.

The authors postulated that priests who sexually offend may be acting out their chronically over-controlled anger and aggression. Thus, while some level of anger and hostility was seen in both normal and offending clergy, these scholars suggest that higher levels of over-controlled hostility correlate with increased chances of clergy acting out in a sexual way with a minor, or with someone in a less powerful position than themselves. Blanchard (1991, p. 238) also reports that anger and hostility might play a role in clergy sexual abuse, and he suggests that power, control, and the need for personal reassurance has also some role to play in these offenses.

My research builds on the existing literature on the relationship between anger and sexual abuse by Catholic clergy, which to date has been under-theorized. One of the consequences of living in an environment in which there is a gap between the rhetoric and the reality, and in which honesty is not the norm regarding personal life and experience, is the development of covert patterns of meeting personal needs. While my research and some of the literature on clergy offenders suggests that loneliness, isolation, and anger must be considered significant in their sexual offending, on their own these factors are not sufficient to "explain" sexual offending by Catholic clergy. This requires more complex analysis, to which I will return in Chapter 10.

Robinson (1994, p. 365) reports that a group of clergy offenders reveals much more concern with authority than a non-offending group. Using various personality tests he found that sexually abusing clergy tended to have higher scores on MMPI-2 measures of authority concerns that the comparison group. Rossetti (1994, p. 4) reports that clergymen who have abused minors have a passive and conforming style of relating. This research is based on his clinical and research work at a treatment program in the United States. Similarly, in their study of 111 sexually abusive clergy, Loftus and Camargo (1993, p. 292) found that Roman Catholic clergy who sexually abuse minors tend to be lonely men, and they are shy and passive in their relationships with other adults.

What is interesting here is how the scholarly work on the personality and biographies of clerical men who have sexually abused minors contrast with the profile of clerical sexual offenders that is presented in popular culture. It is rare to hear that the clerical perpetrator may have been shy or lonely; rather, it is more often said that he was flamboyant or bold, (which of course is true in some cases but not in all). Emotional loneliness and personal isolation are significant features of the biographies of clerical sexual offenders, yet the implications of these factors are rarely considered in public discourses of child sexual abuse by clergy. It is understandable that a hurt and betrayed public is wary of considering any factors that might appear like excuse-making for sexual offenders or that might exonerate sexual offenders from responsibility for their offenses. However, what is also invoked here is a broader international pattern, particularly in the United States, the United Kingdom, and Ireland, in how the crime and the criminal are currently conceived and represented. With increasing emphasis on "moral individualism" and less concern for the context of the lives of the criminal, or for social or political understandings, explanations of crime are based on "a much darker vision of the human condition" than has been the case in previous times (Garland, 2001, p. 15). The criminal is now seen as "culpable, undeserving, and somewhat dangerous," someone from whom the public must be protected (Garland, 2001, p. 175). The result of these changes in the dominant paradigm of crime in the United States, the United Kingdom, and Ireland is that the public discourse is more focused on blaming the perpetrator, silencing his explanations, ignoring root causes, and seeing him punished (Garland, 2001, pp. 130–131). In the case of child sexual offenders it is also thought that they should be subjected to the most rigorous monitoring and constraints on their liberty because of something they could do in the future.

As mentioned earlier, Roman Catholic priests and religious in treatment for sexual offending in Canada were described as ignorant about sexual matters, but this was true for all groups of clergy attending the treatment center, not just those who had abused minors (Loftus & Camargo, 1993, p. 292). Knowledge of the basic physiology of sexuality and of the emotional responses in sexually charged situations appeared to be totally lacking for all participants (Loftus & Camargo, 1993, p. 300). Flakenhain et al. (1999, p. 331) tested 97 Roman Catholic priests and religious brothers who had abused children and found them to be sexually and emotionally underdeveloped. This was a term that Kennedy used in his research with U.S. clergy in 1971.

Several studies report that clergy who have sexually abused minors have experienced sexual abuse themselves in childhood, sometimes by another priest or religious. Figures given are 66% (Robinson, Montana, & Thompson, 1993), 30% to 35% (Connors, 1994), 70% to 80% (Sipe, 1995), 33% to 50% (Valcour, 1990, p. 49), and 66% (Bryant, 1999). The John Jay College (2011, p. 119) reported that the data indicate that the experience of having been sexually abused by an adult while a minor increased the risk that priests would later abuse a child. Six of the nine participants in my research reported a history of sexual abuse, five in childhood and one man in the seminary. Although sexual abuse in childhood can never be accepted as an excuse for sexual offending in adulthood, and many people who experience childhood sexual abuse never abuse anyone, this is an important finding. It is also important that many clergy who had experienced sexual abuse in childhood never discussed these experiences until they were in treatment for sexual offending. Perrillo et al. (2008, p. 611), who analyzed the John Jay (2004) data to try to understand repeat[i] offending by Catholic clergy, found that a history of childhood sexual victimization was found to be one of the strongest predictive variables for clerical men to become repeat offenders. This is an important observation because there is not overall support for this finding in the general literature on other child sexual offenders (Hanson et al., 1993; Hanson & Morton-Bourgon, 2004, 2005). Priests and religious who have experienced childhood sexual abuse may be different in this regard.

In relation to sexual orientation, one study involving 158 Catholic clergy who had sexually abused children and young people found that 44% described themselves as homosexual in orientation, 40% said they were heterosexual, 15% said they were bisexual, and 2% said they were asexual (McGlone, 2002; 2003, p. 115). There is no evidence that sexual identity and sexually abusive behavior have the same origins, and while the majority of priests and religious have abused adolescent boys, the picture does not represent a simple linear trajectory from child sexual abuse of males to homosexuality, or the other way around. In the general child sexual offender field, adult heterosexuality is still reported as the predominant sexual orientation of men who sexually abuse prepubertal children, both boys and girls, while men who abuse adolescent boys are much more likely to have a homosexual orientation (Langevin, Curnoe & Bain, 2000, p. 537; Marshall, 1988, pp. 383–391). However, some men abuse both boys and girls, adolescents and children. Therefore, it is not simply a case of heterosexual men abusing prepubertal girls and homosexual men abusing boys.

The existing literature on sexual abuse by Catholic clergy does not give sufficient prominence to the important issue of what might be referred to as homophobic tendencies within the Catholic Church and in the broader society and how this disables the development of human sexuality and the natural expression of sexual desire and relationship. This is of particular relevance since Catholic sexual teaching sees homosexuality as a dysfunction, and to some extent homophobia is supported by social structures in many jurisdictions. Recent research on identity formation in gay men suggests that homophobia is a particular feature of male gender socialization, and sexual identity development involves a complex range of internalized and externalized male behaviors (Brady, 2008; Cassese, 2001). This is even more so for a group of men who are socialized together into a life of celibate living in an all-male institutional environment. While the literature on child sexual abuse frequently refers to a range of symptoms, such as distrust, shame, guilt, inferiority, confusion, isolation, and despair, that can develop on the part of some individuals who experience abuse (Bass & Davis, 1993; Herman, 1992; Salter, 1995), there is an emerging literature on the impact of sexual abuse on the sexual identity formation in gay men (Cassese, 2001). This literature suggests that experiences of childhood sexual abuse expose the young gay individual to a range of negative mental and physical health symptoms. These effects include suicide (Herrel et al., 1999; Vives, 2002), anxiety and mood disorders (Dillon, 2001), chemical and substance abuse (Gonsiorek, Sell, & Weinrich, 1995; Magel, 2002), and high-risk sexual behavior (Dolezal, 2002; Kalichman et al., 2004; Paul et al., 2001). While this literature sensitizes us to the suffering that can come in the wake of childhood sexual abuse for victims and survivors, and the complexities of this experience for sexual identity formation, particularly for victims and survivors who are also gay, it must also sensitize us to the experiences of Catholic clergy who are not only victims of child sexual abuse but who are also gay as they attempt and sometimes fail to reconcile a gay sexual identity in a Catholic culture that largely sees them as suffering from "dysfunction."

Connors (1994) reports that 45% of clergy sexual offenders have a problem with substance abuse, mainly alcohol. However, this finding should be interpreted with caution, as Connors conducted his research in a treatment center that also had a history of treating priests for alcoholism. Flakenhain et al. (1999, p. 330) suggests that 47% of the clergy sexual offenders in his study in the United States had problems related to alcohol abuse, and some clergy offenders used alcohol as a disinhibitor during their sexual offenses. Loftus and Camargo (1993, p. 292) report no significant history of alcohol abuse in their study of clergy offenders in Canada. Robinson (1994, p. 365) found that sexually abusing clergy tended to have higher scores on measures of addiction problems than the comparison group of non-offending clergy. In my study one man reported a problem with alcohol and with overuse of prescribed medication during the time he was abusing.

Lothstein (1999, p. 59) presented data from his work in the United States to suggest that Roman Catholic clergy sexual offenders may have neuropsychological deficits that are attributable to frontal lobe dysfunction. Langevin (2004, p. 39) reports the presence of endocrine disorders in clergy sexual offenders in the United States. Some men had uncontrolled diabetes (25.8%) and others had thyroid disorders (6.5%). Although such disorders are more common in older people, and clerical sexual offenders tend to be older than other child sexual offenders, the rate of endocrine disorders in clerical sexual offenders was significantly higher than for an age-matched control group (4.2%) and the population at large (5%). According to Langevin

(2004, p. 39), both age and the presence of endocrine disorders appeared to contribute to poor performance on neurocognitive tasks in almost half of the clergy tested.

Religious proscriptions and training are said to play a role in sexual offending by Catholic clergy by a number of scholars of this topic (Connors, 1994; Saradjian & Nobus, 2003; Thomson et al., 1998). Connors (1994) observes that the priest offender typically demonstrates and insists upon strict adherence to liturgical rubrics, while on the other hand he may sexually abuse adolescents without apparent regard for the moral realities involved. Connors (1994) suggests that many clergy offenders who are strict conservatives in their theological views engage in sexual deviance without apparent regard for the implicit contradictions between the ideal and the reality, the theory of morality and their actual moral behavior. Saradjian and Nobus (2003, p. 905) and Thomson et al. (1998, pp. 176–177) report that religious offenders use religion-related beliefs prior to the sexual acts to enable them to overcome inhibitions to offend, and after the offense to reduce guilt and maintain a positive self-image. While these scholars theorize religious beliefs in sexual offending as evidence of cognitive distortions, my interpretation, based on an in-depth examination of the men's narratives, is that religion-related beliefs in sexual offending are more accurately conceptualized as evidence of their experience of the moral and institutional contradictions inherent in the form of clerical masculinity and way of clerical living that are promoted as ideal by the Catholic Church. My study of the subject leads me to think that religious proscriptions are indeed implicated in clerical sexual offending, but far from being evidence of cognitive distortions they are in fact evidence of an institutional logic that is acted out by these men. These ideas will be further discussed later.

It is continually emphasized in the empirical literature on Catholic clergy (Loftus, 1999; McGlone, 2001; Nines, 2006) that very few comprehensive studies exist on the sexual histories and sexual experiences of "normal" clergy and seminarians. This can also be said of clerical perpetrators. The limitations of the available studies that are outlined above, such as small samples and non-matched controls, indicate the need for caution in interpreting these research findings. Despite their limitations, the studies that I have referred to, offer an indication of some of the clinical features of Catholic clergy who have sexually offended against minors. They also allow for comparisons to be made, even tentatively, between the personality features of "normal" clergy and the clerical perpetrators, which offer some small but perhaps significant pointers as to what personality factors, if any, may distinguish these two groups of men.

COMPARING CLERICAL OFFENDERS AND NORMAL CLERGY

The psychological factors that are continually emphasized in the psychological and psychiatric literature to differentiate sexually offending clergy from "normal" clergy are subscales of personality and clinical testing that suggest over-controlled hostility and sexual identity confusion on the part of the clerical perpetrators, although this is simply a matter of degree. Clerical offenders are also thought to be more passive and conforming in their patterns of relating, but again this may be related to over-controlled hostility and an inability or reluctance to deal openly with conflict and anger. Clerical offenders are also thought to have a higher incidence of childhood sexual abuse than "normal" clergy.

Despite these patterns that are highlighted in the literature, such individual or psychological factors alone are insufficient to explain why some clergy sexually offend against minors and why sexual offending by Roman Catholic clergy occurs in the first place. As the results of the John Jay College (2011, p. 3) research concludes, priests with allegations of sexual abuse of minors are not significantly more likely than other priests to have personality or mood disorders. No "psychological, developmental, or behavioral characteristic differentiated priests who abused minors from those who did not" (p. 74). Priests who sexually abused minors did not differ significantly from other priests on psychological or intelligence tests. However, they had vulnerabilities, intimacy deficits and an absence of close personal relationships before and during seminary (p. 5). These social features seem significant and meaningful. The impact of the differences on the subscales of personality and clinical testing as discussed earlier are generally poorly understood and on the face of it do not appear to be clinically significant. These might however be further investigated in future research.

My perspective however is that alternative interpretations to the prevailing model of individual pathology must be explored in our attempts to understand the clerical perpetrator. While McGlone (2001, p. 56) argues for the development of more sensitive psychological assessment instruments to more accurately search for and assess individual pathology, I argue for a broader angle of vision in which to view the problem. Rather than continue the search for the individual pathology that will explain all, in Chapter 10 I set out an alternative analytical framework that offers a point of departure for a more comprehensive explanation of the problem. My work weaves together both individual and systemic dimensions as an attempt to understand and explain and ultimately prevent in as far as possible, sexual abuse by Catholic clergy.

COMPARING CLERICAL AND NON-CLERICAL CHILD SEXUAL OFFENDERS

The psychological literature also provides some tentative data that help compare the psychological profile of clerical offenders with non-clerical child sexual offenders and to suggest some themes. In a number of obvious respects the clerical offender is different from other child sexual offenders. Clerical offenders make a commitment to celibacy, make a vocational commitment to work for the good of God and the community, are trained in the unique environment of an all-male seminary, are subject to one authority, and vow obedience to one supreme head. It is therefore interesting to discover if clergy who commit sexual offenses against minors are different in any respects from other child sexual offenders, and if so in what ways. Within the methodological limitations of the existing data, several studies help with this analysis. Overall, a number of factors are seen to distinguish clerical perpetrators from non-clerical comparisons.

Clerical perpetrators of sexual abuse against minors are older than non clerical offenders (Haywood, Kravitz, Grossman, Wasyliw, & Hardy, 1996, pp. 527–536; Langevin, Curnoe, & Bain, 2000;). They are better educated (Langevin, Curnoe, & Bain, 2000, p. 540) and have a higher IQ (Haywood, Kravitz, Grossman, Wasyliw, & Hardy, 1996, p. 531; Langevin, Curoe, & Bain, 2000; Sullivan & Beech, 2004, p. 49). They are less antisocial and have little history of other kinds of criminal activity (Langevin, Curnoe & Bain, 2000, p. 540; Loftus and Comargo, 1993, pp. 287–303). They are more likely to have abused adolescent boys (Connors, 1994; Haywood, Kravitz, Grossman, Wasyliw, & Hardy, 1996, p. 531). They are more likely than other perpetrators of offenses against minors to report an adult homosexual orientation (Langevin, Curnoe, & Bain, 2000, p. 540; McGlone, 2002). They show a relatively low incidence of general psychopathology (Flakenhain et al., 1999, p. 329; Haywood, Kravitz, Grossman, Wasyliw, & Hardy, 1996, p. 531; Haywood, Kravitz, Wasyliw, Goldberg, & Cavanaugh, 1996, p. 1239). They have fewer victims than other child sexual offenders (Haywood, Kravitz, Grossman, Wasyliw, & Hardy, 1996, p. 531). They have higher rates of endocrine disorders than age-matched child sexual offenders or the population at large (Langevin, 2004, p. 39). They are more sexually under-informed and immature than other child sex offenders (Loftus & Comargo, 1993, p. 297). They report lower sexual drive and have fewer sexual experiences than non-clergy offenders (Flakenhain et al., 1999, p. 329). The majority are accused of past sexual behaviors committed in their 20s or 30s, at least 10 years prior to taking part in some studies (John Jay College., 2004, p. 6). The differences in the profiles of clergy and the non-clergy sexual offenders regarding sexual drive and sexual experiences may be accounted for in part by the formation and socialization experiences of Roman Catholic clerics, since commitment to celibacy involves sexual norms of abstinence and prohibition against all sexual acts and fantasies. Haywood, Kravitz, Grossman, Wasyliw, and Hardy (1996, p. 534) argue that low levels of sexual functioning among clergy offenders, which may be considered the norm among clerics, may be interpreted as dysfunctional for the normal male population. As Loftus points out (1999, p. 16; 2004, p. 88), it is difficult to draw any conclusions in this regard, as research on the sexual lives of "normal" clergy is clearly thin and such research is necessary to establish a baseline of the norm of sexual living across the range of clergy.

The broad consensus in the psychological literature is that Roman Catholic clergy sexual offenders represent an atypical group of child sexual offenders (Kafka, 2004, p. 49; Marshall, 2003) and that situational and contextual factors must be considered significant in their sexual offending (Brenneis, 2001, p. 25; John Jay College, 2011; Marshall, 2003). Sullivan and Beech (2004) include Roman Catholic clergy perpetrators under an umbrella term "professional perpetrators," to argue that clerical perpetrators are not particularly distinguishable from other child sexual offenders in that they use their professional status to gain access to children to abuse (Sullivan & Beech, 2004, p. 49). Having thoroughly analyzed the data gathered on Catholic clergy in the United States, Tallon and Terry (2008, p. 625) conclude it is unlikely that clerical and religious men who have sexually abused minors have specifically chosen a profession in the Catholic Church so they could gain access to children to abuse. My research suggests a similar conclusion (Keenan, 2006). I find no support in the empirical literature for Sullivan and Beech's (2004) conclusion. However, the John Jay College (2011, p. 102) research suggests similarities between clerical offenders and sexual offenders in the general public or in other institutions in the grooming behavior that is said to accompany the onset of abuse. The very concept of "grooming" is itself contested and speaks to a particular theoretical and ideological orientation that requires further critical analysis and deconstruction.

One of the most disturbing features of sexual abuse by Catholic clergy is the number of suicides that have occurred among victims of Catholic clergy and among accused priests themselves (Ferns Report, 2005; Frawley-O'Dea, 2007, p. 53). There are multiple reports of deaths by suicide of many young men who are said to have experienced sexual abuse by Catholic clergy (Frawley-O'Dea, 2007, p. 53). In Ireland and the United States a number of priests and ex-priests have committed suicide after being accused of sexual abuse of minors. There is also anecdotal evidence of the death by suicide of a priest's parent following allegations of the priest's abuses. Frawley-O'Dea (2007, p. 53) also uncovered evidence to suggest that there are murders linked to sexual abuse by Catholic clergy in the United States: in some instances the cleric is the chief suspect and in others he is the victim. When does legitimate anger turn to hatred and violence is a question that is never far away when a sexual crime is committed. What social and psychological measures are necessary to prevent such abuses from descending into ever-increasing spirals of hatred and despair is certainly one of the key questions of our current times. Understanding what the literature has to tell and building our responses on knowledge and compassion may help in this important challenge.

CONCLUDING COMMENTS

The story of sexual abuse by Catholic clergy is indeed a truly sorry one. As one young man who experienced sexual abuse in childhood said to me in court on the day the priest who had abused him in school was jailed: "There are no winners in all of this, only losers." But then, as he reflected some more, he continued: "But all we have is what we have. We all have to live a life. I hope that today will mark a new chapter in mine." I wished that day too that it would for him, and I hope that is has.

In reviewing the literature on "normal" clergy and on clergy who have abused minors, and never straying far from the stories of abuse that emerge in my clinical practice and in the Commissions of Inquiry into child sexual abuse in Ireland (Ferns Report, 2005; Murphy Report, 2009; Ryan Report, 2009), I am continually struck by the pain of the victims' stories that are embedded in all the literature on this subject. The testimonies of men and women who as young boys and girls were assaulted and violated by clerical men, who should have known better, is chillingly moving on every reading.

The representation of the clerical perpetrator that has dominated popular discourse on child sexual abuse in Ireland and the United State is of a middle-aged man who has abused hundreds of young altar-boys, usually by raping them, over many years. The phrase "the pedophile priest" is often used to describe such men and to set them apart as "other" with all the attendant consequences, such as community fear and an unwillingness to have such men live among us. In some instances the men are hunted down and run out of their homes While it is important to note that stories of abuse often tell stories of vandalized innocence, and that stories of vandalized innocence must be re-membered and never forgotten, at the same time, I see limited value in representing the typical clerical perpetrator as a man who abuses hundreds of children by rape when this is not the reality as we know it from the available documents and research. The reality is bleak enough as it is, and it is therefore important not to distort the facts as we know them.

Clerical perpetrators who have abused hundreds of children, and raped some of them, represent a very small but serious group of sexual perpetrators who pose a real danger to children. These men need serious interventions, including significant monitoring and con-straint. However, other clerical men who abused minors sometimes more than up to 20 years ago and have led exemplary lives since then, cannot be classified in the same way; they require a wholly different approach. The point is that clerical men who have sexually abused minors do not constitute a homogeneous group, and while all of the abuses were wrong on every level, there is nothing to be gained by putting all of these men into a similar category and distorting the facts. What we have learned from the empirical literature and the Commissions of Investigation is that a large number of clergy have been responsible for each abusing one or a small number of minors, while a small group of Catholic clergy are responsible for each abusing large numbers of children and adolescents. That any of them abuse one child is of course one child too many. However, little can be served by distorting the profile of the "typical" clerical perpetrator; not for children, not for victims and survivors, not for our communities, and certainly not for the clerical men themselves.

Sipe (1995, p. 134) refers to the sexual abuse crisis as "the tip of the iceberg" when it comes to problems of sexuality for the Roman Catholic Church. When sociological and psychological studies during the late early 1970s, following the exodus of clergy from the Roman Catholic Church, failed to draw the American hierarchy's attention to the poor levels of psychosexual maturity among the Roman Catholic clergy, it could be argued that the sexual abuse problem that the Church now faces has accelerated a simmering problem that has been growing for a very long time and represents a systemic push to bring the sexuality of clergy and its power structures and governance onto the Church's agenda. At the very least, the literature that is reviewed in this chapter, for me at least, suggests that child sexual abuse by Catholic clergy must be considered against the background of the literature on the sexual activities of "normal" clergy and not as an unrelated sphere of clergy activity. The profile of the "normal" clergy that is portrayed in this literature raises important concerns. Insufficiently prepared and inadequately supported in carrying out the tasks of the life they have chosen, the big surprise is why more Catholic clerics are not in trouble, rather than why some are. Individual pathology is insufficient for explaining this complex phenomenon. However, many Catholic clergy who were part of the same organizational culture, and who endured similar deficits in support and training as the clerical perpetrators, never sexually abused anyone. My aim is to systematically move towards a considered explanation for how this occurred and why and how it came to be that those men who did abuse came to act the way they did.

PART TWO

Theorizing Sexual Abuse

4

The Individual as the Unit of Analysis

IT WAS ONCE THOUGHT that sexual abuse of children was rare, but we now know that it is common (McGee et al., 2002). Strangers were once thought to be the main perpetrators, but now we know the majority of perpetrators are known and trusted adults. In a phenomenon of immense complexity, it is mainly those who have a duty to protect who hurt children most. Such adults come from all walks of life. Recent decades have seen an increase in scholarly research on the child sexual offender and on attempts to understand the problem. While the concern of this project is child sexual abuse perpetrated by Catholic clergy, this chapter considers the empirical literature on perpetrators of child sexual abuse in general, since more research has been conducted on non-clerical than on clerical offenders. My aim is to explicate the key theories and concepts that can be helpful when trying to understand the clerical offender. However, as Chapter 3 pointed out, Catholic clergy represent a relatively distinct and atypical group of child sexual offenders whose offending must be considered in relation to the situational and contextual circumstances of their lives as ministers of the Roman Catholic Church (Kafka, 2004; Marshall, 2004). Nonetheless, this chapter on the individual as the unit of analysis is provided to give the reader a platform from which to explore some of the connections and disconnections between sexual abuse outside and inside the Catholic Church.

This and the next two chapters offer the reader a broad theoretical picture of how sexual offending can be accounted for firstly in its individual, and later in its social, and gendered dimensions. Readers who may not have a background in research on sexual offending and sexual socialization might find in these chapters some important concepts that can be used to think about sexual abuse and sexual offending.

The primary focus of the psychological and psychiatric literature on child sexual offending is an individual one, with a strong emphasis on understanding the vulnerability and personality factors that contribute towards an individual's sexual offending. Many psychological theories also acknowledge the social and cultural factors that are implicated in such offending, although the primary emphasis of the psychological and psychiatric literature is more on individual features. While social and cultural factors are seen as providing context for individual sexual offending, the importance of culture and socialization in relation to sexual offending, while acknowledged is often under-theorized. It is important to understand the key debates in this literature because the psychological and psychiatric literature frames much of the current professional and public debate and underlies most therapeutic practice currently engaged with child sexual offenders.

In 1998, Ward and Hudson (p. 47) argued that the major task of all good theory of sexual offending is that it accounts for the onset, development, and maintenance of the problem. However, whether such an all-embracing or totalizing grand theory is possible or even desirable is a moot point, in part because it would need to be sufficiently complex to account for individual particularities and broad enough to have some explanatory merit. At any rate, such an all-embracing theory is some way off, and that might just be a good thing. In the meantime there is a rich program of research under way in the discipline of psychology, involving different kinds of theories focusing on different factors, all of which have a contribution to make to our understanding of sexual offending. A review of the psychological literature on sexual offending shows biological, behavioral, psychodynamic, systemic, feminist, developmental, and social cognitive theories evolving and being refined, and some are linked to active research programs. In the main, however, much psychological research tends to show a preference for biological, psychodynamic, and cognitive-behavioral explanations. Single-factor theories dominated much of the early etiological research on sexual offenders and are still a source of intensive research activity, although they are seen to suffer from too narrow a focus. Ultimately single factor theories are incorporated into more comprehensive theories of sexual offending.

Ward and Hudson (1998, p. 48) identified a number of problems with psychological research and theory development in relation to sexual offending: the main one being a general failure to distinguish between levels of theory and the absence of a meta-level framework that would guide all ongoing theoretical and empirical research. Ward and Hudson set about undertaking this task. To begin, they identified three levels of theory in the sexual offender literature. Level III, which they conceptualize as micro-level theories, are micro models of description which specify the cognitive, behavioral, motivational, and social factors that are associated with the commission of a sexual offence (p. 48). These models are largely descriptive of the offense chain or the relapse process (e.g., Pithers, 1990; Ward, Louden, Hudson, & Marshall, 1995). The second level, which they conceptualize as middle-level or single-factor theories (level II theories), comprises theories that attempt to explain single psychological factors and processes thought to be important in the generation of sexual crime, such as empathy deficits (Marshall, Hudson, Jones, & Fernandez, 1995) or cognitive distortion (Abel, Becker, & Cunningham-Rathner, 1984). At this level of theory development, different aspects of the particular variable are clearly described and the dynamic relationships between the component parts are spelled out (Ward & Hudson, 1998, p. 48).

Level I of Ward and Hudson's (1998, p. 49) meta-theoretical framework, which is conceptualized as multifactorial or comprehensive theories, refer to those theories that attempt to explain the actual offending behavior and account satisfactorily for offense processes (Ward & Hudson, 1998, p. 49) (e.g., Finkelhor, 1984; Marshall & Barbaree, 1990). Level I theories combine single-factor theories with social and situational influences to elaborate more general psychosocial theories of sexual offending.

For Ward and Hudson (1998) a fourth level of the meta-theoretical framework of sexual offending, needs to be developed, which they conceptualize as "mature" or "global" theories. Theories at this level are seen as representing "an advanced form of theoretical development that does not currently exist in the sexual offending domain"; one that were it to exist would act as a guiding ideal for "the integration of theory across all levels" (p. 49). For the purposes of my project I will confine the discussion to single factor and more comprehensive psychosocial theories of sexual offending (level I and level II) with the aim of providing the reader with the broad theoretical concepts that underpin much psychological research on sexual offenders. My aim is not to provide a systematic critique of all the theoretical models in this field.[1]

SINGLE-FACTOR THEORIES OF SEXUAL OFFENDERS

Single-factor theories are best conceived as clusters representing a number of symptoms typically reported in adults who sexually abuse children. These symptoms can be clustered as problems that relate to attachment, intimacy, and loneliness; deviant sexual arousal; emotional regulation; cognitive distortions; and empathy deficits.

Attachment, Intimacy, and Emotional Loneliness

William Marshall (1989, 1993) was one of the first clinical and research psychologists to write about the role of attachment in sexual offending. Drawing on the attachment theory of John Bowlby (1969, 1973, 1979, 1980), Marshall (1989, 1993) studied the hypothesis that men who sexually offend against children failed to establish secure attachment relationships in childhood, and that the intimacy and social competence problems that resulted from such insecure attachment were important in the chain of events leading to a sexual offense against a child. According to Bowlby's theory (1973, p. 78), a child who experiences abusive or neglectful relationships can be skeptical of the emotional availability of other people for him, fearful of emotional closeness, and fearful of disclosing personal feelings. This results in a failure to develop trust in other people and in an impaired sense of personal security and power. For Marshall (1989, p. 495; 1993, p. 113) and others (Ward, Hudson, Marshall, & Siegert, 1995, p. 317), the interpersonal strategies associated with impaired attachment can make it difficult for an individual to develop the skills necessary to establish intimate relationships. Extreme emotional and sometimes social loneliness can result. This literature suggests that childhood attachment problems that lead to an adult's impaired capacity for intimacy are essential links in the developmental chain underlying the emergence of an inappropriate sexual disposition (Garlick, Marshall, & Thornton, 1996; Marshall, 1989, 1993; Ward, Hudson, & Marshall, 1996; Ward, Hudson, Marshall, & Siegert, 1995).

Marshall (1989, p. 492; 1993, p. 113) conceptualized intimacy as a basic human need, arising as a result of evolutionary processes or as a result of sociocultural training. Ward and Stewart (2003, p. 24) also conceptualize intimacy as a basic human need, the absence of which, they say, contributes to levels of unhappiness for the individual and a diminished sense of well-being. Marshall argues (1989, p. 492; 1993, p. 113) that although the preferred level of intimacy differs across individuals, when intimacy deficits persist, chronic loneliness results. According to Marshall (1989, p. 491; 1993, p. 114), one of the consistently observed consequences of prolonged emotional loneliness in adolescents and adults is an increase in aggression. Lonely adults are hypothesized to be more likely than others to act in hostile and aggressive ways (Marshall, 1989, p. 498; 1993, p. 114). According to this theory, emotional loneliness sets the stage for aggressive and self-serving behaviors and makes more attractive those social messages that present individuals as objects, there to meet the needs of individual's willing to take advantage of them (Marshall, 1989, p. 498; 1993, p. 113). Sexual offending is one obvious, but not unique, consequence of such a history, according to this view (Marshall, 1989, p. 498; 1993, p. 114).

Other theorists (Bartholomew & Horowitz, 1991; Sawle & Kear-Colwell, 2001; Smallbone & Dadds, 1998, 2000; Ward, Hudson, & Marshall, 1996) have empirically tested Marshall's (1989, 1993) theory and have extended his initial hypothesis to include not only poor childhood attachments but also poor adult attachments as a key feature of the developmental trajectory of sexual offenders. According to this theory, fear of intimacy and the corresponding loneliness is not solely linked to poor childhood attachments but can also result from poor experiences of intimacy in adulthood. From this perspective, repeated failure on the part of an individual to develop and sustain intimate relationships in adulthood, can be seen, even by an otherwise well-functioning individual, as a sign of personal inadequacy and incompetence, or that the individual is unlovable.

This is an interesting theory as it allows for the conclusion that from a psychological perspective, childhood deprivations in attachment functioning are not the only focus of concern. The failure to develop and sustain intimate relationships in adulthood can also be part of the developmental trajectory of child sexual offenders (Hudson & Ward, 1997; Marsa et al., 2004; Marshall & Mazzucco, 1995; Marshall, Serran, & Cortoni, 2000; McCormack, Hudson, & Ward, 2002; Sawle & Kear-Colwell, 2001; Smallbone & Dadds, 1998, 2000, 2001; Ward, Hudson, & Marshall, 1996). In terms of clergy offenders this is an extremely important consideration, which suggests that intimacy and adult attachment must be an area of focus in exploring clergy offending. This topic will be explored in greater depth later in chapters 7, 8 and 10.

Finkelhor (1984) also understood the influence of attachment in trying to understand why an adult might find it emotionally gratifying to relate sexually to a child. Finkelhor theorizes the possibility of a "fit" between the emotional needs of the adult offender and the characteristics of the child (p. 38). He suggests a number of possibilities: (1) the child sexual offender is arrested in his psychological development and is emotionally immature, experiencing himself as childlike with childish emotional needs that are best met by other children; (2) the child sexual offender feels inadequate in social relationships, and being in relationships with children gives him a feeling of power and control; (3) the child sexual offender needs relationships with children to overcome feelings of shame, humiliation, or powerlessness that originated in a childhood traumatic experience with an adult, and by doing so the child sexual offender is "identifying with the aggressor" (Groth, Hobson, & Gary, 1982, p. 138); (4) the child sexual offender remains in love with himself as a child, in a narcissistic way, and engages only with others who remind him of the lost child he was, or his likeness; and (5) male socialization and male culture encourages men to relate to partners who are younger, smaller, and weaker than themselves, so that the men themselves are dominant and powerful and the initiator in sexual relationships. In this scenario children and childlike women can be seen as "appropriate" objects of sexual interest. Many of these theories have not been empirically tested, and the extent to which any or all of them are relevant to clerical perpetrators is clearly unknown. Some of these theories, however, apply to some offenders and not to others.

Deviant Sexual Preferences

Much of the early psychological literature on sexual offenders emphasized a relationship between deviant sexual preferences and sexual offending (Abel et al., 1984; Freund 1967a, 1967b; Laws & Marshall, 1990; McGuire, Carlisle, & Young, 1965). These preferences were seen as resulting from an accidental pairing of deviant sexual stimuli and sexual arousal at an influential time in an individual's development. According to the thinking, the pairing of deviant sexual stimuli with sexual arousal, accompanied by masturbation to fantasies derived from the original circumstances, is a conditioning process that results in a disposition to engage in deviant sexual acts whenever the opportunity arose or was created (Abel et al., 1984, p. 98). Sexual offenders were also thought to have distinctive sexual preferences that matched their actual offending behaviors. Child abusers were thought to have deviant sexual preferences for children and rapists were thought to have deviant sexual preferences involving forced, nonconsensual sexual relations. This perspective dominates much of the public discourse despite more recent reservations being raised about this theory within the psychological literature.

The theory was based on a number of possible hypotheses: that men who engage in sexually deviant behaviors do so because they prefer them to socially acceptable sexual behaviors; that men engage in sexually deviant behaviors because they are "conditioned" from earlier experiences to do so, or finally that men engage in sexually deviant behaviors because they are suffering from what is described as a paraphilia. Paraphilias have been defined in the *Diagnostic and Statistical Manual of Mental Disorders* (DSM-IV-TR; American Psychiatric Association, 2000, p. 52) as "recurrent, intense sexually arousing fantasies, sexual urges or behaviors, generally around children or non-consenting persons, the suffering or humiliation of oneself or others, or non-human objects." The DSM-IV-TR[2] lists 16 paraphilias, one of which is commonly attributed to men who sexually abuse children: pedophilia. Later in the chapter I will discuss some of the limitations of the psychiatric classification "pedophilia" in its application to most child sexual offenders.

Kafka (1997, 2003) has an understanding of paraphilias which suggests that they originate in the brain, specifically in relation to problems in neurobiological functioning and the operation of several neurotransmitters. This is essentially a biological theory that draws on human and animal studies to try to explain deviant sexual interests. The theory continues to be the subject of neurobiological research and scholarship (Ward, Polaschek, & Beech, 2006, p. 165). This theory has led to the treatment of some sexual offenders with a class of antidepressant drug known as selective serotonin reuptake inhibitors (SSRIs) (p. 165).

The concept of deviant sexual preference has been replaced by the concept of deviant sexual script in the work of Ward and Siegert (2002). Drawing on the work of Money (1993), Ward and Siegert (2002, p. 335) construe the sexual script as a type of "lovemap" or "mental representation" acquired by individuals during development that enables individuals to interpret intimate or sexual encounters in particular ways. The "lovemap" is said to guide subsequent sexual behaviors. In Ward and Siegert's view (2002, p. 336), cultural norms, values, rules, and beliefs are interwoven and eventually integrated into the development of an individual's sexual script. A sexual script sets out when sex is to take place, with whom, what to do, and how to interpret the cues associated with different phases in a sexual encounter. According to this theory (Money, 1993, p. 466; Ward & Siegert, 2002, p. 336), experiences of sexual and/ or emotional trauma early in the child's life may create distortions in the developing sexual script. The distorted sexual script can then lead to sexual encounters with inappropriate partners (e.g., age discrepancy), involving inappropriate behaviors (e.g., deviant or sadistic practices), or within inappropriate contexts (e.g., impersonal sex) (Ward & Siegert, 2002, p. 336). However, as not every child who experiences childhood sexual abuse goes on to sexually offend as an adult, the theory of distorted sexual script offers only a partial explanation for some sexual offending. It is also a theory that has led to much misunderstanding and hurt based on the idea that sexual abuse victims have distorted sexual scripts and can therefore become sexual offenders, a theory that is fundamentally flawed.

In considering questions that link with notions of deviant sexual preference and distorted sexual script and asking why an adult is capable of being sexually aroused by a child, Finkelhor (1984, p. 39) summarizes some of the possible lines of inquiry: (1) child sexual offenders have sexual experiences as children that are intense and either fulfilling or frustrating, which become imprinted and conditioned as a later sexual interest in children; (2) child sexual offenders have experienced sexual trauma as children, which conditions them to adult sex with children or at least provides a model in which sex with children is seen as "acceptable" (e.g., when children grow up in families where they witness other siblings as well as themselves as objects of sexual exploitation); (3) child sexual offenders have earlier experiences of arousal to children that become fixated when incorporated into sexual fantasy, and become increasingly arousing by subsequent masturbatory repetitions; (4) child sexual offenders can attribute sexual motivation in error to an emotional response to children, and once so labeled the responses are reinforced through fantasy and repetition, ultimately leading to more generalized sexual arousal to a particular child or to children in general; (5) child sexual offenders suffer from biological features, such as hormonal or genetic abnormalities, that are hypothesized as predisposing them to develop deviant patterns of arousal (but such abnormalities can be seen as nonspecific in how a person comes to find children arousing); and (6) the availability of pornography involving children can inculcate arousal to children in some adults who might otherwise not be so inclined; (in this way a pattern of sexual arousal to children can be created through repeated exposure to child pornography and to advertising that sexualizes children). In some forms of pornography involving both children and adults, users of adult pornography can also begin to find sexual relations with children sexually arousing. Again, as with much other work in the sexual offender literature, these theories need empirical testing.

Although the view that sexual offenders have distinctive sexual preferences that match their actual offending was not extensively researched (Marshall & Eccles, 1991), this perspective was taken as fact within the psychological community for many years, and encouraged the use of behavioral treatment approaches aimed at changing sexual preferences as an important treatment objective (Hudson, Wales, & Ward, 1998, pp. 22, 23; Laws & Marshall, 2003; Maletzky & Steinhauser, 1998, pp. 105, 106; Marshall & Laws, 2003). The value of such an approach to treatment has now come in for empirical appraisal (Marshall, 1997; Marshall & Eccles, 1991), and the relationship between deviant sexual preferences and sexual offending is not nearly as clear-cut as was originally hypothesized. However, in the minority of cases where a deviant sexual interest in children does exist, Hanson and Bussière (1998, p. 351) found a greater risk of further sexual offending. This finding might explain why some clinicians are still influenced by theories linking deviant sexual preferences and sexual offending and why some treatment programs persist with changing sexual preference as an important treatment goal (Hudson, Wales, & Ward, 1998, pp. 22, 23; Maletzky & Steinhauser, 1998, pp. 105, 106).

A critical review of the literature on the relationship between deviant sexual preferences/ scripts and subsequent child sexual offending suggests the need for caution in linking these two variables in an automatic causal relationship. A focus on the concept of deviant sexual preferences as a possible explanation for child sexual offending would be altogether too limiting, especially since the more recent empirical research (John Jay College, 2011, pp. 99-102; Marshall, 1997, pp. 86ff; Marshall, Anderson, & Fernandez, 2000, p. 125) suggests that many men who abuse children do not have deviant sexual preferences, but that their offending is related to more situational factors and to opportunity. This is even more so when it comes to the sexual abuse of adolescents. In a sample of over 60,000 "normal" adult males, Kafka (2004, p. 52, citing Abel, 2000 [subscriber's section]) reports that heterosexual men who show primary sexual arousal to adult women are also highly likely to show sexual arousal to adolescent girls, as measured by visual reaction time responses. The same pattern has been shown for adult homosexual men in relation to adolescent boys. Kafka argues that sexual arousal to postpubertal adolescents, therefore, cannot of itself represent an inherent pathology, or an example of deviant sexual arousal. Marshall, Hamilton, and Fernandez (2001, p. 126) report that they routinely exclude 20% of random community-based non-offenders from acting as control samples for their research because these people admit to fantasizing about sexual relations with children. However, the consideration of deviant sexual preference cannot be dismissed altogether, since Hanson and Bussière's (1998, p. 351) meta-analysis suggests that there is a greater risk of re-offending when an individual indicates a sexual preference for children. However, those individuals with deviant sexual interests will not commit sexual crimes unless they are willing to hurt others to achieve their goals or can convince themselves that they are not harming their victims or are unable to stop (Hanson & Morton-Bourgon, 2004, p. 1). "Although all sexual offending is socially deviant, not all offenders have an enduring interest in sexual acts that are illegal (e.g., children, rape) (p. 1)." Many stop without ever receiving psychological help.

Emotional Regulation

Problems with emotional regulation and with negative affective states, especially depression and anxiety, have also been highlighted in the psychological literature as acting as facilitators in the chain of events leading to the sexual abuse of a child (Cortini & Marshall, 2001; Knight & Prentky, 1990; Pithers, 1990; Ward, Hudson, & Keenan, 1998). Cortini and Marshall (2001, p. 34) suggest that the presence of powerful negative emotions in child sexual offenders might lead them to use sexual relations with children as a coping strategy. They also suggest that the presence of powerful negative emotions can make it difficult for an individual to inhibit or control any tendencies he might have towards deviant sexual activities (p. 34). Hall and Hirschman (1992) see a strong relationship between negative affective states and the weakening of inhibitors to sexually aggressive behavior (such as victim empathy, guilt, moral conviction, and anxiety regarding prosecution). They argue that the inability to regulate negative emotions functions to inhibit empathy and concern for the child's welfare (p. 20). However, offering an alternative perspective, Hudson, Ward, and McCormack (1999, p. 790) suggest that only a few sexual offenders have problems with emotional self-regulation. Hudson et al. claim that for some individuals, offending is associated with positive emotions, involving explicit and immaculate planning, and that sexual abusing is indicative of a personal choice. The literature linking negative emotional states and child sexual offending is therefore inconclusive, although it cannot be disregarded.

Cognitive Distortions

Beck (1963, p. 324) coined the term *cognitive distortions* to describe "idiosyncratic thought content indicative of distorted or unrealistic conceptualizations." In the sexual offender literature the term *cognitive distortion* is used to refer to maladaptive beliefs and attitudes and problematic thinking styles that are seen to play a role in sexual offenses (Ward, Hudson, Johnston, & Marshall, 1997, p. 480). In relation to sexual offenders, Abel, Becker, and Cunningham-Rathner (1984) defined cognitive distortions as belief systems that supported sexual contact with children, but also as justifications, perceptions and judgments used by the sexual offender to rationalize the child molestation (Abel et al., 1989, p. 137). In cognitive-behavioral therapy "cognitive distortions" are considered to be automatic thoughts or habitual ways of thinking that lead to problematic situations. Abel, Becker, and Cunningham-Rathner (1984) were the first in the sexual offender literature to apply a systematic methodology to the study of cognitive distortions.

Although the term *cognitive distortion* is enshrined in the sexual offender literature, it is a term that has suffered from inconsistent usage and problems of definition (Mann & Beech, 2003, p. 136). An examination of the arguments in relation to cognitive distortions shows a lack of clarity regarding whether cognitive distortions are conscious processes employed by offenders to excuse and justify their behavior, or whether they are unconscious processes adopted by offenders to protect them from shame and guilt. It is not clear either whether cognitive distortions play a causative function in the sexual abuse or a maintenance role after the event: both uses of the term are evident in the literature. Ward and Siegert (2002, p. 341) see cognitive distortions as playing both causative and maintenance functions in sexual offending. Abel et al. (1984) see them as both conscious and unconscious processes used to rationalize abuse. This process allows sexual offenders to prevent or minimize their anxiety, guilt, and loss of self-esteem.

Ward and Keenan (1999) drew on the work of Kelly (1955) to develop a more layered version of cognitive distortion, to try to describe sexual offenders' maladaptive theories of the world and of their victims. They hypothesized that "individuals construct theories about aspects of their world in order to understand, explain and control it" (p. 824). These theories of the world, (implicit theories or sets of core schema), are used like scientific theories by individuals to explain other people's actions and to make predictions about life (Ward, 2000, p. 491). They also underpin the rationale for action. According to this perspective, the implicit theories held by sexual offenders are hypothesized to underlie and generate a range of ideas about themselves, the world, and their victims that are implicated in their sexual offending (Ward, 2000, p. 492; Ward et al., 1999, p. 824).

Implicit theories are said to include: (1) general-level beliefs and assumptions about the nature of people and the world; (2) middle-level beliefs and assumptions dealing with categories of entities such as women and children; and (3) lower-level beliefs and assumptions about a particular victim. According to Ward and Keenan (1999, p. 826), the key beliefs are those at the general and middle level because they persist and constitute the foundation of the offender's interpretations and explanations of the victims' actions and mental states. An individual's implicit theories can change throughout the life course, allowing for the conclusion that from a psychological perspective, one's implicit theories, which may be maladaptive, can be altered through therapeutic interventions or through corrective life experiences. Although the implicit theory idea shows some merit, there has been little research directly investigating its empirical adequacy (Ward, Polaschek, & Beech, 2006).

The whole point of cognitive distortions or maladaptive implicit theories is that they can be understood only against the backdrop of culturally normative thinking. Cognitive distortions are therefore seen as deviant from culturally normative thought. However, as the sociological literature in the next chapter points out, any discussion of normative thinking must also be accompanied by an understanding of the power relations that are at play in the way such knowledge is created (Foucault, 2004, p. 44). When it comes to the human sciences "objective" knowledge does not exist, despite the most rigorous methods of inquiry. Normative judgments therefore cannot be said to represent "objective" reality, but rather they represent merely those practices and customs that are reified over time, often masking the power relations that are at play in their very creation. Normative judgments have the power to act as instruments of oppression (Foucault, 2004, p. 44; White, 2004, p. 124) and like all norms have the power to marginalize people who are seen not to fit in. The term *cognitive distortion* therefore belongs very definitely within a modernist paradigm in which the observer observes the observed in order to evaluate him or her and his or her ideas against pre-existing normative criteria. The observer is seen as the expert with the "correct" knowledge that allows him or her to observe, assess, and judge others without being subjected to the same processes of evaluation and judgment themselves. By definition, the whole concept of cognitive distortion thus involves relations of power that are hidden.

It can be argued that there are ways to interpret the cognitive processes of sexual offenders other than to classify those aspects of their thinking that are out of keeping with what can be regarded as the norm as cognitive distortions. It is possible to use perpetrators' accounts to illuminate the meaning and motivations for their offenses and to understand how they "fitted" or made sense at some level in their lives. We do not need to confine the narratives of sexual offenders to some predetermined category of cognitive distortion by prematurely punctuating their narratives and explanations. In offering this perspective I am not attempting to condone sexual offending but rather to understand the meaning of it and the conditions that gave rise to it from the offender's perspective. By categorizing aspects of a person's story as evidence of cognitive distortion we interrupt the search for meaning and for explanatory understanding.

By abandoning the concept of cognitive distortion while still searching to understand the cognitive processes underlying the perpetrators' thinking (regarding the origins, maintenance, and justification of their sexual offending, and the ideas they hold about themselves, the world and their victims) it becomes possible to get close to the meaning of the events and its internal logic. This in turn helps with prevention and repair. There is little evidence to show whether interventions with sexual offenders that are based on altering cognitive distortions are effective or ineffective in reducing the risk of sexual offending, even though this approach to treatment is included in many sexual offender treatment programs (Ward, Polaschek, & Beech, 2006, p. 131).

Empathy Deficits

The concept of empathy has received considerable attention in the sexual offender literature, with numerous theoretical and research papers on the subject (Covell & Scalora, 2002; Hudson et al., 1993; Marshall et al., 1993; Marshall, Champagne, Brown, & Miller, 1997; Marshall, Hamilton, & Fernandez, 2001; Marshall, Hudson, Jones, & Fernandez, 1995; Marshall & Maric, 1996; Pithers, 1999). In essence, the empathy deficit theory suggests that the sexual offense chain can be influenced by an individual's failure to understand the potentially harmful effects of his behavior on individuals in general or on particular individuals more specifically (Hudson et al., 1993, p. 201; Marshall & Maric, 1996, p. 108). The theory rests on the assumption that having empathic competency can help inhibit any tendency towards harmful behavior (Marshall & Maric, 1996, p. 108).

Despite its strong presence in the literature on sexual offenders, there has been little agreement on the essential elements of empathy and when they are absent (Marshall, Anderson, & Fernandez, 2000, p. 73). The main debates center on whether empathy represents a trait or a state, and how sympathy and empathy can be distinguished. Trait perspectives rest on the idea that people are consistent in their empathic responses; they are in essence empathic people. In this instance, empathy is essentialized as something that belongs in the character of the individual. State perspectives suggest that situational factors determine the nature of the empathic responses: this means that individuals can be empathic in many situations and not in others. While the trait perspective had prominence in the psychological literature for many years, the state perspective is now to the fore, particularly in relation to sexual offenders. Early studies on empathy deficits in child sexual offenders theorized that they lacked empathy in general, in relation to adults and to all children (Marshall, Jones, Hudson, & McDonald, 1993). More recent studies, however, suggest that child sex offenders do not lack empathy in general and that many are empathic in a variety of non-sexual-offense situations; only in relation to their specific child victims are the empathy deficits evident (Marshall, Anderson & Fernandez, 2000, p. 80; Marshall, Hamilton, & Fernandez, 2001; Marshall, Hudson, Jones, & Fernandez, 1995, pp. 99–113).

The sympathy/empathy debate has numerous twists and turns and is complicated by another disagreement over whether empathy represents a purely cognitive response, or an emotional response, or whether it is some combination of both. In response to this debate Marshall (Marshall, 2002, p. 14; Marshall, Hudson, Jones, & Fernandez, 1995, pp. 99–113) outlines a multistage model of empathy that is used in the sexual offender literature, although not without its criticisms. The model consists of four stages, each dependent on the preceding stage. The first stage is seen as emotional recognition, which is the process of identifying, with some degree of accuracy, the emotional state of another person. This usually involves different types of sensory input. In the context of sexual offending, Marshall et al. (1995, 2002) argue that the ability to recognize accurately distress in, for example, the facial expressions of a child or potential victim is a necessary part of the empathic process that could of itself terminate a potential sexual offense.

Stage two is defined as the ability to see and comprehend the world from the other person's perspective. This is known as perspective taking. The main issue here is the degree of similarity between the victim and perpetrator. If the victim is seen as belonging to a group of individuals who are thought to be "different," the empathic response may be inhibited, and it is easier to commit an offense against him or her.

The third stage in the empathic process is the capacity to generate an emotional response that approximates the other person's reaction. This stage is known as empathic responding and involves the ability to respond emotionally to the other person's distress and to experience a feeling of compassion towards him or her. Marshall et al. (1995) argue that emotional replication can occur only if the potential offender (1) has been sufficiently accurate at both stages one and two and (2) has the ability to experience the appropriate emotion. According to this perspective, offenders who have limited access to a range of either emotional language or emotional experiences will have a problem with empathic responses. The fourth stage, is known as empathetic responding, involves the observer's decision to act or not to ameliorate the other person's distress (p. 102). It is also sometimes referred to as sympathetic action. While much literature on the subject suggests that the presence of empathy has an inhibiting effect on aggression, (in that having completed stages one to three accurately, stage four will produce a response to ameliorate the other person's distress), at the same time it is possible for a sexual aggressor who has completed stages one to three accurately, to ignore his perceptions and aggress anyway (Ward, Polaschek, & Beech, 2006, p. 139). While some offenders will ignore the victim's distress, having accurately recorded stages one to three, most won't. For Marshall (Marshall, 2002; Marshall et al., 1995), while a full empathic response involves all four stages of the model, a sympathetic response relies only on the latter two—a feeling of distress or compassion (regardless of how representative it is or not of the other person) that motivates helping action. Marshall et al.'s (1995) empathy model primarily suggests that skills deficits, which are remedial, make an important contribution to why empathy fails in sexual offenders. The strong link between sexual offending and perspective taking (the ability to see and comprehend the world from the other person's perspective) has been demonstrated in several studies (Marshall et al., 2000; Marshall, Hamilton, & Fernandez, 2001; Polaschek, 2003b).

In the decade since Marshall's initial model was published, refinements on the theme of empathy and sexual offending have been the subject of further research. Marshall, Anderson, and Fernandez (2000), in more recent work, have proposed that victim empathy deficits are not the result of empathy problems at all; in fact, the lack of empathy in sexual offenders towards their victims reflects a normal empathy process which comes from the premise that the victim has not been harmed at all. This work suggest that apparent empathy deficits in sexual offenders are no more than faulty thinking about the harmful consequences of their abuse in the first place (p. 85). Others seem to agree (Hanson, 2003; Hilton, 1993). It follows from this research that some sexual offenders do not see the full extent of the harm they are doing to children, while others clearly do. Men who understand the harm they are doing can display indifference or callousness towards their victims. In trying to understand why some offenders fail to recognize the extent of the harm they are causing to children a number of researchers point to the role of shame as an important feature of empathic functioning (Bumby, 2000; Bumby, Marshall, & Langton, 1999; Hanson, 1997b; Roys, 1997; Ward, Hudson, & Marshall, 1994). Bumby's work (2000, p. 151) suggests that offenders are not unaware of the harm they are causing, but rather that they manage their empathic responses to avoid the experience of shame and guilt. Marshall et al. (2000) think that low self-esteem can be an empathy inhibitor in that offenders deny victim harm to protect their already fragile self from further negative self-evaluation. They also go further to suggest that low self-esteem may actually cause sexual aggression through a variety of routes, such as over-reliance on sex for coping with low mood or loneliness. The distinctions between shame and guilt are important here, as both have distinct and separate roles in repeat offending.

Drawing on the work of Tangney (1995, 1996), Bumby (2000, p. 152) describes shame as including "painful and global self-scrutiny, self-consciousness, and perceptions of negative evaluation, all of which create self-oriented distress." Shame goes to the core of one's person-hood. On the other hand, guilt for wrongdoing, while uncomfortable, does not lead to a collapsed identity or to constant negative self-evaluation. Of particular relevance here is the idea that if an offender believes his failure to avoid offending is due to internal factors, such as personal defectiveness, the shame he experiences will actually contribute to an even greater sense of ineffectiveness about preventing offending in the future (Hudson, Ward, & Marshall, 1992). Scholars argue that therapists need to help offenders develop the inner psychological resources to accept the emotional consequences of their behavior (i.e. guilt) without collapsing into self-denigrating shame (Ward, Polaschek, & Beech, 2006, p. 148). If not, some treatments can actually decrease victim empathy by invoking strong shame reactions that increase anger and hostility towards the perceived source (Beckett, Beech, Fisher, & Fordham, 1994). In essence, there are good clinical reasons why offenders need to be helped to move away from shame and towards guilt, accepting the emotional consequences of their offending while at the same time accepting the integrity of their core self. As with many theories of the psychology of the offender, the ones relating to empathy deficits, guilt, and shame require further empirical testing. Despite this, most treatment programs are preoccupied with victim empathy (McGrath et al., 2010), even though there is no evidence that lack of victim empathy is related to sexual recidivism (Hanson & Morton-Bourgon, 2005) or that programs targeting victim empathy reduce the recidivism rates of sexual offenders.

It must be noted before leaving a discussion on empathy that some men who abuse children meet the diagnosis for narcissism. Although a minority, these men are likely to have deficits across a wide range of empathic situations. Usually such men are exceptionally resistant to entering treatment (Ward, Polaschek, & Beech, 2006, p. 150), and if they do they are unlikely to respond to the supportive strategies that enhance self-esteem. Self-esteem enhancement may be counter-indicated at any rate and may be even harmful (p. 150). How to understand and intervene effectively with such offenders requires further theoretical attention.

Used as a relational concept and not one of individual capacity, the concept of empathy can be a useful one when trying to understand how some individuals who are otherwise empathetic do not anticipate the potential effects of their sexually abusive behavior on their victims. Used in a relational manner, the empathy theory suggests that in situations involving the immediate victim, perpetrators of child sexual abuse are at least partially or selectively blind to the possible effects of their actions. My clinical experience suggests the importance of empathy in inhibiting sexual offending in a clergy population. This them will be picked up again in chapter 8.

MULTIFACTORIAL THEORIES OF SEXUAL OFFENDING

As mentioned earlier, a number of scholars have attempted to combine the single psychological factors I have just outlined with social and situational influences to elaborate more comprehensive psychosocial theories of sexual offending. The theories that I will now discuss have been selected because they are the most current or popular ones in the field. It is not my intention to provide a full critique of the adequacy of their theoretical and clinical features and explanatory merits;[3] my aim, rather, is to provide a sense of the theoretical landscape that sets the scene for later discussions on clerical sexual offenders.

Finkelhor's Precondition Model

In attempting to understand what distinguishes abusive from non-abusive men, Finkelhor (1984, p. 53–62) undertook a review of the literature in 1984 that resulted in the precondition model. The precondition model proposes that there are four steps that must be taken before a sexual offense on a child will occur, and these steps must be met in sequence. They involve (1) factors concerning motivation to sexually abuse, (2) factors relating to overcoming internal inhibitions, (3) factors relating to overcoming external inhibitors, and (4) factors relating to overcoming the child's resistance. According to the model, one factor on its own is insufficient to explain how a sexual offense on a child will occur. Finkelhor suggests that abusive men differ from non-abusive men by fulfilling all the preconditions for sexual offending as outlined in his model. Non-abusive men satisfy fewer features.

The precondition model stresses first that in order for a sexual offense on a child to occur, the offender must be motivated. While nonsexual motivations are important, Finkelhor (1984) argues that without consideration of sexual motivation it is difficult to explain why the offense is sexual in nature. He proposes that there are three distinct motives that may give rise to an abuse of a child—emotional congruence, sexual arousal, and blockage—some of which have been discussed above. Emotional congruence is concerned with the way the emotional needs of the offender are met by the child. Congruence implies a "fit" between the needs of the man and what he thinks children or young people can provide. Deviant sexual arousal may be caused by a variety of early learning situations, such as being exposed at a young age to child sexual abuse or pornography. In this scenario, the suggestion is that some individuals acquire entrenched sexual interests in children, and sexual contact with children becomes a way of meeting their sexual and emotional needs. Blockage theories suggest that normally functioning men who experience stress or unusual situations cannot meet their sexual and emotional needs in adaptive ways. A distinction is drawn between developmental blockage, such as fear of intimacy, and situational blockage, such as the lack of suitable sexual and emotional outlets. What happens in these scenarios is that children and young people can become a kind of surrogate partner or a sexual outlet.

According to Finkelhor (1984), the pure fact of being motivated to have sex with a child is unlikely on its own to cause an individual to sexually abuse: he must overcome any personal inhibitions against engaging in sexual acts with children. Why and how some men do this has been answered by a list of possible factors, such as alcohol, impulse disorder, senility, psychosis, failure of the incest mechanism in the family, and the presence of severe stress resulting from such events as loss of job, death of relative, loneliness, lack of intimacy, or sense of personal emptiness. Finkelhor argues that socially entrenched attitudes supportive of patriarchal rights for fathers, such as ownership of children, and a tolerance of sexual interest in children, as displayed in advertising, play a role in undermining a man's attempts to regulate his behavior, allowing him to interpret potential sexual situations with children in self-serving ways.

The next step in Finkelhor's theory involves overcoming the external obstacles that may be present so that an opportunity can be created to sexually abuse the child. This stage can involve either elaborate planning or simply opportunistic behavior. Finkelhor argues that the strategies employed by some men include forming relationships of trust with parents, offering to babysit, securing employment that provides access to children, or coaching children in an activity. The precondition model suggests that some factors make it easier for offenders to overcome the external barriers that usually protect a child from harm. As Chapter 8 points out, the clerical men who participated in my research did not have to go to lengths to create opportunities to abuse children and young people; the power invested in them as adult men and as religious leaders gave them access to the young and the vulnerable as part of their normal ministerial duties.

The final step on the way to offending according to this model is to overcome the child's resistance, based on the idea that wherever there is a sexual offense there is always a parallel story of resistance. At this stage the offender must gain and maintain sexual access to the child, and according to Finkelhor he may employ a number of strategies to do so. Some perpetrators give children gifts, some play sex "games," some establish emotional dependence, and others use threats of violence. Children who are emotionally vulnerable or insecure are thought to be at particular risk. Strategies for overcoming the child's resistance are facilitated in situations where the child has a strong trust in the adult. Finkelhor (1984, p. 61) argues that the lack of sex education and the social powerlessness of children are sociocultural factors that contribute to sexual offenders gaining sexual access to children.

The preconditions model continues to attract interest from scholars and clinicians even many years after it was first conceptualized, but it is dated and other theories, discussed later, are often preferred by a younger generation of clinicians and researchers. The theory has a number of problems that need to be reformulated in the light of current theory and research. In particular, research has shown that many offenders offend while they are engaged in other sexual relationships and activities, which raises doubt about the "blocked" argument that Finkelhor raises. In addition, many have argued that the assumption that we all share internal inhibitions against child sexual abuse is flawed, and this is linked to arguments about the changing nature of childhood, which I discuss in the next chapter. However, despite these significant criticisms, Finkelhor's theory can be useful in the clinical situation. It can provide perpetrators with a framework that helps them to think about their offending in a systematic way. The linking of sociocultural context with the psychology of the offender continues to be one of its strengths.

Marshall and Barbaree's Integrated Theory

To account for the development and maintenance of sexual offending, the integrated theory (Marshall & Barbaree, 1990, pp. 258–271) draws on an interplay between (a) early childhood experiences, including the development of attachment bonds; (b) biological influences, including biological endowment, hormonal changes during adolescence, and the physiology and biochemistry of the brain; (c) sociocultural context, including the social acceptance of interpersonal violence as a way of resolving problems, social acceptance of male dominance, negative attitudes towards women, and the societal acceptance of pornography; and (d) transitory situational factors, including intoxication, strong negative affect (depression, anxiety, boredom, resentment, feeling of deprivation), temporary aimlessness, and the presence of a potential victim. Marshall and Barbaree (1990, p. 258) suggest that advancing an argument for a biological capacity to enact certain behaviors does not mean that they should be accepted as inevitable. In their view, biological endowment simply sets the stage for learning, providing limits and possibilities, rather than determining the outcome.

According to the integrated theory (Marshall & Barbaree, 1990), the developmental background and primary relationship experiences of the child provide the environment in which he learns how to act in pro-social ways. They argue that children who develop in nonnurturing environments often have repeated failure in establishing intimate relationships, which can affect their self-concept and sense of masculinity, leading to strong feelings of anger and resentment. When in a potentially exploitative situation, those men who are chronically vulnerable (as a result of their developmental, social, and conditioning histories) will recognize these situations as an opportunity to offend and, depending on their momentary vulnerability (the effect of transitory factors), they may or may not seize the chance to act in abusive ways. According to this theory, sociocultural factors such as negative images of women or ownership ideas of children are also at play in sexual offending, and some men are more open than others to interpreting such messages in self-serving ways because of their history of emotional vulnerability (Marshall, Anderson, & Fernandez, 2000, p. 30; Marshall & Barbaree, 1990, p. 264).

Resilience, on the other hand, is the capacity to withstand the effects of adversity (Garmezy, 1993; Rutter, 1999) and provides protection against the temptation to offend. Resilience includes attitudes, beliefs, cognitive and behavioral skills, and emotional dispositions (Marshall & Barbaree, 1990, p. 262). These attitudes, beliefs, and skills are not innate, but they can be learned in relationship. Marshall and Barbaree argue that the development of vulnerability to sexually offend corresponds directly to the degree to which there is an absence of any or all of these important skills, attitudes, emotional experiences and capacities. For Marshall and Barbaree (1990, p. 261), the main source of vulnerability is acquired in childhood, mainly with the parents, and a vulnerable individual is more likely than another to create, recognizes, or give into opportunities to sexually offend.

The unifying thread of Marshall and Barbaree's integrated theory concerns the central concepts of vulnerability and resilience. Vulnerability and resilience are hypothesized to develop over the lifespan, and both can be reversed by circumstances or by transitory internal states (1990, p. 257).

Hall and Hirschman's Quadripartite Model

Hall and Hirschman's (1992) quadripartite model of sex offending suggests that while the problem clusters outlined in the early part of this chapter (attachment, loneliness and intimacy deficits; deviant sexual arousal; emotional regulation problems; cognitive distortions and empathy deficits) may contribute to a sexual offense, usually one factor is prominent for each offender and constitutes a primary motive. According to this theory, the activation of one factor (primary motivational precursor) functions to increase the intensity of the others, and this may in turn propel the potential offender above the critical threshold for performing a sexually abusive act. For Hall and Hirschman (p. 18), the prominence of each of these factors is hypothesized to correspond to a particular type of child sexual offender, with each one seen to have distinct treatment needs.

Ward and Siegert's Pathways Model

Another way of understanding how some men commit sexual offenses against children is offered by the pathways model (Ward & Siegert, 2002; Ward & Sorbello, 2003). It suggests that there are five distinct pathways to sexual offending, corresponding roughly to five of the clusters outlined earlier in this chapter: an intimacy deficits pathway, a deviant sexual scripts pathway, an emotional dysregulation pathway, an antisocial cognitions pathway, and a multiple dysfunctional pathway. The pathways model suggests that each pathway involves (a) developmental influences, (b) a core set of causal dysfunctional psychological mechanisms, and (c) opportunity to commit the offense. According to the theory, whether or not an adverse learning event (such as sexual abuse in childhood) results in the development of a dysfunctional psychological mechanism depends on the existence of moderators such as family support. While one dysfunctional mechanism, such as intimacy deficit, is described as taking a leading causal role for each type of offense pathway, all of the other psychological inadequacies are always involved to a minor degree in every sexual crime. However, in what Ward and Siegert (2002, p. 341) refer to as the dysfunctional pathway, there are significant flaws in all four psychological mechanisms (intimacy deficit, deviant sexual script, emotional regulation problems, and antisocial cognitions), and an individual in this latter group is said to represents the true pedophile.

Ward and Beech's Integrated Theory of Sexual Offending

In critiquing all of the above models, Ward and Beech (2006) suggest that the majority of psychological theories of sexual offending tend to focus on the surface level of symptomatology and fail to take account of the fact that human beings are biological creatures. They argue that much of the current theorizing of sexual offending offers "convenient labels for summarising behaviour masquerading as causal mechanisms" (Ward & Beech, 2006, p. 45). They believe that it is not possible to capture the causal origins of dysfunctional sexual behavior without including an analysis of neuropsychological and biological elements. Their integrated theory of sexual offending (Ward & Beech, 2006, p. 50) (or unified theory of sexual offending, Ward, Polaschek, & Beech, 2006, p. 327), which awaits empirical evaluation, is underpinned by the idea that human behavior is generated by the interaction of three sets of factors that are continuously in relationship with each other. These factors are biological factors (influenced by genetic inheritance and brain development), ecological factors (social, cultural and personal circumstances), and neuropsychological factors. According to this theory, sexual offending occurs through the ongoing interaction of these three factors (genes, social learning, and neuropsychological systems), which interact to generate the clinical problems evident in sexual offenders (Ward & Beech, 2006, p. 50). The integrated theory was inspired by a number of sources: "the philosophy of science, current ideas in biology and ecology, neuroscience, developmental psychopathology, and clinical/empirical work in the risk assessment field" (Ward & Beech, 2006, p. 46).

OPPORTUNITY, ROUTINE ACTIVITY, RATIONAL CHOICE, AND SITUATIONAL CRIME PREVENTION

An area of criminological research that is also considered relevant in relation to child sexual abuse and child sexual offenders is that which broadly relates to opportunity, rational choice, and situational considerations. Opportunity theory (Merton, 1957) posits that in any society there are a number of widely shared goals that provide a frame of reference for human aspirations. When an individual has internalized a certain goal and the legitimate means for achieving it are blocked, the individual may resort to illegitimate means to achieve it (Braithwaite, 2007, p. 31). According to opportunity theory, for a crime to be committed, two conditions are necessary: the legitimate means for achieving the goal must be blocked, and illegitimate means for achieving the goal must be open (Cloward & Ohlin, 1960). In other words, there must be illegitimate opportunity. According to this theory, individuals will offend in these kinds of circumstances.

Routine activity approach (Clarke & Felson, 2008, p. 1) makes the distinction between criminal inclinations and criminal events. It is more interested in criminal events than in criminal inclinations. In contrast to much of the literature discussed above routine activity approaches focus on the criminal event as opposed to the offender. Routine activity approach specifies that three minimal elements are required for direct contact predatory crime: a likely offender, a suitable target, and the absence of a suitable guardian against the crime. Routine activity approaches are not concerned with criminal motivation but with the temporal and spatial aspects of crime. The approach suggests that what is important is not criminal motivation but rather the situation and timing of the criminal events (p. 3). This approach is also linked with rational choice perspectives and with situational crime prevention.

Situational crime prevention theorists argue that crime is opportunity-based (Clarke, 1980). The physical environment and situational variables are believed to make particular crimes possible and to determine the timing and location of particular crimes. The aim is to discover the opportunity structures and situational factors that facilitate offending. Situational crime prevention techniques are then applied to identify points of intervention in the environment to reduce the offending. According to this approach offenders have free will and will have weighed up the costs and benefits of the situation before they commit a crime (Cornish and Clarke, 2003). Situational crime prevention approaches claim good support for reducing crime with very little displacement, i.e. offenders will not move to other times and places or to other crimes with no net reduction in offending (Clarke & Felson, 2008, p. 4). In recent criminological theory there is a convergence in several of these approaches to crime and crime reduction; the more important ones are opportunity theory, rational choice, routine activity theory, and situational crime prevention (p. 9).[4]

One argument that draws on routine activities, rational choice, and situational crime prevention suggests that sexual abuse is likely to occur whenever men are put in authority over vulnerable children. This has been observed in volunteer organizations such as the Scouts, residential schools (religious and non-religious), and social service organizations, such as group homes for troubled youth. The response to the problem is to put in place standards and procedures that limit the opportunities for sexual abuse. For example, the Scouts do not allow special groups or secret meetings between the leader and the members of the troop. This literature suggests that sexual abuse has more to do with opportunity for illegitimate activity and lack of opportunity for healthy means of achieving fulfillment. It also connects with theories of closed organizations and how they are more likely than open organizations to give rise to all kinds of abuses of power. This work is important in relation to clerical sexual offenders and I will return to it in Chapter 10.

CHILD SEXUAL OFFENDERS: PSYCHIATRIC CLASSIFICATIONS

The psychiatric literature on child sexual abuse concentrates mainly on classifying the child sexual offender according to the major diagnostic groupings for sexual disorders in the *Diagnostic and Statistical Manual of Mental Disorders of the American Psychiatric Association* (American Psychiatric Association, 1994, 2000). Psychological classifications, which have themselves produced an array of distinctions among the different types of sexual offenders, are often dependent on DSM conceptualizations. Groth, Hobson, and Gary (1982, p. 140) classify child sex offenders into two distinct categories. *Regressed offenders* are described as those people who have a primary sexual preference for adults, but under certain conditions and in certain situations of stress they turn their sexual attention to children and young people. *Fixated offenders* are said to have a longstanding sexual preference for children, and they are said to prefer boys (p. 140).

The *DSM-IV* (APA, 1994) classifies sexual disorders into three subclasses: Sexual Dysfunctions; Disorders Not Otherwise Specified; and Paraphilias. While the first two groups are not of particular relevance for the classification of child sexual offenders, the third category, paraphilia, is. Paraphilia requires the presence of "intense, sexually arousing fantasies, sexual urges, or behaviors" that cause distress or impairment to the person having the condition (APA, 1994, p. 562). The category "paraphilia" includes people who have a preference for using non-human objects for sexual arousal, those who engage in sex under conditions in which a partner suffers or is degraded, or those who engage in repetitive sexual activity with partners who do not give consent. Pedophilia is included in the category "paraphilia."

The diagnostic criteria for pedophilia refers to the presence of recurrent, intense, sexually arousing fantasies, sexual urges, sexual behaviors, or sexual activities lasting not less than 6 months, involving a prepubescent child or children (APA, 1994). According to this diagnosis, the fantasies, sexual urges, or sexual behaviors must cause clinically significant distress or impairment to the pedophilic person in social, occupational, or other important areas of functioning. The pedophilic person must be at least 16 years old and at least 5 years older than the child or children against whom the fantasies or urges are occurring. Pedophilia represents a specific psychiatric classification that locates criminal behavior within a psychiatric frame.

However, unlike pedophilia, which is classified as a psychiatric disorder, sexual attraction to pubescent or postpubescent children in not considered indicative of a psychiatric disorder, and there is no specific classification in the *DSM-IV* for this behavior. Acting on any such attraction is, however, treated as a crime, and individuals who obsessively engage in sexual abuse of postpubescent minors may be diagnosed as suffering from some other disorder, such as obsessive-compulsive disorder (Bennett et al., 2004, p. 13). Some scholars refer to adult men who are sexually attracted to adolescent boys as "ephebophiles." However, the *DSM-IV* does not recognize ephebophilia as a distinct disorder as of now. Hebephilia is thus a newly coined descriptive term for male sexual abuse of adolescent boys and is often used in some literature in relation to clergy who abuse postpubertal boys (Bennett, 2004, p. 13).

Psychiatrists often study human sexuality from three different vantage points: sexual attachment, sexual desire, and reproduction (Beier, 2010, p. 8). Their theory is largely a biological one, linked to evolutionary processes. Attachment is seen as a biological need that requires a bonding situation, which helps towards achieving emotional stability. The structure of sexual preferences is seen as being molded during puberty and thereafter remains unchanged for the rest of our lives. According to Beier, "our desire is focused in terms of the gender of the preferred partner (male, female or both), the stage of physical development of the preferred partner (prepubescent, pubescent, adult) and in terms of the type of interaction, the practices, to which we are inclined" (p. 8). According to this theory, the objects of our desire are fixed in adolescence and are unchangeable thereafter. While the pedophile is said to be sexually responsive to either prepubertal boys or girls or more rarely both sexes, ephebophiles respond to teenage body perceptions. The key point, according to the theory, is that these disorders of sexuality occur in adolescence and are essentially fixed, with individuals who suffer from them having severe inner conflicts as well as the feeling of being "different." This theory has resonance with deviant sexual preference which was discussed earlier.

The use of psychiatric classifications in relation to sexual offenders is really a problematic area and raises much criticism in some of the scholarly literature (Freeman-Longo & Blanchard, 1998, p. 148; Marshall, 1997, p. 169; Polaschek, 2003a, p. 159). In the first place there are definitional difficulties running right through the category "pedophilia"; for instance, what are "intense, sexually arousing urges," when no agreed definition exists in the *DSM-IV* itself for these presentations (Polaschek, 2003a, p. 159)? Similarly, the manual does not specify what symptoms are indicated when "distress and impairment in social functioning" become clinically significant for the offender. This makes the business of diagnosing a wholly subjective matter, but one framed within a context of objective and scientific certainty. Polaschek (p. 159) points out that the clearest evidence of distress or impairment of functioning is more often seen in the *victims* of the sexual offenses, not in the perpetrators.

The diagnostic criteria for pedophilia in the *DSM-IV* (APA, 1994) are problematic in another sense in that they include individuals whose symptoms range from fantasizing about sexual relations with a child to engaging in full-contact sexual abuse. There is some evidence to suggest that many adults who have sexual fantasies about children never commit a sexually abusive act, and Marshall, Hamilton, and Fernandez (2001, p. 126) reported that they routinely exclude 20% of random community-based non-offenders from acting as control samples for their research because these people admit to fantasizing about sexual relations with children. As noted earlier, Kafka (2004, p. 52) reported that in a nonsexual offender sample of over 60,000 "normal" adult men, heterosexual men who show primary sexual arousal to adult women also show sexual arousal to adolescent girls, and the same pattern exists for adult homosexual men towards adolescent boys. Both Kafka (2004, p. 52) and Marshall et al. (2001, p. 126) conclude that the presence of sexual fantasies about children or adolescents cannot be construed as evidence of a psychiatric disorder. For these and other reasons, scholars of sexual offending regard the *DSM-IV* classifications of child sexual offenders with a lot of caution (Marshall, Hamilton, & Fernandez, 2001, p. 126). Marshall (1997, pp. 168, 169) argues in addition that the descriptive features of paraphilia that are specified in the *DSM-IV* (APA, 1994) (e.g., fantasies, urges, distress with symptoms, social and occupational impairment) have no special status in the etiology or management of sexual offenders, and there are no obvious differences in prognosis or treatment between those sexual offenders who meet the criteria for paraphilia and those who do not. Feminists also find the notion of pedophilia problematic, as will be seen later.

The DSM is currently under review for its fifth edition and a working group is charged with revising the diagnoses concerning sexual and gender identity disorders (Blanchard, 2010). Based on the criticisms of the DSM diagnostic criteria for pedophilia on both logical and conceptual grounds and on the fact that the published empirical studies on the reliability and validity of the criteria have produced ambiguous results, the diagnostic criteria for pedophilia are being examined. It is now widely accepted that not all child molesters are pedophiles and not all pedophiles are child molesters (Konopasky & Konopasky, 2000; Seto, 2002). "The existence of paedophiles who never approach a child sexually poses a problem for the distress/impairment criterion" of the current diagnosis of pedophilia (Blanchard, 2010, p. 309). "The existence of persons who have engaged children sexually but do not prefer children poses a problem for the signs/symptoms criterion" (p. 309). The solution to the signs/symptoms criterion involves an answer to the question: How does one use information about sexual acts with children to decide which child molesters are probably pedophiles and which are not? And so the discussion continues thus.

Blanchard's (2010) proposals for remedying the situation suggest a revised set of diagnostic criteria for the *DSM-V*. The proposed criteria (which are continuously being revised as inputs are received from other working groups) include enlarging the boundaries of the diagnosis to include ephebophilia, while preserving the "classic" pedophilia as a specific subtype (p. 313). In relation to the number of separate sexual episodes involving children that must have taken place in order for the adult to be diagnosed as a pedophile, the suggested threshold value is three victims (p. 313). In relation to whether a diagnosis of pedophilia should be applied to cases where the victims are "real children, virtual children and false children" (p. 314), the recommendation is that "for diagnostic purposes, photographed children and impersonated children be treated the same as real children" (p. 314). Such debate continues within the psychiatric profession, and one waits to see the newly revised *DSM-V* and what it has to tell about the new approach to diagnosing men who have perpetrated sexual offenses against children.

Despite the significant criticisms of the *DSM-IV* in relation to sexual offenders, the *DSM-IV* (APA, 1994) is an important instrument in the United States, mainly because insurance companies will not reimburse treatment costs without first receiving clearly defined diagnoses according to certain psychiatric parameters for the insured (Freeman-Longo & Blanchard, 1998, p. 148). This policy means that health care professionals are trained to systematically diagnose all of their patients/clients using *DSM-IV* classifications and psychiatric labeling, the ethics of which must surely be questioned. Freeman-Longo and Blanchard (1998, p. 148) raise the concern that once a person is given a psychiatric label, the diagnosed person and the diagnostic category often become synonymous. Through a process of stigma, the labeled individual becomes synonymous with a pathological identity. In the case of child sexual offenders, this is a most undesirable outcome. When labeling and shaming are combined strategies used to marginalize and objectify one group of individuals from another, the consequences for those individual so labeled can be enormous (Goffman, 1961/1975). In the case of child sexual offenders, there is ample evidence to show the negative consequences of such stigmatizing identities, for child protection, for community harmony, and for the men themselves and their families. This theme is developed further in Chapter 5.

CONCLUDING COMMENTS

Drawing on the history of psychological research on sexual offenders, we must be cautious in advancing empirically based knowledge because of the changing "findings" in the light of the changing horizons in which the theories are constructed and the research conducted. For example, the early literature (Freund, 1967a, 1967b; McGuire, Carlisle, & Young, 1965) emphasized the relationship between deviant sexual preferences and child sexual offending, as sexual offenders were all thought to have distinctive sexual preferences that matched their actual offending. This analysis of the problem led to the widespread use of behavioral treatment approaches aimed at changing sexual preferences, and the theory in which child abusers were thought to prefer sex with children rather than adults significantly shaped the public discourse in which child sexual abuse was narrated. It seems evident from a critical review of the literature above that the concept of deviant sexual preference is a limited one when it comes to understanding child sexual offending, especially since the more recent empirical research (Marshall, 1997) suggests that many men who abuse children do not have deviant sexual preferences, and many men who do have such preferences never abuse children (Abel, 2000; Kafka, 2004, p. 54; Konopasky & Konopasky, 2000; Seto, 2002). However, the consideration of deviant sexual preferences cannot be dismissed altogether, since Hanson and Bussière's (1998, p. 351) meta-analysis suggests that where deviant sexual preferences exist, there is a greater risk of re-offending. The main point is that deviant sexual preferences should not be the primary focus of the discourse or the research on child sexual offenders.

An analysis of the psychological literature on sexual offenders also points to the limitations of single-factor theories in explaining a phenomenon as complex as child sexual abuse. The need to include more social and context-specific factors is highlighted by such a review. While scholars have indeed attempted to combine single-element theories with social factors to develop more comprehensive accounts, it is my impression that psychological or biological factors continue to be privileged over social conditions in such work, with the proper tools of inquiry for thorough sociological analysis poorly applied. It is also important to develop explanations for sexual offending that are particular, localized, and context-specific for particular groups of offenders such as Catholic clergy. Localized accounts can in turn influence the design of focused therapeutic programs for specific client groups that will tailor the therapeutic interventions to meet their specific needs. The need for multidisciplinary and multi-site studies of child sexual offending and child sexual offenders becomes even more apparent as one reviews this literature, especially as the retributive aspects of "law and order" and the public shaming and hunting down of sexual offenders gain momentum.

The psychological perspective, reinterpreted by the popular press, which has become an important educator of the general public, may be inadvertently contributing to the demonizing of individual men, resulting in a situation where those men who are labeled and pathologized as pedophiles capture the public imagination and become modern-day lepers. The influence of psychiatric classifications can be seen in the public discourse, in particular the psychiatric classification "pedophilia," which has become part of everyday language. "The pedophile" has become a creature to be feared and abhorred. Child sexual offenders who are constructed as "pedophiles," a species of being different from other adult men, become the focus of attention in the public sphere, while the home as the site of much sexual abuse for children and women is neglected (Cowburn & Dominelli, 2001, p. 400).

From a psychological perspective, the literature on attachment, intimacy, and loneliness allows us to draw the conclusion that childhood deprivations in attachment functioning are not the only focus of concern when it comes to child sexual offending. The failure to develop and sustain intimate relationships in adulthood can also be part of the developmental trajectory of the child sexual offender. In terms of clergy offenders, this is an extremely important consideration. Whether intimate relationships are avoided for internal reasons (i.e., inability to engage) or external reasons (through a process of clerical socialization), the net effect is the same, the avoidance of intimate relationships, resulting in emotionally lonely people. As will be shown from the narratives of the participants later in this book, the men avoided adult intimate relationships as a way of protecting their vow of celibacy, and as a result they spoke of high levels of emotional loneliness and isolation, psychological factors that are reported as having a role in the genesis of child sexual offending. These issues are fully developed in Chapter 10.

There is broad agreement in the psychological literature that the presence of emotional problems is one of the factors that can influence the development of sexual offending, although the exact role of emotion or emotional regulation in such offenses is less clear. It is not clear whether the presence of strong negative emotions disinhibits the conventional inhibitions against sexual abuse, allowing the perpetrator to overrule his better judgment, or whether powerful negative emotions themselves lead potential offenders into offending as a coping strategy, or both. The assumption that all adults share conventional inhibitions against child sexual abuse as something "natural" is itself a flawed argument that does not take into account the evolving understanding of childhood and of child sexual abuse that has taken place through time.

This chapter indicates that child sexual offending is a complex phenomenon, and psychological theories to explain it continue to evolve. It also points to their limitations, and even their dangers, if applied uncritically. Given the range of competing constructions or "findings" within the discipline of psychology itself, and sufficient stake in their outcomes, in terms of power and prestige, there is brisk competition over whose voice is to be honored and whose findings are to bear the hallmark of "science." Although psychologists have hardly spoken with one voice, it is interesting to note the growing "scientific" emphasis in the discipline (Ward, Polaschek, & Beech, 2006, pp. 1–16). Given the position of power that psychology occupies in the modern world, this development must not slip by uncritically. The charting of the relationship between the biological, the neuropsychological, and what they regard as the ecological can be seen in Ward and Beech's integrated model (2006) as a manifestation of this movement towards a model of "pure science" in the psychology of the sexual offender. I now turn to some of the more critical approaches to understanding child sexual abuse.

5

A Social Approach for Understanding a Social Problem

THE SOCIAL APPROACH for understanding social problems raises different issues than those addressed in the psychological or psychiatric literature. Rather than privileging the individual, sociologists, critical theorists, and social psychologists focus on the complex relationship between the individual, the social, and the linguistic in bringing about certain phenomena. These scholars want to understand the circumstances in which sexual offenses occur, and also how some actions become defined as deviant. They question the role of expert knowledge in the creation of dominant perspectives.

Self-reflexive critique of foundational knowledge has been steadily increasing since the 1900s and can be seen in the history and philosophy of science, the sociology of knowledge, literary theory, hermeneutics, critical theory, the philosophy of history, ethnomethodology, feminist and masculinity theory. As the critique has expanded, many have joined in the search to find new ways of understanding. This "new age of scholarship" (Shotter & Gergen, 1993, p. x) is marked by the inclusion of disparate voices, and it is sharpened by "a sensitivity to the processes by which knowledge claims are made and justified." The new age of scholarship is also marked by a heightened moral concern for the social and political implications of one's perspective and findings, and by a keener appreciation of the communal character of knowledge accumulation and understanding. In essence, a social or critical perspective keeps the contextual, relational, and linguistic constitution of social issues to the fore, and is also mindful of the political and social consequences of particular linguistic constructions in social life.

This perspective is important for the study of sexual abuse by Catholic clergy, as much public and professional commentary has a tendency to individualize the problem, ignoring the political and cultural context in which the abuse and its management takes place, and the professional and political discourses in which the subject is discussed. The topics that are discussed in this chapter, and the questions they raise, provide a corrective to the more individually focused work that was discussed in Chapter 4. This chapter aims to put the "social" back into a consideration of social problems, and in this regard three main topics are central to this endeavor. The discursive constitution of social problems stresses the importance of language and power relations in how social problems take their form. The changing under-standing of child abuse situates the abuse of children in the context of evolving understand-ing of childhood and of sexuality and the family. The section on creating offending identities places discussion of the child sexual offender in the context of wider international debates on how identity is constructed and on crime and criminal policy in general.

THE DISCURSIVE CONSTITUTION OF SOCIAL PHENOMENA
The Importance of Language

Instead of assuming that people's relations with nature and with society are unaffected by the language within which they are formulated, an increasing number of scholars find that these very relations are formulated by the way we talk about them. Scholars argue that lan-guage and its usage are central to the emergence of social problems and to their depiction (Berger & Luckmann, 1991, p. 39; Best, 1995, p. 2; Hacking, 1999, p. 27; Jenkins, 1998, p. 7; Kincaid, 1998, p. 5). Rather than assuming that by the time we come to investigate the sig-nificance of a particular social problem, the "nature" of the problem and the identities of those who inhabit it are both already fixed, these scholars find it more useful to think that both are still in the making, and still open to further change and development. The underlying assumption suggests that how a problem is "languaged" will influence whether or not it will be privileged over other issues and what "core features" will become seen as central to how the problem is understood. Social problems can be open to new ways of seeing and interpret-ing because rather than having a fixed and indisputable essence, their very origins are to be located within communal interchange and within the social processes that are employed to make everyday life intelligible. These patterns of understanding can be reconstituted if for-mulated in a different way (Shotter & Gergen, 1993, p. x). We therefore need not presume that how we see a social problem today, (or how we define the identities of its participants), is "fixed" or "natural"; rather, it is based on "a form of historically dependent intelligibility requiring for its continued sustenance a set of shared understandings" (p. x). It is a moment in an ongoing historical process that may be reconstituted as understandings change. Johnson (1995, p. 20) suggests that the media's use of the "horror" story is a way of gaining privilege for child sexual abuse over other aspects of child maltreatment, child poverty, and child neglect. This is not to suggest that child sexual abuse does not have horrific dimensions for many of the children so abused, just as child neglect, child poverty, and child physical abuse, but the point is that these aspects of child maltreatment are pushed to the back of the public mind because of the preoccupation with child sexual abuse.

Jenkins (1998, p. 9) argues that none of the words or concepts used in relation to child sexual abuse represents a universally accepted "objective" reality. Rather, many of the words used in relation to the maltreatment of children, such as "sexual abuse," "victim," "survivor," "pervert," "pedophile," "molester," are rooted in the attitudes of a particular time, and each carries its ideological baggage. He warns that it seems almost impossible to write on this topic without using language that appears to accept the ideological interpretations of a par-ticular time. In so doing, exploration of other avenues of interpretation is foreclosed. Although it is objectively correct to say that many children are exploited sexually, and this of course must be of public concern, many other assumptions currently taken as objective fact in relation to the complex web of issues surrounding child sexual abuse may or may not be "objectively" correct, including how the identities of the abuse victims and the abuse perpetrators are essentialized as foundationally either good or bad. Different eras have produced different perspectives on this problem, and each era has dealt with it differently. What is interesting is that in each era, the prevailing opinion is supported by professional discourses that present what is being described and proposed as more informed and enlightened than it was in the past. Having researched the history of child sexual abuse, Jenkins (1998) comes to the conclusion that one reality prevails until another replaces it, and each formulation is presented as evolutionary, claiming that the contemporary beliefs are in fact the truth of the situation, whereas the previous ones are not.

It is often argued that recent realizations in relation to child sexual abuse are made possible by the growing accumulation of "objective" knowledge and the lifting of taboos that limited research in the past, and we now have arrived at the truth. This creates a tension in the professional and social field in which those who take this position see others who might have an alternative perspective as being prejudiced or in denial (Hacking, 1999, p. 127; Jenkins, 1998, p. 2; Johnson, 1995, p. 22). Although the existence of child sexual abuse cannot be denied, there are nonetheless many ways of making sense of it and many ways of trying to solve it. It is understandable in a democracy that this will give rise to debate and discussion. However, a particular feature of the child sexual abuse discourse is the attempt to silence one's opponents in such debate, with the accusation that they are in denial about the "reality." Nobody wants to be in denial about the reality of child sexual abuse.

Michael Foucault's (2004, p. 54) understanding of how disciplinary knowledge and disciplinary discourses act in establishing relations of power is important for understanding the social context in which social problems come to be defined in the way that they are. Foucault (2004, p. 54) argues that knowledge and power have become so inseparable that expert disciplines (such as psychology, psychiatry, law, criminology, social work, psychotherapy) can reinforce and reproduce dominant social relations, thereby masking the power relations that are at play. Foucault (2004, pp. 49, 50) conceptualizes discourse as "a group of relations established between institutions, economic and social processes, behavioural patterns, systems of norms, techniques, types of classification and modes of characterization." For Foucault (p. 54), discourses do not merely reflect reality, but in fact they form the reality of which they speak. In the practice of constructing objects, discourses conceal their very own interventions (p. 50). This theory has implications for how the problem of child sexual abuse is construed and discussed, especially with regard to the role played by the professional disciplines.

The Creation of Types

Foucault (1979, p. 191) adopted a hypothesis that all of the disciplines bearing the prefix *psy-* or *psycho-* have their origins in what he regards as a reversal of the political axis of individualization. For a long time, Foucault suggests, "to be looked at, observed, described in detail, followed from day to day by an uninterrupted writing was a privilege" (p. 191). However, that all changed with the disciplinary methods, which reversed this relation and "made of this description a means of control and a method of domination" (p. 191). For Foucault, this turning of real lives into writing is no longer a procedure for the creation of icons and heroes, but rather it serves as a procedure of objectification and subjectification (p. 191). Rose (1993, p. 123) takes up Foucault's thesis to suggest that one of the ways of linking the mental sciences with more general social, ethical, and political transformations is to understand them as "techniques for the disciplining of difference"; as techniques that classify individuals, calibrate their capacities and behaviors, inscribe and record their attributes and deficiencies, and manage their individuality and variability. These practices require the operation of modes of codification of human individuality, which are based on measurements of what it is to be "normal," which once differentiated can make the "abnormal" easily identified.

The systematization of files, case notes, records, and descriptions of individuals is part of this development, in which individuals are identified through profiles consisting of the features of the individual's life that fit the professional agenda. The individual's identity begins to be seen "not through any abstract leap of the philosophical imagination, but through the mundane operation of bureaucratic documentation" (Rose, 1993, p. 126). The psychological test is the principal contribution of psychology toward this process. Based on "the statistical-ization of human variability through the use of the normal curve," the psychological test enables the mathematization of difference (p. 126). The psychological test makes the complex array of individual processes able to be reduced to describable markings by means of a routine procedure. The codification, mathematization, and standardization of difference make the test into a mini-laboratory (p. 26). No longer is it necessary to aggregate people in large institutions to evaluate significant features of behavior; that can be done in a brief period, in a manageable space, at the will of the expert. The call for risk assessments and the search for risk assessment instruments in response to this call form part of the modern management strategies for sexual violations. The expectation of scientific certainty in the attempts to legislate against human risk is one of the most worrying dimensions of this latest development.

It is in this context that Bell warns (2002, p. 84) that the processes or techniques by which child abuse becomes known within the disciplines of psychology, psychiatry, and social work, and the techniques by which the "populations at risk" are constituted, need to be analyzed and understood, and they must always be subject to critical analysis. Offering a Foucauldian analysis, Bell (2002, p. 83) argues that because the *psy-* and *psycho-* disciplines use techniques to gain information about individuals, which is subsequently used to identify and govern others of the same "type," the work of the professional disciplines must always be subject to critique. Their power that society vests in the disciplines to influence the way in which individuals belonging to these "types" are to be understood and treated must not be without control and accountability. The variety of figures that emerge from many of the professional practices associated with the disciplines, including law and child protection professionals, such as "the child abuser," "the pedophile," "the child at risk," "the seductive child," "the colluding mother," "the covering-up bishop," and the changing ways in which certain components are constructed, such as "the victim," "the perpetrator," "the mother of victim," "the denying bishop," must be the subject of continuing analysis and critique in the interest of ethical practice and of justice. Others agree (Bell, 2002; Cowburn & Dominelli, 2001; Hacking, 1999; Haug, 2001; Mercer & Simmonds, 2001). Bell (2002, p. 87) argues that attention must be paid to the techniques that help construct child sexual abuse and the child sexual offender in a particular way, and the power relations that accompany it;

otherwise there is a risk of oppressing and marginalizing. What is important here is that power relations are obscured while the cast of villains are construed and elaborated.

Social Constructionism

Since the publication of Berger and Luckmann's work (1966) on the social construction of reality, there has been a major elaboration of theory that draws connections between social processes, people's life experiences, and an understanding of social realities. Berger and Luckmann (1966) see the achievements of everyday life as a series of interactions that are fluid, multiple, and precariously negotiated. They suggest that when ways of doing or perceiving aspects of social life are tentatively agreed upon, through repetition and a process of reification, they become institutionalized over time and are thought to represent "objective" reality, or the truth of the situation (Berger & Luckmann, 1966, p. 60). However, these "realities" have been shaped and formed by discourses and vested interests. In the process, alternative perspectives are marginalized through the operations of power relations. Although it is clearly not the case that social problems are simple "social constructions," social constructionism offers a way of seeing social problems as containing both "real" and "socially constructed" dimensions (Hacking, 1999, p. 125).

Hacking (1999, p. 125) suggests that when a problem is debated and developed in a social setting with results that have implications for social policy and for the life of a community, this problem is in part socially constructed. However, at the same time the problem is real. Child sexual abuse is one such problem. "Child abuse is real behavior, [it] has not been imagined by activists, and . . . there are innumerable cases of children who have been physically, sexually or emotionally abused" (Hacking, 1999, p. 125). Child sexual offenders are real, too, and they have carried out very real sexual offenses. However, at the same time child sexual abuse and child sexual offenders are also socially constructed, or made and molded into what we believe them to be today through discourse. The term *child abuse* emerged from its forerunner, *child battering*, in 1961, in Denver, Colorado, in the discussions of some authoritative people, pediatricians, who used the term initially to refer to battered babies, but the usage over time has been extended to other abuse situations, acquiring new meanings and implications (Hacking, 1999, p. 125; Kempe & Helfer, 1962). The current usage of the concept of child sexual abuse has evolved since that time, although child–adult sex has a much longer history.

Moral Panic

Cohen (1972) introduced the notion of "moral panics," referring particularly to the Mods and Rockers who had fights on the beaches of English seaside towns in the mid-1960s. He was not so interested in why the Mods and Rockers had fights, but why the social reaction to them was so excessive. In Cohen's view, the reactions and the reporting were widely exaggerated. Cohen argues (2002, p. 1) that every now and then societies appear to be subject to periods of "moral panic," when the novelty of a "condition, episode, person or group of persons emerges to become defined as a threat to societal values and interests." In a moral panic the nature of the problem is presented in a stereotypical fashion by the mass media, and according to Cohen "the moral barricades are manned by editors, Bishops, politicians and other right thinking people" (p. 1). The language of morality and rightness is clearly articulated as "socially accredited experts pronounce their diagnoses and solutions" (p. 1). In essence, the problem is presented in the form of a significant threat to both accepted moral standards and to vulnerable groups and individuals.

Although Cohen's (1972) original moral panic theory has been criticized because of its assumption that the reaction to the original problem is exaggerated, resulting in ill-placed fears, the theory still has something to offer to an analysis of child sexual abuse, especially when it is not used to suggest that the reaction to child sexual abuse is exaggerated (Jenkins, 2009, p. 36). One of the most useful contributions of such an analysis is the idea that coalitions can be formed between formerly opposing forces on matters of public concern, allowing a consensus to emerge on a given issue and resulting in a single, usually heavily policed, discourse to emerge (Haug, 2001, p. 64; Jenkins, 1998, p. 15; Kincaid, 1998). Moral panics about children facing the dangers of sexual abuse are influenced by the changing conceptions of childhood, the child abuse victim, the child sex offender, the consequences of sexual behavior between children and adults, and the range of behaviors deemed prosecutable. Haug (2001, p. 64) argues that in relation to child sexual abuse, the moral panic is fueled by the relentless and detailed descriptions of what happened, by the continuous production of one version of "the truth," by isolating a single culprit, and above all by suggesting that sex is the reason for so much pathology in the individual and in society. These strategies serve to keep the complexities of the issues involved in power, knowledge, sexuality, childhood, adulthood, desire, and the fate of the body off the public and scholarly agenda.

In Jenkins's view (1998, p. 221) a moral panic will evaporate or implode in time, usually through its own internal dynamics. When highly visible miscarriages of justice are publicized, and the public's sense of fairness in justice is offended, often through the work of the arts and the academy, a weakening of the moral panic and its claims begins to occur. However, in Jenkins's view (1998, p. 234), modern concepts of child sexual abuse are linked to what he sees as irreversible social, political, and ideological trends (the vulnerability of children and their need for protection, political and social equality for women, and the power of medico-legal discourses of sexuality), making it likely that contemporary formulations of the child abuse problem will not diminish in the near future (Jenkins, 1998, p. 234).

CHILDHOOD, SEXUALITY, AND CHILD SEXUAL ABUSE
Evolving Understanding of Child Sexual Abuse

Jenkins (1998, p. xi) traced the history of adult–child sex (today known as child sexual abuse) and argues fairly convincingly that although the term *child sexual abuse* has a long history it was not until the mid-1970s that it acquired its present cultural and ideological significance "with all its connotations of betrayal of trust, hidden trauma and denial."[1] This is a concept that has changed over time, and adult–child sex has not always had the same meaning and implications for the child or adult as we have come to accept today. It can of course be also noted that the incest taboo is one of those universal principles that has been a feature of almost every society, in every era through time.

Although Freud and Tardieu wrote about damage to children who had experienced sexual contact with adults, it has only been since the 1970s that this idea has gained professional attention in any real way again (Bolen, 2001, p. 66; Jenkins, 1998, p. 18). For some periods during the 20th century it was not uncommon for some of the clinical literature to suggest that in many cases of adult–child sex the child was the active seducer rather than the one who was "innocently seduced" (Bender et al., 1937, p. 505; Bender et al., 1952, p. 830; De Young, 1982, p. 58; Jenkins, 1998, p. 2). Children were thought to produce such offenses for their own psychological reasons. Such thinking influenced aspects of professional practice in the 1970s. Child sexual abuse was seen as an infrequent occurrence unlikely to cause significant harm to the vast majority of its subjects. Images of sexual offenders have also changed dramatically over time, oscillating between concepts of the benign molester as a defective individual, who was known to all and who was not doing much harm, to the more recent concept of the evil sex fiend, who possesses the most dangerous and sophisticated criminal intellect and who has access to the latest form of technology and communication (Jenkins, 1998, p. 18). The perpetrator of child sexual abuse, once seen as "harmlessly inadequate," is now referred to as a "dangerous predator" (Jenkins, 1998, p. 2). In much public discourse on sexual abuse every child sexual offender is seen as posing danger to every child, in all situations, and his behavior and personhood are often little removed from the worst multiple killer and torturer (Breen, 2004b, p. 9; Hudson, 2005, p. 26; Jenkins, 1998, p. 2). In many Western jurisdictions these shifting attitudes are reflected in changes in attitude toward reporting and prosecuting these crimes. A quick look across the official crime statistics in many Western jurisdictions bears out this fact. Today, the criminal parameters of the problem have come to the fore, with an accompanying approach to child protection that is increasingly legalistic and bureaucratic. In this scenario, the risk paradigm, risk management and public notification of the dangers posed are preferred to the more rehabilitative or reintegrative ideals. Child sexual abuse has acquired a new moral weight, while at the same time sexual offending has become the worst of all possible vices (Hacking, 1999, p. 125; Kincaid, 1998, p. 5). In such circumstances, the child abuse victim is portrayed as damaged for life and the child sexual offender is viewed as the most evil of human beings.

Evolving Understanding of Childhood

In most Western societies, childhood is seen as an age-related phenomenon, which prescribes legal rights and responsibilities to children, and to adults in relation to them. These rights and responsibilities are reflected in the law of the land. Despite these age-related demarcations children grow at different rates both physically and psychologically, and there is no uniformity in how the child is seen throughout the world (Corby, 2000, p. 10). However, through time childhood was not always seen as it is today, and current conceptions of childhood have a direct influence on what it means to be a child, what it means to be a child abuse victim, and what it means to be a child abuse perpetrator.

The most influential work on childhood in the 20th century has been that of Philippe Ariès (1962), a French social historian. In *Centuries of Childhood* (1962, p. 125) Ariès argues that in medieval society the idea of childhood did not exist, but that this was not detrimental to the child. Rather, Ariès thought the opposite was true. In the Middle Ages children mingled with adults as soon as that was physically possible and spent much of their time together in work and play (p. 125). It was from the 17th century onward, with the advent of a form of education dominated by religion-based morality, that children became separated from adults in the way known today. Ariès (1962, p. 126) saw this as a backward step, and he argues that the concept of childhood is a limiting force for children, placing more restrictions on them in their formative years, and placing them more at the mercy of adults, than had previously been the case.

Other scholars (De Mause, 1976, p. 1; Pollock, 1983, p. 7; Wilson, 1984, 183) are not of the same view as Ariès (1962) and argue that he does not have the evidence to back up his wide-ranging claims regarding childhood and family life in the Middle Ages. Some of his critics see the development of the concept of childhood as highly progressive (De Mause, 1976, p. 1; Stone, 1977, p. 70). They argue that such developments heralded a time when children were recognized as a distinct group from adults, and with this came recognition of special rights, based on what was seen as their particular developmental needs and vulnerabilities. Such knowledge, they argue, did much to improve the lot of children. "The further back in history one goes the lower the level of childcare, and the more likely children are to be killed, abandoned, beaten, terrorized and sexually abused" (De Mause, 1976, p. 1).

While scholars of childhood debate these issues and reach varying interpretations of the historical records, it is clear that there is no universal experience of childhood, and there never was. Different eras have produced different constructions of what it means to be a child and on how children are to be socialized. It is also the case that children of different classes, race, and gender have had, and continue to have, widely differing experiences of childhood (Corby, 2000, p. 15). As Davin (1990, p. 10) points out, during the period of industrialization in Britain, as greater sensitivity was shown toward children of the middle classes, appalling working conditions for children of the laboring classes in the mills and factories and on the street were simultaneously accepted. Despite their differences, scholars of childhood appear to come together on an important observation: as societies develop economically there is a tendency for childhood to be extended and to gain more attention as a separate category from adulthood, based on the child's different needs and vulnerabilities (Corby, 2000, p. 12). In this regard, the 20th century has seen the concept of childhood become almost the exclusive preserve of psychology, with childhood experiences seen as a crucial determinative of the human adult character (Dunne & Kelly, 2002, p. 4). This has led to the greater development of child welfare and child protection policies.

In the Irish situation, Buckley, Skehill, and O'Sullivan (1996, p. 12) observed how varying constructions of childhood underpinned social policy since the foundation of the state in 1922, with significant differences in effect. In Ireland, for example, the period up to the 1970s was characterized as the era of the "depraved child," when children, in particular the children of the poor, were seen as in need of discipline and socialization. Childcare interventions were viewed as a means of social control, and children of the poor were taken by the state into the reformatory and industrial schools for education and control (Ryan Report, 2009). In contrast, the 1980s heralded the era of the "deprived child," reflecting the influences of developmental psychology with its emphasis on the emotional and psychological dimensions of childhood, and of the welfare of children (Buckley, 1996, p. 12). Social policy reflected this new perspective, bringing a move away from the industrial and reformatory schools and toward smaller children's units. It also heralded the growth of child and adolescent mental health services and "child guidance" clinics. The 1990s and 2000s also brought a shift in emphasis in how children are conceptualized, and in line with international trends, this era can be considered as the era of the "abused child" and the "sexually abused child," an era that shows no signs of abating (Buckley, 1996, p. 12). While the Irish church and state are currently engaged in honoring the lost childhoods of countless children who were reared in industrial and reformatory schools during the 1950s, 1960s, and 1970s, similar to the "lost generations" in other jurisdictions, such as Australia and Canada, and public attention in the Anglo-Saxon world focuses on the abuses that children suffered at the hands of Catholic clergy during the 1970s, 1980s, and 1990s, countless children live in poverty in Ireland and throughout the world in the year 2010, and services for children with disabilities and those in the care of the Irish state are grossly neglected and underfunded (O'Brien, 2009a; 2009b; 2009c; 2009d; 2009e). This situation lends support for Johnson's thesis (1995) that social issues, including those relating to children, must be construed in a manner that will capture the media's interest so that they can gain privilege over other issues in the social mind and become worthy of social and political intervention.

Childhood, Sexuality, and the Institution of the Family

One aspect of childhood that is under-theorized but that is important in any analysis of child sexual abuse relates to the question of childhood sexuality. Government documents on childhood hardly mention this topic, leading one to suspect that childhood sexuality is a topic that is difficult to discuss. Less than one sentence was devoted to the topic in the Irish *National Children's Strategy* (2000), a document of 140 pages. Scholars of childhood similarly shy away. In attempting to understand sexuality and the child and its implications for child sexual abuse, Haug (2001, p. 61) offers a Foucaudian analysis because it allows her to take a closer look at the interrelationships between such spheres as the family, sexuality, childhood, and law. She points out that one of the peculiarities of the problem of child sexual abuse is that one encounters contradictions almost everywhere, "contradictions [that] are mixed up with society as a whole, with the construction of the family, of sexuality, of childhood and of jurisdiction" (p. 61). For Foucault (1998), traces of modern patterns of sexuality can be linked back to Victorian times, which Ferriter (2009) argues in the case of Irish sexuality is even more complicated. In Victorian times it was believed that children did not have sexuality, but paradoxically they were forbidden to talk about it, and adults closed their eyes and ears whenever children came to show evidence to the contrary (Foucault, 1998, p. 4). For Foucault, these paradoxical features led to a general and studied silence being imposed on childhood sexuality (and on sexuality in general), bringing forth the characteristic features of repression. In effect, childhood sexuality was rendered invisible, as though nonexistent, and by implication "there was nothing to say . . . nothing to see and nothing to know" (p. 4). In Victorian times sexual expression was preserved for the conjugal couple and absorbed into functions of reproduction. A single sexual norm was acknowledged in the public sphere as well as in every household (p. 3). Behavior outside of this enforced model of sexuality carried the suggestion of abnormality. The family had the task of forbidding sex, but such vigilance meant that sex was moved to a central place in the life of the family in an attempt to prevent and control it. The legitimate and procreative model of sexuality imposed itself as a model, enforced the norm, safeguarded the truth, and reserved the right to speak about sex. Silence and secrecy became the rule (p. 4).

Haug (2001, p. 62) argues that silence is the rule when it comes to the subject of sex and particularly sexuality and children, and following Foucault she argues that repression has been "the fundamental link between power, knowledge, and sexuality since the classical age."

For Foucault (1998, p. 19), modern technologies of power, such as the listening techniques, the assumption of causality, the principle of sexuality as omnipresent but in an underdeveloped form, the rules of interpretation, the imperative of rendering sexuality to the domain of the medical, has moved sexuality into something that is thought to be, by nature, susceptible to pathological processes and hence something that calls for therapeutic or normalizing interventions. He argues that sexual repression is now firmly embedded in the regimens of power/knowledge/pleasure that sustain the discourse of sexuality. Further, everything related to unpacking the normative dimensions of sexuality is linked to and conditioned by politics (p. 5). Foucault argues that this stands as the reason why generations have found it difficult to be freed from Victorian constraints, except at significant cost (p. 5). Haug (2001, p. 63) argues that this is the context in which child sexual abuse has taken its current form in public discussion.

While at this point the reader could be forgiven for feeling that a discussion of childhood sexuality in the context of child sexual abuse is purely academic and even dangerous, this topic is far from merely academic in how childhood sexuality and child sexual abuse are currently interlinked, for reasons that go beyond those already discussed. In a wave of new sexual concerns since the 1990s, child protection services are increasingly concerned about "sexual offenses" perpetrated by children. When one considers the limited literature on what constitutes "normal" sexuality for the child, when children are assumed not to have sexuality in the first instance, one encounters some of the problems involved in identifying and understanding what childhood sexual behaviors are to be considered as "abusive." One also becomes concerned about labeling children as "sexual deviants," children who are stigmatized as outside the realm of what is thought to be "normal."

Recent interest in sexual abuses perpetrated by children has led to an evolving psychological literature on normal and abnormal sexual play for children, with lists of symptoms and behaviors that will distinguish one from the other. Scholars are also trying to understand the factors that may lead to the development of problematic sexual behavior in a child (Araji, 1997; Johnson, 2004; Pithers & Gray, 1998;). The term "problematic sexualized behavior" is preferred to the terms "sexual abuse" or "sexual offense" when the "abuse" is perpetrated by a child under the age of 12 years. At the same time, childhood problematic sexualized behavior as an emerging field is dominated by clinical impressions and inferences from adult and adolescent sexual offender research and clinical practice (Hall, 1999). Increasingly children are being considered as suitable for various forms of therapeutic interventions (Taylor, 2003). Never has it been more urgent for honesty to permeate debate on childhood sexuality and for some of the silence to be lifted.

CREATING OFFENDING IDENTITIES
Labeling, Shame, and Stigma

The predominant Western conception of self, which has permeated psychology's understanding of its subject, emphasizes the notion of self as an essential or interior person, capable of being thought about as a separate, more or less integrated and distinctive whole. In this conception of self, the self is seen as something to be discovered, something that is fixed and autonomous, and something that is internal to the individual (Burr, 1995). However, there are other ways of perceiving self, and in much of the critical and sociological literature the self is conceptualized in rather different terms. Here the self is theorized as relational, as a self-in-action, always fluid, always being created and recreated in relationship with others (Goffman, 1963; Hudson, 2005; Mead, 1934). Such a way of conceptualizing self gives rise to the concept of a narrative self, a self that may have a core, physical, and even emotional embodiment, but that is also storied and constructed in language, and in relationship with others (Flaskas, 2002, p. 87; Gergen, 1992; Ward & Marshall, 2007, p. 2; White, 2004).

Mead's (1934) work on labeling and Goffman's (1963) work on stigma describe how identity is constructed through a process of internalization, whereby outside opinion influences an individual's beliefs about himself or herself. Goffman (1959, p. 252) argues that persons are always in a sense presenting themselves; guiding controlled impressions, not necessarily to deceive, but to sustain a sense of self. Ample research indicates that individuals who subscribe to negative self-identity are more likely than those who hold a positive sense of self to live unfulfilling lives (White, 2004, p. 121). Abusive behavior is more likely to occur in individuals who hold a negative sense of identity (Marshall et al., 2000, pp. 48–50). More attention must therefore be paid to the social identity of men who have sexually abused children, especially as it affects their identity conclusions, risks of further offending, and the way in which they are treated by the communities in which they live. It is therefore important to consider the impact of labeling, stigma, and social rejection on the identity formation of sexual offenders if the aim is to prevent and reduce offending. The primary relevance of stigmatization is that it shuns the individual, keeping him as the outcast; a situation some scholars believe can lead to further offending (Karp, 1998, p. 283; Maxwell & Morris, 1999; Soothill & Francis, 1998, pp. 288, 289).

Using Goffman's (1961, 1963) theoretical work on stigma as a conceptual framework, Mercer and Simmonds (2001, pp. 170, 171) argue in relation to sexual abuse perpetrators that "[t]hose individuals who transgress legal and moral codes face a double stigma, typically characterised as a sickness of mind and spirit." In their subsequent treatment by society, there are contradictions everywhere. They are both excluded from the public (for example, they are put into prisons or maximum-security psychiatric institutions), while at the same time they continue to attract widespread public attention (such as a continuous flow of newspaper reports on the details of their offending and their attendance at court). They are both silenced and questioned, in that if they speak they are accused of denial or cover-up, but if they don't they are accused of staying silent. They are both subjects of private secrecy and objects of public scrutiny, in that the public scrutiny and the vilification that follows in fact encourages a culture of secrecy regarding past offending. The cumulative effect of these contradictions is that child sexual offenders are regarded as shameful pariahs and at the same time they are public personae (Mercer & Simmonds, 2001, p. 171). Thus, while society does not know what to do with the known child sexual offenders in its midst, the sexual abuse perpetrators are placed in a double bind: go away but stay; speak but stay silent; hide but be visible.

Scholars argue (Hudson, 2005, p. 55; O'Malley, 1998, p. 1) that once an individual has been labeled as a "sexual offender" the label becomes the most salient part of his identity, at least in terms of how he is perceived by others. Hudson (2005, p. 55) interviewed 32 male sex offenders in prisons in England, 22 of them convicted child sexual offenders. She explored how the participants reacted to public perception of them as sexual offenders and how in turn such public perceptions influenced their lives. The interviewees in her study expressed concern that the very public identification of themselves as sexual offenders made it difficult to establish any other identity. Hence, for them, concealing their offenses and managing their identity became their primary concern. Hudson found evidence to suggest that men were preoccupied with "managing" offending identities and felt they were seen only as sexual offenders, not men with additional histories and life stories (p. 167). She traces these problems back to the misleading portrayal of sexual offenders in the popular media, which ultimately presents all child sexual offenders as a homogeneous mass and penalizes individuals for crimes they might commit in the future. Hudson concludes that in the case of sexual offenders it is not merely the offending actions that are unacceptable to society, but the individuals themselves (p. 55). The offending behavior is disapproved of, but the offender's identity is construed as evil (p. 30). Labeling sexual offenders in such a manner does not serve child protection or the rights of offenders in natural justice.

O'Malley (1998) notes, in the Irish situation, that as soon as a person is formally or informally judged to be a sex offender or child abuser, he is socially classified under that heading only: "The attachment of one of these labels has the effect of obliterating the offender's entire social and personal profile" (p. 1). As soon as a man becomes classified as a sex offender, his earlier achievements and social contributions are deemed irrelevant, and far from being seen as an individual he now belongs to a "type." What matters now is the very sexual nature of the offense and the classification that follows (Bell, 2002, p. 83; Hudson, 2005, p. 26; O'Malley, 1998, p. 1). In most cases, the actual offending behavior of men who abuse minors occupies a very small portion of their lives, although the effect of their offending can of course be wide-reaching. Based on the analyses of the very detailed diaries of a predatory child sexual offender, who had abused over 400 boys over a 20-year period, Marshall (1996b, p. 318) estimated that this man spent 8% of his time offending (including planning and arranging). For many child sexual offenders the time spent offending is much less than 8%. Although this is never an acceptable situation, it means there is much about the perpetrator that can be built on to prevent further abuses. However, when sinister motives are attributed to all of a man's actions and his actions are seen as evidence of a pathological or deviant identity, the effects may be disintegrative in nature in that little or no effort is made to believe that the offender can desist from offending and make good. Little attempt is made to reinforce his membership in the community of law-abiding citizens, long after he has served prison terms and fulfilled community sanctions (Garfinkel, 1956). Instead, many child sex offenders in Ireland and the United Kingdom are hunted down from location to location and in some cases from jurisdiction to jurisdiction.

Social Violence

The use of shaming mechanisms is not new, nor is the use of public humiliation and social disgrace to exact punishment for an offense. Such strategies can be state-led as well as popular responses to sexual offending; both have the same disintegrative or stigmatizing effects. From a critical perspective, these strategies, which are designed to shame offenders into greater respect for the law and create a powerful deterrent to reoffending (Karp, 1998), can be seen as strategies of social or institutional violence, a violence that we have not begun to address in the Western world. While some of the state-led examples of social violence in the United States, can include registration and notification schemes, which are a response to populist calls for punitive responses to sexual crime (Bottoms, 1995), other schemes are much more violent in their impact. In the United States, mandatory self-identification, which mandates the offender to personally inform his neighbors that he is a convicted sexual offender, and community notification schemes, which give the police the power to release details of convicted sexual offenders via the Internet or on posters, are in effect strategies of public exposure and humiliation, although the intent may be to protect the public (Karp, 1998, p. 281). There are numerous examples of shaming strategies imposed by the courts and the probation services in the United States, all of which are designed to bring the crime to the attention of the public so that they may respond with shaming. While part of the intent is to warn potential victims of the potential dangers that an offender may pose, the risk of stigmatizing attached to such penalties is very high (Kelley, 1989, p. 775).

At a more community-based level, public humiliation and shaming strategies are also in evidence, often with the help of the media. The 2000 *News of the World* "name and shame" campaign in England, which also spilled over to Ireland, centered on the "outing" of men suspected and known to have sexually abused minors by printing their photographs, names and addresses, and details of their offending histories in the public press. The aim of this campaign was to name and shame all the child sexual offenders in the United Kingdom and to pressure government into adopting an equivalent of "Megan's Law" from the United States in the United Kingdom, which would provide a greater degree of community notification than had previously been in existence. The media campaign provoked widespread hysteria and vigilante activity culminating in demonstrations outside of people's homes, forcing several families to flee, one man to disappear, and two alleged child sexual offenders to commit suicide (Ashenden, 2002, p. 208).

Far from protecting the community and increasing community safety, such strategies of social violence only serve to label and stigmatize individual offenders and isolate them from their communities (Winick, 1998, p. 539). Such strategies work against the rehabilitative ideal and ultimately may drive many sexual offenders underground (Soothill & Francis, 1998, pp. 288, 289). The aim ought to be to invite sexual offenders or potential sexual offenders to come forth, get help, and be accountable, but such strategies may have the opposite effect. Social violence renders crucial stories about abuse perpetrators' lives invisible, their motivations and intentions bad, their personalities flawed, and their good works suspect. Within the modern-day technologies of power nobody is accountable for inflicting such social violence and social trauma. There is now an emerging literature on human rights for sexual offenders. The reason for this emerging literature is the violation of human rights that is taking place regularly and that can no longer be condoned.

A paradigm shift (Garland, 2001) that has influenced contemporary understanding of crime and the criminal must also be seen as part of the social context in how child sexual abuse and the child sexual offender are currently portrayed in many Western jurisdictions. Since the 1970s the emphasis of crime and crime policy, mainly in the United States and the United Kingdom, has shifted away from welfare to control, and from rehabilitation to punishment (Garland, 2001, pp. 85–89). With increased emphasis on "moral individualism" and less concern for social explanations for crime, individual responsibility replaces social causality in theorizing crime, with explanations of crime based on a vision of the human condition that is dark and unrepenting (p. 15). In official discourses, the criminal is seen as "undeserving and dangerous," someone from whom the public must be protected (p. 175).

While in this approach to crime some attention is paid to victims of crime, an unhelpful dichotomy is simultaneously invoked: being "for" victims is assumed to imply being tough on offenders (p. 11), and helping offenders is assumed to mean being "against" victims. The results of these changes in the United States and the United Kingdom in particular, much of which can also be felt in Ireland, is that criminal justice policies are more focused on blaming the offender, silencing his explanations, ignoring root causes, and seeing wrongdoers punished (pp. 130–131). In this climate, the business of managing and controlling crime is seen as presenting a volatile and dangerous situation for politicians, one in which managing crime, and sexual crime in particular becomes highly "political."

The Media and the Child Sexual Offender

Scholars (Best, 1995a; Breen, 2004a, 2004b; Jenkins, 1996; Kitzinger, 2000) emphasize the role of the print and electronic media in influencing public opinion on sexual offenders and in using shaming techniques and strategies to marginalize and punish. The mass media is said to play a significant role in setting public agendas on a wide variety of issues, and media coverage of a topic can also alter public perception of the central participants in the story (Breen, 2004a, p. 3). While the media can be applauded for helping to support victims of abuse in putting their experiences onto the political and social agenda, the media cannot be applauded for its representation of sexual offenders. In effect, many media commentators fall into the trap that the dichotomous structure offers: if you are with victims, you must be against offenders and the other way round. This dichotomy is at the heart of much media reporting of child sexual abuse.

Best (1995a, p. 8) uses the term *typification* to refer to the process by which claims-makers characterize a problem's nature. Typification is used to give an orientation toward a problem by locating the problem's causes, interpreting the motivations of many of its subjects, and recommending solutions. In most Western societies it has become common to use a medical model to typify social problems, implying sickness or disease, symptoms and treatment, and the idea of cure (Best, 1995a, p. 14). Crime is often typified through the medium of a "melodramatic" model that sees "victims" as exploited by "villains" who must subsequently be rescued by "heroes" (Nelson-Rowe, 1995, p. 84). The media's approach presents child sexual offenders as a homogenous mass that is always and forever a threat to children and from whom the innocent public must be protected, despite research findings that suggest the contrary.

In relation to the coverage of child sexual offenders, it is the use of media templates that is most illuminating. According to Kitzinger (2000, p. 62), media templates are routinely used to emphasize only one clear perspective, to serve as rhetorical shorthand/shortcuts, and to help audiences and producers place stories in a particular context. These templates have a threefold effect: (a) they shape narratives around specific issues, (b) they guide public opinion and discussion, and (c) they set the frame of reference for the future. Even though the events once reported might have long since passed, they continue to carry powerful associations that have long outlived their potential immediate usefulness. The study of media templates allows researchers to develop an understanding of how reality is framed, how various elements of social life are constructed, and how media power is essentially operationalized in society (Breen, 2004a, p. 5). Examples of media templates are "the Wall Street crash of 1929," which serves as a media template for the reporting of financial issues and problems; "Vietnam" for a failed or mired war; and "Watergate" for political scandals (Breen, 2004a, p. 5; Kitzinger, 2000, p. 61). The latter is such a strong template that the suffix "gate" carries its own derived meaning.

The power of media templates lies in their associative force (Breen, 2004a; Kitzinger, 2000). They are used to explain current events, but their main function is to highlight general patterns in particular social problems. The major consequence that follows from the use of media templates is that a strong single discourse dominates, representing "facts" and "truth." However, these "facts" or "truths" have been simplified or distorted and alternative readings of the facts minimized (Kitzinger, 2000). Greer (2003, p. 4) argues that the image of the sexual offender portrayed in the press in Britain is that of an "amoral, manipulative, predatory sociopath" who preys preferably on the most vulnerable. Such imagery succeeds in creating the picture of the sex offender as an inherently different person compared to other members of society. Even legislative and policy responses can be seen as stemming from such perceptions. Hudson (2005, p. 1) argues that the current trend in Britain of taking increasingly punitive measures against sex offenders, both in sentencing and in the community, derives from such created and constructed images. The same can be said about Ireland.

In Ireland, the coverage of sexual abuse by clergy led to the emergence of a new media template, "Brendan Smyth." Father Brendan Smyth, a Norbertine priest, was convicted in June 1994 on 17 counts of sexual abuse of children stretching over 30 years. An investigative journalist, Chris Moore, reporting for Ulster Television showed that the clerical authorities had known for years of Smyth's crimes and had dealt with them simply by moving him on, thereby covering up his abuses (Moore, 1995). A series of political events concerning the mishandling of the case in the Attorney General's office led to political tensions that eventually brought down the government in the republic in 1994 (Moore, 1995). While reporting this case, a new category of sexual offender, "the pedophile priest," was invented by the media (*Boston Globe*, 2002, p. 7; Ferguson, 1995, 248). Furthermore, the media relied heavily on a powerful visual image of Smyth. From the outset, the media repeatedly used the same photograph of Brendan Smyth's bloated and angry face, staring straight into the camera, so that he became "the living embodiment of the greatest demon in modern Ireland" (Ferguson, 1995, p. 249). Long after his death this photograph often accompanied media reports of sexual abuse by other clergy.

Cultural Narratives and Child Sexual Abuse

Kincaid (1998) argues that cultural narratives also shape the particular construction of child sexual abuse and the child sexual offender that dominates the public and professional discourses; in fact, his thesis is that current constructions contribute to the continuation of the problem. Kincaid (p. 8) suggests that in writing on the subject of child sexual abuse, every author feels compelled to state, "[p]lease don't misunderstand me; I know millions of children are sexually molested." He argues that the very feeling of being compelled to ward off such misunderstandings suggests a very narrow range to the current discourse, one that is "conscientiously policed" (p. 8). Only minor variations on a single story can be told, and it is Kincaid's thesis that the story of sexual abuse currently told is in the same domain as the abuse against which it protests. Ultimately children suffer (p. 8). Pointing out that few stories in the Western world are as popular as child abuse, Kincaid (1998, p. 3) asks why sex

offending stories are so popular, what rewards they offer, who will profit from their circula-
tion, and who has to pay the price. Kincaid is less interested in the personal narratives of
individuals than in the cultural narratives that influence ways of seeing children, sexuality,
and sexual boundaries. He maintains that no member of society is ever outside of these
stories but lives within them, playing his or her own unique part in the creation of the
dominant "story" of child sexual abuse (p. 5).

Kincaid's (1998, p. 6) thesis rests on two assumptions: first, the stories being told of child
sexual abuse are serving a function for adults in general, and second, the stories being told of
child sexual abuse keep the subject alive by allowing it to be simultaneously welcomed and
disowned. He argues that Western culture has "enthusiastically sexualized the child while
denying just as enthusiastically that it was doing any such thing" (Kincaid, 1998, p. 13). Child
pageants in the United States and the sexualizing of children in the pop music industry
provide the evidence for this theory. According to Kincaid (p. 20), a society that regards
children as erotic, but also regards an erotic response to children as criminally unimaginable,
has a problem on its hands. In his opinion, the extent of the abuse of children is still denied
because the complexities involved in the interplay of childhood, sexuality, and adulthood are
also denied, while attention is focused on the "monster," who is seen as "other" (Kincaid,
1998, p. 20). Kincaid argues that if a society wants to protect children from sexual abuse and
to understand how the problem is constituted, then the discourse must change to one in
which the problems of child sexual abuse are located within the general adult population
and not with a few individuals who are seen as "flawed" and are identified as "monsters."
Ultimately, a better understanding of the complexities of adult and child sexuality will lead
to greater protection for children (p. 22) and less marginalizing of men. In Kincaid's view,
many children suffer in the current situation: children who are sexually abused and those
who are denied a nurturing relationship with men. Perpetrators of abuse suffer, too, when
they are sentenced to live their lives as "evil monsters" by an unforgiving adult public.

CONCLUDING COMMENTS

The above literature suggests that current constructions of the child sexual offender must be
regarded with caution because they are influenced by power relations, vested interests, professional judgments, and to some extent ideology and emotion. Professional discourses that
help construct the child sexual offender as fundamentally different from the rest of society
unwittingly contribute to the situation where sexual offenders are marginalized and demonized and their human rights violated.

The sociological and critical perspective brings into view the potential dead end that
scholars encounter when we engage in "naturalistic" accounts of the events of everyday life,
including ideas of "the nature" of individuals. Such naturalistic accounts have come to be so
assumed in contemporary understandings of identity and of social problems that it can be
difficult to think outside of them (White, 2000, p. 51). Instead, the refusal to accept such
naturalistic accounts opens the door to endless possibilities and curiosities about how things
came to be the way that they are, and how they can be better. This perspective allows for the
possible complexities involved in child sexual abuse and adult and child sexuality to become
visible. It also creates a space for the complications involved in various social institutions,
such as the family and the body, to be studied. At the same time the law codifies certain

behaviors in the interest of social coexistence, specifying permitted and prohibited behaviors that as part of a normative imperative must also be honored.

A number of contradictions in the ways in which child sexual offenders are treated in Irish society and in the United States also come into view in considering the above literature. Overall, convicted sexual offenders in the United States and in Ireland incur high penalties for their crimes, including terms of imprisonment and lives of alienation and moral condemnation (O'Malley, 1998, p. 1). Paradoxically, many unconvicted sexual perpetrators live within communities that are ignorant of their abusive histories, as evidenced in the difference between the prevalence figures for sexual abuse and the actual number of convictions in both jurisdictions. In effect, sexual offenders are punished for giving themselves up or for telling the truth. This contradictory situation encourages denial of sexual offenses and nondisclosure of sexual crime. In such circumstances the protection of children is weakened and many victims and perpetrators do not get the help they need. Furthermore, the manner in which child sexual offenders are represented as a homogeneous mass that is fundamentally different from the rest of the adult population means that there is overwhelming fear in many communities and calls for harsh penalties for all offenders. Marginalized and alienated, the perpetrators are driven underground (Bell, 2002, p. 84; Hudson, 2005, p. 56). This situation serves neither child protection nor a human rights agenda well. Such approaches, which are intended to protect communities and prevent fear and danger to children, heighten community fear and danger even more. By thinking critically about the discursive constitution of social problems, the need for new ways of understanding and conceptualizing the child sexual offender becomes evident so that children paradoxically can be adequately protected, perpetrators and victims can be adequately cared for, and communities can be made safer places for adults and children.

As I conclude this chapter I am left thinking about the seduction of blame and the attractiveness of individualized explanations for human and social action, particularly in circumstances where the moral fiber of a society is deeply disturbed by something that has occurred (McNamee & Gergen, 1999, p. 50), just as it is in the abuse of children by Catholic clergy. Not only do we wish to blame individuals, those who perpetrated the abuses and those who mishandled the abuse disclosures, but we feel we would be morally remiss if we do not. McNamee and Gergen help me think about the limitations of this blaming tradition and of the alternative models of accountability, that might offer alternatives to the individualised "blame" approach. Braithwaite's (1989) work on reintegrative shaming also offers food for thought.

In many ways it can be argued that the traditional mode of individualizing blame moves towards a truncation of the meaning-making process (McNamee & Gergen, 1999, p. 50) and a neglect of social context and social structure. When we truly understand how social context and social structures influence individual action, we are less swift to point the finger toward individual failing with such authority and unmediated certainty. Western and perhaps modern thought would have us believe that individuals have free will and that every human being has the capacity to act in "responsible" ways (Alexander, 1987, p. 12). The "individual" is both separated out from the group in law and simultaneously protected from the group by the law. In law, individuals are made accountable and responsible for their actions. At the same time, sociologists tell us that there are patterns in the order of life that are deeply structured, which influence the direction in which certain actions can be taken.

They remind us of the complexities of structure and agency for individual action, and the limits of both in explaining human action. Sociologists encourage us to keep both structure and agency in the frame when we are grappling with what is means to be responsible and what it means to be accountable. Feminist moral philosopher and psychologist Hekman (1995) argues for a move away from universal absolutist thinking to a more contextual perspective when considering ethical questions, such as those involved in what it means to be responsible and accountable. Other scholars point to the inadequacy of decontextualized notions of rationality and justice that prevail around the subject of child sexual abuse (Featherstone & Lancaster, 1997, p. 59) and perhaps around the subjects of responsibility and accountability. What McNamee and Gergen (1999) and Featherstone and Lancaster (1997) share is an approach to child sexual offenders that includes a relational context for justice, and one that includes the conscious and unconscious complexity of individuals' intentions (p. 59). Not all bad actions are the result of rational choice or of bad intentions.

When we simply believe that the individual is responsible and therefore to blame and the execution of justice will mean that "he" is "dealt with," "we" can return to our normal lives, believing that the job is well done (McNamee & Gergen, 1999, p. 50). Once the perpetrators are "outed" and taken care of by due process, and they are suitably humiliated in the court of human opinion, the cultural dialog can come to a close and the emotional and relational contextual factors that gave rise to sexual abuse can be ignored. By focusing on "them," "we" don't have to give serious attention to "us." Superficial lip service to social context and social structures will suffice. This tidy means of settling difficult problems means that further discussion or change at a cultural or societal level is seen as unnecessary. The structures that give shape to these problems, and the institutional dimensions to the problem in the political, social, and familial sphere can remain untouched (p. 50). "We" can even feel morally righteous because "we" are not like "them." I am persuaded by McNamee and Gergen's argument in relation to the limitations of the blaming tradition when they argue that "We cease being curious, searching for cooperative means of creating a liveable future together ... We simply go on with life as usual ... until the next atrocity" (p. 50).

Braithwaite's (1989) work on reintegrative shaming offers a different perspective on what it means to work for responsibility and accountability in a society. Braithwaite argues for a model of reintegrative shaming that holds individuals responsible for their actions but in a way that is not marginalizing of them or leading toward individual and social disintegration. The crucial distinction is between shaming that is reintegrative and shaming that is disintegrative or stigmatizing. Reintegrative shaming means that communities will express their disapproval of the bad action and the individual is thus held accountable, but these expressions of disapproval (from the mild to the severe) are followed by gestures of reacceptance into the community. Disintegrative shaming (stigmatization), in contrast, divides communities by creating a class of outcasts (p. 55). Braithwaite reminds us that "much effort is directed at labelling deviance, while little attention is paid to de-labelling, to signifying forgiveness and reintegration, to ensuring that the deviance label is applied to the behaviour rather than the person, and that this is done under the assumption that the disapproved behaviour is transient, performed by an essentially good person" (p. 55). In contrast, stigmatization assigns a deviant identity as a master status to the individual, leaving no doors open for re-entry and reintegration into the community. Braithwaite gives us much to think about in relation to sexual offenders, and in the case of the Catholic church the middle management of bishops and church leaders who acknowledged that they failed so many children.

Not for one moment am I suggesting that individuals who have abused minors should be allowed to act as they will, without regard to the effects of their actions on others. Accepting responsibility for wrongdoing and the punishment imposed by civil society is part of the social contract, and essential for the fair running of democracies. At the same time there are limitations to individualized blame as a useful mechanism for dealing with human failing and relational breakdown. An approach that includes both due process and restorative processes, and that keeps individual agency and social structure in the frame of reference and understanding, offers the best promise for responding to the complexities involved. It is in this context that McNamee and Gergen's (1999, pp. 49–53) proposal for a concept of relational responsibility could also be explored. They propose this concept not as a means of removing punishment, or of judging more accurately or of spreading the blame, but rather as a means of broadening and enriching our collective options for action. They are not attempting to eradicate the individualist tradition altogether, but they are merely suggesting that we fully engage with both the individual and the social at the same time.

McNamee and Gergen (1999) suggest that we move away from the single-identity description of individual lives and break its stranglehold by recognizing that human beings are complex and multidimensional and that even abuse perpetrators are complexly constituted and have many valuable and positive aspects to their lives. They suggest that we turn to an understanding of child sexual abuse that sees it as both real and as being constituted in dialog, and that this takes place within culturally constituted categories. Rather than attempting to close down dialog by speaking with such certainty about complex matters (that are difficult to understand), McNamee and Gergen suggest we sustain enough dialog about these situations and events so that the door to meaning is never fully closed. Through dialog new issues can be raised and insights developed, individually and collectively. They also suggest we stay curious about the potential links between the individual and the social and between individual and group realities. Questions can be asked such as the extent to which, for example, a male offender is speaking to a male tradition of ownership or entitlement that itself requires challenge, or the extent to which a bishop's handling of abuse complaints is speaking to church culture that itself requires challenge? However, on the point of inviting a social dialog about the links between individual action and other groups, McNamee and Gergen recognize that the movement towards individualized blame holds such a powerful sway in contemporary culture that there is no easy means of sharing meaning honestly across these different groups. Once the very real and practical question of who is guilty and who is innocent has to be resolved, the dynamics of accusation and defense are put in motion and "the contours of conflict are established" in a manner that scarcely permits any other form of deliberation more than attack and defense (p. 53). While acknowledging the difficulties in finding alternative spaces for dialog and practices, there is nothing to say that such dialog and practices are not possible. The growth of practices that broadly fall within the spirit of "restorative," "appreciative inquiry," or "public conversations" in other spheres of life could well be explored here.

While the concept and practice of relational responsibility will not bring simple solutions to the problems that child sexual abuse poses, nor is it intended to condone such abuses, it may expand the resources for understanding and for action, and for new ways of going forward. In an era when we can send missiles halfway round the world, and target the "enemy" with extraordinary precision, it seems much more difficult for us to find ways of living collectively that privilege love over war, care over humiliation, and mercy over sacrifice. In my view this is one of the big challenges of our time.

6

Power and Gender

NO STUDY ON CHILD sexual abuse would be complete without attention been given to the literature that emanates from both feminist scholars and from a growing body of research in the field of men's studies, sometimes also known as the study of masculinities. Comprising both dynamic and more enduring features, gender culture consists of practices, norms, values, symbols, rules, language systems, and institutions, in which we are both embedded and in constant and dynamic relationship (Fiske, 2002, p. 85). In essence, we are all born into a culture of practices and meanings that have been laid out by generations, but at the same time we are influencing culture through the dynamics of human relations. For feminists and masculinity theorists, gender, culture, and male socialization are directly implicated in male sexual violence. It is to these topics that we now turn our attention.

THE FEMINIST CRITIQUE

The feminist approach to understanding child sexual abuse is to emphasize power and control, the role of patriarchy, and the gendered context in which the problem comes to be (Cowburn & Dominelli, 2001; Kelly, 1997; Herman, 1981; Mercer & Simmonds, 2001). The feminist analysis maintains that child sexual abuse is intrinsically linked to a system of male supremacy, and early feminists located the problem of sexual violence and sexual abuse firmly within the "normal" patriarchal family and the community of "normal" men (Herman, 1981, p. 177; Kelly, 1997, p. 10). Feminist theory suggests that a distinction cannot always be made between physical and sexual violence against women and children, and both are linked to male domination. Feminists argue that men's violence towards women and children can be seen as an extreme expression of social control, often resulting from a sense of proprietary rights to domestic and sexual services, and a sense of entitlement (Cowburn & Dominelli, 2001, p. 401; Kelly, 1997, p. 10; Mercer & Simmonds, 2001, p. 171). It is the view of many feminists that the practices of male dominance and female subservience are being reinforced through social structures, which are essentially patriarchal, and more particularly through an ideology that assumes that women and children are inferior to men (Cowburn & Dominelli, 2001, p. 401; Kelly, 1997, p. 10; Mercer & Simmonds, 2001, p. 171).

Feminist writings on sexual abuse by Roman Catholic clergy generally make the claim that the institution of the Catholic Church is a system founded upon real or symbolic sexual oppression of the powerless; mainly women and children, and religious beliefs are used to underpin this system of oppression (Condren, 2002; Ranke-Heinemann, 1990). Feminists generally expand the domain of the abuse problems within the Catholic Church to include relationships between clergy and adult women (Fortune, 1994; Kennedy, 2003). Feminist theologians (Ammicht-Quinn, Haker, & Junker Kenny, 2004; Loades, 2001) locate sexual abuse and violence in the patriarchal structure of the whole society, and leaders of the Roman Catholic Church are seen as patriarchal figures who are also participating in gender oppression (Ammicht-Quinn, Haker, & Junker Kenny, 2004, p. 132). The sexual abuse of children by clergy is conceptualized as a misuse of power and a breach of trust (Ammicht-Quinn, Haker, & Junker Kenny, 2004, 132).

The feminist analysis of sexual offending, however, is more varied than is generally appreciated, and the progression in feminist thought over time has been significant. Early or first-wave feminists placed the issues of women and sexuality, gender, and sexual violence on the public agenda, succeeding in challenging the patriarchal ideal and culture and bringing to the fore issues that had heretofore been considered private and taboo. This led to the development of services for women and children and to a proliferation of scholarly and other work on rape and sexual violence. However, as feminists fought hard to change social attitudes, the law, and social structures, ideological splits and tensions began to occur within the movement, and the earlier ideas, which were both liberating and exciting, were taken up by second-wave feminists in a manner that seemed to essentialize, or make as absolutes, some of the core thought and features. Rape and sexual abuse was viewed as a concrete expression of power that men had over women and children, and all men were thought to acquire attitudes and behaviors through culture, and through male socialization, that would directly facilitate sexual offending (Brownmiller, 1975). Child sexual abuse was seen as centering on the patriarchal nature of society and the commitment of the state to maintaining patriarchal relations of power (Waldby, Clancy, Emetchi, & Summerfield, 1989, p. 97). In 1978, following an anti-rape protest in Dublin, Ireland, which ultimately led to the establishment of the Dublin Rape Crisis Centre in 1979, one of the leaders of the protest caused uproar over her reported comments when speaking at that rally: "The streets are ours. We are not looking for jail for men; we are not looking for castration for men. We are not looking for men at all" (Ferriter, 2009, p. 443). Other accounts suggest that she also said, "There were no men on this march tonight and that is why nobody was raped" (Ferriter, 2009, p. 443). The "gender war" had begun in earnest and the dichotomous structure of right and wrong, good and bad, innocent and guilty would play themselves out in the politics of sexual violence. Women were essentialized as good; men were essentialized as bad; and children were essentialized as innocent and good, to be protected by women from men.

The notion of power invoked in this thinking rests on the paradigm of power as domination based on force, which conceptualizes power as a possession and power as something that all men have and which they can exercise over women, either explicitly or implicitly (Lancaster & Lumb, 1999, p. 126). However, this view of power, which sees power as institutionalized in gender, while important, neglects to consider any other dimensions of power, such as power as relational, power as complex and shifting, power that has an unstable existence, and power that is experienced as a result of autonomy, circumstances, opportunities, and knowledge (Ward, Polaschek, & Beech, 2006, p. 171). Other dimensions of power, such as power that is omnipresent in normative structures that regulate and constrain individual freedom, or power that can create consensus, were also excluded (Foucault, 1991). Fisher (2005, p. 13) argues that what happened at this stage in the evolution of feminist thought was that power as domination was recreated within the feminist movement itself. Women's experiences were named and made visible as universalizing definitions of what it was to be a woman and proscriptions of what constituted women's experience began to be applied. Issues of class and race were rendered invisible as women's experiences were cast as all one and the same.

What can be considered as third-wave feminism has now begun to emerge, this time offering a critique of the metaphors and practices of dominance and power that were evident within the second wave, and offering critique of some of the therapeutic practices that emerged from such thought, in particular in relation to domestic violence and sexual violence interventions and work (Fisher, 2005; Lipchik, 1991; Pence, 1999). Third-wave feminists reject some of the earlier feminist perspectives and are skeptical of theories that posit universal explanations that are not sufficiently "self-critical" (Featherstone & Fawcett, 1994, p. 64). These feminists are concerned with identifying the effects of oppression more broadly, and they challenge the notion of gender and power as being fixed and stable. They challenge the essentializing of gender as comprising sets of attributes and characteristics (such as men are aggressive, women are passive), and they argue that the wide variations in attributes and behaviors within gender identity categories were not given due regard in earlier feminist work, which attached "stable and unitary meanings to them" (Featherstone & Fawcett, 1994, p. 73). Instead, third-wave feminists see gender as relational, with masculinity and femininity constituting each other rather than being distinct and oppositional.

Third-wave feminists emphasize the diversity of men and their experiences, attitudes, circumstances, and beliefs. Discourses that identify all men as bad and unable to control their sexual expression and feelings, and all women as good and virtuous, are rejected as theoretically unsound and politically unhelpful in this feminist analysis (Featherstone & Fawcett, 1994). These scholars take issue with the categorization of all men as potential abusers and argue for more elaborate explanations (Featherstone & Lancaster, 1997). They argue that individuals do not inhabit single identity categories that are determinant of behavior, but rather that individuals are much more complexly positioned in life, in relation to race, class, sexual orientation, religion, age, physical appearance, fitness, and mental ability. Third-wave feminists dispute the theory that sees sexual abuse as a simple representation of male power over women and children, and they reject the argument that men abuse because they are men, and to demonstrate the power they have over women and children (Lancaster & Lumb, 1999). Featherstone and Lancaster suggest that earlier feminists still have difficulty taking on board the implications of this thinking for understanding the complexities of men's lives, particularly in relation to debates concerning violence and abuse. "The complexities of acknowledging that a man can be situated in varying ways in relation to the oppressor/ oppressed axis, arguably disturbs the symmetry of the dichotomised analyses which have tended to develop" in relation to sexual offenders (Featherstone & Lancaster, 1997, p. 58). Power, like gender, has relational dimensions, and these later feminists question absolute notions of power as being in the possession of an individual as only one manifestation of power. Power has other manifestations and dimensions.

More recent feminist works on sexual abuse are also critical of some psychological paradigms of explanation and treatment for being what they see as premised on universalist and overtly rationalist assumptions (Featherstone & Lancaster, 1997, p. 51). They argue instead that approaches that see perpetrators of child sexual abuse as a homogenized mass, rationally exercising power, are obscuring the complexity of actual men's lives (p. 52). They suggest that therapeutic approaches that are based on views of abusing men as only rational agents, knowing fully what they are doing in all circumstances, usually ignore psychoanalytic and sociological influences on human behavior (p. 53). They argue that within rationalist frameworks, psychoanalytic understandings such as denial, resistance, projection, and repression have continually been dismissed (p. 54).

An important feature of the feminist literature on child sexual abuse is its positioning towards the concept of pedophilia, the term used to refer to men who have sexually abused a child, as described earlier. Feminists (Cowburn & Dominelli, 2001, p. 400; Kelly, 1997, p. 10; Mercer & Simmonds, 2001, p. 171) argue that current constructions of the pedophile in the popular press, as well as in certain medical and legal discourses, serve only to mask the relevance of gender in men's sexual abuse of women and children. In Kelly's (1997, p. 10) view, once feminists use the term "the pedophile" they move away from recognizing the gender dimension to sexual abuse, and from recognizing men who abuse as "ordinary men," and move towards a view of them as "other," a small minority who are fundamentally different from most men (p. 10). Kelly argues that by conceptualizing men who abuse as pedophiles, attention shifts from the centrality of power to ideas of sexual deviance and pathology. It is her view that the source of the problem of sexual abuse of children lies in the social construction of masculinity, male sexuality, and the family, and the problem does not reside in the realm of "abnormality" (Kelly, 1997, p. 11). Feminists (Cowburn & Dominelli, 2001, p. 401; Kelly, 1997, p. 10; Mercer & Simmonds, 2001, p. 171) also argue that medicalized discourses that focus on the pathology of the offender usually ignore the gendered context of male privilege over women and children. These scholars suggest that discourses that construct men around a polarized dichotomy of "normal" and "deviant," in which ordinary men are thought to assume the role of protector while the deviants are portrayed as predators, represent an unnecessarily simplistic analysis of gender relations, and of the relations of power and dominance that are at play within the domain of masculinity itself (Cowburn & Dominelli, 2001, p. 4000; Kelly, 1997, p. 11; Mercer & Simmonds, 2001, p. 171).

In the weeks following the publication of the Ryan Report (2009) into abuse of children by members of the religious orders who ran residential facilities for children on behalf of the Irish State, an interesting drawing of swords took place between two senior churchmen and a feminist theologian in Ireland (Condren, 2009). This interchange is important for current discussion because of the feminist dimensions and because of the issues the female theologian raised. As will be discussed later, the Ryan Report made for grim reading regarding the depth and extent of the abuses of children that had occurred in Ireland from the 1940s, and it led to an outpouring of public anger towards the religious orders identified in the report (both male and female) as a very upset and angry Irish public took to the newspapers and the airways to have their voices heard. In the mix were the Archbishop of Dublin and a former Professor of moral theology at the Irish seminary in Maynooth.

The Archbishop of Dublin (who was at the time awaiting publication of the Murphy Report into the handling of abuse complaints in his own dioceses, but for the most part referring to a period before he came to office) offered advice to the named religious orders through the pages of the *Irish Times* (Martin, 2009a). He suggested that they must truly try to answer the question that the Ryan Report had put to them: "What happened that you drifted so far away from your own charism?" He believed that the religious orders owed it to "their good members" to try to answer that question thoroughly, honestly, and in a transparent manner. He advised them that their credibility and the credibility and survival of their charism depended on the honesty with which they went about this soul-searching exercise. The Archbishop also admitted then that he himself had known about abuses in the Irish institutions that cared for children, but that he did nothing (like many of the people of Ireland). However, this admission did not stop the Archbishop from feeling able to give advice to the religious orders through the newspapers.

The former professor of moral theology, who was a student of Cardinal Ratzinger, now Pope Benedict XVI, also took to the airwaves. On BBC Northern Ireland's *Sunday Sequence* program (June 6, 2009), he referred to the Religious, who were now being severely criticized, as "the dregs of society" who "never had a genuine commitment to celibacy." This outburst shocked many people in Ireland, and although the retired professor later apologized, in effect the damage was already done. Condren (2009) a feminist theologian herself took to the newspapers, and she didn't hold back. She suggested that both of these men represented a group of senior clerics who had in effect left "the unwanted, the unfortunate, the orphaned" children to the care of the now-accused institutions, and she was unhappy about what she saw as the men's abdication of responsibility for the Irish Church in which such abuses could occur. She accused the senior clerical men of "baying for the blood" of those Religious who had given their lives to the care of the children, many of whom society had also rejected.

In relation to the religious sisters who were now under attack, Condren (2009) said that many religious congregations used small whips every week on their own naked flesh as a form of discipline, often under orders from their superiors. She asked the senior clerical men, whom she also referred to as "clerical hand washers," what effect they thought such practices might have had on the sisters' self-esteem. She argued that women in Ireland, including the religious women, endured a double, if not a triple, colonization when it came to their lives. She suggested a thin line often divided the religious women and those children in their care, who in different ways were both institutionalized and both abused. Condren asked the two senior clerics, "Did you protest against the teachings of a Church that refused women the right to control their own reproduction?" She challenged the men to have recalled to Ireland those clerics who dissented from *Humanae Vitae* and who were "silenced, demoted, exiled and impoverished" to the four corners of the world. Noting that most of the institutional abuse was taking place at a time when women were not even admitted to the study of theology, nor were they encouraged to develop theological competence, Condren asked the clerical men, "What chance did the Sisters of Mercy have of reflecting theologically on their vocations in the light of such exclusions?", something the men were recommending in the light of the Ryan Report.

With these two men now appearing to place a watershed between themselves and the "unfortunate history of Irish Catholicism," Condren (2009) accused the two men of invoking a theology of sacrifice rather than a theology of liberation and of doing what "all the denizens of sacrifice" had done for generations. "You split between good and evil, sacred and profane, holy and damned," she said. She accused the two men of climbing onto the moral high ground at the expense of generations of women and men, most of whom had generously offered their lives to those whom society had consigned to the margins. Condren said the moral high ground must be seen for what it is: "an escape from taking collective responsibility for the violence that permeated every facet of Irish life."

Both clerical men took to the airwaves again following the publication of the Murphy Report (2009) (*Prime Time*, Dec. 1, 2009; *Sunday Sequence*, Dec. 13, 2009; Twomey, 2009, p. 17), this time to give advice to their Episcopal colleagues who were named in the Murphy Report as having failed to respond appropriately to allegations of sexual abuse by clergy. Neither man was involved in the handling of abuse complaints himself during the relevant period; the Archbishop of Dublin worked in the Vatican's diplomatic corps and the former professor of theology lectured in the national seminary in Maynooth.

MASCULINITIES PERSPECTIVES

The phrase "hegemonic masculinity" was coined almost two decades ago by sociologists who were attempting to address some of the issues raised by feminist theories of patriarchy and related debates over the role of men in bringing about change (Carrigan, Connell, & Lee, 1985). Male sex role theory was seen as a limited one for this task, and role theory was also unable to account for the class (Tolson, 1977) and race bias (bell hooks, 1984) that other scholars were beginning to point to, when power is conceptualized solely in terms of sex difference (Connell & Messerschmidt, 2005, p. 831). For some time also power and difference were concepts in the gay liberation movement, which developed a sophisticated analysis of the oppression of men, as well as oppression by men (Altman, 1972). The time was ripe for a new way of theorizing manhood, and the idea of a hierarchy of masculinities grew directly out of this matrix of thought. What emerged in the early version of the theory was the idea of hegemonic masculinity as "the pattern of practices (i.e., things done, not just a set of role expectations of an identity) that allowed men's dominance over women to continue," but that also allowed some men's dominance over other men (Connell, 1987; Connell & Messerschmidt, 2005, p. 832). The term was used, and still is, to distinguish the most honored way of being a man from other subordinated masculinities, which is enacted within the sphere of masculinities itself.

For Connell (1987, 1995), there is more than one form of masculinity, and when one form takes the hegemonic position others are subordinated. This is referred to as the gender order within masculinities (Connell, 1995, pp. 76–78). Although the masculinity in the hegemonic position may not be the most dominant in the statistical sense, it shapes gender practices around men's expectations of how men should behave (Connell, 1995, p. 77). The problem is that hegemonic masculinities can produce an array of models of admired masculine conduct that do not correspond closely to the lives of actual men, thereby creating contradictions (Connell & Messerschmidt, 2005, p. 838). These socially available models of masculinities provide models of relations with women and solutions to problems of gender relations. The theory suggests that hegemonic masculinity is not a fixed character type, but it is the masculinity that occupies the hegemonic position in a given pattern of gender relations (Connell, 1995, p. 76). However, in the early theory, while class, race, and sexual orientation were seen to affect one's positioning on the gender league table, and in turn how one's identity is shaped, the patriarchal dividend, the advantage that men in general gain from the overall subordination of women, was nevertheless assumed to hold its place (pp. 79–80). The theory also suggests the gender order is not fixed and struggles for hegemony can occur, as older forms of masculinity are displaced by new ones, and a more humane, less oppressive means of being a man could become hegemonic. It also suggests that the gender order differs from country to country, culture to culture, and time to time.

In the 20 years that have elapsed since the concept was coined, a vast empirical literature[1] has drawn on the framework of hegemonic masculinity to understand men in various aspects of their lives. The concept has also been taken up by sociologists and criminologists in their attempts to understand and explain sexual crime (Messerschmidt, 1993; Newburn & Stanko, 1994). Messerschmidt (1993) argues that a consideration of competing masculinities provides a better explanation of sexual violence than most common accounts, including the feminist critique. There is also growing recognition of the fact that masculinity cannot be studied as a singular gendered identity category (Brod & Kaufman, 1994, pp. 4, 5; Featherstone & Lancaster, 1997, p. 51; Messerschmidt, 1993, p. 64). Not only do race, class, sexual orientation, religion, age, physical appearance, fitness, and mental ability influence the diversity of men's experiences and their attitudes and beliefs, but for Messerschmidt they also influence a man's way of "doing" masculinity. He argues that men use the resources available to them to assert their gender bias and to show they are "manly," and if the desired masculine outlets are unavailable, crime may become the means for such men to opt for the "gender alternative" (p. 64). "Crime by men is a form of social practice invoked as a resource when other resources are unavailable for accomplishing masculinity" (p. 85). Messerschmidt suggests that by analyzing masculinities, the social scientist begins to understand the socially structured and socially constructed differences among men, and is able to explain why some men engage in crime, including sexual crime.

There is some criticism of the use the term *hegemonic masculinity* in accounting for crime and violence (Collier, 1998; Martin, 1998). The problem is thought to rest with the negative concept of masculinity that is in play, which by force of a circular argument becomes the explanation and the excuse for the criminal behavior (Connell & Messerschmidt, 2005, p. 840). Collier (1998) argues that the central problem rests in the fact that hegemonic masculinity theories excludes positive behavior on the part of men, behaviors that might work in the interest of women and children. However, despite the criticisms, Connell and Messerschmidt suggest (2005, p. 841) there is something to be thought about in the relationship between the socially available models of being man and the daily lives of men and boys, including the mismatches, tensions, and resistances. "It is men's and boy's practical relationships to collective images or models of masculinity, rather than simple reflections of them, that is central to understanding gendered consequences of violence" (Connell & Messerschmidt, 2005, p. 841).

While the theory of hegemonic masculinity has endured for more than two decades, recent times have seen some of its features reformulated in the light of scholarly criticism. Retained is the idea that there is a plurality and a hierarchy of masculinities, based on an abundance of research that supports this idea (Connell & Messerschmidt, 2005, p. 842). Also well supported in the research literature is the idea that the hierarchy of masculinities is a pattern of hegemony, not a pattern of simple domination based on force. The research literature also supports the idea that hegemonic masculinity need not be the most common pattern in the lives of boys and men, but rather that hegemony works through the production of exemplars of masculinity (such as sports stars) that act as symbols of the ideal, despite the fact that most men or boys do not live up to them.

Similar to the developments within third-wave feminism, what has been discarded from the original concept of hegemonic masculinity is the idea that all masculinities and femininities can be seen in a single pattern of power that involves the global dominance of men over women (Connell & Messerschmidt, 2005, p. 846). Instead, what is advocated is a more holistic understanding of the gender hierarchy, recognizing the agency of subordinated groups as much as the power of the dominant groups, and the relationship between them. This reformulation is based on the recommitment to the relational component that is inherent in gender. It also recognizes recent social changes and reconfigurations that are evident in women's identity and practices, especially among younger women, which are being acknowledged by younger men. The focus is now placed on the mutual conditioning of gender dynamics and on the place of other social dynamics (such as race, class, physical ability, sexual orientation) in configuring the gender hierarchy, rather than on men's practices *per se*. What is being reformulated here is a more complex and elaborate understanding of power than the earlier conceptualization of power as domination, located in an individual by virtue of gender. Similar to developments in third-wave feminism, a second form of power, a relational perspective, is being taken into account in understanding gender and power.

A DISCUSSION OF POWER

Lukes (2005) offers a typology of power, comprising three dimensions, that suggests a more elaborate understanding of power than the simple unilateral conceptualization of power as domination, that is popular. In the first representation, power shows up as an overt act of coercion and domination and is seen to be an attribute of an individual or group who act coercively, by virtue of their status in the social structure (Lukes, 2005, p. 16). This is the view of power that is widely purported, and it is based on a structural analysis of social life. Such examples of this view of power might be seen in the following statements: "You are powerful because you are a man [gendered inequality] or because you are a bishop [and you are an agent of the Catholic Church, which is a dominant institution in the world]." In this view of power, power resides in the individual and the focus is on behavior.

The second view of power assumes that power lies in relationships and in the dynamic interaction between individuals and situations. The presumption here is that power manifests itself not only in coercion, but also in the suppression of conflict and difference within relationships (Lukes, 2005, p. 20). In a relational view of power the focus is on the functioning "agency" of both parties. This perspective leads to consideration of the dialectics of power involved in relationships. From a relational perspective, he who appears to be in the power position by virtue of social structural arrangements may actually be in the oppressed position when a relational analysis of power is undertaken.

The third view of power locates power neither in individuals nor in relationships, but in the prevailing discourses (Lukes, 2005, p. 25). Discourses include both linguistic and institutional dimensions and are not merely abstract ideas or ways of talking. Discourses are intimately connected with the way a society is organized and run (Burr, 1995, p. 55). In this view of power, power is having the means to produce consensus. This view of power, which is based on the tyranny of the norm, obscures vested interests and the power relations that are involved in bringing about or "forcing" a consensus view. This third view of power leads to an interest in the strategies involved in marginalizing and alienating those whose views are seen as not "fitting" the dominant agenda, often by means of shaming, undermining, and excluding. These tactics result in a single discourse taking hold.

All three views of power must be involved in any analysis of a subject as complex as child sexual abuse.

CONCLUDING COMMENTS

Aspects of the feminist literature, combined with masculinity studies, have much to offer an analysis of child sexual abuse by Catholic clergy. By emphasizing power and powerlessness in relation to structured social relations, such as the position of a child relative to an adult, or the position of a child relative to a minister of the Catholic Church, feminists and masculinities scholars have brought the power dimension to a discussion that heretofore may have lacked such an analytical frame. More recent feminist theories and scholarship on masculinities have brought something new to this analysis, especially those aspects that suggest that individuals do not inhabit single categories, such as gender, but are much more complexly positioned in life, in relation to race, class, sexual orientation, religion, age, physical appearance, fitness, and mental ability. This recent feminist and masculinities literature gives rise to the idea that power relations are rather more complex than might have been originally suggested, when power was conceptualized solely in terms of domination or coercion. Lukes' typology (2005) helps to elaborate the complexities of power and power relations.

The relevance of Lukes' typology (2005) for a study of Catholic clergy who have sexually abused minors is that it may not be a simple case of clergy always and everywhere being in the power position, even if they were undoubtedly so in relation to the young people whom they abused. In relation to the power of the Catholic Church in Ireland, the "agency" of the Irish people has been emphasized in Ferriter's (2009) recent work on the history of Irish sexuality, in which he suggests that the Irish were in part complicit in their own history of "domination" by the Catholic Church. It was not just a case of a dominant Catholic Church, always imposing its will; at times, a combination of social and economic conservatism coalesced with the newly emerging and more powerful Catholic Church in 20th-century Ireland. Power is complex, and that complexity is played out in the clerical perpetrators' actual lives, particularly in relation to the oppressor/oppressed axis. My way of conceptualizing them is as both powerful and powerless, and it is this constellation and the complexities therein, rather than their power position *per se* (as men and as ministers of the Church), that is seen to contribute to their sexual offending. This issue is picked up again in Chapter 10.

While early feminist work, which sees perpetrators of sexual abuse as a homogeneous gendered group, rationally exercising power and control in the lives of women and children, acts as a reminder of the importance of keeping power and gender in the conceptual frame of analysis, at the same time it fails to help us understand why some men abuse and not others. It also essentializes all men as bad and all women as good, and it blurs women's power in the game of gender politics. In an important article on power and "the promise of innocent places," Fisher (2005, p. 12), a philosopher with a background in the arts and in gay politics who now runs a program in Canada for responding to men's violence against women, makes an illuminating observation: "practices of power work effectively because they promise us something: a productive 'alternative' space in life." His experiences in life and work make him suspicious of the "promise" of "alternative" sites of social justice that are based in binary opposition to sites of "guilt-laden" dominance, because of the assumptions of "innocence" that may be dichotomously cultivated within these alternative sites. In unpacking the meaning of this, and how he came to formulate his thoughts on power and innocence in this manner, Fisher tells how, as a young gay man, he experienced gay men's culture to be constructed as an "innocent" space of "safety, security and 'victim-only' oppression" as he came to terms with his sexuality. However, he argues that the construction of innocence in fact rendered invisible the fact that gay men have personal agency, and also the fact that gay men, just like other individuals who experience oppression in life, can also participate in the exact practices of dominance and power that we often see in larger culture (Fisher, 2004). In Fisher's experience (2005, p. 13), the construction of gay men's "victim-only innocence" did not prepare him for his subsequent experiences of gay men's participation in social practices of power and domination, including sexism, ageism, homophobia, and so on. He includes himself in this description. Fisher's work suggests that the casting of any one site as a site of victim-only innocence is problematic, (except in relation to child–adult relations), as it does not permit the holders of such victim-only innocent identities to view themselves as having personal agency. This is not to negate the importance of structured relations of power, as in adult–child configurations, nor is it meant to undermine the power relations that can be implicated in other social structures (class, race, gender, physical and mental ability, among others).

By definition children are innocent when it comes to sexual behaviors involving adults, which is defined as child sexual abuse. Fisher's work (2005, p. 13) does not undermine this claim. Rather, he is drawing our attention to the folly of believing in "innocent spaces" in the politics of social justice, where power relations are always involved, even if they are rendered invisible by appeals to morality or to right action. Power relations and politics are always involved in larger culture. Just as power and power relations are involved in abuse, so too are power and power relations involved in the politics of abuse. The feminist and masculinities perspectives help us consider the operations of power in coming to understand how child sexual abuse by Catholic clergy came to be, how it was managed by the Church leadership, and how the politics of clerical child sexual abuse are being played out in popular culture.

The literature that is reviewed in this chapter also leads me to the conclusion that in relation to child sexual abuse in the Catholic Church, clerical masculinity is under-theorized. In my view, by understanding clerical masculinities in the plural, and mapping out the critical distinctions within and between clerical masculinities, we may be able to get closer to understanding why some Catholic clergy sexually abuse minors and why others engage in other kinds of consensual and non-consensual sexual "relationships" while other men live the celibate commitment with integrity. As Sipe (2004) points out, celibacy is a valuable part of spiritual life for many individuals, but at the same time forced celibacy as a policy is not unproblematic. By conceptualizing clerical masculinities in the plural I believe a potentially fruitful ground for further research opens up. In Chapter 10 I will develop the contours of an emerging theory in relation to those clerical men who were to become the sexual abuse perpetrators. Before doing so however I will first turn to the narratives of a group of Roman Catholic clerical men who had sexually abused minors and who participated in a research study with me, part of which I report on in the next two chapters. The narratives give the reader a sense of some of the men's reflections on their lives and on the offenses that they had committed.

PART THREE

The Irish Case

ITS CONTEXT AND WIDER IMPLICATIONS

7

Sexuality and Masculinity

WHEN SEXUAL OFFENDERS are demonized and seen as embodied evil, it is understandable that there is little public appetite for hearing what they have to say, particularly about the factors that might be implicated in their sexual offending. It is easy to dismiss their right to speak. However, just as victim accounts have contributed to an increased understanding of child sexual abuse, there is little to suggest that we cannot also learn from listening to the perpetrators. It is for this reason that I undertook an earlier larger study with clerical perpetrators of child sexual offenses and that I present some of the key themes from that research in this section of the book. The men's demographics and some of the ethical considerations involved in undertaking that research are outlined in the Appendix. What is important here is that the study was based on the first-person narratives of the clerical perpetrators and not on clinical accounts. This is a gap in the literature that can be addressed only by going to the men themselves. This is what I did. Only these men can speak with the authority of their experiences, and only they know the factors that led them down the sexually abusive path.

In undertaking this research I adopted a methodology that would both preserve the men's anonymity and at the same time afford an opportunity to conduct qualitative research to the highest academic standards. I believe both have been achieved. In these chapters, the participants are not identified in any way, either by ascribing fictitious names to them or by assigning codes to any part of their narratives. The men's narratives are reported without any identifying details so as to protect their identity and to honor the confidentiality agreement made with them at the outset of the project. Certain aspects of their biographies have also been altered for similar reasons. In agreeing to participate in the research presented here, all of the men expressed the hope that they might be able to give something useful back to the Catholic Church, to society, and most importantly to the children and young people they abused.

The narratives that form the basis of the next two chapters are not presented as justifications or excuses for sexual offending. Rather, they are presented as the men's lived experiences, out of which their abuse of children and young people came to be. Their accounts could be viewed as an ensemble of "conflicting tales, narrative tricks and elaborate fictions" (Weeks, 2005, p. 55) or alternately as stories of human struggle and tragedy that claim the burden of truth for the men who tell them. My attempt in composing this research was to add the voice of the perpetrator to the victim accounts and to the existing literature to try to make sense of how it came to be that Catholic clergy sexually abused children, and to provide a model that could help explain the phenomenon in a comprehensive manner. The men's accounts are part of the elaborate work that went into developing an empirically grounded theory of child sexual abuse by Roman Catholic clergy. They were asked to elaborate on their understanding of their lives, their sexual offending, and the circumstances that gave rise to it, and it is in this context they gave the following accounts. The next two chapters privilege the men's accounts; in the chapter 10 my analysis comes to the fore. My interpretations of the themes that emerge are based on my attempts to get as close as was humanly possible to what it was the men were trying to tell. In this chapter I address the themes that relate to sexuality and the construction of clerical masculinity. In the next chapter I address power, obedience, loneliness and the loss of the self.

A HISTORY OF CHILDHOOD SEXUAL ABUSE

Five of the participants in this research experienced sexual abuse in childhood. One man was sexually violated in a seminary during his time in formation. All of the participants had multiple abusers; one participant was sexually abused by seven different people, two were sexually abused by three different people, and two were sexually abused by two people. A woman was the abuser in two cases. Three of the five participants who experienced childhood sexual abuse did not remember the abusive experiences as traumatic at the time, although they came to know it was wrong and therefore a "shameful secret."

> My next-door neighbor had chickens and I was interested in them . . . I would go in occasionally and feed them with him. On one occasion when I was six years old he got me to masturbate him in the shed. I didn't understand naturally but when he had ejaculated he gave out to me, saying, "Look what you're after doing." I hadn't a notion, I didn't understand . . . When I was eleven years of age I was in the youth club with my friends and there was an older guy. On a few occasions he lay down on top of me and he abused me. It also happened with another older guy when we were away on a camp . . .

As in many situations involving childhood sexual abuse, the men in this research were drawn into secrets by their abusers, leading them to assume responsibility for the sexual "relationship." They believed themselves to be complicit in what was happening and therefore equally culpable. None of the men disclosed these abusive experiences before attending for therapy for sexual offending. The Sexual Abuse and Violence in Ireland Report (McGee et al., 2002, p. 122) indicated that 60% of young men in Ireland who had experienced sexual abuse were particularly unlikely to have disclosed their experience prior to taking part in the SAVI research. The men in the current study did not disclose childhood sexual abuse in the main because they had a conflicted understanding of what was happening to them, and because they felt shame. The men stated that they normalized the experience when they were children, especially if they knew the same thing was happening to other boys in school.

> I never spoke about it. I would never discuss it with anybody until I went to see a counselor about four years ago . . . I don't think the first abuse had any effect on me [the first abuse was when he was a young boy]; the second one did, and I felt very much ashamed about the whole situation. One thing I sort of always feel sad about is because of that I've found myself distancing myself from men in general. I have always felt very uncomfortable with men . . . I found myself distancing from my father as well . . . I also feel really bad that I could not be there for my younger sibling when I saw the same man who abused me also abusing him.
>
> My difficulty about telling or not arose in the context that since I hadn't said no I was implicitly saying yes, and if I had to tell my mother what was happening then I thought I was on the wrong side . . . There was a sense of guilt . . . certainly the second time round, that was a serious problem because you knew what was coming. The second time I knew what was in store for me, and I went . . . it was something I would not discuss . . . It was there, never treated, never handled, just something. The first time that it came up in any context whatsoever was when I came here, 30 to 40 years later.

In this research, the memories of childhood sexual abuse emerged as significant for the participants later in their lives when they began to abuse boys. Four of the men subsequently abused boys using exactly the same techniques as those employed by their own abuser.

> Much of my own sexually abusive behavior later on followed much of the pattern of what I had experienced myself . . . I would tell myself that it was ok and that what was happening was not going to affect these boys . . . I thought it had no effect on me.

None of the men thought about childhood powerlessness in the face of their abusers. It was only since being in therapy for sexual offending that the men fully "realized" that sexual abuse in childhood may have altered how they viewed themselves and how they lived their lives. Even during therapy for sexual offending, one participant felt unsure of whether he was permitted to speak of his childhood abusive experiences. He feared that he might be seen as trying to minimize his sexual offending and evade responsibility for his abusing.

> I am in no way suggesting that such [childhood sexual abuses] minimizes my responsibility for abusing, but it would be wrong if I did not feel a sense of the right to disclose my own experience of abuse. Yet, sometimes I think I have no right to even mention this because I have forfeited this due to my subsequent abusing. I am sure this is not true, but it is the place I often come from. Sometimes I feel like I am no longer a person, I am only a child sexual offender.

His narratives show that when the problem of child sexual abuse is constructed in terms of dichotomies and absolutes, distinctions that naturalize and essentialize the status of victim *or* perpetrator, such as good victim/bad perpetrator, innocent victim/devious perpetrator, there is little room for the complexity of actual men's lives to emerge. When such polarized and dichotomized perspectives on sexual abuse dominate the popular discourse, the view that the same individual can be both good and bad, victim and perpetrator, and act in both innocent and devious ways is not permitted. Fisher elaborates similar complexities in his work in the area of domestic violence (Fisher, 2005). Such dichotomous thinking may actually prevent victims of sexual abuse from coming forward to receive help. It can prevent men who have perpetrated sexual offenses but who are identified in the public discourse as victims from seeking the appropriate help for their sexual offending. The Ryan Report (2009) drew attention to the fact that some boys who were clearly victims of the institutional circumstances in which they were living also sexually abused younger boys in residence with them. The complexities involved in such situations are not helped by simple dichotomies that do not speak to people's real lives.

Two of the participants felt so distinctly impure because of the legacy of childhood sexual abuse that they believed priesthood offered an opportunity to avoid sexuality altogether.

> I grew up believing that I was a very sinful, dirty person. That's how I saw myself and the safest way to be out of this was to find some kind of life in which you didn't have to worry about this stuff. So religious life was the best. In religious life you could do good. I thought as a priest I would do good . . . the whole object was to find someplace where I could do good in spite of feeling so bad . . . I would be safe there.
>
> The abuse left me with mixed feelings. It was pleasurable as well as unpleasant and I felt guilty, also because I couldn't protect my younger brother . . . I was a shy and withdrawn adolescent, I avoided everything to do with sex, even thinking about it. . . entry into religious life enabled me to avoid dealing with the dilemmas posed by sexual development . . . this was not a fully conscious decision, but I now know it to be so.

Five of the men who had experienced sexual abuse could be construed as fitting Ward and Siegert's (2000, p. 336) profile of men who sexually abused minors following a childhood distortion of their sexual script. However, this analysis would offer too simplistic an explanation for the men's sexual offending; many men who experience sexual violence in childhood never sexually abuse anyone. It is true that the men became prematurely sexualized as a result of childhood sexual abuse, and that four of them abused boys using exactly the same techniques as those employed by their own abuser. However, the men in this study were not led by a distorted sexual script to choose an inappropriate context (with children) for sexual activity. On the contrary, the men all knew that a context involving children was not an appropriate one for sexual activity; there was no distorted thinking here. However, as it turns out that is the context in which they sought adult sexual expression. As I discuss later, the reasons for this are complex but in my view are linked to how the men constructed clerical masculinity and the resultant way of "doing" priesthood (see Chapter 10). While it appears that for one man a history of childhood sexual abuse very strongly influenced his sexual offending, childhood experiences of sexual abuse were not given the same significance by the other men.

Several studies have reported that clergy who have sexually abused minors have experienced sexual abuse themselves in childhood, sometimes by another priest or religious, as is the case for two of the men discussed above. Figures cited are 66% (Robinson, Montana, & Thompson, 1993); 30% to 35% (Connors, 1994); 70% to 80% (Sipe, 1995); and 33% to 50%

(Valcour, 1990, p. 49). This is an important finding, and although sexual abuse in childhood can never be accepted as an excuse for sexual offending in adulthood, and many people who experience childhood sexual abuse never abuse anyone, it is important that many clerics who had experienced sexual abuse in childhood had never discussed these experiences until they were in treatment for sexual offending. Perrillo et al. (2008, p. 611), who analyzed the John Jay data to try to understand repeat[1] offending by Catholic clergy, found that a history of childhood sexual victimization was one of the strongest predictive variables for clerical men to become repeat offenders. This is an important observation, as there is not overall support for this finding in the general literature on other child sexual offenders (Hanson et al., 1993; Hanson & Morton-Bourgon, 2004, 2005). Priests and religious who have experienced childhood sexual abuse may be different in this regard. While 57% of priests in the John Jay study (John Jay, 2004, pp. 6–11) had complaints of sexual abuse made against them by one person, priests who had themselves experienced sexual abuse in childhood were seen as particularly at risk for repeat sexual offending. My research points to the possible role of childhood experiences of sexual abuse in repeat offending by Catholic clergy, although again this is only one factor.

What is important about the fact that five of the men in the current study had experienced sexual abuse in childhood is not that they would automatically go on to become abusers, as the public myth would have it, but rather that they entered the seminaries with feelings of shame that rendered them emotionally closed and unable to allow others access to the intimate sphere of their lives. They also believed that the sexual abuse had not caused them harm, but that it reflected negatively on them because of their participation, and in some cases their experiences of sexual pleasure. The abuse had to be kept as a "shameful secret," and it is the corrosive nature of the shame that in my view contributes to the emotional isolation. The men's views on sexual abuse and the accompanying shame, if not "corrected," was set to present problems for them in their priestly and religious lives, when their vocational appointments would give them access to the most intimate spheres of the lives of the young and the vulnerable. It is also clear that two participants, whose motivation for priesthood was in part an attempt to avoid sexuality altogether, needed help to confront such unrealistic aspirations. As the men's experience of seminary life would show, no such honest engagement was fostered, thereby allowing these men to remain "unknown" in the silent and emotionally sterile environment that marked their seminary training and their later priestly lives.

PURITY: A PREREQUISITE FOR PRIESTHOOD AND RELIGIOUS LIFE

Prior to entering the seminary each one of the men in this research had constructed an idea of priesthood or brotherhood that, he believed, would guide his life. The vision was based on ideas of sexual purity and service to God. All of the men came from deeply Catholic backgrounds, and for all of them conscience development in matters of purity and service to God began early in their lives, particularly at home. Their Catholic education, parish sodalities, and altar-server meetings also formed part of the learning environment.

> My conscience formation began at home. However, there was little specific imparting of knowledge and certainly nothing about sexuality, but I had a good idea of what was and was not acceptable moral behavior, that bad language, stealing, telling lies and

being a nuisance to others were unacceptable . . . More specific formation occurred at parish sodalities and altar-servers' meetings, which were weekly. All sort of topics were covered, but the two that made the greatest "impression" and caused the most anxiety were honesty (stealing) and purity. They were singled out for special treatment . . .

I had been told early in life that any sin against chastity was mortal and so very serious. There was no such thing as a venial sin where purity was concerned.

As young men, the participants had a good idea of what was and what was not acceptable moral behavior. However, they had little understanding of sexuality, except that it had something to do with purity, and purity caused considerable anxiety. Talks about purity were given at school, altar-server meetings, and parish sodalities, and they involved references to "bad actions." However, the men's narratives suggest that the instruction on purity was vague, and five of the narratives explicitly indicate that the young men had little understanding of what was involved in purity, except that it had something to do with sex and private bodily parts. It was made clear during their Catholic education that except in the case of marriage, all "bad actions" and "bad thoughts" were mortal sins (unlike stealing, where small amounts were simply venial sins), which for Catholics in mid-20th-century Ireland was an extremely serious matter, with implications of condemnation to hell for all eternity (Fagan, 2009, p. 24; Inglis, 1998, p. 2). To avoid committing mortal sin, one needed to refrain from sexual thoughts, feelings, desires, and actions—or suffer the consequence. Living a life of purity and avoiding sexuality brought a lot of fear and shame, especially when one could not "control" one's sexual thoughts. The men also believed that purity was a central tenet of worthiness for priesthood or religious life.

Even sexual thoughts were seriously wrong for me. There was this terrible feeling of guilt whenever they surfaced, especially in my teenage years. I knew in my mind that these could not be sinful unless I acted on them, but the sense of guilt was strong . . . During my third year in school I became quite troubled after a severe talk on purity during a retreat and as a result became extremely scrupulous in these areas. Even a thought, or listening to a dirty joke caused very strong feelings of guilt and shame . . . the sense of guilt was quite physical.

Before reaching puberty I was happily able to ignore the issue since it was not relevant to me, but then purity became a constant worry.

The above narratives indicate that the men felt deeply troubled for much of their adolescent lives with concerns about bad thoughts and "bad actions," and they had little information regarding sexuality, as they tried to prepare their pathway into priesthood or religious life. In effect some of the men believe that they took a vow of celibacy around the time they were taking their first state examinations, at 16 years, when their wish to become priests or brothers led them to stifle any feelings that might arise where girls or relationships with other young people were concerned.

Unconsciously I tried to become a sexless person.

I grew up on a farm and the first real sense I got about sexuality was from the animal point of view . . . I had a great curiosity but I never talked about it with anyone when I was growing up . . . I was 19 or 20 when I started to put all the facts together.

When I began to have sexual feelings as a teenager a lot of fear and anxiety built up around this issue and a lot of nervous energy was put into suppressing sexual thoughts and feelings so that there would be no bad actions. Sometimes I agonized over whether I willfully entertained the bad thoughts that came to my mind. At school I kept my distance whenever other boys were talking dirty. I was curious to know more but terrified of crossing the sin barrier. By my late teens I had formed a conscience that was in harmony with Church teaching and I was able to remain true to that conscience in all major respects. However, I can see now that I had shelved the issue of facing the reality that I was a sexual being. It was very much a case of avoidance and suppression. It was in this state that I began seminary formation.

As Inglis (1998) points out, Ireland of the 1950s and 1960s was a place of sexual repression and sexual fear, largely influenced by the powerful position occupied by the Roman Catholic Church, which had a monopoly on morality. The narratives of the men in this research confirm this perspective of a sexually repressive Ireland, especially during their adolescent years. However, while Ferriter (2009) shows that sexual repression in Ireland was also accompanied by sexual transgressions, and that the Irish, while sexually repressed, were not nearly as passively compliant with regard to Catholic moral teaching as earlier research seems to suggest, sexual purity and Catholic moral teaching certainly were unmediated by any other factors for the men who participated in my research. It is notable that the men became even more troubled by sexuality during their years in formation for priesthood and religious life, particularly as they heard the messages of sexual purity and sexual sin further reinforced by their professors and mentors. The two aspects of sexuality that were particularly troubling during their seminary education were again purity and now masturbation. Shame for even thinking about it always had to be confessed.

Sex was dirty and sinful and we needed to purify ourselves.
The over-abiding experience I had as regards sexuality was that it was sinful. This was primarily learned in school but it continued in the seminary . . . It was the forbidden fruit . . . It was a struggle for survival about the guilt factor.
Every week we had two lectures from a priest from the Diocese, who is long since dead, and I tell you everything about sex was bad, bad, bad. Then you also had the hygiene and sanitation lectures, which spoke of going out with women you could get VD [venereal disease].
I often went to confession three or four times a week just so as to feel ok . . . Would I or wouldn't I, did I or didn't I, what did I think? Never about touching, always about thinking . . . I didn't know how to get rid of this thing. I was ashamed of myself for having to go and repeat the same things again in confession over and over and over again. It was all about sexuality. I believe we lived in the seminary as though there was no other commandment . . . there was only one thing in morality and that was sex . . . Nothing else mattered. There was nothing else moral. Everything else was just something else. So the word morality was sex. Nothing to do with justice, nothing to do with any other thing, it had to do with sex.

The men learned that purity, like celibacy, was a "gift" from God, and they tried the recommended lessons of praying to the Blessed Virgin for the gift of purity and saying three

Hail Mary prayers in the morning to cure all bad thoughts and desires. The problem was that they had to ask and pray for the "gift," but when they didn't receive it, the failure was internalized. "They" had failed to receive the gift because of their unworthiness. Further spirals of prayer and personal failure, shame, and guilt became the norm.

> It was always stressed that we remain pure. We were encouraged to pray to Our Blessed Virgin for the gift of purity. We mustn't offend against purity even by our speech. We must avoid all impure thoughts. In my early years I don't ever remember being told that such thoughts would just come to us, that they were natural . . . I fought off any visual thoughts that came to my mind. I stifled all sexual feelings.
>
> Saying your three Hail Marys for purity every morning and evening was the cure for all bad thoughts and desire.
>
> I can remember going through all sorts of Sheehan's Apologetics at the time [this is a reference to Canon Sheehan, who was a stern and orthodox significant Catholic figure], rather than the catechism, trying to find some kind of words to say what was happening . . . the things that were going on in your mind, the attractions, the desire, this was the area of scruples. You were not supposed to be like that.

Fagan (2009, p. 23) points out the effect that Jansenism had on Irish Catholicism, for the scrupulosity and fear that accompanied much of it. In this regard, Irish young men in training for priesthood and religious life were a captive audience, and to some extent they still are today. The negative views of sexuality propagated by the most distinguished theologians of the Catholic Church provided rich soil for fear, anxiety, and scrupulosity, especially when accompanied by ideas of an authoritarian and punishing God, who could see into the depths of the seminarian's or priest's subconscious mind and his shameful thoughts and feelings. While some things have changed in relation to the image of God that is now propagated by the Catholic Church, little has changed in relation to its teaching on sexuality, a teaching that some theologians describe as "bad theology" (Fagan, 2009, p. 14) or "seriously warped" (Dorr, 2009, p. 111).

Within the seminary environment, masturbation was known as "self-abuse," and this was highly problematic for all of the men because it contravened their understanding of purity and chastity. Six of them were in their 30s before they first masturbated.

> I began to wonder if I was guilty of murder, like was the sperm like a human being? There were all sorts of anxiety going through my mind. In my theology the question came up regarding Church teaching on the matter. They used to say to us if somebody comes to confession and says they have masturbated, you have to say it's a sin, because if they did it a number of times it would become a habit, then they are under severe stress, and this could cause it as well, so there may be a whole lot of complications.
>
> In the mid-1960s there was a great atmosphere in the place and the Vatican Council was beginning to have its effects on religious life and on the Church. I threw myself into the life and into the studies. It was during this time when I moved to another house that I found a gay magazine and had my first experience of sexual excitement and masturbation. I was filled with guilt and terrified. How would I get confession? Who would I tell? Would I be thrown out? I heard one of the others talking about a priest

who was very approachable in confession and so I went to him and confessed my sin. Naturally I resolved it would never happen again. But this new-found pleasure and sexual excitement was strong and I enjoyed it.

In a scholarly work on a cultural history of masturbation, Laqueur (2003) suggests that St. Thomas Aquinas saw crimes against nature as part of a spectrum that would lead to a slippery slope of human degeneration, and masturbation represented one such crime. This teaching had its presence felt in Catholic moral theology for a long time to come. However, for Laqueur, the cultural history of solitary sex articulates a story of the relation of the body to passion, desire, and selfhood. It is a step towards self-discovery, a part of the making of the modern self. It is also intimately bound up with the power to create and the process of self-making (p. 69). In effect, it could be argued that masturbatory practices are linked to sexuality and identity formation. However, it is still part of an approach to pleasure that the Church seems to abhor, and the advocates of a particular form of purity attempt to stifle interest in this most available of sins. This was certainly the case for the participants in my research.

One man questioned whether Church leaders had ever considered the idea that many priests were troubled by masturbation. He lamented the absence of open dialogue between lower-ranking clergy and those within positions of authority in the Catholic Church on matters relating to sexuality and clergy. This does not concern him now, as his life is increasingly outside of an institutional Church that has no place for him.

> In the Church's teaching on masturbation there is such ambivalence and such double dealing . . . I sat in the confessional for 25 years and would know that well up to a few years ago . . . this is not breaking the seal, I think it would be a common fact that . . . one of the major problems or one of the major sins for priests and religious . . . would be the whole thing of masturbation, and yet on the other hand . . . the Church that sets moral standards must be aware of what's going on in men's [priests'] lives, because the very people who are legislators must be themselves . . . [pause] have problems with this too, they couldn't but be as human as everybody else . . . we have grown up with such moral sort of blinkers.

It emerges from the men's narratives that, as seminarians, they accepted what they were taught regarding the theology of sexuality, purity, and celibacy and they tried to live by such teachings. They did not argue with two thousand years of the theology of sexuality, delivered in an academic manner, by professors of moral theology who had devoted their lives to the study of this subject. The men in my study reported that they did not have the language, a particular theological language, to debate the issues with their professors.

> Unfortunately, in my case and in many others, the moral theology was taught by men who had no experience of the real world. They based their teaching totally on Canon Law, whereas moral theology should have concentrated on how men and women can live a good moral life. It should not have been lists of case studies—that was for legal people—but on the experience of people who tried to live out the Gospel. The professor ideally should have had ample experience of the confessional so that he could use

his experience to get the students to think about life themes and not the Canon Laws. Unfortunately I had a Canon Lawyer who treated all human activity as a lawyer, giving the reaction between two mythical people, Caius and Bertha! Emotion and feeling never entered the equation. Sin was breaking Canon Law, rather than insulting God or others.

It was within this seminary environment that the men's idea of what it was to be a "good" priest or brother was perfected. One aspect of this involved sexuality. The good priest would exclude sexuality from his thinking and behavior, become sexless, avoid intimate relationships with women, and avoid "particular friendships" with men in order to live a chaste and celibate life.

Although I had a strong sense of curiosity and an instinct to discover what was involved [in sexual relationships] this was strongly outweighed by the fear of breaching the strong moral code instilled in me about sexual behavior. My strategy was to exclude it from my thinking and my behavior, probably on the basis that what was out of mind would not have to be dealt with.

We were encouraged not to have female friends, in fact the expected attitude could be summed up in the diktat that we were reminded about continuously, never to be "*solus cum sola*," never be alone, with a woman. If I was driving a car my grown-up sister was expected to sit in the back.

I had a rather mechanical approach to celibacy, avoid relationships and there will be no problem. I took a rational line by excluding not alone marriage and sexual intimacy, but also any kind of close relationship, seeing this as placing myself in a situation which could lead to conflict with celibacy. This had the effect of creating in me emotional isolation as well as a long-established approach of subjecting emotion to logic. This, in turn, made it impossible for me to confide in anyone about emotional matters, especially when problems did arise for me . . . however, this emotional distancing was learned in childhood and is not a consequence of the celibacy issue alone.

The atmosphere in seminaries was described by the men as one of strict surveillance by authorities and seminarians alike, a surveillance mainly as to how seminarians "performed" as potential future priests and religious. Particular attention was paid to how one dressed, talked, walked, and attended to the required religious and educational activities. Being on time was especially important. Even among fellow seminarians, there was no discussion of sexuality, intimacy, relationships, closeness, touch, or fulfillment, all the aspects of life that the men in this study now consider as being important. The men described their seminary training as having a focus on conformity to the institution and education to orthodoxy. Women were to be distrusted, the Blessed Virgin was to be revered as the ideal model of womanhood, and friendships with men were to be avoided. Issues were presented in black-and-white terms. Ranson (2002a, p. 394) also makes this point and argues that such an environment does not foster a spirit of open disclosure regarding one's sexual or any other struggle. Lest readers think that such a time is confined to the past, data I gathered from younger priests and former priests, who were in Irish seminaries in the 1980s and 1990s, much later than the clerical perpetrators who participated in my original study, confirm that although some things have changed, much remains to be done. Later I will discuss what I learned from those men.

> Life was routine and like clockwork. It was a strict and restrictive regime. There was never any discussion about sexuality in any real sense. Perhaps some of my fellow novices were more tuned into sex education than I was, but there was an innocence and unreality about it all. While we got lectures on the vows [poverty, chastity, and obedience] and community, the information was purely academic. There was no mention of feelings, attraction, intimacy, frustration, or what it was like to be human and a priest. Everything was for the honor and glory of God. I was swept along in the tide of prayer, meditation, liturgy, music, routine, and all the other activities that were part of the formation program. As students we talked about everything else except about ourselves as persons and especially about our most intimate and basic needs as human beings.

The implication for the participants in my research of developing a view of sexuality based solely on purity was that sexuality became something dark, dirty, and unclean, which was to be feared, rather than enjoyed or embraced, albeit in a celibate form. This approach to sexuality, which focused more on an ethic of purity and property rather than an ethic of love, justice, or goodness, was to have profound effects not only on these men (and on the children they abused) but also on generations of Catholics who believed in it. Not only did this theology of sexual morality contribute to a deep-seated suspicion and distrust of women, it also contributed to a distrust of the body that has marred Christian sexual ethics for far too long. It also compounded the duality of spirit and matter that has plagued Christian thought for generations (see for example Fagan, 2009, pp. 14–24; Flannery, 2009, pp. 162–170; Robinson, 2007, pp. 175–200). The Catholic Church has a very poor record of trying to heal this split; if anything, it has made it worse. This view of sexuality also led to a gap between the reality of the men's actual experiences of living and the ideal theoretical world of moral theology. This split which had begun to occur for them during their adolescent years, as they prepared for lives as priests and religious, became fully operationalized during their years in formation for priesthood and religious brotherhood. This gap became a fertile place for the growth of shame-based identities. It was in this institutional environment that the men perfected their education in denial and concealment of sexual thought, emotion, and desire. Other Irish men of similar years, despite the sexually repressive atmosphere of Catholic Ireland of the 1950s, 1960s, and 1970s, got on with their lives and loved and learned within the context of intimate relationships. This was not permitted for Catholic clergy.

MAN OF REASON: INTELLECTUAL UNDERSTANDING OF SEXUAL LIFE

The narratives of four of the participants indicate how much they subjected their sexual and emotional life to a process of intellectualization, a process that they also perfected during their time in the seminary. However, three of the men stress that they already had some vulnerability in the area of emotional intimacy when they entered the seminary. The intellectualization of sexuality and emotion was a theme that was brought up time and again in my research. This theme is also reported in other research on clergy, which suggests that priests and religious have an understanding of their celibate commitment that seems overly intellectualized (Connors, 1994; Loftus, 1999; Sipe, 1995, 2003). The narratives of the men in the current study suggest that the only inputs on sexuality they received during their seminary formation were from retreat directors and moral theology professors, and this knowledge was presented in an intellectual manner. The men did not allow this knowledge to impinge upon them beyond the level of the intellect, nor were they encouraged to do so. None of them entered into personal dialogue with anyone during their seminary years about how sexuality fitted into their overall lives. However, like many adults of the times, all of the men that I interviewed said sexuality would have been a very uncomfortable subject to discuss. This does not mean that seminaries should have avoided the issue, particularly as they were sending these men out to minister to the young and the vulnerable. The nine men took the view that it was sufficient that they had already decided that sexual activity was not going to be part of their lives, and they were resolved to observe the obligations of celibacy and chastity. The narratives indicate that the men never faced sexuality in an honest way, nor did they consider how it would interface with the human reality of their vow of celibacy— that is, until they had to face the realities of life following ordination or profession. The men had an academic and intellectual understanding of sexuality and celibacy when leaving the seminaries.

> It was all about surrendering ourselves to God. God would give us the graces we needed since He was calling us to follow Him in priesthood and religious life. Chastity was primarily tied in with celibacy, as it was intrinsically part of religious life . . .
> I had never taken it [sexuality and the implications of celibacy] from the closet, dusted it down, and faced it squarely. It does appear that I left the seminary in much the same state as I had entered it, for as long as temptation remained at bay I was able to cope and my conscience was clear. On reflection I can see that my approach to chastity was all part of the pattern of my tendency to govern my life, from a young age, on the basis of intellectual considerations and the will of others, to the exclusion of my own feelings and emotional needs. What was correct was more important than how any action or omission affected my happiness.

For some, the sexual "awakening" happened when it was already too late.

> I believe that sexual awakening happened in me when the die was cast, when I had actually reached my goal of priesthood. It was then I began to relax a bit. Unfortunately, partly because of my strict earlier experiences and partly because I believed that boys were safe as far as celibacy was concerned, I began to take an interest in them.

CELIBATE COMMITMENT WITHOUT ADEQUATE PERSONAL AWARENESS

All of the men in this research said that they freely accepted their vow of celibacy and that had celibacy been an option at the time, they might still have opted for a celibate commitment. The men now reflect on how little they understood about themselves and their emotional lives when taking on the commitment at that time. During their seminary years the men conditioned themselves to abstinence, for the love of God and for the good of others, as part of what was required of them to do God's work on earth. All of them accepted celibacy freely as a "gift" or a "sacrifice" and none of them blames the vow of celibacy for their sexual abusing. They do, however, believe they were inadequately prepared emotionally and sexually for such a commitment, and they believe they were unrealistic in thinking they could walk this path alone. The seminary did not appear to either support or challenge them sufficiently to face themselves honestly regarding their emotional and sexual lives.

I was sexually ignorant and naïve, and while I realized I would never be married I did not give too much thought to the importance of intimacy, closeness, deep friendship, sharing my most intimate thoughts, feelings, and desires with others.

There was a belief that if you played a lot of games you would be free from sexual drives and desires. I was not a games person, so I was in disaster land . . . Huge numbers of my colleagues left between 1966 and 1972. It never seemed to dawn on the authorities that celibacy was the central issue for most of them. Time and marriage has proved this.

"Never let a woman cry on your shoulder," we were told.

I was highly idealistic and could not foresee that I would have difficulty in making the sacrifice of abstention from sex as part of my commitment to God and the Church. Sexuality and its absence were seen by me in a religious context, and the promise of chastity was freely embraced by me. With hindsight I can say that given my retarded emotional development, including the failure to integrate a sense of sexuality into my sense of self, my expectations were not realistic. I did not have a sense of reality about my own emotional life and the possible difficulties that could arise . . . Celibacy was conveyed to me as part of the sacrifice made for the good of others and received by me as a positive thing. At the time it was embraced I did not consider celibacy an unrealistic commitment and I was not one of those who promoted the abolition of celibacy. I was happy to take on the duty as a sacrifice, but now realize there was little real awareness of the implications of this for my personal happiness. In a way, the question of my personal happiness in the vocation I had chosen was irrelevant.

Five of the nine men reflected that when they accepted the vow of chastity and made a commitment to celibate living they had no way of knowing how difficult life-long abstinence from sexual relations could be. Eight of the nine men had no sexual experience in consenting adult relationships whatsoever before entering the seminary.

The common good came first. "Go and give your best" was the answer to celibacy, and God would provide all that you need. You will find every satisfaction and fulfillment in doing what is expected of you.

Realizing that one can never have a full grasp of what the future holds when one makes a commitment, and this is also the case in respect of clergy, one participant noted that in his particular case, the decision to take a vow of celibacy was completely beyond his grasp at the time because of his emotional naïvety and "retarded emotional development." This was a decision that was to have serious consequences for him and for the children he abused.

With hindsight I can say that insofar as there was anything unrealistic about my acceptance of celibacy it was not the commitment itself, or intellectual knowledge of what was involved, but rather the inadequacy of my personal development and my absence of awareness of this. The sidelining of any reflection on my emotional life prevented a practical understanding of the consequences of the commitment to celibacy. The fact that I was totally inexperienced sexually and tended to rationalize it from my life made it impossible for me to understand what this would entail in practice.

The absence of adequate personal awareness is striking in the men's accounts, as is the fact that their training was so highly focused on educating them intellectually and theologically, at the expense of personal and human development.

HOMOSEXUALITY: CONCEALING "DYSFUNCTION"

For six of the men in this study, the project of priesthood or religious brotherhood was more explicitly sexualized than for other men because they were defined as deviant by a heteronormative culture and dysfunctional by their own Church. They lacked institutional support to help them find their way as homosexual men and priests and brothers—by that I mean that in the 1950s, 1960s, and 1970s the institutional Catholic Church and the seminaries did not have a space for a "gay masculinity." Many of the men feared abandonment, if they were to be discovered. Without institutional support the project of constructing sexual identity and priesthood as a gay man was a concealed affair, an individual and isolated journey. The religious and cultural mores of their day made acknowledging homosexuality something they could not contemplate.

Part of the strategy for surviving such a situation lay in denying their sexual orientation, even to themselves, while calling on God in prayer that one's greatest fear might not be realized. It is clear from the narratives of the men who were of a homosexual orientation that life was at times difficult, especially during formation. In all cases, acknowledgement of their homosexuality came late in the men's lives, sometimes during therapy for sexual offending.

I was aware that I had an attraction to boys of my own age. I believed it was only a phase and it would pass. I was ashamed and terrified to tell anyone . . . In the seminary I felt so ashamed, and so afraid . . . the whole attitude in moral theology and in the Church's thinking on homosexuality was so rigid that I was terrified of what was going on inside me. There were times when I saw myself as a freak.

It was only during my last year as a clerical student that I knew what a homosexual was, even though I had known in theory what homosexual sins were well before this. I never questioned my own sexuality. I always took it for granted that I was as normal as the rest of my friends, I just didn't associate with girls because I was a clerical student and later a priest. The word "gay" wasn't used back then. It was only at the age of 50 years that I began to realize that I was either bisexual or homosexual, but I was slow even to admit this . . . It was only then that I first asked myself the question. I suspected that I was on the homosexual side of the continuum, but did not want to admit it.

On one occasion one of the participants took steps to end his life, mainly because he could not cope with homosexuality, masturbation, and feelings of shame resulting from his experiences of childhood sexual abuse.

There was no reason not to kill myself over it [homosexuality] because to be it meant I would go to hell . . . there was no point in living . . . I couldn't reconcile in myself at that stage the whole thing of good and evil. I was in secondary school, I was dating, I was praying. I was in a constant battle to be pure and to be good. I was constantly throwing the ball up in the air and saying I would be good, in other words I would not be gay and I would stop masturbating . . . I was fighting homosexuality and masturbation and I thought I was damned and I would go to hell. I thought my life was finished and it never started.

The men in the research who struggled with homosexuality believe that their efforts to conceal and repress their sexual orientation had the opposite effect to the one desired. Concealing required the continuous monitoring of their behavior and emotions to avoid being unmasked, and in effect the process of concealing became an exercise in hypervigilance. The very process of purging oneself of sexuality in effect kept it even more present and alive. This process of concealment and hypervigilance, which began in adolescence, continued during their seminary years and into their priestly and religious lives.

There is some suggestion that in the post-Vatican-II period, in the 1980s and 1990s, a "gay subculture" began to develop in some seminaries in the Western world (Bennett et al., 2004, p. 29), although one participant, who was ordained in the 1980s and who struggled with homosexuality, did not refer to any such gay subculture. Non-offending clergy who were also in Irish seminaries in the 1980s and 1990s said in fact that homosexuality was carefully policed. It is not clear what effect the presence of such a "gay subculture" might have had for the individuals in this research, were it to have existed. Perhaps it might have provided the support they needed, although subcultures rarely contribute to the healthy running of institutions, particularly when they are covert and closeted. Subcultures can be negative and lead to bullying and abuses of power. The idea of a gay subculture is now used in a negative sense in some literature to suggest that homosexual men are taking over the seminaries (Bennett et al., 2004, p. 29) or to demonstrate an inherent contradiction within the Catholic Church, which is alleged to ignore the gay subculture within its ranks while simultaneously referring to homosexuality as dysfunction (Berry, 2000, p. xxii).

One unhappy outcome of such a simplistic analysis of homosexuality and priesthood can be seen in recent Vatican policy on homosexuality, whereby men of a homosexual orientation are effectively not considered welcome into the priesthood (Congregation for Catholic Education, 2005; Gallagher, 2006, p. 67; Hannon, 2006, p. 75). The Vatican line makes a distinction between homosexual orientation and homosexual behavior. It suggests that it is not the potential candidate's homosexual orientation *per se* that is the problem but rather any history he had of previous sexual activity. Prospective candidates must be recovered or "cleansed" from his previous sexual behavior before becoming worthy to become a priest or religious. While this policy represents current Catholic sexual ethics, it also amounts to a Catholic social teaching that is clearly under pressure. At any rate, the men's fears of being unmasked and their need to conceal their homosexuality were "justified," when now, in a time of greater understanding at the social level, and legal acceptance of homosexuality as a life choice, the Catholic Church is effectively closing its doors to homosexual men. Some commentators argue that homosexual clergy are being unfairly blamed for the problem of child sexual abuse within the Roman Catholic Church (*Boston Globe*, 2002, p. 170; Frawley-O'Dea, 2007, p. 122).

A MASCULINITY WITH SOME NON-MANLY FEATURES

The narratives of seven of the men in this research highlight other specific experiences in childhood and adolescence that may have constrained them in how they construed masculinity and their evolving sense of a gendered self, such as medical conditions affecting self-image, circumcision, and inadequacy on the sports field, constraints that were added to by their seminary experiences. Connell (2005, p. 13) argues, "Since masculinities are by definition the configuration of practice associated with the social position of men, the life-histories of boys are the main site of their construction." As many of the men in this study entered seminaries during their adolescent years, the sphere of the seminary is considered an additional site for the construction of masculinity for the men in this research. Messner (2002) points out that body practices, including sports, are now almost as important as sexuality as a site of masculinity formation. Connell agrees (2005, p. 15) that sports are increasingly presented to young men as "a site of masculine camaraderie, a source of identity, an arena of competition for prestige, and a possible career." From the narratives of the men in this research, eight of whom were young men in the 1950s and 1960s, this emphasis on sports as an arena of male gender socialization is not a new phenomenon.

It is interesting to note that the men in this research continued their distant relationship with sports when they were ordained as priests or professed as religious brothers. While two men were involved in coaching boys' sports teams, only one man attended Gaelic Athletics Association (GAA) matches with other priests on any kind of a regular basis, and none of the men belonged to a golfing fraternity consisting of other priests. Priests and religious in Ireland often cite the sporting networks of the GAA and the golfing fraternity as a site of friendship with other priests and a site of social and emotional support. The extent to which this is in fact the case has not been researched. At any rate, the men in this research did not take advantage of such fraternal opportunities. Most of the men chose solitary activities, such as music, photography, reading, and pastoral activities involving their ministry, for their social outlet.

The lack of sexual experience and sexual knowledge did not emerge as a source of inadequate masculinity for any of the men in this research, despite Connell's (2005, p. 14) view that the physical and the sexual are hugely significant in the creation of masculinity. Connell (2005, p. 14) argues that physical strength and sexual prowess are often a source of pride and a claim to masculine honor, especially for adolescent boys. In Connell's (2005, p. 14) view, current hegemonic masculinity discourse treats adult heterosexuality as natural, and becoming heterosexual as a complex learning of interpersonal skills and identities, as well as sexual techniques. What is interesting to note, therefore, is that lack of sexual experience was not seen at the time by the men as a particular problem as they moved from boyhood to manhood. It is now understood by them to have been a big loss.

One possible explanation for this situation might be that at that particular time, the 1950s, 1960s, and early 1970s, hegemonic masculinity in Ireland was essentially rural and based heavily around the family, marriage, and celibacy (Ferguson, 2001, p. 120). The celibate priest was the role model for Irish masculinity, and Irish Catholic masculinity was especially expressed in terms of sexual purity and chastity (Ferguson, 2001, p. 122). The lack of sexual experience or a commitment to a life of celibacy was therefore more likely to contribute to a sense of strong masculinity rather than to an inadequate one. The sense of inadequate masculinity experienced by the men in this research was derived, therefore, initially at least, from sources other than their lack of sexual experience, such as childhood sexual abuse, medical conditions, circumcision, and weakness on the sports field and in traditional male competitive sports. However, concerns of sexuality became apparent soon after the men were ordained or professed, when the realities of celibate living led to isolation and loneliness in an Ireland that was fast becoming secularized, influenced by the sexual revolution of the 1970s and the feminist critique, and in a Catholic Church that was living through the changes brought by the post-conciliar period (Inglis, 1998). During this period the hierarchy of masculinities in Ireland was also altering, with celibate masculinity swiftly moving into the least acceptable way to practice masculinity. This changing Ireland brought with it challenges and dilemmas for Irish clergy.

A CULTURE OF SECRECY AND DENIAL

In drawing together the men's reflections on sexuality and its link to sexual abuse, all of the nine men referenced a struggle with sexuality in their lives and with physical and emotional intimacy within the context of their celibate vocation. One man specifically spoke of sexual arousal in the presence of adolescent boys.

> My attraction to young boys was ambivalent—I so much wanted to help them, but I wound up . . . looking forward to meeting them. I was attracted to young-looking novices like myself and still suffered appallingly from scruples, right up to the big day [ordination]. Nothing untoward took place then . . . But there were so many safeguards and dire predictions of particular friendships going awry that all such feelings towards other seminarians were stuffed and later confessed . . . Things began to unravel shortly after I was appointed to a boys' school.

All of the men spoke of sexual issues and the need for physical intimacy during their years in the priesthood. These feelings in relation to adults were feared and concealed and in some cases denied and ignored. As Chapter 8 shows, the men also concealed their emotional and physical loneliness and emotional vulnerability. Many of the men placed their sexual abusing as a battle between their desire and their will—the urge for physical and sexual touch and their controlled and reasoned minds. For some of the men the battle was initially fought in their own private intellectual world. Others deluded themselves.

> I enjoyed what I liked to think at the time was this intimacy, this touching and that . . . there was this vulnerable kid that I wanted to show affection to, but I enjoyed the tenderness myself, and when I got the pleasure the first time I waited for some days to pass and I called him again . . . and again . . . this became something very clearly planned . . . There was the sexual pleasure side of it and the warmth and the intimacy, and I should have directed it in other ways but at the time I didn't.

The men tried to suppress and dismiss the reality of their sexual desires and the need for physical and emotional intimacy by rational argument. They did not feel equipped to deal with their sexual feelings and the need for intimacy, and as the narratives indicate, they did not know how to negotiate professional and personal boundaries within a celibate commitment. Sexual feelings or loneliness did not fit with their idea of priesthood and celibacy. Their narratives indicate that they could not express these thoughts or feelings to anyone.

> I said often to myself there must be some way, there must be some way where I can be comfortable and have friendships without having, you know, having to go to bed with someone, or having intercourse or that, and the whole area of touch, of showing affection. There must be some way I could be comfortable with people without going through guilt and having to run off to confession or whatever . . . for me this is all tied up with the area of intimacy, of trust, of recognizing that relationships don't have to be sexual in the sense of genital contact . . . I knew nothing about real intimacy and boundaries . . . the thought that I could have a close and deep relationship with some person or persons without it being sexual was something that never surfaced in discussions or formation.

All the narratives suggest that the men felt isolated in their sexual struggles. Each man felt he was unusual or unnatural or different from every other priest and religious brother in this regard. All of the men believed that there was not one other man in the priesthood or in religious life who had similar sexual struggles. They believed that no one else was going through the same "fire and brimstone." And for this group of men at least they did not feel there was a place to go to talk about it. They internalized the shame. The clerical culture of silence and denial, within the seminaries in the first place and in priestly and religious life later on, contributed to this silent existence. The men felt isolated in their struggles, and apart from their confessor nobody knew what was going on in their lives.

All of the narratives suggest that while some of the men stopped abusing for many months at a time and did nothing out of fear of mortal sin, fear of God, or fear of being found out, ultimately "all sense of morality went out the window" and sexual and emotional desire won the battle again. In attempting to "make sense" of their sexual abusing some of the men felt they were looking for "something" that they could not fully identify because of the business of trying to conceal, even to themselves, the fact that they had sexual, physical, and emotional needs. One man believed that after years of depression and loneliness the first moment someone showed interest in him, he latched onto them, in the wrong way.

> I think it [the abuse] was basically the neglect of a whole lot of things, neglect of even taking care of myself, worrying about needless things, being under pressure and probably not even realizing that there was depression there, not sleeping right, not eating right, and I would put myself down, not saying a whole pile to anybody but doing a whole lot of things, and being there for everybody, and couldn't say no to anyone . . . and of course not having the, we'll say, comradeship of other priests, and being alone and lonely. I recognize all these things now and I would say that my biggest fault was that the first person that came along and showed a personal interest in me, I took advantage of. He was boy who needed my help.

THE PERSPECTIVES OF NON-OFFENDING CLERGY

What is interesting in a changing Ireland with regard to sexuality is how little real change has been effected in Irish seminaries in preparing clerics for this new world. Because the clerical perpetrators whose narratives are discussed above were in Irish seminaries during the 1960s and 1970s, it might be easy to discount their experiences as not being relevant to today, or being tainted because of their abuse histories. The suggestion is also often made that things have significantly changed in Irish seminaries since that time (Ferns Report, 2005; Murphy Report, 2009). Although it is indeed true that *Pastores Dabo Vobis* (1992) brought changes to seminary curriculum, with human and pastoral formation now included as subjects of study, my clinical work with seminarians and clergy led me to question how much change had really occurred in practice as a result of the new curriculum. For these reasons I decided to interview two clerics and two former clerics, for comparative purposes, all of whom agreed to complete questionnaires on their seminary experiences in Ireland in the late 1980s and 1990s and on their lives as ordained Catholic priests in the 1990s and 2000s (some 20 years later than the clerical perpetrators). While these interviews and questionnaires were initially intended to provide additional information for me alongside my clinical experience, and in many ways as a corrective to it, and the men were chosen because of their interest in my work broadly and their willingness to complete the questionnaires; what they uncovered is so pertinent to the current debate that I sought permission to include their narratives in the body of this book. All agreed. To do justice to their experiences I will quote in part directly from their narratives. While there are significant similarities in the narratives, there are also some slight differences, representing the fact that the men attended different seminaries in Ireland in the 1980s and 1990s. Today there is one major seminary in the south of Ireland and one in the north of Ireland.

By the 1980s an effort was being made to improve the training for Catholic clergy in Irish seminaries, and this change can be seen as incremental, with each few years adding a little more human and pastoral formation to the curriculum, and this continues up until today. However, some features of seminary life seemed more enduring, according to these participants: women portrayed as temptress; few laypeople involved in the training; homosexuality carefully monitored; child sexual abuse never mentioned until the late 1990s; little real preparation for the complexities involved in establishing a healthy emotional life within the context of establishing and maintaining professional boundaries. "The Blessed Virgin Mary and prayer were to be the focus of female intimacy." Hobbies and interests were encouraged to deal with loneliness, as were involvement in priestly fellowships and brotherhood, prayer retreats, class reunions, and spiritual direction. The men were encouraged to be honest with their spiritual directors, but the consensus view was that sexuality was not a comfortable topic of conversation.

When it came to moral theology, the men in this section of my research suggested that issues tended to be relayed in black-and-white terms, moral theology was presented in terms of rules and regulations, and the emotional support and empathy necessary for living the clerical celibate life was frequently lacking. However, there was a small shift in the approach taken to the teaching of moral theology during 1980s and 1990s, when two types of professors emerged in other disciplines: one group was described as strict, conservative, and reserved, and the other group was more liberal and more tolerant of open discussion and debate. However, a rule-based theology was always in the background. "It was very clear that theology was a means to an end and that the primary goal was simply to become priests." "I went into the seminary at 18 and seven years later I left at still aged 18, but 25 years old. No growing up was done, no mechanism to evaluate ideas with any of the normal experiences and longings that belong at that stage of life. Everything was suppressed."

MASCULINITY AND IRISH CATHOLIC CLERICAL IDENTITY

Some important observations can be made in the light of the narratives of the clerical men who abused minors about sexuality and masculinity and its relationship to their subsequent sexual offending. The Irish "take" on masculinity and sexuality provides an interesting context marker for such an analysis. At the time that the men in this research were developing psychologically and sexually, transitioning from boyhood to manhood and entering into religious and clerical life, masculinity in Ireland was essentially rural, heavily based around the family, marriage, and celibacy (Ferguson, 2001, p. 120). The Catholic hierarchy expected strict adherence to compulsory celibacy, and the Irish form of hegemonic masculinity was based around celibacy. The celibate priest was the role model for Irish masculinity. The sole purpose of sexual activity was procreation; pleasure was not on the agenda (Ferguson, 2001, p. 120). Irish Catholic masculinity was especially expressed in terms of sexual purity and chastity (p. 122), and as their narratives suggest, the participants in the current study drew heavily on such understanding of masculinity and sexuality. The disciplined, chaste, hard-working man was expected to go on to become the God-fearing priest or the good breadwinning father (p. 122), and having a priest in the family brought special cultural kudos, being seen as a reflection on the good Irish Catholic mother (Inglis, 1998).

Between home and school, most Irish Catholic children developed a Catholic *habitus* (Bourdieu, 1977, p. 82; Inglis, 1998, pp. 57–61), a deeply embodied, almost automatic way of being spiritual and moral that became like second nature, creating a Catholic identity and a way of behaving and interpreting the world. While being Catholic was a fundamental part of the social and personal identity of most Irish people, who happened to be Catholic, for boys who wished to become priests or religious, the Catholic way of understanding oneself and of being seen by others was even more extreme, as the narratives of the men in this research indicate. The effects of the total and totalizing institution of the Catholic seminaries just reinforced what was already in effect, an Irish Catholic *habitus*. This helps explain why, even though many Catholics may no longer practice as regularly as their parents or adhere to fundamental teachings of the Church, they still regard themselves as belonging to an Irish Catholic heritage (Demerath, 2001). In effect, most Irish people are "hard-wired" as Catholic. It also explains why, despite all they have endured as Catholic priests in the wake of the revelations of sexual abuse, including laicization, the men in this research remained and remain loyal to the institution of the Roman Catholic Church.

Anthropologists, ethnographers, and other commentators on Ireland have often pointed out how the Irish were repressed sexually (Brody, 1973; Humphreys, 1966; Messenger, 1969; Rigert, 2008; Scheper-Hughes, 2001; Scheper-Hughes & Devine, 2003), but a recent work on the subject suggests that the history of Irish sexuality is more complex than earlier works seem to indicate (Ferriter, 2009). Perhaps for reasons to do with Irish history and its relationship with Britain, Irish sexuality seems to have embodied that of middle-class Victorian Britain (Ferriter, 2009, p. 23; Inglis, 2005, p. 14). While Victorians were "divided and contradictory" in their attitudes towards sexual morality (Copeley, 1992, p. 79; Ferriter, 2009, p. 26), there is a suggestion that for some, sex was seen as something dark and primeval, involving anarchic and explosive instincts that knew no values, possessed no morality, and had no sense of good or evil (Inglis, 2005, p. 15). However, it is hard to generalize about the issue because of the varying perspectives. Inglis (2005, p. 16) suggests from his reading of the literature that the progress from savagery to civilization depended on the subjugation of sex. Foucault (2004) observed that as one of the main strategies for civilizing society, sex was banned from sight and conversation, and moved from being frank, open, and honest to being secretive, hidden, problematized, and scientifically studied. However, Ferrriter (2009) consistently emphasizes the individual resistance (agency features) to cultural norms (social structure) that was evident from his reading of the relevant papers. In part, this debate centers on the relative influence of structure and agency on individual action.

While the Victorian mentality also influenced sexuality in Britain and the United States, it appears that the Victorian mentality seemed to penetrate the minds and bodies of the Irish more deeply and lasted far longer than its British or American counterparts (Ferriter, 2009, p. 25; Inglis, 2005, p. 10). While this situation can in part be explained by the fact that there were few alternative or resistant discourses to the dominant obsession with purity, in what was predominantly a monocultural, mainly Catholic country (Ferriter, 2009, p. 545; Inglis, 2005, p. 10), it would not be true to say there was no resistance. By uncovering state papers, court records, and documents of voluntary organizations as well as biographies, diaries, letters, and literature in researching the history of Irish sexuality, Ferriter (2009, p. 24) raises doubts about the absence of variety of discourses of sexuality in Ireland. There were certainly "delusions about Irish sexual purity," which proved to be quite durable (Ferriter, 2009, p. 546), and there were sexual transgressions.

Ferriter (2009, p. 545) describes the continuities in Irish sexuality during the 20th century as "a concern with outward conventions, a decidedly middle-class discourse about sexuality, [and] deep strains of homophobia and misogyny." Drawing on the work of Clark (2008, p. 2), Ferriter suggests that in Ireland as in Europe, attempts by the authorities, clerical and lay, to manage sexual desire have frequently failed. For Ferriter, the Irish are regarded as having indulged in "twilight moments" (a phrase coined by Clark in her book *Desire,* 2008, pp. 6–7), when activities seen as shameful or dishonorable were nonetheless indulged in.

It cannot be denied that an Irish Catholic sexuality that was built on purity, chastity, virginity, modesty, and piety left the Irish psyche with a sense of shame and embarrassment about sexual practices, feelings, and emotions at the same time as they indulged in their "twilight moments." In 20th-century Ireland, there was an "avowedly Catholic ethos, oppression and watchfulness" at the same time as there was no shortage of illicit sexual behavior (Ferriter, 2009, p. 546). As we now know, some of it concerned the clergy themselves, who were in fact the moral police. Birth control was illegal in Ireland until 1976. Heterosexuality was regarded as fixed, and homosexuality was illegal until 1996. For Catholic clergy, whose mission it was to develop these regimes of chastity and sanctity, the messages were well and truly embodied, splitting for some the personal from the public persona as they engaged in illicit sexuality themselves. The clergy in my research, who learned the lessons of purity, chastity, virginity, modesty, and piety in their own homes and schools, were further indoctrinated during their seminary formation by professors of theology and senior clerics who themselves had learned the orthodoxy well. Shame and guilt regarding bodily matters went hand and hand with such Catholic sexual *habitus.* This necessitated increased vigilance for sins against purity, as chastity had to be imposed on their own and other Irish bodies (Fagan, 2009; Flannery, 1999; Inglis, 1998, 2005). This central objective was achieved primarily through greater adherence to the teachings and practices of the Catholic Church, and for those men whose life ambition it was to become servers of God, the teachings were even more stringently reinforced. The denial and silencing of sex was part of a wider program within their seminary education of denying and sacrificing the self. The rejection of enjoyment, pleasure, and desire obtained enormous cultural purchase in the Ireland of the time, and Catholic celibates were elite. The rigorous regime of sexual censorship that was part of the Irish concern with outward appearances necessitated the supervisory eyes of priests, nuns, brothers, teachers, and parents. Joni Mitchell's song *Come in from the Cold* captures life for such religious police, who also imposed harsh penalties for those who sexually transgressed the dominant moral code, especially women. Women who transgressed the sexual code (or those so designated by the authorities) were incarcerated in mental asylums and Magdalene homes for "fallen women" who had given birth to children out of wedlock; some of whom remained there for the rest of their lives (Inglis, 2002, p. 6; 2005, p. 29; Smyth, 2007). In other instances the babies of "fallen women" were sent abroad to Australia and the United States for adoption.

Despite the resistances along the way, and there have been many, since the late 1990s sex and sexuality has begun to be perceived, understood, and embodied in radically different ways in Ireland, although there is still considerable disagreement about the parameters of sexual choice, freedom, and liberation (see for example Ferriter, 2009; Inglis, 1998, 2005). And just as in the old sexual regimes in Ireland, where there were transgressions and transgressors, so too in the new. In the old regime the greatest scorn and punishment was reserved for the single woman who became pregnant outside of marriage and for the unmarried mother who failed to hide her shame (Inglis, 2005, 2002). And it was the Catholic Church, through its teachings, censures, and prohibitions enacted by priests, nuns, and brothers, that orchestrated this regime, but not always against the will of the people (Ferriter, 2009; Inglis, 2005). Other transgressors, "men who frequent prostitutes, or make young unmarried women pregnant," and others who engaged in forbidden sexual acts were not stigmatized with deviant identities (Ferriter, 2009, p. 546). However, today the new sexual regime in Ireland is orchestrated by the media, and the greatest transgressors are those priests and religious brothers who have molested and abused young children (Inglis, 1998, 2005). The hunting down of such priests is part of the wider process of demonizing, castigating, and shaming those who earlier sought to deny sexual pleasure. But there is more to it. The individual and institutionalized hypocrisy regarding Catholic celibate masculinity that the current crisis in the Catholic Church has given rise to is hard to take by the Irish people, who are beginning to think that children and young people were part of the cost to keep its appearances alive. In a climate that has seen a change in Irish hegemonic femininity and masculinity, a clerical celibate masculinity is now one that raises social suspicion.

Masculinity for the Irish male is undergoing a significant process of change, one that is also affecting clergy. And child sexual abuse by clergy is one of the key areas where gender and power relations are being reconfigured in Ireland (Ferguson, 1995, 2001). While an assumption of compulsory heterosexuality is now at the core of how Irish hegemonic masculinity is constructed, and Irish men have been "sexualized," Ferguson (2001, p. 123) argues that it is celibate masculinity that has been left to carry the weight of social disapproval and interrogation. Celibate sexuality can now be regarded as a marginalized masculinity. However, when it comes to child sexual abuse, Ferguson (1995, p. 254) believes that the current discourses involve a desexualization and "un-gendering" of men as fathers, in that the problem of sexual offending is not discussed by law or the State as a problem of maleness, masculinity, or male sexuality. At the same time, sexual abuse by clergy has involved the exact opposite: priests, religious brothers, and the Roman Catholic Church have undergone a dramatic process of sexualization. Ferguson (1995, p. 250) sees this situation as resulting from the hegemonic gender order in which the construction of the "pedophile priest" serves to force attention away from the fundamental issue that men from all social backgrounds commit such crimes of violence and that these crimes are policed by a range of organizations that are male dominated. This is similar to the feminist arguments outlined earlier. Ferguson's view (1995, pp. 250–254) suggests that by deflecting attention away from sexual abuse by heterosexual men, the normative structures of the patriarchal society are left unchallenged and clerical celibacy as an authentic form of masculinity is marginalized. He argues that the debates in relation to sexual abuse by Catholic clergy must be seen in the context of discourses of men and masculinities and the dynamics of sexuality, organization, and power in society in general, and not just within the Catholic Church.

Ferguson (2001, p. 123) dismisses any consideration of a possible role for clerical celibacy in sexual offending by Catholic clergy, arguing that clerical celibacy and child sexual abuse are unrelated. Otherwise one subscribes to the male sexual drive discourse, which rests on the assumption that men must have sex and if they do not they will visit their urges on those people in a less powerful position, including children. Ferguson also seems to suggest that an anticlerical agenda may be at play in Ireland and the United States when the debate on clergy sexual abuse is constructed in terms of clerical celibacy. While Ferguson makes important arguments it is premature to dismiss clerical celibacy as an authentic area for research in relation to sexual abuse by Catholic clergy. Clerical celibacy as a form of masculinity is full of contradictions that need unpacking, consideration, and perhaps even reconfiguration if it is to be livable in the 21st century. Arthurs, Ferguson, and Grace (1995, p. 459) argue that members of the clergy in Ireland are undergoing a general crisis not only in relation to the sexual abuse issue but also in relation to masculinity, and celibate masculinity in particular. Something more than the traditional ways of being clergymen is required (p. 460). I arrive at a similar conclusion.

It emerges in my research that the clerical masculinity that is in the hegemonic position is particularly problematic for Catholic clergy, as they fail to live up to its idealized form. Following Connell (1987, 1995, 2005), I am using this term to distinguish the most honored way of being a clerical man from other subordinated clerical masculinities, which is enacted within the sphere of clerical masculinities itself. When one type takes the hegemonic position, others are subordinated. Although the masculinity in the hegemonic position may not be the most dominant, in the statistical sense it shapes clerical men's practices around how they should behave. The problem is that hegemonic masculinities can produce an array of models of admired clerical masculine conduct that do not correspond closely to the lives of actual men, thereby creating many contradictions (Connell & Messerschmidt, 2005, p. 838). These socially available models of clerical masculinities provide models of relations with women, with children, and with other men. The research literature also supports the idea that hegemonic masculinity need not be the most common pattern in the lives of boys and men, but rather that hegemony works by producing exemplars of masculinity that act as symbols of the ideal, even though that most men do not live up to them. I am adopting this theory for use in relation to clerical men and to help explain the range of sexual and other behaviors that are becoming evident and how individual clergy "do" celibacy and "do" priest-hood or religious life. This analysis, might provide us with a sense of how clerics see and understand themselves as Catholic priests and brothers in their everyday life, and how being a Catholic priest or religious permeates their personal, family, social, and work existence. By understanding the differences in clerical masculinities and their various elements and mech-anisms, I suggest we may get somewhere closer to understanding priesthood and religious brotherhood and how these men live their lives. I return to this discussion in Chapter 10.

CONCLUDING COMMENTS

All the clerical perpetrators who took part in this research battled with sexuality during their priesthood or religious brotherhood. The problems related to deeply embodied shame, emerging from a sexual ethic that rendered bodies bad and every sexual thought, feeling, and action sin. Poorly prepared for a life of celibate living and lacking the skills necessary to develop intimate relationships safely within the context of a celibate commitment, the men denied their need for intimacy and male sexual expression, or concealed their needs from others, in particular from other clergy. The split between the "reality" of their actual experi-ences of living and the "ideal" theoretical world of moral theology, which had begun to occur during adolescence, was fully operationalized during their years in formation for priesthood and religious life. Other studies (Bennett and Catholic Review Board, 2004; Goode, 2003; Ranson, 2002a) note the inability of some Church leaders and formation staff to educate and mentor their young seminarians and clerics in the skills necessary for a life of celibacy. Many of the men in leadership positions were themselves formed in a different era that denied them, too, the opportunity for sexual and emotional honesty, and poorly equipped them for the pastoral tasks involved in educating their young clerics, humanly, spiritually, and pastorally.

Lessons in denial and concealment were perfected in the highly policed environment of the seminary, where the individual's inclinations to conceal sexual thoughts and desires and the system's messages of sexual purity and denial of the sexual came together in a perceptible alignment, bringing the individual and the institution together in seamless harmony. From the narratives outlined above it is possible to say that the men in this study emerged from Irish seminaries, after many years of study for the priesthood and religious brotherhood, worse off than when they entered. Fear of sexuality resulting in denial of sexual need appeared to be reinforced. In their efforts to conceal and repress their sexuality, some of the men became preoccupied with sex. For all of them sex was the main sin. The very process of purg-ing oneself of sexuality kept it even more present and alive, especially for the men of a homo-sexual orientation, who feared that they would be unmasked. The fact that personal issues, such as a history of childhood sexual abuse or a struggle with homosexuality, were not addressed during their seminary education points to a failure on the part of the institutional Church in helping seminarians and novices turn areas of potential personal vulnerability into areas of personal strength and resilience. Although childhood sexual abuse was not openly acknowledged in Ireland during those years, and seminary professors can be excused for not knowing the men's histories, the fact that few personal spaces existed in Irish semi-naries for men to discuss the issues that affected their lives made sure that nothing of a per-sonal nature would receive due attention. In the 1980s and 1990s little had changed, and my experience teaches me that little has changed even today. Making a commitment to a life of celibate living without adequate self-awareness was based on a theology of sexuality with the split between matter and spirit at its core, and on a notion of spirituality that was devoid of the human realities of young men's lives, especially when their newfound lives would give them powerful access to the young and the vulnerable. As it turns out, such inadequate preparation for the celibate life and inadequate support and supervision in subsequently living it would have devastating consequences for them and for the children they abused.

Robinson (2007, p. 174) suggests that it is in the field of sexuality, above all others, that the Catholic Church is in danger of denying its own basic principles regarding "the goodness of God's creation." He asks: If everything and everyone is made in the image and likeness of God, then why not sex, too? Devoid of a relational, a love, a justice, or a goodness ethic, Catholic sexual teaching is still based on notions of purity and property, both of which developed from a particular cultural and historical reading of the Bible and the relevant teachings and documents (Ranson, 2008). What current Catholic moral theology has left us with is a deep-seated bias against women on the subject of sex; notions of purity based on hygiene, cleanliness, and dirt in relation to sex and sexuality; a property ethic in Christian life and in some ideas of the family; distrust of the body; and a sexuality that is caught up with the duality of spirit and matter (Robinson, 2007, p. 193–194). Much of this thinking involves rules made by men that are grossly unfair to women and debasing to men. It is also based on relative values of a particular cultural and historical time that have been turned into absolutes. Current Vatican policy is unwilling to review these issues because of the charge of "moral relativism." As Robinson observes, "sexuality is always ambiguous and paradoxical and there is nothing quite like it in human life to mock our rationality and give lie to our claims of calm control" (Robinson, 2007, p. 196). "When we begin to speak of morality in this field we must tread lightly and carefully" (p. 196). If child sexual abuse by Catholic clergy does not get the Roman line on sexuality and power moving, then I am not sure what will. It is to other aspects of the men's lives that I now turn.

8

Organized Irresponsibility (II)

CLERICAL ELITES, RULES, OBEDIENCE, AND LONELINESS

WHEN GIVING EVIDENCE in cases related to clerical sexual abuse, clerics occasionally appeal to the Church doctrine of "mental reservation" as a defense to justify not telling the truth (Doyle, 2010). Some have claimed that "mental reservation" is a legitimate doctrine used by the Church for centuries, which has grown out of the common Catholic teaching about when it is permissible to lie (Murphy Report, 2009). It is believed that it is a legitimate justification for lying when the person subjectively decides the conditions to do so are present. While Catholic social teaching says it is never allowable to tell a lie, the traditional doctrine also says that people can, under an obligation to keep secrets faithfully, fulfill that duty by saying what is false. In essence, it amounts to something like not telling the whole truth, by playing with words. In the doctrine of strict mental reservation the speaker mentally adds some qualification to the words he utters, and the words, together with the mental qualification, make a true statement in accordance with fact. On the other hand, in the doctrine of a wide mental reservation, the qualification comes from the ambiguity of the words themselves, or from the circumstances of time, place, or person in which they are uttered (Doyle, 2010). Ethics and morality scholars of many religions, both ancient and modern, have accepted this position. In the Murphy Report (2009) into child sexual abuse in Ireland, one of Ireland's senior prelates explained the importance of the concept, which in the words of the Commission "permits a churchman knowingly to convey a misleading impression to another person without being guilty of lying." While this senior prelate explained its use in his handling of some cases of abuse by clergy, I also had experienced its use with some clerics who have perpetrated such abuses. It was often that I commented, "If I don't ask the right question in exactly the correct terms, I won't get the right answer." On other days, I referred to "the drip system." While I thought this was to do with defensiveness on the part of clerical men who were in treatment for sexual offending, now I know their positioning was utterly consistent with the doctrine of mental reservation.

However, in trying to understand why and how Catholic clergy sexually abuse minors and in attempting to find answers to my questions, the days of mental reservation have passed for the group of men who participated in my research, and what I believe has emerged is their true understanding of their lives and how it came to be that they sexually abused minors. I wanted to know how the men gave themselves permission to engage in this behavior and how they squared it with their conscience. I wanted to know how they overcame the child's resistance and what they did to avoid detection. I also wanted to discover how the abuse had continued for so long, and what factors had maintained it. It is with these questions in mind that I turn again to the men's accounts.

The literature on the psychology of the sexual offender is clear: while sexual motivation is always present to a greater or lesser extent in all sexual offenses, other factors must not be neglected in any analysis of how a sexual offense come to be (Finkelhor, 1984, p. 54; Marshall 1989, 1993; Ward, Hudson, & Marshall, 1996; Ward, Hudson, Marshall, & Siegert, 1995, p. 317). Factors relating to nonsexual motivation, power, opportunity, and the social context in which the offense occurs have also been identified as significant. In this chapter I wish to address these themes and how they were presented in the men's accounts.

FEAR AND OBEDIENCE

Boszormenyi-Nagy and Spark (1973, p. 151) argue that the process of "parentification" within the family can be an important influence on the development of the caregiver role, and Stalfa (1994, p. 374) argues that this is a feature of the childhood experience of many priests and religious. Nagy and Spark argue that through this process of parentification children are recruited into premature responsibility within the family in order to support the real or perceived inadequacies in the functioning of the parents. In such cases the child "parents" the parents. Mehl (1990) produced data to suggest that many candidates for Catholic ministry have traumatic family histories, including physical and sexual abuse and addiction. He suggests that the subsequent style of caring by Catholic clergy is characterized by over-responsibility for others and lack of care for self. Benyei (1998, p. 37) argues that a high percentage of Roman Catholic clergy come from family backgrounds that result in tendencies towards low self-esteem, reluctance to trust others, and reluctance to admit to personal neediness, pain, or the need for help. Benyei (1998, p. 37) describes such clergy as "other-directed" in that they minimize their own need for care and attention and privilege the needs of others.

All the participants in my research described themselves as having been quiet and subservient children. In seven of the nine homes as children they were punished by verbal disapproval or by verbal outbursts. Five men describe early childhood relationships characterized by parental disapproval and shame, especially at failing to meet parental expectations. The children learned to keep a distance, largely to protect themselves from potential disapproval and rejection. Four of them also began to relate to others in a submissive and self-effacing way. Listening to each other's reflections in the course of this research moved one man to spontaneously draw some comparisons between his own and other men's lives.

Much in X's life parallels my own . . . There is so much in common, it makes me wonder. We found our needs in those who needed us, the children we worked with.

While attending to their needs we were really confusing theirs with our own, a recipe for disaster for everyone. This symbiotic relationship has been our undoing. In the context of our repressive upbringing, I think about how vulnerable children really are, not just to abuse and corruption, but to the lifestyle and habits of parents—behavior that children take as normative, but I now see as stultifying and dysfunctional. Children are largely unquestioning.

What is important here is the men's understanding of obedience in entering into priestly and religious life, as obedience is one of the central features of governance for the Roman Catholic Church in exercising authority.

All of the participants describe their period in the seminary as a time when they focused on rules and regulations, conformity to the system, obedience to superiors, and what was and was not an acceptable way to be a priest or religious. Their narratives suggest that understanding themselves as men was marginalized in favor of learning what was expected of them in order to become good priests or brothers. The men can be seen as having exchanged their personal voice for a communal one, at a time when their personal voice was merely developing, during their late adolescence and early adulthood. This process is reported in other writings by Irish clergy (Cosgrave, 2001; Flannery, 1999), with the implication that when individual identity is subsumed into that of the larger organization, the scene is set for potential conflict and adversarial relationships later in life, usually at a covert level. Even the one participant who as a late vocation soon became fearful of authority, and particularly of the bishop.

The participants developed a rigid understanding of "obedience" and lived their lives quietly, avoiding overt conflict and a questioning mind. They would not consider breaking even the simplest rule, such as turning up late for prayer. The prize of ordination or profession guaranteed submission during their seminary training, and they believed that to speak up or speak out was not conducive to attaining that goal. This established a pattern that was to continue into their priestly and brotherly lives for the majority of the men, although two gained a different reputation. One man seems to have been quite outspoken, and even overtly intolerant and critical of others, but not his superiors, earning him the reputation of being awkward and arrogant, which it sounds like he was. Another was authoritative in the public exercise of his role, covering over his deep frustration. Obeying superiors became part of what all the men tried to do, because they knew this was expected. This submission was particularly evident when it came to vocational appointments.

Conforming to what was expected was how I learned to win acceptance. I lived my life quietly and in a somewhat isolated way. It is only with hindsight that I can see how much was lacking in my life at an emotional level.

It was a fear of sin that prevented me from expressing myself . . . I was also afraid to rock the boat . . . I did not have the confidence . . . I was afraid all my life of saying the wrong thing or doing the wrong thing. I generally would say nothing, but would let it go . . . in my early days in priesthood I would just keep my head low and sort of took whatever came . . . You didn't have the freedom of speech.

"We cannot always choose where we want to be" was what I was told when I queried this appointment . . . "Go and give your best for God" was always the answer "and God would provide all that you need" ... I realize now there was an anger building up in me that would eventually catch up with me.

Three of the men accepted appointments on the basis of "obedience" that they did not want. This was also the case with senior Church figures in Ireland, some of whom were plucked from academia and thrust into jobs for which they were obviously unsuited but felt compelled to take. While I have no evidence on which to base any views on how the senior prelates handled this call to obedience, for four of the clerical perpetrators in my research, it became a source of anger and animosity. Outwardly compliant but inwardly hostile, the anger, lack of job satisfaction, and lack of personal autonomy did not find expression except in covert ways. For the other five men who did not register their anger, even to themselves, this life of submission was to contribute to what I am calling the "soul death" of the self. Two of these five men became depressed and weary. Confronting or challenging bishops or senior Church leaders was anathema. Two men even believed that the superiors had God on their side.

But, of course, I mean mmm, our rules always said that superiors were guided by the Holy Spirit, and while I might think that the Holy Spirit is dozing, I never made bold enough to say there could be another opinion or that the Holy Spirit couldn't work through other people as well ... While I mightn't be convinced of something the superior said, I didn't challenge it either ...

In retrospect, frustration is a word and a feeling that was at the heart of many of our lives. The image is that of being caged in and seeking every opportunity and method of breaking out.

It was like the kettle boiling.

How often did I hear about the power of God's holy will? How often did I hear that and that you take up your cross? ... look at all the other crosses I've put on other people's backs, simply because ... that's the reality.

You were in a place and you didn't want to be there, you never actually dealt with it, you were frustrated and angry, you tried to make the most of a bad deal and try to move on, but you're under stress, you're under pressure and you never discuss the situation with anyone that you are a frustrated priest.

The problem with the whole approach to obedience that was encouraged and accepted by the participants during their training was that it kept them like children in an institution that rewarded compliance. Such relational requirements posed obstacles to maturity and to ensuring that an autonomous functioning individual, healthy and relationally mature, would emerge. Instead, the men had little or no say in the major decisions that were to affect their lives and were kept relationally immature, with an understanding of obedience and authority that went only one way: upwards. The men were responsible to the bishop, who was to be feared. The laity, on the lower rung of the ladder, held less concern. The emphasis on obedience to bishops or religious superiors was not confined to the Church in Ireland. As one Australian priest put it when taking part in *Background Briefing* on ABC radio, on March 7, 2010: "See, if you've got 250 parish priests in Melbourne diocese, for example, who

I feel for strongly, I call them the *desaparecidos*—the ones who have disappeared. Because in fact the bishops have come in and the senior clergy and blown a whistle, and told us all that we have to behave as clones. Now that's the end of the individualism in the Roman Catholic clergy." He added, "They've disappeared into their goddamn burrows, like rabbits."

Kelly (1998, p. 315) found in his treatment program for sexually abusive Roman Catholic clergy in the United States that some of the men had struggles with Church leaders that fueled their anger, an anger that was implicated in their subsequent sexual offending. In Kelly's view, the abuse of power by Roman Catholic clergy can be seen as a displacement of their struggle with religious leaders, as the "impotent" man finds an arena in which he can feel potent (p. 315). As can be seen from their narratives, the relationship between anger with Church leaders and sexual abuse of minors is rather more complex for the men in my study than Kelly's work (1998, p. 315) would suggest. Theories of displacement do not adequately explain their sexual acting out, but something about the power/powerlessness dichotomy seems more likely. This idea is further analyzed later in the chapter. For six of the men in my study, the unexpressed anger and lack of personal agency also contributed to chronic feelings of sadness and dejection and a weariness of life that at times amounted to depression.

EMOTIONAL LONELINESS

According to Connell (2002, p. 80), male emotion and sensitivities in general are subject to strong surveillance and curtailment, and sites of surveillance for male emotional expression include the home, the school, and the peer group. The seminary provided an additional site of surveillance for male emotional expression for the participants in my research. For these men, concealing their sexual and emotional loneliness and not disclosing their emotional distress was something they did. All of the men lacked the skill required to negotiate boundaries around sexual and emotional intimacy, especially within the context of their celibate vocation. In fact, the men thought they were to avoid intimacy with adults altogether. They had difficulty using social supports and they avoided disclosing emotional distress. Severe emotional and sometimes physical loneliness resulted.

> Boundaries did not seem to be a word that we were familiar with or that we know anything about . . . The thought that I could have a close and deep relationship with some person without it being sexual was something that never surfaced in discussion or formation.
>
> Emotions were to be distrusted; for example, we were told that anger was sinful. I eventually learned that this was not true—anger itself is morally neutral, it is the inappropriate acting out of anger that could be wrong.
>
> I didn't fit into cliques in the seminary and when I was ordained and moved out into a parish I was on my own . . . you are living a lie, really. I can see a thread through the whole thing, a fear of talking about anything intimate. I had no friends that I could go and talk to . . . I suppose most diocesan priests will say the same to you . . . Priesthood was my choice but my dream didn't come through. I couldn't tell anybody . . . I was upset and lonely, there was fear and confusion and I didn't know what to do. All sense of purpose had gone. My life had gone to rock bottom . . . That's the way I felt.

In truth I never even consciously considered that I had emotional needs. It would be true to say that I had never been in touch with my inner self and emotions. Yet I cannot say that I was aware of being deeply unhappy because of this ... It was only the reality of independent living, away from the constraints of family and the seminary, that brought a sort of "awakening" that I had needs other than intellectual. The reality was that my emotional life and my sexual urges and the need for intimacy could not simply be suppressed or dismissed by rational argument alone.

Communicating psychological distress or conflict was regarded as taboo among the men. They regarded this as something they were unable to do, either because they lacked the skill, the language, the necessary confidence, or because it was something priests and religious did not do. Other people and their troubles had to be privileged over themselves and their feelings.

It was only when I came to therapy that I learned a language that I could communicate about my feelings.

While I was always a lonely and isolated person my dark secret exacerbated this and I kept people at a distance, until a few good adult friends later in my life. I was not comfortable with myself, so how could I be comfortable with others?

For all of the men in my study, nondisclosure of emotional upset or loneliness in their religious communities or dioceses was linked to the structure of the community and to the culture of nondisclosure that they saw prevailing within priestly and religious life. They felt that no space existed for emotional displays or for emotional disclosure. Community discussions and meetings were always about organization, finances, and planning liturgy. Later for diocesan men, some deanery meetings held even less promise (although it appears that today deanery meetings offer good support to clerical men). There did not seem to be time for discussion about life or how the men were coping. Balboni (1998) noted similar findings in her research with the Bishop's Conference in the United States: everything was discussed except the important issues of the day. Several studies (Cozzens, 2004; Papesh, 2004; Ranson, 2002a, 2002b) report this finding in which clergy, even religious priests and brothers living communally, cannot communicate openly with each other. The men in my research seemed to suggest that community living was a continuation of the secretive and closed clerical world of the seminary, and that each man was on his own. Issues of living were silenced or denied.

The atmosphere surrounding our training and later in our living was one of medieval times and we lived in some cases like medieval monks. Sometimes I think the Dean in the seminary, who was harsh, was also a victim of the regime he had to interpret and impose. We were constrained from communicating openly and honestly and this carried on into our community living.

Nondisclosure of emotional distress to family members was linked to the role that the men played in their families' lives. Their role as priest or religious brother gave them a special position as comforter during family crises or bereavements, and "holy" man on sacramental occasions.

All of the seven priests in this study administered religious sacraments to family and friends. The men adopted outward positions of happiness and serenity vis-à-vis their families of origin (in particular their mothers), regardless of how they were feeling internally. Nondisclosure of their sexual offending was linked to potential loss of status and to shame. The men also feared the consequences of such disclosures for themselves and their families. They also did not want to give their families the burden of such a terrible knowing. It was only when the media threatened disclosure or prior to first court appearances that many of the men first disclosed their sexual offending to their families. Few families of clerics came to the family support group that was running at the treatment center, although the families came for help and support from therapists once the sexual abuse disclosures were publicly known and sometimes when court proceedings were imminent.

Some of the men were aware that nondisclosure of emotional distress was not good for them, while other men denied emotional loneliness and distress, even to themselves, until they had begun to abuse children. For all of them, seeking professional help was not considered something they could do, and this became even more significant once the abusing had begun. This contrasts with McGlone's (2001, p. 119) finding that clergy in general are beginning to seek help for their problems, such as loneliness, sexuality, and depression.

> I was too ashamed and embarrassed to look for advice. I tried to work it out for myself and so things didn't change . . . I was a perfectionist and never wanted to admit that I would do wrong.
>
> It was clear that by my own power I was unable to break the habit. Therefore, reason suggests I needed expert help. This troubled and disturbed me, but the fear of disclosure was so immense that I could not conceive of revealing the secret to anyone. Rationally I can say that seeking help would have been a test of the sincerity of my remorse and repentance, but psychologically this was impossible for me . . .

Earlier I suggested that one of the consistently observed consequences of prolonged emotional loneliness is an increase in aggression, and lonely adults are more likely than other people to be hostile and aggressive (Marshall, 1989, p. 491; 1993, p. 114). Emotional loneliness sets the stage for self-serving behaviors, of which sexual offending is one obvious, but not the only, consequence (Marshall, 1989, p. 491; 1993, p. 114; Ward, Hudson, & Keenan, 1998, p. 153). Lonely adults are also more likely to use inappropriate sex as a way of coping, or in some cases as a way of punishing someone else, not the child (Ward, Hudson, & Keenan, 1998, p. 153). As the Australian priest put it when taking part in *Background Briefing* on ABC radio on March 7, 2010: "The more you leave a person on his/her own, the more chance you have that he or she will go backwards to being either the child they never were, or the adolescent they never had a chance to be." He felt the institution was not geared to helping individual clergymen develop to their optimum as people. For some of the men who participated in my research, the inability to find solutions to the conflicts that existed within themselves or with their Church leaders gave way to entitlement arguments for sexual abuse. Other clerics have also suggested that the clerical culture itself creates a culture of entitlement "as the priest is ontologically transformed and therefore feels automatically entitled to respect and social advantage for simply being a cleric and not for any earned merit" (Smyth, 2009, p. 472).

I wanted to hold this kid and I wanted to feel the warmth. I wanted that, and on the other hand there was also I think an element or sort of thing of, over there, those bloody ones on my back [colleagues and superiors]. They don't appreciate what I am doing. I am going to have a little bit of comfort. I broke through the wall like a bull-dozer ... This is alright, I said, it won't harm him [the boy], so there were times when I was saying, you shouldn't do this, and I could have stopped, I know I could, but so I didn't ... I'm still trying to understand it.

The collapse of an increasingly fragile self-identity with a possible loss of their life's work and priesthood was more than the clerical perpetrators could contemplate, and they feared this if they were to disclose their problems. They had to keep up the image in order to preserve their priesthood and religious vocation. Constant performative work was required to project an image of rationality and strength, when the private internal struggles intensified and with it a collapsing self-identity. For many of the men, working hard and striving for excellence in the performance of many aspects of their priesthood allowed them to "compensate" for the abuses they were perpetrating. It also helped them in a sense suppress, even from themselves, "the terrible realization" of their problems. While at one level working excessively in itself posed additional stresses, given the underlying context of emotional distress and social isolation, at another level the feedback and affirmation for the work done well became necessary to sustain a fragile and collapsing identity.

There was certainly denial about the gravity of my situation. I did feel a sense of shame but I derived a false sense of worthiness from my work achievements and popularity ... There was a lot of ambivalence in my thinking.

By my mid 30s I had everything, as other people outside saw it ... I had a car, I had two secretaries, I had three rooms ... yet having all of that, this loneliness, this isolation, this feeling of inferiority ... in spite of all the success I was not able to say I'm not really interested in that at all, I just want to be me ... I was trying to meet what other people expected of me, I don't mean to throw the blame on them, but it was all an image.

Problems with emotional life and emotional regulation are noted in the sexual offender literature as providing a pathway into sexual offending for some men (Ward & Sorbello, 2003, p. 16). Some individuals are thought to have problems identifying emotion, they lack an emotional vocabulary, they may have difficulty modulating negative emotions, or in some cases they have difficulty using social supports in times of emotional distress (Ward, Hudson, & Keenan, 1998, p. 153). According to this theory (Ward & Sorbello, 2003, p. 16), the inability to manage emotion might lead an individual either to become disinhibited or to opportunistically use sexual relations with a child as a strategy to meet their emotional and sexual needs. Emotional rather than sexual factors are hypothesized to drive the choice of sexual outlet. According to this thinking, men whose abusing is propelled by emotional factors are more likely to prefer sex with age-appropriate partners but will engage in the sexual abuse of a child when emotionally stressed (Ward & Sorbello, 2003, p. 16).

The narratives of the clerical perpetrators in my research indeed show that their emotional life was highly "regulated," but not in the sense that Ward and Sorbello (2003) had in mind. While Ward and Sorbello stress the significance of managing emotional responses and avoiding volatility, the men in my research were regulated from above, trying to become rational rather than emotional beings. My research shows that the participants had difficulty in identifying emotions, in part because they lacked the "permission" or the courage to speak about emotions or become emotionally engaged, given the clerical culture of the time and their training. They also lacked an emotional vocabulary. All of them had learned an approach that involved subjecting emotions to a process of intellectualization and rational argument. While they were taught in the seminaries to ignore their emotional lives, for some of the men the idea of not showing emotions goes back much further than their seminary years. These men learned in their early lives that "boys don't cry" and in some cases that "anger will not be tolerated." For these men concealing emotions was seen as "the safe way, the only way" to negotiate life. For all of the men in my research, a lifestyle of submission and severe emotional loneliness, accompanied by a history of shame, generated feelings of frustration and anger that were likely to influence their behavior as long as the feelings remained unacknowledged and pervasive.

My analysis is that their early life experiences and their understanding of what it meant to be a good priest or brother combined to produce a particular way of "doing" priesthood or brotherhood that left the men isolated, lonely, and in some cases frustrated. Despite the differences in their early childhood experiences, it is notable that all of them learned similar ways of "performing" priesthood or brotherhood, which involved a submissive style of relating, avoidance of emotional disclosure of distress, and avoidance of intimate relationships. Although some of the men entered the seminaries with well-tried patterns of concealing emotions, for all of the men the seminary reinforced such behaviors rather than offering an important corrective. The men were not helped to develop resilience against any such future emotional vulnerability, and in fact the seminary messages appeared to reinforce the idea that avoiding emotional disclosure and adopting a submissive style of relating was a prerequisite for being a good priest or brother. Here, what can be seen is a coming together of the individual and the system in a seeming affiliation that would ultimately serve neither man nor Church well. Most adults, who may have vulnerabilities with regard to emotional intimacy in adult life, often learn these skills in the rough-and-tumble of adolescent and adult life, with a few good friends and with loving partners. The men in this research had no such experience. Instead, the restricted seminary life and sterile environment in which they tried to mature from boyhood to manhood and to adult maturity simply stifled emotional growth rather than promote it. Subsequent clerical life merely presented a continuation of a lonely and emotionally isolated existence, devoid of honest engagement within the great fraternity of clerical men.

THE CONFIDING SPACE: GOD AND THE CONFESSIONAL

Ward and Stewart (2003, p. 25) stress the importance of networks and friendships for men's health and well-being. However, what is apparent from the narratives of the participants in my research is that even when they lived in religious communities or had contact with their families of origin, their pattern of emotional isolation was maintained. The confessional was the main place of respite and support from their emotional conflicts and loneliness. Non-offending clerics have said that confession was suggested as the most appropriate site to bring their sexual and emotional concerns. The confessors were carefully selected for their important job.

> The only ones who must have sensed what I was going through were my confessors— they were carefully selected by me, and time and time again I recounted my temptations and falls, my scruples and shame. They after all were bound to a strict code of secrecy. I was known personally to them all. They were my lifelines.

The word "secrecy" is interesting in this man's account. For all of the clerical perpetrators, the confession made bearable what was for them, at times, a complex site of paradox, contradiction, and ambiguity in which their self-identity and performance were at odds, and the performance of integrity was severely undermined. As the gap between their self-identity and the performance of their ministry widened, and their sense of personal integrity deteriorated, the men continued a pattern they had learned early in their lives in their Irish Catholic homes and schools, a pattern that was reinforced during their formation: they turned to the confessional and to God. Interestingly, they did not turn to spiritual direction. The anonymity and confidentiality of the confessional became an important avenue for disclosure of sexual and emotional distress and ultimately for disclosure of sexual offending. Eight of them disclosed their sexual abusing in the confessional. The confessional became a space for them between the ideal and the reality. It was also a secret conversational space, not only of forgiveness but also of "externalizing" the issues in "safety."

> After each abusive occurrence I felt full of guilt and at the earliest opportunity I sought to confess and receive absolution. While this was well intentioned there is a sense in which it was a mechanical process, but it effected a degree of relief and a feeling of a new beginning. There was always a resolution that it would not occur again—and yet experience should have told me that that was an unrealistic purpose of amendment given my awareness of my inclinations and that opportunity was frequently presented. With hindsight I can say that deep down I realized that I would not be able to keep that resolution. It seemed impossible for me to prevent my desires from overcoming my will. Long periods could elapse without abusive behavior, depending on the amount of work, social activities, and level of contentment, but eventually the urge for the pleasure took control of reason and in the heat of the moment all sense of morality of the activity went out the window. At that point there was no question of my evaluating the morality of what was imminent. The desire for inappropriate intimacy was overpowering and all thoughts of earlier purpose of amendment were discarded from my mind.
>
> There were times of guilt, shame, and fear that I would get caught but I used confession to clean the slate. I minimized everything in this area . . . convincing myself that I would never do it again, especially after confession. It seemed to ease my conscience that I was truly making an effort to change and to stop . . . and going to confession and being able to couch it in such a way that you know I didn't have to give the full story, until one day towards perhaps the second last abuse I went to confession and this man absolutely just went for me . . . he just said to me, "you know what you are doing is not alone morally wrong, but it is a criminal act."

In all the times I confessed to abusing a minor I can only remember one occasion when I got a reprimand or advice not to do this thing. In a strange way the sacramental confession let us off the hook rather lightly, and perhaps allowed us to minimize what was really happening . . . Perhaps I minimized in my accounts, but I do not think so. I certainly agonized as to how to present the abuse, and maybe the language used probably veiled the horror of the action. It was not open denial, but maybe it was not unadulterated truth either. The practice allowed us to feel that the disapproval and shame we experienced in telling was only short-lived and never likely to be discussed anywhere except there. Not confronted adequately we experienced only a short duration of guilt and no sense of responsibility for how we hurt others, only the alleviation of our own guilt and shame.

Receiving confession played a role in easing the men's conscience in coping with the moral dilemmas following episodes of abusing, and it provided a site of respite from guilt. For some of the men it also helped them think that they were making an effort to change. As the men oscillated between a sense of "self" and "false-self" that at times undermined their stability and sense of security, the confessional became a site that provided respite from such a conflicted existence. The men did not turn to spiritual direction for a variety of reasons.

I did not seek spiritual direction. To have talked to a professional at an early stage (spiritual or otherwise) and had supportive help may have prevented the "growth" of the problem. However, a combination of "minimization," shame, and the terrifying thought of disclosure made any request for help psychologically impossible. The only disclosure was the minimum required for the integrity of the sacrament of penance.

Spiritual direction was . . . something that was not part of my formal training or ongoing lifestyle . . . Without doubt, the most powerful experience of spiritual direction for me was during my time in prison. When all the supports . . . were suddenly taken away from me I was faced with such real, frightening, and challenging questions, as "Is there a God?" "God, where are you?" and "Do I believe?"

The narratives of the men indicate that they drew on the familiar spiritual resources of God, prayer, and the confessional, but not spiritual direction, more than any other resource, to survive the conflicted and colliding sites that they inhabited, such as those of manhood/priesthood (or religious brotherhood); sexual being/celibate commitment; emotional need/emotionally needed; powerful/powerless. They had differing views on how God would see their abusing, and while they knew God would not approve of their behavior, the men's narratives consistently indicate that without a belief that God would understand and help them, many of the men could not have survived the conflicted lives they were living.

I felt that He [God] was the only one who could understand that my behavior was rooted in the human weakness of one who desired to live the Christian life and not in an evil will . . . Had I not had this image of an understanding and merciful God, life would have been hopeless for me in the context of my constant falls.

I would pray and pray that I would change and be resolute in my desire to change.

Organized Irresponsibility (II)

The men relied a lot on God to help prevent their total disintegration, especially when they began abusing boys. Most of them imagined God as a friend in whom they could acknowledge vulnerability and share their struggles, but some of them even tried to keep their abusing from God, so great was their shame. The participants elaborate the complexity of their relationship with God, especially during the years that they were abusing.

> I knew that God alone had a total perception of who and what I was. I knew that while I could cover up my behavior from people I could not hide from God. I knew that after each offence I was genuinely remorseful and sought forgiveness in the Sacrament of Penance. I knew that God was aware that, at that time, I had a purpose of amendment. Yet I was faced with the fact that a genuine repentance could not be reconciled with the repetitious nature of the behavior... How could God accept the authenticity of my remorse when I was not taking steps to deal with the compulsion which was causing me to sin?... I suppose I resolved this issue by falling back on my belief that the God who could understand my failures could also understand why I could not seek help to avoid these falls. However, I was highly ambivalent about this and can now see the use of this rationalization to enable me to preserve my relationship with God, the one thing that prevented total disintegration.
>
> I think in my early years I associated God as the one always watching me who would punish me if I did wrong or even what I felt to be wrong. It took me quite a while to accept that God was one who loved me "warts and all" and loved me in spite of my weaknesses. But I think I even tried to hide from Him the doubtful things I did, really the bad things I did. There were times I was quite upset with myself, and the way I was going. This would occur to me at the time of a retreat and I would be determined to change. Often the retreat was during the summer holidays when there were no boys around and I may go away to do a few weeks' parish work. I suppose the resolution got forgotten when I got back to school. But I knew God would forgive me if I repented and did my best. I suppose I excused myself too easily and minimized what I was doing. Dare I say it, I may have normalized it... I now worry about the idea of God that the boys I abused are left with.
>
> In my early life for me it was very much the God-fear thing, especially regarding sexuality and masturbation. As a confessor I was open in that whole area for other people, but not for myself... Later I believed that God would understand, that God is love, that He is a loving and merciful father and not the ogre of the Redemptorists' preaching... God was the father of the Prodigal Son and I saw myself as fitting into the parable. He was kind and compassionate, loving and forgiving. He was not the God of wrath and condemnation. He was always willing to forgive. He was always available in confession and his mercy was always there for the taking. God had sent Jesus to call sinners to repentance and I was one of those.

The narratives show that their belief in God sustained the participants through some difficult times. They believed that God, who was aware they were struggling to be good, would love them in spite of their weaknesses if they sought forgiveness, were genuinely remorseful, and did their best not to abuse again. God was always available in confession. The men saw themselves as sinners, and they tried to repent. God and the confessional provided the key site of support and hope for them, especially when they were abusing boys. However, the narratives also give rise to some important observations regarding the function of confession. It is notable that only one confessor on one occasion, among the many times that the men disclosed their abusive behavior in confession, pointed out the criminal nature of the sexual abuse. The very process of confession itself might therefore be seen as having enabled the abuse to continue, not only in how the men used the secrecy and safety of the confessional space to resolve the issues of guilt, but also in the fact that within the walls of confession, the problem of sexual abuse of children was contained. While the *Catechism of the Catholic Church* (1994) makes clear that the seal is a fundamental aspect of the theology of the sacrament of confession, and it is not the function of the confessor to judge the confessant, nonetheless no pathway existed for this important information of abuse by clergy, which was emerging in the confessional, to flow back into the system, to alert the Church hierarchy to a growing problem. The fact that the problem was individualized at the level of the confessional is an important feature of abuse by clergy.

OVERCOMING MORAL CONSCIENCE

As part of my attempts to understand those factors that enabled clerical men to sexually abuse minors, the men were asked to describe their understanding of moral conscience and to describe how their understanding of moral conscience fitted or conflicted with their sexually abusive behavior.

My underlying rational conviction was that the behavior was not ok. I knew that it was contrary to the system of morality I had been taught. To some extent that teaching had been internalized, but certainly not sufficiently to enable me to realize the nature and effects of my "invasion" of a young person. My principal focus was on the moral aspect of the behavior and not on the personal/psychological consequences for the young person. I was certainly aware that the more "gross" actions possible would not alone have breached the moral order, but would also have been extremely traumatic . . . The intention to hurt was not in my mind and what I considered would clearly do so was not on my "agenda." I had deep moral inhibitions about advancing to more "degrading" activity. So, despite my realization that the behavior in which I was already engaging was wrong, anything further would have been "a step too far." By "minimizing" the behavior (such as saying it is only touching!) I persuaded myself that while there was a moral breach, the harm to the young person was minimal. The fact that the other person did not object was a factor in my "justification" of the behavior in that there was a sort of tacit assent to the "intrusion." This was dishonest and distorted thinking, because the fact is that I had already ensured submission by targeting only those whom I believed would be compliant. I knew in my heart that the fact that the person showed no enthusiasm whatever was sufficient sign of unwillingness. So there was much double-thinking going on. The question of the age difference and the incapacity of a young person to make any kind of decision in this regard I never considered.

I really twisted my conscience to go along with my actions. I convinced myself that these actions were not morally serious. I think all this justification gave me a very poor attitude to personal boundaries and that my conscience was very distorted in this area of life.

I made the distinction between venial and mortal sin. Because of my minimization I opted for the venial category ... I know I did not realize how serious and damaging my behavior was and would become.

The scenario was always the same, get the boys to accept me touching their thighs up their trousers in a classroom or in my office. Always I would be aroused but I fought off ejaculation. In fact I cannot remember ejaculating on any occasion. That would have been a serious sin and difficult to explain in confession ... I did not think about justice to the individual ... it was about how far did you go with yourself in the process, before committing a sin. The individual was not considered ... I did not go to orgasm and I did not ejaculate ... and this thinking was compounded when you went through the process of confession. What was seen was what you did and not the individual ... that was my way of giving myself permission.

Minimizing the seriousness and harm of what I was doing was also the key to getting around conscience.

What is interesting here is the revelation that when they were abusing, the clerical perpetrators focused on the moral or sin aspects of their behavior and not on the personal or psychological consequences for the young person. All of the men thought first about breaches of the moral code and focused on the sexual "act" rather than on the consequences for the young person. They adopted an approach to morality that was based on rules and rational thought rather than personal or relational engagement. It was possible to bargain with the rule-book without putting themselves in the shoes of the child. Some perpetrators persuaded themselves that while there was a moral breach, it was minor when compared to other sex acts. Their thinking was accompanied by minimizations that the behavior in which they were engaged was "only touching." By focusing on the "act" and not on the impact of the actions for the young person, one participant believed that more "gross" actions, compared to the ones in which he was engaged, would not just have been a significant moral breach, but would also have been traumatic for the young person. By focusing on the "act" and his part in it, another participant prevented himself from ejaculating, because this would have been a graver sin.

While one could be forgiven for believing that these men suffered from distorted thinking, in fact the opposite may well be the case. From their study of Catholic sexual ethics they understood sexual sin as direct offense against God but not as a direct offense against a person, who happened to be on the receiving end of the sex "act," and who was a minor. It was on God that they focused their concerns, not on the child they were abusing. This can at one level be seen as in harmony with Catholic moral teaching. A purity ethic rather than a relational ethic predominates. The perpetrators also bargained with the rule, and while all sexual sins are equally mortal in Catholic moral theology, some perpetrators made up their own ranking system of gradations of harm, while others saw all sex "acts" as one and the same. Those perpetrators who engaged in what could be regarded as the least intrusive abuses, such as touching, compared to the more intrusive fellatio or buggery (although bearing in mind that the subjective experience of the victim is always what matters), were those perpetrators who had a gradation system of sexual sins in place. Touching, although harmful, was lower on the sin scale than the more intrusive sexual acts, which were regarded as more serious and therefore more "sinful." An internal logic applied, accompanied by rationalizations and justifications that "fitted" with their clerical perspective.

Dorr (2000, p. 13) points out that in his 7 years of the study of moral theology for the priesthood, several further years of study for a doctorate in moral theology, and several subsequent years of teaching moral theology in a seminary, he never heard or read anything about child sexual abuse. Sex with a child was left off the list of sexual sins despite Canon 1395[1] specifically forbidding the sexual abuse of children and minors (Canon Law Society of America, 1983). Dorr (2000, pp. 13, 14) suspects that the absence of mention of child sexual abuse among the sexual sins can be partly explained in terms of a fundamental flaw in Catholic moral theology, which is still defended by some Church authorities today. According to Catholic moral theology, certain acts are seen as intrinsically evil, independently of their consequences (p. 14); sexual sins are in this category. Within the domain of moral theology attention is directed to the nature of the act itself, and not to the consequences of such action (p. 14). Sexual activity between a man and a woman is seen as a different kind of sin from sexual activity between people of the same gender, and sex between a human and an animal is seen as yet another kind of sin. In Dorr's view, moral theologians overlooked child sexual abuse as a sexual sin because they were listing the different kinds of sexual sin in purely physical terms. Putting this crudely, Dorr claims the focus of their attention was on "what organ of what body was put into what part of another body" (p. 13). The theologians were thinking more of bodies than people, and for them the fact that the other body was that of a child was not relevant to the otherwise sinful act itself.

The narratives also show that the men adopted a legalist-orthodox approach to morality, a view of morality based on adherence to rules and regulations (Inglis, 1998, p. 22). This amounted to an externally defined morality that was devoid of internal and critical reflection and engagement. It was also marked by the absence of a relational ethic. This legalistic-orthodox approach to morality was not unusual to find in Irish people during the 19th and 20th century. Influenced by the doctrine of the Council of Trent and run by the powerful Church in Ireland, its influence on Catholic clergy was particularly problematic because of the depth of its penetration and its perseverance.

A legalistic-orthodox approach to morality is based primarily on the belief that salvation is the preserve of the Church and is attained through performance of good work and strict observance of Church rules and regulations (Inglis, 1998, p. 30). The main informing beliefs are that this life is not important and is only a preparation for the next; salvation is achieved by avoiding sin; being holy involves denying oneself and serving others; and there is no salvation outside of the Church (Flannery, 1999, p. 15). This type of morality creates docile, obedient subjects who live with an anxiety and fear about fulfilling duties exactly as the rulebook dictates (Inglis, 1998, p. 32). The rules of God and the regulations of the Church are to be followed in a disciplined way. This is *the simple faith* that dominated much Irish Catholicism of the 19th and 20th centuries (Inglis, 1998, p. 21). At the heart of it lies a strong orthodox belief in God, Christ, and Our Lady, a high level of religious and devotional practice, and an unquestioning handing over of one's moral reasoning to the institutional Church.

What is important in the context of sexual abuse by clergy is that within this approach to morality, individuals were not encouraged to question and were not encouraged to reflect for themselves (Inglis, 1998, p. 35). Questions of morality were left in the hands of the bishops and the pope, and moral lapses were solved by attendance at confession. Individuals were not encouraged to derive a code of moral behavior from a reading and analysis of the Bible but rather from the norms and regulations the Church had derived for them. How the rules and regulations were applied in practice was not to be disputed, and individual interpretation of the rules was similarly discouraged. In this way, a powerful Irish Church hierarchy, in a largely monocultural homogenous society, produced a docile population regarding matters of faith and morals. This was even more the case within the Irish Catholic clergy, which for historical reasons attracted to the top men who would toe the Roman line (see Fuller, 2002).

My clinical observations and research indicate that those clerical men who went on to commit sexual violations were more inclined than other clergy to be strict rule-keepers, "systems" men, high on religious and devotional practice and unquestioning of the institutional Church. Unable to break little rules safely or critically question the very institutional rules and practices that were crippling them emotionally, the men went on to break bigger rules of social conduct, with dire consequences for themselves and countless others, most especially children. Equipped with a rule-book based on fear, that was even more restrictive for Catholic clergy than for the laity, and unschooled in the art of critical engagement, the men attempted to live by the rules until the life became impossible to live. The men's narratives show how their attempts to covertly subvert the rules that they could not overtly challenge, within the context of their lives as adult men and devoted clergy, were not insignificant in their subsequent sexual offending. A morality that was based on a rule-book had consequences for these men and for the children they abused. By focusing on the rule-book that provided an almost automatic list of responses to sin, the men did not engage with moral behavior in specific terms, in specific situations, regardless of what the apparent rules seemed to suggest or omit. Their responses were "logical" and "intellectual" and devoid of emotional or self-reflective engagement. In the psychological literature, the facility to put oneself in the shoes of the other, cognitively and emotionally, is regarded as empathy.

The more psychologically based bargaining strategies that the men employed to overcome their moral conscience, when abusing involved a number of minimizations and justifications. They minimized the behavior: "it is only touching." They minimized the harm done. They labeled what they were doing as "curiosity." Some of them construed the abuse as "affection" or "friendship." They construed the boys' lack of verbal protest as indicating agreement and "consent." One perpetrator told himself he was weak and not to blame for the condition, as God had made him that way. Others believed it was less harmful to the priesthood to have sex with boys than to have adult relationships. They used excuses for finding "some little satisfaction and solace." One priest convinced himself he was helping the boys, while another saw sex with the boy as a payoff for other work done. All of the participants resolved never do it again, especially after confession. The narratives demonstrate the extent to which the men were able to convince themselves of their motivations, of the boys' "consent," and of the lack of harm being done to the boys.

Eight of the men now recognize their rationalizations for what they were, the contradictions in their behavior, and the double thinking they used to enable the abusing to continue.

The narratives indicate how they tried to keep such "insights" at bay, even from themselves, during those years of abusing.

> I kept on pretending that it was the other person who wanted the relationship . . . The one thing I could never admit to myself was that I was causing pain because I bloody well knew that if I allowed myself think I was causing pain it was this that would have caused me to stop. . . I can turn around now and say I feel all the pain and that I understand what the victims went through. I wish to Christ I could, but I'm not sure any of us have it or can ever have it. All I can say is I am sorry, this should not have happened.
>
> I now realize that he never said a word because he was afraid. He was afraid of me.
>
> The tendency was to blame the boy for not stopping you, and I think some people still do that after all these years.
>
> In 1985 I read an article in *Time* magazine and others in the newspapers and it really opened my eyes. I became aware of all the devastation and whether the child was 16, 17, 18, or 19 it would be the same as if he were 11 . . . No one could tell me otherwise. I stopped that day.

Eight of the nine participants demonstrated that they came to realize the effects of the abuse on their young victims, although as one participant pointed out, he was not sure that men who had abused could ever fully appreciate what it must have been like for those young people. The perpetrators could only draw on their own experiences of abuse and listen carefully to the stories that victims of abuse were telling, both by way of the treatment program and the media. The perpetrators felt a sense of sadness and regret for the hurt they had caused to the boys and the one girl. They also felt guilty and in some cases shameful for the crimes committed.

> Since my therapy experiences I know the terrible effects sex abuse has on young people as they grow up. They feel dirty, violated, losing their childhood, emotionally insecure, the list goes on. It really troubles me now that I caused such hardship . . . I had no idea at the time that I was going to cause so much hurt. This really saddens me. I can't undo the damage. When I think about these activities now I feel a great sense of shame. Now I realize that I sinned grievously and continually ask the Lord for healing for the victims and forgiveness for myself.

The participants were also aware of the vulnerability and exposure of the victims who had been abused in a classroom or boarding school environment, particularly vis-à-vis other boys in class who knew the abuse was taking place. The perpetrators see such action as another effect of abuse. The narratives suggest the participants believe the boys they abused were caught in a world of secrecy and silence, which was an isolating experience for the child. At the time of their abusing the men relied upon the silence of the child and an atmosphere of secrecy to ensure that the child would not disclose and that the abuses would not be discovered.

> I was . . . the all-powerful, sitting up in his big office . . . and sometimes I think of what kind of effect it had on the other kids when I called a kid up to my room. I am sure

some of those kids must have been saying, "the bloody bastard . . . if he comes near me, am I going to be next?" What I now see is what the kid must have gone through coming up to my office . . . It was only when I looked back at my own abuse that I recognized that when I would be called out of the class there would be sniggers and smiles from the other fellows in the class . . . I can only think of the things that must have been said to that young man, that young child, as he went back to the classroom.

What is happening to the child is another form of abuse when other kids know that he is your victim . . . what exactly is he thinking about himself, and by the same token where was he to go, who was he to talk to . . . where do all these feelings go? If a child cannot talk to its parents I can see now exactly what happens: it creates or cements something into existence between the child and his parents, in that he cannot talk to them. It gives it permanence. I feel terribly ashamed of what I have done because many of the kids I abused were in the position of not telling their parents. You were banking on the fact that they couldn't or wouldn't or didn't talk about it . . . It is so . . . sad.

One participant reflected on how he felt many years earlier when boys he had abused had reported the abuse to their parents and he was subsequently moved to another ministry. He felt ashamed at the thoughts he had at the time about the boys and their families.

The trust these kids, these boys, had in me . . . the boys' parents spoke to me at the time about how they felt . . . here at this time of their lives I had destroyed them. What had I done to their families? And do you know, I am ashamed to say, but that in some ways at that time I was almost saying: "give me another chance." I didn't say that to them, but that was in my own thinking . . . Now I think about the upset, the anger, the parental stress, and how distressed those children were.

The narratives of the men indicate that they were now also aware of the ripple effects of sexual abuse on other people as well as on their immediate victims. In particular they were concerned about the victims' families, their own families, other priests and religious, the Church leaders, their friends, and the laity.

POWER AND OPPORTUNITY

It was not difficult for the participants in my research to overcome any external obstacles that existed to abusing, as their lives as Roman Catholic ministers gave them a role in the community in which they were trusted (Inglis, 1998, p. 2; Kirby, 1984, p. 56; McDonagh, 1995, p. 5). Their work gave them unlimited access to children, families, and vulnerable adults. The men were often alone with young people as part of their vocational and priestly ministries, giving them ample opportunity to abuse young people, if that was indeed their intention. The men's opportunity to abuse was helped by a number of factors: (1) the power position they occupied both as adults and as ministers of the Roman Catholic Church in Ireland, which itself occupied a strong power base in Irish society (Inglis, 1998; Kirby, 1984; McDonagh, 1995, p. 5); (2) the effects of clericalism on the men themselves and on the Catholic laity; and (3) the lack of support, supervision, and accountability for lower-ranking clergy within the structures of the Roman Catholic Church. The Church's mishandling of abuse complaints played an important role in maintaining the problem once it had begun. While gaining access to young people was therefore not a problem for the men who participated in this research, nonetheless they needed to conceal their abusing from the children's parents and from their superiors in order to be seen as worthy ministers.

Power as Adult and as Roman Catholic Minister

Because of their work in parishes, hospitals, schools, and youth clubs and on youth holidays and youth retreats, all of the men in this study were involved in situations involving unsupervised access to children. This situation has a long and established tradition, and the relationship between bishop, priest, or brother and the people was one of trust and reverence (Inglis, 1998, p. 2; Kirby, 1984, p. 259; McDonagh, 1995, p. 5). Trust existed as part of the social relations between the Roman Catholic Church and the people, and the pastoral privileges of the priest were closely associated with celibacy (Kirby, 1984, p. 259). Celibate priests and religious men were presumed by the people to be free from the usual sexual desires and to live in perfect chastity (Kirby, 1984, p. 259). Within such a social context, parents believed that children were safe with clergy, and they even believed their sons would benefit from involvement with the holy men (*States of Fear*, 1999; *Suing the Pope*, 2002). In some situations, parents allowed clergy into the private sphere of the family and children were allowed to spend time alone or on vacation with the family's clergy friends (*States of Fear*, 1999; *Suing the Pope*, 2002). Within such a cultural and vocational environment priests and brothers had unlimited opportunity to abuse young people if that was their intention. Their teaching and pastoral roles gave them unlimited access to young people. Without such a role, other men who abuse minors have first to establish the route to access potential victims. This was not the case for the men in this study.

Clergy as Elite; Clericalism and the Catholic Laity

In Ireland, from the 1960s to the early 1990s, the period in which the men in this study were abusing minors, clerics were presumed to be superior to laity and closer to God, and in this sense they formed an elite within the Roman Catholic Church (Doyle, 2003, p. 209). Clerics saw themselves as set apart and set above. The laity viewed them as God's men on earth. An attitude also prevailed that it was sinful to make any unkind accusation against a priest or bishop (Doyle, 2003, p. 209; Wills, 2000, pp. 177, 179). An extension of this attitude was the belief that the priests and bishops could and would do no wrong. While other factors, such as shame and fear, may have been involved in why victims of clergy abuse did not report such abuses in the past, the belief that priests and religious could do wrong no contributed to this situation (Doyle, 2004, p. 34; Fahy, 1999; Madden, 2004). Such a belief and privileged position in Irish society also enabled the priests and religious brothers in this study to dismiss the idea that the boys they abused would tell.

Lack of Supervision and Accountability

The participants in this research worked within a model of accountability in which, in theory, the laity and lower clergy were accountable to the bishops and the bishops were accountable to the pope. The accountability structures were loose and the men were largely both unsupervised and unsupported in the exercise of their duties. The men themselves also seemed to interpret accountability in terms of delivering services (e.g., number of Masses, a good homily, good teaching and devotions), and they did not think of accountability in terms of the kinds of ethical or personal relations that they engaged in with the people to whom they ministered.

> I always felt very accountable in "delivering the goods"—good teachers, excellent results, good PR—but not in the other side of the coin.

This hierarchical model of one-way accountability had no checks and balances, and the men were free upon leaving the seminary to practice and minister unsupported and unsupervised in most cases. The lack of support and supervision was especially felt in the first 5 to 10 years of ministry, during which time many of the men first abused boys. The men rarely met their bishops or leaders for mentoring or advice as they learned to "sink or swim" outside the protective structures of the seminary and their families, within a context of the newfound power conferred on them at ordination and final profession.

Other studies also found that clergy lack both support and supervision in the exercise of their ministerial duties (Bennett et al., 2004; Cozzens, 2004; Goode et al., 2003). Poorly prepared for and unsupported in many of the pastoral situations they encountered and poorly prepared humanly for the celibate commitment they had made, the narratives of the men in this study show that it was not long before the challenges of celibacy and loneliness and the need for intimacy arose for seven of the nine participants, accompanied by a newfound power and unlimited access to children and young people. When young people became the men's main source of personal connection, in some cases their only close "friends," it was only a matter of time before the men violated their professional boundaries and sexually abused some of the boys. Without adequate support structures and within a culture of denial and secrecy, the men did not admit to colleagues or superiors what was in fact occurring in their lives and in their ministries. All of the men denied the reality of the boundary violations, even to themselves. Without adequate professional supervision in the exercise of their duties, it was also possible for the problems to go undetected for a very long time.

Church Handling of Abuse Complaints

The actions taken by Church leaders following the initial complaints of sexual abuse made against the men in this study further contributed, however unwittingly, to the maintenance of the problem. It is evident from the men's accounts and from a review of the literature that not only did the Church leaders fail to fully engage with the victims' complaints or to deal adequately with the offending clergy, but also that they failed to undertake a comprehensive analysis of the problem to understand what it was all about. In this they were failed by leadership from the Vatican. Each leader appears to have adopted a defensive position in relation to his diocese or religious order, thus ensuring that information would not be shared or the problem would not be comprehensively investigated.

There is no suggestion in any of the men's narratives that their abusive behavior was encouraged or condoned by their superiors. On the contrary, the men in this study were encouraged to seek full repentance for their "sin" and to change their ways, and in some instances the men were sent for psychological or psychiatric assessments. However, despite such assessments few of the men received what could be regarded as comprehensive sexual offender treatment until several instances of abuse had been disclosed over many years. Some men had one or two consultations with a psychiatrist in the earlier years. However, because Church leaders left the men's priesthood (or brotherhood) intact and at the same time failed to provide adequate support and supervision for them, the men's greatest fears (which was dismissal from the clerical state) were alleviated and they returned effectively to an unchanged situation, albeit in most cases to a different geographical site in which to minister. By seeing the problem of child sexual abuse as an individual one, initially in terms of sin and later of pathology, the possible systemic dimensions to the problem, such as sexuality and celibacy, accountability, governance structures, and lack of support and supervision, were not recognized or addressed. All of the nine men in this study were reassigned to further ministries following their abuse disclosures, often involving children; in eight of the nine cases the men went on to abuse further young people. At most, the men's narratives indicate that moving them around merely slowed the process of abusing until the men got to know their new context, new parishes, and new families; it did not end the abuse.

During the 1990s, following the renewed wave of publicity that sexual abuse in the Catholic Church received in the United States and the Anglophone world, all of the men who participated in this research were removed from their ministries and sent for sexual offender treatment. While some had ceased offending of their own accord for several years prior to attending treatment, to the best of my knowledge none of the men who participated in this research has ever abused a minor since participating in treatment.

CONSCIENCE AND GOOD JUDGMENT

The narratives of the men, as described above, indicate that a failure in moral judgment and in conscience functioning contributed to their sexual offending. Stilwell (2003, p. 5) argues that sexual offending always represents a failure in conscience functioning. According to political philosopher Hannah Arendt (2003, p. 44), who reported on the Eichmann trials following the Second World War, and who undertook significant scholarly work on totalitarianism and totalitarian regimes, the precondition for the kind of judgment that is necessary to prevent wrongdoing is not a highly developed intelligence or sophistication in moral matters, but rather a disposition to live with others and explicitly with oneself and to engage in an ongoing silent dialogue with oneself, especially about the consequences of one's actions for another. This kind of thinking is not technical and does not concern theoretical problems and is "not like the thought process of pure reasoning" (Arendt, 2003, p. 44). The power of good judgment rests on a potential agreement with others in whose place we put ourselves before we act. Judgment involves an internal dialogue between a person and himself, but this dialogue always finds itself in an anticipated communication with others, with whom the individual knows he must finally come to face and to agree. Judgment needs the special presence of others "in whose place" one must think, and whose perspectives one must take into consideration (p. 44). When related to the participants in my research, the kind of judgment that was required was that the men put themselves in the place of the child, knowing that agreement on the sexual act that was imminent could never take place, by definition, and ask themselves what the child's parents (as adults, who had guardianship of the child) would reply on the child's behalf if they knew what the cleric was about to do.

An all-male institutional seminary environment in which the participants were cocooned in the intellectual and theoretical pursuits of knowledge and morality, unmediated by honest discussion about and engagement with the actual realities of human life, did not provide an environment in which to make good moral judgments. On the contrary, such an environment led to denial and deceit as individuals tried to live up to the "ideal" and to deny the actual "realities" of their own and other people's lives. To help seminarians make good moral judgments, not only would an opportunity for internal reflection and honest dialogue be required, but also an environment that would take into account the anticipated consequences for another of one's actions, in very particular and specific ways, seminarians need exposure to and immersion in the pastoral realities of their own and other people's lives (a conclusion that is based on Arendt's work). As Arendt (2003, p. 44) points out, making good judgments is far from theoretical or abstract; it is very specific and very personal. (In the psychological literature this process is referred to as empathy (Marshall, 2002; Fernandez, 2002)). In contrast, the men in my study describe their learning environment as one in which moral theology was taught and learned in an academic manner and intellectualized by them as though consisting of a set of learned or innate rules that they could generally apply. Based on the insights developed by Arendt (2003), I believe such a seminary environment would not equip its students to make good judgments. The ability to make good judgments is personal, specific, and very particular.

The men in this study understood well the rule-book on morality, but they were unable to make good moral judgments in situations that required self-reflection, personal awareness, and the ability to put themselves in the shoes of the other. The seminary and clerical culture that the men describe in this study, in which honest dialogue between the men and their seminary professors, bishops, superiors, and laypeople was discouraged, failed to bring the participants to a point at which they would make good judgments. It even appears to have encouraged an approach to morality that was devoid of internal reflection, personal awareness, and the importance of seeing each situation as requiring a unique response—perhaps by default and unintentionally, or maybe as a form of controlling men's minds. Hill (1997, p. 156) wonders about the kind of education that seminaries provide and about the forms of authority in religious life and the power it confers. He fears that the answer points to only one thing: that clergy are taught that they owe obedience to those in authority over them, and accountability to those under them does not seem to be considered. He says that there is hardly a word about "how authority should be exercised, about the obligations that go with power and the moral limits to its use" (p. 156).

A seminary training that did not encourage the seminarians to recognize their own power position and their own emotions, much less those of children, and see things from the other person's perspective did not provide them with the skills that they would require for ministering to the young and the vulnerable. The seminary, with its lack of emphasis on personal awareness, personal reflection, and human engagement, was not a context in which the men in my research could develop emotionally and relationally. A theoretical and intellectual education was never going to prepare them for the level of human engagement that their vocational life would demand. (This of course is not to say that they are not responsible for the actions they took.)

Hirschman's (1970) analysis of exit, voice, and loyalty can be helpful when considering why the clergy in my research deceived themselves and others in the way that they did when it came to their sexual abuse of children. According to Hirschman (p. 93), individuals in organizations where there are high fees for entering (such as clerical and religious life, where a long period of training is involved, as well as commitment to chastity and obedience) and stiff penalties for exiting (such as the shame of being a "failed" priest, which until recently in Ireland incurred considerable social stigma) may have a considerable stake in self-deception, particularly when they do not have sufficient say in decisions that affect their lives. The absence of "voice" and the fear of "exit" can inevitably lead to self-deception, denial, and secrecy on the part of its members (Hirschman, 1970, p. 93). Such was the case for the men in my study. As the gap widened between the reality of their lives and their attempts to live up to the "ideal" that was demanded by their understanding of what it meant to "do" priesthood or religious brotherhood according to their interpretation of the rules and regulations, a space existed in which it was possible for them to rationalize even the most unacceptable of human behavior.

THE PERSPECTIVES OF NON-OFFENDING CLERGY

It is interesting to note that my research with non-abusive clerics and former clerics also provides important information on seminary and clerical culture and the focus on obedience, rule-keeping, and hierarchical authority. While I mentioned earlier that the seminary formation in celibacy seems to have undergone some small improvements during the 1980s and 1990s; the same cannot be said for clerical culture and the system of authority that was being practiced or preached. The seminary culture was presented as one of absolute conformity to superiors, "without question." There was "a culture of hard work, study, spiritual discipline, oppression and paranoia." "There was a big emphasis on attending morning prayers and Mass, which was the main focus of the day." Potential students were regularly monitored, and if poor attendance at these exercises was detected, they were severely reprimanded. However, "it was also clear that there were different rules for different people. Those that the Dean liked could break rules at will, go to the pub, be late for Mass, return later to college, while everybody else could suffer his wrath." There was a strong culture of gossip, and every relationship and every friendship was scrutinized by everybody else. "There was a culture of paranoia as students gradually did not trust each other." While some seminarians developed very good friendships with other students, overall there was a sense of superficiality, and serious issues were seldom discussed. Clerical culture "emphasizes loyalty and conformity to the brotherhood. When this is adhered to, elevation and promotion in the ranks becomes imminent." Mandatory celibacy allows clerical culture to thrive, according to these men, because without a separate life outside of priesthood, all of a man's energy and identity goes into the clerical role. Unfortunately, "it appears that many clergy seldom have a strong personal identity apart from being a priest, which is one of the contradictions built into the job." I will return to this subject later.

My research with these clerics and former clerics tells me that initially the men were very trusting of "the system," both the local Church and the institution of the Catholic Church more universally, when they entered into seminaries as young men. However, as time went on they became reserved and upset and often disillusioned by what they experienced and witnessed. At the same time "the cruel and oppressive nature of the system cultivated a culture of resilience and determination to succeed." "The fact that there was such an emphasis on the common good and a disregard for individual needs was quite concerning as the seminary training developed." "It operated like a business model and students were a product that had to be modeled and reshaped to go out and preach the 'word of God' to the world." "They certainly had no interest in us beyond being ordination fodder. They knew nothing about us for the most part and certainly were not interested. I always had the sense that they were men chosen for their orthodoxy rather than their learning, and they were much more concerned with the Church than with people." While some seminary staff were identified as approachable and kind, most were distant, and engagement between seminarians and staff was at an academic or supervisory level, such as times when students needed to seek special permissions or make special requests. The conclusion seems to have been that "you had to play the system in order to survive, and it was important to try and make yourself anonymous if possible and keep a low profile."

"Speaking one's mind was the thing most likely to have somebody told they were unsuitable for the priesthood." One man observed there was absolutely no effort made to inculcate any kind of critical thinking in the student body; "in fact the opposite obtained." In a hierarchical system of seniority and a contrasting culture of subordination, there were a lot of unwritten rules of do's and don'ts and poor systemic accountability. My research with these men and my clinical experience suggest that some seminarians are hurt by some of the relationships of power involved this process, and they have no place to go to have their hurts addressed because of the imbalance of power and the goal of ordination.

While all of the men felt there is a need for much more support for clergy, they also indicated that the relationship with the bishops depended on the personality and leadership style of the man in the position. One man summed up the relationship between priests and bishops as "cautious, mutually respectful (mutually fearful?)." It was emphasized that the bishops have a significant power in the lives of Irish clergy. Irish priests are dependent on those in authority because priests have no proper salary structure and no security of tenure when it comes to accommodation (this is not the case in the operations of the Catholic Church in other countries). Two of the men whose narratives I report here voluntarily left the priesthood after many years of ministry. When I asked them why they had left, one man simply and quite poignantly replied, "loneliness."

CONCLUDING COMMENTS

The clerical men who went on to become perpetrators of child sexual abuse and who participated in my research constructed their priestly or religious vocation on fear: fear of breaking a celibate commitment and fear of displeasing others. The accompanying way of "doing" priesthood involved strategies for their attempts to live a chaste and obedient life, such as adopting a submissive way of relating to others, avoiding relationships with women, and avoiding particular friendships with men. Such strategies produced poor adult attachments, a fear of emotional and physical intimacy, and prolonged emotional loneliness. The narratives suggest that the men avoided adult relationships as a way of protecting their priesthood or religious vocation and as a way of protecting their celibate commitment. Most of them employed a construct of priesthood or brotherhood in which all pathways to sexual or emotional engagement with adult women or men were closed. Unsure of how to negotiate the complex intersection of personal and professional boundaries within the parameters of a celibate vocational commitment, the men avoided relationships with adults altogether. Some of them denied the depths of the personal struggle, even to themselves, until it was already too late and they had begun to abuse boys. Overall, it seems that in trying to abide by rules that were impossible to live, the men became isolated and chronically lonely, despite being part of a community or diocese, while some of them even at times appeared to be gregarious and popular in the priestly role.

The issue of obedience is an important one when it comes to sexual abuse by Catholic clergy because it appears not only to be implicated in giving way to abuse in the first place, but also in how the hierarchy dealt with abuse complaints. The issue of blind loyalty to the institution goes to the heart of the sexual abuse issue for the Catholic Church, and my research suggests that just as senior prelates were and are expected to be loyal to the Roman line or suffer the consequences (see Geoff Robinson's experience [2007] in Chapter 9), so too is loyalty to the bishop expected of the priests. Apart from stifling debate, the culture of obedience becomes a culture of deference that is devoid of honest dialogue. By adopting a submissive style of interacting, the clerical perpetrators gained acceptance from their seminary professors, and later their bishops and superiors, and social approval from the communities they served. However, years of submission and unacknowledged loneliness also gave way to deep feelings of resentment and anger that were not acknowledged or expressed.

The confessional emerges as not only providing a site of support and respite from the conflicted lives that many of the men were living, but as also serving a function in enabling the abuse to continue. The confessional allowed the men to resolve the issues of guilt resulting from their abusing, and it contained the problem of clergy sexual abuse within the walls and the seal of the confessional. No pathway existed for this important information, which was emerging in the confessional, to flow back into the system to alert the Church hierarchy to a growing problem. This is something that Church leaders may wish to review in the future, as the knowledge of abuse by clergy must have been in the system years earlier than it emerged in public, especially since all of the men in this study confessed to their abusing, sometimes up to several times a week, over a period of at least 20 years. When one combines this conclusion with the literature that was examined in Chapter 1 on the level of knowledge that Church leaders had about sexual abuse by clergy, it is safe to conclude that the Roman Catholic Church had within its systemic "ears" knowledge that priests were abusing boys and girls years earlier than when they first admitted. By failing to use the "ears" of the confessional to "catch" the collective problems of clergy, without in any way breaking the seal, a significant source of information is constrained that otherwise could improve the lives of many suffering clergy and prevent abuse of children. It emerges in this study that just as the confessional was an outlet for personal conflict, guilt, and shame, the abuse was an outlet for unmet sexual and intimacy needs. Both were conducted in secret.

Despite enduring similar conditions in both the educational environment and the environment of clerical life, many clerics did not turn to children to meet their emotional needs, nor did they sexually abuse minors. It is to this issue that I turn in Chapter 10. I will attempt to draw the contours of a framework that might help us think about why some clergy turn to minors to meet their sexual (and emotional) needs and thus abuse them, while others do not.

To reduce the answer to this complex issue to mere psychopathology is not borne out by the available data, much of which was discussed in Chapter 3. I will also draw a multilevel systemic framework of child sexual abuse within the Catholic Church, which I propose is the most meaningful way in which to analyze and understand the problem. However, I wish now to turn to the Church's handling of abuse complaints.

9

The Handling of Abuse Complaints

CHILD SEXUAL ABUSE within the Catholic Church has two interlocking dimensions: the fact that the abuse occurred at all, and the way the problem was managed once it came to light. While relatively little is understood about the clerical perpetrators and the causes and context of the problem, the bulk of attention has focused on the Church's handling of abuse complaints and its response to those abused in Ireland, the United Kingdom, the United States, Canada, Australia, and more recently in Europe. While it is not publicly known how every bishop in the world handled this issue when faced with it, and therefore it is wrong to speak of "the" bishops as though they are one and the same, at the same time, in those cases that have been subject to investigation in Ireland and the United States and those reported elsewhere, there appears to be some remarkable consistency in the patterns that can be discerned in the Church response to the abuse complaints.

In attempting to analyze the response of the Catholic Church to sexual abuse by Catholic clergy, we must remember that little research has attempted to understand the bishops' perspectives on this subject or to distinguish the emotional, personal, and vocational factors within their professional and religious networks that may have influenced their decision-making at local and at broader organizational levels. Little research has attempted to follow the bishops' learning curve and to analyze the points and junctures at which their thinking changed, and why this occurred. While it is clear that some changes were forced upon the bishops and the Catholic Church by the pressure of the media, to assume that it was only media pressure that brought about such changes may be to obscure the facts and the "truth". It is an important truth however that the voices and narratives of victims and survivors (sometimes through the media) were very influential in encouraging the bishops and the dioceses to change their response patterns by bringing the diocesan leaders to an understanding of the harm done by sexual abuse. In the absence of primary research with the hierarchy of the Roman Catholic Church, public opinion is influenced by the revelations of the official investigations into the handling of abuse complaints in a number of countries, including Ireland and the United States, and by the published accounts that are adding to the fast-accumulating recorded history of the subject. These accounts are becoming reified as accepted explanations of why the bishops responded as they did, leaving many questions unanswered and many avenues unexplored, as we will see as this chapter evolves. The conventional explanation of the hierarchy's response to the problem of sexual abuse in the Catholic Church has become a theory of "cover-up"—a theory the simplicity of which is intuitively compelling and socially supported. However this theory also requires further scholarly analysis.

The gap in the data on this topic is important, as the data on which to base good analysis are hard to come by. In other organizations where there are allegations of wrongdoing, the power, boundaries, and secrecy of the organization have either restricted or completely prevented researchers from gaining access to information about leadership and decision-making (Vaughan, 1997, p. 36). I am not sure if scholars have been interested in undertaking research on decision-making in the Catholic Church up until now or if they have been similarly prevented from gaining access, but at any rate, little scholarship that includes the perspective of the decision-makers exists on this topic. The information that is available on the Church's handling of abuse complaints is at best a partial record of what took place, and much of the current analysis is constrained by data that are as yet untapped or missing. Similar to what Vaughan discovered in reports on other organizations, I suspect that there are critical conversations never recorded and critical individuals not fully consulted (including bishops now accused of failing children); problems with recall and memory by many of the individuals whose work is under microscopic and public scrutiny, including Church leaders, health and medical personnel, and members of the legal and criminal justice system; and perhaps even documents undiscovered or missing. When we add to this the pressures, relationships, norms, and moral climate that often typify human organizations and in which public inquiries and Commissions of Investigation are conducted, I think we can glimpse the reasons for being cautious in our current interpretations and for believing that the final word has not yet been written on the Church's handling of abuse complaints.

We can also only imagine the effect of being personally involved and implicated in the trauma that childhood sexual abuse has brought for so many individuals and in being part of the leadership of the Catholic Church that is charged with contributing to this problem. It is difficult to assess the effects of this trauma on all of the key participants—the victims, the perpetrators, their families, the Church leaders, and the general community—as the post-abuse accounts are being told. However, from my work with abuse victims, abuse perpetrators, and a number of bishops involved in the situation, it is clear to me that the post-abuse accounting period is extremely traumatic for most people associated with it, in different ways.

In this chapter, I revisit some of the questions raised in relation to the response of the Catholic hierarchy to child sexual abuse since the 1960s. To facilitate this discussion I draw on a number of Irish reports and sources, such as three government-commissioned reports into the handling of sexual abuse by the Church hierarchy in Ireland (Ferns Report, 2005; Murphy Report, 2009; Ryan Report, 2009); a number of official reports from the United States (Office of the Attorney General, Commonwealth of Massachusetts, 2003; Office of the Attorney General, New Hampshire, 2003; Office of the Grand Jury, Philadelphia, 2005, 2011; State of Maine, Office of the Attorney, 2004; Suffolk County Supreme Court Special Grand Jury, 2002; Westchester County Grand Jury, 2002); two studies that involved first-person interviews with bishops in relation to their handling of abuse complaints, one in the United States (Balboni, 1998) and one in Ireland (Goode, McGee, & O'Boyle, 2003); the work of the *Boston Globe* investigative journalists into the handling of abuse complaints in the Archdiocese of Boston (*Boston Globe*, 2002); and the work of Bishop Geoffrey Robinson (2007), who was appointed in 1994 by the Australian bishops to a position of leadership in responding to revelations of abuse in the Australian Catholic Church, a position he held for 9 years. Other works are consulted as necessary. I also draw on my professional experience in this field. My attempt in this chapter is to restore social context to this issue and to raise some questions about the conventional interpretations that are reified in current explanations. My suggestion is that the decision-making processes used in the Catholic Church in relation to handling the abuse problem are more complex than the published accounts or media representations suggest. My concern is that in isolating individuals from their systemic context as the objects of blame, further injustices may be perpetrated this time in the name of justice.

THE IRISH CHURCH RESPONSE TO SEXUAL ABUSE FROM THE 1990S

The Irish Catholic Church comprises 26 dioceses, each managed by a bishop; in larger dioceses, auxiliary bishops in the past were appointed to support the bishop's work (sometimes today Vicars are appointed to support the bishop rather than auxiliaries). In Ireland until recent times there were 32 bishops in total. Although the Republic of Ireland comprises 26 counties and there are 6 Northern counties that are under British rule, for the purposes of the Catholic Church, the entire island of Ireland functions as the Irish Catholic Church. Northern and Southern bishops come together in the Irish Episcopal Conference. In line with the structure of the Catholic Church, each bishop functions independently of the others. In addition, there are a number of religious orders that come under the auspices of the Conference of Religious of Ireland (CORI) and some religious orders come together as the Irish Missionary Union (IMU).

While the evidence suggests that there were problems with clerical abuse of minors dating back to the 1960s and before, in Ireland, in the early 1990s the Irish Catholic hierarchy began to address the problem of sexual abuse in the Catholic Church in a more concerted manner than they had done previously, partly influenced by events in the United States. In the early 1990s they set up an expert committee to offer advice on guidelines for the protection of children within each diocese. The results of these deliberations were published in *Child Sexual Abuse: Framework for a Church Response* (Irish Catholic Bishops Advisory Committee on Child Sexual Abuse by Priests and Religious, 1996). This document became known as the Framework Document, and a committee was set up with an Episcopal chairperson in 1996 to consider any issues relevant to its implementation. The idea was that the document would guide the practices of the Irish bishops and the religious leaders in all matters relating to victims of abuse, child protection, and clerical offenders. The Framework Document included the recommendation that all sexual abuse allegations regarding Catholic clergy would be referred to the civil authorities.

However, when the document was sent to Rome for ratification, some problems arose. According to one senior cleric, who was Chancellor of the Archdiocese of Dublin: "Rome had reservations about its policy of reporting to the civil authorities. The basis of the reservation was that the making of a report put the reputation and good name of a priest at risk" (Murphy Report, 2009, p. 122). A second senior cleric, who was also once Chancellor of the Archdiocese of Dublin, stated that "the Congregation for the Clergy in Rome had studied the document in detail and emphasized to the Irish bishops that it must conform to the canonical norms in force" (p. 122). According to the Monsignor, the Congregation found that "the text contains procedures and dispositions which are contrary to canonical discipline. In particular 'mandatory reporting' gives rise to serious reservations of both a moral and a canonical nature" (p. 122). The Monsignor said that the Congregation regarded the document "as merely a study document" (p. 122).

In 1999, the implementation committee was replaced by a new one on child abuse, chaired by a different Episcopal chairman, Bishop Eamonn Walsh. The principal role of this committee was to liaise with the Government's Commission to Inquire into Child Abuse in the Religious-run Institutions, which had been forecast by the Government at the time. The committee was also instrumental in establishing a Child Protection Office for the Irish Bishops' Conference in July 2001, which would serve all dioceses in Ireland and Northern Ireland. CORI also established a National Child Protection Office to help the religious congregations who were members of CORI in their responses to child sexual abuse by religious in Ireland. In 2003 the Archdiocese of Dublin set up its own Child Protection Office, independent of the Child Protection Service of the Bishops' Conference. The Archdiocese said it required its own structures because of the size of the Archdiocese. In 2001, Bishop Walsh's committee on child abuse commissioned an independent study to examine the psychological, social, and faith impact of child sexual abuse by clergy in Ireland, the experiences of disclosure, and the Church's response, and to make recommendations for its future management. The results of the study were published in *Time to Listen* (Goode, McGee, & O'Boyle, 2003). The Irish Episcopal Conference and two religious orders also made a financial contribution towards the costs involved in conducting research with clerical perpetrators.[1]

However, while progress was being made at some levels in attending to the abuse problem in the Irish Catholic Church by these interventions, and the Church's main activity focused on the responses to abuse disclosures and the management of the problem, the tsunami of complaints continued to pour in, and many contained accounts of the inadequate handling of child sexual abuse complaints by the Church authorities years earlier. The screening of several television documentaries, the public testimonies of victims and survivors who had been abused as children by clerics, and the public outcry that followed propelled the Catholic hierarchy into further action. Among other things, the hierarchy was accused of continuing to deny the extent of the problem and of responding to the problem only when they were under pressure from the media to do so—an accusation that had some validity. In April 2002, in a proactive move, the Irish Bishops' Conference announced a nationwide independent audit into the handling of all complaints of child sexual abuse by diocesan priests or religious in diocesan appointments dating back to 1940. Judge Gillian Hussey was appointed to chair the audit. This was an important initiative, and Judge Hussey appointed a robust committee to help her in such an important undertaking. Had the work of this committee been completed as a forthright attempt to examine and address the extent of the problem, it might have helped restore some credibility to the leaders of the Church in Ireland. However, in December 2002 the work on this audit ceased suddenly with a statement from Judge Hussey that the work of her committee was terminating. Around this time the Irish Minister for Justice, Equality and Law Reform announced that he was preparing legislation that would provide a statutory basis for a new mechanism to investigate matters of significant and urgent public importance. Judge Hussey suggested that as such a scheme would include the handling of clerical sexual abuse, she believed her audit would be duplicating the work of the State. Terminating the audit was in my view one of the biggest mistakes that the Catholic Church in Ireland made at this time. We still do not have the data on the extent of the problem of sexual abuse by clergy in Ireland; data that are emerging much more slowly on "the drip" system. It was not until 2004 that the Government's new legislation was enacted as the *Commission of Investigation Act* 2004, and not until 2006 that a Commission of Investigation was announced under this legislation into the handling of abuse complaints in the Catholic Archdiocese of Dublin, which reported in 2009.

In 2005, the Irish Bishops' Conference, CORI, and the IMU joined together and commissioned another study into child protection and the handling of abuse complaints, this time to provide a comprehensive and unified approach to child protection across the Catholic Church in Ireland, including the dioceses, religious orders and the Irish missionary unions. It was realized that a unified one-Church approach to dealing with child sexual abuse was required, as the Church leadership knew they would continually be judged by the behavior of its weakest member. Known as the Lynott Committee, the findings were reported in *Our Children, Our Church* (Irish Bishops' Conference et al., 2005). This document would replace *Child Sexual Abuse: Framework for a Church Response* (Irish Catholic Bishops Advisory Committee on Child Sexual Abuse by Priests and Religious, 1996) as the guiding document on child protection for the Church in Ireland.

In 2006 the three commissioning bodies (Bishops' Conference, CORI, IMU) appointed a Board of Child Protection, headed by a retired judge, to oversee the implementation of child protection services across the Catholic Church in Ireland. This committee led to the closure of the two existing national child protection offices (the one for the Episcopal Conference and the one for CORI) and the development of a new service including child protection, to be known as the National Board for Safeguarding Children. Yet another new set of guidelines and protocols for the handling of abuse complaints were introduced by the National Board for Safeguarding Children in 2009, replacing or displacing *Our Children Our Church* (2005). This time, in line with similar developments in the United Kingdom and the United States, all Church authorities who wished to be part of this child safeguarding policy had to sign a commitment that they would implement the policy. In a new departure, the names of those Church authorities who failed to sign the commitment would be made public, as would the failure of any Church authority to comply with the policies that might be uncovered in periodic audits. In adopting this new procedure the Catholic Church approved a policy of "name-and-shame" as the way to ensure compliance with "best practice." The Church in Ireland also made some improvements in the seminary programs based on the initiatives announced by the Vatican on the use of psychology in screening and preparing candidates for the priesthood (Congregation for Catholic Education, 2008).

In 1997, the religious orders also established a free Helpline and face-to-face counseling service for survivors of abuse, with some funding from some bishops, which was known as Faoiseamh. Between 1997 and 2011 the Faoiseamh Counselling Service provided face-to-face counseling to nearly 4000 persons as well as providing Helpline support to over 15000 survivors of clerical and religious abuse. In 2011 this service was replaced by a new Towards Healing service which was established following consultation between the Irish Catholic Bishops' Conference, CORI, the IMU, Faoiseamh and Survivor Groups. The new service was designed to ensure that survivors of clerical and religious abuse receive counseling and other support services in a more holistic manner than heretofore. The funding of this new service now involves an arrangement between the Bishops' Conference, CORI and the IMU (Irish Catholic Bishops' Conference, 2011).

IRISH STATE RESPONSES TO THE CHURCH HANDLING OF SEXUAL ABUSE

In 2000 the Irish Government established the Commission to Inquire into Child Abuse to investigate the abuse of children in institutions run by the religious orders on behalf of the State. Two different pieces of legislation, the *Commission to Inquire into Child Abuse Act* (2000) and the *Commission to Inquire into Child Abuse (Amendment) Act* (2005), gave the Commission its powers. The Government also initiated a "redress scheme" under the *Residential Institutions Redress Act* (2002) to financially compensate the victims of the residential institutions. In 2002, following public outcry about sexual abuse in the Diocese of Ferns, an inquiry was set up into the handling of abuse complaints by the Church hierarchy and the statutory authorities in the Diocese of Ferns. The Ferns Inquiry presented its findings in 2005. In 2006, a State commission was established to investigate the handling of abuse complaints in the Archdiocese of Dublin. The Commission's work was framed by the *Commissions of Investigation Act* 2004, a new piece of legislation designed to find an efficient and cost-effective means of conducting public inquiries in Ireland. The Dublin Commission presented its findings in November 2009, also known as the Murphy Report. Another commission of inquiry in the Diocese of Cloyne, reported in 2011, amid calls for the Government to extend the work of the commissions of inquiry to all Catholic dioceses in Ireland.

In what follows I will outline some of the key findings of three of the four Irish commissions of inquiry/investigation into the handling of sexual abuse complaints by the Catholic hierarchy, and I also offer some commentary on the commissions and their work. As undertaking a comprehensive scholarly analysis of these reports would be beyond the scope of the current project and would involve revisiting the original data and the participants, what I raise in this chapter are merely questions about some of the interpretations that the commissions made on the basis of the available data. My argument is that while the Irish commissions of inquiry put details of sexual abuse by clergy and the handling of such abuses by the Church hierarchy into the public domain in a manner not done previously, thus vindicating the victims' accounts of their experiences and offering the Irish people and the Catholic Church much to consider about themselves and their history, the Ferns and Murphy reports in particular failed to show the diversity of views amongst many of the participants, primarily the professionals involved and the Church hierarchy and the effects of their distinctive social locations on their understandings. What this diversity can reveal when executed carefully is not untruths but multiple meanings, and thus multiple truths depending on where one is located in the social system. In the Ferns (2005) and Murphy (2009) reports in particular, such critical work is not included in the frame of analysis, leading both more in the direction of leveling blame than in the direction of critical understanding. One of the serious limitations of the these reports is their failure to offer a comparative analysis of child protection practices in other domains in Ireland during the relevant period. The Ryan Report (2009), on the other hand, represents a much more comprehensive undertaking and for the first time in Ireland produced substantial evidence as to the existence and extent of child abuse in its broadest terms (including physical, sexual, and emotional abuse and neglect) of Ireland's children of the poor in the child-care institutions of the 20th century. However, there are other aspects of the Ryan Report that warrant further scholarly analysis, but that is beyond the scope of my particular contribution.

The Ferns Inquiry

The Ferns Inquiry, chaired by Mr. Justice Francis D. Murphy, a former judge of the Supreme Court, identified approximately 100 complaints against 21 priests operating under the aegis of the Diocese of Ferns, in a period of approximately 40 years up to 2002 (Ferns Report, 2005, p. 2). It investigated the work of three bishops during this time. It found that prior to 1980, one bishop removed two priests against whom allegations of abuse had been made "without taking steps to protect other children from the dangers which the priests presented" (p. 250). The men were sent to a diocese in England without the authorities there being told of the men's histories. It found that the bishop regarded the priests who abused children as guilty of moral misconduct but did not appear to have recognized the wrongdoing as a serious criminal offense (p. 250). It found that neither the medical and health care community nor the bishop appreciated the damage that child sexual abuse can cause to its victims. It found the bishop's decision to restore the two offending priests to their former positions after a 2-year period of "penance" to be ill advised: "To do so without supervision or monitoring was neither adequate nor appropriate" (p. 250). Both perpetrators went on to subsequently abuse further children. The inquiry also found that even when allegations of sexual abuse were made against two seminarians, the men were accepted for ordination. When these two men abused again after ordination and the bishop sent them for assessment (reflecting the developing understanding of the nature of child sexual abuse), he failed to act on the reports. The inquiry concluded that the bishop felt bound to appoint any priest ordained for his diocese to a curacy, regardless of his suitability (p. 251).

In the case of a second bishop who replaced the first in 1984, the report concluded that this bishop sent offending clergy, or those who had aroused suspicions about their propensities to abuse children, to a psychologist or psychiatrist for assessment and treatment if necessary (p. 251), and they praised this development. However, they noted that the bishop was "unable or unwilling to implement the medical advice which he received" when it came to the priests' fitness to practice (p. 251). The inquiry also uncovered evidence to suggest that the bishop had not given the medical experts the full history of priests against whom previous allegations had been made (p. 251). What is of course key here, but something to which we do not know the answer, is the bishop's account of why he took such action, and whether his motivation was to deliberately mislead the assessing practitioner or whether some other motivation guided this practice. By the late 1980s the bishop was also of the view that the appropriate response to an allegation of child sexual abuse was to have the accused priest step aside from active ministry, pending a determination of the allegation made against him. However, the report suggests that the bishop was consistently unable to achieve this objective (p. 251).

While acknowledging that the bishop dealt with some very difficult clergy who were unwilling to follow his requests to step aside, in the majority of cases the inquiry found that the bishop failed to remove these men, due to his conviction that "it would be unjust to remove a priest on the basis of an allegation that was not corroborated or substantiated by what he considered to be convincing evidence" (p. 251). The report notes the bishop believed "that he could not and should not take an action which would necessarily damage the repu-tation of one of his priests without convincing evidence of their guilt" (pp. 254–255). In any event, the report concluded that "he did not prioritise child protection in his response" (p. 255). The report noted that the bishop was "rightly conscious of the need to protect the good name and reputation of his clergy but he failed to recognise the paramount need to protect children as a matter of urgency, from potential abusers" (p. 251). It also noted that "using Canon Law to force a priest to step aside from active ministry was difficult in circum-stances where that law was unclear and untried" (p. 254). Despite the context and the difficul-ties involved in these situations, the bishop was seen to have failed and to have put children at risk. He resigned in 2002, prior to the publication of the Ferns Report, following a television documentary regarding the handling of sexual abuse complaints in the Diocese of Ferns.

In the case of the third bishop, who was appointed as the Apostolic Administrator of the Diocese of Ferns in 2002, after the resignation of the previous bishop, the inquiry found that this bishop was prepared to ask a priest to step aside from active ministry where he had a "reasonable suspicion" that a child had been abused (p. 252). While rumor or suspicion ema-nating from a single source might not in itself be sufficient grounds for this action, the bishop said he would note it and if he received any further information of untoward behavior on the part of the priest, he would act immediately. The inquiry found that seven of the eight priests whom the bishop asked to stand aside did so. The one priest who refused to do so, following an application by the bishop to Rome, was the subject of a dismissal. While the inquiry noted this action as the bishop not having to involve his powers under canon law to stand aside a priest from active ministry, the bishop nonetheless used some powers to apply to Rome for the man's dismissal. It was beginning to be clear that Vatican policy on dismissal was changing since 2001, when previously the only route to censure was the cumbersome canonical trial, which was now being replaced by other swifter routes to censure that were being authorized by the Congregation for the Doctrine of the Faith, which took over the management of child sexual abuse cases in 2001.

Overall, the Ferns Report (2005, p. 256) noted that since the appointment of the Apostolic Administrator to the Diocese of Ferns in 2002, the approach to the problem of sexual abuse by clergy in the Diocese of Ferns and the responses to it reflected a more efficient manage-ment of the diocese, as well as a clearer understanding on the part of the clergy of the need to respond promptly and efficiently to allegations of child sexual abuse. The report included much commentary on the management of the diocese. For example, it praised the new record-keeping system and suggested that the failure of previous successive bishops to create and preserve proper records of allegations of child sexual abuse in the past had prevented them from being able to access important information about priests and therefore of being able to manage well. It also found that the failure to operate a transparent complaints proce-dure for members of the public wishing to express child protection concerns regarding a priest of the diocese had also been a problem in the past. This was corrected since 2002. The Church authorities or those acting on their behalf in the diocese now provided more sympa-thetic listening to people making allegations of misconduct against their colleagues than they had done in the past.

The inquiry believed that a culture of secrecy, fear of causing scandal, and a lack of under-standing of the dynamics of child sexual abuse within the Catholic Church had prevented clergy in the past from identifying and passing on information about child sexual abuse to their superiors and the civil authorities, and all of this was now being corrected (Ferns Report, 2005, p. 256). It found that Church and State response to allegations or suspicions of child sexual abuse "developed over the period of time considered by this Inquiry" (p. 254). In 2009, following the publication of the Murphy Report (2009) into the handling of abuse complaints in the Archdiocese of Dublin, the bishop who had been the Apostolic Administrator in Ferns and who was so highly praised for his work by the Ferns Inquiry Team was forced to tender his resignation following extensive media pressure to do so for his part as an auxiliary bishop in the Archdiocese of Dublin, when complaints of child sexual abuse were mishandled many years earlier. In 2010 the Pope declined to accept the bishop's offer of resignation (see Allen, 2010d, for further discussion on Episcopal resignations). A priest of the Ferns Diocese died by suicide in March 1999 just before facing charges relating to the sexual abuse of minors.

The Commission to Inquire into Child Abuse in Ireland

The Commission to Inquire into Child Abuse was established in 2000 to investigate the abuse of children in institutions run by the religious orders on behalf of the Irish State. Part of its remit was concerned with establishing whether abuse had occurred, and the nature and scale of that abuse. Eighteen religious orders were involved in this commission's inquiry. A feature of the Irish State since its foundation has been the involvement of the religious orders in developing and running social and welfare services for the Irish people, some on behalf of the State. These include schools, hospitals, child-care facilities, and facilities for the physically and mentally disabled. Mrs. Justice Laffoy, the first chairman of the commission, resigned in 2003 in controversial circumstances of tension between the Commission and the Government (Reid, 2003). The new chairperson, Mr. Sean Ryan, SC, who has since been promoted to the rank of judge, took over the chair of the commission in 2003. The report of this commission's work is hereafter referred to as the Ryan Report (2009).

The Ryan commission examined an extensive range of documents, consulted with experts, and held oral sessions in which witnesses gave testimony in private to a confidential committee or publicly to an investigation committee. Witnesses who gave evidence included many of the former residents of the institutions who could choose to give evidence to a Confidential or an Investigative Committee, as well as some of the staff or former staff, and the current leadership of the named religious orders. While the Ryan commission also investigated physical and emotional abuse and neglect of the children of the institutions, I will confine my commentary to those findings relating to sexual abuse primarily, as this is most relevant to the current discussion.

The confidential committee heard 1,090 witness reports relating to the period between 1914 and 2000, of which 23 referred to abuse experienced prior to the 1930s or after the 1990s (Ryan Report, 2009, Vol. 3, pp. 12–13). Witnesses who attended hearings with the confidential committee chose to give their evidence in confidence, and their evidence was uncontested. Approximately half of all the confidential committee witnesses reported experiences of sexual abuse (p. 13). In some instances it occurred only once, but in other cases the abuse was more prolonged and chronic. The secretive nature of the abuse was continually emphasized by the witnesses, who described contact and non-contact sexual abuse by religious and lay staff, by other boys and co-residents, and by professionals and others, both within and external to the institutions. The "others" included volunteer workers, visitors, work placement employers, foster parents, and others who had unsupervised contact with the children and young people in the course of everyday events. Some witnesses said that when they disclosed abuse they were subjected to severe reproach by those who had responsibility for their care and protection. Female witnesses in particular described being told that they were responsible for the sexual abuse they experienced, both by their abuser and by those to whom they disclosed the abuse (p. 13).

Putting the evidence from the confidential committee and the investigation committee together, the Ryan Report (2009, Vol. 4, p. 19) arrived at a number of conclusions. The report concluded that physical and emotional abuse and neglect of children were features of the institutions. Sexual abuse occurred in many of them, particularly those relating to boys. Schools were run in a severe and regimented manner that imposed unreasonable demands and oppressive discipline on the children and staff. The large-scale institutionalization that was a response to a 19th-century way of viewing certain problems (in some cases relating to the children of the poor) was outdated and incapable of meeting the needs of children. The defects of the system were exacerbated by the way in which the congregations managed them. It noted a culture of deference in Ireland during the period, which manifested itself in the deferential and submissive attitude of the Department of Education towards the congregations who were in charge of running the institutions. In effect, this deferential attitude compromised the Department's statutory duty to inspect and monitor the schools and how they were being managed.

The Ryan Report (2009, p. Vol. 3, p. 21) concluded that sexual abuse was endemic in boys' institutions. The situation in girls' institutions was different, and although girls were sexually abused by male employees or other outside visitors, sexual abuse was not systemic in girls' institutions. In boys' institutions, perpetrators of abuse were able to operate undetected for long periods, sometimes at the core of the institution. The report concluded that cases of sexual abuse were managed with a view to the risk of public disclosure and consequent damage to the reputation of the institution and the congregation. This policy resulted in protection of the perpetrator. Importantly, the report concluded that laypeople who were discovered to have sexually abused children were reported to the police, but congregation members who were found to be abusing were dealt with internally. The difference in treatment of lay and religious perpetrators led the commission to believe that in one congregation, the congregational authorities were aware of the seriousness of the offense of child sexual abuse and of its criminal parameters, yet there was a reluctance to confront religious who offended in this way (p. 21). On occasions when the Department of Education was informed, it colluded in the silence (Ryan Report, 2009, Vol. 3, p. 23).

The congregations asserted that during the period of the inquiry, knowledge of sexual abuse was not as available in society as it is today, and that sexual abuse and the priest's or brother's sexual acts with children were seen as a moral failing on his part. The commission did not accept this explanation, in the light of the above. One particular congregation also had on file documents relating to long-term offenders who often repeatedly abused children wherever they were working. The response of the religious authorities to evidence of sexual abuse was to transfer the offender to another location, where in many instances he re-offended. The commission believed that the congregation was concerned about the potential for scandal and the bad publicity that would ensue should such abuse become public knowledge.

The Ryan Commission presented evidence to suggest that although sexual abuse was known by the religious authorities to be a persistent problem in male religious organizations throughout the relevant period, "every instance was treated in isolation and in secrecy by the authorities and there was no attempt to address the underlying systemic nature of the problem" (Ryan Report, 2009, p. Vol. 3, p. 22). The commission found that authoritarian management systems prevented staff from disclosing sexual abuse where it might be known, and this served to perpetuate abuse. It also found that when older boys sexually abused younger boys the system did not deal well with the issue, and the victims were punished as severely as the perpetrators, inevitably leading to conditions in which boys learned to suffer in silence rather than report the abuse and face punishment. The sexual abuse of girls was generally taken seriously by the religious sisters. Lay staff members who perpetrated sexual abuse were dismissed when the abuses were discovered. Girls who experienced sexual abuse were more likely to be abused when they visited host families for holidays or visits. Like many victims of childhood sexual abuse during this period, the children did not feel able to report the abuses for fear of disbelief and punishment.

Commission of Investigation Report into the Catholic Archdiocese of Dublin

Following several television documentaries discussing abuse by clergy and following intensive lobbying by victims and survivors of abuse, the Dublin Archdiocese Commission of Investigation was established in 2006 to report on the handling by the Irish Church and State of a representative sample of allegations and suspicions of child sexual abuse against clerics operating under the aegis of the Archdiocese of Dublin over the period 1975 to 2004. The commission was chaired by Judge Yvonne Murphy, a judge of the Circuit Court. This commission was different from the Ryan Commission in that while the Ryan Commission was concerned with establishing whether abuse had occurred and the nature and scale of that abuse, the Murphy Commission had no such remit. Notwithstanding this fact, the report states that "it is abundantly clear, from the Commission's investigation as revealed in the cases of the 46 priests in the representative sample, that child sexual abuse by clerics was widespread" (p. 2). The commission received information about complaints, suspicions, or knowledge of child sexual abuse pertaining to 172 named priests and 11 unnamed priests during the relevant period. Of these priests, 102 came under the commission's remit. It sampled 46 cases and did an in-depth investigation into approximately 320 complaints against these priests. During the relevant period there were four archbishops in the Dublin archdiocese and six auxiliary bishops, all of whose work came under the remit of the commission.

The commission suggested that in 1981, the then Archbishop of Dublin had "a clear understanding of both the recidivist nature of child sexual abusers and the effects of such abuse on children" when he referred a priest to a treatment facility in the United Kingdom (Murphy Report, 2009, p. 6). It suggested that all the archbishops and auxiliary bishops in Dublin in the period covered by the commission were aware of some complaints of child sexual abuse against clergy. Some of the officials who worked in the chancellery also knew of the fact of abuse from the early 1980s. The commission also found that when priests knew of instances of abuse that had occurred "the vast majority simply chose to turn a blind eye" (p. 7), a finding with which many priests simply disagree. The commission heavily criticized the bishops and auxiliary bishops of the archdiocese, apart from the current office holder who was appointed in 2004. The commission found that despite the participation of the previous bishops and the named auxiliary bishops in civil society and the fact that some of them held civil and canonical legal qualifications, it was only in 1995 that officials in the Archdiocese of Dublin first began to notify the civil authorities and the police of complaints of child sexual abuse against its priests. The report did not contextualize this finding in relation to reporting practices in other organizations and institutions in Ireland for child sexual offenses during the relevant period.

In relation to canon law, the commission reported that there were varying interpretations and conflicting opinions on canon law rules in relation to child sexual abuse within the archdiocese, and in effect canon law appears to have fallen into disuse and disrespect during the mid-20th century (Murphy Report, 2009, pp. 7–8). The commission found, however, that those aspects of canon law that were of concern to many of the officials were the provisions that dealt with "secrecy" (p. 8). One manifestation of this concern was the refusal of the officials of the archdiocese to acknowledge or recognize an allegation of child sexual abuse unless it was made in strong and explicit terms. The Murphy team suggested that in one case where a bishop heard of suspicions regarding a priest's behavior, the bishop did not take the steps of asking the complainant precisely what was involved, nor did he go to the priest for information (p. 8). Why the bishop took such action or failed to take other action raises important questions that require further analysis.

In relation to the handling of the clerical perpetrators, the Murphy Report (2009) suggested that offending priests were moved around to different ministries with little or no disclosure of their past offending. Why this policy prevailed in so many cases also requires unpacking; the "cover up" theory currently prevails. Some perpetrators were sent for assessment and therapy. However, in terms of the management of the problem within the archdiocese, the commission suggested that the problem as a whole did not seem to have been discussed openly by the archbishop and his auxiliaries until the 1990s. For most of the time covered by the commission's remit, they suggested there was nothing resembling a management structure (p. 15) and there was poor communication between the archbishop and his auxiliaries. According to the commission, the auxiliary bishops appeared to have had a role akin to that of deputy chief executives of a company, but they did not have the clarity of responsibility or power that such a position would normally entail (p. 15). It is not clear what this finding means in terms of the culpability or responsibility therefore of the auxiliaries. Neither is it made precisely clear how decisions were made within the archdiocese and the dynamics of the relationships that existed between the relevant archbishops and the auxiliaries.

The Murphy Commission came to the conclusion that all the archbishops and many of the auxiliary bishops in the Archdiocese of Dublin handled complaints of child sexual abuse badly in the period covered by the commission's work (p. 10). It found that at least until the mid-1990s, the archdiocese was preoccupied with "the maintenance of secrecy, the avoidance of scandal, the protection of the reputation of the Church, and the preservation of its assets. All other considerations, including the welfare of children and justice for victims, were subordinated to these priorities" (p. 10). The report stated that "[c]omplainants were often met with denial, arrogance and cover-up and with incompetence and incomprehension in some cases" (p. 10). Like the Diocese of Ferns, the Murphy Report found evidence that the Archdiocese of Dublin improved its practices in responding to child sexual abuse from the start of the implementation of the Church's Framework Document in 1996.

Although it took some time for the structures and procedures to be fully implemented, the situation improved considerably in 2003 with the establishment of the Child Protection Service. In the Cloyne Report (2011) which was published in the days just prior to this book going to press it was noted that the Church's own guidelines on responding to and reporting abuse had not been complied with in that diocese.

Following the publication of the Murphy Report, four of the auxiliary bishops named in the report offered their resignation, and one retired bishop who had some pastoral duties within the archdiocese was stepped aside by the current Archbishop of Dublin. One former auxiliary, now a bishop in another diocese, refused to offer his resignation, and one retired cardinal, who was an archbishop in the Archdiocese of Dublin during the period covered by the Murphy Report (2009), had no change in his status. In an interesting turn of events, the Pope accepted the offer of resignation of two of the former auxiliary bishops and refused to accept the offer of resignation of two others. It is not clear why the Pontiff took this approach to the offers of resignation. Unsurprisingly, that decision was not received well by the victims' groups, who felt that by rejecting the resignations of the two bishops, the Pope was "rubbing more salt into already deep and still fresh wounds of thousands of child sex abuse victims and millions of betrayed Catholics" (Blaine, 2010). The decision was not received well either by the Irish media, who felt that the decision was sending contradictory messages and that it undermined the authority of the current Archbishop of Dublin, who had been very vocal in voicing his anger over how sexual abuse had been handled in the past by his Episcopal colleagues.[2]

Fallout from the Commissions of Investigation in Ireland

The scale of the sexual abuse uncovered in the Ferns Report (2005), the Ryan Report (2009), the Murphy Report (2009) and the Cloyne Report (2011) is extreme, both in depth and in detail, and it is clear that children suffered greatly. They and their parents did not feel heard or responded to well by the Church leaders. There were also consistencies in the pattern of responses to abuse complaints by the leadership of the Catholic Church in Ireland. Also some priests in the Dublin Archdiocese and the Diocese of Ferns were accused of abusing very few individuals (although any abuse is one too many) and a smaller number of priests were accused of, or admitted to, abusing larger numbers of children. This pattern is also reported by the John Jay College report (2004, 2006, 2011) regarding abuse by Catholic clergy in the United States.

Since the publication of these reports in Ireland, there has been an outpouring of public outrage and anger, and the topic of sexual abuse within the Catholic Church is never far off the public agenda. The Irish people found various outlets to give expression to their outrage, such as participating in radio and television programs, writing in newspapers, organizing protests at the residence of the Papal Nuncio, protesting at gatherings of the Episcopal Conference, setting up a website to help individuals to decommission their membership of the Catholic Church, and organizing a boycott of Mass. Victims of sexual abuse by Catholic clergy also received rewards from various organizations for their bravery and public service in bringing the abuses to light.

Following the publication of the Ryan Report (2009) and the public outcry that followed, all of the 18 named religious orders entered into ongoing negotiation with the Government to increase their share of the contribution towards monetary redress for former residents of institutions run by the congregations. Under a 2002 indemnity agreement, the congregations had contributed €128 million towards the Government's redress scheme, but in the outcry that followed the publication of the Ryan Report and the negotiations that followed, it is understood that the total amount so far offered by the congregations is €348.51 million, in addition to their initial contribution (McGarry, 2010c). Latest reports suggest the Irish Government is seeking a further €200 million from the congregations in addition to what they have already offered (McGarry, 2010c). The final cost of the response to residential institutional abuse is estimated to reach €1.36 billion (McGarry, 2010c). The Irish Government plans to set up a statutory fund of €110 million for former residents of the institutions.

The findings of the Murphy Report (2009) created tensions within the leadership of the Archdiocese of Dublin and within the Irish Episcopal Conference itself. The position taken by the Archbishop of Dublin in accepting unequivocally the findings of the Murphy Report, a stance applauded by the Irish media and large sections of the Irish public, was not seen in the same light by many of his Episcopal colleagues. It was suggested by a retired auxiliary bishop of Dublin that the Archbishop of Dublin was unfair in his criticism of the bishops. "You were out of the Diocese for thirty-one years and had no idea how traumatic it was for those of us who had to deal with allegations without protocols or guidelines or experience in the matter of child sexual abuse," he said (for full coverage see O'Sullivan, 2010, p. 1). The retired auxiliary bishop had a point here in suggesting how easy it is for bishops and senior clerics who were not involved in managing cases of child sexual abuse to judge those who were, and in doing so to point the finger of blame at individuals. As the current Archbishop of Dublin fell into this category, his condemnation of the bishops was particularly hurtful, although the Archbishop's stance in general on child sexual abuse within the Catholic Church has been singled out by commentators as "remarkably free of the defensive and excuse-ridden responses that we have heard in the United States for more than two decades" (*National Catholic Reporter*, 2010b). While it is true that the current Archbishop of Dublin has been particularly outspoken in his commentary on the wrongs of the past, and in his support and compassion for survivors and it is important never to forget past failings, by singling out individuals for blame when the problem is clearly one of institutional and systemic proportions, it could well be that the Archbishop himself is failing to grasp the full extent of the problem in all of its systemic dimensions. It may well be that all the participants in this sorry tale need to be met with compassion and understanding.

DOCUMENTS ON THE ROLE OF THE VATICAN

On Jan. 17, 2011, the Irish national broadcaster RTE aired a television documentary, *Would You Believe,* in which the reporter, Mick Peelo, revealed documents to show how the Vatican blocked the Irish bishops' efforts to improve child protection and bring clerical men who had abused minors to justice in Ireland. Peelo also argued that members of the Vatican were every bit as inept in their own handling of abuse as those Irish bishops who now stand accused. In his letter to the Irish Catholics in 2010 Pope Benedict XVI blamed the Irish bishops for their mishandling of "unspeakable crimes" by priests. The role of the Vatican was not even mentioned. I took part in this RTE documentary, and I have seen the following documents to which Peelo refers.

On Jan. 31, 1997, a strictly confidential letter was sent to the members of the Irish Episcopal Conference from the Apostolic Nuncio, Luciano Storero. The letter said that the Congregation for the Clergy attentively studied the complex question of sexual abuse of minors by clerics and the document *Child Sexual Abuse: Framework for a Church Response,* which had been published by the Irish Bishops' Advisory Committee in 1996. The congregation emphasized to the Irish bishops that the text of the Framework Document (1996) contained "procedures and dispositions which appear contrary to canonical discipline and which, if applied, could invalidate the acts of the same bishops who are attempting to put a stop to these problems. If such procedures were to be followed by the bishops and there were cases of eventual hierarchical recourse lodged at the Holy See, the results could be highly embarrassing and detrimental to those same Diocesan authorities." The letter went on to suggest that the issue of mandatory reporting gave rise to serious reservations of both "a moral and a canonical nature." The letter concluded by referring to the Framework Document (1996) as "merely a study document" and not an official document of the Episcopal Conference. The Nuncio reminded the Irish bishops that he was directed to inform the individual bishops of Ireland "of the preoccupations of the Congregation in its regard, underlying that in the sad cases of accusations of sexual abuse by clerics, the procedures established by the Code of Canon Law must be meticulously followed under pain of invalidity of the acts involved if the priest so punished were to make hierarchical recourse against his bishop."

Just when the Irish bishops were beginning to come to grips with how to deal with the clerical sexual abuse problem, Rome intervened and tried to enforce Vatican policy, as directed by the Congregation for the Clergy, which warned the Irish bishops to put the interests of the priest first. Victims were not mentioned. The *Would You Believe* documentary suggested that this letter threatened Irish bishops that if they followed their new child protection guidelines, it would support the accused priest if he were to appeal to its authority. A second letter, which I have also seen, from March 1997 reiterates the concerns of the Congregation for the Clergy: "Lacking congruence with canonical norms and other aspects of our discipline, Episcopal acts, based on the abovementioned policies and procedures could be canonically null, with consequent negative impact on the same Episcopal authority which is, at the same time, trying to deal effectively with the serious and delicate problems of sexual abuse."

The *Would You Believe* documentary disclosed that in 1998 the Cardinal Prefect for the Congregation for the Clergy, Castrillon Hoyos, and his officials came to Sligo in Ireland to meet with the Irish hierarchy. It was a difficult meeting. Peelo's information is that Cardinal Hoyos told the Irish bishops that Vatican policy was to defend the rights of the accused priest. In 1999, the Irish bishops were called to a meeting at the Congregation for the Clergy in Rome and were told by Cardinal Hoyos to be "fathers to your priests, not policemen!" While this is an important and complex matter, in the face of what they were experiencing, Peelo reported that the Irish bishops were furious at the Vatican's attitude. The Irish bishops' policies were vigorously opposed by Cardinal Hoyos, putting the Irish bishops in direct conflict with Rome. This was to result in major problems for the Irish bishops, as time has revealed.

In responding to the revelations made in the Jan. 31, 1997, letter from the Vatican to the Irish bishops, and of the interventions of Cardinal Hoyos, Father Federico Lombardi, the Vatican spokesman, defended the letter, saying it aimed to ensure that bishops fully followed

Church law for dealing with accusations against clergy so as to avoid a situation in which an abusive priest could be returned to ministry on a technicality resulting from his bishop's mishandling of the process (Wooden, 2011). Lombardi failed to point out how inadequate the then norms of canon law (Church law) had been for dealing with the problem of abuse, a situation that necessitated revision of the norms many times since 2001. Lombardi did not acknowledge the problems the Irish bishops faced at the time, and their efforts to address the problem in their Framework Document (1996). Neither did he refer to their "meetings" with Cardinal Hoyos. Lombardi also plays down the letter's concern regarding mandatory reporting, saying the concerns related to the sacrament of confession (Allen, 2001), but this is something that makes no sense in light of the problems the Framework Document (1996) was attempting to address. It is more likely the concerns mentioned in the letter refer to the priest's right to protect his good name, a point emphasized by Cardinal Hoyos in his subsequent meetings with the Irish bishops. Lombardi stated current Vatican policy, saying the Vatican makes clear to bishops that in their policies for dealing with abuse accusations "they must respect the laws of their country" (Wooden, 2011).

John Allen of the *National Catholic Reporter* (2011) was also less than sympathetic to the Irish bishops' case, arguing that it is not clear if the judgment of the Congregation for the Clergy (and therefore Cardinal Hoyos) could be considered binding Vatican policy by itself, perhaps hinting the Irish bishops were unnecessarily Vatican compliant. To support his case Allen argues that when the American sex abuse norms came up for Vatican approval in 2002, several different departments were involved in the discussions and the objections voiced by the Congregation for the Clergy did not prevail. However, in proffering such an argument Allen fails to acknowledge the significance of 2001, when the Congregation for the Doctrine of the Faith and Cardinal Joseph Ratzinger took over control of sex abuse cases. From then on Cardinal Ratzinger was to fight a battle that he would ultimately win in bringing about some changes in Vatican policy in relation to clerical sexual abuse and in so doing curtail the power of the Congregation of the Clergy in relation to sexual abuse.

The Vatican has never acknowledged its role in the problem of clerical sexual abuse in Ireland or that in 1997 it obstructed Irish bishops who were trying to deal with clerical perpetrators in difficult circumstances, trying to develop right policies and practices for responding pastorally to victims, deal justly with clerical perpetrators, and ensure that such abuses would not occur again. As one contributor to the *Would You Believe* documentary put it: "I felt they [the Irish bishops] were caught in a pincer movement, if you like, between conflicting messages . . . In a way we weren't well served by Rome in this whole situation." In effect, the Vatican intervention contributed to a culture of fear and confusion on the part of the Irish bishops, whose authority to lead their priests and dioceses could be undermined by Rome if an accused priest successfully appealed a bishop's decision to Rome, not because of insufficient evidence of abuse but on canonical or technical grounds. This point was made by Bishop Brendan Comiskey in his report to the Ferns Inquiry (1995). The *Would You Believe* documentary uncovered evidence to suggest that on at least two occasions the Vatican overturned decisions by Irish ecclesiastical tribunals that recommended laicizing abusive clerics. The program also revealed that a senior Irish bishop threatened to resign after an alleged abuser priest's appeal was upheld by the Vatican.

Would You Believe raised the question whether there was a culture within the Vatican that put the rights of abusive priests over and above the rights of victims and their families.

The documentary cites cases from the United States to suggest that even Pope Benedict himself and the current Secretary of State, Cardinal Bertone, when they led the Congregation for the Doctrine of the Faith, did exactly what the Irish bishops are today being blamed for doing: they did not follow the long-established norms of canon law (which had fallen into disuse following the Second Vatican Council, as discussed earlier), and they appeared to put the reputation of the Church and the avoidance of scandal over the concerns for the victims.

By 2001, Cardinal Ratzinger began to realize the gravity of the problem and the difficulties bishops were having with the culture within the Vatican. Over time, Cardinal Ratzinger, now Pope Benedict XVI, has taken on this issue and instituted significant changes in policy and canon law to tip the balance in favor of the victims. It may be that this balance has swung too much in another direction, compromising the rights of clergy, but that analysis is work for another day and requires a critical systemic overview of the current Church responses. The *Would You Believe* program questioned whether real and lasting renewal could happen in the Catholic Church if questions were not addressed regarding the Vatican's role in this sad, sorry saga?

The Pope's Letter to the Catholics of Ireland

In response to the Murphy Report (2009) and the Ryan Report (2009) and the public outcry that followed, Pope Benedict XVI took the step of writing a pastoral letter to the Catholic people of Ireland. Among other things, the Pope's letter contained harsh words for the Irish bishops: "It cannot be denied that some of you and your predecessors failed, at times grievously, to apply the long-established norms of Canon Law to the crime of child abuse. Serious mistakes were made in responding to allegations. I recognize how difficult it was to grasp the extent and complexity of the problem, to obtain reliable information and to make the right decisions in the light of conflicting expert advice. Nevertheless, it must be admitted that grave errors of judgment were made and failures of leadership occurred" (Pastoral letter of the Holy Father Pope Benedict XVI to the Catholics of Ireland, 2010).

What is interesting in the context of the Pope's pastoral letter to the Irish people is his failure to mention in any way the role of the Vatican or the Congregation for the Clergy or the Congregation for the Doctrine of the Faith in the handling of abuse complaints. He suggests that the failure to apply the norms of canon law lay at the feet of the Irish bishops, a finding not fully supported either by the Murphy Report (2009) or the Ferns Report (2005), which both found the provisions of canon law to be anything but clear. When Pope Benedict XVI also suggested to the Irish bishops that they needed "self-examination, inner purification and spiritual renewal" carried out with complete honesty and transparency to restore the respect and good will of the Irish people towards the Church, I am sure he could not have foreseen the intensive scrutiny that his own ministry would be subjected to regarding his handling of abuse complaints during his time as bishop of Munich (1977–1982), as Prefect for the Congregation of the Doctrine of the Faith (1982–2005), and as Pope since 2005. He was aware that pressure was mounting as the German abuse situation was already unfolding, but I am sure nobody could have foreseen the extent to which the pressure would mount on the Pope personally.

Neither could anyone have foreseen the statement that would be made by the Taoiseach of Ireland (Prime Minister) in the Irish Dáil (Parliament) on July 20th in responding to a motion on the report of the Commission of Investigation into the Catholic Diocese of

Cloyne (2011). "The revelations of the Cloyne report have brought the Government, Irish Catholics and the Vatican to an unprecedented juncture. It's fair to say that after the Ryan and Murphy Reports Ireland is, perhaps, unshockable when it comes to the abuse of children. But Cloyne has proved to be of a different order. Because for the first time in Ireland, a report into child sexual-abuse exposes an attempt by the Holy See, to frustrate an Inquiry in a sovereign, democratic republic . . . the Cloyne Report excavates the dysfunction, disconnection, elitism . . . the narcissism . . . that dominate the culture of the Vatican to this day. The rape and torture of children were downplayed or 'managed' to uphold instead, the primacy of the institution, its power, standing and 'reputation'. Far from listening to evidence of humiliation and betrayal with St. Benedict's "ear of the heart" . . . the Vatican's reaction was to parse and analyse it with the gimlet eye of a canon lawyer. This calculated, withering position being the polar opposite of the radicalism, humility and compassion upon which the Roman Church was founded. . . . The Government awaits the considered response of the Holy See. . . . This is the 'Republic' of Ireland 2011. . . . But if the Vatican needs to get its house in order, so does this State. . . . For far too long Ireland has neglected its children" (Department of Taoiseach, 2011).

OVERVIEW OF AMERICAN AND IRISH REPORTS

Following revelations of sexual abuse of children by Catholic clergy in the United States, a number of reports of grand juries and attorneys general investigated the issues involved, focusing in particular on the hierarchy's response to the problem in several dioceses (Office of the Attorney General, Commonwealth of Massachusetts, 2003 [hereafter known as Boston Report]; Office of the Attorney General, New Hampshire, 2003 [hereafter known as Manchester Report]; Office of the Grand Jury, Philadelphia, 2005, 2011 [hereafter known as Philadelphia Report 2005, Philadelphia Report 2011]; State of Maine, Office of the Attorney, 2004 [hereafter known as Maine Report]; Suffolk County Supreme Court Special Grand Jury, 200-2[hereafter known as Suffolk Report]; Westchester County Grand Jury, 2002 [hereafter known as Westchester Report]). Common themes can be determined from an examination of these reports, themes that are also noted in the Irish reports on the same topic. There are also some variations that are specific to local conditions. Further scholarship is seriously required on this topic, in particular a scholarly analysis of the relational systems surrounding the decision-making process within the Catholic Church. However, for the purposes of this chapter the broad themes that can be detected in the Church's handling of abuse complaints as presented by the commissions of investigation and the reports of attorneys general and grand juries, will now be broadly summarized. Some of the work of investigative journalists will also be referred to for this purpose.

Awareness of Abuse Prior to the Crisis of the 1990s

Documentation is now available indicating that in many of the cases of clergy sexual abuse, the Church authorities were aware of the priest's past sexual activities long before the crisis began to emerge in the 1990s (*Boston Globe*, 2002, p. 74; Boston Report, 2003, p. 25; Ferns Report, 2005; Goode et al., 2003, pp. 174–178, Manchester Report, 2003; Murphy Report, 2009; Philadelphia Report, 2005; Raftery and O'Sullivan, 1999, p. 256; Ryan Report, 2009; Suffolk Report, 2002; Westchester Report, 2002).

Trauma for Child Victims

All of the reports suggest that sexual abuse and/or misconduct by a member of the clergy had shattering psychological effects on the victims (see for example Ferns Report, 2005; Maine Report, 2005; Murphy Report, 2009; Ryan Report, 2009; Westchester Report, 2002). While no two victims reacted in exactly the same way, patterns were detected. In some cases, even some 30 years after the abuses, some reports suggest that time had still not provided relief from the psychological trauma of the crime (Westchester Report, 2002; Ryan Report, 2009). The fact that the perpetrator was often regarded as a family friend and was seen by the child or young person as God's representative on earth often added to the trauma experience. Victims and their families reported in many cases that they did not promptly report the abuses because they viewed the priest as next to God and that he could do no wrong (Westchester Report, 2002).

Poor Communication with Victims Following Abuse Complaints

Several reports suggest that there was often a failure in communication between the religious institution and the victim or his or her family once the initial complaint was made. This added to the frustration and trauma (Murphy Report, 2009; Westchester Report, 2002). Many victims and their families reported that they were often dismissed or ignored by Church authorities (*Boston Globe*, 2002, p. 78; Ferns Report, 2005; Goode et al., 2003, pp. 80–82; Murphy Report, 2009; Ryan Report, 2009; Westchester Report, 2002). Many victims and survivors stated that the response of Church leaders added to their feelings of hurt (Goode et al., 2003, pp. 80–82; Ryan Report, 2009). Some survivors reported that Church personnel really were not interested in hearing their complaint and often did not take it seriously (Ferns Report, 2005; Goode et al., 2003, p. 81; Murphy, 2009; Ryan Report, 2009). Other complainants felt that they did not experience understanding, warmth, or compassion from those to whom they reported the abuse (Goode et al., 2003, p. 81). However, some victims had positive experiences with Church personnel when they disclosed abuse and were shown compassion and understanding, and even the kindest gesture would be remembered for years afterwards (Goode et al., 2003, p. 82; Ryan Report, 2009, p. 15).

Religious Institutions Failed to Report Complaints of Abuse to the Civil Authorities

In none of the cases reviewed by the grand jury in Westchester, New York (Westchester Report, 2002), in which the religious institution received an allegation of sexual abuse or misconduct was the information passed on to law enforcement authorities. Non reporting is noted in all the reports under consideration (see for example Boston Report, 2003, p. 52; Suffolk Report, 2002, p. 119). As a result, these offenses were never prosecuted, as they were barred by the statute of limitations. In the Boston situation the investigative team found that officials of the archdiocese did not provide all the relevant information to law enforcement authorities during criminal investigations, when such were undertaken (Boston Report, 2003, p. 57). Many victims and family members who testified to the various commissions and inquiries stated that the religious institution never recommended that they report the abuse to law enforcement officials.

Approach to Clerical Offenders Changed Over Time

Frequently prior to the 1980s abusive priests were allowed to continue in ministry, in many cases without treatment. The problem was dealt with by passing the offender on to a new parish or location. In the 1980s, moving the perpetrator was often accompanied by some form of psychological or psychiatric evaluation and to what is referred to in some reports as "superficial treatment" (Westchester Report, 2002, p. 8). Following a period of administrative duties many offenders were transferred back to local communities, often with full ministerial duties. However, the new parish or location was rarely briefed on the perpetrators' past history (Boston Report, 2003; Ferns Report, 2005; Ryan Report, 2009; Murphy Report, 2009; Suffolk Report, 2002; Westchester Report, 2002).

From the early 1990s onwards, assessment and treatment for clerical offenders seems to have become the norm. In some instances treatment of abusive priests was often provided in centers dealing exclusively with troubled clergy. Some treatment programs allowed the abusive priests to continue in unsupervised pastoral ministry in neighboring parishes, where they committed further sexual crimes (Bassett, 1994, p. 30; *Boston Globe*, 2002, p. 173). While this was not widespread practice, the very fact that it happened gives an indication of the thinking of some centers that treated offending clerics during the 1970s and 1980s.

While Church leaders began to see the importance of comprehensive sex offender treatment from the 1990s onwards, it is evident that part of their earlier motivation for sending clergy for assessment was for the bishop to establish the priest's suitability for returning to ministry. The Ferns Report (2005, p. 251) suggested that having sought medical advice, the bishop was "unable or unwilling to implement the medical advice which he received" when it came to the priest's fitness to practice (p. 251). This charge is not leveled against all bishops, but it seems clear that the bishops had great difficulty in removing their priests from ministry permanently, even when they were being advised to do so. While this practice began to change in the mid-1990s, it was one with which many bishops had difficulty. The *Boston Globe* (2002) uncovered evidence to suggest that some Church leaders in the United States "shopped around" for medical/psychological advice when it came to placing men back in ministry following histories of abusing children, until they met with advice that served their purposes.

It appears both in the United States and Ireland that in certain cases the bishops did not give the medical and treating personnel the full history of the priests against whom allegations had been made (Ferns Report, 2005, p. 251; Lothstein, 2004a, p. 128; Murphy Report, 2009; Suffolk Report, 2002; Westchester Report, 2002). While some bishops dispute this claim in relation to particular cases, others do not. At the very least, some bishops did not give full information to the referring doctor or psychologist. Sometimes this happened because the relevant personnel, either the bishop or the Director of Priest Personnel, did not review prior psychiatric evaluations and letters of complaint about sexually abusive priests that were in the priest's personnel folder. In other cases the bishop or senior diocesan personnel did not know of the priest's past history because he was never told (Murphy Report, 2009; Suffolk Report, 2002, p. 108). In yet other situations there may have been more sinister motivations for not disclosing the offender's full sexual offending history, as suggested by some commentators, such as maintaining secrecy and protecting the institution.

Until the 1980s the problem of sexual abuse by priests was treated as a moral one, with some offenders sent for retreats and periods of "penance" to help them deal with their problem (Ferns Report, 2005, p. 250). There is evidence to suggest that during the 1980s the problem began to be seen as a psychological one, and offenders were sent for assessment and treatment (Balboni, 1998, p. 7; Ferns Report, 2005; Goode et al., 2003, p. 177; Westchester Report, 2002). Only in the mid-1990s were the criminal aspects of the problem acted upon in some cases that came to the notice of the Church authorities in Ireland and the United States. However, in one religious order in Ireland, allegations of sexual abuse against lay staff were reported to the authorities even in earlier times, whereas allegations of abuse against members of the religious order were dealt with internally (Ryan Report, 2009).

Several reports commented on the poor supervision that clerical offenders received by the religious institutions, even when it was known that a particular individual had a history of sexually abusing minors (Boston Report, 2003; Ferns Report, 2005; Murphy Report, 2009; Suffolk Report, 2002; Westchester Report, 2002). The Westchester Report (2002) suggested that the diocesan authorities knew that known offenders were taking children away on overnight trips and they did nothing. The Suffolk Report (2002, p. 128) suggested that policy guidelines developed after 1992 were rarely adhered to. However, following extensive investigation of sexual abuse by Catholic clergy in the United States, the John Jay College (2011, p. 119) reported that the diocesan responses to abusive priests changed substantially over the sixty-year period addressed in the study. Abusive priests were increasingly less likely to be returned to active ministry and the diocesan personnel experienced less confusion or difficulty about the available options open to them in such circumstances (such as suspension, laicization, reinstatement). By the mid 1980s the American bishops had been made aware of child sexual abuse of minors by the victims and survivors and the work of investigative journalists as well as other reflections and learning. The John Jay College reported that when diocesan leaders responded to acts of abuse in the past, the focus had been on the priests and not the victims. Some diocesan leaders were "innovators" who led the organizational change to address the problems (p. 119). Others however were "laggards" and were slow to respond to organizational change (p. 19).

Claims for Compensation Were Settled on Condition of Confidentiality

In many instances victims were offered counseling after an allegation was made, but many reports suggest that confidentiality agreements accompanied the offer of counseling and compensation (see for example Maine Report, 2004, p. 11; Suffolk Report, 2002, p. 173; Westchester Report, 2002, p. 11). In some cases, confidentiality agreements barred the victim from reporting the sexual abuse and misconduct to law enforcement officials or the general public (Maine Report, 2004, p. 11). While confidentiality agreements can be routine part of civil lawsuit settlements, their use in preventing the investigation and prosecution of potential criminal activity was seen as injurious to the victims and their families and to the protection of other potential child victims. They were also seen to serve the interests of the religious authorities in ensuring the continued secrecy of clerical sexual abuse.

Legal Defense of Allegations

Many of the reports noted that religious institutions routinely questioned the veracity of the victims' claims, even in the face of substantial evidence of abuse, including in some cases multiple allegations from different victims against a single offender (see for example Westchester Report, 2002). Some reports suggested that the response of priests in the diocesan hierarchies to allegations of sexual abuse was not pastoral, despite the tone of some of the policy documents (see for example the Suffolk Report, 2002, p. 106). Several reports commented on the preparedness of the Church authorities to commit enormous financial resources to defend legal liability in relation to abuse by its clergy (Murphy Report, 2009;

Ryan Report, 2009; Suffolk Report, 2002). What were described as "aggressive legal strate-gies" were employed to defeat and discourage lawsuits, even when there was evidence of abuse (Suffolk Report, 2002, p. 106).

Sexual Abuse in the Seminaries

There are reported cases in Ireland (Ferns Report, 2005, p. 240) and in the United States (Sipe, 1999, p. 115; Stearns et al., 1993, p. 20) of seminarians who were subjected to sexual abuse by priests and religious during their formation. In December 1993, an independent board of inquiry suggested that 12 priests out of 44 at a minor Franciscan seminary in Santa Barbara, California, had been sexually active with the students, all of whom were boys 11 to 17 years old (Stearns et al., 1993, p. 20). The alleged abuse lasted over a period of 23 years, from 1964 to 1987. Sipe (1995, p. 140; 1999, p. 115) reports that sexual approaches were made to 10% of clergy by seminary faculty during their studies for priesthood and religious life. In Ireland, the Ferns Report (2005, pp. 240, 241) uncovered allegations and confirmed cases of sexual abuse of boys and young men 11 to 17 years old during the 1980s and 1990s in St. Peter's College in Wexford, which was also a junior seminary until the 1980s. Allegations of sexual abuse were also made against one senior dean in an Irish diocesan seminary in Maynooth by a number of men who had been clerical students under his care in the 1980s. Some of these latter claims were not fully substantiated (Ferns Report, 2005, pp. 174–183, 241).

Conclusions of the Reports

Several reports noted bad management, poor record-keeping, poor complaints procedures, poor communication between diocesan personnel, poor demarcation of the lines of respon-sibility and power, poor education of the clergy in the dynamics of child sexual abuse, and lack of sympathetic listening by Church authorities to people making allegations of abuse or misconduct as contributing to the failure of the Church authorities to adequately respond to child sexual abuse by Catholic clergy (Ferns Report, 2005; Murphy Report, 2009). Diocesan authorities were often accused of failing to conduct meaningful investigation of sexual abuse complaints (Boston Report, 2003, p. 57; Philadelphia Report, 2005).

All reports noted a change in the early 1990s in the United States (the John Jay College, (2011, p.119) suggests the change can be detected by the mid 1980s) and in the mid-1990s in Ireland in the development of written protocols and guidelines for handling cases involving the sexual abuse of children by priests. However, some reports suggest that even when dioc-esan policies were in place, they were often not followed, even in the post-1992 situation (Suffolk Report, 2002). The Cloyne Report (2011) found that Church policies were not fol-lowed in that diocese in 2000s. Diocesan officials were also accused of frequently ignoring the advice of the professionals they hired to evaluate priests accused of sexually abusing chil-dren, especially when it came to returning the priest to ministry (Suffolk Report, 2002, p. 132).The Ryan Report (2009) cited authoritarian management systems in the institutions as preventing disclosures of sexual abuse by staff, which served to perpetuate the abuse. While the Ferns Report (2005) found that many low-ranking clergy did not know or under-stand anything about child sexual abuse in the period under its investigation, which they saw as a failing on the part of the Church authorities, the Murphy Report (2009) thought that some priests were aware that instances of abuse had occurred and "the vast majority simply chose to turn a blind eye" (p. 7). This claim was noted in other works on abuse by clergy in the United States (Frawley-O'Dea, 2004, p. 135) but is one that is vehemently contested by many clergy in Ireland, who feel completely wronged by the accusation. The Suffolk report (2002, p. 118) interpreted lapses in the memory of priests involved in personnel management regarding events relating to sexual abuse by some of their colleagues as demonstrating "a lack of concern on the part of these priests for the issues; they were simply not memorable."

In interpreting the evidence before them and coming to conclusions regarding the handling of sexual abuse complaints against Catholic clergy, it was not unusual for the Commissions of Investigation, the attorneys general, and the grand juries to condemn the Catholic Church authorities in the strongest terms and to level accusations at the diocese in general or, in the case of Ireland and Philadelphia, at certain named key personnel (Ferns Report, 2005; Murphy Report, 2009; Philadelphia Report, 2005, Philadelphia Report, 2011). In the Boston situation the report concluded that the widespread sexual abuse of children in the Archdiocese of Boston was due to "an institutional acceptance of abuse and a massive and pervasive failure of leadership" (Boston Report, 2003, p. 73). The report suggested that for at least six decades, the diocesan authorities in the archdiocese operated "with tragically misguided priorities. They chose to protect the image and reputation of their institution rather than the safety and wellbeing of the children entrusted to their care" (p. 73). The report concluded that diocesan officials acted with "a misguided devotion to secrecy" (p. 73). These conclusions were replicated in all the reports studied. The dioceses were seen as having orchestrated efforts to protect abusing clergy from investigation, arrest, and prosecution by civil authorities, and by so doing to protect the religious institutions from adverse publicity that might have affected their economic welfare (see for example Suffolk Report, 2002, p. 122; Westchester Report, 2002, p. 7). All the reports suggested that in contravention of its own teaching, the Catholic Church put children at risk.

In all cases, officials of the investigated dioceses were seen as having failed in their responsibility to protect children, and in effect the investigated dioceses were all found to have endangered the welfare of children. Diocesan officials were seen as having ignored credible complaints about the sexually abusive behavior of priests in the past and as having failed to act on obvious warning signs of sexual abuse, such as instances of priests having children in their private rooms in the rectory overnight, or the priest drinking alcohol with underage children or exposing them to pornography (see for example Suffolk Report, 2002, p. 172).

The Manchester Report (2003, p. 1) suggested that there was evidence to prove a criminal violation of the child endangerment legislation against the diocese. The Suffolk Report (2002, p. 174) suggested that the conduct of certain diocesan officials would have warranted criminal prosecution but for the fact that the existing statutes were inadequate. The Boston Report (2003) did not produce sufficient evidence to suggest that the diocese or its senior managers should be charged with crimes under the relevant state law (Boston Report, 2003, p. 21). The Maine Report (2004, p. 3) found no criminal liability on the part of the bishop, the diocese, or its administrative staff. The Westchester Report (2002, p. 13) suggested that the legislation required amendment to ensure that mandatory reporting laws include the notification of offenses by clergy and that the reckless supervision by employers of employees known to have harmed children result in criminal penalties. The Philadelphia grand jury (Philadelphia Report, 2005) concluded in 2005 that state legislation was not defined in such a way as to allow criminal sanctions to be brought against the leaders of the archdiocese for the manner in which they responded to abuse complaints. In effect, having explored a variety of possible charges at that time, including endangering the welfare of children, corruption of minors, victim/witness intimidation, hindering apprehension, and obstruction of justice, they found that no criminal charges could be brought against the leaders of the Philadelphia archdiocese (Philadelphia Report, 2005). With regard to the archdiocese itself, while Pennsylvania law does establish the possibility of corporate criminal liability for institutional misconduct, the Archdiocese of Philadelphia was not organized as a legal corporation and therefore was immune from such liability. However, in 2011 the Philadelphia Grand Jury came to a different conclusion regarding criminal charges that could be brought against the leaders of the archdiocese when they investigated further allegations of sexual abuse by Catholic clergy (Philadelphia Report, 2011). This time the Grand Jury recommended charging the Secretary for Clergy for the Archdiocese of Philadelphia with two counts of endangering the welfare of a child. The bishops and auxiliary bishops who were named in the Murphy Report (2009) in Ireland have also been bquestioned by the Irish police force, An Garda Síochána, as to their part in the handling of abuse complaints.

In the Manchester diocese the attorney general's office was prepared to present indictments to the Hillsborough County grand jury charging the diocese with multiple counts of endangering the welfare of a minor in violation of the legislation (Manchester Report, 2003, p. 1). However, the diocese entered into agreement with the state that ended criminal proceedings. The diocese acknowledged that the state had evidence likely to sustain a conviction against the diocese for child endangerment and entered into agreement to comply with several conditions that would "safeguard children, ensure transparency regarding both its prior and future conduct, and create a system of accountability" going forward (p. 2). The state felt that the agreement with the diocese accomplished greater protection of children than would have resulted from a criminal trial and conviction.

While the reports into the handling of sexual abuse complaints by leaders of the Catholic Church at the level of bishop or religious superior can only be regarded as deeply shocking, it may also be the case that the published accounts can also be seen as historic records that may be distorted by retrospective analyses and hindsight. Scholars of the sociology of organizations teach us that when observers who know the results of organizational actions try to make sense of them retrospectively, they tend to see two kinds of analytical sequences (Starbuck & Milliken, 1988, p. 38; Vaughan, 1996, p. 69). In starting with attempts to explain bad results, observers seek incorrect action, flawed analyses, and failures that led to the bad outcome. Starbuck and Milliken suggest that nearly all explanations of crisis, disaster, or organizational failure single out how managers "failed to spot major environmental threats or opportunities, failed to heed well-founded warnings, assessed risks improperly, or adhered to outdated goals or beliefs" (p. 38). When it comes to organizational successes, managerial vision, wise risk-taking, and intelligent goals are often celebrated (Vaughan, 1996, p. 69). For Vaughan, these two analytical sequences lead to a selective focus that oversimplifies what happened. Firstly, the attention is focused on individual decision-makers, with middle-management understanding seen as the cause of the organizational outcomes. Secondly, "they obliterate the complexity and ambiguity of the task environments that people once faced" (p. 69).

Geertz (1973, pp. 14–17) tells us that understanding a people's culture exposes their normalness, and that true understanding and explanation will come about only when we set the decisions and actions that are of concern within the context of the organization's own cultural frame. There is further scholarly work to be done on this aspect of the sexual abuse crisis within the Catholic Church, and while the commissions of inquiry, Reports of the Grand Juries and the commission reports in both the United States and Ireland have begun an important process of investigation, much remains to be done. It appears to me that the final word on the Church's handling of abuse complaints is far from written.

EXPLANATIONS FOR THE CHURCH'S RESPONSE TO THE PROBLEM OF CLERICAL SEXUAL ABUSE

Balboni (1998) (United States) and Goode et al. (2003, p. 123) (Ireland) conducted first-person research into the bishops' handling of abuse complaints and spoke to a number of bishops in this regard. On the basis of their work they report that the bishops initially viewed the problem of sexual abuse by clergy as one of private moral failing and a breach of discipline that called for spiritual solutions, such as prayer, penance, and/or a retreat. Seen through this lens, the bishops believed in confidentiality (Balboni, 1998). Balboni (1998) argues that because of their familiarity with the seal of confession, Church leaders were scrupulous in keeping confidential any allegation of wrongdoing. The Murphy commission found that the code of canon law places a very high value on the secrecy of the canonical process (Murphy Report, 2009, p. 77). The obligation to secrecy was described as a "secret of the Holy Office' in the 1922/1962 documents *Crimen Sollicitationis* (which will be discussed later), the penalty for breach of which was excommunication. Breach of secrecy was also a sin that could be absolved only by a bishop (Murphy Report, 2009, p. 77). All of the commissions of investigation into the handling of abuse complaints in both the United States and Ireland describe what they saw as a culture of secrecy as contributing to the problem (see Ferns Report, 2005; Murphy Report, 2009; Office of the Attorney General, Commonwealth of Massachusetts, 2003).

In explaining their handling of abuse complaints, some bishops argued that they misunderstood confidentiality and secrecy and that they treated allegations of sexual abuse against clergy with the utmost confidentiality, believing this to be the right way to approach the issue (Goode et al., 2003, p. 176). Many bishops developed what they thought was a trusting relationship with all of their priests and treated the priest offender with the same level of confidentiality as they would any other priest who had a personal problem. At the same time an obligation to secrecy/confidentiality on the part of the bishops in the canonical process could also have undoubtedly constituted an inhibition on the reporting of child abuse to the civil authorities and to others, as the Murphy Report (2009, p. 77) found. Some bishops and Church leaders now see this as a major pastoral mistake on their part (Goode et al., 2003, p. 176).

Some bishops saw their first obligation as the preservation of the institution of the Catholic Church, and from this perspective it was not acceptable to expose any weakness in the Church; to do so was perceived as a sign of infidelity (Balboni, 1998; Goode et al., 2003, p. 167). Balboni (1998) argues that the American bishops appeared to be united in their loyalty to the Catholic Church (a particular version of Church obviously), and similar to the Ryan Report (2009) and the Murphy Report (2009) the bishops were committed to the preservation of its good name and reputation. The bishops handled the disclosure of the priests' abuses in the way that they did for another reason too: because they had a personal resonance with priesthood and all that it meant; they could not easily dislodge abusive priests from their priesthoods, regardless of what powers they had or otherwise in canon law.

The bishops saw a vocation to the priesthood as permanent and irrevocable and did all in their power to salvage the priesthood of the offending cleric (Balboni, 1998). The idea of salvaging priesthood was something that had an intense and personal meaning for Church leaders, since they themselves understood what it meant to make a personal commitment to clerical or religious life (Goode et al., 2003, p. 177). One bishop explained in a personal communication to me: "It is very difficult for someone who is a celibate himself not to be influenced by that [salvaging the priesthood] when dealing with priests. Your whole identity is tied up with your ministry; your ministry is your life. One of the reasons for that is celibacy. I believed at the time that if we took away his ministry that we would take away his life. I didn't want to do that" (Irish bishop, personal communication, August 2003). The suggestion is that no bishop wanted to take away the "erring" priest's life. I believe this partly explains why so many bishops found it difficult to remove the offending cleric from ministry, even when clear complaints were made against him, and why the bishops moved the offending cleric around to give him every chance to redeem and reform himself. In taking this action, some Church leaders took a restorative rather than a punitive approach to the offender. They were willing to trust the word of the perpetrator, who hadn't disclosed the extent of his offending and who promised not to re-offend. In doing so, the bishops did not take account of the harm that was being done to children, not only by the abuses that had already occurred, but the possible abuses that could occur in the future.

Virtually all survivors who gave evidence to the Murphy Report (2009, p. 57) stated that when they first complained to the Church authorities, they wanted the abuser removed from ministry so that he could no longer use his status to abuse children. As events have also shown, the Church leadership did not countenance that victims of abuse by clergy would have a problem with the offender returning to priestly ministry some time later. Even if a guarantee could be given that the priest would never abuse again, which by definition could not be given. It may well be that this was an evolving situation, which the leadership of the Church saw as a matter for them alone to decide, with reference to canon law and Vatican direction, and not, as turned out to be the case, with reference to the victims of sexual abuse and the media who supported them in effectively campaigning for all clerical offenders to be removed from clerical ministry permanently. Permanent removal of sexually offending clergy from ministry now appears to be Vatican policy, a policy that has been evolving since 2002 when the American bishops secured Vatican agreement for their norms for sexual abuse. The norms included a "one strike and you're out policy" for a 5-year period only, but in 2006 the Congregation for Bishops announced that a slightly modified version of the American norms was now agreed on a permanent basis (Allen, 2010a).

It was the failure of the diocesan authorities to deal with their concerns regarding the continued ministry of abuse perpetrators that most distressed many parents who spoke to the Dublin archdiocesan authorities, according to the Murphy Report (2009, p. 57). It is clear that the suffering and the stress of survivors was often related to the fact that their abuser was still functioning as a cleric and might therefore be a threat to other children. It is also clear that removing a cleric permanently from ministry was a source of great stress and anxiety for the bishops. A clear breakdown in the relationship between the survivors and their parents on one side and the bishops or church leaders on the other can now be seen in many of these scenarios. Clarity regarding what the key individuals involved wanted and needed at all levels does not seem to have been achieved.

Preventing scandal was also put forward as an explanation for many of the decisions taken by Church leaders in relation to sexual abuse allegations against clergy (Balboni, 1998; Goode et al. 2003, p. 166). Preventing scandal was an important function of Church leaders as they saw it, because giving scandal was seen as a serious sin (Balboni, 1998; Goode et al., 2003, p. 166). The approach, based on a "theology of scandal," implied that giving scandal would undermine the faith of the people and the credibility of the Church. Church leaders believed that they must protect the people from being scandalized by the fact of the abuse of children by clergy. They believed it was better for everyone if this information did not reach the public realm (Goode et al., 2003, p. 92). Some Church leaders even believed that giving scandal was theologically akin to leading other people into sin (p. 167). Balboni (1998) reports that some of the bishops in her study said that the parents of victims also wanted to prevent scandal and often just wanted the perpetrator taken care of so that he would not do it again.

As part of their explanations for why they acted in the way that they did, Church leaders in the United States reported that the presence of lawyers for the dioceses, victims, and insurance companies negatively affected the way they responded to clergy abuse allegations (Balboni, 1998). They believe that the legal emphasis took them away from a pastoral perspective. It is interesting to note that the commissions of inquiry in Ireland, all of which were chaired by eminent judges, do not give this topic due attention. The absence of analysis of the role of the legal profession for the dioceses, the victims, and the insurance companies is a gap in current understanding. My view is that lawyers played a significant role in how the Church hierarchy handled abuse complaints and in the actions that victims took, and as in many other areas of life in the United States and Ireland, a culture of litigation developed rather than a culture of understanding or healing. However, this is not simply a case of "greedy lawyers" exploiting the suffering of victims, as some have suggested. In many instances, victims of clerical abuse were forced into taking legal action to have their voices heard (Balboni & Bishop, 2010). On the Church side, Church leaders were not compelled to act on the legal advice given if it contradicted their value system and their "better" judgment. The issue here involves the limitations of the law for healing and for adequate redress, both of which are important and require further empirical work.

One of the sad ironies of our times is the belief that we can correct the breakdown in relationships and right the wrongs of the past through the medium of the law. While the criminal and civil law has a lot to offer, time and again we encounter its limitations in crimes that involve a breakdown in relationships, and disappointment inevitably arises subsequent to criminal and civil proceedings, even when the law is fully applied (O'Malley, 2009; Balboni & Bishop, 2010). This is where the practices involved in restorative justice and conflict resolution have a lot to offer, both of which are underused in the area of sexual abuse involving Catholic clergy. It is not to say that restorative practices would be used instead of criminal or civil proceedings, but as one of a variety of models that could be applied. Some combination of retributive and restorative paradigms of justice might offer a useful way forward. This is a topic to which I will return.

THE LEARNING CURVE

Church leaders have argued that the mistakes made in the handling of abuse complaints by them were due to sheer ignorance on their part and a general lack of awareness about the pervasiveness of child sexual abuse (Goode et al., 2003, p. 170). They argued that they were on a steep learning curve. The Murphy Report (2009, p. 6) rejected the view that the bishops in the Archdiocese of Dublin were on a learning curve, based on the commission's evidence that the Archbishop of Dublin took out insurance in 1987 to ensure against the cost of any liability that might arise from child sexual abuse by clergy, at a time when the archbishop and his predecessors had information on abuse by at least 17 priests operating under the aegis of the Dublin archdiocese. The commission took the view that this event, and the rationale for it, plus the existing knowledge on the 17 cases is inconsistent with the view that the archdiocesan officials were still on a learning curve at dates later than 1987, or that "they were lacking in an appreciation in the phenomenon of clerical child sex abuse" (p. 6).

The Murphy Report (2009) also presented evidence that the Irish authorities, such as the office of the Director of Public Prosecution (pp. 93–98), the Gardaí (Irish police) (pp. 82–84), and the social workers charged with child protection (pp. 86–87), were developing and refining their practices in relation to child sexual abuse during the period that the Commission investigated. The Ferns Report (2005) presented evidence that led that inquiry team to conclude that neither the medical and health care community nor the bishop appreciated the damage that child sexual abuse can cause to its victims (p. 250). In the light of this evidence from Murphy and Ferns, the conclusion of the Murphy Report (2009, p. 6) that the bishops of Ireland were not on a similar learning curve to other medical, social work, and criminal justice professionals does not hold up well to scrutiny even on the basis of its own internal logic. It is abundantly evident from the Murphy Report that at several key moments in Irish life, advances taking place in the Western world in relation to child abuse were influencing social policy and legislative developments in Ireland. The expansion of research in the social sciences and in psychiatry was leading to better ways of understanding and responding to victims of sexual abuse and to abuse perpetrators, and the Western world was learning from the victims who spoke openly about their experiences. Internationally it is recognized that child protection services have been developing at quite a pace since the 1980s, 1990s, and 2000s, and a review of the literature shows that child protection services are becomingly increasingly legalistic and bureaucratic as the criminal parameters of sexual abuse of children are becoming increasingly recognized, emphasized, and legislated for. To suggest that the priests and bishops in the Archdiocese of Dublin were out of step with the state of knowledge in the world at the time, and in fact that they were more knowledgeable, is not borne out by the available facts or by empirical research. That the bishops of the Archdiocese of Dublin knew of cases of abuse and that they took out insurance on the basis of this knowledge is beyond doubt. However, to suggest that they were not on a learning curve regarding the handling of abuse complaints is quite something else and does not logically make sense in light of the evidence.

The bishops also argue that the more they did to understand the problem, the more confused they became (Goode et al., 2003, p. 170). They attribute this lack of clarity to the professional confusion that already existed among professional experts in the field (Goode et al., 2003, p. 170). However, many experts were quick to argue back that they had not been given all the information in the first instance (Lothstein, 2004a, p. 128), indicating that Church leaders concealed even from the treatment providers the extent of a man's abusive history. The same claim was made by a medical witness who gave evidence to the Murphy Report and by some treatment providers in Ireland who were responding to the report's publication.

Where this practice was engaged by bishops, either willfully to mislead or out of ignorance of the gravity of the issues at hand, it was wrong. At the same time, it is a weak argument on the part of professionals to suggest that any mistakes on their part could be attributed to the bishops' unwillingness to tell them everything. Professionals working in the area of sexual offending know full well it is an area that is surrounded by secrecy and shame, and this relates not only to the abuse perpetrators but also to many of the people involved in the close network of relationships with them. Why any treatment providers would assume that they had been handed over all the information, without going searching and asking the right questions, and without undertaking systemic assessments, including conversations with as many people as possible who are pertinent to the situation, speaks to an approach to assessment and therapy that has outlived its usefulness. It points to the need for full systemic assessments in all instances of sexual abuse by Catholic clergy, and indeed of all sexual abuse, as a more useful way forward.

The argument that Church leaders did not fully understand the pervasiveness of the problem of sexual abuse by Roman Catholic clergy is somewhat weakened in the Irish context by the fact that Church leaders took out insurance in the 1980s specifically to cover the cost of compensation claims by people who had been abused by clergy. However, it is abundantly clear that they did not fully understand or investigate the systemic dimensions of the abuse problem, which was and to some extent still is seen as an individualized problem—of initially sinful and more recently "flawed" individuals. The bishops did not address the problem as a national or an international one that required international and systemic analysis and solutions (Balboni, 1998). In many ways the situation remains the same today, despite the cross-cultural, cross-border pattern of abuses by Catholic clergy that continues to unfold. Despite the fact that the English-speaking bishops met every 2 years from the mid-1990s to update each other and share knowledge on the unfolding events in their countries, what was remarkably absent was Vatican leadership on a problem that was becoming apparent all around the world (Robinson, 2007, p. 8).

While the response to abuse complaints by the leadership of the Catholic Church in several countries continues to improve, empirical work on the causes and contexts of the problem on an international level continues to be neglected. The American bishops commissioned a number of studies on sexual abuse by clergy: one on the extent of the problem (reported by the John Jay College [2004, 2006]) and another on the causes and contexts of the problem (which reported in 2011). The Pontifical Academy for Life, in collaboration with other organs of the Holy See, organized a symposium in 2003 on sexual abuse of children and young people by Catholic priests and religious, which was addressed by some experts in the field of child sexual abuse. However, overall there has been little empirical work commissioned by the Holy See to understand how these problems came to be, either the abuse in the first place or the mishandling of abuse complaints in the second, nor is there an attempt to understand, through research, the Church-specific conditions that might favor sexual abuse. It may well be that nobody wants to know the results of such research, as the necessity for change in aspects of the institution may be indicated.

On the basis of the available evidence it appears to me that the Irish bishops were on a steep learning curve, and they still are. The next lesson that must be learned is one about uniting in their efforts in bringing power to bear on the Holy See and on their local conferences to undertake multidisciplinary, multi-site empirical research, qualitative and quantitative (similar to my own and the John Jay studies) in an attempt to understand all of the factors that led to the current situation. Part of such scholarship should also involve research with "normal" clergy, the Church hierarchy, and the Church decision-makers, as well as with the clerical perpetrators and the survivors of abuse by Catholic clergy in trying to find more hopeful ways forward.

THE ROLE OF CANON LAW

Before analyzing the role of canon law in relation to sexual abuse by clergy, I will briefly outline some of the key provisions as I understand them in relation to sexual abuse of children (for additional information, see the Congregation for the Doctrine of the Faith, 2010, Historical Introduction).

The 1917 Code of Canon Law recognized the existence of a number of canonical crimes or "delicts," which were reserved for handling by the Sacred Congregation of the Sacred Office (in 1965, it changed its name to the Congregation for the Doctrine of the Faith). In 1922, the pope also issued *Crimen Sollictationis* (1922), giving local dioceses and tribunals detailed instructions regarding the procedures to be adopted when dealing with the canonical crime of solicitation. The crime of solicitation concerned the abuse of the sacrament of penance by a priest who solicited the penitent to sin against the sixth commandment.[3] This involved the sin of adultery. The crime of solicitation was considered as most serious, and to accuse a priest of such a crime was also considered one of the most serious accusations one could bring against a Catholic priest. According to the Vatican's own briefing notes on canon law (The Congregation for the Doctrine of the Faith, 2010), *Crimen Sollictationis* (1922) was mainly intended to "establish a procedure that responded to the singularly delicate situation that is a sacramental confession." However, it also included a short section on same-sex clerical misconduct, *crimen pessimum*, and determined that procedures for solicitation cases would be used for *crimen pessimum* cases too, with whatever adaptations were necessary in relation to the nature of individual cases.

In 1983, the new Code of Canon Law was promulgated by Pope John Paul II, and cases concerning the crime of solicitation remained within the remit of the Congregation for the Doctrine of the Faith. The 1983 code also updated the area of clerical misconduct. Canon 1395 of the 1983 code (p. 2) states that "a cleric who in another way has committed an offense against the sixth commandment of the Decalogue [the Ten Commandments] . . . with a minor below the age of 16 years, is to be punished with just penalties, not excluding dismissal from the clerical state if the case so warrants." The 1983 code also provided procedures for investigating allegations of sexual wrongdoing (Canon Law Society, 1983, Canons 1717–1719). The canonical norm states that bishops are obliged to investigate reports of clerical misconduct by means of a "preliminary investigation" (Canon Law Society, 1983, Canons 1717–1719).

It is worth noting that Canons 1341 and 1342 gave discretion to the superior or the ordinary (usually the bishop) to determine whether there should be a penal procedure after a preliminary investigation (Canon 1717), and whether to follow an administrative or a judicial procedure (Canon 1718). This discretion was qualified by the code's preference for judicial procedure to protect the better right of the defense (Canons 1342, 1; 221, 3) (Beal, Coriden, & Green, 2000, p. 1559). Before making a decision regarding an administrative or judicial route, the bishop could also consider whether it would be expedient, with the parties' consent, for himself to make a decision about the question of harm. While the purpose of this power appears to have been to avoid useless or unnecessary trials, the power appears to have offered the bishops some discretion in how they responded to cases of misconduct and gave them the possibility of issuing a pastoral admonition. Pastoral admonition was not regarded in canon law as a punishment but as a warning. This warning preceded actual punishment. Punishments resulted from an administrative disciplinary process (which could impose a temporary suspension on the offending cleric but not permanent dismissal from the clerical state) or from a full canonical trial (which had powers to order dismissal from the clerical state, sometimes referred to as laicization). Dismissal from the clerical state could also be issued by direct order of the pope. Priests who were disciplined as a result of an administrative disciplinary process or as a result of a full canonical trial could appeal their sentences to Rome.

It is not really clear from the Code of Canon Law (1983) what a pastoral admonition would actually amount to in practice, but it appears that this is one of the routes many bishops opted for when dealing with offending clergy, often encouraging them to repent and sending them off for retreats and in some cases for assessment and therapy. In practice, in some cases where offending clerics were temporarily removed from ministry following allegations of abuse, many were reassigned to new parishes and new ministries very quickly, often without the new parish being informed of the priest's history. In other cases, particularly from the mid-1990s onwards, offending priests were not reassigned without some legal and medical opinion. Some offending clerics seem not to have been admonished or disciplined at all, for reasons that are only partially explained.

The options chosen by bishops for dealing with offending clerics are now considered to have been wrong, especially in relation to repeat offenders. Catholic bishops and church leaders are currently heavily criticized for not putting offending clergy through the rigors of a full canonical trial that might have led to dismissal from the clerical state. The bishops are also criticized for not reporting allegations of sexual abuse against clergy to the civil authorities, particularly in the decades prior to the revelation of the sexual abuse scandals.

In 2001, Pope John Paul II issued a new list of canonical delicts to be dealt with by the Congregation for the Doctrine of the Faith. Sexual abuse of minors (under the age of 18) by Catholic clergy was included among them. From 2001 onwards it thus became clear that the Congregation for the Doctrine of the Faith would be the body at the level of the Vatican that would deal with cases of child sexual abuse by Catholic clergy. The instruction *Crimen Sollictationis* (1922) was also replaced with a new instruction: *Sacramentorum Sanctitatis Tutela* (2001). A letter, *De Delictis Gravioribus* (2001), signed by Cardinal Ratzinger, Prefect for the Congregation of the Faith (now Pope Benedict XVI), informed bishops of the new law and the new procedures. The gravest crimes, reserved for the Congregation of the Doctrine of the Faith, were specified in the letter. They included crimes against the sacrament of the Eucharist, crimes against the sacrament of penance, and crimes against morality, including sexual abuse of minors. The procedural norms to be followed in cases involving sexual abuse of minors were spelled out clearly (in my opinion for the first time), and all cases were to be reported to the Congregation for the Doctrine of the Faith, which would either deal with the cases themselves or indicate to the bishop the course of action that needed to be taken (The Congregation for the Doctrine of the Faith, 2010). In 2010, 9 years after the promulgation of the *Sacramentorum Sanctitatis Tutela* (2001), the Congregation for the Doctrine of the Faith issued changes to these norms in light of the gathering controversies and criticisms of canon law in relation to child sexual abuse. The text currently in force was approved by Pope Benedict XVI on May 21, 2010.

Canon lawyer Tom Doyle (2004, pp. 26, 28) has consistently argued that the 1983 Code of Canon Law and its 1917 predecessor contained the legal means to effectively confront and deal with sexual abuse by clergy. The failure to deal with the problem, Doyle argues, was not the fault of the law itself but of those charged with implementing it, namely the bishops and the Vatican officials. This is a view shared by those who argue that sexual abuse is and always was a crime under canon law (Martin, 2009b), and occasionally the Vatican likes to remind the bishops of this fact (see the Pope's letter to the Catholic People of Ireland, 2009). Citing specific canons from the Code (Canon Law Society, 1983, Canon 1395, Canons 1717–1719), Doyle argues that the sexual abuse of children and minors was always specifically forbidden by the Code of Canon Law (Canon 1395), which also provided clear and detailed procedures for investigating allegations of sexual wrongdoings (Canons 1717–1719).

While Doyle (2004) and others (see Martin, 2009b; Pope's letter to the Catholic People of Ireland) represent the case of canon law for dealing with cases of sexual abuse as fairly simple and straightforward, laying the blame at the feet of the bishops primarily for its non-enforcement, evidence produced by the commissions of investigation and inquiry in Ireland (Ferns Report, 2005; Murphy Report, 2009) suggests that canon law was not nearly as simple or clear-cut in its operational detail as Doyle and others seem to suggest. The Ferns inquiry found that "using Canon Law to force a priest to step aside from active ministry was difficult in circumstances where that law was unclear and untried" (Ferns Report, 2005, p. 254). The same report also found evidence that at least on three separate occasions the bishop had sought canon law advice in an intention to remove priests who had allegations of child sexual abuse made against them from the ministry, but that canon law advice did not help him in achieving this goal (p. 45). The Ferns inquiry team found that "having regard to the emphasis placed by Canon Law on the duty to protect the good name of alleged abusers," it was not surprising that the bishop adopted a view that was in keeping with this principle (p. 45). The inquiry also found that experience over time (in my view, particularly since 2001 with direct interventions and clarifications from Rome) solved some of these problems.

The Murphy Report (2009, p. 58) found that it was not easy to provide a coherent description of the relevant parts of canon law that related to child sexual abuse. This is because canon law had been in a state of flux from the 1960s onwards, "making it difficult for experts to know what the law is or where it is to be found" (p. 58). While canon law was the prime instrument of governance in the Catholic Church for many centuries, the Murphy commission heard evidence to the effect that the system suffered an enormous loss of confidence in the 1960s and seems to have fallen into neglect, especially after Vatican II (pp. 59–60): "Even the best attempts of competent people to discover the norms which, according to Canon Law, should be applied to cases of sexual abuse were in vain" (Murphy Report, 2009, p. 78). When the new and revised code was promulgated in 1983, following years of work on the revisions to the 1917 code, the Murphy commission found that it was not clear, either not even to canonists. What its effects were on older decrees or sources of law, including the procedural rules that were issued in the document *Crimen Sollicitationis* (1922) (and which was slightly modified in 1962) (p. 61) remained poorly defined. Nor was it clear to what extent *Crimen Sollicitationis* (1922) related to child sexual abuse that took place outside of the confessional and was therefore not dealt with under the delict of solicitation.

Prior to 2001, the Congregation for the Doctrine of the Faith was involved only in those cases where the alleged sex abuse occurred in the context of the confessional, since a canonical tribunal within that congregation handled all cases involving abuse within the sacrament of penance (Allen, 2010c). That is how the Congregation for the Doctrine of the Faith ended up dealing with the case of Father Marcel Maciel Degollado, the founder of the Legionaries of Christ, and why the officials of the Milwaukee archdiocese directed the case of Father Lawrence Murphy to that congregation (Allen, 2010c). The case involving Murphy led to accusations that Pope Benedict XVI himself had failed to act in this case when he was prefect for the Congregation for the Doctrine of the Faith (Goodstein, 2010), a claim vehemently refuted by Vatican officials (Brundage, 2010; Lombardi, 2010) and other clerics (Twomey, 2010).

Prior to 2001, the time that the Congregation for the Doctrine of the Faith took a lead role in the management of sexual abuse cases, it was never clear who in Rome dealt with cases involving sexual abuse by clergy. Canonical trials were extremely slow and cumbersome, and in some cases bishops had cases returned from Rome with their decisions overturned, as in some cases where priests had successfully appealed the bishop's decisions on canonical grounds (see case of Bishop Donal Wuerl vs. Father Anthony Cipolla, reported in Allen, 2010c; Ferns Report, 2005, p. 45). While the Vatican has been keen to point out that the canonical processes involved in handling clerical misconduct had been decentralized following the promulgation of the 1983 code (The Congregation for the Doctrine of the Faith, 2010, Historical Introduction), in my view this represents an attempt to abdicate responsibility for the systemic failures and to hold the bishops entirely responsible. As the Ferns Report (2005) suggested, the bishops were watchful of Rome and the Congregation for the Clergy, who had an interest in preserving the good name of clergy. When it came to taking action, no bishop wanted to bring the wrath of Rome on him or appear to be so incompetent. Some bishops believed that a poor outcome from Rome would affect their credibility and standing in the diocese and would actually diminish the ability to deliver effective ministry (Ferns Report, 2005, p. 45). Having been involved in discussions on child sexual abuse with canon lawyers during the 1990s and early 2000s, I believe that interpretations of the canon law contained conflicting and contradictory opinion on what was and what was not permitted.

In October 2006, Doyle claimed in a BBC documentary, *Sex Crimes and the Vatican*, that the Church directive *Crimen Sollicitationis* (1962) imposed an oath of secrecy in relation to the child victim, the priest, and any witness in an abuse case. Breaking the oath could result in excommunication. Doyle maintained that the directive was "indicative of a worldwide policy of absolute secrecy and control of all cases of sexual abuse by the clergy." The following week, the Vatican news reporter for the *National Catholic Reporter*, John Allen (2006), discussed the documentary. He said that *Crimen Sollicitationis* (1922/1962) was extremely obscure; that it went out of force in 1983; and that it had nothing to do with the question of cooperation with police or civil authorities. Doyle (2006) offered a response the following week, maintaining that Allen was wrong to claim that the instruction was no longer in force after the promulgation of the Code of Canon Law in 1983, and that *Crimen Sollicitationis* (1922/1962) remained in force until May 2001, when Pope John Paul II promulgated *Sacramentorum Sanctitatis Tutela* (2001). Doyle (2006) continued: "Although I was a consultant to the producers of the documentary, I am afraid that some of the distinctions I have made about the 1962 document have been lost. I do not believe now nor have I ever believed it to be proof of an explicit conspiracy, in the conventional sense, engineered by top Vatican officials, to cover up cases of clergy sexual abuse. I do not believe that the Vatican or any group of bishops needed a conspiracy."

Irish canon lawyer Dr. Michael Mullaney insisted that the directive *Crimen Sollicitationis* (1922/1962) was about abuses within the sacrament of penance and the manner in which such abuses were to be treated (Ferriter, 2009, p. 402). If someone complained about inappropriate behavior of a priest in a confessional, then the confessional priest and those dealing with the complaint had to treat the problem in a confessional manner, because of the seal of confession (some might say in a secretive or confidential manner). However, according to Mullaney, this did not prevent the complainant from bringing the complaint to the civil authorities if a crime had been committed. The Murphy commission (Murphy Report, 2009, p. 61) found that the main problem with these procedural rules was that virtually no one knew anything about them, including those who were supposed to implement them. Of those who did know something, nobody knew if they were still valid. The Murphy commission concluded that in an unusual situation, a document setting out the canonical procedures for dealing with child sexual abuse by clergy existed, but virtually no one knew of its existence or how to use it: "This was an obvious problem in an era when a large number of clerics were being accused of criminal offences" (p. 60).

The new set of instructions, *Sacramentorum Sanctitatas Tutela* (2001), represented a major change in Vatican policy. It provided that all allegations of child sexual abuse that had reached "a semblance of truth" should be directly referred to the Congregation for the Doctrine of the Faith in Rome, which would either elect to deal with the matter itself or advise the bishop on the appropriate action to take (Allen 2010c; The Congregation for the Doctrine of the Faith, 2010, Historical Introduction; Murphy Report, 2009, p. 64). The policy was adopted to ensure that a unified approach would be taken in dealing with complaints of child sexual abuse against clergy throughout the Roman Catholic world (Murphy Report, 2009, p. 64). However, the policy was soon modified when "Rome was unable to deal with the vast number of referrals" (p. 64).

Both *Sacramentorum Sanctitatis Tutela* (2001) and *De Delictis Gravioribus* (2001) reminded the bishops of their duties in relation to secrecy and confidentiality, which Vatican sources insist applied only to the Church's internal disciplinary procedures and did not preclude any bishop from reporting cases of child sexual abuse to the civil authorities in their various jurisdictions (Allen, 2010c; The Congregation for the Doctrine of the Faith, 2010, Historical Note). Interestingly, however, although *Sacramentorum Sanctitatas Tutela* (2001) did not preclude bishops from reporting sexual abuse allegations against clergy to the civil authorities, it did not encourage them to engage openly with the public about these matters either; nor did it mention the civil authorities. In fact, there was no reference at all to broader society or the public at large either in the letter *De Delictis Gravioribus* (2001) from the Prefect of the Congregation for the Doctrine of the Faith, Cardinal Ratzinger or in *Sacramentorum Sanctitatis Tutela* (2001). This omission is important, given that during the reign of Pope John Paul II bishops found it extremely difficult to get clear guidance from the Holy See in relation to child sexual abuse and what exactly to do with clerics who had sexually abused minors (Robinson, 2007). It appears even more illuminating when one thinks about the context of an increased public awareness of the criminal parameters of child sexual abuse.

The bishops' failure to report their clerical colleagues to the civil authorities may well be linked to a range of factors, such as clericalism and the tendency to put the interests of the ordained above the non-ordained, or the lack of appreciation on the part of the bishops of the criminal parameters of the issues involved. However, it might also be the result of that very human tendency to favor those one knows, even when they have done something wrong. I am convinced that one of the motivations for the bishops in their response to clerics who abused was the fact that they identified with their fellow priests. In the most human of human ways they wanted to protect them from exposure and humiliation. That is not to excuse the bishops for not listening well enough to the child victims or for ignoring the voices of the abused and their families, but this observation adds another dimension to the complex relational picture of why and how the bishops responded as they did to sexual abuse by clergy, and how some clergy were returned to ministries in which they went on to abuse further children.

In the light of the Roman line that was being taken during all of this period, the comments of the Archbishop of Dublin (Martin, 2009b, p. 15) at the press conference following the launch of the Murphy Report (2009) that "the sexual abuse of a child is and always was a crime in civil law; it is and always was a crime in Canon Law" might be just a little too simple and polemical, and a little hard to take for those bishops who struggled for years with the complexities of cases, not being sure where next to turn for advice. The Archbishop, who is undoubtedly "a man of good intentions" (Dorgan, 2009, p. 14), committed to restoring the Catholic Church in contemporary Ireland in difficult times, might be wise at the same time to consider his own advice that "there is no room for revisionism regarding the norms and procedures that were in place" (2009, p. 15). He is right on this. What he and others fail to acknowledge is that the mishandling of sexual abuse complaints by the Church hierarchy is and was systemic. In most cases the failure to act represents a systems failure of significant proportions, over and above the responsibilities of individual bishops. By "systemic" I suggest a failure of leadership and of the relational governance that went right to the top. In my view, the bishops' "failures" lay not in their noncompliance with institutional norms but rather in the opposite: the bishops' failures lay in their conformity with the institutional culture.

Doyle's (2006) certainty of the provisions of canon law may well also be evident in hindsight, but the disorganized chaos that appears to more accurately describe canon law since the mid-1960s may better depict the environment in which the bishops in Ireland, were trying to manage cases. This is not to exonerate anyone who failed in his duty to respond appropriately to complaints of child sexual abuse by Catholic clergy, or to respond appropriately and with compassion to the victims of such abuses, especially if there is evidence to suggest the endangerment of children. However, it does highlight the complexities involved for the majority of bishops in managing cases, which is important in the interest of fairness, perspective, and ethical justice. It is to the role of the papal leadership and the Vatican bureaucracy that I now turn.

THE ROLE OF THE VATICAN

The pope is the supreme legislator for the Catholic Church and all of its members. Only he can create and change law on a universal or worldwide level. Many of these laws are found in legal codes or in papal decrees. Canon 331 (Canon Law Society, 1983) makes clear that "the office uniquely committed by the Lord to Peter, the first of the Apostles, and to be transmitted to his successors, abides in the bishop of the Church of Rome. The Pope is the head of the College of bishops, the Vicar of Christ and the Pastor of the universal Church here on earth." Consequently, by virtue of his office, the pope has supreme, full, immediate, and universal ordinary power in the Church, and he can always freely exercise his power. Canon 331.1 (Canon Law Society, 1983) also makes clear that by virtue of his office, the Roman pontiff not only has power over the universal Church, but also has preeminent ordinary power over all particular Churches and their groupings. There is neither appeal nor recourse against a judgment or decree of the Roman pontiff (Canon 333.3). Priests have a duty of obedience to their bishop, and bishops must take an oath of fidelity to the Pope (Murphy Report, 2009, p. 49).

Australian Bishop Geoff Robinson was appointed in 1994 by the Australian bishops to a leadership position in responding to revelations of child sexual abuse in the Australian Catholic Church. He held this position for 9 years. I met him first when I made a presentation to the English-speaking bishops in 1998. My talk was on caring for the clergy left "holding the parish." We had just previously had a case in Ireland where reporters and television cameras had arrived at a Sunday Mass to video a young curate giving his homily. This was on the Sunday of the week in which it had been made public that one of the parish clergy had been involved in sexually abusing minors. Some parishioners removed the television crew from the church, and I was concerned about clerics in these situations, left "carrying the parish," particularly in divisive situations, where some parishioners believed "all" clergy must have known about the priest's abusive past and covered it up, and other parishioners didn't believe the allegations at all. Priests caught in these difficult situations experience severe stress and sometimes even threats if they were seen to be in support of or against the abusive cleric. My presentation was on this topic. In any event, I met Geoff Robinson and out of a large group of bishops, he stood out for me. I was impressed by his honesty and his determination, but mostly I was impressed by his search to find the right way forward for all—for the victims, for the perpetrators, for the entire Church of the People of God. I will tell a little of his experience to give shape to my discussion on the role of the Vatican in the handling of child sexual abuse cases.

In his official position as the person coordinating the Australian Church's response to child sexual abuse, Bishop Robinson (2007, p. 20) says he passed through three stages. Firstly, he tried to be a good human being, a good Christian, and a good priest. He soon realized that this was not enough, and so in stage two he began to listen to as many victims as he could so as to learn from them and from their experiences. During stage three, when he began to have strong resonances with the feelings and experiences of the victims, he remembered, some 2 years after he had been appointed to the position, and some half a century after it had occurred, that he too had experienced sexual abuse in childhood, and he became conscious of the effect it had had on him (p. 21). He believes his problems with the Church's response to the revelations of sexual abuse flow from all of these experiences. As coordinator of the Australian Church's response to sexual abuse by clergy he also looked for "compassionate leadership" from Pope John Paul II in responding to the issues that were unfolding. The silence from Rome was disturbing. Robinson began to find it difficult to accept the requirement that he give submission of mind and will to the writings of the Pope, (which he felt was an increasing requirement of being a bishop under John Paul II, as papal power

became increasingly centralized), especially when he experienced "the failure to give leadership in a crisis" from Rome, and that this failure in leadership "seemed to count for little"
(p. 21). Robinson felt that as well as giving submission to the writings of the Pope, the
demand was being made that he give submission to the silence from Rome on child sexual
abuse too, and this he could not do.

At a public meeting in 1996, Bishop Robinson responded to a victim's question by saying
he was not happy with the level of support the bishops were receiving from Rome. He
responded honestly and in good faith, following which he received an official letter on Aug.
7, 1996. The letter expressed "the ongoing concern of the Congregation for Bishops that you
have in recent months expressed views that are seriously critical of the magisterial teaching
and discipline of the Church" (Robinson, 2007, p. 21). The bishop was told that "in a recent
audience, the Holy Father [then John Paul II] has been fully apprised of your public position
on these issues and He has shown 'serious preoccupation in your regard'" (p. 21). Two
months later, on Oct. 16, 1996, Bishop Robinson received another letter, this time informing him that "[t]he relevant documentation will be forwarded, for its information and
review, to the Congregation for the Doctrine of the Faith," which Bishop Robinson took to
mean that he was suspected of some form of heresy (p. 21). While personally hurt, it also led
Bishop Robinson to the conclusion that an authority that had to be defended in as heavy-
handed as manner as this, when all he was doing was giving a truthful reply to a room full of
victims and journalists, must have had serious doubts about its own responses to the problem. Bishop Robinson eventually felt he could not continue to be a bishop of a Church
about which he had so many reservations. He resigned from his office as Auxiliary Bishop of
Sydney and began to write a book on the foundations of sex and power in the Catholic
Church (p. 22).

Robinson became disillusioned with some aspects of the Church in relation to the abuse
issue, typified by his conviction that "a number of people, at every level, were seeking to
'manage' the problem and make it 'go away' rather than truly confront and eradicate it"
(Robinson, 2007, p. 8). He came to the unshakable conviction that there must be profound
and enduring change. "In particular, there must be change on the two subjects of *power* and
sex" (p. 8). Robinson proposes a way forward for the Catholic Church, "one that is not contrary to the mind of Jesus Christ" (p. 22). It contains ideas for a renewed and reinvigorated
Church, and one that accepts and confronts the causes of child sexual abuse by Catholic
clergy and does not try to simply manage it away.

Before ordination every bishop is required to take an oath of fidelity to the pope. Bishops
take this oath seriously. From what is in the public domain it seems that bishops are quickly
reminded of it if they step out of line (Ferriter, 2009, p. 533; Robinson, 2007, p. 126). The
pope is immensely powerful in holding the Catholic Church together, and a bishop who
criticizes "would feel, and would be made to feel, that he was performing the unthinkable act
of abandoning the rock" (Robinson, 2007, p. 126). Bishops are expected to be loyal to individual popes and to their teachings (p. 126). Consequently, if bishops are not happy with the
way things are done in Rome, the unhappiness will usually be directed towards a cardinal or
official, but never towards the pope (p. 126).

According to Robinson (2007, p. 126), international meetings of the bishops do not occur
unless they are controlled by Vatican officials, leaving it difficult for bishops to organize
together to formulate policy or to act as one. "No bishop would wish to create an atmosphere

of the bishops on one side against the Pope on the other" (p. 126). According to Robinson, there are many degrees of unhappiness with Rome among the College of Bishops, for different reasons, which is understandable, but a bishop who criticizes Rome could easily be left high and dry by his fellow bishops (p. 126). Far from being the all-powerful bishops that these men are in their own jurisdictions and dioceses, when it comes to Rome and the Holy See, it is unlikely that they speak their minds. This may have been different when the Irish bishops met with the pope and Vatican officials in 2010 in relation to child sexual abuse in Ireland. It also seems to have been the case that the American bishops spoke their minds in 2002 amid the flood of complaints of sexual abuse by Catholic clergy that was tearing the American Church apart.

In relation to child sexual abuse and the Vatican, it must be remembered that since the 1970s there have been two pontiffs in charge: John Paul II (1978–2005) and Benedict XVI, who was appointed as pope in 2005. While both administrations are separate in relation to the governance of child sexual abuse, in part they overlap, as Pope Benedict XVI was prefect for the Congregation of the Doctrine of the Faith from 1982 until 2005 and for much of the papacy of John Paul II.

Pope John Paul II

In relation to John Paul II, it is being acknowledged that his reign left much to be desired in relation to dealing effectively with child sexual abuse by clergy (France, 2004; Berry & Renner, 2004; Podles, 2008; Robinson, 2007). For far too long he stayed silent on the matter, and failed to issue directives and guidance to bishops in light of an emerging problem, when clearly *Crimen Sollicitationis* (1922) and the canonical judicial processes that were provided for in canon law were proving unsatisfactory for modern conditions. It is also clear that "Rome" was overruling decisions of some Irish bishops on appeal by Irish clergy, potentially compromising the bishop's authority in the eyes of his priests, and indicating where Rome stood on the matter (Ferns Report, 2005). Allen (2010c) suggests that to the extent that anyone was tracking the sex abuse issue at the level of policy in Rome, it was the Congregation for Clergy, "whose main interest usually seemed to be defending the due process rights of accused priests." It must also be remembered that Pope John Paul II is seen as having been responsible for censuring many Catholic theologians who were dismissed from their positions, causing deep rivers of hurt that are still like open wounds in the Catholic Church today. John Paul II also had a mistrust of empiricism, leaving Catholic moral teaching devoid of the latest critical theological, biological, psychological, and sociological conceptualizations of sexuality and gender and of all that is most obvious about human development (Dominion, 1998, p. 12; 2007, p. 12; Frawley-O'Dea, 2004, p. 126; Green, 1997, p. 219; Sipe, 1995, p. 5). Despite this, in 2003 the Church hierarchy invited a panel of experts on child sexual abuse to a consultation at the Vatican (Hanson et al., 2004). It is my understanding that Cardinal Ratzinger, then prefect for the Congregation of the Faith and now Pope Benedict XVI, was in attendance for at least part of the symposium, a view that was confirmed by one of the participants at the consultation.[4]

While there are many aspects of John Paul II's papacy for which he is revered and which are considered very important for the Catholic Church, it is his failure to take decisive action in relation to child sexual abuse by Catholic clergy for which he is often criticized. His handling

of the two cases of child sexual abuse that he was called upon to directly handle is most telling of his attitude to child sexual abuse by clergy at the time. The cases involve Vienna's
Cardinal Hans Hermann Groër and Marcial Maciel Degollado, founder of the Legionaries
of Christ. Both cases have been well documented (Agnew, 2010b; Berry & Renner, 2004,
pp. 227–232; France, 2004, p. 258; Podles, 2008, pp. 234–237).

Hans Hermann Groër was a Benedictine monk, known for his devotion to Our Lady of
Fatima. In 1986 he was consecrated Archbishop of Vienna and in 1988 he was named as a
Cardinal (Berry & Renner, 2004, p. 288). Some commentators suggest that these appoint-
ments came despite the fact that allegations of abuse had been made against Hans Hermann
Groër by a number of seminarians (Barry & Renner, 2004, p. 229; Czernin, 1998, p. 20;
Podles, 2008, p. 235). It is also important that he denied the allegations. However, in 1995
further allegations of abuse were made against the Cardinal by a number of former seminar-
ians and monks who accused him of having molested them during their time in a seminary.
Cardinal Groër did not accept the allegations but offered his resignation as Archbishop of
Vienna, following mounting public pressure that was causing serious problems for the
Church in Austria (Berry & Renner, 2004, pp. 230, 231; Podles, 2008, p. 235). John Paul II
is seen as having remained silent and of failing to give adequate direction, even when this
issue was causing divisions in the Church in Austria. He is also seen as having been slow to
intervene directly in the Cardinal's case, despite the numerous allegations of abuse that were
mounting against him (Berry & Renner, 2004, p. 231; Podles, 2008, pp. 235, 237). Cardinal
Groër died in exile in 2003 (Podles, 2008, p. 235). According to some commentators (Berry
& Renner, 2004, p. 232; Podles, 2008, p. 237), John Paul's actions in this case suggest a
Vatican policy that failed to acknowledge or address the gravity of the issues involved in
sexual abuse by Catholic clergy.

In relation to Maciel, accusations that he had abused members of his order had circulated
for decades, but again Pope John Paul II is seen as having failed to deal with the accusations
of abuse against him (Berry & Renner, 2004, pp. 209–221). Victims tried to get the Vatican
to investigate the case against him many times, but on all occasions they were unsuccessful
(Donadio, 2010b). However, in 1998 Maciel was accused not only of abuse but of absolving
his victims in the confessional. This allegation put the case in the lap of the Congregation for
the Doctrine of the Faith, since its disciplinary section at the time handled serious offenses
under canon law, including abuse of the sacrament of penance (Allen, 2010a). As a noted
and beloved friend of Pope John Paul II, the case of Maciel brings to light the involvement
of both past and current pontiffs, John Paul II as pope and Cardinal Ratzinger as prefect for
the Congregation of the Doctrine of the Faith at that time. The complaint languished until
2001 (causing untold anguish for the survivors), when the crisis in the United States put new
pressure on the Vatican to act on sexual abuse issues across the board (Allen, 2010a).
Although an investigation was launched, no action was taken against Maciel for at least
another 4 years. By then it was the new, Pope Benedict XVI, who took action. Maciel was
barred from public ministry and instructed to live a life of prayer and penance. Maciel died
in 2008. Critics of the Vatican say Maciel was protected by influential Vatican patrons, up
to and including John Paul II himself (Allen, 2010a). In contrast, some see the removal of
Maciel as an indication of the intention of the new pope, Benedict XVI, to act decisively in
cases of sexual abuse against clergy. It may of course the case have been that the new pontiff
could no longer ignore the fact that sexual abuse by clergy was reported across the world and

was fast becoming recognized as a global Church problem that required papal leadership and intervention.

Pope Benedict XVI

According to Allen (2010a), Cardinal Ratzinger "always had an exalted theology of the priesthood, and little patience for priests who sullied their office. Yet for more than two decades after his arrival in Rome in 1981, there's no evidence that he broke with the standard Vatican attitude at the time—that while priests may do reprehensible things, talk of a 'crisis' was the product of a media and legal campaign to wound the Church." Cardinal Ratzinger is seen as having changed his perspective during the early 2000s. Allen (2010a, 2010c) regards the turning point for the then Cardinal Ratzinger as coming in 2003–2004, when he and the Congregation for the Doctrine of the Faith became centrally involved in the management of abuse cases under the direction of *Sacramentorum Sanctitatis Tutela* (2001). *Sacramentum Sanctitais Tutela* for the first time assigned juridical responsibility for certain grave crimes under canon law, including child sexual abuse, to the Congregation for the Doctrine of the Faith, which was headed by the then Cardinal Ratzinger, now Pope Benedict XVI. As already noted, prior to that time the Congregation for the Doctrine of the Faith managed cases concerning solicitation in the confessional, offences against the sacrament of penance (Allen, 2010a).

From sometime early in the 2000s Cardinal Ratzinger found a speedy way to authorize immediate action in cases involving accused priests, many of whom were swiftly removed from ministry or suffered expulsion from the priesthood without the necessity for the canonical trial (Allen, 2010c). Allen (2010c) suggests that Cardinal Ratzinger and his deputies "sometimes squared off against other departments which regarded the 'zero tolerance' policy as an over-reaction, not to mention a distortion of the Church's centuries-long tradition, in which punishments are supposed to fit the crime, and in which tremendous discretion is usually left in the hands of bishops and other superiors to mete out discipline." In his time as pope, Benedict XVI appears to have continued with such decisive action at several levels, meeting victims, meeting bishops, and in his pastoral letter to the Irish Catholics encouraging the Irish bishops and Church leaders to cooperate with the civil authorities in regards to clerics who have abused minors (Pastoral Letter to the Irish People from Pope Benedict, March 20, 2010). He has also acted directly in a number of abuse cases, including the case of Maciel, and he ordered apostolic investigations and visitations, such as an apostolic investigation of the Legionaries, and an apostolic visitation of certain dioceses in Ireland, as well as other seminaries and religious congregations. In addition, Benedict XVI has asked that bishops would draw on the discipline of psychology in screening and preparing the clergy for ministry (Congregation for Catholic Education, 2008).

Despite the innovations brought by Pope Benedict XVI in the handling of abuse cases, his past from time to time raises questions about his suitability to lead the Catholic Church, leading the Catholic newspaper the *National Catholic Reporter* in an important editorial in 2010 to ask the pontiff to directly answer the questions about his own role in managing cases as Archbishop of Munich (1977–1982), as prefect of the Congregation for the Doctrine of the Faith (1982–2005), and as pope (2005–present) (*National Catholic Reporter*, 2010a).

This they argue is necessary in the interest of complete transparency in times of "the largest institutional crisis in centuries, possibly in Church history."

In an open letter to the bishops of the world, Hans Küng (2010, p. 15), a former colleague of Pope Benedict XVI, wrote about the role of the Vatican in the current situation facing the Catholic Church. "There is no denying the fact that the worldwide system of covering up cases of sexual crimes committed by clerics was engineered by the Roman Congregation for the Doctrine of the Faith under Cardinal Ratzinger (1981–2005). During the reign of Pope John Paul II, that Congregation had already taken charge of all such cases under oath of strictest silence. Ratzinger himself, on May 18th, 2001, sent a solemn document to all the bishops dealing with severe crimes (*'epistula de delictis gravioribus'*), in which cases of abuse were sealed under the *'secretum pontificium,'* the violation of which could entail grave ecclesiastical penalties" (Küng, 2010, p. 15). In effect, Küng and Doyle's reading of the situation regarding the oath of silence that was placed on bishops is similar, but these claims are countered in the strongest terms by Vatican officials. Amid such significant claims and counterclaims regarding the meaning and relevance of these documents and the calls to secrecy that are at the basis of the charge of "cover-up," understanding what it means to take responsibility and to be accountable in situations of collective wrongdoing or omission takes very different forms.

While Pope Benedict XVI's record on child sexual abuse since his election in 2005 may indicate a man who has tried to address the problem (Allen, 2010a) and he may even have done all the right things in relation to the clerical perpetrators and in responding to victims, in the politics of clerical child sexual abuse there are two issues that continue to be of importance. First in adopting strict policies for dealing with abusive clergy, in the eyes of some of his critics, Pope Benedict has tackled only part of the problem (Berry, 2009, p. 13). So far he has not been seen to adopt any new accountability mechanisms for "erring" bishops, and with few exceptions bishops have not been asked to resign (Allen, 2010a; Berry, 2009). At the same time, it is hard to see where justice would lie if the Vatican turned on its bishops for their failures in relation to handling abuse complaints when some of the evidence seems to point to failures on the part of the Vatican too and to the varying interpretations of secrecy— if not so much in the reign of Pope Benedict XVI as pope, certainly in the reign of his predecessor. However Allen argues (2010a) that "as long as the perception is that the Catholic Church has fixed its priest problem but not its bishops' problem, many people will see the job half done. Secondly, in the politics of clerical child sexual abuse and in an increasingly hostile public atmosphere, it is the past rather than the present that seems to matter, and there appears to be no respite for those who have learned important lessons in responding to survivors and in dealing with abusive clergy. If this situation continues as it is, it may well be a case of the last man standing that will ultimately lead the Catholic Church, and based on the current pattern of disclosures, he may well be a bishop who was not involved in the handling of abuse cases prior to the mid 1990s.

What is clear at the very least from the evidence thus far available is that there was an extraordinary absence of guidance or direction from Pope John Paul II for the bishops at the time on matters relating to child sexual abuse. At the same time, the requirement of secrecy in regard to the conduct of canonical trials was sacrosanct. The absence of any reference to civil authorities is also notable at the same time as the emphasis on the rights of the accused priest prevailed in Rome. In the absence of Roman direction that reflected the gravity of the situation, it seems that many bishops reacted according to older values rather than with a new mind to meet the new problem (Robinson, 2007, p. 8). "The older values have for a thousand years included secrecy, the covering over of problems and the protection of the good name of the Church" (p. 8). Had John Paul II spoken early in the crisis, had he invited victims into dialogue, had he given direction to the bishops for openness and honesty and for cooperation with the civil authorities, had he tried to get to the bottom of what was driving Catholic clergy across the world to sexually abuse minors, then it is likely that the Catholic Church might be at the point of confronting the problem of sexual abuse by clergy rather than simply reacting to it. While the current pontiff has an opportunity to make significant differences in this regard, and he has made certain inroads, in particular in meeting with victims and in encouraging the bishops to cooperate with the civil authorities; in relation to getting to the bottom of what is driving Catholic clergy to sexually abuse minors, and what are the Church-specific conditions that might favor sexual abuse, so far the indications are that it is a return to orthodoxy. Secularism and moral relativism are two of the current pontiff's concerns. In failing to acknowledge the Vatican's role in the mishandling of abuse complaints in his letter to the people of Ireland, the pontiff has also missed an opportunity to acknowledge the problem in all of its dimensions.

The Roman line "which speaks with the voice of thunder when it suits, would now have it that individual bishops are more or less independent medieval princelings. Ours when it suits us; on their own when that suits us, is the message from the Pontiff and the *Curia*" (Dorgan, 2009, p. 14). The suggestion that Vatican documents contained instruction to secrecy in the handling of abuse complaints, with the contingent lack of encouragement to the bishops to report abuse complaints to the civil authorities in those jurisdictions in which such reporting was required, is at the heart of the current crisis. While spokesmen for the Vatican say the secrecy or confidentiality aspects of the documents related only to the canonical process, others disagree. This is a central issue in the current politics of clerical child sexual abuse that is unlikely to go away easily. While the bishops acknowledge their part in the inadequate handling of abuse by clergy, the Vatican has not admitted to any such failure (see Pastoral Letter, 2010). In a particular irony of the times, the pontiff may be unable to do so "for legal reasons," given that two unique cases *O'Bryan v. Holy See* and *Doe v. Holy See* work their way through the U.S. judicial system, challenging the Vatican and its leadership's claim of sovereign immunity in clerical sexual abuse cases in the United States. What is at issue is whether an exception to immunity can be established if it is instituted that a particular priest who was abusive is seen as an agent of the Vatican (Smyth, 2009). *Doe* raises questions about the Vatican's financial liability in clerical abuse cases, questioning its monetary obligations as the employer of sexually abusive clergy (Formicola, 2011. p. 2). *O'Bryan* brought suit for financial damages against the Holy See and also petitioned the court for the right to dispose leading church personnel, including the pope, about the handling of clerical sexual abuse cases (p. 2). It may be that more such test cases will follow.

Relationship Between the Vatican and the Local Bishops

This is an issue that brings up both the relationship between the Vatican and local churches and also the distinction between the Vatican as Church and the Holy See as a sovereign state. The Vatican has pleaded sovereign immunity with respect to being sued in the courts in the United States (Robertson, 2010; Smyth, 2009). However some of the current legal challenges in the United States are based on attempts to establish the authority of the Vatican over national Churches and to prove that priests and bishops, whom it appoints, are actually its agents in a legal sense (Formicola, 2011; Smyth, 2009). The remarkable special position of the Catholic Church in international law is also reflected both in the diplomatic immunity of its nuncios and in its position at the United Nations. Unlike any other religious organization or nongovernmental organization (NGOs), the Holy See (not the Vatican state) participates in the business of the UN as a "non-member state permanent observer," a designation that entitles it to participate but not vote in the General Assembly. It is allowed in practice also to both attend and vote at UN-sponsored international conferences. Because such meetings operate by consensus, the Holy See has played an important, some argue deeply reactionary, role in debates on a wide range of social policy issues, from population control, to the rights of women, to AIDS. That has prompted a campaign led by the U.S. organization Catholics for Choice to have the status and rights of the Holy See at the UN reduced to that of any other observer NGO (Smyth, 2009).

Doyle (2004, p. 30) suggests that the mishandling of abuse cases goes to the very nature of the Catholic Church's governmental system. He describes the response of the hierarchy as full of "fear, secrecy and arrogance" (p.30). In his view clericalism can be seen as part of an explanation for the inadequate response of the hierarchy to clerical sexual abuse, in which the clergy see themselves not only as set apart but also as set above (p. 34). At the same time, the evidence seems to suggest that the bishops operated in one of the worst crisis facing the Catholic Church within a highly centralized system without leadership on one of the most important moral issues to face the Catholic Church in the late 20th century.

So why didn't the bishops speak out, and why didn't they challenge the Pope and the Vatican officials at the time? Surely men of such power and privilege were able to speak when they needed, especially when they were never found wanting in most of their dioceses in using their authority to manage the clergy and direct the Catholic laity? Robinson gives clues to the possible answer. "This is not an easy question to answer. I can only say that it is a combination of loyalty, love and fear" (Robinson, 2007, p. 126). "Bishops love the Church and gave their lives for it, and they are aware that a stand-up, knock-down fight between a group of bishops and the Vatican would bring great harm to the Church" (p. 127). As in Robinson's case, it may well be that when a bishop seriously begins to question Catholic moral teaching and the operations of power within the Catholic Church, he ultimately ends up questioning his own role in an organization that gives absolute power to one man, a power that eventually silences him from using his better judgment and speaking what he believes to be true. How individual and systemic responsibility and accountability are played out in these scenarios is of course at the heart of the current issue.

In relation to the culture of clericalism in which priests and religious are set apart and set above, and in this sense seen as superior to the laity, many of the reports into the handling of abuse complaints show these features. Conway, a theologian (2004, p. 75), argues that one's interpretation of the theology of priesthood can support or resist the privileged positioning of the priest over people. In Conway's view, when priests and bishops adopt a model of priesthood as *repraesentatio Christi*, which originated with the Council of Trent, the differences between priests and the laity are amplified. In contrast, when priests and bishops adopt a model of priesthood as *repraesentatio ecclesiae*, which developed during the Second Vatican

Council, the communion of the priest and the people is what is to the fore. In this latter model of priesthood, the priest and bishop are in the service of the people and not of the institution. However, when the sacramental system is constructed in such a way that the sacraments, the traditional means of salvation for Roman Catholics, are ministered by clerics who are the authority figures who control access to them, the priest will be set apart almost by definition, as "closer to God." It is very easy to come to the conclusion on the basis of the unfolding evidence that the roots of some of the current crisis lie buried not just in Catholic moral thought or the manner in which power is exercised in the Catholic Church, but in ecclesiology and in the answer to a central and core question. Is this a Church of the clergy or is this a Church of the People of God? The practical responses to this fundamental question will determine not only how the Catholic Church responds to the past but also how it goes forward into the future.

A CULTURE OF OBEDIENCE

Writing in the *National Catholic Reporter,* Chittister (2010) addresses a central issue in the sexual abuse crisis for the Catholic Church, including the bishops' handling of abuse complaints, the unmasking of which she argues requires serious changes in the Catholic Church. She is referring to the culture of obedience. Chittister's main argument is that beyond the problems of sexual repression and institutional face-saving that the sexual abuse crisis gives rise to in the Catholic Church, "the dilemma that really threatens the future of the Church is a distorted notion of the vow of obedience and the tension it creates between loyalty to the Gospel and loyalty to the institution." One case involving the Irish primate brought this issue into sharp focus. A man with "a good heart and a good reputation," he took testimony from two young boys abused by an abusive priest, Father Brendan Smyth in 1975, at the end of which the boys were vowed to silence (Chittister, 2010). Although some steps were taken against Smyth he went on to abuse many more children for another 18 years. The cardinal said nothing about this case other than to his bishop ever again, despite the fact that the Smyth case was instrumental in bringing down an Irish government, and the cardinal was centrally involved in the Irish Church's response to child sexual abuse for more than a decade. When asked why he failed to give evidence of a crime, the cardinal's answer, according to Chittister, is "the Nuremberg defense: He was only following orders; he did not have the responsibility to make any reports other than to his bishop; he was only the note-taker."

While feeling sympathy for the cardinal who was challenged to resign, Chittister (2010) asks: "why would a good man with a good heart, as he surely is, think twice about his responsibility to take moral and legal steps to stop a child predator from preying on more children everywhere?" She answers her own question. The answer is a simple one: "It is that the kind of 'blind obedience' once theologized as the ultimate step to holiness, is itself blind. It blinds a person to the insights and foresight and moral perspective of anyone other than an authority figure." For Chittister, blind obedience is a misuse of the human soul in the name of religious commitment. "It makes moral children of the adults from whom moral agency is required." It acts as an assault on moral conscience. It makes the priests and religious beholden to laws of the manmade human institution and the individuals who occupy the positions of power, rather than to the law of God. Critical debate or discussion is regarded as breach of obedience. For Chittister, going forward, in order for members of the Catholic community to be able to presume that key Church personnel are imbued with a strong conscience and a commitment to the public welfare, the Catholic Church needs to address its theology of obedience, so that "those of a good heart can become real moral leaders rather than simply agents of the institution."

When a bifurcation of loyalties requires a bishop to put canon law above civil law and moral law, it may well be, according to Chittister (2010), the leaders of the faith community become one of its greatest dangers, especially when it comes to the credibility and morality of the Church itself. In this sense, I think Chittister gets to an important issue. Loyalty and obedience to the institution and to the pope influenced the bishops' decisions when it came to the handling of child sexual abuse. In the absence of leadership, in the case of John Paul II, and the disorganized chaos that was canon law, they floundered and became even more conforming "systems men" rather than questioning the culture and turning to the civil authorities for help. While it is clear that it is not helpful to evaluate the past by today's standards or levels of awareness (Cloyne and Philadelphia will be judged by contemporary levels of knowldege), and this is certainly a problem in dealing with history and historical cases of child abuse, the role of obedience in the current crisis of child sexual abuse hitting the Catholic Church cannot be underestimated. Earlier, I addressed the role of obedience and how it operated in a different way in the lives of those men who became the clerical perpetrators.

POPE BENEDICT XVI'S ANALYSIS OF CHILD SEXUAL ABUSE BY CATHOLIC CLERGY

On Nov. 23, 2010, a 6-hour recorded conversation between Pope Benedict XVI and a journalist, Peter Seewald, was published in the form of a book (Seewald, 2010) on a range of topics pertinent to faith, the Catholic Church, and society. Never before in the history of the Catholic Church had a pontiff answered questions in the form of a personal, direct interview; it marked a new development. The discussion is illuminating for its faith and clarity, its humanity on many topics and its unflinching orthodoxy on others, (at times in a manner that can appear devoid of compassion in particular in relation to homosexuality). I now refer to some of Pope Benedict's latest reflections on child sexual abuse and the Catholic Church.

Referring as he often does to sexual abuse in the Catholic Church as "so much filth" (Seewald, 2010, p. 23), Pope Benedict experienced the great crisis of child sexual abuse during his papacy as almost like "the crater of a volcano" (p. 23). "Above all the priesthood suddenly seemed to be a place of shame and every priest was under the suspicion of being one like that too" (p. 23). However, the crisis was not entirely unexpected for Pope Benedict because of his previous work on child sexual abuse with the Congregation for the Doctrine of the Faith. Nonetheless, occurring on the scale that it did was, he says, "an unprecedented shock" (p. 24).

The pope sees sexual abuse by Catholic clergy as a particularly serious sin, and he likens it to the parable of the wheat and the weeds: "the Lord told us also that among the wheat there will be weeds—but that the seed, his seed, will nevertheless continue to grow" (p. 25). The pontiff sees the problem of child sexual abuse by Catholic clergy as a problem of individuals—caused by sickness (p. 38), sin (p. 30), or evil (p. 35)—that he sets in a context of the problem of relativism in which "nothing intrinsically evil exists" (p. 38). "Pedophilia is first rather a sickness of individuals, but the fact that it could become so active and so widespread was linked also to an intellectual climate through which the foundations of moral theology, good and evil, became open to question in the Church". Good and evil became interchangeable: "they were no longer absolutely clear opposites" (p. 38). The causes of abuse touch on "the *mysterium iniquitatis,* the mystery of evil" (p. 35).

The pope wonders what clerical men who have sexually abused minors think of in the morning when they go to the altar to offer the Holy Sacrifice. The pontiff wonders if such men actually go to confession (p. 35). My research and clinical experience can answer that question: many clerical men who have sexually abused minors do indeed go to confession, often many times a week, and for some it is their relationship with God that prevents them from total disintegration. In time, it might serve the Church well if the current pontiff met with some clerical perpetrators to hear about their lives and times and how it came to be that they sexually abused minors. The Catholic Church might also usefully commission a global scholarly in-depth study into the lives and experiences of such clerical men, because their stories and narratives might well help inform the Church's program of reform.

It is in his treatise of the relationship between love and punishment that the pope's attitude to clerical men who have sexually abused minors is both telling and I suggest also limited. "We have to learn all over again that love for the sinner and love for the person who has been harmed are correctly balanced if I punish the sinner in the form that is possible and appropriate" (p. 26). While punishing sinners is regarded as showing love, there is no hint as to when the punishment is served. As Pope Benedict sees it, the law and the need for punishment were obscured during the 1960s in favor of a narrow concept of love, which he sees as part of the problem (p. 26). The pontiff rightly emphasizes the need for charity towards victims of sexual abuse by clergy and the need to do everything to help victims cope with what they have experienced (p. 28). However, there is less leadership given on the need to show charity towards clerical perpetrators, or of helping them cope with their life situations, in a world in which they are fast becoming the modern-day lepers.

In relation to the global Church's response to the problem, Pope Benedict cites the Archbishop of Dublin. "He [the Archbishop of Dublin] said that ecclesiastical penal law functioned until the late 1950's: admittedly it was not perfect—there is much to criticize about it—but nevertheless it was applied. After the mid-sixties, however, it was simply not applied any more. The prevailing mentality was that the Church must not be a Church of laws but, rather, a Church of love; she must not punish. Thus the awareness that punishment can be an act of love ceased to exist. This led to an odd darkening of the mind, even in very good people" (p. 26). Here Pope Benedict sees the errors made in the handling of abuse complaints by the Church hierarchy again as a failure of individuals, individuals whose minds were "darkened" by their failure to link punishment and love, or who had decoupled the relationship between love and punishment and reinterpreted the need for love in the Catholic Church in new ways. The systemic impact of Vatican II on the application of the norms of canon law and the general upheaval that was experienced in the Church worldwide in the wake of the Second Vatican Council is set aside in favor of individual failing.

Pope Benedict XVI has a tendency to see the global Church problem of sexual abuse by Catholic clergy in a compartmentalized manner, on a county-by-country basis. In the American situation the response was eventually to issue revised, stricter norms and to improve collaboration between the secular and the ecclesiastical authorities. The pontiff was surprised that abuse existed on the scale that it did in Germany. Ireland's problems were, as he saw them, "altogether specific" (p. 24). "[T]here is a self-enclosed Catholic society, so to speak, which remained true to its faith despite centuries of oppression, but which, then, evidently certain attitudes were also able to develop" (p. 24).

Pope Benedict reiterates that in October 2006, in his address to the bishops of Ireland, he called on them to bring "the truth to light" and to ensure that the principles of law and justice were fully respected. Above all he says that he encouraged the bishops of Ireland to bring healing to the victims (p. 24). It is not fully clear if the pontiff is referring only to the Church in Ireland when he suggests that "we must examine thoroughly how it was possible for that to happen, and at the same time what can be done so that something like that does not happen again" (p. 25). Pope Benedict does suggest that the points made in his public address to the Catholics of Ireland must also be applied further, although this needs further elaboration and clarification. The apostolic visitation to Ireland, which Pope Benedict announced in May 2010 and which began in January 2011, is consistent with a view that the Church in Ireland in particular needed examination. This examination could well benefit from additional social science research, the findings of which could supplement those of the apostolic visitation the results of which will hopefully be released in the public domain. Pope Benedict wonders in hindsight if at the time of the American crisis it might have been Rome's duty to say to all the other countries of the world, "Find out whether you are in the same situation." The pontiff reflects that "maybe we should have done that" (p. 26).

The pope's current approach to dealing with the problem of sexual abuse by Catholic clergy is two-pronged: respond better to abuse complaints, "more precisely and correctly to the situation" (p. 32), and ensure as much as possible that abuse no longer happens. In this regard, the pope encourages his bishops to take care of victims and help them heal; screen candidates for the priesthood carefully (to prevent such potential abusers from gaining entry); punish perpetrators and bar them from the opportunity to repeat such abuses; tighten the penal processes for responding to abusive clergy, and improve the formation process to include a "positive formation in true chastity and in dealing correctly with one's own sexuality and that of others" (p. 32). On the role of theology in the action plan, the pope suggests that "theologically as well there is certainly much to be developed and an appropriate climate to be created" (p. 32). Unfortunately Pope Benedict does not elaborate what he means by this, apart from strengthening the distinctions between good and evil, punishment and love. At a more Church-wide level the pontiff believes the whole faith community should become involved "in thinking about vocations and promoting them and being attentive to individuals" who may follow this path in life (p. 32). The pontiff also believes that there must be positive measures to create "a spiritual climate in which these things can be eliminated, overcome, and as far as possible precluded" (p. 32). The pope emphasizes the need for purification and conversion and for "interior renewal, transformation, humility and penance" (p. 34).

A number of observations must be made on the above framework for understanding sexual abuse within the Catholic Church and the resultant program of action. The pontiff leaves out of his sphere of analysis a number of human factors that limit the confidence one can have in his full understanding of or approach to the problem. However, the spiritual aspects of the Holy Father's vision, as the leader of the Catholic Church, cannot be denied.

The human factors that I would like to see Pope Benedict pay more attention to in his attempts to understand the conditions in which sexual abuse by Catholic clergy became possible and in which the Church leaders responded as they did include the institutional conditions in which clerical men live and are trained work; the theology of sexuality, including clerical celibacy; Church governance and the exercise of power, authority, and obedience; clerical culture, the template for which is set in the seminaries; the distinctions between the ordained and non-ordained, which arises from the "ontological change" that is said to occur in an individual at ordination; and finally the model of Church in which the ordained and laity are not equal by virtue of baptism but are distinguished by virtue of ordination, thereby creating two Churches within the one: an elite Church of the ordained and a second-order Church of the laity.

As reform in seminary training is becoming a popular notion for the current pontiff and a point with which I agree, this understanding warrants further comment. If seminary training in chastity and sexuality was remiss in the past and is in need of reform, as suggested by Pope Benedict himself and reported in the John Jay Causes and Context Study (2011), perhaps a less condemnatory approach to generations of clerical men who were failed by such formation systems and who went on to become abuse perpetrators might be more forthcoming; not in terms of offering jobs but in terms of offering hope. Following the logic of the pontiff's own program of reform, if seminaries failed generations of clergy, then this fact needs to be accommodated in a systemic model of causality. Instead of casting such men aside as sick or sinners or evil, perhaps Pope Benedict XVI and those Church leaders courageous enough to do so in current times might take the opportunity to give leadership to the Christian world on what it means to fail, and where redemption is to be found in the face of such significant human failing. This is not to offer excuses for clerical perpetrators of sexual abuse against minors, or to suggest that the pontiff find new ministries for such men within the priesthood, but it is to suggest that an ideal opportunity exists for global leadership on the complexities of the human condition and of human failing, on the redemptive story and on how erring individuals might be more compassionately embraced and understood and helped in the world. If some say compassion or misguided compassion was part of the problem in the past I say lack of it is part of the problem in the present.

In outlining his understanding of the conditions that contributed to sexual abuse by Catholic clergy in Ireland, in his pastoral letter to the Catholics of Ireland (2010), Pope Benedict also referred to "a tendency in society to favour the clergy and other authority figures, and a misplaced concern for the reputation of the Church and the avoidance of scandal, resulting in failure to apply existing canonical penalties and to safeguard the dignity of every person" (p. 189). Pope Benedict's reluctance to fully acknowledge the role of the papacy, the Vatican, and the *Curia* in the local and global Church's failure in relation to sexual abuse by Catholic clergy, at both a preventive and a responsive level, on several continents and for several decades, is perhaps the most serious failing in his analysis, despite his undoubted achievements. Pope Benedict does acknowledge that in the case of Marcial Maciel Degollado, the founder of the Legionnaires of Christ, "unfortunately we addressed these things very slowly and late" (p. 38).

As the RTE documentary *Would You Believe*, which was screened on Jan. 17, 2011, showed, documents exist to suggest that in the Irish case, the Vatican played a significant role in shaping the response of the Irish bishops to the problem. In what is now being cast by

Rome as the failure of a number of named individual Irish bishops, in fact the RTE documentary suggests much more systemic complicity, a theory that matches my own research on the subject, and that was argued earlier in this book. In the interest of truth, justice, and ultimately renewal, such systemic involvement in what might not be a cover-up, as is popularly charged, but more reasonably might be regarded as mistakes, misplaced loyalty, and errors of judgment, must finally be acknowledged.

CONCLUDING COMMENTS

The bishops' handling of complaints of child sexual abuse cannot be seen outside of the context of canon law, their oath of allegiance to the pope, the manner in which authority is exercised in the Catholic Church, and the relationship between bishops and priests. Effectively, the relationship between the Holy See and the bishops can be characterized as one of deference and obedience. Even if a bishop believes the Roman line is wrong, Church politics and Church governance effectively thwart all efforts of reform. The moral dilemmas involved in navigating this terrain must be immense for bishops who do not subscribe to orthodoxy, or who make efforts to encourage institutional change for modern conditions.

The dilemmas for bishops with regard to their allegiance to the pope in relation to child sexual abuse by Catholic clergy was compounded by the fact that in most Western democracies, civil law takes precedence over canon law in running the affairs of the state. In Ireland, where there was little separation between Church and State until the late 20th century, and in which State institutions adopted a deferential attitude towards the Catholic Church (Ryan Report, 2009), the child sexual abuse crisis was to bring a number of issues into sharp focus for the Catholic bishops of Ireland. Used to dealing with the State on matters of morality, child sexual abuse was to provide a whole new configuration of Church–State relations, something that had already begun to happen in Ireland for sure but that was heralded along by the child sexual abuse scandals. The problem of child sexual abuse brought the interface of Church and State or Church and laity together in ways that had not happened like this before. Child sexual abuse did not only involve the laity, such as contraception and divorce, which although these issues were of immense concern to the Church leaders from a morality perspective, they did not directly affect the daily lived behavior of clergy; child sexual abuse did. Child sexual abuse involved both clergy and laity and later the hierarchy in direct "intimate" and "power" relations. It was not an issue that the Church leadership could refuse to acknowledge or one that could be dealt with internally, although at times they tried to do both. What was different about child sexual abuse was that it inextricably linked the clergy and laity, Church and State, and canon and civil law in an interminable problem that also involved sexual morality and Church governance. Most importantly there were child victims on the end of this matrix who were supported by the media, to have their voices heard.[5] It is my belief that neither the clerical perpetrators nor the Church hierarchy ever believed that the survivors and their families would "go public," such was the hold that clericalism had on these men. This scenario was not confined to Ireland.

The complex relationship between the bishop and the priest, in which the bishop was the shepherd as well as the enforcer, made for human as well as leadership problems in the decisions that many bishops faced. Even if the Irish bishops had understood the full criminal and civil parameters of the problem of child sexual abuse (and further research is required on that topic), the fact that the Vatican had not endorsed *Child Sexual Abuse: Framework for a Church Response* (1996) when the Irish bishops sent it to Rome for approval, the organized chaos that best describes canon law at the time, and the relational network and complex responsibilities that were often involved in these roles, the Irish bishops, and perhaps those in other parts of the world, were left floundering with very little help from Rome. In fact they were left in unclear waters regarding what Rome expected of them when it came to dealing with clerics who had sexually offended against minors, except for something about "confidentiality" and "secrecy". That many such offenders, particularly repeat offenders, were moved around and left in ministries that unintentionally or in ignorance gave them further access to children, where they re-offended, is part of a systemic problem of sexual abuse within the Catholic Church, requiring systemic solutions at many levels—institutional, organizational, and cognitive.

Internationally, child sexual abuse has become an axis for seeking reform in many issues that have at once to do with relationships between Church and State, civil and canon codes, and clergy and the laity. When the Bishop of Kildare and Leighlin said, on his resignation following the publication of the Murphy Report (2009) in Dublin, that in hindsight he should have confronted the prevailing culture, he was saying something important. However, on his own, particularly as an auxiliary bishop, he was never going to be successful in changing the culture then but he could do something about it right now. For a man who professed such insight he is remarkably quiet since his resignation on what exactly needs to change and what he can do to change it. It is only through organized efforts that this cultural change is possible, and the evidence shows that the bishops are as heterogeneous a group of men as any other. In an irony of the current situation, it may well be that the greatest impetus to change in the Catholic Church going forward will turn out to be child sexual abuse by Catholic clergy, and the strength that survivors of abuse have had in challenging the system that failed them.

Since the mid-1990s, the response to survivors of abuse has improved somewhat in Ireland and the United States (and maybe in other jurisdictions too), although much remains to be done. I hear constantly from survivors who are still left without responses for far too long when they report allegations of historical abuse to the various instruments of the Church's infrastructure. This notwithstanding there have been some changes as the Church in several jurisdictions tries to adopt a better approach to the management of child abuse cases. At the same time, it is important to consider the limitations of the Church's new superstructures for child protection. If the new practices and protocols have improved the response to the problem at one level, they have created others at another level. The chief casualties of the new situation are the clergy themselves, the relationships between bishops and priests and the rights of Catholic clergy who are falsely accused. It is always important that organizations take extreme care in managing systemic change, as change in one part of the system will produce changes in all others, raising the potential for unforeseen problems in the attempt to resolve the original problem. This is exactly what is happening now in the Catholic Church.

10

Understanding and Explaining Child Sexual Abuse within the Catholic Church

GENDER, POWER, ORGANIZATIONAL CULTURE

INTRODUCTION

The question "why" is often asked in Western culture and in much psychological and sociological scholarship, particularly in relation to highly complex problems that produce wells of manmade hurt. In attempting to understand why certain events occur and why individuals and groups behave as they do the search for explanation is often to the fore. In many Western countries no longer are social problems seen as the act or will of God as they were in pre-modern times. Rather, since the Enlightenment there has been an increasing move towards understanding the part played by social structures and human agency in how social problems come to be and if and how they can be prevented. There are multiple ways of understanding and multiple ways of responding, and all approaches are influenced by philosophy, ontology and epistemology.

Within social science research it is accepted that philosophical and epistemological orientation influences not only a researcher's methodology and his or her research claims but also the manner in which theory is constructed. Those social scientists who adopt a modernist or positivist orientation tend to emphasize generalization, universality, rationality, and stability. From this perspective the goal of social science research is to seek out causal relationships that will explain and predict human behavior with as much certainty as possible (Hollis, 1999, p. 41).

An alternative social science perspective involves a more reflexive, constructionist, and interpretive approach, sometimes referred to as postmodernist and poststructuralist perspectives, based on the idea that the goal of social science research is not to seek explanations based on "scientific" laws or causal relationships, but rather to understand social phenomena from the point of view of the social agent, in which all "findings" are provisional and tentative and influenced by subjectivity and philosophical orientation. Research from a postmodernist and interpretive perspective emphasizes positionalities, partialities, instabilities, and situatedness (Clarke, 2005). Instead of focusing on the causes of behavior, what is sought is the meaning of action. From this perspective no claims of certainty or "universal truth" are made, as every research account is seen as provisional, holding out the possibility for multiple interpretations. Far from being "objective," the researcher is also seen as part of what is finally produced.

I referred to some of the philosophical and epistemological debates in relation to social science research in my introductory chapter. At this point, I merely wish to restate my own philosophical positioning and my orientation to theory construction. My work can be located primarily within the interpretive tradition that highlights understanding, explanation, and explanatory interpretation. My aim is not to develop fixed categories or explanatory theory that can be regarded as foundational truth or that can explain all. Rather, my attempt is to offer one way of understanding sexual abuse within the Catholic Church that, in effect, is co-constructed; combining the participants' understanding of their situation and my interpretation of all that I have come to know about the topic. This account is not fixed or final but can inform the work of practitioners and scholars as they compare and contrast their own versions with that which is produced in my work. Having said that, my research also attempts to deal with provisional knowledge within a context of empirical and academic rigor. This does not amount to a choice between one "truth" and relativism, science and art, certainty and uncertainty. Instead, elements of all epistemologies are drawn upon in my attempts to understand sexual abuse within the Catholic Church. Just as within most spheres of complex human life, all perspectives have their place. I make no big claims for the explanations I offer, nor am I claiming truth status for my theory. Rather, I am presenting my interpretations based on the research that I undertook; as such, they represent one perspective.

This chapter begins by making the case for a gendered perspective on child sexual abuse and by extension on sexual abuse by Catholic clergy. Initially I thematically elucidate a number of broad structural and institutional conditions that emerged as significant in the lives the clerical perpetrators; all of which are implicated in their sexual offending. As readers will see, many of these conditions relate also to Catholic clergy more generally and not just the clerical perpetrators. Therefore, further theoretical refinement is necessary. This I undertake by turning to the dynamic factors that I believe distinguish clerics who become abuse perpetrators from those who do not. For this analytical work I draw on the insights of Erving Goffman (1975/1961), which facilitates a discussion of seminary formation and how clerical identity is construed. A gendered theory of sexual abuse by Catholic clergy is developed in which the clerical perpetrator is conceptualized as part of a more layered and complex theory of clerical masculinities.

Building on my understanding of the clerical perpetrators, I then turn attention to the institutional and societal dimensions of child sexual abuse in the Catholic Church, interweaving my understanding of the clerical perpetrators with the social, cultural and organizational factors that I have encountered, to develop a multi-layered framework for understanding sexual abuse by Catholic clergy in Ireland. While this framework acts as an exemplar of sexual abuse within the Catholic Church more broadly (and will benefit from elaboration in the light of new or emerging data and insights), what is presented here is an attempt to conceptualize the issues involved in a meaningful way and to develop some useful understandings.

GENDER AND SEXUAL ABUSE

In much of the literature on sexual violence and child sexual abuse, the invisibility or erasure of gender from evolving conceptualizations and resultant public policy is notable. By ignoring the gendered nature of the phenomenon and by excluding the socially available ways of being male from critical analysis, our understanding of the subject is limited and confined to individualized psychological formulations, theories of risk, and theories of "evil" that lack sociological import or critique. This represents a gap in current scholarship and in potential knowledge and sources of inspiration. It narrows our range of possibilities when it comes to prevention and repair.

A cursory look at global trends in violence and even the briefest review of the empirical literature on sexual abuse cannot but lead one to the view that "[m]ale violence, sexual or otherwise, is not the unusual behaviour of a few 'odd' individuals, neither is it an expression of overwhelming biological urges: it is a product of the social world in which we live" (Cowburn et al., 1992, pp. 281–282). By extension, I will argue that sexual abuse by Catholic clergy is not the unusual behavior of a few 'odd' individuals or an expression of overwhelming biological urge; rather it is the product of the social world and the organizational structures in which these men live and work. Most people who sexually harm others are male, yet as Cowburn (2010, p. 229) discovered, many therapeutic programs for sexual offenders appear to give little recognition to issues of gender, or particularly to the enactment of masculinities. Women also sexually offend against minors but do so in vastly fewer numbers, as far as current scholarship indicates (Saradjian, 1996). Some publications explicitly concerned with the management of sexual offenders make no mention of men or masculinity or masculinities or gender in their index (Cowburn, 2010, p. 229). In my analysis of the clerical perpetrators and of child sexual abuse within the Catholic Church (a highly gendered organization), gender, power, and organizational culture are at the heart of the matter.

As outlined in Chapter 6, recent years have seen a major expansion of studies on men and masculinities, which has given rise to a number of developments in our understanding of men. One development signals a move away from a notion of singular masculinity that is fixed and biologically and psychologically determined to a more differentiated interrogation of masculinities in the plural (see Hearn, 2010, for review). This move allows for consideration of the different forms of structural, collective, and individual practices and relations in which men engage. In essence, the thinking suggests there is not only one model of manhood in any society. By thinking in terms of multiple masculinities we are open to consider not only men's ways of relating to women but also their relationships with other men and the interconnections of gender with other social considerations, such as age, class, race, ethnicity, nationality, disability, religion, and sexual orientation. By thinking in terms of multiple masculinities we are forced to consider power relations, materially and discursively, not only between men and women but also between men. Connell (1995) argues in his theory of hegemonic masculinity (as discussed in Chapter 6) that not all masculinities are equal and that there are hierarchies of social power among men in the project of patriarchy.

The concept of hegemonic masculinity (Connell, 1995) is a useful one. It has been refined and qualified over recent years and continues to promote a range of conceptual questions (see Chapter 6 and Hearn, 2010, for a useful overview). It has also drawn our attention to an exploration of the meaning of bodily integrity in relation to boys' and adult men's practices.

Mac an Ghaill (1994, p. 9) identified the complex and dominant influences of "compulsory heterosexuality, misogyny and homophobia" on secondary school boys and their understanding of masculinity. The challenge of our times is to develop male sexuality that is not rooted in or associated with misogyny, since a close relationship between misogyny and male sexuality is seen to underpin some harmful sexual relationships and behaviors (Cowburn, 2010, p. 240). Hearn (2010, p. 174) argues that as well as considering hegemonic masculinity and its impact on men's lives, the hegemony of men in relation to women must not be overlooked. This is essentially a reminder that in any discussion of gender and especially of hegemonic masculinity the question of power and the role of patriarchy in Western gender relations is always kept in view.

Milner (2004) offers a cautionary note in relation to gender and its role in sexual and other violence. She advises that demonizing men (by virtue of gender) is not at all helpful; at the same time trying to separate the "predators" from the "protectors" has its limitations (Cowburn & Dominelli, 2001). Any reductionist theory can contribute to social injustice, especially because of the manner in which much social theory is taken up in popular culture and presented as "fact" or "truth". Theory must be sensitive to context. Following Milner (2004, p. 95), while gender sensitivity is critical in theory construction and in practice, to place gender theory above other features of an individual's frame of reference (such as class, race, age, physical ability, and sexual orientation) is to demonstrate lack of theoretical sensitivity to the complexity of gender relations and of men's lives. The oppressor/oppressed axis is complex, and analytical attention must always be paid to the multiple ways in which individuals are complexly positioned in life in relation to the power/powerlessness axis. Gender is only one feature of such complex positioning; race, class, age, sexual orientation, and physical ability are others. While hegemonic masculinity (currently heterosexual masculinity) will always shift to defend its privileges, the gender debate and its relationship to child sexual violence requires more thorough deconstruction and analysis than merely pointing to hegemonic masculinity. At the very least we know that in relation to children and young people, men can relate positively (in terms of care), functionally (in terms of work), and negatively (in terms of violence and abuse and neglect) (Hearn & Pringle, 2006, p. 367). We also know there are two other gendered ways in which men relate to children: in the gendering of children themselves and in how men relate to women (p. 367). Child abuse and the role of gender must consider not only men and their relationships with children but also men and their relations with women. This treatise of masculinity and gender and its relationship to child sexual abuse has implications for understanding the clerical perpetrator.

THE CLERICAL PERPETRATOR: THEMES, TENSIONS, AND PARADOXES

A number of themes, tensions, and paradoxes, some of which relate to gender, masculinity, power and organizational culture emerged in my research with clerical perpetrators, which I suggest must be considered relevant as we attempt to understand how some Catholic clergy went down a sexually abusive path. While many of these themes relate to Catholic clergy in general, their particular role in sexual abuse by Catholic clergy will be identified. These themes are grouped as the theology of clerical sexuality, the interplay of power and powerlessness, the clerical role, moral theology and moral judgment, and emotional loneliness and isolation.

The Theology of Clerical Sexuality

Male sexual identity is a primary requirement for priesthood of the Roman Catholic Church, yet male sexual identity cannot be evident in actual experience, as seminarians and clerical men learn to live in a "no man's land" a place where gendered male sexual expression is prohibited (*Catechism of the Catholic Church*, 1994, p. 1577). Since the Council of Trent (1545–1563), a manualized approach to clerical sexual expression has dominated Catholic moral thought, based on a series of moral rules and regulations. In an attempt to control clerical male sexual expression, sexual activity, and erotic sexual desire have been calcified and set as one (Gallagher, 2011). In effect, sexual activity must be eliminated altogether and sexual desire must be sublimated.

At ordination and sacred consecration, priests and male religious vow to act out a maleness in which sexual arousal is a problem to be overcome and penetration is forbidden (Gordon, 2004, p. 104). According to Catholic moral teaching, every sexual thought, word, desire, and action outside of marriage is mortally sinful (*Catechism of the Catholic Church*, 1994, pp. 2331–2364). Homosexuality is regarded as dysfunction (*Catechism of the Catholic Church*, 1994, pp. 2357–2359). Chastity and purity encourage an "apprenticeship in self-mastery" (*Catechism of the Catholic Church*, 1994, pp. 2337–2356). Sexual sins are considered "grave matter." My research suggests that in proposing such an approach to clerical sexual ethics, which I believe to be part of the current crisis for the Catholic Church, insufficient attention has been paid to generations of clergy who have attempted and in many cases failed to live according to such moral norms. In effect, attempts to control sexual desire and sexual activity have led to sex-obsessed lives of terror, in which the body is disavowed, sexual desire is a problem to be overcome, and the moral superiority of vowed virginity is presumed.

While it is clear that men can grow to mature manhood and have fulfilling lives without fathering children and without sexual engagement, others cannot. For some men, the loss of that opportunity is especially problematic and a personal burden, especially if the loss is in part imposed. Despite this knowing, celibacy is not open for debate in the Catholic Church and it is rarely conceptualized in seminary formation as a major human "loss,". No grieving is facilitated or takes place. Instead, celibacy is presented as a "gift" or part of the "sacrifice" and is largely presented in religious or spiritual terms. The losses of male sexual expression and fatherhood are largely ignored. A degendered version of Christ Jesus and a sanitized version of Christian history and theology are presented, based on one reading of Scripture that is presented as "truth" rather than a version that offers multiple interpretations. A theology of sacrifice eclipses all human considerations.

Current approaches to formation for priesthood teach clergy that they lose nothing by committing to a life of celibate living, but in fact that they receive a gift from God. Given that they must pray for the gift, failure in this regard is often internalized as personal unworthiness or personal failure, especially by those men who ultimately became the clerical perpetrators. Clerical men and vowed religious who were fortunate enough to have been formed in more enlightened theology (mainly because they were fortunate to meet enlightened theologians) and who developed sufficient insight to mourn the loss of male sexual intimacy and of a potential family, adapted and redirected their generative strivings into productive lives, including strivings to protect and watch over the young and vulnerable (Frawley-O'Dea,

2004, p. 132). Psycho-sexual and emotional maturity and adequate relational support to live the clerical life facilitated this process. Other clergy neither achieved such psychosexual maturity nor had adequate relational support to live emotionally and sexually healthy lives.

Clerical culture involves a silence on matters of sexuality and loss, and little space is afforded to articulate these concerns. Clerics and former clerics told me that many of their contemporaries drink heavily to compensate, others gamble, others use their power "to lord it over people," and many engage in physical relationships with "consenting" adults. The clerical perpetrators who participated in my research could not openly acknowledge the reality of their sexual lives and losses, even long before they had to begun to abuse minors. Nor could they deal appropriately with the losses that clerical life would bring. Rather, these men continually sought that which they could not have, attempting to sublimate and deny sexual desire and control sexual expression.

My research suggests that celibacy is not the problem that gives rise to sexual abuse of minors by Roman Catholic clergy (although an open discussion of its role in the Catholic Church is long overdue), but a Catholic sexual ethic and theology of priesthood that "problematizes" the body and erotic sexual desire and emphasizes chastity and purity over a relational ethic for living may be. This theology of sexuality contributes to self-hatred, shame, and personal failure, and needs serious theological examination and revision. The theologies of self-mortification and sacrifice, which add to the problem, contribute to the unhelpful split between and "spirit" and "matter." Such a split has had severe consequences for the Christian tradition for centuries and is even evident in priesthood today. The role of such an unhelpful disregard for the embodied experience of ordained and consecrated men in the sexual abuse crisis emanates from the manner in which this split has become institutionalized in celibate culture, and even idealized as the model of perfection of clerical male sanctity (Ranson, 2002a, p. 391). In essence, the body is disavowed and the spirit is idealized. When one adds the practices of self-flagellation into this mix, practices that mark the biographies of some of the participants in my research, at least in the early part of their clerical and religious lives, the unhealthy disregard for the mortified and sacrificed body that emerges from these and many other clerical narratives begs an important question: Not why did so many clergy sexually act out in the way they did, but rather why didn't more of them do so? It is out of this complex set of sexual, emotional, and gender-based conditions that the sexual abuse of minors in the Catholic Church emerges.

Interplay of Power and Powerlessness

A second contradiction that marks the biographies and stories of the clerical perpetrators who participated in my research centers on the structural conditions that kept them inherently powerless while at the same time setting them apart from and above other non-ordained or non-consecrated religious men and women. This contradiction emanates from the theology of priesthood that dominated and continues to dominate the Catholic Church and the ecclesiology (model of Church) that it gives rise to. Essentially, while formation and the structure of clerical life kept the men sexually and relationally immature, ordination and sacred consecration set them apart as elite, superior to other men. This also applies to other clerical men.

At ordination, a priest's hands and his whole being are made sacred and he is conferred with extraordinary powers to administer the sacraments, transform lives, and forgive sin, powers that belong to him alone as a priest (*Catechism of the Catholic Church*, 1994, pp. 1544–1568; Gordon, 2004, p. 105). For vowed religious, while the same sacred powers are not bestowed at consecration, the sense of sacredness of the chosen life comes from the idea that they have been "called" by God for this sacred role. Catholic tradition (which supports the moral superiority of vowed chastity and the discipline of celibacy), and clericalism (which positions clergy as superior to Catholic laity, not least because of their celibate commitments and their powers as sacramental ministers), sustain and foster this perspective (Doyle, 2003, p. 209). At the heart of what I believe to be problematic is the notion of the ontological change that underpins the theology of priesthood and the ecclesiology that it fosters.

In a program on ABC National Radio in Australia (*Background Briefing*, March 7, 2010), the following extract from a book on priesthood , written by Bishop Porteous (2008), an Australian Bishop and until 2008 a rector of an Australian seminary in Sydney, illustrates succinctly the point I wish to make. Bishop Porteous describes the changes that occur at ordination: "A man once ordained is ontologically changed. He is a priest. Something mysterious happens. It is an action of grace, and something quite real . . . The priesthood is not just the deputing of an individual to take on a particular role. It is more than a function; it is a radical reorienting of the whole reality of the person. He is changed at the level of his being . . . Ordination is not just the power to exercise the priestly office in the Church; it is such a transformation of the person that a distinctly priestly character can be identified in him." In this vision of priesthood, which can also be seen in the writings of Popes John Paul II and Benedict XVI (Donovan, 2009), the priest is not alone an instrument of God, nor a minister of the sacraments; he is essentially changed. He acts in *Persona Christi,* not as a mere instrument of Christ's work but rather as Christ's real image and representative (Ryan, 2011; Conway, 2004). In this theology of priesthood, it is little wonder that priesthood is construed by clergy and laity alike as a personal gift and a permanent sacred calling that is irreversible, rather than as a gift of service to the community (Ryan, 2011).

Emerging from Irish seminaries, it is no surprise that generations of otherwise disempowered seminarians became convinced that they were set apart and set above the Catholic laity by virtue of ordination. It is no surprise that even despite intentionality, such clerics subscribed to a dual model of Church in which clergy were elite and laity subordinate. One former (non-abusing) priest remarked to me: "It was an extraordinary experience to move from being a student for a seven-year period to being a priest thereafter. We had one noticeable professor who did not associate directly with students, but once you were elevated to the level of priesthood, his demeanor automatically changed." Many of the men who participated in my research, along with other clergy, experienced the ontological change at ordination as a privilege rather than as something that would prove to be problematic once they were back living in the real world of priesthood. Other scholars report similar conclusions (Frawley-O'Dea, 2004, p. 130). Some priests have told me that they experienced such ontological change as a burden.

Even the reforms of the Second Vatican Council (1962–1965), which tried to humanize many aspects of the Roman Catholic Church, did not resolve the emotional and sexual contradictions and dilemmas of clerical life. Its attempts to chart a new theology of priesthood were also left floundering. While the messages of the Council led priests and religious to an understanding that their lives must not be devoid of intimacy, little guidance was offered as to how such intimacy was to be achieved within the boundaries that the pastoral and spiritual dimensions of priesthood or religious life would require. Within such a context, boundary violations, including sexual violations, were inevitable. Papesh (2004, p. 98), himself a priest, argues that maintaining appropriate professional boundaries is a constant source of concern for Catholic clergy. He suggests that to manage professional boundaries adequately, the only true friends a priest or religious can ever have are those of his family, fellow priests, and friends from the time before he entered clerical or religious life.

I am coming to the view that the ontological change that belongs to a particular theology of priesthood sets otherwise healthy men, who have chosen a life of priestly and consecrated service, apart from ordinary men, in an unhealthy manner. Such thinking also breathes a dominant culture of autocratic clericalism that gives rise to a paradigm of Church (or an ecclesiology) that is far removed from the participative Church of the People of God. Far from baptism bestowing equality as the rite of passage and as the vision, current ecclesiology suggests a dual model of Church in which the Church of the clergy is superior and more "holy" than the Church of the laity. Apart from ignoring the role of baptism in bestowing equality on all of the People of God and the role of the Holy Spirit, which in Christian tradition is said to fill the faith community and guide its work, current ecclesiology, of which clericalism is both a consequence and a cause, gives rise to the very conditions that enabled the sexual abuse of minors to occur in the first place and to go undetected for far too long.

In the public sphere, clergy appear independent in the exercise of their duties and powerful in the minds of the public (Doyle, 2003, 2004; Inglis, 1998; Kirby, 1984). Traditionally the priest in Ireland was given respect and could do no wrong—at least that was the popular belief during the period in which the participants in my research were active in ministry. However, despite experiencing the trappings of such a dominant power position in the public realm, the clerical perpetrators in my research indicated that personal powerlessness, lack of autonomy, loneliness and frustration in the private sphere were very much part of daily life. Their narratives and my clinical experience suggests that the Catholic Church in Ireland operates a governance structure in which Catholic clergy can be dominated in the private sphere by a system of clerical hierarchical governance that is not transparent and not accountable. Relationships with superiors, particularly regarding vocational appointments were especially problematic for the priests and religious brothers who participated in my research. The theology of obedience contributed to this situation. Seven of the participants felt alienated from Church leaders. However, two men acknowledged exceptional support and help given by their bishops when their sexual offending histories began to be uncovered in the 1980s. Other research on Roman Catholic clergy in Ireland found that the most important source of stress for priests was their relationships with Church leaders (Lane, 1997, p. 22). The fact that Irish priests are dependent on their bishop for accommodation and salary contributes to the power imbalance.

My research suggests that their stance of affable submissiveness, particularly towards superiors, diminished the clerical perpetrators' sense of personal authority and autonomy and overshadowed much of their conscious awareness of their power as adult men and as Church ministers. In other words, the men appeared to have little awareness of the context from which and in which they operated. Their training had taught them to think of power in one direction only; upwards. The emphasis was on the obedience they owed to people who had authority and power over them; not about how authority should be exercised by them, the obligations that accompany such power and authority, and the moral limits to its uses (Hill, 1997).

In these circumstances the men could relate easily to children and young people, whom their narratives indicate they saw as "friends" and "equals." Children and young people thus became the receptors for adults' needs and feelings. It does not appear to be the case that the abuse perpetrated by the men in my study was about gaining power *over* the victims in order to feel "human" or masculine or powerful. In fact, in the personal sphere the men saw the victims as equal to them, capable of saying yes or no to their advances. This was part of the problem. To be sure the men knew they were in the power position in the public exercise of their ministries as a teacher or priest, and they knew they could call children at will from classrooms or other venues and that the child would have no option but to come. However, at the level of the sexual and the emotional, their narratives paradoxically indicate that they saw children and young people as potential "friends" and "equals." Thus, it was the men's interpretation of "equality", their blindness to power in the sexual and emotional sphere (i.e. their sexual and emotional immaturity) and their lack of understanding of childhood vulnerability and sexuality that was part of their problem.

In a manner that might be difficult for many adults to comprehend, the clerical perpetrators did not countenance adequately the power imbalances that were involved in their "relationships" and "friendships" with children and young people in the private sphere. Their principal preoccupation was one of personal and individualized inner conflict and distress, mainly related to celibacy, sexuality and inner emotional turmoil and frustration. Many of the men did not feel powerful, despite the power positions they occupied in the communities in which they worked and in the minds of the Irish laity.

The clerical perpetrators lived out of an unreflective script of private powerlessness whilst ministering in a site of unsupervised and unchallenged public dominance. This paradox is at the core of their sexual offending. A feeling of private powerlessness that eclipsed an awareness of the power context from which and in which they operated, as adult males and as ministers of the Catholic Church, became a deadly combination of circumstances that resulted in the sexual abuse of minors. This is at the heart of the abuse issue for Roman Catholic clergy. The picture of power relations is therefore a complex one. The clerical perpetrators were both powerful and powerless and it is this constellation, rather than their power position *per se* that is seen as contributing to their sexual offending.

Whilst no excuses can be made for their sexual offending, in attempting to explain their actions at the level of power, I have come to the following conclusion: their experiences of powerlessness in the private sphere combined with their idea of power as accountability upwards, were devoid of facilitated introspection, as they were left unsupervised, unsupported and unchallenged to minister in a site of unregulated public power. It is this dynamic of power/powerlessness that is implicated in their sexual offending. In such circumstances the sexual abuse of children in the private realm functioned to preserve the priesthood in the public sphere; that is as long as the secrecy was maintained.

The concept of "emotional congruence with children" has been well described in the psychological literature on sexual offenders as a correlate of child molestation (Wilson, 1999) and as a risk factor for sexual recidivism (Mann, Hanson, & Thornton, 2010). The motivation for such emotional congruence may be allied to emotional immaturity and/or to lack of opportunity for healthy adult engagement. Jenks (1996) suggests that in conditions of instability, such as those found where sources of adult attachment are weakened, children can become the repository for feelings of stability that cannot be attained elsewhere. In the case of the clerical perpetrators, while some men developed "friendships" with children and young people prior to any abusive ideation, in other scenarios the abuse was much more opportunistic.

Cossins (2000) suggests the power/powerlessness axis is implicated in sexual offending, and although I agree with this analysis, Cossins' interpretation of power and powerlessness is different from mine. Cossins believes that child sexual offending is the method by which some men alleviate experiences of powerlessness to establish their masculinity, a theory that is similar to some of the masculinities theorists (Messerschmidt, 1993). In this case, the drive is to have power *over* the victim to feel powerful as part of the project of masculinity. My view is that in the case of Catholic clergy, the power/powerlessness dynamic works in a different way.

The Clerical Role and Identity

A third issue that I believe forms part of the complex web of conditions that gave rise to sexual offending by clerical men relates to their understanding and expectations of the clerical role and to how they were to live. The combination of the divine aspects of clerical maleness, a sacrificial approach to the body that bordered on fear and self-hatred, and the denied reality of their actual sexual and emotional lives was addressed in ways that could not be sustained. In particular, the men over-identified with the public dimensions of their role and lived their lives as though the role represented their whole identity. Always on duty, everyone was a potential "soul" to be saved. The priest was always a priest, whether visiting his mother, having dinner at home, or celebrating the Eucharist. Such over-identification with the priestly or religious role contributed to his problems.

The clerical perpetrators who participated in my research described their lives as having no boundary between their clerical identity and their identity as male human beings. Their clerical identity defined who they were and how they lived. There was no functional distinction between their work and their personal lives. They lived and worked and worked and lived, helping other individuals negotiate their spiritual lives and their relationships with God. In attempting to be good clergymen they felt compelled to put aside their own emotional, physical, and sexual needs. However, this was an impossible and unrealistic expectation, and one that would lead them into boundary violations of the worst kind. Adopting singular hobbies, such as music or painting or additional pastoral work, the men were in a sense "always available" for the public, always available to do God's work. Unacknowledged depression and burnout were to result. While ordination or religious sacred consecration marked a change in their external status, the narratives suggest that eight of the nine men felt they were working towards priesthood or religious brotherhood almost all of their conscious lives. During this time, much of their psychological and sexual growth and development was overshadowed by their vocational "calling." These men, while appearing to be loved by those to whom they ministered, were completely unknown to anyone at all.

Part of the over-identification with the priestly and religious role, which is a problem not just for the clerical perpetrators, is theologically driven, based on the ontological change at ordination, the notion of sacred "calling" (that differs from the "calling" of the laity) and the irreversibility of the priestly vocation.[1] As currently constructed, significant skill and support is required to enable the young cleric to discern the distinctions between his theological status (that one is always a priest) and his social and emotional status (that life cannot be lived healthily through this role alone). This task necessitates good personal awareness, a strong sense of personhood and identity, and a deep understanding of the power and social complexities inherent in priestly and religious life. These conditions are necessary if appropriate boundary-making is to be the norm (Ranson, 2010, personal communication[2]).

For many priests, over-identification with the role is a big problem, that eventually leads to compromised integrity and a split between the public persona and the private reality. It can also give rise to individual and institutional hypocrisy in which one set of behaviors is proclaimed in public while another is practiced in private. Clerics and former clerics have often drawn my attention to the double life that some clerics live, and figures produced by Sipe (1995, 2003) and others (McGlone, 2001; Nines, 2006), which were discussed in Chapter 3, support such an assertion. The space between the twin tracks of such double lives holds the potential for alcoholism, alienation, depression, despair, and inappropriate sexual acting out.

Moral Theology and Moral Judgment

A fourth issue that I see as significant in relation to the life conditions that gave rise to sexual abuse by Catholic clergy relates to problems in making good judgments, particularly in relation to sexuality and children. For helping me understand these processes more clearly I have found the work of Arendt (2003) to be particularly helpful. As Arendt observed (2003, p. 44), the precondition for the kind of judgment that is necessary to prevent wrongdoing is not a highly developed intelligence or sophistication in moral matters, but rather a disposition to live with others and explicitly with oneself in which one can engage in an ongoing silent dialogue with oneself, especially about the consequences of one's actions for another. Judgment needs the special presence of others "in whose place" one must think, and whose perspectives one must take into consideration (Arendt, 2003, p. 44). In the psychological literature this process is referred to as "perspective taking," one of the essential steps in demonstrating empathy (Fernandez, 2002; Marshall, 2002). Following Arendt I have come to the conclusion that a moral education that is overly intellectualized and technical and focuses primarily on theoretical or abstract problems does not equip its students to make good moral judgments.

For the participants in my research, the lack of personal awareness, the absence of real and honest dialogue with others, the lack of a reflective space in which to face their lives honestly and openly, and a legalistic-orthodox approach to morality (Inglis, 1998, p. 22) dominated their clerical education. Obedience to the law of the Church was seen as the way in which to win favor with God and Church, whereas breaches of the law constituted sin. This legalistic understanding of moral obligation was devoid of a relational ethic. The men's narratives show how they negotiated with the Church's moral rules regarding the parameters of sexual sin when they began abusing, such as preventing ejaculation, or focusing on the level of intrusion of the sex "act" and not on the child (see Chapter 7). This method of making moral judgments is consistent with a legalistic-orthodox approach to morality, one that is externally determined based on rules and regulations rather than internally constituted, based on an individually principled ethic. Although the participants in my research tried to convince themselves at the time that the consequences of their actions were not severe for the young people, they were deeply concerned about the sin aspects of their behavior, focusing on the act, less on the person. However, such "matters of conscience" could be attended to in confession, where they were met by confessors who were trained in the same legalistic-orthodox tradition. Eight of the nine participants in my study confessed their abusing on many occasions in confession, acknowledging "sin" or "wrongdoing." Within the safe and secretive space of the confessional the men received absolution from sin, relief from guilt, and a fresh start.

Absent from the men's education was an approach to morality, conscience, and ethics in which moral judgment could be based on reasoned debate, personal reflection, emotional expression, empathic concern, and a relational principle that would encourage the capacity to put oneself in the shoes of the other, in whose place one could feel. The narratives of the men suggest instead that they had learned a morality that relied solely on moral absolutes and a theoretical understanding of morality. They were also well versed in Church rules and regulations and they bargained with these. Far from the notion that the sexual abuse crisis in the Catholic Church suggests the need for further articulation of moral absolutes (see Pope Benedict XVI in Seewald, 2010), my research in fact suggests the opposite. The clerical perpetrators were not ignorant of the moral absolutes of Catholic moral thought, and they did their absolute best to live by such moral norms. The problem was that the norms were impossible to live, and the men lacked the requisite emotional and relational intelligence to enable them to make good judgments when knowledge of moral absolutes did not provide answers to the human complexities of life that they encountered. This is not to say that there is not room for some moral absolutes. However, knowledge of moral absolutes is insufficient in itself to enable good moral judgment. The narratives of the participants in my research demonstrate that the men were able to bend Church and moral rules and regulations to suit their purposes without ever having to look the child honestly in the eye or face themselves in the mirror, with the child and his parents in view, and try to convince the child and his parents that what they (the clerical perpetrators) were doing to the child was "right". The lack of emotional engagement with matters to do with children, emotion and sexuality and the lack of preparation for the judgments that they would ultimately have to make in the personal and pastoral spheres of their clerical lives are evident in the men's accounts.

According to Arendt (2003, p. 44), when conscience functions in an automatic way as though through the possession of a set of prelearned rules in which every new situation or experience is prejudged into a certain category, then acts of wrongdoing are a distinct possibility. Avoiding wrongdoing involves an individually principled ethic that is internally motivated rather than externally driven. Exercising good judgment requires internal reflection, reasoned debate, and dialogue with the other in imagination, in whose place one must stand in anticipation. In Arendt's view (2003, p. 44), the people who did not participate in the Holocaust, even when ordered to do so, were the ones who were capable of judging for themselves, not because they held a better system of values than those who participated in the Holocaust, or because the standards of right and wrong were more firmly planted in their minds and conscience (p. 44). The non-participants in the Holocaust were those people whose conscience did not function in an automatic way, as though possessing a set of learned or innate rules, which they then applied to all situations (p. 44). The non-participants were reflective. They asked themselves to what extent they could live in peace having carried out certain deeds on their fellow men (p. 44). They asked themselves how they would face the man they would destroy and at the same time continue to face themselves honestly (Arendt, 2003, p. 44). Their judgments were far from theoretical or abstract; they were very specific and very personal (p. 44). In essence, (1) the habit of examining and reflecting upon whatever comes to pass; (2) the activity of "thinking in specifics" regarding the particulars of life situations ; and (3) the practice of thinking of others "in whose place" one must think and anticipate represent the act of making good judgments (p. 189).

For Arendt (2003, p. 160), the practice of making good judgments in the manner in which she describes could be such as to condition men against wrongdoing. A critical moral theology and a socially and emotionally mature clergy could enhance such circumstance. However, in the case of the participants in my research, the opposite was in fact what happened. A seminary structure and content devoid of personal awareness, personal reflection, an individual principled ethic and a critical moral theology was simply inadequate in preparing the clerical perpetrators in my research for the level of human engagement that their vocational life would demand and for the complex moral judgments that they would ultimately be called upon to make. It is out of this scenario that the sexual abuse of minors became possible at the level of conscience.

Emotional Loneliness and Isolation

The final theme that cannot be ignored in attempting to understand the conditions that gave rise to sexual abuse by Catholic clergy are emotional loneliness and isolation. Catholic clergy are thought to belong to a brotherhood of men, yet many live lives of emotional isolation. Although clerics believe that by giving up their lives to follow Jesus and leaving their families to join a diocese or religious order they will belong to an eternal fraternity of men who will always stand by each other (as also noted by Greeley, 2004, p. 107), the reality is in fact quite different. Social loneliness can be a consequence of the geographical changes that accompany clerical appointments (often without being asked) and suffered by most at different times. However, emotional loneliness and emotional isolation are quite different. Much of these can be traced back to the template of silence, secrecy and self neglect that perhaps unintendedly was fostered in Irish seminaries. By privileging the performative aspects of priesthood and religious life at the enormous expense of honest relationship and self care, generations of clergy were left devoid of the tools to develop appropriate sexual and emotional health within the complexities of a celibate vocation.

Fresh from the constraints of seminary life and away from the support and constraints of family and seminary colleagues, many of the young and functionally immature men who emerged from Irish seminaries of the 1970s and 1980s were put in charge of adolescents with whom they could identify. All of the participants in my research were assigned to ministries involving youth, in schools and parishes, following ordination or sacred consecration, without the necessary pastoral, sexual, or psychological maturity required for working with the young and the vulnerable. Lonely and unsupported and often in first appointments and with older, occasionally "alcoholic" or otherwise "unwell" priests, the "youthful" priest or brother was soon to develop the heretofore prohibited "particular friendships" of his seminary training with some of the teenage boys to whom he ministered. It was only a matter of time before his freer self emerged and with it a need for intimacy, touch, acknowledgement, love, emotional regard, and sexual expression. In the United States Celenza (2004, p. 218) found a similar pattern in her work with clergy. The celibate clerical man, lonely and unsupported, yet elevated and idealized within the structural power imbalance of the pastoral relationship with children, eventually broke his vows, sometimes after some years, and crossed the "sin barrier." Having done so once, he continued to do so again and again, sometimes seeking out similar opportunities to "feel alive." Unfortunately for him and his victims, he was able to do so again and again in a pattern that continued initially undetected and later detected for far too long. While such scenarios can never be presented as an excuse for sexual offending, it was within these contexts that many clerical men sexually abused minors, as their sexual and relational desires that were otherwise unrecognized and unlanguaged became evident, as these isolated but powerful men learned about "real" life and relational living.

THEORIZING THE CLERICAL PERPETRATOR: TOWARDS A GENDERED THEORY

In trying to understand those clerical men who had sexually abused minors and in trying to offer an explanation, but not an excuse, for their sexual offending, I have come to believe that an analysis of gender and sexual abuse and clerical masculinity and its construction offers some promise. In my work on this subject I have come to believe that many of the modes of life available to Catholic clergy can serve to impoverish, delude, and alienate them. I have also come to believe that clerical structures can distort the men's relationships with women and with one another. My thesis is that the men who were to become the abuse perpetrators were trapped in a particular model of clerical masculinity in which they became captives of choices that ultimately were not satisfying for them. Without attempting in any way to make excuses for their sexual offending but in an attempt to understand it, I began to wonder if the clerical perpetrators became "violent" and cruel to children (even if not in many cases overtly so), because of the systematic "violence" and cruelty that was done to their bodies and spirits in the course of their lives as young clerical males. I wondered if in being hurt, they had become hurters.

Clerical Masculinities and Sexual Abuse

In the gender order suggested by Connell (1995), clerical masculinity, meaning celibate masculinity, is in the marginalized position relative to other masculinities in the dominant hierarchy of masculinities. The gender order which comprises heterosexual and sexually active masculinity (which is in the hegemonic position), heterosexual and sexually inactive masculinity (which is complicit), homosexual masculinity (a subordinated masculinity), and celibate masculinity (which is regarded as a marginalized masculinity). It is possible to borrow Connell's framework and apply it to the subgroup of masculinities known as celibate clerical masculinity to make some useful inferences about different ways of embodying clerical masculinity and of "doing" priesthood and religious brotherhood and to conceptualize a hierarchy of clerical masculinities. From this perspective, clerical masculinity is best conceptualized as clerical masculinities in the plural, and it is my thesis that one form of clerical masculinity is more likely than others in the hierarchy of clerical masculinities to give rise to the sexual abuse of minors. This form of clerical masculinity, which I name as "Perfect Celibate Clerical Masculinity," is in the idealized and hegemonic position and is supported in clerical culture and seminary training.

All clerics adopt and integrate a clerical identity as they attempt to embody priesthood or religious brotherhood. For many students of priesthood this process begins in the seminary, but for many others it is a process that begins in imagination, long before entry into a formal formation process. A number of theological and social factors influence this process, factors that are interpreted by individuals through their own cognitive lens. This in turn gives rise to different versions of clerical masculinity and to how priesthood or religious brotherhood is to be embodied. Different interpretations of clerical masculinity underpin what it means to be a good clerical man and in turn how priesthood or religious brotherhood is to be performed. In this manner, a number of clerical masculinities can be identified, each permitting and constraining certain behaviors, including sexual behaviors, and influencing certain ideas regarding how to live as good clergymen. A hierarchy of clerical masculinities emerges from this scenario through social and power relations. However, it would be wrong to see this schema as consisting of absolute types into which individuals fit neatly. Instead, the "types" are offered as representative of a broad range of features that help in conceptualizing these complex phenomena.

Perfect Celibate Clerical Masculinity is the form of masculinity that is in the hegemonic position and promoted by the Catholic Church as the "ideal" type. It is a version of clerical masculinity in which perfection is the goal and perfect celibacy and chastity is the norm. Perfect Celibate Clerical Masculinity invites ways of living premised on emotional, social, and sexual perfection. Human transgressions and failure to achieve perfection are seen as personal failures or sinful weakness. Other versions of clerical masculinity (which I call Compassionate Celibate Clerical Masculinity, Incongruous Celibate Clerical Masculinity and a version that is built on very deep faith and holiness) invoke ways of "doing" priesthood and religious brotherhood and ways of achieving intimacy and male sexual expression that are less inclined to hold perfection as the norm and are therefore less condemnatory and more understanding of the individuals involved. These alternative models of priesthood and clerical identity do not lead to criminal behavior, even if the practices in the intimate and sexual sphere often break the norms and disciplinary codes of priestly and religious life. Models of priesthood and clerical identity based on Perfect Celibate Clerical Masculinity produce the pool of clergy out of which the clerical perpetrators emerge.

Those clerics who adopt a Compassionate Celibate Clerical Masculinity experience themselves as emotional and sexual as well as spiritual beings that embody their maleness as part of their lives, even if awareness of body brings "trouble" in the face of the celibate commitment. These men seek out emotional and at times sexual relationships with other adults, women or men, which they understand as part of the project of their humanity. Although they experience guilt and conflict because of their breaches of Church discipline, they are able to forgive themselves for their transgressions, without shame and severe damage to self-esteem and respect. Although these men experience guilt, they do not live with shame-based identities. They have friends of both sexes and they "do their best" in their approach to their work, often working too hard, which is rarely motivated by a need to compensate for private shame.

Those clerics who adopt an approach to clerical masculinity based on an Incongruous Celibate Clerical Masculinity are similar to the Compassionate group in many respects, except that when these men engage in sexual relationships with adults, they experience no guilt at all. These men rationalize their double life as part of the project of "mature adulthood." Overtly compliant but internally resistant, Church discipline is seen as the problem to be overcome by these men, who live their lives in silent transgression. Like many other clergy, they work too hard, but not as compensation for shame. These men do not live with shame-based identities.

While other forms of clerical masculinity can be further developed and more richly described, the point of mentioning the four that I do, with particular emphasis on Perfect Celibate Clerical Masculinity, is to indicate how the form of clerical masculinity that one embodies gives rise to a host of attitudes and subsequent behaviors, some of which result in negative consequences for the young and the vulnerable as well as for the cleric himself.

Perfect Celibate Clerical Masculinity

Perfect Celibate Clerical Masculinity sees the identity of the priest or religious brother as based on the priestly or religious role, and gender or maleness is merely a secondary consideration. Within such a construct, the individual is priest or religious brother first and only secondly is he a man. According to this template, masculinity is based on purity and chastity. Celibacy is seen as a gift from God, for which the individual must pray. Sex and sexual expression is construed as a set of "acts," and the list of sexual sins is based on lists of rules and regulations regarding the sex "acts." Sexual desire and emotional intimacy are seen as less relevant for priests and religious brothers than they are for other individuals. Women and girls are seen as a threat to the celibate commitment. Intimacy with men is also construed as threat, in particular because of underlying Church policy on homosexuality, which can link with homophobic ideation. Clergy are seen as set apart and set above. Being set apart and set above is a burden that is worn heavily but it also confers an institutional power in society; men who construct clerical masculinity along these lines are aware of this and benefit from it. Human perfection is the aim in serving God, and failing to achieve perfection is interpreted as personal failure and must be covered up.

My research with clerical perpetrators who have attempted to live priesthood or religious brotherhood according to the norms of Perfect Celibate Clerical Masculinity suggests that a number of sub-themes specifically can be identified. In general, members of this group believe in self-denial and self-abasement, and the priest's personal happiness is not seen as relevant. Fulfillment is thought to come solely from doing God's work. Although the men know they are doing wrong in abusing children, they believe children and adolescents will not be "harmed" by sexual acts, or at least not too much, unless the "acts" are especially "intrusive." These men have a list of behaviors at where to draw the line regarding sexual intrusions, usually involving touching. Clericalism helps them to assume that children will never disclose, even if at the time the men would not see what they were doing as sexual abuse.

In terms of lifestyle and environment, the man who embodies a model of Perfect Celibate Clerical Masculinity avoids and denies sexuality and sexual desire. He tries to become "holy and detached" and "sexless." He avoids relationships with women and friendships with men.

He has few close friendships within the clergy and no close adult friendships. He feels lonely and unfulfilled. He conceals emotional distress and turns his attention to God and the needs of others. He works too hard and strives for excellence and perfection in his public ministry. He lacks supervision and support. He is outwardly a rule-keeper, whose rigid adherence to rules and regulations is devoid of internal reflection and emotional engagement. He adopts a subservient position in relationships, particularly towards Church leadership. Many of these men live overtly quiet and compliant lives. However, an outwardly compliant demeanor masks an underlying unhappiness and discontent, which is not expressed. Life takes off on twin tracks. The internal struggle and the public personae are compartmentalized. He learns to live in "no man's land," a place where gendered identity is avoided.

At a psychological level, the man who embodies Perfect Celibate Clerical Masculinity as a way of "doing" priesthood and religious brotherhood intellectualizes his emotion. He denies anger and resentment. He feels lonely and emotionally isolated. He feels disconnected from the brotherhood of priests and is more likely to be emotionally connected to young people, who become like "friends". He feels connected to and interested in those to whom he ministers and is often seen as a very good priest. He internalizes shame and personal failure in living a life of internal conflict and struggle. He lives with a form of depression and a weariness of life and he becomes "soul dead." For some men who embody Perfect Celibate Clerical Masculinity, children and adolescents are both "friends" and emotionally connected, while other children and adolescents are a means to a sexual end.

As outliers, a small number of men in this group center on the self. Their personal happiness and ambitions are seen as important and they are more likely to commit the more intrusive sexually abusive acts by believing that children and adolescents have sexuality and can and do give consent. They act in passive-aggressive ways, becoming gregarious and even provocative towards those in authority, adopting an overtly passive-aggressive way of relating. These men are inclined to act out in quite "risky" and provocative ways. For them, children and adolescents at generally kept at an emotional distance, but children and adolescents become sexually a means to an end. Clergy whose clerical masculinity is based on Perfect Celibate Clerical Masculinity also abuse vulnerable adults, as well as, or instead of minors. The choice of victim is more likely related to opportunity than to other features.

The problem with Perfect Celibate Clerical Masculinity as a hegemonic masculinity in the Catholic Church is not that it is built on a system of inherent tensions and paradox, but rather that to hold the tension between the paradoxes requires significant skill. Both seminary training and the support and supervision systems for clergy are remiss in this regard, failing to equip Catholic clergy with the skills necessary for navigating healthily such complexity. The lack of care that was provided for young clergy who were often preoccupied with learning the ministerial tasks of their first vocational appointment without adequate mentoring, support or supervision, must be seen as part of the systemic genesis of the problem of sexual abuse by clergy. Leaving young clerical men to manage blindly in an increasingly secular world of increased complexity, with the rulebook of moral theology as the only guide, is not only inadequate as preparation for such a life but is also negligent. It is not surprising that men who interpreted the messages of Perfect Celibate Clerical Masculinity literally and rigidly, and who tried to cope with its inherent tensions by resorting to the default position of avoiding human intimacy altogether and avoiding honest emotional expression and human connection, were doomed to fail in achieving their goal. The failure to achieve perfection inevitably led to further isolation for the men who participated in my research, and this isolation ultimately gave way to further shame. We know that shame underpins much sexual offending.

Even if humans can live healthily without sexual relations, and theorists of all persuasions continually debate such considerations, there is no disputing the fact that humans simply cannot live without intimacy (Marshall, 1989, p. 492; 1993, p. 113; Ward & Stewart, 2003, p. 24). Simply put, individuals who feel good about themselves and are able to engage in constructive relationships do not need to engage in destructive behaviors, including the abuse and hurt of minors.

It is my contention that children and young people were chosen for sexual and emotional expression by the participants in my research because they believed that all routes to adult sexual and emotional relationships were closed to them as part of the project of clerical life. In addition, their highly gendered organization failed to prepare them for the power positions they would occupy as adult men and as ordained ministers of the Catholic Church. Despite the idealized and unrealistic aspirations they held of themselves and their ministries, sooner or later, when their interior selves and their public commitments came into sharp conflict, their way of living gave way to the sexual abuse of minors.

What is important here is the first occasion on which the sexual abuse took place. My research suggests that this often occurred not in premeditated ways but in ways that were unintended, almost at times "by accident." However, after the first abusive occasion, while many clerical men never abuse again, for the participants in my research who did, the sexual experience had its own momentum and was reinforced dramatically in a number of ways. The "buzz," the cure for loneliness and the new interest that sex and sexual expression provided in the life of the otherwise "dead" man, took over as he began the journey of trying to accommodate in his thinking and his conscience this new-found secret world that would keep him "alive," although conflicted. This secret world had to be balanced with the fact that all the clerical perpetrators knew they were doing wrong. In this they adopted the usual psychological mechanisms that all humans adopt in maintaining bad behavior; denial, minimization, rationalization, justifications.

I suggest that the particular form of clerical masculinity that is embodied by individual clergy enables and constrains how the individual lives, and it provides a template for what sexual behaviors or intimate relationships will be rationalized and enacted—and with what degree of guilt or regret. That some clerics turn to children and young people for sexual and emotional contact, while others turn to vulnerable women, religious women, "consenting" adults, Internet technologies, or indeed to spirituality and God to meet their emotional and sexual needs, speaks to the different forms of clerical masculinity that underpin each man's embodiment of clerical life and to his way of performing priesthood or religious brotherhood in which Perfect Celibate Clerical Masculinity is in the hegemonic position.

SURVIVING CLERICAL PERFECTION: DISTINGUISHING
CLERGY FROM EACH OTHER

While popular culture and some professional discourses would have us believe that the disease of pedophilia singularly distinguishes clergy who abuse minors from those who do not, my research does not support this conclusion. In fact, it is my experience that many clerical men who sexually abuse minors do not fit the psychiatric classification of pedophilia at all. Research conducted by the John Jay College (2004, 2006, 2011) in the United States concurs, arguing that whatever else is propelling sexual abuse by Catholic clergy, it is not pedophilia (Smith et al., 2008, p. 580; Tallon & Terry, 2008, p. 625). I wish to offer another explanation for how we can understand the factors that distinguish those clerics who abuse minors from those who do not, partly by asking a different question. The usual question—Why do some clerics sexually abuse children and adolescents when others who may have had a similar training and life circumstance do not?—is replaced by what I consider to be more useful one: What happens to some clerical men that enables them lose contact with self during the course of formation and priestly life so that they become candidates for rigidly adopting a lifestyle that is clearly impossible to live and in which they end up sexually abusing minors? In essence, I am asking how it happens that some Catholic clergy "buy into" the model of Perfect Celibate Clerical Masculinity as an ideal type and how others resist this in favor of adopting other more socially acceptable, if not fully Church acceptable, models of living as clerical men in which they meet their sexual and emotional needs in socially acceptable ways.

To answer this question I return to Goffman's (1975/1961) concept of total institutions and to the work that I set out in Chapter 2, in which I conceptualized seminaries as total and totalizing institutions. In doing so, following Goffman (1975/1961, p. 22), I conceptualize Catholic seminaries, and their role in socializing clergy, and the governance structures of the Catholic Church as a form of social hybrid—part residential community, part formal social organization—that acts as a "forcing house for changing persons," each as "a natural experiment on what can be done to the self." My suggestion is that the degree to which the individual responds to or resists the institution's attempts to undermine and change the self will determine the extent to which he develops and maintains a sense of authentic or real self and identity, independent of the clerical role. This in turn influences the ideas he develops about himself, the kind of lifestyle and environmental contexts that are acceptable to him, and his requirements for taking care of his psychological and emotional well-being.

It is my thesis that those men who became the abuse perpetrators were rule-keepers by and large who were molded by their seminary experiences and experiences of clerical life, losing their personal selves and integrity in their attempts to embody a Perfect Celibate Clerical Masculine identity. Other seminarians and clerical men found ways to keep some distance, some elbow room, between themselves and that with which the institution and its promoters assumed they should be identified (Goffman, 1975/1961, p. 279). These latter men erected defenses against the institution's power to mold the self, and in this sense these men became "stance-taking entities," individuals who took up a position "somewhere between identification with an organization and opposition to it," always ready at the slightest pressure to regain the balance by shifting their involvement in either direction, either more towards the self or towards the institution's requirements (p. 280). In contrast, the clerical men who became the abuse perpetrators did not resist the pull of the model of priesthood that was in the hegemonic position, even in small ways, and the mortification of self and personal identity that it required. Instead, their sense of selfhood arose through the status that the role provided, while their personal identities, which were merely "in formation" by virtue of their age and in some cases personal vulnerability, resulting from histories of childhood abuse, shame, and struggle with sexual orientation, were lost or hidden in the new achievement.

Goffman (1975/1961, pp. 60–65) offers a typology which suggests four lines of adaptation that are open to individuals to manage the tension between the "home world" and the "institutional world" when one enters a total institution, such as a Catholic seminary or religious life. These represent ways of managing the tensions between individual identity and institutional identity. In religious institutions where the seminarians are there voluntarily because they feel they have gotten "the call," the conversion to the institution's principles has already taken place, and it only the seminarian's intimate world, the world of the self, identity, emotion, and self-discipline, that is to be re-defined (p. 110). In religious institutions the self is under scrutiny, and Goffman's four lines of adaptation are useful in helping us understand how seminarians and young clerics manage the tensions between their evolving selves, identities, dreams, and hopes and the ideal institutional identity for priesthood or religious brotherhood (Perfect Celibate Clerical Masculinity) that is presented.

Adaptation strategies include "situational withdrawal," whereby the person disengages from all interactions except for the most basic of body requirements (Goffman, 1961, pp. 60–65). Generally this does not work for seminarians, but it does for some clergy following ordination and sacred consecration, as they completely withdraw from the life world of the Church, in spirit if not in body, finding support largely outside of official Church structures. A second adaptation strategy involves adopting an "intransigent line," whereby the individual openly challenges the rules and regulations. Seminarians who are intransigent are often asked to leave, and following ordination or sacred consecration intransigent clerics are barely tolerated. These men often cause problems for themselves and their authorities. A third adaptation strategy open to seminarians and clerics is "colonization," whereby the individual adapts to "a stable, relatively contented existence," using the home world and that which is known and familiar as a point of reference to support the attractiveness of the new world or institutional norms and expectations. By adopting this strategy, any tension between the two worlds is significantly reduced (p. 62). These men keep the link between the home identity and the institutional identity in smooth harmony. The fourth adaptation strategy open to the young cleric or seminarian is that of "conversion," whereby the newcomer appears to adopt the official view of him and tries to act out the role of the perfect recruit. These men become perfect seminarians and priests, converted to the institutional role and identity, losing connection with individual identity that is often merely taking shape (by virtue of age, vulnerability and life experience). The difference between the colonized individual and the converted one is that the colonized individual builds as much of a free community for himself as possible and keeps links with his "former world" using the limited facilities available, while the convert takes a more disciplined moralistic line, presenting himself as someone whose institutional enthusiasm is always in evidence.

It is this latter group of men who become what they think the institution wants and rigidly apply the institutional rules, losing contact with self and integrity in the goal of becoming perfect priests and religious. In so doing they win approval from superiors and bishops and later the communities they serve, but at great personal cost to their psychosocial and sexual health and personal integrity. It is my theory that these are the men who are most at risk for becoming the abuse perpetrators, and it is out of this pool of men that the clerical perpetrators emerge.

For some seminarians, contact with the home world, level of maturity, age, experience, or just pure luck sometimes in having a wise mentor provides immunization against the bleak world of the institution and its demands for the mortification of the self. They adapt to the institutional demands for self-mortification in clever and mature ways, developing alternative models of priesthood, either by sheer luck, pure intellect, or sheer cunning, or for reasons to do with psychological and emotional resilience. These men either adapt the rules of Perfect Celibate Clerical Masculinity in line with their own spiritual meanings and requirements or they develop alternative models of Clerical Masculinity, such as Compassionate Celibate Clerical Masculinity or Incongruous Celibate Clerical Masculinity, as previously discussed. These alternative clerical masculinities help them deal with the complexities of priestly and religious life in more fluid and less rigid ways which can help them from boundary violations of the worst kind. In contrast, those men who embody Perfect Celibate Clerical Masculinity as the template for priesthood and religious life, often do so for reasons to do with sheer naïvety, sheer idealism, or psychological and emotional vulnerability. In such circumstances the protective factors that are necessary to help them mediate the home world and the institutional demands in a healthy manner are either not easily available or are not activated until it is too late. By the time they come to realize that Perfect Celibate Clerical Masculinity is built on a way of living that is impossible to achieve, the failure has been internalized as personal, something that contributes to a shame-based priestly existence, out of which the sexual abuse of minors arises.

A NEW THEOLOGY OF CLERICAL MASCULINITY

My research suggests there is an emerging challenge for a new masculine theology of priesthood and religious life that will reach beyond isolation and fear towards a masculinity that is appropriate for a world framed by multiculturalism, feminism, gay sexuality, and the developing partnership of world faiths, ethical stances, and ecological consciousness (Pryce, 1996, p. 94). The task is for all men to learn to develop masculinities in which they may fully participate in the ongoing creation and recreation of spiritual and sexual integrity, met with sincerity and honesty. This important work needs to be engaged by theologians and social scientists with an interest in ending male sexual violence, including that perpetrated by clerical men. It is a project in which the ontological change at ordination will require honest theological and social scientific interrogation. In such theological scholarship, perhaps a more symbolic and a less literal reading of some of the great documents of the early Churches will hold clues and answers to current problems. It is also a project that might reasonably involve a look to the human face of God and of Jesus Christ (that is for as long as only men can be ordained to the priesthood). This is not Jesus as the Church conventionally presents him, a man without sexuality, who is hardly a bodily being (Pryce, 1996, p. 103). Theological and social scientific reflection might reasonably look to the Jesus as the artists of the Renaissance represented him, a Jesus who is fully human and takes a full physical form (Pryce, 1996, p. 103). A new theology of priesthood and clerical masculinity will need to incorporate a strong interaction between the natural law and recent social scientific development and understandings. While a full exploration of a new theology of priesthood is beyond the scope of the current project, such an undertaking is long overdue. If the sexual abuse crisis in the Catholic Church has served to surface the issues of gender, power, the theology of priesthood, and organizational culture, it can also be said that the organizational

Church has failed thus far to begin to address these important structural, theological, and organizational issues.

THEORIZING SEXUAL ABUSE AND THE CATHOLIC CHURCH: A MULTILEVEL RELATIONAL AND CONTEXTUAL FRAMEWORK

Having attempted to understand the cognitive and social circumstances of the individual perpetrators that have contributed to their sexual offending, I now wish to turn attention to the broader organizational and institutional contexts that are also part of the sexual abuse crisis for the Catholic Church in Ireland and worldwide. It is not my intention to arrive at a neat theory that will explain all in simple terms, nor is my intent to excuse the clerical perpetrators of responsibility for their wrongdoing. Rather, I propose a contextual and relational understanding of this multifaceted problem that involves multiple levels of operation and effect. Despite popular accounts, I do not see sexual abuse by Catholic clergy as a problem of "flawed" individuals or of overwhelming sexual drive. Rather, I see the problem as a complex one, involving a number of subject positions that are enacted within a web of theological, sociological, psychological, and historical considerations. From this perspective, sexual abuse within the Catholic Church is seen as a breakdown in relationships within a gendered context of power relations, organizational culture, theological deliberation, and social conditions. The behavior, emotions, ideas, and understandings of individuals at different levels within the local Church organization, interlinked relationally across time, interact with universal Church norms and practices and with local economic, social, and cultural conditions to produce the local distinctions that mark the "identity" of the problem in different national Churches. However, universally the same core themes emerge across all Catholic Churches worldwide. The Irish Church in the context of the global Catholic Church is the case study undertaken in my work, as an exemplar of child sexual abuse within the universal Catholic Church more broadly.

When detailed knowledge of the Church administration, the institution of the Catholic Church, and the Irish social context are linked to the personal narratives of some offenders, and in fact each reflects back on the other, what emerges is that the individual, the organizational, and the institutional dimensions are actually influencing each other and are bound together in particular dynamic relations. It also becomes evident that there are obvious and noticeable links between what happens on the grand scale of things and on the local level. Such observations might reveal that the classic micro/macro distinction is a rather artificial construction and that the interplay of personal agency and social structure must always be kept simultaneously in view in trying to make sense of social phenomena.

THE FEATURES OF A MULTILEVEL RELATIONAL AND CONTEXTUAL FRAMEWORK

At the first level in a multilevel relational and contextual framework for understanding child sexual abuse within the Catholic Church is the breakdown in the fiduciary relationship between the clerical perpetrator and the abuse victim. Children and their families believed they would be safe, and they were not. The factors that contributed to such a relational breakdown on the part of the clerical perpetrator have been discussed above, and as already outlined they speak to institutional as well as relational and psychological constituencies. It would be repetitive at this point to elaborate these circumstances further.

At the second level of the framework is the relational context that existed between the Catholic clergy and the people of Ireland. What is important here are the relational networks that existed between the clergy and the laity and the principles and beliefs that defined them. The role played by the Catholic Church in the Irish history of emancipation from Britain a time, when the Irish Church was more influenced by local conditions than by Rome, gave priests and religious men and women a special standing in the eyes of a Catholic laity. In addition, the revered position of clerical celibacy, in what was essentially a conservative and predominantly Catholic country, added to the special status of the Catholic clergy. The laity subscribed to the theory that priests and religious were called by God for a special mission, and that they were superior to other men (Conway, 2004; Doyle, 2003; Kirby, 1984). Catholic clergy were seen as "super" human beings who could do no wrong in a recursive relationship that was fostered by both clergy and laity. These factors rendered the priest and religious "safe" in the eyes of a Catholic laity who were blind to or ignored the issues of Catholic male sexual expression and intimate relational living for clergy. A culture of deference marked these relational interactions.

The Murphy (2009) and Ryan (2009) reports suggested that in some situations "normal" clergy and Catholic laity were bystanders to the abuses of children that were occurring; even if full knowledge of the extent or depth of the abuses was incomplete. It is likely that child sexual abuse was the last thing on the minds of non-abusive clerics and the majority of the Catholic laity at the time. However, a culture in which the Catholic clergy were idealized and idolized, and in which their illusivity and denied sexual status were revered rather than in any way potentially problematic for some must be considered as part of the relational context that contributed to the pattern of sexual violations that took place in the Catholic Church in Ireland.

For their part, "normal" clergy did not "witness with awareness" to the unusual behavior of their clerical colleagues (which we now know led to the abuse of minors)—such as being alone in their rooms with children for long periods of time, or having "friendships" with children and young people in the absence of more adult relationships. A general pattern of clerical relating, which was devoid of honest engagement and based more on secrecy and denial of male sexual expression and emotion, contributed to this situation. The template for such an approach to clerical relational interaction was set for the most part in the emotionally sterile environment of the Irish seminary.

In relation to the Irish laity, the Ferns (2005), Murphy (2009), and Ryan (2009) reports strongly suggest that Irish officials in State departments were directly involved in the mishandling of abuse complaints against Catholic clergy. These reports point to the failure of various State personnel and government departments to deal effectively with child sexual abuse. The Ryan Report (2009) speaks of a culture of deference towards the Catholic Church that permeated Irish life. The civil authorities in Ireland are charged with ignoring survivors of sexual abuse in their attempts to get justice and help. The reports highlight failures on the part of the Irish Gárda (the Irish police force), the Irish Health Services, the Department of Health and Education, and many other bodies responsible for the care of children in their responses to sexual abuse generally and by Catholic clergy in particular. It is clear that just like the accused bishops, neither the Irish civil servants nor the Irish political class responded adequately to the sexual abuse of children by Irish Catholic clergy. In what is a sad fact of Irish social history Irish children were simply not a priority. Numerous examples that go beyond the Catholic Church demonstrate this point (see for example Irish Council for Civil Liberties, 1988; McGuinness, 1993). In Ireland we have not yet begun to examine the practices of many other organizations such as schools, social services or other health professionals to get a picture of the practices of other organizations in relation to children in Ireland during the relevant period. I would argue that we have all failed Irish children and sadly we are still failing them (see for example O'Brien, 2009a, 2009b, 2009c, 20009d, 2009e).

It is a fact of life that the knowledge we have today about child sexual abuse in relation to, both survivors and perpetrators, is deeper and more richly described than was available in the 1960s, 1970s, 1980s, and early 1990s. Nonetheless, while it is unfair to judge historical events in the light of contemporary knowledge, a pattern of relationships and contexts existed in which it is hard to conclude anything other than the fact that the Irish Catholic adult laity and non-abusing clergy were psychologically, socioculturally, and relationally part of a context in which child sexual abuse was enacted outside and within the Catholic Church. No one in Ireland stands outside of the responsibility and accountability dock on this matter, despite one's relative positioning on the continuum of knowing. However, all that appear available are individual models of accountability which do not adequately address the societal and systemic dynamic components of the problem. In the dialectics of blame it is usual for blame to shift around in line with power relations, as pointing fingers at others and away from self masks or deflects the pain of such a terrible knowing as to one's part in the sorrow and abuse of so many children.

At the third level of framework for understanding the relational and structural conditions that gave rise to sexual abuse by Catholic clergy in Ireland, I place the local Church organization and its relational governance. This in turn was influenced by Rome. While Chapter 9 treated this subject in depth, my analysis is weakened by the lack of empirical scholarship on the decision-making processes within the Catholic Church. Very little is known about how exactly decisions are made in the Catholic Church. In the Archdiocese of Dublin, this issue is particularly relevant, particularly in relation to its history of management of child sexual abuse allegations. While all the auxiliary bishops as well as the previous archbishops who handled sexual abuse complaints stand accused of mishandling, and some have lost their clerical ministries because of this, the history of decision-making in this local organization has yet to be written, particularly regarding the relationships and interactions that existed between the auxiliaries and their bishop. In calling for the "truth" to be told, this is another part of the truth that must be understood. Only time will tell if former bishops and auxiliary bishops in Ireland will be willing to participate in ongoing research.

Chapter 9 mapped out some of the psychological, relational, and institutional forces that were at play at an organizational and institutional level of the problem's definition and context. Based on that analysis the management of sexual abuse by the Catholic hierarchy contributed, albeit unwittingly, to a climate in which some clerical perpetrators continued to abuse minors as Irish Church leaders struggled within their own organizational context at home and in Rome to face honestly the problems that were emerging. Just as in the United States, insiders were engaged but outsiders were rebuffed as information about sexual abuse within the Catholic Church was tightly controlled (John Jay College, 2011, pp. 119). It is also abundantly clear that some Irish bishops and auxiliary bishops were innovators, doing all in their power to develop right practices and processes to address the problems to the best of their ability. This did not prevent such men from being publicly alienated in both the public or Church sphere when their earlier limitations were exposed.

At the same time there were also those bishops who not alone lagged behind, but who acted defensively and worked against some of their more innovative Episcopal colleagues as they tried to deal with the problem. Despite the rhetoric of child safeguarding, I am not convinced that there are not still those bishops who drag their heels. Delay in responding to abuse complaints is one obvious and current representation of this. Nonetheless, with inadequate preparation for such work and with limited knowledge of the extent and dimensions of the problem in the past, the bishops of Ireland failed to deal adequately with the survivors of abuse and with the clerical perpetrators. Again this is just another sad fact of Irish social history. While much public commentary sees the failure of the Irish bishops as a problem of deliberate and intentional "cover-up" that amounts to criminality, this conclusion, while understandably laden with anger, requires further in-depth analysis. In is a known feature of social life that organizations and social institutions often work to project the best image in public for a variety of motivations, usually in their own organizational interest. This managing of public image often includes covering over, minimizing, or deflecting attention from the organization's unpalatable features or failings, and may not involve intentional criminality. Managing one's image is not confined to the Catholic Church.

However, while some would argue that managing its image ought not to have been high on the priority list of the Catholic Church during the problem years, but that responding to survivors and perpetrators ought to have been, little research has been able to explain the thinking behind such image management with any kind of meaningful depth. The theology of scandal, while helpful, is only a partial explanation. For me, the thread of the explanation for such Episcopal behavior lies in the thesis that in the minds of the hierarchy there were two models of Church, a church of the clergy which was important, and had to be protected and a church of the laity which mattered less. In a most sad paradox, the problems in the church of the clergy had to be hidden from its most faithful followers in the Church of the laity, some of whom were in fact its very victims.

At a fourth level of the framework I place the relationship between Church and State, canon and civil law (including criminal law). It is increasingly evident that the relationships between Church and State and canon and civil law are implicated in many jurisdictions where the problem of sexual abuse by Catholic clergy has come to light and where these issues are being debated. This applies across a continuum from predominantly secular countries to countries where religion is strong. In almost every jurisdiction in which abuse by Catholic clergy has been reported, the scandal of abuse of children has engendered national debate about religious education, single-sex institutions, the role of celibacy, women and ordination, governance of the Catholic Church, and Church–State relations. These relational and structural long-term ruminations are certainly a consequence of the sexual abuse crisis. In the Irish situation the State's failure to adequately legislate for the protection of Irish children sits alongside the Church's failure to adequately protect them when they were in their care.

The multilevel framework suggests that action at all levels of the Church system is required if the problem of sexual abuse in the Catholic Church is to be adequately addressed. Unfortunately, apart from the changes in norms and protocols that are taking place within the Catholic Church for responding to abuse complaints and for helping survivors, the more structural issues at the heart of the matter continue to be ignored by the institutional Church. My wish is that such institutional stonewalling and fortress mentality will eventually be graced by wisdom and inspiration.

CONCLUDING COMMENTS

In my attempts to understand the clerical perpetrator and to offer some explanation for his actions, in addition to drawing on masculinity theories much of the theoretical work discussed earlier in the book has been particularly relevant. Marshall's (1998) work on attachment has been helpful in drawing attention to the importance of developing and sustaining intimate relationships in adulthood, the absence of which has been detected in the developmental trajectory of child sexual abuse perpetrators. In terms of clerical offenders this is an extremely important consideration. Whether intimate relationships are avoided for reasons to do with lack of skill or because of how the role of cleric is construed, the net effect is the same: the avoidance of intimate relationships resulting in severe emotional loneliness. The clerical men who participated in my research avoided adult intimate relationships as a way of protecting their vow of celibacy and as a result experienced extremes of emotional loneliness and isolation, psychological factors that are reported as having a role in the genesis of child sexual offending.

Marshall, Anderson, and Fernandez's (2000) work on shame and its links to empathy has also a particular relevance for clerical perpetrators and for my consideration of judgment. Marshall et al.'s work proposes that sexual offenders who lack empathy for their victims are doing so not because of an empathy problem but because of a belief that the victim has not been harmed. In trying to understand why some perpetrators fail to recognize the extent of the harm they are causing to children, a number of researchers point to the role of shame as an important construct with respect to empathic functioning (Bumby, 2000; Bumby, Marshall, & Langton, 1999; Hanson, 1997b; Roys, 1997; Ward, Hudson, & Marshall, 1994). Bumby (2000, p. 151) argues not that perpetrators are unaware of the harm they are causing to their victims, but rather that they manage their empathic responses to avoid the experience of shame and guilt. This is evident in the narratives of clerical perpetrators. Marshall et al. (2000) think that low self-esteem can be an empathy inhibitor for sexual offenders, in that they deny victim harm to protect their already fragile self from further negative self-evaluation. Marshall et al. further suggest that low self-esteem may actually cause sexual aggression through a variety of routes, such as over-reliance on sex for coping with low mood or loneliness. Shame-based identities underpin my reflections on the link between the failure to achieve Perfect Celibate Clerical Masculinity and child sexual offending.

The major thesis of my work is that sexual abuse is inevitable given the meaning system that is taught by the Catholic Church and to which many priests adhere. The contradictions force failure and increase shame and a way of living that encourages sexually deviant behavior. The narratives of the clerical perpetrators, when linked with the detailed knowledge of the Church's administration already presented, strengthen this case. One counterargument could arise from opportunity theory (which was discussed in Chapter 4), which suggests that abuse has more to do with blocked legal routes to achieve personal needs and goals and the availability of illegal or illicit routes to do so. Opportunity says little about psychological, organizational, or social conditions apart from those that concern opportunity. Extrapolating from opportunity theory, abuse by Catholic clergy has more to do with opportunity than it has to do with the moral teaching of the Church, with priests' masculinity, or with Church structure and organization. While such understanding is important, it is also limited when one considers the narratives of the clerical perpetrators and the detailed knowledge of the institutional and governmental administration of the Catholic Church that has been presented. However, opportunity theory appears to underpin the Church's obsession with instigating new procedures and protocols for policing the clergy and for responding to abuse complaints, to the neglect of the more psychological, organizational and structural dimensions of the problem.

While opportunity is certainly important in understanding how if not why sexual offenses occur, with implications for controlling the kinds of access that particular adults have to children, at the same time we must recognize that opportunity theory also emphasis the importance of having "legal" routes by which to fulfill one's needs and goals. In the case of Catholic clergy opportunity theory highlights the need for both a safe and healthy climate in which the sexual and emotional needs of Catholic clergy can be "legally" expressed in respectful and honest ways as well as the need for situational prevention models which can disturb access and opportunity for sexually harmful behavior in the future (John Jay, 2011, p.120).

The failure of the institutional Catholic Church in using the young men who were willing to devote their lives to it as ordained fodder, to be sent out to service the masses of hungry souls, cannot be ignored in coming to an understanding of how some Catholic clergy came to be abuse perpetrators. The pressures to be superhuman and to be "ideal" or "perfect" clergy were only matched by the systemic neglect of the realities of their actual lives, both in their training and afterwards, as they became deferentially loyal and ultimately disloyal soldiers in the business of serving an institution and a Catholic laity in preaching the word of God. The "business model" in which seminarians were a product to be modeled and reshaped to go out and preach the Word failed generations of Catholic clergy and the children whom some of them abused, and it must be seen as significant in the sexual abuse crisis. The inadequate training for clergy and the grossly inadequate supports and supervisions afforded to them in living the clerical life in modern times continue to be seriously underestimated in understanding the conditions against which the sexual abuse of minors by Catholic clergy must be seen.

My belief is that all the men who participated in my research tried to remain good and faithful priests and brothers as they lived in a battlefield of opposing forces of denied sexuality, emotional need, learned rationality, and intellectualization of physical, sexual, and emotional life. When the numerous strategies employed to resolve this war failed, including a spiritual and prayer life of surrender to and belief in God, the men in my research engaged in a complex web of psychological and moral bargaining, built on a rigid adherence to rules and regulations, untouched by human love, to justify "stealing" sex from children, making children the sacrificial lambs in the continuance of this performance of priesthood. In choosing children and young people as sexual and emotional "partners" in some instances, and opportunistically for sex in others, the public image of celibate priesthood or religious brotherhood remained intact, priesthood was preserved, the private emotional and sexual turmoil was temporarily settled, as silence was guaranteed by the "voiceless" and in some cases "unaware" children. Such an approach to life found a way to prevail within a gendered culture of institutional hypocrisy and secrecy. In such a climate of institutional denial there was inadequate preparation for clerical power and its moral limits, inadequate support in living the celibate life, and inadequate vocational supervision and accountability. When children began to speak out and the public persona and private worlds of the perpetrators collided, only then did many of the clerical perpetrators surrender to the impossibility of their conflicted lives. When the adult children began to speak through the help of the media, only then did the institutional Church begin to really listen. The institutional Church has yet to address the necessary institutional and structural issues that the sexual abuse crisis has brought to the surface.

The narratives of the participants in my research led to the finding that motivation for abusing children is complex, and the many dimensions of why the men abused minors are best described as stories of contradiction and ambivalence, double thinking and justification, concealment and denial. These stories represent conscious and unconscious processes that have become clear only with the benefit of hindsight and in conversation with others. For many of the men who took part in this study their stories are of winning and losing in a battlefield of complex emotions, forbidden desires, concealed truths, and spiritual desperation. In such circumstances the sexual abuse of children in the private realm functioned to preserve the priesthood in the public sphere—that is, as long as the secrecy was maintained.

Despite the allure of simple explanations of child sexual abuse by clergy, such as individual deviance or pathology, the research that is presented and drawn upon in this book suggests the need for a broader lens through which to view the problem, one that includes understanding the complex web of relationships, emotions, and beliefs, power relations, theology of priesthood, and current ecclesiology in which child sexual abuse within the Catholic Church came to be enacted. It is my view that the conditions that gave rise to the abuse of children and vulnerable adults by workers within the Catholic Church are the very conditions that give rise also to abuse of workers by other, perhaps more powerful workers within the same organizational Church system. My analysis suggests the need for multilevel interventions if the problem of sexual abuse within the Catholic Church is to be comprehensively addressed. In so doing we may go some way towards healing the myriad of lives that have been affected by the sexual abuse crisis in the Roman Catholic Church.

Conclusion

PROSPECTS, VISIONS, AGENDAS

IN SETTING OUT on the journey of research for this book I was clear that I wanted to achieve an in-depth understanding of child sexual abuse within the Catholic Church that would include the views of the clerical perpetrators, set against the background of the relevant reports and literature on the topic. In undertaking this task I wanted to develop a model of performance that would help conceptualize, but never justify, sexual abuse within the Catholic Church. I also wanted to understand how the clerical men made sense of their lives and how they made meaning of their sexual abuse of minors. While I set about devising a rigorous methodology that would enable me to achieve these aims, I recognized at same time that the dialogue with the clerical perpetrators must be interpreted in light of the context in which the research was conducted. I acknowledge that in themselves the men's narratives do not represent objective facts but are only their subjective accounts, which in turn have been subjected to my interpretation (and there can never be, of course, a final or correct interpretation). Nonetheless, the stories told by the men are seen by me still as representing the accounts of their lived experience. These are the stories of their lives, and they are of course subjectively as valid for them and the way they tell them as for any other person. Bearing this in mind, the stories that emerge in the context of this book are somewhere between objective fact and subjective remembering. It is for the reader to judge the authenticity of the stories that are presented in this work and the possible transferability of their meaning and my interpretation of them to other similar contexts.

In adopting this approach to the research I wanted to leave open a space for other parts of the story of sexual abuse within the Catholic Church that are as yet unlanguaged, much less understood, to emerge and be incorporated into the unfolding narrative. Such stories could in turn change the whole landscape of interpretation in relation to clerical perpetrators and the Church leadership, and how we view them. By adopting such a position of tentative understanding, the space is left open for time and circumstance to influence and reconsider what we know. What cannot change or be forgotten however, is our knowledge and understanding of how so many children were sexually abused by Catholic clergy throughout the world, and how their pleas for help fell on deaf ears or were responded to poorly by countless leaders of the Catholic Church and by many adults who failed them.

The research that is presented in this book marks a departure from previous works on Roman Catholic clergy who have sexually abused minors and it does so in a number of respects. Previous research and scholarly works had a tendency to think in terms of us-versus-them distinctions, basing the analysis almost exclusively on third-party study and interpretation. In contrast, this book places in the foreground the first-person narratives of nine Roman Catholic clergy who have sexually abused minors, in a way that very little other work on the subject has done before. The men's narratives are engaged with, in depth and detail, against the background of the relevant literature and an understanding of the organizational structures and dynamics of the Catholic Church. This approach brings forth important issues for consideration. When the individual and the institutional dimensions of the problem are brought together what becomes evident is how the individual perpetrators, the bishops and religious leaders, the lower-ranking clergy and the Catholic laity are interconnected in a web of interacting dynamics and relationships that contributed to the evolution and maintenance of the problem. The individual and the institutional dimensions, when studied all together, reflect beliefs and values that form part of the problem—beliefs and values that are usually obscured from view when one focuses solely on individual action (or when one gets lost in the discourse of pedophilia). The complex relationship between the individual, the institution, culture and language is strongly emphasized in my work. The ways in which responsibility and accountability are taken up in such dynamic interactions are at the heart of concerns for victims and survivors: who is taking responsibility and who is accountable in the face of such collective wrongdoing and neglect?

We know from hearing the survivor accounts that many suffered enormously, and their pain was intensified by the responses of the Church hierarchy to their complaints. It is evident from the many survivor accounts that criticism, disbelief, humiliation, and fear were part of their experience in trying to have their stories heard. We know also from the survivor accounts of how the resistance of civil society to listen to their pleas compounded their problems. We know in Ireland of the failure of many instruments of the state to privilege the children, in what has been described as a culture of deference to the Catholic Church (Ryan Report, 2009). We know from survivor accounts that alienation from the Church is now common (Balboni & Bishop, 2010). Survivors continually demonstrate that the realization that the Church had betrayed their trust and that clergy had stolen their childhood innocence was and still is crushing for them. What models of relational or community responsibility are available to us in these circumstances, what do they mean and how can they be operationalized? Is individualism, and individualized models of responsibility and accountability all that we can draw on in the face of such collective failure?

Although nothing can excuse their sexual offending as we attempt to understand and explain, my research offers a map of the small compromises that ordinary clerical men made on the road to abusing minors. To this extent, the accounts of sexual offending presented in this work are more confronting than other accounts of sexual abuse by Catholic clergy, mainly because it can no longer be just about "pedophile priests," but maybe ordinary men. The problems for the men who participated in my research lay in the gap between the ideal and the reality of clerical masculinity and in their adaptation to these circumstances.

With the absence of voice in the running of their lives in an institution that was built on fear, authority and obedience, the fear of giving voice to psychosexual and emotional conflict was temporarily resolved by resorting to unhealthy and ultimately abusive relationships with minors. An understanding of authority that was devoid of a theology of power, in which the focus was on the oppressive forces of being "under" authority rather than on the obligations that go with having authority "over," contributed to this situation.

When the gap widened between the reality of their psychosexual lives and the "ideal" of what they believed were the requirements of embodying perfect celibate clerical masculinity (an "ideal" that was impossible to live), it became possible for the clerical perpetrators to rationalize even the most unacceptable of behaviors, including the sexual abuse of minors. Ultimately, personal integrity and loyalty to the institution, to which they had given their lives, were compromised as they used the private underworld of sexual "relations" with minors, opportunistically and in more considered ways, to maintain an outward appearance of "normality" and perfection. This way of living could be maintained only by self and other deception in the context of a guilt-alleviating secret confessional system, for as long as the secrecy was maintained. The men who participated in my research were not in themselves "bad" men, rather, they were trying to be "perfect" priests; attempting to embody celibate clerical masculinity (as the ideal type described in chapter 10) founded on an idea of perfection with all the unreality that it entailed. In the event, their lives both imploded and exploded, resulting in many people getting hurt, including children and young people; the ramifications of which cannot be overstated.

The response of the Catholic Church to the crisis of sexual abuse within the Church in many countries has been organizational and procedural in emphasis, attempting to remedy gaps and reduce future risk by putting in place new policies, procedures, and mechanisms for dealing with the problem. Although these innovations may play some role in increasing the protection of children and vulnerable adults within the Catholic Church, they are equally unlikely to remedy the factors that underpin such abuses. Some of the changes have indeed produced unforeseen consequences in other parts of the organization, creating problems that are not insignificant. First, new groups of casualties are emerging, primarily priests who are falsely accused. Although few have an appetite for thinking about priests who are falsely accused, who are regarded as "collateral damage" against the background of such abuse by clergy, I am concerned about this group of men whose lives are devastated by such occurrences. Interestingly, it is not the complaints that do the damage; rather, it is how they are handled by their own authorities. The relationships between bishops and the clergy are also at an all-time low, certainly in Ireland (Duffy, 2009; Hoban, 2009). Nobody knows what the consequence of this state of affairs will be in time to come.

Second, the manner in which some former perpetrators are treated by the Church authorities (not to mention popular culture) also gives rise for concern. Despite the popular view that the Catholic Church is "light" on perpetrators, my experience is that the raw and barely concealed anger that clerical perpetrators encounter from some of their former leaders and colleagues, regardless of whether they remain within the fold or are laicized (sometimes they remain linked because of financial support arrangements in the case of older men), makes life almost intolerable. My attempt here is not in any way to detract from the pain of survivors; merely to say that much pain surrounds this difficult topic. Neither is it my intention to suggest that priests or Church hierarchy have not a right to be angry with their former abusive colleagues. They do of course have such a right. However, when anger is not attended to in the proper forum, it spills out everywhere, permeating the public discourse in an unhelpful manner especially if it comes from Church leaders who ought to know better. There are many aspects of the problem that warrant further study, some of which I have briefly alluded to, as the risk is high for new injustices to be perpetrated within the Catholic Church and within the social sphere, this time in the name of justice.

Apart from the models that I have proposed in this work for understanding the clerical perpetrator and for conceptualizing child sexual abuse within the Catholic Church, there are a whole range of related topics, which would exceed the limits of this project were I to discuss them in detail. However, while this is not the place to discuss these themes at length, I would at least like to hint at their dimensions and the potential impact of these themes in how to deal with abuse. Their dimensions are mainly of a philosophical-theoretical, political-moral, theological, rehabilitative, and justice type. I will end with a final word on witnessing, hope, and repair.

PHILOSOPHICAL-THEORETICAL CONSIDERATIONS

There is no need to play an empirical "number game" to detect and sense the uniqueness of abuse by Catholic clergy and why it caused such moral outcry. The gaps between preaching water while drinking wine, between the rhetoric of love and the reality of abuse, between the presumption of celibacy and the reality of sexual violations, have brought the trust that once existed between the all-powerful clergy and the all-believing Catholic laity into sharp decline. The Church's handling of abuse complaints and the position of the Vatican vis-à-vis its role in this situation have contributed further to the breakdown in relations, leading some commentators to refer to a "crisis of credibility" in the Catholic Church that has not been experienced since the Reformation (Küng, 2010, p. 15).

Cruelty and hypocrisy cannot be measured, nor are they empirically verifiable, yet they do exist. We know that the unique dimensions of clerical abuse and how they link to the institutional dimensions of the Catholic Church lie exactly in the gap between the rhetoric and the reality, no matter what else is seen to apply. In Ireland, at least three further factors are important: (1) the previously unchallenged moral and religious monopoly of the Catholic Church (despite a recent decline among churchgoers, Ireland is still next to the United States and Poland in terms of religious adherence), (2) the complete failure of state control and oversight, and (3) the indifference of large parts of Irish society to the plight of children, particularly the children of the poor. This is not the place to discuss all of the dimensions of church, state, and civil society and how they relate to each other. In my concluding remarks I will limit myself to one: the institutional dimensions of the Catholic Church and how institutional hypocrisy is linked to cruelty. Is there a relationship between cruelty and hypocrisy? How can we consider these issues specifically in the context of an institution like the Catholic Church?

Very few political philosophers, and not too many theologians, have attempted to think systematically about the formative and educational experiences and what it means to receive the right psychological constitution and attitude that will help citizens to make good moral choices and to avoid cruelty and suffering. This is clearly a challenge in the education of clergy and in conscience development. Particularly when it comes to distinguishing between what is morally right and what is wrong, citizenship education can be the most complex and challenging task, despite some of the moral simplicity and moral absolutism that emerges not only from some of the dogma of the Catholic Church, but also in another form from the new arbiters of morality, mainly in sections of the media. For the specific context of the Catholic Church it is not my intention to try to produce answers, but only to hint at the right problems. The problems that need to be addressed comprehensively but that can only be hinted at here can be summarized in the following set of questions: What exactly is the relationship between cruelty and hypocrisy, and which form does it take, specifically in the context of an institution like the Catholic Church? How can an institution like the Catholic Church ensure that its candidates for priesthood and religious brotherhood receive the right psychological constitution and attitude that will help them make good moral choices and avoid cruelty and suffering? When will such formation programs include a theology of power in which authority in the Catholic Church is reconfigured to include not just an understanding of the obligations when "under" authority but also an understanding of the responsibilities of those "in" authority? When will the Catholic Church provide an appropriate support infrastructure for its clergy, respecting personal autonomy and individual conscience? Can an institution that purports to have moral monopoly, and that re-enacts its monopoly daily through its rituals, ever reach a situation where rhetoric and practice can meet? In other words, can the Catholic perception and suggested practice of sexual mores for clergy ever be reconciled with the demands of biology, psychology, and social and intimate bonding?

If the answer to the last question is indeed positive (as the Church seems to argue), another question arises: is the aim of spiritual salvation worth the sexual sacrifice? Or are not the means and ends totally out of synch for modern conditions? Is it not cruel to demand lifelong sexual abstention from human beings, despite all the research hinting at serious problems with such lifelong practices, especially when not voluntarily chosen? Against easily available scientific and social scientific knowledge and advice, the Church still continues to teach and train (how?) its clergy to abstain sexually. Knowing that such demands of sexual abstention are totally unrealistic, this is exactly where one aspect of institutional hypocrisy comes in as an explanation. The Church still promotes an institutional practice that is bound to fail. Cruelty and abuse are bound to arise from such impossible tasks. The power and control game (control men's bodies and you control their minds) has turned into a cynical exercise against better knowledge. Just for the purpose of order and maintaining the very institution, human lives are now sacrificed and destroyed, lives that include the identifiable victims of Catholic clergy, whose stories of pain resound around the world, but lives that also include the clergy themselves. Making celibacy mandatory for all Catholic clergy no longer serves anyone well. Celibacy could indeed be optional for individuals who wish to choose it, for reasons of belief, spirituality or faith, without the problems that accompany its mandatory companion.

POLITICAL-MORAL CONCERNS

There are, secondly, questions that relate to the political-moral context in which sexual abuse by Catholic clergy is currently understood. In a world in which not all relational breakdown and all human failings can be legislated for, and where errors, bad judgments, misguided loyalty, and all the wrong motivations have contributed to enduring cruelty and suffering of others, there exists a moral vacuum. The dearth of models or frameworks for understanding and responding to relational or collective responsibility is seriously problematic in a world in which individualism dominates and in which legal responsibility is centered on the individual. No language exists for responsibilities and accountabilities that go beyond the individual, the terms "individual" and "responsibility" being almost bound as one. How in the face of such intellectual and moral deficit can we think and act in ways that reflect relational and communal responsibilities especially when individual, organizational, institutional and societal relations overlap and interrelate to bring forth the problem?

In the absence of suitable legal or social models for addressing relational or communal responsibilities (and I would argue in the absence of a suitable language to discuss same) we resort to a form of moral responsibility based yet again on an individualized perspective. The "name-and-shame" morality, which dominates much public debate in Ireland is usually fought out in the court of public opinion, is often given expression in media outlets in which everything seems to be fair game. The advances in technology, which make the most local of failings fodder for international commentary, contribute to this situation. The name-and-shame morality dominates much public debate on sexual abuse by Catholic clergy.

The name-and-shame morality works when the atypical is elevated to the typical through a concerted appeal to stereotypes (see Scraton, 2002). "They" are all regarded as the same, and at the level of the worst of cases. Although every sexual violation is one too many and we must continually take a stand against it, collapsing all men who have perpetrated abuse into the same homogenized group serves to nourish the stereotype and incite hatred rather than facilitate appropriate responses. The morality of name-and-shame is at its most potent when it is the only perspective that dominates. By being tough on individual causality and consequences, seemingly with no place for social or organizational context (or by merely paying lip service to it), the moral vacuum can be filled with a sense of superior moral individualism premised on notions of rational choice. We are all free agents; we take the consequences of our actions! In these situations the morality tale responds to the media hype. Exceptions are used, even exploited, to play the morality card, a card that trumps all others (Scraton, 2002). More often than not, short-term opportunism is used to satiate hunger for revenge, all of course used in the name of morality. Absolute prescriptions are administered regarding the correct moral action in the light of one's failings; the complexity of competing interests and material struggles often hidden or misrepresented. When such a singular discourse takes hold, "morality" is taken for granted, as though only one interpretation exists. We all know what is moral and what is the right thing to do! No explanation is needed. Defying relativity and presuming consensus suffices (Scraton, 2002, p. 43). One version of this populist morality tale is that the only acceptable "confession" is one in which the person accepts complete and unmediated blame.

When applied to the bishops in Ireland, this form of populist morality translates into the expectation that every bishop who was part of a diocese in which abuse took place, regardless of his current commitment to safety, should resign on "moral" grounds. It is not good enough that he acknowledges failure and even tries to make amends; in the new morality there is no room for explanation for making amends or for understanding context. He did wrong; he should go! The very certainty of such approaches to "right" over "wrong" exposes the simplicity and simple-mindedness of such moral absolutes. There are no gray areas, no contradictions, and no different "ways of seeing" (Scraton, 2002, p. 43). From this position it becomes all too easy to slide into the construction of "otherness," rejecting "their" "moral" definitions, decisions, and actions or not being willing to listen or understand. Such behavior, dressed up as "moral," is not only destructive to maintaining social bonds and a sense of communal security but is also lacking any intellectual or moral depth, and yet it takes pride of place in the politics of child sexual abuse. Bizarre as it may sound, the Catholic Church in Ireland has joined in supporting the name-and-shame movement within its own Safeguarding Children's office. The deficits in moral thought in that particular institution have never been more apparent.

While moral absolutes might be attractive to the Catholic Church, and in my view contributes to some of its problems, the very same processes are taking hold within popular culture, especially when the abuse of children by Catholic clergy is defined and popularized by those who then occupy the moral high ground. These comments are in no way an attempt to underestimate the hurt that has been endured by many survivors of sexual abuse by Catholic clergy throughout the world or to suggest that the history and memory of such trauma and injury can or should be forgotten. On the contrary, the public knowing of such hurt and trauma must always be remembered and the work of finding innovative and creative responses to the hurt and remembering must be part of the social imperative. However, at the level of explanation, I am merely suggesting that in all complex situations, the reality of the abuse that was caused, and how it got to be so bad, will be understood in different ways by different participants in the process, and all of the individuals involved and their perspectives must form part of the human story.

To deny anyone voice is to deny the most basic; that is in part why the survivors have been hurt for so long by the Catholic Church and the societies who closed their ears. However, in the current politics of morality it may even be the case that in some circumstances the experience of survivors and the lives of perpetrators are exploited in a form of political gameplaying, especially when "all" victims are seen as the same and "all" perpetrators are too. In the current politics of morality the moral identifications follow a similar pattern to the well-worn pattern of moral determinations propagated by the Catholic Church (albeit with different sins and transgressions) and against which society is now revolting. Part of the problem lies in the failure of those moral absolutes to relate to the human condition and to the reality of human life and failing. What appears to be happening in popular culture is that new moral guardians are merely replacing the old, and the new guardians of morality are not those with access to pulpits and education, but those with prime access to technology. Commercial interests may also be in play.

At the same time we cannot descend into moral relativism, a situation in which everything goes and in which there is no "right" action. This is where reasoned debate, philosophical inquiry, and critical theology are required, peppered with some sense of mercy rather than the dominant theology of sacrifice. No matter how we proceed regarding sexual abuse by Catholic clergy, whether through secular or religious means, or both, the promotion of moral purpose and moral renewal is vacuous when not linked to context. Outside of context, all human action is rendered unintelligible and can lead to dark visions of the human condition. Against such prospective negativity I hold that learning, understanding, and continually exploring the ethics for communal and social relations offers the only lasting safeguard against a descent into "moral chaos" or a new form of moral dictatorship.

When questions of responsibility and accountability are resolved by recourse to the law, such as when a criminal act is committed, one aspect of moral responsibility is seen to be laid to rest, even in situations of historical abuse where the complexities of time, memory, and retrospective justice apply. However, in the case of clerical abusers, current experience teaches that accepting responsibility for past abuses, accepting the rigors of the criminal law, repenting for such abuses and indicating a willingness to make amends are insufficient to gain re-entry as a member of the human community. Public vilification, humiliation, and ostracism are also penalties that apply, and there is no release date. Homeless in a world that has no place for them, the societal "cover-up" is that we too move these men around. Just as the Church hierarchy moved clerical perpetrators around from diocese to diocese in the past, so does civil society now. The state's rhetoric of management of sexual offenders, particularly in the Anglophone world, is usually about control rather than well-being, and in civil society nobody wants "them" in their backyard. In many instances, men with whom I have worked have been run out of their homes and run out of their country without as much as a peep from the political caste, human rights defenders, or indeed the leadership of the Catholic Church. If such practices continue with men who have abused children, who are welcome almost nowhere, we will soon have a tier of moving folk, mainly men, who live in the unknown underworld of no man's land. I cannot see how such an approach to the problem is likely to make anyone safer—not to mention the human rights violations that are involved.

THE NEED FOR A CRITICAL THEOLOGY

A third issue that I wish to raise is the need for a new, more critical theology. The essential tension at the heart of the Catholic Church is between Catholicism as a moral and social proposition on the one hand and the power apparatus the Church has turned into on the other (Dorgan, 2009, p. 14). Sometimes set as the tension between the divine message and the human institution that helps to spread the Word, the problem is that the human institution is now regarded as having moved far away from the moral and social proposition that gave birth to it. In its current form the institutional structures that helped to interpret and deliver the message are no longer meaningful or sustainable. The energy that is put into maintaining this version of the Church is indeed remarkable. There have been and always will be attempts at returning to a "true spirit" of the Church by arguing that the institutional Church has become too powerful, and promoting theological alternatives. This is where critical theology and liberal practice, as promoted by theologians from Rahner (1982) to Metz (1980), come in. However, revelations of child sexual abuse by Catholic clergy have once again brought this tension to center stage, with a force that bears the hallmark of previous critical times. Judging from the public outcry by Catholics throughout the Western world, including the clergy themselves, the abuse problem by clergy, and the response to abuse by the Church hierarchy and the Vatican, is one that will be settled only by structural reform, a new more critical theology and a new ecclesiology. Apologies repeated at regular intervals, shame-filled speeches by senior clerics, compensation for victims, defrocking of clerical perpetrators, and resignations of bishops, although welcomed by some commentators as important, will not solve the problems that the Catholic Church now faces. No one individual, not even the pope, no matter how sincere or well intentioned, is likely to diffuse the contradictions that have been building up within the Catholic Church for a very long time. Anything less than structural reform and a new model of the Church will be seen in the minds of many believers as a missed opportunity. Anything less than structural reform will be seen as a crisis weathered rather than a crisis transformed.

Despite the changes in the Catholic Church since Vatican II, it is still difficult for many clerics and laity to move away from definitions of "the Church" as belonging primarily to the clergy to a notion of the Church that is much less defined by traditional political structures. Even the language of clergy and laity is problematic, as it keeps the basic distinctions between the ordained and the non-ordained as foundational. Increasingly the terminology "lay" and "laity" as part of the ordinary vocabulary of the Catholic Church is proving to be problematic. For a multitude of reasons the program of Vatican II, which envisaged a more collegial Church with active lay participation and a better balance of power between the papacy and local churches or branches, has for the most part not been realized (O'Hanlon, 2010a, 2010b). However, the mixed theologies that are evident in the documents of the Council suggest that perhaps an over-reliance on Vatican II is not where the Church needs to go (Ryan, 2009). The rich significance of the Church's theology of Church has yet to be realized. While the post-Vatican II Church emphasized the theology of Church as the Church of the People of God, with all Church members sharing in the ministry of Christ, there are problems in matching this theology with the lived experience of "Church." Part of the difficulty lies in the very teachings of Vatican II itself, particularly the ecclesiological dualism that it contains (pp. 588–589). As various Church historians and theologians have articulated, there are many good reasons, not least the emergence of a more globalized world, for a centralized papacy, but not one without checks and balances and appropriate accountability structures. I cannot see how anything less than a Third Vatican Council, and at the very least a Synod for the Church in Ireland (and perhaps other countries) will adequately address the complex but nevertheless urgent issues involved in considering a new ecclesiology, partly brought to a head by the child abuse crisis. Other issues, such as sexuality, the position of women, and inter-religious dialogue, are also in need of reformulation. As the archbishops of Dublin noted in a recent interview (McGarry, 2010b), "occasionally you have these seismic moments when you have a real change ... a qualitative leap to a different view of Church." It appears to me that the seismic moment has arrived for a wider consultative process, in which a different view of Church can be envisioned, orthodoxy can be questioned, and a more representative and accountable Church can emerge from the current crisis. While reform at individual church level is of course important, nothing short of radical and structural institutional reform will suffice in current times.

A MULTILEVEL RELATIONAL APPROACH TO THERAPY AND REHABILITATION

Based on the research presented in this book, I propose a particular way of thinking about the problem of sexual abuse by clergy that offers a future framework for the work of rehabilitation. It is a model that is not dominated by a preoccupation with the past alone, but one that is also concerned with present and future too. This does not imply that the past offenses and the history of abusing are not important, nor that they are not seriously examined in all their dimensions, but rather that the methodology involves a constant back-and-forth movement between present, past, and future, in which past, present, and future are constantly interwoven between people, through conversation, and through their imagining, envisioning, and anticipating (Lang, 2003). Rather than focusing on trying to prevent bad things from occurring, a future focus places emphasis on possibilities and a movement from past learning to positive action to positive outcome. This approach to therapeutic work finds support in psychotherapeutic research, which stresses the importance of hope, expectation, and a belief in possibilities for bringing about positive therapeutic change (Snyder, Michael & Cheavens, 2005, p. 181).

Traditional approaches to therapy and rehabilitation with clergy who have abused minors have focused exclusively on individual offenders. The findings discussed in this book suggest that an alternative approach could prove to be useful. My proposal is that individually focused therapy and rehabilitation programs be replaced by ones that are based on the multilevel relational framework. Within the multilevel relational approach to therapy and rehabilitation, all participants pertinent to the given situation are invited to come together in different compositions and caucuses, for different forms of facilitated dialogue and analogical relational work, for as long as is necessary until the problem is resolved. Within the various centers of dialogue and relational work (which draws on a multitude of verbal and non-verbal therapeutic approaches), issues such as protection, accountability, punishment, and reparation are addressed. Such forums aim to draw in all the individuals who are involved when a particular problem of sexual abuse is disclosed. As such it could include the clerical perpetrators and their families, the survivors and their families (when and wherever the survivor sees fit), Church personnel, and state professionals. Within such forums, in which meaningful dialogue and relational work is facilitated in different configurations, the moral and ethical issues pertinent to all participants are respected. The aim of the work is that children can be made safe and put beyond harm and perpetrators can resign from their abusive ways and put themselves above suspicion (Lang, 2003).

A series of meetings of the entire multilevel-relational system, supplemented by caucus groups for particular members, and a special therapy group for the clerical perpetrators would provide the structure for this multilevel dialogical and relational work. The groups would work individually and collectively together over time until everyone's concerns have been adequately addressed. This approach to therapy is influenced by therapeutic ideas emanating from the field of systemic therapy (such as Anderson & Goolishian, 1988; Byrne & McCarthy, 1988; Lang, 2003; Waldergrave, Tamasese, Tuhaka, & Campbell, 2003) and from restorative and transformative principles (Zehr, 1990). The therapeutic or rehabilitative program would work alongside the criminal and civil law.

I advocate this approach to rehabilitation and therapy in cases of sexual abuse by Catholic clergy, in order to take account of the multilevel relational and contextual framework for understanding sexual abuse within the Catholic Church and to take account of the extended web of human suffering that emerges from such abuses. All individuals affected by the problem are offered a forum for dialogue and relational healing. My experience suggests that when therapeutic and rehabilitative services mirror the divisions that occur in the social field of concern in relation to complex human and social problems, such as sexual abuse, and in some cases become oppositional, taking positions in almost opposing camps, the isolation and marginalization of both survivors and perpetrators in the social field are amplified and entrenched. In addition, the work of rehabilitation falls short. When therapeutic services contribute to a divided social field there can be unintended consequences; the survivor's unanswered questions and needs that can often only be met by a form of mediated dialogue or innovative process with the perpetrator are left unaddressed and perpetrator's need and desire to make amends and repair the harm done are ignored. It is also the case that even low-risk offenders who have completed therapy and served custodial sentences are "exiled at home" and marginalized by Church and society; in effect they are welcomed almost nowhere.

An approach to therapy and rehabilitation that does not contribute to such social divisions and that is based on the idea of an expanded social systems approach (Byrne & McCarthy, 1988) minimizes the possibility of marginalization and alienation and it respects the systemic context in which the sexual offending by Catholic clergy takes place. At the same time it facilitates a dialogical and relational space in which the issues pertaining to responsibilities and accountabilities can be addressed. By dialoguing within the multilevel relational field, the systemic changes that are required as part of the commitment to put all children beyond risk and abuse perpetrators above suspicion are more likely to be achieved, as all voices are honored and accountabilities are rendered visible and transparent. Such therapeutic processes can work in partnership with statutory child protection agencies and state-led criminal and civil justice systems.

TOWARDS TRANSFORMATIVE JUSTICE

In a study released in 2010 on the experiences and motivations of 22 men and women who entered into mass tort litigation against the Catholic Church in the United States, primarily the Archdiocese of Boston, as well as 13 plaintiffs' attorneys and other legal advocates, Balboni and Bishop (2010) offer some illuminating insights. While the study highlights the capacity for litigation to transform the personal and social identities of the litigants it also points to some of the limitations of criminal and civil law (or retributive justice) when it comes to recovering from the trauma of child sexual abuse and finding a way forward. It is to this research and to some suggestions for restorative or transformative processes that I now wish to turn.

Balboni and Bishop's research (2010) indicates that part of the participants' motivations for pursuing tort proceedings was very personal. They wished to finally believe something that had been a struggle; that the sexual abuse had occurred. By taking civil proceedings the survivors hoped to put to rest questions they had about their own memories, and to have others acknowledge their victimization (p. 140). Participants had trouble believing their own memories, so incongruous and confusing had been their experience. They also wished to give back responsibility for the wrongdoing to the offender, as several of them reported that they had been told (or told themselves) that they were responsible for the abuse (p. 143). Balboni and Bishop suggest that the difference between contacting a therapist and contacting an attorney lay in the attorney's role. Through the litigation process the attorneys had the capacity to establish both the plaintiff's innocence and also the defendant's responsibility. Not only did this mean that the abuse victims were believed, but that someone else believed they had been so badly wronged that they had a right to demand redress.

Another motivation for taking class action was the desire to establish the truth for others and to build a community of survivors (Balboni and Bishop, 2010, p. 145). The opportunity to connect and provide mutual support was very important. In almost all cases, individual survivors sensed or knew that he or she was not the only victim of a particular cleric. In coming together they hoped they would be vindicated in the eyes of the community by exposing the hypocrisy of the Church. The participants indicated that they wanted to undermine the legitimacy of the Catholic Church as a moral institution by demonstrating the wrongs perpetrated by some of its members and leaders (p. 147). The participants in this research wanted to force the Church to own up to its history of neglect, secretive behavior, and deceit and to take the consequences of its failings (p. 149). The inequality in power and prestige between the victims and the priest, the survivors and the Catholic Church made this process difficult.

Balboni and Bishop's research (2010) demonstrates the power of class action to influence the social and personal identities of the participants as a result of taking back power, exercising personal agency and engaging in generative activities, such as helping other survivors. At the same time the research highlights the folly of seeing litigation as a panacea for recovery from personal injury. Litigation in fact, was more a beginning than an end for the participants in Balboni and Bishop's study (p. 151). Many of the participants hated to see the litigation come to a close, not because they enjoyed the dispute but because they feared that settlement would quiet their newfound voices. They wanted to continue the dialogue that had begun and did not want the conversation to be over. They wanted to continue in dialogue about protecting children, building awareness about sexual offenders, and about abuses in the Catholic Church.

In an unfortunate postscript to the original goals of taking the class action and despite the personal and social transformations that had occurred, these law suits often left the participants feeling "at best, underwhelmed, at worst, used or duped by lawyers in the quest for money" (Balboni & Bishop, 2010, p. 151). The participants reported that in the end the litigation became "about the money," despite their aspirations and goals relating to truth and justice and creating supportive communities for survivors (p. 151). The researchers suggest this happened not because the survivors wanted it to be so, but because the attorneys had turned the negotiations into a language of monetary currency. Since the final settlement amount was set in advance of the legal mediation, "the survivors came to see themselves in a zero-sum game that not only put a price on their pain, but ranked them by who was the most 'damaged' ... and they detested the idea that they were now competing with their peers for their settlement" (p. 151). The centrality of money at the conclusion of these suits was seen by the participants as a bitter pill because their original goals and hopes extended far beyond monetary settlements. Similar experiences have been reported privately by survivors of the reformatory and industrial schools in Ireland, on their experiences of the Institutional Redress Board, whose job it was to allocate monetary compensation for their pain and trauma. The situation is ongoing and is made all the more difficult by a confidentiality agreement that was enforced on the survivors, this time not by the Catholic Church but by the Irish state who prohibits the survivors from discussing their experiences of the Redress Board in a public forum.

Legal proceedings of a civil nature can serve a number of useful purposes for victims of sexual crime, as Balboni and Bishop's research (2010) indicates, and criminal proceedings can lead to punishment of the offender. However, it is a mistake to encourage the assumption that the initiation and conclusion of legal proceedings, whether civil or criminal, can provide a complete resolution to the varieties of injury, hurt, loss, and harm that have resulted from past abuses (O'Malley, 2009, p. 103). Such false hopes or promises lead to deep wells of disappointment for survivors, perpetrators and for their families and communities. It may well be that we have so far paid insufficient attention to the long-term needs of survivors and perpetrators of sexual offenses and perhaps the time has come when we need to ask them what else must be done.

Leaving survivors for a moment and turning to perpetrators, Maruna (2001), who has undertaken research on desistance from crime very convincingly demonstrates the importance of personal and social identity and self narrative in understanding how offenders desist from crime and reform their lives. In a process he characterizes as "making good," Maruna's research demonstrates that offenders are more likely to desist from further offending when they can rewrite a shameful past as a prelude to a more productive and worthy life (something which Maruna (p. 87) calls the "redemptive script"), and when they are facilitated to go on to more generative activities, such as helping other offenders or participating in the community in productive ways. For Maruna, individuals who can make sense of their lives and their behaviors as less about their "core" selves and more about the environment in which they have lived, are more able to redeem themselves and become more empowered, enhanced, and ennobled. Importantly, while the catalyst for change is sometimes seen as an outside force, such as criminal proceedings or therapy, desistance almost always seems to come from within and how one sees and narrates the self. As one of Maruna's participants observed "You become what you want to become" (p. 96). One of the priest participants in my own study reported that he had more personal freedom in prison than he had had in all his years prior to that point, mainly because he had "found himself." This is a form of "redemptive script" that is helpful in the project of reform. "Condemnation scripts" have the opposite effect. To my knowledge, the man who participated in my research mentioned above has not re-offended in twenty years.

Maruna's research (2001) helps us understand the importance of the personal narrative and the redemptive script, such as "finding oneself again," or "for the first time" for desistance. It also helps us understand the role of generative activities in desistance, which help with righting the wrongs (as much as possible), making restitution, providing fulfillment, and providing social legitimacy (Maruna, 2001, pp. 119–123). It is in this context that the social process of shaming and stigmatizing and refusing former offenders re-entry to the fold of the human community again (especially following adjudication by the criminal justice system and on completion of therapy) are not only unhelpful but foolish. Such exclusionary policies and practices are also humanly cruel and verge on human rights violations.

Drawing on some of the works outlined above, if we put together the importance of personal and social identity for survivors and the redemptive script for perpetrators, and the generative needs of both in overcoming trauma, or in the project of making good it seems to me logical that a social and psychological space must be created for this work to take place. If we add to this scenario what I imagine to be the interest of many Church leaders who wish to find ways of repairing their mistakes and wrongdoing, not via sensationalist newspapers or headline-searching commercial TV stations, the stage is set for restorative or transformative possibilities. It is here that I see the potential for restorative practices, perhaps even transformative practices, in which no person is disqualified and the experience of all is held and honored.

"Restorative practices" is basically an umbrella term for work that covers a wide range of approaches that are used for working in situations involving trauma and relational breakdown (Gavrielides & Coker, 2005; Morris & Maxwell, 2003; Noll & Harvey, 2008; Umbreit, 1994; Umbreit, Bradshaw & Coates, 1999). Restorative work is guided by a number of core principles: that crime is a violation of people and of interpersonal relationships; that violations create obligations; and that the central obligation is to put right the wrongs (Zehr, 1996: 19). The goals of "restorative" and "transformative" work are to address harm, address causes and to seek to right the wrongs. The work is embedded in a Human Rights Framework in which dignity and respect for all are at its core. The work is generally future-focused, remembering and healing the past, in the present, and making possible a peaceful and respectful future. The aim is to enable both victims and offenders and all of those people whose lives are interconnected through unwelcomed traumatic events, to turn their tragedies around and find fulfilling and peaceful ways to go forward.

Restorative practices are only possible when the survivor desires it and is open to communication and when the perpetrator admits to wrongdoing. The extent of the personal injury is always acknowledged. Restoring a sense of worth after trauma or wrongdoing is facilitated in ways that does not diminish the other but rather enhances the worth of self. Recent experiments in restorative justice strive for social and personal healing by restoring the worth of all parties through acknowledgement, apology and forgiveness (a full exploration of which is beyond the scope of the current project, but I just want to hint at their possible uses in sexual abuse within the Catholic Church). Some initiatives for responding to very serious social problems have also drawn on restorative principles and practices, such as in the Truth and Reconciliation Commissions of South Africa (Villa Vincenzo, 1999) and in responding to paramilitary violence in Northern Ireland (McEvoy & Mika, 2001). However, since there are few precedents in relation to sexual abuse, and political and cultural circumstances are always particular, it is fair to say that both the South African and the Northern Ireland examples are not easily copied or exportable.

Restorative practices have a lot to offer in the aftermath of sexual abuse by Catholic clergy, as long as they are conceived alongside and not instead of the criminal and civil law proceedings. Some attempts are being made to bring restorative processes to bear in cases involving sexual abuse by clergy, particularly in some parts of the United States (Noll & Harvey, 2008, p. 395). The approach encourages responsibility and accountability for past behavior but also focuses on a future for all. Memories of past injuries, physical or psychological, are part of the process and there is something to be said for victims having the right to forget and perpetrators an obligation to remember. Done well this can be a desirable outcome. However, at the same time nobody wants or should be confined to living only in the past. If true, this is perhaps why creating futures might actually turn out to be a noble undertaking. I believe this is a practice that we need to take a closer look at. As Zehr observed (1985, p. 80): "Retributive justice defines justice the Roman way, as right rules" and it measures justice by the intention and process. Restorative justice defines justice the Hebrew way, "as right relationship measured by the outcome." Restorative practices always require skilled facilitation.

HOPE, RECONCILLIATION AND REPAIR

It is hard to live without hope and the chances of repair. As Socrates knew, life without meaning and a life that's neither examined nor understood is not worth living. So what must it be like to be exiled in a seemingly meaningless and hopeless place of existence in which no one wants to understand and few appear to care and even less strive for repair? This homeless place of no man's land is what many abuse survivors and perpetrators of sexual crime describe in the wake of sexual abuse disclosures. This awareness leads me to a reconsideration of hope, reconciliation and despair.

In much public debate on sexual abuse by Catholic clergy individual psychic processes are privileged over social and relational context, "deficit" thinking prevails against resourcefulness, and pathology is prioritized over making sense. This equally applies to victims, perpetrators and the Church leadership. In the politics of child sexual abuse within the Catholic Church individuals and their lives get lost or used. Within such social and political discourses there is little space for hope, reconcilliation and repair. While the extent of the suffering involved in sexual abuse can never be underestimated and must not be forgotten, the absence of hope or the potential for reconciliation and repair contributes in no small way towards the growing web of human suffering and pain. The imperative is to respond creatively and compassionately so as to stand in witness with all of those who try to rebuild their lives; recovering from trauma, and / or accommodating the reality of having acted abusively or having failed.

First, I will turn to hope. Western ideas of hope view it as a feeling, usually as an achievement of the individual alone, and this premise underpins much empirical work on the psychology of hope (Snyder, Michael & Cheavens, 2005). From this perspective, responsibility for the achievement of hope rests with the individual. However, such a perspective does not always bring the desired effect. Expecting people to achieve hope when they are feeling low of spirit not only seems foolish but may also be downright irresponsible (Weingarten, 2007, p. 14). Despair is a more likely outcome. An alternative perspective of hope is predicated on the idea that hope is something we "do" with other people, and far from being the responsibility of individuals, "doing" hope is the responsibility of the community (p. 14). Within this perspective there are "hope tasks" for the hopeless and for those who witness their despair. The main task for individuals who feel hopeless is to resist isolation, and the task for those who witness their despair is to refuse indifference (p. 15).

The forgiveness literature (see for example Muller-Fahrenholz, 1997; Tomm, 2002) also offers pointers as to a possible direction for the work of healing and reconciliation. Reconciliation, which is always regarded as a major interpersonal achievement, involves complex human processes often enacted through apology and forgiveness work. However, the personal and interpersonal challenges are immense and must not be underestimated. Then again, the evidence for good outcome in relation to such transformative processes is fast accumulating and might make this work something worth considering in relation to sexual violations (Restorative Justice Council, 2010). The discussion in the literature on repair is also helpful. However, achieving meaningful repair is no easy task. Some medical and psychoanalytic-inspired literature has tried to address the question from an individual perspective in the context of trauma and traumatic experiences (Frankl, 2004; Friedlander, 1979; Lifton, 2000; Niederland & Krystal, 1971). But more recently there has been a resurging debate, mainly among sociologists and historians, that looks at social and cultural constellations and settings, that might make it possible to identify possibilities for repair (Alexander et al., 2004; Stein, 2007). All of this literature may point to future possibilities for responding further to the needs of survivors and perpetrators and the networks and communities affected by child sexual abuse by Catholic clergy. It also has reach beyond this particular cohort.

Lack of hope is evident and chances for reconciliation and repair are still minimal, particularly in the many countries that have experienced the problem of sexual abuse in general and by Catholic clergy in particular. Perpetrators are seen as "embodied evil," and victims are seen as "damaged for life." The risks of further abuses are often exaggerated within the public discourse, and the resultant fear can overwhelm hope and interfere with constructive action and much-needed repair work. Fearful of losing voice that was so hard won, victims of abuse fear being silenced again. Similarly voiceless in a society that has reduced their identity to the single description of "abuser," former clerical perpetrators return to isolation. Under such conditions it can be difficult for individuals to cope. The imperative is for groups of individuals to work together to diminish that fear and to resist the powerful pull of hate (Weingarten, 2007: 20).

Providing a helping infrastructure for reconciliation and restorative action does not mean to suggest that we blindly ignore the re-offense potential of men who have abused children or that we do not work to protect children. It *is* to suggest that we move the lens through which we view the problem from individual to community, from fear and hate to hope and repair, and that we seek solutions that will put all children beyond risk and that will give abuse perpetrators a way to take their place in the human community again. Central to this activity is an understanding of the problem in all its complexity, based on very deep introspection, honest dialogue, and an elaborate concept of human rights and social justice. The general lack of thought at the social and political level regarding the problem of child sexual abuse in the Anglophone world is disturbing. Often populist agendas and "solutions" seem to compound the very problems they are trying to overcome. Both clerical perpetrators and abuse victims are caught in such restricted fields of social and political vision.

Kathe Weingarten (2007, p. 22) tells us that "[h]ope is a resource. We hoard it at our peril ... It is a human rights issue. Just as food, water, and security must be equitably distributed, so too, must hope. Whether we offer or receive, co-create or imagine, we can all participate in doing hope." Nelson Mandela was right, and hinted at the right direction, when he advised that a nation should not be judged by how it treats its highest citizens, but by how it treats those who are seen as its lowest. I wish we could come to a situation where this also applies to the cases I have discussed in this work.

My hope is that this book will offer an opportunity to see the issue of sexual abuse by Catholic clergy in a new light, using the contextual issues, historical experience, original narratives, and psychological, social, and critical theory to open up a new perspective at this crucial time. By expanding the horizons of our knowledge and reflection, it may be that the men who have participated in this research can achieve an important milestone on our behalf. It is clear that the Catholic Church represents a politico-religious amalgam, the political dimensions of which have been a shock to the people of "*the simple faith*" and to me as I got deeper into understanding its workings. At the same time the Catholic Church is a human system, making and molding the lives of its many believers. In my work I have attempted to incorporate both.

When the problem of child sexual abuse is constructed in terms of dichotomies and such polarized perspectives dominate the popular discourse, the view that the same individual can be both good and bad, victim and perpetrator, and act in both innocent and devious ways is not articulated or comprehensively situated in the complexity of human life and living. In a world where words and labels matter, it behooves all of us to look beyond the label. In the research that is presented in this book, "the "monster" spoke and it had a human voice."

Appendix

THE PARTICIPANTS IN THE RESEARCH

The main data that are presented on the clerical perpetrators were gathered from the men themselves, and details were verified against data contained in the men's case files and in Books of Evidence, prepared in the course of criminal proceedings. The reader's attention is drawn to the fact that the primary research that was undertaken with the clerical perpetrators and that is presented in this book represents a small part of an earlier work. The research that is presented here was not conducted for the purposes of this book alone. The methodology was designed for the original study in such a manner as to preserve the anonymity of the participants and to safeguard their welfare. I realized that by participating in sensitive research on a topic of public importance the participants in my research were in fact offering something back, and my attempt was to enable them to do so without risk to themselves. Concern for the dignity and respect of individual participants is at the heart of research ethics and one of the important ways in which this principle is codified is through the principle of informed consent. Another is in protecting the identity of the individual participants. In undertaking this research my aim was at all times to safeguard the men's welfare and preserve their anonymity and to help them tell their stories in a manner that might help towards a deeper understanding of the phenomena and ultimately towards prevention of further sexual abuse of minors by Roman Catholic clergy. This appendix does not describe the methodology or design of the original study in detail but does give the reader an overview of the research participants and of the ethical complexities involved in undertaking such research and in how they were dealt with.

AN OVERVIEW OF THE RESEARCH PARTICIPANTS

Seven Roman Catholic priests, one religious brother, and one Christian brother participated in this research. Two of the priests were secular clergy and five were religious order priests, although one was working in a diocesan parish ministry. All of the participants, bar one, were older than late 50s when they participated in the research. One man was in his 40s. Seven of the men were convicted in the criminal courts for the offenses they perpetrated. The victims involved in two cases did not wish to pursue criminal charges. None of the men function any longer as clerics of a diocese or religious order. One man does light errands for his religious community, and the other men were retired or laicized.

The gender of the victim was not a feature of selection for participation in this study. However, all of the victims were male, except in one case where one man abused an adolescent girl. In six cases the boys were 12 to 18 years old; in two cases the boys were 14 to 18 years old; one man sexually abused boys who were 8 to 14 years old. One man also abused or attempted to abuse up to five seminarians, who were in their early 20s. In two cases, the men abused boys by touching the boys' genitalia. Neither of these two men ever disrobed or got a boy to touch him. The abuses consisted of the men touching the boys, sometimes inside and sometimes outside of their clothing. In these cases, no other forms of sexual abuse took place. In the other seven cases the range of sexual behaviors extended right across the sexually abusive spectrum.

The abuses took place in the boys' homes, in the priests' homes or rooms, in their offices, in cars, in schools, in the boys' dormitories, and in youth and children's facilities. The John Jay study (2004, 8) reports that abuses by clerical perpetrators in the United States are also alleged to have occurred in a variety of locations, including the priest's home or parish residence (40.9%), in a church (16.3%), in the victim's home (16.3%), in a vacation home (10.3%), in school (10.3%), and in a car (9.8%). In less than 10% of the allegations the abuse occurred in other locations, such as a hotel room or on a Church outing. In my research with the clerical perpetrators there are no allegations of abuse having taken place in a church, but one man is alleged to have abused boys in a shed on Church grounds. The boarding school environment was their home for many children who were abused by the men in this research. These children were dependent on the adults in the school environment to take care of them in *loco parentis*. Some children describe the absolute desolation they felt during the abusive times, when trapped in boarding schools, without the immediate support of parents.

Two of the men admitted to abusing up to 25 minors over the course of their ministries; others abused fewer children. One man abused or attempted to abuse up to five seminarians. While one man first abused a boy during his studies for the priesthood, the majority of the men, eight in all, began abusing some years after ordination, but mostly within 5 to 10 years. The main point is that seven of the nine men were in their late 20s before they began abusing, one man abused at an earlier age when he was still a seminarian, and another man, who was a late vocation to the priesthood, was older before he first abused. This finding is similar to the John Jay College report and is important because clerical men are generally older than other child sexual offenders when they first abuse.

The frequency of the abuses also shows some interesting patterns. Some abuses can be classified as "opportunistic" and were "once-offs." In other cases the abuses were more planned and took place on a number of occasions with the same boy. Some men admitted to abusing a boy for a prolonged period, often lasting up to 3 years. If the duration of abusive behavior is calculated by using the date of the first incident of abuse and the date of the most recent reported incident, in seven of the cases the men abused boys and young people for a period of up to 20 years; one man abused for a period of 15 years and the younger man abused boys over a 10-year period. It is important to note, however, that these figures do not necessarily represent continuous abusive activity.

SELECTING THE PARTICIPANTS

At the time the study began, the men who were approached to participate in the research had admitted to the abuse of minors and were attending therapy at a treatment facility in Ireland. At that time, clergy and non-clergy participants attending the treatment program were treated in separate therapy groups. I was involved as co-therapist in all of the clergy groups that were running at the time in the center. One group of clergy participants were approached and asked whether they would be willing to volunteer for the research that would be undertaken. The particular group of clergy that were selected consisted of those clergymen who had a long record in taking part in the treatment program, with the exception of one man. These men were selected because I believed they would be in a good position to reflect honestly and openly on the questions posed, as they had spent on average 18 months in outpatient therapy at the time that the research began, and in my opinion they were beyond the point of trying to cover up their abuses or be dishonest with themselves or each other. This group of men were living through a critical time in their lives; some were awaiting legal proceedings and they had all lost their clerical ministries.

While a group setting may be quite a constraining environment for some people, and may even be a force in preventing some from discussing intimate matters, I believed that this would not be so for the men in this research. I was aware from the therapeutic relationship that many of the barriers to intimate and personal disclosure had already been broken down and overcome by the participants in this particular group during the previous months when they worked together in therapy. I was also of the view that the one man who had spent a merely a short period in treatment before participating in the study would be encouraged and brought along by the other men's participation, and by the depth of their conversation. I was aware from my clinical work of the richness of the conversation that can be stimulated in a group setting, a richness that would be enhanced by inviting the men to ask questions of each other and comment on each other's responses, as part of the research process. The questions that the men posed to each other and the comments they made on each other's accounts and explanations served to generate an even greater profusion of important data. By generating the research data initially in a group setting, I was also able to follow up and interview particular individuals later in the course of the research to clarify ideas that were emerging and to fill in gaps in the analytical work. Theoretical sampling facilitated this process.

ETHICAL CONSIDERATIONS

A number of ethical and epistemological concerns arose in conducting this research, all of which were addressed to the fullest extent possible. The main concerns centered on a number of questions: Are clients in therapy free to give informed consent to participate in research, especially when the person asking them to participate is one of their therapists? What are the implications for the therapist/client relationship when this relationship temporarily changes to researcher/researched? Can reporting client narratives in a research project compromise the participants' confidentiality? And as I was both an insider and an outsider to the research under investigation, given that I was intimately acquainted with the research participants through the therapeutic relationship, would I be able to be sufficiently outside in order to look inside and vice-versa, and how could I be both inside and outside and use this positioning to further the research aims?

Collecting qualitative data from clients in therapy can be intrusive and demanding no matter what methods the researcher uses, and these issues had to be addressed (McLeod, 2001, p. 15). In this study a number of steps were taken to address the ethical concerns in the following ways.

The Question of Informed Consent

Given the inequalities of power that are present by definition in the therapeutic relationship, with its potential for manipulation and control (McLeod, 2001, p. 18) I was concerned that the clients who were approached to participate in the research might feel obliged to agree to do so or be afraid to refuse. With this concern in mind, a number of safeguards that would ensure that the participants were free to give informed consent were agreed upon between the director of the therapy center, the co-worker in the therapy group, and myself.

Firstly, the idea and purpose of the study was outlined to the selected participants as a group and the proposed research methodology and methods of data generation and analysis were outlined. Issues of confidentiality were spelled out. The participants were given time to think about the proposal and further discussion took place one week later. Confidentiality and fear of identification emerged as real concerns for the group members and included questions regarding the storing and disposal of the research data. Given that the research was being conducted in a small country, with a small group of men, this concern was indeed understandable. No changes in the methods were found to be necessary after the men stated that they merely wanted to voice their anxieties and to seek further reassurances about the research process.

Following these group discussions I met all the potential participants individually. These individual meetings offered potential participants an opportunity to discuss any reservations they had about participating in the study but felt they could not raise in a group setting. It was also used to assess whether any individual was being pressured inadvertently by other group members to participate in the research. The participants were told that I would keep any individual objections confidential, so that no person would be compromised, if he wished not to participate. The men were told that if any group member objected to participating in the research, I would move to another of the groups at the treatment center to seek participants for the study. No individual problems with participation were identified. Thus, individually and collectively, the men indicated their willingness to participate in the study.

As a final safeguard to ensure free and informed consent, the participants had a meeting without the researcher, with the co-therapist in the treatment program, to discuss their involvement in the project. Full participation in the study was affirmed. All participants were given a signed declaration guaranteeing confidentiality and were afforded an opportunity to withdraw their consent at any stage. No participant withdrew consent at any stage of the research. When the requirements of the Ethics Committee of the treatment center were met, the study was given the final approval to proceed.

From Therapy Client to Research Participant

Conducting research with men engaged in psychotherapy creates changes in the therapist/client relationship and therefore this issue had to be addressed. It was important that the men and I understood the ethical distinctions between participating in therapy and participating in research. These changes were managed in this study in the following manner.

For the duration of the initial phases of the research the group interviews were conducted for the purpose of the study and my focus was on the research. My role was firmly that of a researcher in the group conversations and interviews. This was explained to the group participants. However, once the initial batch of data had been generated the group reformed as a therapy group, and the co-therapist and I resumed our roles as therapists to the group of men. The men went on to complete their treatment and I continued with my research analysis. Some 18 months later, I moved employment from the therapy center to an academic appointment, by which time many of the men had graduated from the treatment program or were imprisoned.

As the research progressed I reconnected with the participants in various locations and interviewed some of the men individually in order to clarify aspects of my analysis and seek further comment on particular themes that were emerging. This time I returned as the researcher. However, the fact that I had once been their therapist, at a critical moment in their lives, clearly influenced the subsequent relationships. The frankness with which the men shared important and sensitive aspects of their lives may be related to the "trust" that existed from the therapeutic relationship.

The main difference between the therapeutic and the research processes for the men in this research centered on confidentiality and the purpose of the conversations that were taking place. The data gathered during the research conversations would be analyzed and presented in a public forum, unlike the content of the therapeutic conversations, which would not. For these reasons, I committed to giving the men feedback on the research as it progressed, and to giving them the penultimate draft of the study for feedback and appraisal and to eliminate any biographical or identifying personal details, which is what I did. It is just part of the original study that is reported in this book.

Potential Compromise of Confidentiality in Reporting Client Narratives

To overcome the final ethical consideration, that of the potential compromise of confidentiality that is involved when client narratives are reported in a research project, I selected a methodology that would minimize the risks of such breaches occurring. The methodology allowed for the research participants to be involved in the study until its completion and I adopted a process of going back to the research participants many times during the lifetime of the study, and finally with the penultimate draft, for their recommendations on the removal or amendment of any of their biographical or identifying details that they felt might compromise their confidentiality. This method of returning to the participants throughout the lifetime of the research also served purposes beyond the preservation of the participants' confidentiality; it helped me to follow up on ideas that emerged in the early analysis of the data and it facilitated increased respondent validity.

When the penultimate draft of the analyzed data was written, copies were given to six of the nine research participants for comments and appraisal. One man was deceased and two were unable to participate. This practice was adopted for ethical reasons and to act as a validity check of a kind. I had promised the participants at the outset of the study that they would have access to the research findings before the final account was published to check that confidentiality was not breached and to offer comments that would keep the analysis grounded in their narratives. The men were invited to check that the final document did not contain any identifying details that would amount to a breach of confidentiality. They were asked to consider this fact also on behalf of the men who were unable to participate or were deceased. The men were also invited to write comments in red ink on hard copies of the analyzed text and to give an overall impression of each chapter. All six participants gave detailed responses to the copy. Occasionally individual men made additional comments on a particular argument in general or suggested a refinement that related to his own unique case. For example, in one case the participant commented that his history of emotional loneliness did not begin when he entered the seminary, but rather that while he became even more lonely during his seminary training, his emotional loneliness had its origins in his childhood and in his family of origin (see Chapter 9). In another case one participant felt that his history of childhood sexual abuse had had profound effects on his life and subsequent offending, in contrast to other men, where this was not the case (see Chapter 8). In three cases the men asked for a small biographical detail to be omitted that might compromise their confidentiality. The process of going back to research participants was in keeping with the general orientation of the study. However, the argument for going back to the research participants with tentative results and refining them in the light of the participants' reactions as an attempt to increase validity is not unproblematic (Mason, 2002, p. 193; Silverman, 2000, p. 177). The problem arises if a privileged status is attributed to the respondents' accounts (Mason, 2002, p. 177; Silverman, 2000, p. 177). This did not arise in my research and the men's reflections on the analyzed data were woven into the final analysis and were treated as yet another source of data and insight. The final interpretations are mine.

NOTES

INTRODUCTION

1. It is not surprising, therefore, that offenders describe their sexual abuse in terms of failing to recognize victim harm because that is the message that the larger society is trying to communicate to them through their therapists. Most treatment programs are preoccupied with victim empathy (McGrath et al., 2010), despite there being no evidence that (a) lack of victim empathy is related to sexual recidivism (Hanson & Morton-Bourgon, 2005) or that (b) programs that target victim empathy have an impact on reducing the recidivism rates of sexual offenders. Who knows: perhaps priest offenders are different.

CHAPTER 1

1. In canon law some offenses are time-barred after a certain period, meaning that complaints made after the relevant time cannot be investigated. This is known as the period of prescription. Until 2001, the period of prescription for many offenses, including child sexual offenses, was 5 years. In 2001, Rome extended the time for making a complaint of sexual abuse to 10 years, and in the case of a minor this ran not from the last offense but from the victim's 18th birthday. In 2002 the Pope made a further concession when he granted the CDF the faculty to derogate from the period of prescription on a case-by-case basis. From then onwards, complaints dating back a period of 10 years or more could be investigated on a discretionary basis.

2. The Conference of Bishops, also known as the Episcopal Conference, is "the assembly of the Bishops of a country or of a certain territory, exercising together certain pastoral offices for Christ's faithful of that territory ... Plenary meetings of the Episcopal Conferences are to be held at least once a year, and moreover as often as special circumstances require, in accordance with the provisions of the statutes" (Canon 453, Canon Law Society of Great Britain and Ireland, 1983).

While the Conference cannot interfere with each bishop's direct link to Rome, it does speak on behalf of the entire body of bishops and, with the permission of Rome, it can issue directions on minor matters within dioceses, such as some liturgical innovations (Doyle, Sipe, & Wall, 2006, p. 334). See the glossary of terms for further elaboration.

3. See, for example, http://www.bishop-accountability.org/AbuseTracker.

4. Personal communication, January 2010, Karen Terry (U.S.), Friedemann Pfafflin (Germany), Karl Hanson (Canada), Tony Robinson (Australia), John Loftus (U.S.), Richard Sipe (U.S.).

5. The data used in this study were archival and came from diocesan personnel files. It is not a census of all reported cases of child sexual abuse within the Anglican Church in Australia, but it does survey most. All 23 dioceses were invited to participate; 17 dioceses took part. Of the 6 dioceses that were not involved, 3 rural dioceses declined to participate and the remaining 3 were omitted because they did not have relevant cases. Of the dioceses that did participate, not all cases could be analyzed. For example, in Adelaide only about 75% of files could be analyzed due to staffing constraints. In Sydney and Newcastle, a small number of files were not accessible, for example because they were with lawyers. However, the study covers the vast majority of the known cases that were within the scope of the 17 dioceses that participated.

6. For brief overview of sexual abuse in other religious institutions see John Jay College (2011 pp. 20-22).

7. See for example Boyle, 1994; Bringer, Brackenridge & Johnston, 2001; Colton, Roberts and Vanstone, 2010; Finkelhor & Williams, 1988; Gallagher, 2000; Gonsiorek, 1995; Margolin, 1991; McCarthy, 2009; Moulden, Firestone and Wexler, 2007; Shakeshaft, 2004; Sullivan & Beech, 2004; Utting, 1998.

8. Personal communication, Friedemann Pfafflin (Germany), January 2010.

9. Personal communication, January 2010, Karen Terry (U.S.), Friedemann Pfafflin (Germany), Karl Hanson (Canada), Tony Robinson (Australia), John Loftus (U.S.).

10. See Chapter 9 for a fuller discussion of this case.

CHAPTER 2

1. A pre-Christian and early Christian religious movement teaching that salvation comes by learning esoteric spiritual truths that free humanity from the material world, which this movement believed to be evil.

2. Rigorism was constituted by a systematic discipline, surveillance, and sexualization of the body.

3. Legalism is the ethical attitude that holds moral conduct to be a matter of rule-following. A legalistic perspective takes a law-and-order approach to morality in which external sources of authority are used as sufficient justification of moral judgments.

4. The interested reader is referred to Sipe's website: http://www.richardsipe.com/

5. For a fuller discussion of the importance of technology and the *Curia* in promoting papal power, see Robinson, 2007, pp. 127–129.

6. For a fuller discussion of the plurality of communal self-understandings that are contained in the various documents of the New Testament, see Sanks, 1997, pp. 45–52.

CHAPTER 3

1. Repeat offending is seen as similar to recidivism in the John Jay study, although I would argue that it is different. Most research on repeat sexual offending focuses on recidivism—a form of repeat offending in which additional acts of sexual abuse occur after some form of correctional intervention, such as incarceration or participation in a treatment program. Some studies define recidivism as a new charge; others define it as a new conviction. Whatever the case, the idea of recidivism is that an offender has re-offended following an intervention. The John Jay team members interpret the reporting of the allegation as an intervention for the purposes of their analysis of repeat offending, whereas my understanding of recidivism is that the intervention must be of a significant magnitude, involving apprehension or treatment.

CHAPTER 4

1. Readers who are interested in following up further on level I, II, and III theories of sexual offending and a critique of the same are referred to Ward, T., Devon, L., Polaschek, L., & Beech, T. (2006). *Theories of Sexual Offending.* Chichester: Wiley and Sons.

2. The following are the paraphilias described in the DSM-IV-TR (APA, 2000): exhibitionism, fetishism, frotteurism, sexual sadism, sexual masochism, transvestic fetishism, voyeurism, pedophilia, and paraphilia (not otherwise specified), which includes: obscene phone calling, necrophilia (corpses), zoophilia (animals), partialism (exclusive focus on specific body parts), coprophilia (feces), klismaphilia (enemas), and urophilia (urine). Polaschek (2003) notes that rape is omitted from this classification scheme unless it fits the diagnostic criteria for sexual sadism.

3. Readers who wish to undertake such an analysis might like to consult Ward, T., Polaschek, L. L., & Beech, A. R. (2006). *Theories of Sexual Offending.* Chichester: Wiley.

4. Readers who wish to follow up further on these criminological theories might consult Clarke, R., & Felson, M. (2008) (Eds.). *Routine Activity and Rational Choice. Advances in Criminological Theory, Vol. 5.* New Brunswick, NJ: Transaction Publishers.

CHAPTER 5

1. For a fuller discussion of the history of the concept see Jenkins (1998) and for institutional practices of pederasty see Bleibtreu-Ehrenberg (1990) and Ames & Houston (1990).

CHAPTER 6

1. See for example Skelton (1993), who used the term to understand teacher strategies and identities among physical education teachers; Messner (1992) and Messner & Sabo (1990), who used the term in their analysis of men and sport; Sabo & Gordon (1995), who used the concepts of hegemonic and subordinated masculinities to help understand men's health practices and risk-taking sexual behavior; and Barrett (1996), who used the term in his research on the military.

CHAPTER 7

1. Repeat offending is seen as similar to recidivism in the John Jay study, although I would argue that it is different. Most research on repeat sexual offending focuses on recidivism, a form of

repeat offending in which additional acts of sexual abuse occur after some form of correctional intervention, such as incarceration or participation in a treatment program. Some studies define recidivism as a new charge, others as a new conviction. Whatever the case, the idea of recidivism is that an offender has re-offended following an intervention. The John Jay team members interpret the reporting of the allegation as an intervention for the purposes of their analysis of repeat offending, whereas my understanding of recidivism is that the intervention must be of a significant magnitude, involving apprehension or treatment.

CHAPTER 8

1. Canon 1395 states: "A cleric who has offended . . . against the sixth commandment of the Decalogue [the Ten Commandments] . . . with a minor under the age of 16 years is to be punished with just penalties, not excluding dismissal from the clerical state if the case so warrants."

CHAPTER 9

1. A part of this research is reported in this book in Chapters 7 and 8.

2. For a discussion on why the Vatican is always reluctant to see a bishop resign under fire, see Allen (2010d).

3. The Sixth Commandment of the Catechism of the Catholic Church states, "You shall not commit adultery." The commandment also means that "everyone who looks at a woman lustfully has already committed adultery with her in his heart."

4. I am indebted to one of the reviewers of this manuscript, who as a participant in the 2003 Vatican consultation, can confirm that the then Cardinal Ratzinger, now Pope Benedict XVI, was in attendance for some of the proceedings.

5. In Chapter 5 I outlined some of the limitations of the media reporting of sexual abuse, especially in relation to clerical perpetrators. While there are also problems with how victims are portrayed in the media for many survivors, the work of the media in Ireland and the United States in bringing child sexual abuse onto the public agenda and in supporting survivors to do so cannot be underestimated.

CHAPTER 10

1. As an aside, recent Vatican policy seems to have rendered ambiguous the irreversible status of priesthood in relation to clerical perpetrators, in an example of some of the incoherent policies that the sexual abuse crisis is provoking in Vatican circles.

2. I met David Ranson in Sydney in February 2010 and discussed some of these ideas, for which I am very grateful.

GLOSSARY

ABSOLUTION: "Absolution takes away sin, but it does not remedy all the disorders sin has caused. Raised up from sin, the sinner must still recover his full spiritual health by doing something more to make amends for the sin: he must 'make satisfaction for' or 'expiate' his sins. This satisfaction is also called 'penance'" (*Catechism of the Catholic Church*, 1994, p. 1459).

ADOLESCENT: A person who is in the process of developing from a child into an adult (*Concise Oxford English Dictionary*, 2002). In this work an adolescent is considered to be a person between the ages of 13 and 18 years, also referred to as a young person.

ALTAR: The center of the Church; the place on which the Mass is celebrated; the place where "the sacrifice of the Cross is made present under sacramental signs. The altar is also the table of the Lord, to which the People of God are invited" (*Catechism of the Catholic Church*, 1994, p. 1182).

ALTAR-SERVER: A person who assists the priest on the altar when he celebrates the Mass. Altar-servers can be male or female and are usually young people, although not always.

ALTAR-SERVER'S MEETINGS: Meetings held for the purpose of training the altar-servers for the tasks involved in serving at Mass. These meetings are usually held for young altar-servers, such as young people under the age of 18.

ANATHEMA: From a Greek word meaning "a thing devoted to evil," it refers to "something that one vehemently dislikes, a formal curse of the Church, excommunicating a person or denouncing a doctrine" (*Concise Oxford English Dictionary*, 2002).

BISHOP: "By divine institution, Bishops succeed the Apostles through the Holy Spirit who is given to them. They are constituted Pastors in the Church, to be the teachers of doctrine, the priests of sacred worship and the ministers of governance. By their Episcopal consecration, Bishops receive, together with the office of sanctifying, the offices also of teaching and of ruling, which however, by their nature, can be exercised only in hierarchical communication with the head of the College [the pope] and its members" (Canon 375, Canon Law Society of Great Britain and Ireland, 1983). "Bishops to whom the care of a given Diocese is entrusted are called diocesan Bishops" (Canon 376, Canon Law Society of Great Britain and Ireland, 1983).

CANON LAW: The body of laws governing the Roman Catholic Church of the Latin Rite (Canon 1, Canon Law Society of Great Britain and Ireland, 1983). The first official and complete code was promulgated in 1917 and remained in effect until 1983 when, following the Second Vatican Council, a revised code was published.

CATECHISM: An organized presentation of Church teaching on faith and morals in language that is intelligible to the average person (Doyle, Sipe, & Wall, 2006, p. 332).

CELIBACY: The state of a person who abstains from marriage and from sexual relations for religious reasons (*Concise Oxford Dictionary*, 2002). All Roman Catholic priests are obliged to make a vow or a promise of celibacy. This promise includes the commitment to "perfect and perpetual chastity" (Canon 277, Canon Law Society of Great Britain and Ireland, 1983). Celibacy is regarded as "a special gift of God by which sacred ministers can more easily remain close to Christ with an undivided heart, and can dedicate themselves more freely to the service of God and their neighbour. Clerics are to behave with due prudence in relation to persons whose company can be a danger to their obligation of preserving continence or can lead to scandal of the faithful" (Canon 277, Canon Law Society of Great Britain and Ireland, 1983).

CHASTITY: "Chastity is a moral virtue. It is also a gift from God, a *grace,* a fruit of spiritual effort. All baptized people are called to chastity. All Christ's faithful are called to lead a chaste life in keeping with their particular states of life" (*Catechism of the Catholic Church,* 1994, pp. 2345–2348). Some Christians profess virginity or consecrated celibacy, while others who may be married live in a way that is prescribed for all by the moral law—that is, they are expected to remain chaste by not involving themselves in immoral sexual behavior.

CHILD: A young human being below the age of full physical development (*Concise Oxford English Dictionary*, 2002). In this study a child refers to a person of 12 years or under. An adolescent is from 13–18 years; both are called "minors."

CHILD SEXUAL ABUSE: It is difficult to achieve a commonly accepted definition of child sexual abuse because it has been used in diverse ways in legal, social, and clinical settings and its meaning and implications have changed over time (Jenkins, 1998). However, in this study if a person alleges that he or she has been hurt or violated in a sexual way in their contact, with the alleged perpetrator and the allegation is validated, then this is a situation in which child sexual abuse is seen to exist.

CHRISTIAN BROTHER: A religious brother who is a member of the Irish Congregation of the Christian Brothers, a religious institution (Canon 607, Canon Law Society of Great Britain and Ireland, 1983). He professes vows of chastity, poverty, and obedience and is obliged to observe the state of celibacy.

CHURCH: In this study, the Roman Catholic Church of the Latin Rite, unless specified otherwise.

CLERGY: In this study, secular and religious priests, religious brothers, and bishops.

COLLEGE OF BISHOPS: Part of the Church governance, the College of Bishops is the subject of supreme power in the Church, but only in union with the Roman pontiff. The College of

Bishops exercises its power over the universal Church in Ecumenical Councils. Its decrees do not oblige unless approved by the Roman pontiff.

CONFERENCE OF BISHOPS: The Conference of Bishops, also known as the Episcopal Conference, is "the assembly of the Bishops of a country or of a certain territory, exercising together certain pastoral offices for Christ's faithful of that territory. By forms and means of apostolate suited to the circumstances of time and place, it is to promote, in accordance with the law, that greater good which the Church offers to all people" (Canon 447, Canon Law Society of Great Britain and Ireland, 1983). The Conference of Bishops is a permanent institution. Each Episcopal Conference draws up its own statutes, which are reviewed by the pope. In the statutes, arrangements for plenary meetings of the Conference are set out, and provision is made for a permanent committee of bishops, for a general secretary of the Conference, and for other offices and commissions that in the judgment of the Conference are necessary to help it more effectively achieve its purposes (Canon 451, Canon Law Society of Great Britain and Ireland, 1983). "Plenary meetings of the Episcopal Conferences are to be held at least once a year, and moreover as often as special circumstances require, in accordance with the provisions of the statutes" (Canon 453, Canon Law Society of Great Britain and Ireland, 1983). While the Conference cannot interfere with each bishop's direct link to Rome, it does speak on behalf of the entire body of bishops and, with the permission of Rome, it can issue directions on minor maters within dioceses, such as some liturgical innovations (Doyle, Sipe, & Wall, 2006, p. 334).

CONFESSION: An admission of guilt for wrongdoing by a penitent to a priest in the course of receiving the sacrament of penance, now called the sacrament of reconciliation. "In the sacrament of penance the faithful who confess their sins to a lawful minister, are sorry for their sins and have a purpose of amendment, receive from God, through the absolution given by that minister, forgiveness of sins they have committed after baptism, and at the same time they are reconciled with the Church" (Canon 959, Canon Law Society of Great Britain and Ireland, 1983). "In hearing confessions the priest is to remember that he is at once both judge and healer, and that he is constituted by God as a minister of both divine justice and divine mercy, so that he may contribute to the honour of God and the salvation of souls" (Canon 978, Canon Law Society of Great Britain and Ireland, 1983). "In asking questions the priest is to act with prudence and discretion, taking into account the condition and the age of the penitent, and he is to refrain from enquiring the name of a partner in sin" (Canon 979, Canon Law Society of Great Britain and Ireland, 1983).

DEACON: The lowest rank in the order of the hierarchy that governs the Catholic Church. Until recently, the diaconate was reserved for men on their way to the priesthood. Vatican II restored the permanent diaconate for men who may be married before they are ordained. However, members of the permanent diaconate may not marry after ordination (Doyle, Sipe, & Wall, 2006, p. 335).

DIOCESE: A group of Catholic people entrusted to a bishop to be nurtured pastorally and spiritually by him in such a way that, remaining close to its pastor and gathered by him through the Gospel and the Eucharist in the Holy Spirit, it constitutes a particular Church (Canon 369, Canon Law Society of Great Britain and Ireland, 1983). A diocese is often bounded by a particular geographical territorial boundary (Canon 372, Canon Law Society of Great Britain and Ireland, 1983). Dioceses are divided into parishes, usually each with its own priest or priests as pastor or pastors.

FORMATION: The training process undertaken by those who wish to become ministers of the Church. Young men who intend to become priests receive the appropriate religious formation and instruction in the duties proper to the priesthood in a major seminary (Canon 235, Canon Law Society of Great Britain and Ireland, 1983). Men wishing to become religious priests or brothers receive their religious formation and instruction in Houses of Formation.

INCARDINATION: The process whereby a priest is affiliated with a particular diocese. Every cleric must be incardinated in a particular church or in an institute of consecrated life or a society that has this faculty. In this way, "wandering" clergy are in no way allowed (Canon 265, Canon Law Society of Great Britain and Ireland, 1983).

INCIDENCE: The number of new cases of a particular event or behavior occurring over a particular period of time, usually 1 year.

LAICIZATION: The process whereby the Vatican returns a member of the hierarchy to the ranks of the laity. Laicization can be requested by a cleric or imposed by a court or the pope as a punishment for a serious ecclesiastical crime (Canon 290, Canon Law Society of Great Britain and Ireland, 1983).

MINOR: In canon law (Canon 97, Canon Law Society of Great Britain and Ireland, 1983), "[a] person who has completed the eighteenth year of age has attained majority: below this age a person is a minor." In this work a minor refers to any person under the age of 18 years and thus includes both children and young people.

NOVICE: A person who has just begun his training for life as a religious within a religious institute.

NOVITIATE: "The purpose of the novitiate, by which life in a [religious] institute begins, is to give the novices a greater understanding of their divine vocation, and of their vocation to that institute" (Canon 646, Canon Law Society of Great Britain and Ireland, 1983).

ORDINATION: The action of ordaining someone in Holy Orders (*Concise Oxford English Dictionary*, 2002).

PARISH: A small administrative district with its own church and clergy (*Concise Oxford English Dictionary*, 2002).

PARTICULAR FRIENDSHIPS: Particularly close friendships between two men; often thought of in terms of homosexual relationships.

POPE: The supreme legislator for the Catholic Church and all of its members. Only he can create and change law on a universal or worldwide level. Many of these laws are found in legal codes or in papal decrees. The office uniquely committed by the Lord to Peter, the first of the Apostles, and to be transmitted to his successors abides in the Bishop of the Church of Rome. He is the head of the College of Bishops, the Vicar of Christ, and the Pastor of the universal Church here on earth. By virtue of his office, he has supreme, full, immediate, and universal ordinary power in the Church and can always freely exercise his power (Canon 331). By virtue of his office, the Roman pontiff not only has power over the universal Church, but also has preeminent ordinary power over all particular Churches and their groupings (Canon 331.1). There is neither appeal nor recourse against a judgment or decree of the Roman Pontiff (Canon 333.3).

PREVALENCE: The proportion of a population that has experienced a particular event or behavior.

REDEMPTORIST: The Redemptorist Order, an order of religious priests, brothers and religious sisters.

RELIGIOUS: By vows or other sacred bonds, in accordance with the laws of their own orders or institutes, religious are men or women who profess publicly to make vows of chastity, poverty, and obedience (Canon 573, Canon Law Society of Great Britain and Ireland, 1983). The vow of chastity involves the obligation of perfect continence observed in celibacy (Canon 599). Religious find the rule of life in following Christ as proposed in the Gospel and as expressed in the constitutions of their own institutes (Canon 662). Religious reside in their own religious houses and observe a common life (Canon 665). Some religious are also ordained to the priesthood and are referred to in this study as religious priests. Religious who are not ordained are referred to as religious brothers or religious sisters.

RELIGIOUS BROTHER: A layperson who is a member of a religious institute (Canon 607, Canon Law Society of Great Britain and Ireland, 1983). He too is consecrated to God and the Church's salvific mission through the profession of the evangelical counsels of poverty, chastity, and obedience (Canon 207).

RELIGIOUS PRIEST: A priest who is incardinated into a particular religious institute (Canons 607, 265). He is consecrated to God and the Church's mission of salvation through the profession of the evangelical counsels of poverty, chastity, and obedience.

RETREAT: A period or place of seclusion for the purposes of prayer and meditation (*Concise Oxford English Dictionary*, 2002).

ROMAN CATHOLIC CHURCH: The Latin Church, which comprises the worldwide group of Christians who accept the pope, who is the Bishop of Rome, as their spiritual leader. The Church is divided into administrative units known as dioceses, entrusted to the care of a bishop (Canon 369, Canon Law Society of Great Britain and Ireland, 1983). Each diocese is divided into parishes, which are defined in accordance with Canon 515. Each parish has its own parish priest and sometimes one or more curates or other priests in residence. Alongside the hierarchical structure of the Roman Catholic Church, there are many religious institutes of men and women, often referred to as religious orders, each with their own internal government, independent of the diocesan bishop. However, in matters of public worship or pastoral activities, religious may be subject to the supervision of diocesan bishops (Canon 678).

ROMAN *CURIA*: The pope conducts the business of the universal Church through the Roman *Curia*, which acts in his name and with his authority for the good and service of the Church. The *Curia* is composed of the Secretariat of State or Papal Secretariat, the Council for the public affairs of the Church, the Congregations, the Tribunals, and other Institutes of the Roman Catholic Church (Canon 360, Canon Law Society of Great Britain and Ireland, 1983).

SCHOLASTICATE: Period of formation for members of a religious order who are between the novitiate and the priesthood.

SEAL OF CONFESSION: "The sacramental seal [of confession] is inviolable. Accordingly, it is absolutely wrong for a confessor in any way to betray the penitent, for any reason whatsoever, whether by word or in any other fashion" (Canon 983, Canon Law Society of Great Britain and Ireland, 1983). "The confessor is wholly forbidden to use knowledge acquired in confession to the detriment of the penitent, even when all danger of disclosure is excluded. A person who is in authority may not in any way, for the purpose of external governance, use knowledge about sins which has at any time come to him from the hearing of confessions" (Canon 984, Canon Law Society of Great Britain and Ireland, 1983).

SECULAR PRIEST: A secular priest or diocesan priest is an ordained man who has been incardinated into a particular diocese (Canon 265, Canon Law Society of Great Britain and Ireland, 1983). He works under the leadership and authority of the bishop of that particular diocese (Canon 369). He has a special obligation to show reverence and obedience to the pope and to his ordinary (bishop) (Canon 273). He is obliged to observe perfect and perpetual continence for the sake of the kingdom of heaven, and is therefore bound to celibacy (Canon 277). Secular priests often live alone; sometimes they share a house with other diocesan clergy.

SEMINARY: An undergraduate- or graduate-level place of residence and training for young male candidates for the Roman Catholic priesthood.

SEMINARIAN: A young man in training for Catholic priesthood.

SODALITY: A Roman Catholic religious fraternity or association (*Concise Oxford English Dictionary*, 2002).

VATICAN: The palace and official residence of the pope in Rome (*Concise Oxford Dictionary*, 2002). Vatican City is a 44-acre sovereign state in Rome, established in 1929 by the Lateran Treaty with Italy. Most of the administration of the Catholic Church is conducted within its boundaries (Doyle, Sipe, & Wall, 2006, p. 341).

REFERENCES

Abel, G. C. (2000). www.abelscreen.com Abel Screen Inc., March 27 (subscribers' section).

Abel, G. C., Becker, J. V., & Cunningham-Rathner, J. (1984). Complications, consent, and cognitions in sex between children and adults. *International Journal of Law and Psychiatry, 7*, 89–103.

Abel, G. C., Becker, J. V., Mittelman, M., Cunningham-Rathner, J., Rouleau, J. L., & Murphy, W. D. (1987). Self-reported sex crimes of non-incarcerated paraphiliacs. *Journal of Interpersonal Violence, 2*(1), 3–25.

Abel, G. C., Gore, D. K., Holland, C. L., Camp, N., Becker, J., & Rathner, J. (1989). The measurement of cognitive distortions of child molesters. *Annals of Sex Research, 2*, 135–153.

Abel, G. C., & Osborne, C. (1992). The paraphilias: The extent and nature of sexually deviant and criminal behaviour. *Clinical Forensic Psychiatry, 15*(3), 675–867.

Agar, M. (1980). *The Professional Stranger: An Informal Introduction to Ethnography.* New York: Academic Press.

Agnew, P. (1994). Bishops to discuss child sex case, says Cardinal. *Irish Times,* p. 3, Oct. 26.

Agnew, P. (2010a). Papal meeting set to bring scandal closer to Vatican. *Irish Times,* March 12.

Agnew, P. (2010b). Abuse scandal ratchets up pressure on Vatican as Pope visits Malta. *Irish Times,* April 17. Available online at www.irishtimes.ie, accessed April 17, 2010.

Alexander, J., Eyerman, R., Giesen, B., Smelser, N., & Sztompka, P. (2004). *Cultural Trauma and Collective Identity.* Berkeley, CA: University of California Press.

Alexander, J. C. (1987). "What is theory?" In J. C Alexander. *Twenty Lectures—Sociological Theory since World War II* (pp. 1–21). New York: Columbia University Press.

Alexander, J. C. (2003). *The Meanings of Social Life: A Cultural Sociology.* New York: Oxford University Press.

Alexander, J. C (2004). *Cultural Trauma and Collective Identity.* Berkeley, CA: University of California Press.

Allen, G. (1989). A Church in crisis: sex scandals shake Newfoundlanders' faith. *Maclean's* (Canada), p. 66, Nov. 27.

Allen, J. Jr. (2004). Clergy sexual abuse in the American Catholic Church: The view from the Vatican. In T. G. Plante (Ed.), *Sin against the Innocents. Sexual Abuse by Priests and the Role of the Catholic Church* (pp. 13–24). Westport, CT, London: Praeger.

Allen, J. Jr. (2006). Fr. Tom Doyle on "Crimen Sollicitationis." *National Catholic Reporter,* Oct. 12.

Allen, J. Jr. (2010a). Will Ratzinger's past trump Benedict's present? *National Catholic Reporter,* March 17. Online version, http://ncronline.org/, accessed March 17, 2010.

Allen, J. Jr. (2010b). Memo to Munich: Get it out now! *National Catholic Reporter,* March 19. Online version, http://ncronline.org/, accessed March 19, 2010.

Allen, J. Jr. (2010c). Keeping the record straight on Benedict and the crisis. *National Catholic Reporter,* March 26. Online version, http://ncronline.org/, accessed March 26, 2010.

Allen, J. Jr. (2010d). Why Rome scorns resignations and a great week for wonks. *National Catholic Reporter,* Aug. 13. Online version, http://ncronline.org/, accessed August 13, 2010.

Allen, J. Jr. (2011). Is Vatican letter on abuse a "smoking gun"? *National Catholic Reporter,* Jan. 19th. Available at http://ncronline.org/blogs/ncr-today/vatican-letter-abuse-smoking-gun, accessed Jan. 21, 2011.

Altman, D. (1972). *Homosexual: Oppression and Liberation.* Sydney, Australia: Angus and Roberston.

American Psychiatric Association (1994). *Diagnostic and Statistical Manual of Mental Disorders: IV,* Washington, DC: American Psychiatric Association.

American Psychiatric Association (2000). *Diagnostic and Statistical Manual of Mental Disorders IV, text revised,* Washington, DC: American Psychiatric Association.

Ames, M., & Houston, D. (1990). Legal, social and biological definitions of pedophilia. *Archives of Sexual Behaviour,* 19(4), 333–342.

Ammicht-Quinn, R., Haker, H., & Junker Kenny, M. (2004). Introduction. In R. Ammicht-Quinn, H. Haker, & M. Junker Kenny (Eds.), *The Structural Betrayal of Trust.* 3. London: Concilium.

Anderson, H., & Goolishian, H. (1988). Human systems as linguistic systems: preliminary and evolving ideas about the implications for clinical theory. *Family Process,* 27, 371–393.

Anglophone Episcopal Consultation on Child Protection at the Vatican in Rome. (2007). May.

Archdiocese of St. John's, Newfoundland. (1990). *Archdiocesan Commission of Inquiry into Sexual Abuse of Children by Members of the Clergy.*

Araji, S. K. (1997). *Sexually Aggressive Children: Coming to Understand Them.* Thousand Oaks, CA: Sage Publications.

Arendt, H. (2000). *The Portable Hannah Arendt* (edited with an introduction by Peter Baehr). New York: Penguin Classics.

Arendt, H. (2003). *Responsibility and Judgement* (edited with an introduction by Jerome Kohn). New York: Schocken Books.

Ariés, P. (1962). *Centuries of Childhood.* Harmondsworth: Penguin.

Arthurs, H., Ferguson, H., & Grace, E. (1995). Celibacy, secrecy and the lives of men. *Doctrine and Life,* 45(7), 471–480.

Asay, T., & Lambert, M. (2005). The empirical case for the common factors in therapy: Quantitative findings. In M. Hubble, B. Duncan, & S. Miller (Eds.), *The Heart and Soul of*

Change. What Works in Therapy (10th ed., pp. 33–56). Washington, DC: American Psychological Association.

Ashenden, S (2002). Policing Perversion: The Contemporary Governance of Paedophilia, *Journal for Cultural Research, 6 (* 1&2), 197-222

Associated Press (2010). Cardinals claim Pope hit by "hate" campaign. *New Zealand Herald,* April 8, p. A14.

Association for the Treatment of Sexual Abusers (1993). *The ATSA Practitioner's Handbook.* Lake Oswego, OR: Author.

Association for the Treatment of Sexual Abusers (2001). *Civil commitment of sexually violent offenders.* http://www.atsa.com/ppcivilcommit.html, retrieved July 8, 2002.

Australian Catholic Bishops' Conference (1996). *Towards Healing: Principles and Procedures in Responding to Complaints of Sexual Abuse against Personnel of the Catholic Church in Australia.* Hectorville, Australia.

Australian Catholic Bishops' Conference (1999). *Integrity in Ministry: A Document of Principles and Standards for Catholic Clergy and Religious in Australia.*

Background Briefing. (2010). ABC National Radio, Australia. Broadcast March 7. Available at http://www.abc.net.au/rn/backgroundbriefing/

Balboni, B. S. (1998). *Through the "Lens" of the Organizational Culture Perspective: A Descriptive Study of American Catholic Bishops' Understanding of Clergy Sexual Molestation and Abuse of Children and Adolescents.* Unpublished PhD thesis, Northeastern University, Boston, Massachusetts. Available at http://www.Bishop-accountability.org/resources/resource-files/reports/BalboniLensTitle.htm, accessed 10/1/07.

Balboni, J. M., & Bishop, D. M. (2010). Transformative justice: survivor perspectives on clergy sexual abuse litigation. *Contemporary Justice Review,* 13(2), 133–154.

Barrett, F. J. (1996). The organizational construction of hegemonic masculinity: the case of the U.S. Navy. *Gender, Work and Organization,* 3(3), 129–142.

Bartholomew, K., & Horowitz, L. M. (1991). Attachment styles among adults: A test of a four category model. *Journal of Personality and Social Psychology,* 61, 226–244.

Bartlett, E. (1989). The aftershock of Mount Cashel. *Western Report,* p. 46, Nov. 6.

Bass, E., & Davis, L. (1993). *Beginning to Heal.* London: Cedar.

Batchelor, A., & Horvath, A. (2005). The therapeutic relationship. In M. Hubble, B. Duncan, & S. Miller (Eds.), *The Heart and Soul of Change. What Works in Therapy* (10th ed., pp. 133–178). Washington, DC: The American Psychological Association.

Bateson, G. (1972). *Steps to an Ecology of the Mind.* New York: Ballantine Books.

Bateson, G. (1980). *Mind and Nature: A Necessary Unity.* New York: Bantam Books.

Baumeister, R. F. (1990). Suicide as escape from self. *Psychological Review,* 97, 90–113.

Beal, J., Coriden, J., & Green, T. (2000) (Eds.) *New Commentary on the Code of Canon Law.* New York: Paulist Press.

Bean, P. & Melville, J (1989). *Lost Children of the Empire.* London: Harper Collins.

Beattie, T. (2009). *Between the Devil and the Deep Blue Sea: Catholicism, Sex and Society in Changing Perspective.* Talk given at St. Mary's Church, Haddington Road, Dublin, Nov. 5.

Beck, A. T (1963). Thinking and depression: I. Idiosyncratic content and cognitive distortions. *Archives of General Psychiatry,* 9(4), 324-333.

Beckett, R., Beech, A., Fisher, D., & Fordham, A. S. (1994). *Community-Based Treatment for Sex Offenders. An Evaluation of Seven Treatment Programmes.* London: Home Office.

Behl, L. E., Conyngham, H. A., & May, P. F. (2003). Trends in child maltreatment literature. *Child Abuse and Neglect*, 27, 215–229.

Beier, K. M. (2010). Why does child sex-abuse happen? *The Tablet*, March 13, p. 8.

Bell, V. (2002). The vigilant(e) parent and the paedophile: The *News of the World* campaign 2000 and the contemporary governmentality of child sexual abuse. *Feminist Theory*, 3(1), 83–102.

Bender, L (1948). Genesis of Hostility in Children. *The American Journal of Psychiatry*, 105, 241-245.

Bennett, R., and the staff of the National Review Board for the Protection of Children and Young People (2004). *A Report on the Crisis in the Catholic Church in the United States*. Washington, DC: The United States Conference of Catholic Bishops.

Benyei, C. R. (1998). *Understanding Clergy Misconduct in Religious Systems. Scapegoating, Family Secrets and the Abuse of Power*. New York: The Hayworth Pastoral Press.

Berger, P., & Luckmann, T. (1991/1966). *The Social Construction of Reality. A Treatise in the Sociology of Knowledge*. Harmondsworth: Penguin Books.

Berlin, F. S., & Krout, E. W. (1986). Pedophilia: Diagnostic concepts, treatment, and ethical considerations. *American Journal of Forensic Psychiatry*, 7(1), 13–30.

Berlin, F. S., & Meinecke, C. F. (1981). Treatment of sex offenders with antiandrogenic medication: Conceptualization, review of treatment modalities, and preliminary findings. *American Journal of Psychiatry*, 138(5), 601–607.

Berry, J. (2000/1992). *Lead Us Not into Temptation, Catholic Priests and The Sexual Abuse of Children*. New York: Doubleday.

Berry, J. (2009). Papal princes immune to censure. *The Irish Times*, Dec. 4, p. 13.

Berry, J., & Renner, G. (2004). *Vows of Silence. The Abuse of Power in the Papacy of John Paul II*. New York: Free Press.

Best, J. (1995a). Typification and social problem construction. In J. Best. (Ed.), *Images of Issues, Typifying Contemporary Social Problems*. (pp. 1–16) New York: Walter de Gruyter.

Best, J. (Ed.) (1995b). *Images of Issues, Typifying Contemporary Social Problems*. New York: Walter de Gruyter.

Bieler, L. (1963). *The Irish Penitentials*. Dublin: Institute for Advanced Studies.

Blaine, B. (2010). SNAP blasts Pope for "rubbing salt into wounds" [press release, Aug. 11]. Available at: http://www.snapnetwork.org/snap_statements/2010_statements/081110_snap_blasts_pope_for_rubbing_salt_into_wounds.htm

Blanchard, G. T. (1991). Sexually abusive clergymen: A conceptual framework for intervention and recovery. *Pastoral Psychology*, 39, 237–245.

Blanchard, P. (1954). *The Irish and Catholic Power*. London: Derek Verschoyle.

Blanchard, R. (2010). The DSM diagnostic criteria for pedophilia. *Archives of Sexual Behaviour*, 39(2), 304–316.

Bleibtreu-Ehrenberg, G. (1990). Pederasty among primitives: Institutional initiation and cultic prostitution. *Journal of Homosexuality*, 20(1–2), 13–30.

Blumer, H. (1969). *Symbolic Interactionism: Perspectives and Methods*. Engelwood Cliffs, NJ: Prentice Hall.

Bolen, R. M (2001), *Child Sexual Abuse; Its Scope and Our Failure*. New York: Kluwer Academic, Plenum Publishers.

Bolen, R., & Scannapieco, M. (1999). Prevalence of child sexual abuse: A corrective meta-analysis. *Social Services Review*, 73, 281–313.

Bourdieu, P (1977). *Outline of a Theory of Practice*. Cambridge: Cambridge University Press.

Boston Globe Investigative Staff (2002). *Betrayal: The Crisis in the Catholic Church*. Boston: Little Brown.

Boswell, J. (1990). *The Kindness of Strangers: The Abandonment of Children in Western Europe from Late Antiquity to the Renaissance*. New York: Vintage.

Boszormenyi-Nagy, I., & Spark, G. (1973). *Invisible loyalties: Reciprocity in Intergenerational Family Therapy*. Oxford, England: Harper & Row.

Bottoms, A. E. (1995). Crime and insecurity in the city. In C. Fijnaut, J. Goethals, T. Peters, & L. Walgrave (Eds.), *Change in Society, Crime and Criminal Justice*. The Hague: Kluwer.

Bowlby, J. (1969). *Attachment and Loss: Volume 1, Attachment*. London: Hogarth.

Bowlby, J. (1973). *Attachment and Loss: Volume 2, Separation*. London: Hogarth.

Bowlby, J. (1979). *Attachment and Loss: Volume 3, Sadness and Depression*. London: Hogarth.

Bowlby, J. (1980). *The Making and Breaking of Affectional Bonds*. London: Tavistock.

Boyle, P (1994). *Scout's Honor: Sexual Abuse in America's Most Trusted Institution*. Rocklin, CA: Prima Publishing.

Brady, S. (2008). The impact of sexual abuse on sexual identity formation in gay men. *Journal of Child Sexual Abuse,* 17(3–4), 359–376.

Bradshaw and Coates, 1999;

Braithwaite, J. (1989/ 2007). *Crime, Shame and Reintegration*. Cambridge: Cambridge University Press.

Breen, M. (2004a). Rethinking Power: An Analysis of Media Coverage of Sexual Abuse in Ireland, the UK and the U.S.A. In M. Kearney (Ed.). *Postmodernism: The Global Moment. Tokyo: Conference Kogaluin University*. March 9th – 11th .

Breen, M. (2004b). Depraved Paedos and Other Beasts: The media portrayal of child sexual abusers in Ireland and the UK. In P. Yoder & P. M. Kreuter (Eds.), *Monsters and the Monstrous: Myths and Metaphors of Enduring Evil*. Inter

Brenneis, M. (2001). Personality characteristics of clergy and of psychologically impaired clergy: A review of the literature. *American Journal of Pastoral Counselling,* 4(77), 7–13.

Bringer, J. D., Brackenridge, C. H. & Johnston, L. H (2001). The Name of the Game: A Review of Sexual Exploitation of Females in Sport. *Current Women's Health Reports,* 1 (3), 225-231.

Brod, H., & Kaufman, M. (1994). Introduction. In H. Brod & H. Kaufman (Eds.), *Theorising Masculinities*. London: Sage.

Brody, H. (1973). *Inishkillane: Change and Decline in the West of Ireland*. Harmondsworth, Middlesex: Allen Lane.

Broken Rites Australia (2009). Black-collar crime. Available at http://brokenrites.alphalink.com.au/nletter/bccrime.html, accessed Feb. 10, 2009.

Brown, R. (1984). *The Churches the Apostles Left Behind*. New York: Paulist Press.

Brown, R., Fitzmyer, J., & Murphy, R. (1990) (Eds.). *The New Jerome Biblical Commentary*. Englewood Cliffs, NJ: Prentice-Hall.

Brown, R., & Meier, J. (1983). *Antioch and Rome: New Testament Cradles of Catholic Christianity*. New York: Paulist Press.

Brown, V. (1995). Does Fr. Cleary's conduct really matter? *Irish Times,* p. 14, June 28.

Brownmiller, S. (1975). *Against Our Will: Men, Women and Rape*. New York: Simon and Schuster.

Brundage, X, (2010). Update: Milwaukee church judge clarifies case of abusive priest, Fr. Murphy. *Catholic Anchor,* March 29, http://catholicanchor.org/wordpress/?p=601, accessed March 30, 2010.

Bruni, F. (2010). At the Vatican, Up against the World. *New York Times,* March 26. Online version. Available from http://www.nytimes.com/, accessed March 26, 2010.

Bryant, C. (1999). Psychological treatment of priest sex offenders. In T. G. Plante (Ed.), *Bless Me Father For I Have Sinned: Perspectives on Sexual Abuse Committed by Roman Catholic Priests* (pp. 87–110). Westport, CT: Praeger /Greenwood.

Buckley, H., Skehill, C., & O'Sullivan, E. (1997). *Child Protection Practices in Ireland. A Case Study.* Dublin: Oak Tree Press.

Bumby, K. M. (2000). Empathy inhibition, intimacy deficits and attachment difficulties in sex offenders. In D. R. Laws, S. M. Hudson, & T. Ward (Eds.), *Remaking Relapse Prevention with Sex Offenders: A Sourcebook* (pp. 143–166). Thousand Oaks, CA: Sage.

Bumby, K. M., & Hansen, D. J. (1997). Intimacy deficits, fear of intimacy and loneliness among sexual offenders. *Criminal Justice and Behaviour,* 24(3), 315–331.

Bumby, K. M., Marshall, W. L., & Langton, C. M. (1999). A theoretical model of the influence of shame and guilt on sexual offending. In B. K. Schwartz (Eds.), *The Sex Offender: Theoretical Advances, Treating Special Populations, and Legal Developments* (Vol. 3). Kingston, NJ: Civic Research Institute.

Burck, C. (2005). Comparing qualitative research methodologies for systemic research: the use of grounded theory, discourse analysis and narrative analysis. *Journal of Family Therapy,* 27, 237–262.

Burkett, E., & Bruni, F. (1993). *A Gospel of Shame.* New York: Penguin Books.

Burr, V. (1995). *An Introduction to Social Constructionism.* London and New York: Routledge.

Bush, S. S., Connell, M. A., & Denny, R. L. (2006). *Ethical Practice in Forensic Psychology: A Systematic Model for Decision Making.* Washington, DC: American Psychological Association.

Byrne, N. O'R., & McCarthy, I. C (1988). Moving statutes: re-questioning ambivalence through ambiguous discourse. In V. Kenny (Ed.), Radical constructivism, autopoiesis and psychotherapy. *The Irish Journal of Psychology [Special Issue],* 9(1), 173–182.

Byrne, N. O'R., & McCarthy, I. C. (1998). Marginal illuminations. A fifth province approach to intracultural issues in an Irish context. In McGoldrick, M. (Ed.), *Re-Visioning Family Therapy: Race, Culture and Gender in Clinical Practice* (pp. 387–403). New York: Guilford Publications.

Byrne, N. O'R., & McCarthy, I. C. (1999). Feminism, politics and power in therapeutic discourse: fragments from the fifth province. In I. Parker (Ed.), *Deconstructing Psychotherapy* (pp. 87–102). London: Sage.

Cafardi, N. (2008). *Before Dallas.* New York: Paulist Press

Calvert, S. (1993). Three revolutions later . . . Working to empower clients who have been abused by their therapist. *Professional Sexual Abuse. Dulwich Centre Newsletter,* 3, 4, 7–12.

Camargo, R. J. (1997). Factor, cluster and discriminate analyses of data on sexually active clergy: The molesters of youth identified. *American Journal of Forensic Psychology,* 15(2), 5–24.

Camargo, R. J., & Loftus, J. A. (1992). *Child Sexual Abuse Among Troubled Clergy: A Descriptive Study.* Paper presented at the 100th Annual Convention of the American Psychological Association, Washington, DC.

Camargo, R. J., & Loftus, J. A. (1993). *Clergy Sexual Involvement with Young People.* Paper presented at the 101st Annual Convention of the American Psychological Association, Toronto.

Canadian Conference of Catholic Bishops (1992). *From Pain to Hope: Report of the Ad Hoc Committee on Child Sexual Abuse.* Ottawa.

Canon Law Society of Great Britain and Ireland (1983). *The Code of Canon Law* (English translation). Great Britain: Collins.

Cardinal Secrets. (2002). RTE Television Documentary.

Caritas in Veritate. Available from http://www.vatican.va/holy_father/benedict_xvi/encyclicals/documents/hf_ben-xvi_enc_20090629_caritas-in-veritate_en.html, accessed 10/04/2010.

Carrigan, T., Connell, R. W., & Lee. J. (1985). Toward a new sociology of masculinity. *Theory and Society,* 14(5), 551–604.

Carroll, J. (1992). Bishops must now "focus on accountability and truth." *Irish Times,* p. 3, July 1.

Cassese, J. (2001). Introduction: Integrating the experience of childhood sexual trauma in gay men. In J. Cassese (Ed.), *Gay Men and Childhood Sexual Trauma: Integrating the Shattered Self* (pp. 1–17). Binghamton, NY: The Haworth Press.

Cassese, J. (2001). (Ed.). *Gay Men and Childhood Sexual Trauma: Integrating the Shattered Self.* Binghamton, NY: The Haworth Press.

Catechism of the Catholic Church (1994). Dublin: Veritas Publications.

Catholic Bishops Conference of England and Wales (2001). *A Programme for Action: Final Report of the Independent Review on Child Protection in the Catholic Church in England and Wales.* (The Nolan Report).

Catholics for a Free Choice (2002). *The Holy See and the Convention on the Rights of the Child. A Shadow Report.* Available at www.BishopAccountability.org

Celenza, A. (2004). Sexual misconduct in the Clergy. The Search for the Father. *Studies in Gender and Sexuality,* 5(2), 213–232.

Charmaz, K. (1995). Grounded theory. In J. A. Smith, R. Harré, & L.V. Langenhove (Eds.), *Rethinking Methods in Psychology* (pp. 27–49). London: Sage.

Charmaz, K. (2000). Grounded theory: objectivist and constructivist methods. In N. K. Denzin & Y. S. Lincoln. (Eds.), *Handbook of Qualitative Research* (2nd ed.). Thousand Oaks, CA, and London: Sage Publications.

Charmaz, K. (2006). *Constructing Grounded Theory. A Practical Guide Through Qualitative Analysis.* London: Sage.

Check, J. V. P., Perlman, D., & Malamuth, N. M. (1985). Loneliness and aggressive behaviour. *Journal of Sexual and Personal Relationships,* 2, 243–252.

Child Protection Services of the Catholic Bishop's Conference of England and Wales (2006). Annual *Report.* Available at www.copca.org.uk, accessed 01/05/2007.

Chittister, J. (2010). Divided loyalties: an incredible situation. *National Catholic Reporter.* March 17. Online http://ncronline.org/, accessed March 17.

Chopko, M. & Stinski, B (1992). Restoring trust and faith: human rights abuses do happen. *Human Rights* 19, 22-26.

Churchill, R. P. (2006). *Human Rights and Global Diversity.* Upper Saddle River, NJ: Pearson Prentice Hall.

Clancy, S. (2010). *The Trauma Myth: The Truth about Sexual Abuse of Children and its Aftermath.* New York: Basic Books.

Clark, A. (2008). *Desire: A History of European Sexuality.* London: Routledge.

Clarke, A. E. (2005). *Situational Analysis: Grounded Theory after the Postmodern Turn.* Thousand Oaks, CA: Sage.

Clarke, R (1980). Situational Crime Prevention: Theory and Practice, *British Journal of Criminology*, 20 (2), 136-147.

Clarke, R., & Felson, M. (2008) (Eds.). *Routine Activity and Rational Choice. Advances in Criminological Theory, Vol. 5*. New Brunswick, NJ: Transaction Publishers.

Cloward, R., & Ohlin, L. (1960). *Delinquency and Opportunity: A Theory of Delinquent Gangs*. Glencoe, IL: Free Press.

Cloyne Report (2011). Report by Commission of Investigation into the Catholic Diocese of Cloyne (2011). Available at http://www.justice.ie/en/JELR/Pages/Cloyne_Rpt Accessed 25ᵗʰ July 2011.

Code of Canon Law (1983) (English translation). Great Britain: Collins.

Coghlan, D. (1992). Taoiseach says referendum on abortion go ahead. *Irish Times*, p. 1, June 5.

Cohen, P. (1972). Subcultural conflict in working class community. *Working Papers in Cultural Studies*, No. 2, Centre for Contemporary Cultural Studies, University of Birmingham.

Cohen, S. (2002/1972). *Folk Devils and Moral Panics: The Creation of the Mods and Rockers* (3rd ed.). London: Routledge.

Coldrey, B. M. (2000). *Religious Life without Integrity*. Melbourne: Tamanirak Press. Available at www.BishopAccountability.org, accessed March 16, 2006.

Coldrey, B. M. (2004). *A Christian Apocalypse: The Sexual Abuse Crisis in the Catholic Church, 1984-2004*. Melbourne, Australia. Tamanarak Press.

Coleridge, M (2010). Roots of the Scandal "Go Deep and Wide". *National Catholic Reporter*. August 18ᵗʰ. Available at http://ncronline.org/news/accountability/roots-scandal-go-deep-and-wide accessed 18ᵗʰ August.

Colgan, I. F. (1991). *The Fifth Province Model: Father-Daughter Incest Disclosure and Systemic Consultation*. PhD thesis, University College Dublin.

Collier, R. (1998). *Masculinities, Crime and Criminology: Men, Heterosexuality and the Criminal(ised) Other*. London: Sage.

Colton, M., Roberts, S. & Vanstone, M (2010). Sexual Abuse by Men who Work with Children. *Journal of Child Sexual Abuse, 19* (3), 345-364.

Commissions of Investigation Act (2004). Dublin: Government Publications.

Commission on Child Abuse Report (2009). Dublin: Government Publications (Also referred to as the Ryan Report).

Commission to Inquire into Child Abuse Act (2000). Dublin: Government Publications, the Stationary Office.

Commission to Inquire into Child Abuse Amendment Act (2005). Dublin: Government Publications, the Stationary Office.

Condren, M. (2002). *The Serpent and the Goddess* (2nd ed.). Dublin: New Island Books.

Condren, M. (2009). Church figures cannot be allowed blame abuse on those without "real" vocations. *Irish Times*, June 12. Available online at www.irishtimes.ie, Accessed June 13, 2009.

Congregation for Catholic Education. (2005). *Instruction Concerning the Criteria for the Discernment of Vocations with regard to Persons with Homosexual Tendencies in view of their Admission to the Seminary and to Holy Orders*. Congregation for Catholic Education. Nov. 4th. Translation to be found on Vatican website, www.vatican.va, accessed Nov. 10, 2005.

Congregation for Catholic Education, (2008). *Guidelines for the Use of Psychology in the Admission and Formation of Candidates for the Priesthood*. Accessed June 15, 2009. Available at http://www.vatican.va/roman_curia/Congregations/ccatheduc/documents/rc_con_ccatheduc_doc_20080628_orientamenti_en.html

Connell, R. W. (1987). *Gender and Power*. Sydney, Australia: Allen and Unwin.

Connell, R. W. (1995). *Masculinities*. Cambridge: Polity Press.

Connell, R. W. (2002). *Gender*. Cambridge: Polity Press.

Connell, R. W. (2005). Growing up masculine: rethinking the significance of adolescence in the making of masculinities. In A. Cleary (Ed.), *Masculinities. Irish Journal of Sociology [special issue]*, 14(2), 11–28.

Connell, R. W., & Messerschmidt, J. W. (2005). Hegemonic masculinity. Rethinking the concept. *Gender and Society*, 19(6), 829–859.

Connolly, S. J (1982). *Priests and People in Pre-famine Ireland, 1780-1845*. Dublin and New York: Gill & MacMillan.

Connors, C. (1994). *Keynote address to National Catholic Council on Alcoholism*. Washington, DC: St. Luke's Institute. Unpublished paper.

Conway, E. (2004). Operative theologies of priesthood: Have they contributed to child sexual abuse? In R. Ammicht-Quinn, H. Haker, & M. Junker-Kenny, (eds.), *The Structural Betrayal of Trust*. London: Concilium.

Corby, B. (2000). *Child Abuse: Towards a Knowledge Base*. Milton Keynes: Open University Press.

Corkery, J. (2009a). *Joseph Ratzinger's Theological Ideas. Wise Cautions and Legitimate Hopes*. Dublin: Dominican Publications; North America: Paulist Press.

Corkery, J. (2009b). Joseph Ratzinger on liberation theology: what did he say? Why did he say it? What can be said about it? In P. Claffey & J. Egan (Eds.), *Movement or Moment? Assessing Liberation Theology Forty Years after Medellin* (pp. 183–202). Oxford, New York, Wien: Peter Lang.

Coriden, J. A. (1991). *Introduction to Canon Law*. New York: Paulist Press.

Coriden, J. A., Green, T. J., & Heintschel D. E (1985). *The Code of Canon Law: a text and commentary*. New York: Paulist Press.

Cornish, D. & Clarke, R.V (2003). Opportunities, Precipitators and Criminal Decisions: A Reply to Wortley's Critique of Situational Crime Prevention. *Crime Prevention Studies* 16, 41–96.

Cornwell, J. (2001). *Breaking Faith: Can the Catholic Church Save Itself?* New York: Penguin Compass.

Cortini, F., & Marshall, W. L. (2001). Sex as a coping strategy and its relationship to juvenile sexual history and intimacy in sexual offenders. *Sexual Abuse: A Journal of Research and Treatment*, 13(1), 27–43.

Cosgrave, W. (2001). *Christian Living Today. Essays in Moral and Pastoral Theology*. Dublin: The Columba Press.

Cossins, A. (2000). *Masculinities, Sexualities and Child Sexual Abuse*. The Hague: Kluwer Law International.

Costain Schou, K., & Hewison, J. (1994). Issues of interpretive methodology. The utility and scope of grounded theory in contextual research. *Human Systems. The Journal of Systemic Consultation and Management*, 5, 45–68.

Costain Schou, K., & Hewison, J. (1998). Health psychology and discourse. Personal accounts as social texts in grounded theory. *Journal of Health Psychology*, 3(3), 297–311.

Covell, C. N., & Scalora, M. J. (2002). Empathic deficits in sexual offenders. An integration of affective, social and cognitive constructs. *Aggression and Violent Behaviour*, 7, 251–270.

Cowburn, M. (1998). A man's world: Gender issues in working with male sex offenders in prison, *Howard Journal*, 37(3), 234–251.

Cowburn, M. (2010). Invisible men: Social reactions to male sexual coercion—bringing men and masculinities into community safety and public policy. *Critical Social Policy*, 30(2), 225–244.

Cowburn, M., & Dominelli, L. (1998). Moving beyond litigation and positivism: Another approach to accusations of sexual abuse. *British Journal of Social Work*, 28(4), 525–543.

Cowburn, M., & Dominelli, L. (2001). Masking hegemonic masculinity: reconstructing the paedophile as the dangerous stranger. *British Journal of Social Work*, 31, 399–415.

Cowburn, M., Wilson, C., with Loewenstein, P. (1992). *Changing Men: A Practice Guide in Working with Adult Male Sex Offenders*. Nottingham: Nottingham Probation Service.

Coyle, A., & Kitzinger, C. (Eds.) (2002). *Lesbian and Gay Psychology. New Perspectives*. Oxford: Blackwell.

Cozzens, D. (2000). *The Changing Face of Priesthood. A Reflection on the Priest's Crisis of Soul*. Collegeville, MN: Liturgical Press.

Cozzens, D. (2002). *Sacred Silence. Denial and the Crisis in the Church*. Collegeville, MN: Liturgical Press.

Crimen Sollicitationis. Translation available at http://www.vatican.va/resources/index_en.htm

Curran, C. E. (1988). Catholic social and sexual teaching: a methodological comparison. *Theology Today*, 44.4. Accessed at http://theologytoday.ptsem.edu/search/index-browse.htm

Curran, C. E. (1991). A century of Catholic social teaching. *Theology Today*, 48.2. Accessed at http://theologytoday.ptsem.edu/jul1991/v48-2-article3.htm

Curran, C. E. (2002). *Catholic Social Teaching, 1891–Present: A Historical, Theological and Ethical Analysis*. Washington, DC: Georgetown University Press.

Cusack, J. (1992). Garda file on "X" case to be sent to DPP's office. *Irish Times*, p. 2, June 4.

Czernin, H. (1998). *Das Buch Groër: Eine Kirchenchronik*. Vienna: Wieser Verlag.

Daly, K. (2006). Restorative justice and sexual assault: an archival study of court and conference cases. *British Journal of Criminology*, 46, 334–356.

Dardis, J. (2000). Speaking of scandal. *Studies*, 49(356), 309–319.

Davie, G. (1994). *Religion in Britain since 1945—Believing without Belonging*. Oxford: Blackwell.

Davies, K. (1994). *When Innocence Trembles: The Christian Brothers Orphanage Tragedy*. Sydney: Angus and Robertson.

Davin, A (1990). The precocity of poverty. In *The Proceedings of the Conference on Historical Perspectives on Childhood*. University of Trondheim.

Dear Daughter. (1996) RTE, Documentary broadcast by RTE on 22 February.

De Mause, L (1976). *The History of Childhood*. London: Souvenir Press.

Dempsey, P. (Ed.) (1992). Report to the Cardinal's Commission on Clergy Sexual Misconduct with Minors. (Report to the Cardinal Archbishop of the Chicago Roman Catholic Archdiocese, June 15, 1992.). Available at www.BishopAccountability.org, accessed March 20, 2006.

Demerath, N. J. (2001). *Crossing the Gods: World Religions and Worldly Politics*. New Brunswick, NJ: Rutgers University Press.

Denzin, N. K. (2000). The practices and politics of interpretation. In N. K. Denzin & Y. S. Lincoln. (2000). (Eds.) *Handbook of Qualitative Research* (2nd ed.) Thousand Oaks and London: Sage Publications.

Denzin, N. K., & Lincoln, Y. S. (2000). Introduction. The discipline and practice of qualitative research. In N. K. Denzin & Y. S. Lincoln. (2000). (Eds.), *Handbook of Qualitative Research* (2nd ed.). Thousand Oaks and London: Sage Publications.

Denzin, N. K., & Lincoln, Y. S. (2000). (Eds.) *Handbook of Qualitative Research* (2nd ed.). Thousand Oaks and London: Sage Publications.

Department of Health and Children (2000). *The National Children's Strategy. Our Children, Their Lives*. Dublin: Government Publications, Stationary Office.

Department of Justice (1993). *A Proposal for a Structured Psychological Treatment Programme for Sex Offenders: Discussion Document*. Dublin: Government Publications, Stationery Office.

Department of the Taoiseach (2011). *Statement by the Taoiseach on the Dáil Motion on the report of the Commission of Investigation into the Catholic Diocese of Cloyne, in Dáil Éireann*. Available at http://www.taoiseach.gov.ie/eng/Government_Press_Office/Taoiseach's_ Speeches_20111/Statement_by_the_Taoiseach_on_the_Dáil_Motion_on_the_report_of_ the_Commission_of_Investigation_into_the_Catholic_Diocese_of_Cloyne,_in_Dáil_ Éireann,_.html Accessed 25th July 2011.

De Swaan, A. (1990). *The Management of Normality: Critical Essays in Health and Welfare*. New York: Routledge.

De Young, M. (1982). Innocent seducer or innocently seduced? The role of the child incest victim. *Journal of Clinical Psychology*, 11, 56–60.

Dillon, J. (2001). Internalised homophobia, attributions of blame and psychological distress among lesbians, gay and bisexual trauma victims. *Dissertation Abstracts International*, 62 (4–B).

Dokecki, P. (2004). *The Clergy Sexual Abuse Crisis*. Washington, DC: Georgetown University Press.

Dolezal, C. (2002). Childhood sexual experiences and the perception of abuse among Latino men who have sex with men. *Journal of Sex Research*, 39, 165–173.

Dominelli, L. (1989). Betrayal of trust: A feminist analysis of power relationships in incest abuse and its relevance for social work practice, *British Journal of Social Work*, 19, 291–307.

Dominion, J. (1998). How psychology can help our spirituality. *Priests and People*, April, 129–133.

Dominion, J. (2007). Journey of love, not law. *The Tablet*, pp. 12–13. April 4.

Donadio, R. (2010a). Pope may be at crossroads on abuse, forced to reconcile policy and works. *New York Times*, March 26. Online version available at http://www.nytimes.com/, accessed March 26, 2010.

Donadio, R. (2010b). Catholic order admits its founder abused boys over decades. *New York Times*, March 26. Online version available at http://www.nytimes.com/, accessed March 26, 2010.

Donovan, D. (2009). *Fr. Daniel Donovan Reviews Bishop Julian Posteous' Book on Priest and Priesthood*. Available at http://www.catholica.com.au/gc2/dd/016_dd_271009.php, accessed 01/03/2011.

Donovan, D. (2010). Sydney priest and former lecturer at the Australian Catholic University, speaking on *Background Briefing*, ABC Radio National, Australia, March 7.

Dorgan, T. (2009). Scandals could undermine the church's foundations. *The Irish Times*, p. 14.

Dorr, D. (2000). Sexual abuse and spiritual abuse. *The Furrow*, 51(10), 523–531.

Dorr, D. (2009). Who was responsible? In T. Flannery (2009). (Ed.), *Responding to the Ryan Report* (pp. 111–121). Dublin: The Columba Press.

Downes, D. (1999). Crime and deviance. In S. Taylor, *Sociology, Issues and Debates* (pp. 231–252). Dublin: Macmillan.

Doyle, P. (2002). *The God Squad: The Bestselling Story of One Child's Triumph over Adversity.* Transworld Publishers.

Doyle, T. P. (2003). Roman Catholic clericalism, religious duress and clergy abuse. *Pastoral Psychology*, 51, 189–231.

Doyle, T. P. (2004). Canon Law and the clergy sex abuse crisis: The failure from above. In T. G. Plante (Ed.), *Sin against the Innocents. Sexual Abuse by Priests and the Role of the Catholic Church* (pp. 25–38). Westport, CT, London: Praeger.

Doyle, T. P. (2006). Fr. Tom Doyle on *"Crimen Sollicitationis."* *National Catholic Reporter*, Oct. 12.

Doyle, T. P. (2010). *The Doctrine of Mental Reservation.* Available from http://www.richardsipe. com/Doyle/1993-2007/2006-11-19-Doyle-Mental_reservation.pdf accessed Jan. 6, 2010.

Doyle, T. P., Sipe, A. W. R., & Wall, P. J. (2006). *Sex, Priests and Secret Codes. The Catholic Church's 2000-year Paper Trail of Sexual Abuse.* Los Angeles: Volt Press.

Draucker, C. B., Martsolf, D. S., Ross, R., & Rusk, T. (2007). Theoretical sampling and category development in grounded theory. *Qualitative Health Research,* 17(8), 1137–1148.

Driver, J. (2006). *Ethics: The Fundamentals.* Oxford, UK: Blackwell Publishing

Dublin Archdiocese Commission of Investigation. (2006). March.

Duffy, E. (2004). *Faith of Our Fathers.* London, New York: Continuum.

Duffy, E. (2009). Presbyteral collegiality: precedents and horizons. *The Jurist,* 69, 116–154.

Dulwich Centre Publications (2000). (Eds). *Reflections on Narrative Practices: Interviews and Essays.* Adelaide: Dulwich Centre Publications.

Dulwich Centre Publications (2003). (Eds.). *Responding to Violence. A Collection of Papers Relating to Child Sexual Abuse and Violence in Intimate Relationships.* Adelaide, South Australia: Dulwich Centre Publications.

Dunn, P. J (1990). *Priesthood: A re-examination of the Roman Catholic theology of the presbyterate.* New York, NY: Alba House.

Dunne, J., & Kelly, J. (2002). *Childhood and Its Discontents: The First Seamus Heaney Lectures.* Dublin: Liffey Press.

Durkheim, E. (1952/1897). *Suicide: A Study in Sociology.* London: Routledge and Kegan Paul.

Eldridge, H., & Wyre, R. (1998). The Lucy Faithfull Foundation Residential Program for Sexual Offenders. In W. L. Marshall & Y. M. Fernandez. (Eds.). *Sourcebook of Treatment Programs for Sexual Offenders* (pp. 79–93). New York and London: Plenum Press.

Fagan, S. (2009). The Abuse and our bad theology. In T. Flannery (2009). (Ed.), *Responding to the Ryan Report* (pp. 14–25). Dublin: The Columba Press.

Fahey, T. (2007). Population. In Sara O'Sullivan (Ed.), *Contemporary Ireland. A Sociological Map* (pp. 13–29). Dublin: UCD Press.

Fahy, B. (1999). *Freedom of Angels: Surviving Goldenbridge Orphanage.* Dublin: O'Brien Press.

Feathrestone, B., & Fawcett, B. (1994). Feminism and child abuse: opening up some possibilities? *Critical Social Policy,* 42, 61–80.

Featherstone, B., & Lancaster, E. (1997). Contemplating the unthinkable: Men who sexually abuse children. *Critical Social Policy,* 17(4), 51–71.

Felder, F., & Heagle, J. (2002). Time for Bishops to listen, take ordinary Catholics seriously. *National Catholic Reporter Online.* Available at www.Natcath.org, accessed May 20, 2006.

Ferguson, H. (1994). Past neglect returns to haunt us in Smyth case. *Irish Times,* p. 12, Oct. 18.

Ferguson, H. (1995). The paedophile priest. A deconstruction. *Studies,* 84(335), 247–256.

Ferguson, H. (1998). McColgan case: A different era. *Irish Times.* Jan. 26.

Ferguson, H. (2000). States of fear, child abuse and Irish society. *Doctrine and Life,* 50(1), 20–30.

Ferguson, H. (2001). Men and masculinities in late-modern Ireland. In B. Pease & K. Pringle (Eds.), *A Man's World. Changing Men's Practices in a Globalised World.* New York: Palgrave.

Ferguson, K. J. (2007). A Protestant approach to clergy sexual abuse. In M.G. Frawley-O'Dea & V. Goldner (Eds.), *Predatory Priests, Silenced Victims. The Sexual Abuse Crisis and The Catholic Church* (pp. 189–195). New Jersey and London: The Analytic Press.

Fernandez, Y., & Serran, G. (2002). Empathy training for therapists and clients. In Y. Fernandez (Ed.), *In their Shoes: Examining the Issue of Empathy and Its Place in the Treatment of Offenders* (pp. 110–131). Oklahoma: Wood "N" Barnes Publishing.

Ferns Report (2005). Delivered to the Minister for Health and Children, Ireland.

Ferriter, D. (2009). *Occasions of Sin. Sex and Society in Modern Ireland.* London: Profile Books.

Fichter, J. H. (1974). *Organisation Man in the Church.* Cambridge, MA: Schenkman Company.

Finkelhor, D. (1982). Sexual abuse: A sociological perspective. *Child Abuse and Neglect,* 6, 95–102

Finkelhor, D. (1984). *Child Sexual Abuse: New Theory and Research.* New York: Free Press.

Finkelhor, D. (1994). The international epidemiology of child sexual abuse. *Child Abuse and Neglect,* 18, 409–417.

Finkelhor, D., Hotaling, G., Lewis, I. A., & Smith, C. (1990). Sexual abuse in a national survey of adult men and women: Prevalence, characteristics and risk factors. *Child Abuse and Neglect,* 14, 19–28.

Finkelhor, D. & Williams, L (1988). *Nursery Crimes: A Study of Sexual Abuse in Daycare.* Newbury Park, CA: Sage.

Fisher, A. (2004). *Narrative Possibilities for Unpacking Homophobia.* Keynote address presented at the International Summer School of Narrative Practice, Dulwich Centre, Adelaide, South Australia.

Fisher, A. (2005). Power and the promise of innocent places. *Narrative Network News,* pp. 12–14. Adelaide, South Australia: Dulwich Centre Publications.

Fiske, A. P. (2002). Using individualism and collectivism to compare cultures—a critique of the validity and measurement of the constructs: Comment on Oyserman et al., 2002. *Psychological Bulletin,* 128, 78–88.

Flakenhain, M. A. (1999). Cluster analysis of child sexual offenders: A validation with Roman Catholic priests and brothers. *Sexual Addiction and Compulsivity,* 6, 317–336.

Flannery, T. (1999). *From the Inside: A Priest's View of the Catholic Church.* Cork: Mercier Press.

Flannery, T. (2009). (Ed.) *Responding to the Ryan Report.* Dublin: The Columba Press.

Flannery, T. (2009). Some ideas on a new approach to Catholic social teaching. In T. Flannery, (2009). (Ed.), *Responding to the Ryan Report* (p. 162–171). Dublin: The Columba Press.

Flaskas, C. (2002). *Family Therapy beyond Postmodernism: Practice Challenges Theory.* Hove and New York: Brunner-Routledge, Taylor and Francis Group.

Fleming, P., Lauber-Fleming, S., & Matousek, M. (2007). *Broken Trust. Stories of Pain, Hope and Healing from Clerical Abuse Survivors and Abusers.* New York: The Crossroad Publishing Company.

Flick, U., von Kardorff, E., & Steinke, I. (2004). What is qualitative research? An introduction to the field. In U. Flick, E. von Kardorff, & I. Steinke. (Eds.), *A Companion to Qualitative Research.* (pp. 3–12). London and Thousand Oaks: Sage.

Flick, U., von Kardorff, E., & Steinke I. (Eds.)(2004). *A Companion to Qualitative Research*. London and Thousand Oaks: Sage.

Fones, C. S. L., Levine, S. B., Althof, S. E., & Risen, C. B. (1999). The sexual struggles of 23 clergymen: A follow-up study. *Journal of Sex and Marital Therapy*, 25, 183–195.

Formicola, J. (2011). Catholic Clerical Sexual Abuse: Effects on Vatican Sovereignty and Papal Power. *Journal of Church and State*. Advance Access, June. DOI: 10.1093/jcs/crs028

Fortune, M. (1992). *Is Nothing Sacred? When Sex Invades the Pastoral Relationship*. San Francisco: Harper.

Fortune, M. (1994). Is nothing sacred? The betrayal of the ministerial or teaching relationship. *Journal of Feminist Studies in Religion*, 10(1), 17–24.

Foucault, M. (1979). *Discipline and Punish: The Birth of the Prison*. London: Allen Lane.

Foucault, M. (1988). The dangerous individual. In L Kritzman (Ed.), *Politics, Philosophy, Culture: Interviews and Other Writings 1977–1984* (pp. 125–151). New York: Routledge.

Foucault, M. (1990). *The Care of Self. The History of Sexuality: 3* (translated by Robert Hurley). London: Penguin.

Foucault, M. (1991). *Discipline and Punish. The Birth of the Prison*. UK: Penguin Books.

Foucault, M. (1992). *The Use of Pleasure. The History of Sexuality: 2* (translated by Robert Hurley). London: Penguin.

Foucault, M. (1998). *The Will to Knowledge. The History of Sexuality: 1* (translated by Robert Hurley). London: Penguin.

Foucault, M. (2004). *The Archaeology of Knowledge* (translated by A. M. Sheridan Smith; first published in 1969; first published in English in 1972; 6th ed.). London: Routledge Classics.

Fox, T. C (2011). Richard Sipe's Insight on the John Jay report. *Denver Catholic Network*. May 19th.

France, D. (2004). *Our Fathers: The Secret Life of the Catholic Church in an Age of Scandal*. New York: Broadway Books.

Francis, P. C., & Turner, N. R. (1995). Sexual misconduct within the Christian Church: Who are the perpetrators and those they victimize? *Counselling and Values*, 39, 218–228.

Frankl, V. (2004). *Man's Search for Meaning*, New York: Random House.

Franklin, 1992, p. 2; on ecclesiological records chapter 1

Frawley-O'Dea, M. G. (2004). Psychosocial anatomy of the Catholic sexual abuse scandal. *Studies in Gender and Sexuality*, 5(2), 121–137.

Frawley-O'Dea, M. G. (2007). *Perversion of Power. Sexual Abuse in the Catholic Church*. Nashville: Vanderbilt University Press.

Frawley-O'Dea, M. G., & Goldner, V. (2007) (Eds.). *Predatory Priests, Silenced Victims. The Sexual Abuse Crisis and The Catholic Church*. New Jersey and London: The Analytic Press.

Freeden, M. (1991). *Rights*. Minneapolis, MN: University of Minnesota Press.

Freeman-Longo, R. E., & Blanchard, G. T. (1998). *Sexual Abuse in America: Epidemic of the 21st century*. Vermont: The Safer Society Press.

Freund, K. (1967a). Diagnosing homo- or heterosexuality and erotic age preferences by means of a psycho physiological test. *Behaviour Research and Therapy*, 5, 209–228.

Feund, K. (1967b). Erotic preferences in pedophilia. *Behaviour Research and Therapy*, 5, 339–348.

Friedlander, S. (1979). *History and Psychoanalysis*. New Jersey: Henry Holt and Company.

Fuller, L. (2002). *Irish Catholicism since 1950: The Undoing of a Culture*. Dublin: Gill and Macmillan.

Gadamer, H. G. (1981). *Reason in the Age of Science* (F. G. Lawrence, Translator). Cambridge: MIT Press.

Gadamer, H. G. (2003). *Truth and Method* (2nd rev. ed.) New York: Continuum.

Gallagher, B (2000). The Extent and Nature of Known Cases of Institutional Child Sexual Abuse. *British Journal of Social Work,* 30, 795-817

Gallagher, R. (2006). Can gay men be priests? *The Furrow,* 57(2), 67–74.

Gallagher, R (2011). Church Authority and Sexual Morality. Paper presented at *Church: A Culture of Abusive Relationships?* Conference organized by Irish Theological Association in All Hallows College, Drumcondra, Dublin. March 18th – March 19th.

Garfinkel, H. (1956). Conditions of successful degradation ceremonies. *American Journal of Criminology,* 61, 420.

Garland, D (2001). *The Culture of Control. Crime and Social Order in Contemporary Society.* Chicago: The University of Chicago Press.

Garlick, Y., Marshall, W. L., & Thornton, D. (1996). Intimacy deficits and attribution of blame among sexual offenders. *Legal and Criminological Psychology,* 1, 251–258.

Garmezy, N. (1993). Children in poverty: resilience despite risk. *Psychiatry,* 56(1), 127–136.

Gavrielides, T., & Coker, D. (2005). Restoring faith: Resolving the Roman Catholic Church's sexual scandals through restorative justice. *Contemporary Justice Review,* 18(4), 345–365.

Gay, P. (1998). *The Bourgeois Experience: The Pleasure Wars.* Vol. 5. London: Harper Collins.

Geertz, C. (1973). *The Interpretation of Cultures: Selected Essays.* New York: Basic Books.

Geertz, C. (1979). From the native's point of view: On the nature of anthropological understanding. In P. Rabinow & W. M. Sullivan (Eds.), *Interpretive Social Science: A Reader* (pp. 225–241). Berkeley: University of California Press.

George, W. H., & Marlatt, A. G. (1989). Introduction. In R. D. Laws. (Ed.), *Relapse Prevention with Sex Offenders.* New York: The Guilford Press.

Gergen, K. (1985). The social constructionist movement in modern psychology. *American Psychologist,* 40, 266–275.

Gergen, K. (1992). Social constructionism in question. *Human Systems,* 3, 163–182.

Gergen, K. (1993). Warranting voice and the elaboration of the self. In J. Shotter & K. Gergen, *Texts of Identity* (pp.70–81). London: Sage.

Gibson, D. (2003). *The Coming Catholic Church: How the Faithful are Shaping a New American Catholicism.* San Francisco: Harper.

Gilun, J. (1992). Definitions, methodologies and methods in qualitative family research. In J. Gilgun, K. Daly, & G. Handel (Eds.), *Qualitative Methods in Family Research.* Newbury Park: Sage.

Glaser, B. G. (1978). *Theoretical Sensitivity: Advances in Grounded Theory.* Mill Valley, CA: The Sociology Press.

Glaser, B. G., & Strauss, A. L. (1967). *The Discovery of Grounded Theory.* New York: Aldine De Gruyter.

Goffman, E. (1961). *Asylums:* Essays on the Social Situation of Mental Patients and Other Inmates. New York: Anchor Books (Doubleday).

Goffman, E. (1963). *Stigma. Notes on the Management of Spoiled Identity.* New Jersey: Penguin Books.

Goldner, V. (2004). Introduction: the sexual abuse crisis and the Catholic Church. Gender, sexuality, power and discourse. *Studies in Gender and Sexuality,* 5(1), 1–9.

Gonsiorek, J. C. (Ed.) (1995). *Breach of Trust: Sexual Exploitation by Health Care Professionals and Clergy*. London: Sage Publications.

Gonsiorek, J. C. (1999). Forensic psychological evaluations in clergy abuse. In T. G. Plante (Ed.), *Bless Me Father for I Have Sinned: Perspectives on Sexual Abuse Committed by Roman Catholic Priests* (pp. 27–57). Westport, CT, London: Praeger.

Gonsiorek, J. C. (2004). Barriers to responding to the clergy sexual abuse crisis within the Roman Catholic Church. In T. G. Plante (Ed.), *Sin against the Innocents. Sexual Abuse by Priests and the Role of the Catholic Church* (pp. 139–153). Westport, CT, London: Praeger.

Gonsiorek, J., Sell, R., & Weinrich, J. (1995). Definition and measurement of sexual orientation. *Suicide and Life Threatening Behaviour*, 25, 40–51.

Goode, H., McGee, H., & O'Boyle, C. (2003). *Time to Listen, Confronting Child Sexual Abuse By Catholic Clergy In Ireland*. Dublin: The Liffey Press.

Goodstein, L. (2003). Decades of damage: Trail of pain in Church crisis leads to nearly every Diocese. *New York Times*, 1–6, Jan. 12.

Goodstein, L. (2010). Vatican declined to defrock U.S. priest who abused boys. *New York Times*, March 24. Online version available at http://www.nytimes.com/, accessed March 24, 2010.

Gordon, M. (2004). The priestly phallus. A study in iconography. *Studies in Gender and Sexuality*, 5(1), 103–111.

Greeley, A. M. (1972a). *Priests in the United States: Reflections on a Survey*. Garden City, NY: Doubleday.

Greeley, A. M. (1972b). *The Catholic Priest in the United States: Sociological Investigations*. Washington, DC: United States Catholic Conference.

Greeley, A. M. (1993). How serious is the problem of sexual abuse by clergy? *America*, 168(10), 6–10.

Greeley, A. M. (2000). How prevalent is clerical sexual abuse? *Doctrine and Life*, 50(2), 66–71.

Greeley, A. M. (2004). *Priests: A Calling in Crisis*. Chicago and London: University of Chicago Press.

Green, S. (1997). Psychology and the quest for the spiritual. *Doctrine and Life*, 47(4), 218–227.

Greer, C. (2003). *Sex Crime and the Media: Sex Offending and the Press in a Divided Society*. Devon: Willan.

Groth, A. N., & Birnbaum, H. J. (1978). Adult sexual orientation and attraction to underage persons. *Archives of Sexual Behaviour*, 7(3), 175–181.

Groth, N. A., Hobson, W.F., & Gary, T. S. (1982). The child molester: Clinical observations. *Journal of Social Work and Human Sexuality*, 1(1–2), 129–143.

Habermas, J. (1971). Technology and science as "ideology." In J. Shapiro.(Trans). *Towards a Rational Society*. Boston: Beacon Press.

Hacking, I. (1999). *The Social Construction of What?* Cambridge, MA, and London: Harvard University Press.

Hall, D. K. (1999). Book reviews. *Canadian Journal of Human Sexuality*, 18(1), Spring.

Hall, G. C. N. (1995). Sexual offender recidivism revisited: A meta-analysis of recent treatment studies. *Journal of Consulting and Clinical Psychology*, 63, 802–809.

Hall, G. C. N., & Hirschman, R. (1991). Towards a theory of sexual aggression: A quadripartite model. *Journal of Consulting and Clinical Psychology*, 59, 662–669.

Hall, G. C. N., & Hirschman, R. (1992). Sexual aggression against children: A conceptual perspective of etiology. *Criminal Justice and Behaviour*, 19, 8–23.

Hanmer, J. (1994). Men, power and the exploitation of women. In J. Hearn & D. Morgan (Eds), *Men, Masculinities and Social Theory*. London: Unwin Hyman Ltd.

Hannon, P. (2006). Can gay men be priests? *The Furrow*, 57(2), 74–80.

Hanson, R. K. (1997a). *The Development of a Brief Actuarial Risk Scale for Sexual Offence Recidivism*. User Report 1997–04. Ottawa: Department of the Solicitor General of Canada. Available at http://www.defenseforsvp.com/Resources/Hanson_Static-99/RRASOR.pdf

Hanson, R. K. (1997b). Invoking sympathy—assessment and treatment of empathy deficits among sexual offenders. In B. K. Schwartz & H. R. Cellini (Eds.), *The Sex Offender: New Insights, Treatment Innovations and Legal Developments* (Vol. 2). Kingston, NJ: Civic Research Institute.

Hanson, R. K. (1998). What do we know about sex offender risk assessment? *Psychology, Public Policy and Law*, 4(3), 50–72.

Hanson, R. K. (2003). Empathy deficits of sexual offenders: a conceptual model. *Journal of Sexual Aggression*, 9, 13–23.

Hanson, R. K (2010). Personal communication.

Hanson, R. K., & Bussière, M. T. (1998). Predicting relapse: A meta-analysis of sexual offender recidivism studies. *Journal of Counselling and Clinical Psychology*, 66(2), 348–362.

Hanson, R. K., Gizzarelli, R., & Scott, H. (1994). The attitudes of incest offenders. Special entitlement and acceptance of sex with children. *Criminal Justice and Behaviour*, 21(2), 187–202.

Hanson, R. K., Gordon, A., Harris, A. J. R., Marques, J. K., Murphy, W., Quinsey, V. L., & Seto, M. C. (2002). First report of the collaborative outcome data project on the effectiveness of psychological treatment for sex offenders. *Sexual Abuse: A Journal of Research and Treatment*, 14(2), 169–193.

Hanson, R. K., & Morton-Bourgon, K. E. (2004). *Predictors of Sexual Recidivism: An Updated Meta- Analysis* (Research Report, No. 2004–02). Ottawa, Canada: Public Safety and Emergency Preparedness Canada.

Hanson, R. K., & Morton-Bourgon, K. E. (2005). The characteristics of persistent sexual offenders: A meta-analysis of recidivism studies. *Journal of Consulting and Clinical Psychology*, 73, 1154–1163.

Hanson, R. K., Morton-Bourgon, K. E., & Harris, A. J. R. (2003). Sexual offender recidivism risk. What we know and what we need to know. *Annals New York Academy of Sciences*, 989, 154–166.

Hanson, R. K., Pfafflin, F., & Lutz, M. (2004). (Eds.) *Sexual Abuse In the Catholic Church. Scientific and Legal Perspectives*. Vatican City: Libreria Editrice Vaticana.

Hanson, R. K., Steffy, R. A., & Gauthier, R. (1993). Long-term recidivism of child molesters. *Journal of Consulting and Clinical Psychology*, 61, 646–652.

Hanson, R. K., & Thornton, D. (2000). Improving risk assessments for sex offenders: A comparison of three actuarial scales. *Law and Human Behaviour*, 24, 119–136.

Hare-Mustin, R. T. (1993). Cries and whispers: A case of therapist abuse of a patient. *Professional Sexual Abuse. Dulwich Centre Newsletter*, 3(4), 27–32.

Harris, M. (1990). *Unholy Orders: Tragedy at Mount Cashel*. Toronto: Penguin.

Hart, C. (1998). *Doing a Literature Review*. London: Sage Publications.

Hart, S. D., Laws, R. D., & Kropp, R.P. (2003). The promise and the peril of sex offender risk assessment. In T. Ward, R. D. Laws, & S. Hudson (Eds.), *Sexual Deviance: Issues and Controversies* (pp. 207–225). Thousand Oaks, CA: Sage.

Haug, F. (2001). Sexual deregulation or, the child abuser as hero in neoliberalism. *Feminist Theory*, 2(1), 55–78.

Haugaard, J. J., & Emery, R. E. (1989). Methodological issues in child sexual abuse research. *Child Abuse and Neglect*, 13, 89–100.

Hayashino, D. S., Wurtele, S. K., & Klebe, K. J. (1995). Child molesters: An examination of cognitive factors. *Journal of Interpersonal Violence*, 10(1), 106–116.

Haywood, T. W., Kravitz, H. M., Grossman, L. S., Wasyliw, O. E., & Hardy, D. W. (1996). Psychological aspects of sexual functioning among cleric and noncleric alleged sex offenders. *Child Abuse and Neglect*, 20, 527–536.

Haywood, T. W., Kravitz, H. M., Wasyliw, O. E., Goldberg, J., & Cavanaugh, J. L. (1996). Cycles of abuse and psychopathology in cleric and noncleric molesters of children and adolescents. *Child Abuse and Neglect*, 20, 1233–1243.

Hearn, J. (2010). Reflecting on men and social policy: Contemporary critical debates and implications for social policy. *Critical Social Policy*, 30(2), 165–188.

Hearn, J., & Pringle, K. (2006). Men, masculinities and children: some European perspectives. *Critical Social Policy*, 26(2), 365–389.

Hekman, S. (1995). *Moral Voices, Moral Selves: Carol Gilligan and Feminist Moral Theory.* Cambridge: Polity Press.

Hederman, M. P., & Kearney, R. (1977). Editorial, art and politics. *The Cranebag: Book of Irish Studies*, 1977–1981, 1(1), 10–12. Dublin: Blackwater Press.

Hegarty, K. (1996). Celibacy falling away in practice if not in doctrine. *Irish Times*, Sept. 21.

Herman, J. L & (1981). *Father Daughter Incest.* Cambridge, MA, and London: Harvard University Press.

Herman, J. L. (1992). *Trauma and Recovery: From Domestic Abuse to Political Terror.* U.S.A: Basic Books.

Herrel, R., Goldberg, J., True, W., Ramakrishman, V., Lyons, M., Ostrow, D., et al. (1999). Sexual orientation and suicidality: A co-twin control study in adult men. *Archives of General Psychiatry*, 56, 867–874.

Hervieu-Léger (2000). *Religion as a Chain of Memory.* Cambridge: Polity.

Hervieu-Léger (2003). Individualism, the validation of faith and the social nature of religion in modernity. In R. Fenn (Ed.), *The Blackwell Companion to Sociology of Religion* (pp. 161–175). Oxford: Blackwell.

Hidalgo, M. (2007). *Sexual Abuse and the Culture of Catholicism.* New York: The Haworth Maltreatment and Trauma Press.

Hill, E. (1997). Obedience, authority and responsibility. *Doctrine and Life*, 47(3), 155–159.

Hilton, N. Z. (1993). Childhood sexual victimization and lack of empathy of child molesters' explanation or excuse? *International Journal of Offender Therapy and Comparative Criminology*, 37, 287–296.

Hirschman, A. O. (1970). *Exit, Voice and Loyalty. Responses to Decline in Firma, Organizations and States.* Cambridge MA: Harvard University Press.

Hoban, B. (2009). A time for courage. *The Furrow, A Journal for the Contemporary Church*, 60(6), 342–354.

Hoban, B (2010). A New Association of Catholic Priests. *The Furrow, A Journal for the Contemporary Church*, 61(9), 483 -.

Hoge, D. (2002). *The First Five Years: A Study of Newly Ordained Catholic Priests.* Collegeville, MN: Liturgical Press.

Hoge, D., & Wenger, J. (2003). *Evolving Visions of the Priesthood: Changes from Vatican II to the Turn of the New Century.* Collegeville, MN: Liturgical Press.

Hollis, M. (1999). *The Philosophy of the Social Science. An Introduction.* Cambridge: Cambridge University Press.

hooks, bell. (1984). *Feminist Theory: From Margin to Center.* Boston: South End.

Hubble, M., Duncan, B., & Miller, S. (2005). Introduction. In M. Hubble, B. Duncan, & S. Miller (Eds), *The Heart and Soul of Change. What Works in Therapy* (pp. 1–32). Washington, DC: American Psychological Association.

Hudson, K. (2005). *Offending Identities. Sex Offenders' Perspectives on their Treatment and Management.* Devon: Willan Publishing.

Hudson, P. E. (1997). Spirituality as a component in a treatment program for sexually addicted Roman Catholic clergy. *Counselling and Values, 41,* 174–183.

Hudson, S. M., Marshall, W. L., Wales, D., McDonald, E., Bakker, L. W. and McLean, A. (1993). Emotional recognition skills in sex offenders. *Annals of Sex Research, 6,* 199–211.

Hudson, S. M., Wales, D. S., & Ward, T. (1998). Kia Marma: a treatment program for child molesters in New Zealand. In W. L. Marshall, Y. Fernandez, S. M. Hudson, & T. Ward. (Eds.), *Sourcebook of Treatment Programs for Sexual Offenders* (pp. 17–28). New York and London: Plenum Press.

Hudson, S. M., & Ward, T. (1997). Intimacy, loneliness and attachment styles in sexual offenders. *Journal of Interpersonal Violence, 12,* 323–339.

Hudson, S. M., Ward, T., Marshall, W. L (1992). The abstinence violation effect in sex offenders: A reformulation. *Behaviour Research and Therapy, 30,* 435-441.

Hudson, S. M., Ward, T., & McCormack, J. (1999). Offence pathways in sexual offenders. *Journal of Interpersonal Violence, 14,* 779–798.

Humphreys, A. (1966). *New Dubliners.* New York: Fordham University Press.

Hydén, M., & McCarthy, I.C. (1994). Woman battering and father–daughter incest disclosure: discourses of denial and acknowledgement. *Discourse and Society,* 5(4), 543–565.

Inglis, T. (1997). Foucault, Bourdieu and the field of Irish sexuality. *Irish Journal of Sociology, 6,* 5–28.

Inglis, T. (1998). *Moral Monopoly. The Rise and Fall of the Catholic Church in Modern Ireland* (2nd ed.). Dublin: University College Dublin Press.

Inglis, T. (2002). Sexual transgressions and scapegoats: a case study from modern Ireland. *Sexualities,* 5, 5–24.

Inglis, T. (2005). Origins and legacies of Irish prudery: sexuality and social control in modern Ireland. *Eire-Ireland,* 40(3 & 4), 9–37.

Inglis, T. (2007a). Catholic identity in contemporary Ireland: belief and belonging to tradition. *Journal of Contemporary Religion, 2,* 205–220.

Inglis, T. (2007b). Individualisation and secularisation in Catholic Ireland. In S. O'Sullivan (Ed.), *Contemporary Ireland. A Sociological Map* (pp. 67–82). Dublin: UCD Press.

Irish Bishops' Conference, The Conference of Religious of Ireland, The Irish Missionary Union (2005). *Our Children, Our Church. Child Protection Policies and Procedures for the Catholic Church in Ireland.* (The Lynott Committee) Dublin: Veritas.

Irish Catholic Bishops' Advisory Committee on Child Sexual Abuse by Priests and Religious (1996). *Child Sexual Abuse: A Framework for a Church Response*. Dublin: Veritas Publications.

Irish Catholic Bishops' Conference (2011). *Towards Healing. The Launch of New Counselling and Support Service for Survivors of Clerical and Religious Abuse*. Available at http://www.catholicbishops.ie/2011/02/04/towards-healing-the-launch-of-new-counselling-and-support-service-for-survivors-of-clerical-and-religious-abuse/ accessed May 20th 2011

Irish Council for Civil Liberties (1988). *Report of the Child Sexual Abuse Working Party*. Dublin: The Irish Council for Civil Liberties.

Isely, P. J. (1997). Clergy sexual abuse and the Catholic Church: An historical and contemporary review. *Pastoral Psychology*, 45, 277–299.

Isely, P. J., & Isely, P. (1990). The sexual abuse of male children by church personnel: Intervention and prevention. *Pastoral Psychology*, 39(2), 85–99.

James, W. (1997). *The Varieties of Religious Experience* (introduction by Reinhold Niebuhr). New York: Simon and Schuster Inc.

Jamieson, S., & Marshall, W. L. (2000). Attachment style and violence in child molesters. *Journal of Sexual Aggression*, 5(2), 88–98.

Janesick, V. J. (2000). In N. K. Denzin & Y. S. Lincoln. (Eds.), *Handbook of Qualitative Research* (2nd ed., pp. 379–400). Thousand Oaks and London: Sage Publications.Jay, E. (1980). *The Church: Its Changing Image through Twenty Centuries*. Atlanta: John Knox Press.

Jenkins, A. (1990). *Invitations to Responsibility. The Therapeutic Engagement of Men Who Are Violent and Abusive*. South Australia: Dulwich Centre Publications.

Jenkins, P. (1995). Clergy sexual abuse: The symbolic politics of a social problem. in J. Best (Ed.), *Images of Issues, Typifying Contemporary Social Problems* (pp. 105–130). New York: Aldine De Gruyter.

Jenkins, P. (1996). *Paedophiles and Priests. Anatomy of a Contemporary Crisis*. New York: Oxford University Press.

Jenkins, P. (1998). *Moral Panic. Changing Concepts of the Child Molester in Modern America*. New Haven and London: Yale University Press.

Jenkins, P. (2002). The proper view on 'paedophile priests.' *Our Sunday Visitor*. Retrieved from *www.catholicmatters.com*

Jenkins, P. (2003). *The New Anti-Catholicism. The Last Acceptable Prejudice*. New York: Oxford University Press.

Jenkins, P. (2009). Failure to launch. Why do some social issues fail to detonate moral panics? *British Journal of Criminology*, 49, 35–47.

Jenks, C. (1996). *Childhood*. London: Routledge.

Jenny, C., Roesier, T., & Poyer, K. (1994). Are children at risk for sexual abuse by homosexuals? *Pediatrics*, 94, 41–44.

John Jay College of Criminal Justice (2004). *The Nature and Scope of Sexual Abuse of Minors by Catholic Priests and Deacons in the United States, 1950–2002*. Washington, DC: United States Conference of Catholic Bishops (Also referred to by name of primary author, see Terry et al., 2004).

John Jay College (2006). *Supplementary Report. The Nature and Scope of Sexual Abuse of Minors by Catholic Priests and Deacons in the United States, 1950–2002*. Washington, DC: United States Conference of Catholic Bishops.

John Jay College (2011). The Causes and Context of Sexual Abuse of Minors by Catholic Priests in the United States, 1950-2010. A Report Presented to the United States Conference of

Catholic Bishops by the John Jay College Research Team. Washington, DC: United States Conference of Catholic Bishops. Available at http://www.usccb.org/mr/causes-and-context. shtml Acessed May 26th 2011.

Johnson, J. M. (1995). Horror stories and the construction of child abuse. In J. Best. (Ed.), *Images of Issues. Typifying Contemporary Social Problems*. New York: Aldine De Gruyter.

Johnson, T. C. (1998). Children who molest. In W. Marshall & Y. Fernandez (Eds.), *Sourcebook of Treatment Programs for Sexual Offenders* (pp. 337–352). New York: Plenum Press.

Kafka, M. (1997). A monoamine hypothesis for the pathophysiology of paraphilic disorder. *Archives of Sexual Behaviour, 26*, 343–358.

Kafka, M. (2003). The monoamine hypothesis for the pathophysiology of paraphilic disorders. In R. Prentky, E. Janus, M. Seto, & A. W. Burgess (Eds.), Understanding and managing sexually coercive behaviour. *Annals of the New York Academy of Sciences, 989*, 86–94.

Kafka, M. (2004). Sexual molesters of adolescents, ephebophilia and Catholic clergy: A review and synthesis. In R. K. Hanson, F. Pfäfflin, & M. Lütz (Eds.), *Sexual Abuse in the Catholic Church: Scientific and Legal Perspectives* (pp. 51–59). Vatican City: Libreria Editrice Vaticana.

Kalichman, S., Gore-Felton, C., Benotsch, E., Cage, M., & Rompa, D. (2004). Trauma symptoms, sexual behaviours and substance abuse: Correlates of childhood sexual abuse and HIV risk among men who have sex with men. *Journal of Child Sexual Abuse, 13*(1), 1–15.

Karp, D. R. (1998). The judicial and the judicious use of shame penalties. *Crime and Delinquency,* 44, 277.

Kearney, P. A., Byrne, N. O'R., & McCarthy, I. C. (1989). Just metaphors: Marginal illuminations in a colonial retreat. *Family Therapy Case Studies, 4*(1), 17–31.

Keddy, P. J., Erdberg, P., & Sammon, S. D. (1990). The psychological assessment of Catholic clergy and religious referred for residential treatment. *Pastoral Psychology, 38*(3), 147–159.

Keenan, M. (1998). Narrative therapy with men who have sexually abused children. *Irish Journal of Psychology, Special Issue,* 1, 136–151.

Keenan, M. (2006). The institution and the individual—child sexual abuse by clergy. *The Furrow. A Journal for the Contemporary Church, 57*(1), 3–8.

Keenan, M. (2009). "Them and Us": The Clerical Child Sex Offender as "Other". In T. Flannery (Ed.). *Responding to the Ryan Report* (pp. 180–231).Dublin: Columba Press.

Keenan, T., & Ward, T. (2000). A theory of mind perspective on cognitive, affective, and intimacy deficits in child sexual offenders. *Sexual Abuse: A Journal of Research and Treatment,* 12(1), 49–60.

Kelle, U. (2004). Computer-assisted analysis of qualitative data. In U. Flick, E. von Kardorff, & I. Steinke. (Eds.), *A Companion to Qualitative Research* (pp. 276–283). London and Thousand Oaks: Sage.

Kelley, R. K. (1989). Comment. Sentenced to wear the scarlet letter: judicial innovations in sentencing. *Dickinson Law Review,* 1, 759.

Kelly, A. F. (1998). Clergy offenders. In W. L. Marshall (Ed.), *Sourcebook of Treatment Programs for Sexual Offenders* (pp. 303–318). New York: Plenum Press.

Kelly, G. A. (1955). *The Psychology of Personal Constructs*. New York: Norton.

Kelly, L. (1997). Weasel words: Paedophiles and the cycle of abuse. *Nota News,* 22, 9–19.

Kempe, H. C., & Helfer, A. T. (1962). The battered child syndrome. *Journal of the American Medical Association,* 18(1).

Kennedy, E. (1971). *The Catholic Priest in the United States: Psychological Investigations*. Washington DC: United States Catholic Conference.

Kennedy, E. & Heckler, V.J (n.d.) *The Loyola Psychological Study of the Ministry and Life of the American Priest.* Washington, DC: National Conference of Catholic Bishops.

Kennedy, E. (1977). Telephone interviews and email correspondence, 1997–1998 (unpublished) cited in S. Balboni (1998). *Through the Lens of the Organizational Culture Perspective: A Descriptive Study of American Catholic Bishops' Understanding of Clergy Sexual Molestation and Abuse of Children and Adolescents.* PhD thesis, Northeastern University, Boston, Massachusetts, U.S.A. Available on *www.BishopAccountability.org* Accessed 10/01/2007.

Kennedy, E. (2001). *The Unhealed Wound. The Church and Human Sexuality.* New York: St Martin's Press.

Kennedy, G. (1992). Trocaire funds down by 60%. *Irish Times,* p. 1, June 17.

Kennedy, M. (2003). Sexual abuse of women by priests and ministers to whom they go for pastoral care and support. *Feminist Theology: The Journal of the Britain and Ireland School of Feminist Theology,* 11(2), 226–235.

Kenny, V. (Ed.) (1988). Radical constructivism, autopoiesis and psychotherapy. *The Irish Journal of Psychology [special issue],* 9, 1.

Kincaid, J. R. (1998). *Erotic Innocence. The Culture of Child Molesting.* Durham and London: Duke University Press.

Kirby, P. (1984). *Is Irish Catholicism Dying?* Dublin: The Mercier Press.

Kitayama, S., & Markus, H. R. (1999). Yin and yang of the Japanese self: the cultural psychology of personality coherence. In Y. Shoda (Ed.), *The Coherence of Personality: Social Cognitive Bases of Personality Consistency, Variability, and Organization* (pp. 242–302). New York: Guilford Press.

Kitzinger, J (1999) The ultimate neighbour from hell: Media framing of paedophiles. In B. Franklin (Ed.), *Social Policy, the Media and Misrepresentation.* London: Routledge.

Kitzinger, J. (2000). Media templates: patterns of association and the (re)construction of meaning over time. *Media, Culture and Society,* 22(1), 61–84.

Knight, R. A., & Prentky, R. A. (1990). Classifying sexual offenders: The development and corroboration of taxonomic models. In W. L. Marshall, D. R. Laws, & H. E. Barbaree (Eds), *Handbook of Sexual Assault: Issues, Theories and Treatment of the Offender* (pp. 209–229). New York: Plenum.

Knopp, F. H. (1984). *Retraining Adult Sex Offenders: Methods and Models.* Vermont: The Safer Society Press.

Konopasky, R., & Konopasky, A. (2000). Remaking penile plethysmography. In D. R. Laws, S. M. Hudson, & T. Ward (Eds.), *Remaking Relapse Prevention with Sex Offenders* (pp. 257–284). London: Sage Publications.

Koss, M. P., Bachar, K. J., & Hopkins, C. Q. (2003). Restorative justice for sexual violence: Repairing victims, building community and holding offenders accountable. *Annals New York Academy of Sciences,* 989, 384–396.

Krebs, T. (1998). Church structures that facilitate paedophilia among Roman Catholic clergy. In A. Shupe (Ed.), *Wolves within the Fold: Religious Leadership and Abuses of Power* (pp.15–32). New Brunswick, NJ: Rutgers University Press.

Krenik, Rev. T. W. (1999). *Formation For Priestly Celibacy: A Resource Book.* St. Paul, MN: The Saint Paul Seminary, School of Divinity of the University of St. Thomas.

Krugman, R. (1996). The media and public awareness of child abuse and neglect: It's time for a change. *Child Abuse and Neglect, The International Journal,* 20(4), 259–260.

Kuhn, T. (1962). *The Structure of Scientific Revolutions*. Chicago: The University of Chicago Press.

Küng, H. (2003). *The Catholic Church. A Short History* (translated by John Bowden, 2nd ed.). New York: Modern Library.

Küng, H. (2010). Church in worst credibility crisis since the Reformation, theologian tells Bishops. *The Irish Times,* April 16, p. 15.

Kvale, S. (1996). *InterViews. An Introduction to Qualitative Research Interviewing*. Thousand Oaks and London: Sage.

Laaser, M. R. (1991). Sexual addiction and the clergy. *Pastoral Psychology,* 39, 213–235.

Laeuchli, S. (1972). *Power and Sexuality: The Emergence of Canon Law at the Synod of Elvira*. Philadelphia: Temple University Press.

Lambert, M. J. (1992). Implications of outcome research for psychotherapy integration. In J. C. Norcross & M. R. Goldfried (Eds.), *Handbook of Psychotherapy Integration* (pp. 94–129). New York: Basic Books.

Lancaster, E., & Lumb, J. (1999). Bridging the gap: feminist theory and practice reality in work with perpetrators of child sexual abuse. *Child and Family Social Work,* 4, 119–129.

Lane, D. (Ed.). (1997). *Reading the Signs of the Times. A Survey of Priests in Dublin*. Dublin: Veritas.

Lang, P. (2003). *Putting Children Beyond Risk and Perpetrators Beyond Suspicion*. Workshop held in Department of Social Policy and Social Work, University College Dublin. April.

Lang, P., & McAdam, E. (1997). Narrative-ating: Future dreams in present living. *Human Systems: The Journal of Systemic Consultation and Management [special issue],* 8(1), 3–12.

Langevin, R. (2004). Who engages in sexual behaviour with children? Are clergy who commit sexual offences different from other sex offenders? In R. K. Hanson, F. Pfäfflin, & M. Lütz. (Eds.), *Sexual Abuse in the Catholic Church: Scientific and Legal Perspectives* (pp. 24–43). Vatican City: Libreria Editrice Vaticana.

Langevin, R., Curnoe, S., & Bain, J. (2000). A study of clerics who commit sexual offences: Are they different from other sexual offenders? *Child Abuse and Neglect,* 24, 535–545.

Laqueur, T. W. (2003). *Solitary Sex: A Cultural History of Masturbation*. New York: Zone Books.

Lash, N. (2008). *Theology for Pilgrims*. London: Darton, Longman and Todd.

Lawler, R., Boyle, J., & May, W. (1998). *Catholic Sexual Ethics. A Summary, Explanation and Defense*. Indiana: Our Sunday Visitor Publishing Division, Our Sunday Visitor, Inc.

Laws, D. R. (1989). (Ed.). *Relapse Prevention with Sex Offenders*. New York: The Guilford Press.

Laws, D. R. (1999). Relapse prevention: The state of the art. *Journal of Interpersonal Violence,* 14, 285–302.

Laws, D. R., & Marshall, W. L. (1990). A conditioning theory of the etiology and maintenance of deviant sexual preferences and behaviour. In W. L. Marshall, D. R. Laws, & H. E. Barbaree (Eds.), *Handbook of Sexual Assault: Issues, Theories and Treatment of the Offender* (pp. 209–229). New York: Plenum Press.

Laws, D. R., & Marshall, W. L. (2003). A brief history of behavioural and cognitive behavioural approaches to sex offenders. Part 1. Early developments. *Sexual Abuse: A Journal of Research and Treatment,* 15, 75–92.

Lepenies, W. (1988). *Between Literature and Science: The Rise of Sociology*. Cambridge: Cambridge University Press.

Lepenies, W. (1997). *Benimm und Erkenntnis* [Moral Behaviour and Epistemology]. Frankfurt: Suhrkamp.

L'Estrange, S. (2005). *Catholicism and Capitalist Social Order in Ireland, 1907–1973. An Historical and Institutionalist Analysis.* Unpublished PhD thesis, Queen's University Belfast.

Lifton, R. J. (2000). *The Nazi Doctors.* New York: Basic Books

Lincoln, Y. S., & Guba, E. G. (2000). Paradigmatic controversies, contradictions, and emerging confluences. In N. Denzin & Y. Lincoln (Eds.), *Handbook of Qualitative Research* (2nd ed.). London: Sage.

Linden, I. (1997). *Liberation Theology: Coming of Age?* London: CIIR.

Lipchik, E. (1991). Spouse abuse: Challenging the party line. *Networker*, May/June, 59–63. Dulwich Centre Publications.

Lippke, R. L. (2002). Toward a theory of prisoners' rights. *Ratio Juris*, 15, 122–145.

Loades, A. (2001). *Feminist Theology. Voices from the Past.* Cambridge: Polity Press.

Lofland, J. (1969). *Deviance and Identity.* Englewood Cliffs, NJ: Prentice Hall.

Loftus, J. A. (1999). Sexuality in priesthood: Noli me tangere. In T.G. Plante (Ed.), *Bless Me Father for I Have Sinned* (pp. 7–19). Westport, CT, London: Praeger.

Loftus, J. A. (2004). What have we learned? Implications for future research and formation. In T. G. Plante (Ed.), *Sin against the Innocents. Sexual Abuse by Priests and the Role of the Catholic Church* (pp. 85–96). Westport, CT, London: Praeger.

Loftus, J. A., & Camargo, R.J. (1993). Treating the clergy. *Annals of Sex Research*, 6, 287–303.

Lombardi, F. (2010). Statement of the Director of the Holy See Press Office, Fr. Federico Lombardi, S.J., concerning the Murphy Case, March 24, 2010. Accessed March 15, *http://www. vatican.va/resources/index_en.htm*

Lothstein, L. (1999). Neuropsychological findings in clergy who sexually abuse. In T. G. Plante, *Bless Me Father for I Have Sinned* (pp. 59–85). Westport, CT, London: Praeger/Greenwood.

Lothstein, L. (2004a). The relationship between the treatment facilities and the church hierarchy: forensic issues and future considerations. In T. G. Plante. (Ed.), *Sin Against The Innocents. Sexual Abuse by Priests and the Role of the Catholic Church* (pp. 123–138). Westport, CT, London: Praeger.

Lothstein, L. (2004b). Men of the flesh: the evaluation and treatment of sexually abusing priests. *Studies in Gender and Sexuality*, 5, 167–195.

Lukes, S. (2005). *Power: A Radical View.* London: Palgrave Macmillan.

Lumen Gentium (1964). *Dogmatic Constitution of the Church.* Promulgated by His Holiness Pope Paul VI. Available at *http://www.vatican.va/archive/hist_councils/ii_vatican_council/ documents/vat-ii_const_19641121_lumen-gentium_en.html*

Mac an Ghaill, M. (1994). *The Making of Men: Masculinities, Sexualities and Schooling.* Buckingham: Open University Press.

MacCartaigh, S. (1995). Couple made their own marriage vow. *Irish Times*, p. 7, June 26.

MacIntyre, D., & Carr, A. (1999). The epidemiology of child sexual abuse. *Journal of Child Centred Practice*, 6(1), 57–85.

MacMillan, H. L., Fleming, J. E., Trocmé, N., Boyle, M. H., Wong, M., et al. (1997). Prevalence of child physical and sexual abuse in the community: Results from the Ontario Health Supplement. *JAMA*, 278, 131–135.

Madden, A. (2003). *Altar Boy. A Story of Life after Abuse.* Ireland: Penguin

Madden, J. E. (1990). *Personality and Occupational Stress in Roman Catholic Priests.* Doctoral dissertation, Ohio State University.

Magel, N. (2002). Psychosocial predictors of health risk taking behaviours in gay men. *Dissertation Abstracts International*, 63(5-B), 2593.

Maletzky, B. M. (2002). A 25-year follow-up of cognitive behavioural therapy with 7,275 sexual offenders. *Behaviour Modification, 26*, 123–148.

Maletzky, B. M., & Steinhauser, C. (1998). The Portland Sexual Abuse Clinic. In W. L. Marshall, Y. Fernandez, S. M. Hudson, & T. Ward. (Eds.), *Sourcebook of Treatment Programs for Sexual Offenders* (pp. 105–116). New York and London: Plenum Press.

Mann, R., & Beech, A. (2003). Cognitive distortions, schemas and implicit theories. In T. Ward, R. D. Laws, & S. M. Hudson (Eds.), *Sexual Deviance. Issues and Controversies.* Thousand Oaks, CA: Sage Publications.

Mann, R., Hanson, R., & Thornton, D. (2010). Assessing risk for sexual recidivism: Some proposals on the nature of psychologically meaningful risk factors. *Sexual Abuse: A Journal of Research and Treatment, 22*(2), 191–217.

Margolin, L. (1991). Child Sexual Abuse by Nonrelated Caregivers. *Child Abuse & Neglect, 15* (3), 213-221.

Marques, J. K., Nelson, C., Alarcon, J. M., & Day, D. M. (2000). Prevention of relapse in sex offenders: What we learned from the SOTEP's experimental treatment program. In D.R. Laws (Ed.), *Remaking Relapse Prevention with Sex Offenders* (pp. 321–340). California: Sage Publications.

Marsa, F., O'Reilly, G., Carr, A., Murphy, P., O'Sullivan, M., Cotter, A., & Hevey, D. (2004). Attachment styles and psychological profiles of child sex offenders in Ireland. *Journal of Interpersonal Violence, 19*(2), 228–251.

Marshall, P. (1997). The Prevalence of Convictions for Sexual Offending. *Research Findings, no. 55.* Croydon, UK: Home Office Research and Statistics Directorate.

Marshall, W. L. (1989). Invited essay: Intimacy, loneliness, and sexual offenders. *Behaviour Research and Therapy,* 27(5), 491–503.

Marshall, W. L. (1993). The role of attachments, intimacy, and loneliness in the etiology and maintenance of sexual offending. *Sexual and Marital Therapy,* 8(2), 109–121.

Marshall, W. L. (1996a). The enhancement of intimacy and the reduction of loneliness among child molesters. *Journal of Family Violence,* 11(3), 219–235.

Marshall. W. L. (1996b). The sexual offender: monster, victim or everyman? *Sexual Abuse: A Journal of Research and Treatment,* 8(4), 317–335.

Marshall, W. L. (1997). The relationship between self-esteem and deviant sexual arousal in non-familial child molesters. *Behaviour Modification,* 21, 86–96.

Marshall, W. L. (2002). Historical foundations and current conceptualisations of empathy. In Y. Fernandez (Ed.), *In their Shoes: Examining the Issue of Empathy and Its Place in the Treatment of Offenders* (pp. 36–52). Oklahoma: Wood "N" Barnes Publishing.

Marshall, W. L. (2003). *Consulting at the Vatican.* Keynote address given at the Annual Research and Treatment Conference of the Association for the Treatment of Sexual Abusers. St. Louis, Missouri. October.

Marshall, W. L. (2004). Cognitive behavioural treatment of child molesters. In R. K. Hanson, F. Pfafflin, & M. Lutz, (2004). (Eds.). *Sexual Abuse In the Catholic Church. Scientific and Legal Perspectives* (pp. 97–114). Vatican City: Libreria Editrice Vaticana.

Marshall, W., Anderson, D., & Champagne, F. (1997). Self-esteem and its relationship to sexual offending. *Psychology, Crime, Law,* 3, 161–186

Marshall, W., Anderson, D., & Fernandez, Y. (2000). *Cognitive Behavioural Treatment of Sexual Offenders* (2nd ed.). England: Wiley and Sons.

Marshall, W. L., & Barbaree H. E. (1990). An integrated theory of sexual offending. In W. L. Marshall, D. R. Laws, & H. E. Barbaree (1990), *Handbook of Sexual Assault, Issues, Theories and Treatment of the Offender* (pp. 257–275). New York: Plenum Press.

Marshall, W. L., Bryce, P., Hudson, S. M., Ward, T., & Moth, B. (1996). The enhancement of empathy and the reduction of loneliness among child molesters. *Journal of Family Violence,* 11, 219–235.

Marshall, W. L., Champagne, F., Brown, C., & Miller, S. (1997). Empathy, intimacy, loneliness and self-esteem in nonfamilial child molesters: A brief report. *Journal of Child Sexual Abuse,* 6(3), 87–98.

Marshall, W. L., Cripps, E., Anderson, D., & Cortoni, F. A. (1999). Self-esteem and coping strategies in child molesters. *Journal of Interpersonal Violence,* 14(9), 955–962.

Marshall, W. L., & Eccles, A. (1991). Issues in clinical practice with sex offenders. *Journal of Interpersonal Violence,* 6, 68–93.

Marshall, W. L., Fernandez, Y. M., Hudson, S. M., & Ward, T. (Eds.) (1998). *Sourcebook of Treatment Programs for Sexual Offenders.* New York and London: Plenum.

Marshall, W. L., Hamilton, K., & Fernandez, Y. (2001). Empathy deficits and cognitive distortions in child molesters. *Sexual Abuse: A Journal of Research and Treatment,* 13, 123–130.

Marshall, W. L., Hudson, S. M., Jones, R., & Fernandez, Y. M. (1995). Empathy in sex offenders. *Clinical Psychology Review,* 15, 99–113.

Marshall, W. L., Jones, R. J., Hudson, S. M., & McDonald, E. (1993). Generalised empathy in child molesters. *Journal of Child Sexual Abuse,* 2(4), 61–68.

Marshall, W. L., & Laws, D. R. (2003). A brief history of behavioural and cognitive behavioural approaches to sex offenders. Part 2. The modern era. *Sexual Abuse: A Journal of Research and Treatment,* 15, 93–120.

Marshall, W. L., Laws D. R., & Barbaree, H. E. (1990). *Handbook of Sexual Assault, Issues, Theories and Treatment of the Offender.* New York: Plenum Press.

Marshall, W. L., & Maric, A. (1996). Cognitive and emotional components of generalised empathy deficits in child molesters. *Journal of Child Sexual Abuse,* 5(2), 101–110.

Marshall, W. L., & Mazzucco, A. (1995). Self-esteem and parental attachments in child molesters. *Sexual Abuse: A Journal of Research and Therapy,* 7(4), 279–285.

Marshall, W. L., Serran, G. A., & Cortoni, F. A. (2000). Childhood attachments, sexual abuse and their relationship to adult coping in child molesters. *Sexual Abuse: A Journal of Research and Treatment,* 12(1), 17–26.

Martin, D. (2009a). Tarnished orders have a last chance at redemption. *The Irish Times,* May 25. Online at *www.irishtimes.ie,* accessed May 25, 2009.

Martin, D. (2009b). I am aware that no words of apology will ever be enough. *Irish Independent,* Nov. 27, p. 15.

Martin, D. (2010). *John Henry Newman: Faith and Reason. The Ireland of Newman—the Ireland of today.* Popili Meeting, Rimini, August 24. Available at *http://www.dublindiocese.ie/index. php?option=com_content&task=view&id=2011&Itemid=372*

Martin, M., & McIntyre, L. (1994). *Readings in the Philosophy of Social Science.* A Bradford Book. Cambridge MA and London: MIT Press.

Martin, P. Y. (1998). Why can't a man be more like a woman? Reflections on Connell's masculinities. *Gender and Society,* 12(4), 472–474.

Maruna, S. (2001). *Making Good. How Ex-Convicts Reform and Rebuild Their Lives.* Washington, DC: American Psychological Association.

Mason, J. (2002). *Qualitative Researching*. London, Thousand Oaks: Sage.

Maxwell, G., & Morris, A. (1999). *Understanding Re-offending*. Institute of Criminology, Victoria University of Wellington.

McAdam, E., & Hannah, C. (1991). Violence–Part 2: Creating the best context to work with clients who have found themselves in violent situations. In H. G. Hanks, E. McAdam, & C. Hannah (Eds.), *Human Systems. The Journal of Systemic Consultation and Management. Special Issue. Systemic Approaches to Child Maltreatment,* 2(3–4), 217–226.

McAdams, D. P. (1993). *The Stories We Live by. Personal Myths and the Making of the Self.* New York and London: The Guilford Press.

McAlinden, A. (2007). *The Shaming of Sexual Offenders: Risk, Retribution and Reintegration.* Oxford: Hart Publishing.

McAlinden, A. (2008). Restorative justice as a response to sexual offending: addressing the failings of current punitive approaches. *Sexual Offender Treatment,* 3(1), 1–12. Online journal available at *www.iatso.org* Accessed 10/08/2009.

McCall, D. (2002). Sex and the clergy. *Sexual Addiction and Compulsivity,* 9, 89–95.

McCarthy, I. C. (2002). The spirit of the fifth province: an ancient metaphor for a new millenium. In *Celebration of the Fifth Province, Feedback: The Magazine of the Family Therapy Association of Ireland,* 9(2), 10–13.

McCarthy, I. C., & Byrne, N. O'R. (1988). Mistaken love: conversations on the problem of incest in an Irish context. *Family Process,* 27, 181–199.

McCarthy, J (2009). *Deep Deception: Ireland's Swimming Scandals.* Dublin: O'Brien Press Ltd.

McCormack, J., Hudson, S. M., & Ward, T. (2002). Sexual offenders' perceptions of their early interpersonal relationships: an attachment perspective. *The Journal of Sex Research,* 39(2), 85–93.

McCarthy, P. (2009). The Murphy Report – a Personal Assessment. *The Furrow, A Journal of the Contemporary Church.* 61, (2), 71.

McDonagh, E. (1995). The winter name of the Church. *The Furrow,* 46(1), 3–12.

McDowell, M. (1998). Facing up to sex crime. *Sunday Independent.* June 28, p. 4.

McEvoy, K., & Mika, H. (2001). Policing, punishment and praxis: restorative justice and non-violent alternatives to paramilitary punishments in Northern Ireland. *Policing and Society,* 11, 359–382.

McGarry, P. (1994). Reviews of the week. *Irish Times,* Oct. 22, p. 2.

McGarry, P. (2002). Bishop doubts Comiskey's resignation was right. *Irish Times.* April 3, p. 5.

McGarry, P. (2010a). *Tonight with Vincent Brown.* March 10. Aired on TV3, Ireland.

McGarry, P. (2010b). Pope's pastoral letter likely before Lent, says prelate. *Irish Times,* Jan. 2. Online *www.irishtimes.ie,* accessed Jan. 2, 2010.

McGarry, P. (2010c). Further €200m sought from religious. *Irish Times,* April 16. Online at *www.irishtimes.ie,* accessed April 16, 2010.

McGarry, P. (2010d). Abuse victims to celebrate Reformation Day at Vatican. *Irish Times,* Aug. 21, p. 7.

McGee, H., Garavan, R., de Barra, M., Byrne, J., & Conroy, R. (2002). *The SAVI Report: Sexual Abuse and Violence in Ireland. A National Study of Irish Experiences, Beliefs and Attitudes Concerning Sexual Violence.* Dublin: The Liffey Press.

McGlone, G. J. (2001). *Sexually Offending and Non-offending Roman Catholic Priests: Characterization and Analysis.* Unpublished dissertation. California School of Professional Psychology, San Diego.

McGlone, G. J. (2003). Prevalence and incidence of Roman Catholic clerical sex offenders. *Sexual Offending and Compulsivity,* 10, 111–121.

McGlone, G. J., Viglione, D. J., & Geary, B. (2002). *Data from One Treatment Center in U.S.A (N=150) Who Have Sexually Offended.* Presented at the Annual Research and Treatment Conference of the Association for the Treatment of Sexual Abusers, Montreal. October.

McGrath, R., Cumming, G., Burchard, B., Zeoli, S., & Ellerby, L. (2010). *Current Practices and Emerging Trends in Sexual Abuser Management.* The Safer Society 2009 North American Survey. Vermont: The Safer Society Press. Available at *www.safersociety.org*

McGrath, T. G. (1990). The Tridentine evolution of modern Irish Catholicism, 1563–1962: A re-examination of the "Devotional Revolution" thesis. In Reamonn O Muiri, (Ed.), *Irish Church History Today: Cumann Seanchais Ard Mhacha Seminar* (pp. 84–99). March. Armagh.

McGuinness, C. (1993). *Report of the Kilkenny Incest Investigation.* Dublin: Stationery Office.

McGuire, R. J., Carlisle, J. M., & Young, B. G. (1965). Sexual deviations as conditioned behaviour: A hypothesis. *Behavioural Research and Therapy,* 2, 185–190.

McKay, S. (1998). *Sophia's Story.* Dublin: Gill and MacMillan.

McLeod, J. (2001). *Qualitative Research in Counselling and Psychotherapy.* London: Sage.

McNamee, S., Gergen, K., & Associates (1999). *Relational Responsibility. Resources for Sustainable Dialogue.* Thousand Oaks, CA: Sage Publications, Inc.

McNamee, S., Gergen, K., & Associates (1999). A case in point. In S. McNamee, K. Gergen, & Associates (1999). *Relational Responsibility. Resources for Sustainable Dialogue* (pp. 49–56). Thousand Oaks, CA: Sage Publications, Inc.

Mead, G. H. (1934). *Mind, Self and Society.* Chicago: University of Chicago Press.

Mehl, G. (1990). *The Quality of Ministerial Candidates from a Counsellor's Perspective.* Lancaster Career Development Centre. Unpublished paper.

Méndez, C. L., Coddou, F., & Maturana, H. (1988). The bringing forth of pathology. in V. Kenny (ed.). Radical Constructivism, Autopoiesis and Psychotherapy. *The Irish Journal of Psychology [special issue],* 9(1), 144–172.

Mercado, C., Tallon, J., & Terry, K. (2008). Persistent sexual abusers in the Catholic church. An examination of characteristics and offence patterns. *Criminal Justice and Behaviour,* 35(5), 629–642.

Mercer, D., & Simmonds, T. (2001). The mentally disordered offender. Looking-glass monsters: reflections of the paedophile in popular culture. In T. Mason, C. Carisle, C. Walkins, & E. Whitehead (Eds.), *Stigma and Social Exclusion in Healthcare* (pp. 170–181). London and New York: Routledge.

Merton, R (1936). The Unanticipated Consequences of Purposive Social Action. *American Sociological Review,* 1 (6), pp. 894–904.

Merton, R (1940). Bureaucratic Structures and Personality. *Social Forces,* 18 (4), pp. 560–568.

Merton, R. (1957). *Social Theory and Social Structure.* Glencoe, IL: Free Press.

Merton, R., & Barber, E. (2004). *The Travels and Adventures of Serendipity*: Princeton, NJ: Princeton University Press.

Messenger, J. (1969). *Innis Beag.* New York: Holt Rinehart and Winston.

Messerschmidt, J. W. (1993). *Masculinities and Crime. Critique and Reconceptualisation of Theory.* U.S.A: Rowman and Littlefield Inc.

Messner, M. A. (1992). *Power at Play: Sports and the Problem of Masculinity.* Boston: Beacon.

Messner, M. A. (2002). *Taking the Field: Women, Men and Sport.* Minneapolis: University of Minnesota Press.

Messner, M. A., & Sabo, D. (1990). *Sport, Men and the Gender Order: Critical Feminist Perspectives.* Champaign, IL: Human Kinetics Books.

Metz, J. B. (1980). *Faith in History and Society. Towards a Practical Fundamental Theology.* New York: The Seabury Press. A Crossroads Book.

Mickens, R. (2000). The Vatican: It's still a man's world. *Priest and People*, 14(8/9), 323–327.

Miles, M., & Huberman, A. (1994). *Qualitative Data Analysis.* London: Sage.

Miller, P. A., & Eisenberg, N. (1988). The relation of empathy to aggression and anti-social behaviour. *Psychological Bulletin*, 103, 324–344.

Milner, J. (2004). From "disappearing" to "demonised": the effects on men and women of professional interventions based on challenging men who are violent. *Critical Social Policy*, 24(1), 79–101.

Mishler, E. G. (1991). Representing discourse: the rhetoric of transcription. *Journal of Narrative and Life History*, 1, 255–280.

Money, J. (1986). *Love Maps: Clinical Concepts of Sexual/Erotic Health and Pathology. Paraphilia and Gender Transposition in Childhood, Adolescence, and Maturity.* New York: Irvington Press.

Money, J. (1993). Development of paraphilia in childhood and adolescence. *Sexual and Gender Identity Disorders*, 2(3), 463–475.

Moore, C. (1995). *Betrayal of Trust, the Father Brendan Smyth Affair and the Catholic Church.* Dublin: Marino Books.

Morris, A., & Maxwell, G. (2003). Restorative justice for adult offenders: The New Zealand experience. In L. Walgrave (Ed.), *Repositioning Restorative Justice.* Devon: Willan Publishing.

Moulden, H. M., Firestone, P. & Wexler, A. E (2007). Child Care Providers Who Commit Sexual Offences: A Description of Offender, Offence, and Victim Characteristics. *International Journal of Offender Therapy and Comparative Criminology*, 51 (4), 384-406.

Mouton, F. R., Doyle, T. P., & Peterson, M. (1985). The problem of sexual molestation by Roman Catholic clergy: Meeting the problem in a comprehensive and responsible manner. Unpublished paper given to the United States Conference of Catholic Bishops. Available from *www. BishopAccountability.org*, accessed 05/06/2006.

Müller-Fahenholz, G (1997). *The Art of Forgiveness: Theological Reflections on Healing and Reconciliation.* Geneva: WCC Publications.

Murdock Smith, L. (2007). Women priests and clergy sexual misconduct. In M.G. Frawley-O'Dea & V. Goldner, (Eds.), *Predatory Priests, Silenced Victims. The Sexual Abuse Crisis and The Catholic Church* (pp. 195–203). New Jersey and London: The Analytic Press.

National Catholic Reporter (2010a). Credibility gap: pope needs to answer questions. *National Catholic Reporter.* Editorial, March 26. Online version available at *http://ncronline.org/*, accessed March 26, 2010.

National Catholic Reporter (2010b). A few in the Hierarchy show honesty and courage. *National Catholic Reporter.* Editorial, Aug. 18. Online version available at *http://ncronline.org/*, accessed August 18, 2010.

Nelson-Rowe, S. (1995). The moral drama of multicultural education. In J. Best. (Ed.), *Images of Issues, Typifying Contemporary Social Problems.* New York: Walter de Gruyter.

New York Times. (2010). The pope and the pedophilia scandal [editorial]. March 24, 2010. Online at http://www.nytimes.com/, accessed March 24, 2010.

Newburn, T., & Stanko, E.A. (1994). *Just Boys Doing Business? Men, Masculinities and Crime.* New York: Routledge.

Nic Ghiolla Phádraig, M. (1976). *Religion in Ireland: preliminary analysis.* Social Studies 5(2), pp. 113-180.

Nic Ghiolla Phádraig, M. (1988). Ireland—the exception that proves two rules. In T. Gannon (Ed.), *World Catholicism in Transition.* London: Macmillan.

Nic Ghiolla Phádraig, M. (2009). Religion in Ireland: No longer an exception? *Research Update,* 64. Available online at http://www.ark.ac.uk/publications/updates/update64.pdf

Niederland, W., & Krystal, H. (1971). *Psychic Traumatization: Aftereffects in Individuals and Communities* (International Psychiatry Clinics, 8, (1)). Little Brown and Company.

Nines, J. (2006). *Sexuality Attitudes and the Priesthood.* Unpublished PhD thesis, School of Human Service Profession, Widener University.

North Western Health Board. (1998). *West of Ireland Farmer Case: Report of the Review Group.* North Western Health Board.

Noll, D. E., & Harvey, L. (2008). Restorative mediation: the application of restorative justice practice and philosophy to clergy sexual abuse cases. *Journal of Child Sexual Abuse,* 17(3–4), 377–396.

Noyes, T. (1997). *Broken Vows, Broken Trust: Understanding Clergy Sexual Misconduct.* Unpublished PhD thesis, The Union Institute.

Nussbaum, M. (2006). *Frontiers of Justice: Disability, Nationality, Species-membership.* Cambridge, UK: The Belknap Press of Harvard University Press.

Oakley, F., & Russett, B. (Eds). (2004). *Governance, Accountability and the Future of the Catholic Church.* London and New York: Continuum.

O'Brien, C. (2009a). Twenty dead and 6500 at risk of abuse: The State's children today. *Irish Times,* May 23, p. 7.

O'Brien, C. (2009b). Lack of inspections leaves thousands in care vulnerable to abuse—groups. *Irish Times,* May 23, p. 7.

O'Brien, C. (2009c). HSE to review child deaths in care over decade. *Irish Times,* July 6, p. 5.

O'Brien, C. (2009d). Children still at risk, says ombudsman. *Irish Times,* July 1, p. 6.

O'Brien, C. (2009e). State's aftercare "responsibility" for young. *Irish Times,* June 4, p. 8.

Office of the Attorney General, Commonwealth of Massachusetts (2003). *The Sexual Abuse of Children in the Roman Catholic Archdiocese of Boston.* Report available at www.BishopAccountability.org, accessed 10/01/2009.

Office of the Attorney General of New Hampshire (2003). *Report on the Investigation of the Diocese of Manchester.* Available at www.BishopAccountability.org, accessed May 6, 2010.

Office of the Attorney General, State of Maine (2004). *A Report by the Attorney General on the Allegations of Sexual Abuse of Children by Priests and Other Clergy Members Associated with the Roman Catholic Church in Maine.* Available at www.BishopAccountability.org, accessed May 6, 2010.

Office of the Grand Jury, Philadelphia (2005). *Report of the Grand Jury into Sexual Abuse of Minors by Clergy in the Philadelphia Archdiocese.* Available at www.BishopAccountability.org, accessed May 6, 2010.

Office of the Grand Jury, Philadelphia (2011). *Investigation of Sexual Abuse by Clergy II.* Available at http://www.phila.gov/districtattorney/PDFs/clergyAbuse2-finalReport.pdf, accessed May 10th

Ogles, B., Anderson, T., & Lunnen, K. (2005). The contribution of models and techniques to therapeutic efficacy: Contradictions between professional trends and clinical research. In M. Hubble, B. Duncan, & S. Miller (Eds.), *The Heart and Soul of Change. What Works in Therapy* (10th ed., pp. 201–226). Washington, DC: American Psychological Association.

O'Gorman, C. (2010). *Beyond Belief: Abuse by His Priest, Betrayed by His Church—The Story of the Boy who Sued the Pope*. Hodder Paperback.

O'Halloran, M. (1994). Irish judges need to take part in wider dialogue for penal reform. *Irish Times,* Sept. 16, p. 6.

O'Hanlon, G. (2010a). Ireland's nettles that need to be grasped. *The Tablet,* Feb. 13, pp. 4–6.

O'Hanlon, G. (2010b). A response to the Murphy Report. *The Furrow,* 61(2), 82–90.

O'Mahony, P. (1996). *Criminal Chaos. Seven Crises in Irish Criminal Justice.* Dublin: Round Hall, Sweet and Maxwell.

O'Malley, T. (1996). *Sexual Offences. Law, Policy and Punishment.* Dublin: Round Hall, Sweet and Maxwell.

O'Malley, T. (1998). Opening remarks. *Conference on Treatment of Sex Offenders.* Irish Penal Reform Trust. Dublin, Nov. 14.

O'Malley, T. (2009). Responding to institutional abuse: the law and its limits. In T. Flannery (Ed.), *Responding to the Ryan Report* (pp. 95–110). Dublin: The Columba Press.

O'Meara, T. (2004). *God in the World. A Guide to Karl Rahner's Theology.* Collegeville, MN: The Liturgical Press.

O'Morain, P. (1994). Tendency to keep quiet about abuse needs to be overcome. *Irish Times,* Sept. 20, p. 12.

Orend, B. (2002). *Human Rights: Concepts and Context.* Ontario, Canada: Broadview Press.

O'Sullivan, (2010). Dublin divided. *The Irish Catholic,* Jan. 28, p. 1.

O'Toole, F. (1994a). Tracing Fr. Brendan's 40 years of child abuse. *Irish Times,* Oct. 8, p. 5.

O'Toole, F. (1994b). Events that shook pillars of power may assist peace. *Irish Times,* Nov. 19, p. 6.

Papesh, M. (2004). *Clerical Culture, Contradiction and Transformation.* Collegeville, MN: Liturgical Press.

Parkinson, P., Oates, K., & Jayakody, A. (2009). *Study of Reported Child Sexual Abuse in the Anglican Church.*

Parton, N. (1985). *The politics of child abuse.* London: Macmillan.

Pastoral letter of His Holiness Benedict XVI to the Catholics of Ireland, (2010). March 19. http://www.vatican.va/holy_father/benedict_xvi/letters/2010/documents/hf_ben-xvi_let_20100319_church-ireland_en.html, accessed March 20, 2010.

Pastores Dabo Vobis: Apostolic Exhortation of his Holiness John Paul II on the Formation of Priests (1992). London: Catholic Truth Society.

Patton, M. Q. (1987). *How to Use Qualitative Methods in Evaluation.* Newbury Park, London: Sage.

Paul, J., Catania, J., Pollack, L., & Stall, R. (2001). Understanding childhood sexual abuse as a predictor of sexual risk taking among men who have sex with men: The Urban Men's Health Study. *Child Abuse and Neglect,* 25, 557–584.

Paulson, J. E. (1988). The clinical and canonical considerations in cases of paedophilia: The Bishops' role. *Studia Canonica,* 22, 77–124.

Payer, P. J. (1982). *Book on Gomorrah: An Eleventh-century Treatise against Clerical Homosexual Practices.* Waterloo, Ontario, Canada: Wilfrid Laurier University Press.

Pelto, P. J., & Pelto, G. H. (1978). Ethnography: the fieldwork enterprise. In J. J. Honigmann (Ed.), *Handbook of Social and Cultural Anthropology*. Chicago: Rand McNally.

Pence, E. (1999). Some thoughts on philosophy. In E. Pence & M. Shepard (Eds.), *Coordinating Community Responses to Domestic Violence: Lessons from Duluth and Beyond*. Thousand Oaks, CA: Sage.

Perillo, A., Mercado, C., & Terry, K. (2008). Repeat offending, victim gender and extent of victim relationship in Catholic Church sexual abusers. Implications for risk assessment. *Criminal Justice and Behaviour,* 35(5), 600–614.

Piquero, A., Piquero, N., Terry, K. Youstin, T., & Nobles, M. (2008). Uncollaring the criminal. Understanding the criminal careers of criminal clerics. *Criminal Justice and Behaviour,* 35(5), 583–599.

Pithers, W. D. (1990). Relapse prevention with sexual aggressors: A method for maintaining therapeutic gain and enhancing external supervision. In W. L. Marshall, D. R. Laws, & H. E. Barbaree (Eds.), *Handbook of Sexual Assault: Issues, Theories and Treatment of the Offender* (pp. 343–362). New York: Plenum.

Pithers, W. D. (1999). Empathy. definition, enhancement and relevance to the treatment of sexual abusers. *Journal of Interpersonal Violence,* 14(3), 257–284.

Pithers, W., & Gray, A (1998). The other half of the story: Children with sexual behaviour problems. *Psychology, Public Policy and Law,* 4, 200–217.

Plante, T. G. (1996). Catholic priests who sexually abuse minors: Why do we hear so much yet know so little? *Pastoral Psychology,* 44(5), 305–310.

Plante, T. G. (Ed.) (1999). *Bless Me Father for I Have Sinned*. Westport, CT, London: Praeger/Greenwood.

Plante, T. G. (2003). Priests behaving badly: what do we know about priest sex offenders? *Sexual Addiction and Compulsivity,* 9, 93–97.

Plante, T. G. (Ed.) (2004). *Sin Against The Innocents. Sexual Abuse by Priests and the Role of the Catholic Church*. Westport, CT, London: Praeger.

Plante, T. G., & Boccaccini, M. T. (1997). Personality expectations and perceptions of Roman Catholic clergy members. *Pastoral Psychology,* 45(4), 301–315.

Plante, T. G., Manuel, G., & Bryant, C. (1994). *Catholic Priests who Sexually Abuse Minors: Intervention, Assessment and Treatment*. Paper presented at the 13th annual conference of the Association for the Treatment of Sexual Abusers, San Francisco, CA.

Plante, T. G., Manuel, G., & Bryant, C. (1996). Personality and cognitive functioning among hospitalised sexual offending Roman Catholic priests. *Pastoral Psychology,* 45(2), 129–139.

Plante, T. G., Manuel, G., & Tandez, J. (1996). Personality characteristics of successful applicants to the priesthood. *Pastoral Psychology,* 45(1), 29–40.

Porteous, J. (2008). *After the Heart of God: The Life and Ministry of Priests at the Beginning of the Third Millennium*. Australia: Connor Court Publishing.

Podles, L. (2008). *Sacrilege. Sexual Abuse in the Catholic Church*. U.S.: Crossland Press.

Polaschek, D. L. L. (2003a). The classification of sex offenders. In T. Ward, D. R. Laws, & S. M. Hudson (Eds.), *Sexual Deviance: Issues and Controversies* (pp. 154–171). Thousand Oaks, CA: Sage.

Polaschek, D. L. L (2003b). Empathy and victim empathy. In T. Ward, D. R. Laws, & S. M. Hudson (Eds.), *Sexual Deviance: Issues and Controversies* (pp.172–189). Thousand Oaks, CA: Sage.

Pollak, A. (1994). Church in Ireland wakes up to clerical sex abuse of children. *Irish Times,* Oct. 11, p. 11.

Pollock, L. (1983). *Forgotten Children: Parent-Child Relations from 1500 to 1900.* Cambridge: Cambridge University Press.

Popper, K (1959). *The Logic of Scientific Discovery.* London: Hutchinson

Prime Time, RTE Television (2009). Katie Hannon reports that Bishop Donal Murray is under pressure to resign following the report of the Commission of Investigation into the Catholic Archdiocese of Dublin (Dec. 1). Available at http://www.rte.ie/news/av/2009/1201/abuse_av2659744.html

Pryce, M. (1996). *Finding a Voice. Men, Women and the Community of the Church.* London: SCM Press Ltd.

Quinn, D. (2005). 241 clerics accused of sex abuse over four decades. *Irish Independent,* Oct. 28, pp. 26–27.

Raftery, M. (2010). *Tonight with Vincent Brown,* March 10, aired on TV3Ireland.

Raftery, M., & O'Sullivan, E. (1999). *Suffer the Little Children.* Dublin: New Island.

Ragin, C., & Becker, H. (1992). *What is a case? Exploring the Foundations of Social Inquiry.* Cambridge and New York: Cambridge University Press.

Rahner, K. (1982). *Foundations of Christian Faith. An Introduction to the Idea of Christianity.* New York: The Crossroads Publishing Company.

Ramde, H. (2010). Pope sued by man claiming Vatican knew about school abuse priest. *Irish Independent,* April 23.

Rank, M. (1992). The blending of qualitative and quantitative methods in understanding child-bearing among welfare recipients. In J. Gilun, K. Daly, & G. Handel, (Eds.), *Qualitative Methods in Family Research.* Newbury Park: Sage.

Ranke-Heinemann, U. (1990). *Eunuchs for Heaven. The Catholic Church and Sexuality* (translated by John Brownjohn). London: Andre Deutsch Ltd.

Ranson, D. (1999). Conversation and conversion—professional misconduct in the Catholic Church. *The Furrow,* 50(12), 660–665.

Ranson, D. (2000). Sexual abuse—implications for initial formation. *The Furrow,* 51(4), 223–229.

Ranson, D. (2002a). The climate of sexual abuse. *The Furrow,* 53(7/8), 387–397.

Ranson, D. (2002b). Priest: public, personal and private. *The Furrow,* 53(4), 219–227.

Ranson, D. (2008). What does the Bible say about sex? *The Furrow,* 59(9), 477–486.

Ranson, D. (2010). Personal communication, Feb. 2.

Reason, P., & Rowan J. (1996) (Eds.). *Human Inquiry. A Sourcebook of New Paradigm Research.* Chichester: Wiley.

Reason, P., & Rowan J. (1996). Issues of validity in new paradigm research. In P. Reason & J. Rowan. (Eds.), *Human Inquiry. A Sourcebook of New Paradigm Research* (pp. 239–252). Chichester: Wiley.

Reder, P., Duncan, S., & Gray, M. (1993). *Beyond Blame. Child Abuse Tragedies Revisited.* London: Routledge.

Reese, T. J. (1996). *Inside the Vatican: The Politics and Organization of the Catholic Church.* Cambridge: Harvard University Press.

Reformation.com (2010). Available at www.reformation.com/ Accessed July 20th 2010.

Reid, L. (2003). Resignation of Laffoy to be examined by various committees. *The Irish Times,* Sept. 8.

Report by the Commission of Investigation into the Catholic Archdiocese of Dublin (2009). Available at http://www.justice.ie/en/JELR/Pages/PB09000504 Accessed 28/02/2011 (Also known as The Murphy Report).

Report of the Commission to Inquire into Child Abuse (2009). Dublin: Government Stationary Office. Also available at http://www.childabusecommission.com/rpt/pdfs/ Accessed 28/02/2011. (Also known as the Ryan Report).

Report by Commission of Investigation into the Catholic Diocese of Cloyne (2011). Available at http://www.justice.ie/en/JELR/Pages/Cloyne_Rpt Accessed 25th July 2011.

Residential Institutions Redress Board (2002). *Residential Institutions Redress Act* (2002). Dublin: Government Publications.

Restorative Justice Council (2010). *Restorative Justice Works.* Available at http://www.restorative-justice.org.uk/ Accessed May 4th 2011.

Richards, A. (2007). Clergy sexual misconduct: Episcopal and Roman Catholic clergy. In M. G. Frawley-O'Dea & V. Goldner, (Eds.), *Predatory Priests, Silenced Victims. The Sexual Abuse Crisis and The Catholic Church* (pp. 195–203). New Jersey and London: The Analytic Press.

Richardson, V. (2000). Writing: a method of inquiry. In N. K. Denzin & Y. S. Lincoln. (Eds.), *Handbook of Qualitative Research* (2nd ed., pp. 923–948). Thousand Oaks and London: Sage Publications.

Riessman, C. K. (1993). *Narrative Analysis.* Newbury Park, CA, and London: Sage.

Rigert, J. (2008). *An Irish Tragedy: How Sex Abuse by Irish Priests helped to Cripple the Catholic Church.* New York: Crosslands Press.

Roberts, T. (2011). Critics point to John Jay study's limitations. *National Catholic Reporter,* May 23rd. Available at http://ncronline.org/news/accountability/critics-point-john-jay-studys-limitations accessed 23rd May.

Robertson, G (2010). *The Case Of The Pope: Vatican Accountability for Human Rights Abuse.* London: Penguin Books.

Robinson, G. (2007). *Confronting Power and Sex in the Church. Reclaiming the Spirit of Jesus.* Australia: John Garratt Publishing.

Robinson, E. A., (1994). *Shadows of the Lantern Bearers: A Study of Sexually Troubled Clergy.* Unpublished doctoral thesis, Loyola College, Maryland.

Robinson, E. A., Montana, S., & Thompson, G. (1993). *A Descriptive Study of Sexually Troubled Clergy.* Paper presented at the Annual Research and Treatment Conference of the Association for the Treatment of Sexual Abusers. Boston, November.

Rose, N. (1993). Individualizing psychology. In J. Shotter & K. Gergen. *Texts of Identity* (pp. 119–132). London: Sage.

Rossetti, S. J. (1990) (Ed.). *Slayer of the Soul: Child Sexual Abuse and the Catholic Church.* Mystic, CT: Twenty-Third Publications.

Rossetti, S. J. (1994). Some red flags for child sexual abuse. *Human Development,* 15(Winter), 1–10.

Rossetti, S. J. (1995). The impact of child sexual abuse on attitudes toward God and the Catholic Church. *Child Abuse and Neglect,* 19, 1469–1481.

Rossetti, S. J. (1996). *A Tragic Grace. The Catholic Church and Child Sexual Abuse.* Collegeville, MN: The Liturgical Press.

Rossetti, S. J. (2002a). The Catholic Church and child sexual abuse. *America,* 186, 8–16.

Rossetti, S. J. (2002b). The Catholic Church and child sexual abuse. Paper presented at the 21st Annual Conference of the Association for the Treatment of Sexual Abusers, Montreal, Quebec, Canada.

Rossetti, S. J. (2004). Remarks made during conference *Sexual Abuse In the Catholic Church: Scientific and Legal Perspectives*. Vatican City.

Rossetti, S. J., & Coleman, G. D. (1997). Psychology and the church's teaching on homosexuality. *America*, 17(13), 6–23.

Rossetti, S. J., & Lothstein, L. M. (1990). Myths of the child molester. In S. J. Rossetti (Ed.), *Slayer of the Soul: Child Sexual Abuse and the Catholic Church*. (pp. 9–18). Mystic, CT: Twenty-Third Publications.

Royal Commission of Inquiry into the Response of the Newfoundland Criminal Justice System to Complaints (1992). (2 vols.) Office of the Queen's Printer, St. John's, Newfoundland.

Roys, D. T. (1997). Empirical and theoretical considerations of empathy in sex offenders. *International Journal of Offender Therapy and Comparative Criminology*, 41, 53–64.

Russell, D. E. H. (1983). The incidence and prevalence of intra-familial sexual abuse of female children. *Child Abuse and Neglect*, 7, 133–146.

Rutter, M. (1999). Resilience concepts and findings: implications for family therapy. *Journal of Family Therapy*, 21(2), 119–144.

Ryan, F. (2009). A theology of ministry. *The Furrow. A Journal for the Contemporary Church*, 60(11), 588–595.

Ryan, F. (2011). Images of God, Images of Priesthood. Paper presented at *Church: A Culture of Abusive Relationships?* Conference organized by Irish Theological Association in All Hallows College, Drumcondra, Dublin. March 18th – March 19th.

Salter, A. (1995). *Transforming Trauma. A Guide to Understanding and Treating Adult Survivors of Child Sexual Abuse*. London, New Delhi: Sage.

Salter, A (2003). *Predators, Paedophiles, Rapists and Other Sex Offenders: Who They Are, How They Operate, and How We Can Protect Ourselves and Our Children*. New York: Basic Books.

Sanday, P. R. (1981). *Female Power and Male Dominance*. Cambridge: Cambridge University Press.

Sanks, T. H. (1997). *Salt, Leaven and Light. The Community Called Church*. New York: The Crossroads Publishing Company.

Saradjian, A., & Nobus, D. (2003). Cognitive distortions of religious professionals who sexually abuse children. *Journal of Interpersonal Violence*, 18(8), 905–923.

Sawle, G. A., & Kear-Colwell, J. (2001). Adult attachment style and paedophilia: A developmental perspective. *International Journal of Offender Therapy and Comparative Criminology*, 45(1), 32–50.

Scheper-Hughes, N. (2001). *Saints, Scholars and Schizophrenics: Mental Illness in Rural Ireland*. Berkeley: University of California Press.

Scheper-Hughes, N., & Devine, J. (2003). Priestly celibacy and child sexual abuse. *Sexualities*, 6(15), 15–40.

Schmidt, G. (1991). The debate in pedophilia: Forward. *Journal of Homosexuality*, 20(1–2), 1–4.

Schmidt, C. (2005). The analysis of semi-structured interviews. In U. Flick, E. von Kardorff, & I. Steinke. (Eds.), *A Companion to Qualitative Research* (pp. 253–258). London and Thousand Oaks: Sage.

Schneider, P. (2010). Benedict's fragile church. *New York Times*, March 22. Accessed at http://www.nytimes.com/2010/03/23/opinion/23Schneider.html?_r=1&ref=ireland on March 23, 2010.

Schoenherr, R. (2002). *Goodbye Father* (edited with an introduction by David Yamane). Oxford and New York: Oxford University Press.

Schwandt, T. A. (2000). Three epistemological stances for qualitative inquiry: interpretivism, hermeneutics and social constructionism. In N. K. Denzin & Y. S. Lincoln. (Eds.), *Handbook of Qualitative Research* (2nd cd., pp. 189–214). Thousand Oaks and London: Sage Publications.

Scraton, P. (1997) (Ed.). *Childhood in Crisis*. London and New York: Routledge, Taylor and Francis Group.

Scraton, P. (2002) (Ed.). *Beyond September 11. An Anthology of Dissent*. UK: Pluto Press.

Seale, C. (2000). Using computers to analyse qualitative data. In D. Silverman. *Doing Qualitative Research. A Practical Handbook*. London, Thousand Oaks: Sage.

Seewald, P. (2010). *Light of the World: The Pope, the Church and the Sign of the Times* (translated by M. J. Miller & A. J. Walker). London: Catholic Truth Society; San Francisco: Ignatius Press.

Segal, L. (1990). *Slow Motion: Changing Men, Changing Masculinities*. London: Virago.

Seto, M. (2002). Precisely defining pedophilia. *Archives of Sexual Behaviour*, 31, 498–499.

Sex Crime and the Vatican. Panorama Documentary. BBC One, shown Oct. 1, 2006.

Shakeshaft, C. (2004). *Educator Sexual Misconduct with Students: A Synthesis of Existing Literature on Prevalence*. Planning and Evaluation Service, Office of the Undersecretary, US Department of Education.

Shaw, I. (2002). How lay are lay beliefs? *Health (London)*, 6, 287–299.

Shaw, I., & Gould, N. (2001). *Qualitative Research In Social Work*. London: Sage Publications.

Sheridan, K. (1995). Sympathy for a priest turns cold eyed analysis. *Irish Times*, July 1, p. 7.

Shotter, J. (1993). Social accountability and the social construction of "you." In J. Shotter & K. Gergen, *Texts of Identity* (pp. 133–152). London: Sage.

Shotter, J., & Gergen, K. (1993). *Texts of Identity*. London: Sage.

Shotter, J., & Gergen, K. (1993). Preface and introduction. In J. Shotter & K. Gergen. *Texts of Identity* (pp. ix–xi). London: Sage.

Shupe, A. (1995). *In the Name of All That's Holy. A Theory of Clergy Malfeasance*. Westport, CT, London: Praeger.

Shupe, A. (1998) (Ed.). *Wolves within the Fold. Religious Leadership and Abuses of Power*. New Brunswick, NJ, and London: Rutgers University Press.

Silverman, D. (2000). *Doing Qualitative Research. A Practical Handbook*. London, Thousand Oaks: Sage.

Sipe, A. W. R. (1990). *A Secret World: Sexuality and the Search for Celibacy*. New York: Brunner/Maxel Inc.

Sipe, A. W. R. (1995). *Sex, Priests, and Power: Anatomy of a Crisis*. London: Cassell.

Sipe, A. W. R. (1996). *Celibacy: A Way of Loving, Living and Serving*. New York: Brunner/Maxel Inc.

Sipe, A. W. R. (1998). Clergy abuse in Ireland. In A. Shupe (Ed.), *Wolves Within the Fold: Religious Leadership and Abuses of Power* (pp. 133–151). New Brunswick, NJ: Rutgers University Press.

Sipe, A. W. R. (1999). The problem of prevention in clergy sexual abuse. In T. G. Plante (Ed.), *Bless Me Father for I Have Sinned* (pp. 111–134). Westport, CT, London: Praeger.

Sipe, A. W. R. (2003). *Celibacy in Crisis. A Secret World Revisited*. New York: Brunner Routledge.

Sipe, A. W. R. (2004). The crisis of sexual abuse and the celibate/sexual agenda of the Catholic Church. In T. G. Plante (Ed.), *Sin Against the Innocents. Sexual Abuse by Priests and the Role of the Catholic Church* (pp. 61–71). Westport, CT, London: Praeger.

Sismondo, S. (2009). *An Introduction to Science and Technology Studies* (2nd ed.). London: Wiley and Sons.

Skelton, A. (1993). On becoming a male physical education teacher: The informal culture of students and the construction of hegemonic masculinity. *Gender and Education,* 5(3), 289–303.

Smallbone, S. W., & Dadds, M. R. (1998). Childhood attachment and adult attachment in incarcerated adult male sex offenders. *Journal of Interpersonal Violence,* 13(5), 555–573.

Smallbone, S. W., & Dadds, M. R. (2000). Attachment and coercive sexual behaviour. *Sexual Abuse: A Journal of Research and Treatment,* 12(1), 3–15.

Smallbone, S. W., & Dadds, M. R. (2001). Further evidence of a relationship between attachment insecurity and coercive sexual behaviour in nonoffenders. *Journal of Interpersonal Violence,* 16(1), 22–35.

Smith, B. (2003). Nuns as sexual victims get little notice. *St. Louis Post–Dispatch,* Jan. 4.

Smith, M., Rengifo, A., & Vollman, B. (2008). Trajectories of abuse and disclosure. Child sexual abuse by Catholic priests. *Criminal Justice and Behaviour,* 35(5), 570–582.

Smyth, D. (2009). The Pirate Island—clerical culture and sexual abuse. *The Furrow,* 60(9), 471–474.

Smyth, J. (2007). *Ireland's Magdalen Laundries and the Nation's Architecture of Containment.* Indiana: University of Notre Dame Press.

Smyth, P. (2009). Vatican's right to immunity being tested. *Irish Times,* Dec. 19. www.irishtimes.ie, accessed Dec. 19, 2009.

Smyth, S. (1995). Angry Fr. Cleary "Wife" tells all in new book. *Irish Times,* Sept. 20.

Snyder, C., Michael. S., & Cheavens, J. (2005). Hope as a psychotherapeutic foundation of common factors, placebos and expectancies. In M. Hubble, B. Duncan, & S. Miller (Eds.). *The Heart and Soul of Change. What Works in Therapy* (10th ed., pp. 179–200). Washington, DC: American Psychological Association.

Spear, L. (1979). *The Treatment of Sexual Sin in the Irish Latin Penitential Literature.* PhD dissertation, University of Toronto.

Songy, D. G. (2003). Psychological and spiritual treatment of Roman Catholic clergy offenders. *Sexual Addiction and Compulsivity,* 10, 123–137.

Soothill, K., & Francis, B. (1998). Poisoned chalice or just deserts? The Sex Offenders Act, 1997. *Journal of Forensic Psychiatry,* 9, 281.

Spohn, W. C. (2004). Episcopal responsibility for the sexual abuse crisis. In T. G. Plante (Ed.), *Sin Against the Innocents. Sexual Abuse by Priests and the Role of the Catholic Church* (pp. 155–168). Westport, CT, London: Praeger.

Stagmaman, D. (1999). *Authority in the Church.* Collegeville, MN: The Liturgical Press.

States of Fear. (1999). RTE Television Documentary, May 11.

Stalfa, F. J. (1994). Vocation as autobiography: Family of origin influences in the caregiving role in ministry. *Journal of Pastoral Care,* 48(4), 370–380.

Starbuck, W., & Milliken, F. (1988). Executives' perpetual filters: what they notice and how they make sense. In D. Hambrick (Ed.), *The Executive Effect.* Greenwich, CT: JAI.

Statistical Yearbook of Ireland (2008). Available at: www.cso.ie/releasespublications/statistial_yearbook_ireland_2008.htm

Stauss, A. L., & Corbin, J. A. (1990). *Basics of Qualitative Research: Grounded Theory Procedures and Techniques.* Newbury Park, CA: Sage.

Stearns, G. B., Baggerley-Mar, K., Merlin, E., Bonner, D., & Higgins, R. (1993). *Report to Father Joseph P. Chinnici, OFM, Provincial Minister, Province of St. Barbara. Independent Board of Inquiry Regarding St Anthony's Seminary*, November.

Steier, F. (1991). (Ed.) *Research and Reflexivity*. London: Sage.

Steier, F. (1991). Introduction: research as self-reflexivity, self-reflexivity as social process. In F. Steier (Ed.), *Research and Reflexivity* (pp. 1–11). London: Sage.

Stein, A. (2007). Trauma stories, identity work, and the politics of recognition. In J. M. Gerson & D. L. Wolf (Eds.), *Sociology Confronts the Holocaust*. Durham: Duke University Press.

Steinfels, P. (2002). Extent of abuse in church not understood. *New York Times*. May 4. Retrieved from http://www.nytimes.com/, accessed June 2, 2004.

Steinfels, P. (2003). *A People Adrift: The Crisis of the Roman Catholic Church in America*. New York: Simon and Schuster.

Steinke, I. (2004). Quality criteria in qualitative research. In U. Flick, E. von Kardorff, & I. Steinke. (Eds.), *A Companion to Qualitative Research* (pp. 184–190). London and Thousand Oaks: Sage.

Stermac, L. E., & Segal, Z. V. (1989). Adult sexual contact with children: An examination of cognitive factors. *Behaviour Therapy*, 20, 573–584.

Stermac, L. E., Segal, Z. V., & Gillis, R. (1990). Social and cultural factors in sexual assault. In W. L. Marshall, D. R. Laws, &d H. E. Barbaree (Eds.), *Handbook of Sexual Assault: Issues, Theories and Treatment of the Offender* (pp. 143–159). New York: Plenum Press.

Stearns, F. B., Baggerley-Mar, K., Merlin, E., Bonner, D & Higgins R. (1993). Report to Father Joseph P. Chinnici O.F.M. Provincial Minister, Province of St. Barbara. Independent Board of Inquiry Regarding St. Anthony's Seminary, Santa Barbara, California (November).

Stein, A (2007). Trauma Stories, Identity Work and the Politics of Recognition. In J. M. Gerson, & D. L Wolf (Eds.), Sociology Confronts the Holocaust: memories and identities in Jewish diasporas. Durham & London: Duke University Press Books.

Stilwell, B. (2003). Foreword. In N. Delson. *Using Conscience as a Guide. Enhancing Sex Offender Treatment In The Moral Domain*. Holyoke, MA: Neari Press.

Stone, L. (1977). *The Family, Sex and Marriage in England 1500–1800*. London: Weidenfeld and Nicolson.

Strauss, A. L., & Corbin, J. A. (1990). *Basics of Qualitative Research: Grounded Theory Procedures and Techniques*. Newbury Park, CA: Sage.

Suffer Little Children. (1994). Ulster Television.

Suffolk County Supreme Court Special Grand Jury (2002). *Grand Jury Report*. Available at http://www.weirdload.com/grandjury.pdf accessed May 6, 2010.

Suing the Pope. (2002). RTE and BBC Television Documentary

Sullivan, J., & Beech, A. (2002). Professional perpetrators. Sex offenders who use their employment to target and sexually abuse the children with whom they work. *Child Abuse Review*, 11, 153–167.

Sullivan, J., & Beech, A. (2004). A comparative study of demographic data relating to intra- and extra-familial child sexual abusers and professional perpetrators. *Journal of Sexual Aggression*, 10(1), 39–50.

Sunday Sequence, Radio Ulster. *Pope's student Fr Vincent Twomey condemns Bishops*. Dec. 13. Available at http://news.bbc.co.uk/2/hi/uk_news/northern_ireland/8410497.stm

Survivors for Justice(n.d.). Avaliable at www.survivorsforjustice.org/Gui/Content.aspx?Page=Home

Tallman, K., & Bohart, A. (2005). The client as a common factor: Clients as self-healers. In M. Hubble, B. Duncan, & S. Miller (Eds.), *The Heart and Soul of Change. What Works in Therapy* (10th ed., pp. 91–132). Washington, DC: American Psychological Association.

Tallon, J., & Terry, K. (2008). Analyzing paraphilic activity, specializations and generalizations in priests who sexually abused minors. *Criminal Justice and Behaviour, 35*(5), 615–628.

Tangney, J. P. (1995). Shame and guilt in interpersonal relationships. In J. P. Tangney & K. W. Fisher (Eds.), *Self-Conscious Emotions: Shame, Guilt, Embarrassment, and Pride* (pp. 114–139). New York: Guilford Press.

Tangney, J. P. (1996). Conceptual and methodological issues in the assessment of shame and guilt. *Behaviour Research and Therapy, 34*, 741–754.

Taylor, I. (1997). *Developing Learning in Professional Education: Partnerships for Practice*. Milton Keynes: SRHE and Open University Press.

Taylor, J. (1996). Catholic Bishops say sorry to Australian victims of sex abuse. *International News*. April 28.

Taylor, J. F. (2003). Children and young people accused of child sexual abuse: A study within a community. *Journal of Sexual Aggression, 9*(1), 57–70.

Taylor, S. (Ed.) (1999). *Sociology. Issues and Debates*. London: Macmillan.

Terry, K. (2008). Stained glass: The nature and scope of child sexual abuse in the Catholic Church. *Criminal Justice and Behaviour, 35*(5), 549–569.

Terry, K., & the Staff of the John Jay College of Criminal Justice. (2004). *The Nature and Scope of the Problem of Sexual Abuse of Minors by Priests and Deacons*. Washington, DC: United States Conference of Catholic Bishops.

Terry, K., & Ackerman, A. (2008). Child sexual abuse in the Catholic Church: How situational crime prevention strategies can help create safe environments. *Criminal Justice and Behaviour, 35*, 643–657.

Thavis, J. (2010). CDF official details response to sex abuse. *National Catholic Reporter*, March 16. Online at http://ncronline.org/, accessed March 16, 2010.

The Awareness Center. Available at www.theawarenesscenter.org

The Congregation for the Doctrine of the Faith (2010). Historical Introduction. *The Norms of the Motu Proprio "Sacramentorum Sanctitatis Tutela"* (2001). Available at http://www.vatican.va/resources/resources_introd-storica_en.html

The Jewish Week(n.d.). Available at www.thejewishweek.com

The Tablet (2010). Too little too late? March 20, 2010. Online at www.thetablet.com, accessed March 20, 2010.

Thompson, C. (1999). Qualitative research into nurse decision making: Factors for consideration in theoretical sampling. *Qualitative Health Research, 9*(6), 815–828.

Thomson, J. G., Marolla, J. A., & Bromley, D. G. (1998). Disclaimers and accounts in cases of Catholic priests accused of pedophilia. In A. Shupe. (Ed.), *Wolves within the Fold. Religious Leadership and Abuses of Power* (pp. 175–190). New Brunswick, NJ, and London: Rutgers University Press.

Todd, N., & Wade, A. (2003). Coming to terms with violence and resistance: from a language of effects to a language of responses. In T. Strong & D. Pare (Eds.), *Furthering Talk: Advances in the Discursive Therapies*. New York: Kluwer.

Toibín, C. (1995). Dublin's epiphany. *New Yorker*, April 3, p. 45.

Tolson, A. (1977). *The Limits of Masculinity*. London: Tavistock.

Travers, M. (2001). *Qualitative Research Through Case Studies*. London, Thousand Oaks: Sage.

Tomm, K (2002). Enabling Forgiveness and Reconciliation in Family Therapy. *The International Journal of Narrative Therapy and Community Work*. Adelaide: Australia.

Turner, S., & Turner, F. (1990). *The Impossible Science: An Institutional Analysis of American Sociology*. New York: Sage.

Twomey, V. (2009). Response to clerical child abuse report. *Irish Times*, Dec. 3, p. 17.

Twomey, V. (2010). Recent attacks on pope not justified by evidence. *Irish Times,* April 2. Accessed online at www.irishtimes.ie on April 2, 2010.

Umbreit, M. (1994). *Victim Meets the Offender: The Impact of Restorative Justice and Mediation*. Monsey, NY: Criminal Justice Press.

Umbreit, M., Bradshaw, W., & Coates, R. B. (1999). Victims of severe violence meet the offender: restorative justice through dialogue. *International Review of Victimology*, 6, 321–343.

Valcour, F. (1990). The treatment of child sex abusers in the Church. In S. J. Rossetti. (Ed.), *Slayer of the Soul: Child Sexual Abuse and the Catholic Church* (pp. 45–66). Mystic, CT: Twenty-Third Publications.

Vaughan, D. (1997). *The Challenger Launch Decision. Risky Technology, Culture and Deviance at NASA*. Chicago and London: The University of Chicago Press.

Vaughan, D. (1999). The dark side of organizations: mistake, misconduct and disaster. *Annual Review of Sociology*, 25, 271–305.

Vaughan, D. (2006). The social shaping of commission reports. *Sociological Forum*.

Vess, J. (2009). Fear and loathing in public policy: Ethical issues in laws for sex offenders. *Aggression and Violent Behaviour*, 14, 264–272.

Villa Vincenzo, C. (1999). A different kind of justice: the South African Truth and Reconciliation Commission. *Contemporary Justice Review*, 1, 403–428.

Vital Statistics (2003). Available at http://www.cso.ie/releasespublications/pr_bdm.htm

Vives, A. (2002). The psychological sequelae of victimization based on sexual orientation: A structural equation model of predicting suicidality among lesbian and gay young adults. *Dissertation Abstracts International*, 62(12–B).

Wade, A. (1997). Small acts of living: everyday resistance to violence and other forms of oppression. *Journal of Contemporary Family Therapy*, 19(1), 23–39.

Waldby, C., Clancy, A., Emetchi, J., & Summerfield, C. (1989). Theoretical perspectives on father-daughter incest. In E. Drier & A. Droisen (Eds.), *Child Sexual Abuse: Feminist Perspectives* (pp. 88–106). Basingstoke: Macmillan.

Waldergrave, C., Tamasese, K., Tuhaka F., & Campbell, W. (2003). *Just Therapy: A Journey. A Collection of Papers from the Just Therapy Team, New Zealand*. South Australia: Dulwich Centre Publications.

Walker, R. (1985) (Ed.). *Applied Qualitative Research*. Aldershot: Gower.

Ward, T. (2001). Hall and Hirschman's quadripartite model of child sexual abuse: A critique. *Psychology, Crime and Law*, 7, 291–307.

Ward, T. (2009a). Dignity and human rights in correctional practice. *European Journal of Probation*, 1(2), 110–123.

Ward, T., & Beech, A. (2006). An integrated theory of sexual offending. *Aggression and Violent Behaviour*, 11, 44–63.

Ward, T., & Birgden, A. (2007). Human rights and correctional clinical practice. *Aggression and Violent Behaviour*, 12, 628–643.

Ward, T., & Hudson, S. M. (1998). The construction and development of theory in the sexual offending area: A meta-theoretical framework. *Sexual Abuse: A Journal of Research and Treatment*, 10, 47–63.

Ward, T., & Hudson, S. M. (2001). A critique of Finkelhor's precondition model of child sexual abuse. *Psychology, Crime and Law*, 7, 333–350.

Ward, T., Hudson, S. M., Johnston, L., & Marshall, W. (1997). Cognitive distortions in sex offenders: An integrative review. *Clinical Psychology Review*, 17, 479–507.

Ward, T., Hudson, S. M., & Keenan, T. (1998). A self-regulation model of the sexual offence process. *Sexual Abuse: A Journal of Research and Treatment*, 10, 141–157.

Ward, T., Hudson, S. M., & Marshall, W. (1994). The abstinence violation effect in child molesters. *Behaviour Research and Therapy*, 32, 431–437.

Ward, T., Hudson, S. M., & Marshall, W. (1996). Attachment styles in sex offenders: A preliminary study. *Journal of Sex Research*, 33, 17–26.

Ward, T., Hudson, S. M., Marshall, W. L., & Siegert, R. (1995). Attachment style and intimacy deficits in sex offenders: A theoretical framework. *Sexual Abuse: A Journal of Research and Treatment*. 7, 317–335.

Ward, T., & Keenan, T. (1999). Child molester's implicit theories. *Journal of Interpersonal Violence*, 14, 821–838.

Ward, T., Keenan, T., & Hudson, S. M. (2000). Understanding cognitive, affective, and intimacy deficits in sexual offenders: A developmental perspective. *Aggression and Violent Behaviour*, 5(1), 41–62.

Ward, T., & Langlands, R. (2009). Repairing the rupture: Restorative justice and offender rehabilitation. *Aggression and Violent Behaviour*, 14, 205–214.

Ward, T., Laws, D. R., &. Hudson, S. M. (2003). (Eds.). *Sexual Deviance, Issues and Controversies*. London and New Delhi: Sage Publications.

Ward, T., Louden, K., Hudson, S., & Marshall, W. (1995). A descriptive model of the offense chain for child molesters. *Journal of Interpersonal Violence*, 10, 452–472.

Ward, T., & Marshall. W. L. (2007). Narrative identity and offender rehabilitation. *International Journal of Offender Therapy and Comparative Criminology*, 6(51), 279–297.

Ward, T., & Moreton, G. (2008). Moral repair with offenders: ethical issues arising from victimization experiences. *Sexual Abuse: A Journal of Research and Treatment*, 20, 305–322.

Ward, T., Polaschek, D. L. L., & Beech, A. R. (2006). *Theories of Sexual Offending*. Chichester: Wiley.

Ward, T., & Siegert, R. J. (2002). Towards a comprehensive theory of child sexual abuse: A theory knitting perspective. *Psychology, Crime and Law*, 9, 319–351.

Ward, T., & Sorbello, L. (2003). Explaining child sexual abuse: Integration and elaboration. In. T. Ward, D. R. Laws, & S. M. Hudson, (Eds.), *Sexual Deviance, Issues and Controversies* (pp. 3–20). Thousand Oaks CA: Sage Publications.

Ward, T., & Stewart, C. A. (2003). Good lives and the rehabilitation of sexual offenders. In T. Ward, D. R. Laws, & S. M. Hudson (Eds.), *Sexual Deviance, Issues and Controversies* (pp. 21–44). Thousand Oaks CA: Sage.

Wasyliw, O. E., Benn, A. F., Grossman, L. S., & Haywood, T. W. (1998). Detection of minimization of psychopathology on the Rorschach in cleric and noncleric alleged sex offenders. *Assessment*, 5, 389–397.

Weber, M. (1978). In: R. Guenther and C. Wittich (Eds.), *Economy and Society* (2nd ed.). Berkeley, CA: University of California Press.

Weeks, J. (2005). Fallen heroes? All about men. *Journal of Sociology. Special Edition on Masculinities* (edited by Anne Cleary). The Sociological Association of Ireland.

Weigel, G. (2003). *The Courage to be Catholic: Crisis, Reform, and the Future of the Church.* New York: Basic Books.

Weingarten, K. (1998). The small and the ordinary: the daily practice of a postmodern narrative therapy. *Family Process,* 37, 3–15.

Weingarten, K. (2003). *Common Shock. Witnessing Violence Every Day: How We Are Harmed, How We Can Heal.* New York: Dutton.

Weingarten, K (2007). Hope in a time of Global Despair. In C. Flaskas, I. McCarthy and J. Sheehan (Eds.). *Hope and Despair in Narrative and Family Therapy: Adversity, Forgiveness and Reconciliation* (pp. 13-23). London: Routledge. Taylor and Francis Group.

Weitzman, E. A. (2000). In N. K. Denzin & Y. S. Lincoln. (Eds.), *Handbook of Qualitative Research* (2nd ed., pp. 803–820). Thousand Oaks and London: Sage Publications.

Westchester County Grand Jury (2002). *Report of the Westchester County Grand Jury Concerning Complaints of Sexual Abuse and Misconduct against Minors by Members of the Clergy.* Available at www.BishopAccountability.org, accessed May 6, 2010.

White, M. (1986). Negative explanation, restraint and double description: A template for family therapy. *Family Process,* 22, 255–273.

White, M. (2000). Re-engaging with history: The absent but implicit. In Dulwich Centre Publications, *Reflections on Narrative Practices: Interviews and Essays* (pp. 35–58). Adelaide: Dulwich Centre Publications.

White, M. (2004a). *Narrative Practice and Exotic Lives: Resurrecting Diversity in Everyday Life.* Adelaide, South Australia: Dulwich Centre Publications.

White, M. (2004b). Working with people who are suffering the consequences of multiple trauma: A narrative perspective. *International Journal of Narrative Therapy and Community Work,* 1, 45–76.

White, M., & Epston, D. (1990). *Narrative Means to Therapeutic Ends.* New York: Norton.

White, M., & Terry, K. (2008). Child sexual abuse in the Catholic Church. Revisiting the rotten apple explanation. *Criminal Justice and Behaviour,* 35(5), 658–678.

White, S. (2001). Auto-ethnography as reflexive inquiry: The research act as self-surveillance. In I. Shaw & N. Gould, (Eds.), *Qualitative Research In Social Work* (pp. 101–115). London: Sage Publications.

White, W. (1993). A systems perspective on sexual exploitation of clients by professional helpers. *Professional Sexual Abuse. Dulwich Centre Newsletter,* 3(4), 77–88.

White, W. (1995). A systems perspective on sexual exploitation of clients by professional helpers. In J. C. Gonsiorek. *Breach of Trust. Sexual Exploitation by Health Care Professionals and Clergy* (pp. 176–192). Thousand Oaks, London: Sage.

Whyte, J. H. (1980). *Church and State in Modern Ireland 1923–1979* (2nd ed.). Dublin: Gill and MacMillan.

Wild, R. (1990). The pastoral letters. In R. Brown, J. Fitzmyer, & R. Murphy (Eds.), *The New Jerome Biblical Commentary.* Englewood Cliffs, NJ: Prentice-Hall.

Wills, G. (2000). *Papal Sin.* New York: Doubleday.

Wilson, R. J. (1999). Emotional congruence in sexual offenders against children. *Sexual Abuse: A Journal of Research and Treatment,* 1, 33–47.

Wilson, S. (1984). The myth of motherhood: The historical view of European child rearing. *Social History,* 9, 181–198.

Winick, B. J. (1998). Sex offender law in the 1990's: A therapeutic jurisprudence analysis. *Psychology, Public Policy and Law, 4* (1/2), pp. 505-570.

Wyre, R. (1996). Personal communication on a visit to the Lucy Faithfull Treatment Programme, Birmingham, England.

Wolfe, A. (1989). *Whose Keeper? Social Science and Moral Obligation.* Berkeley and Los Angeles: University of California Press.

World Religious Statistics (2006). Major religions ranked by size. Available at http://www. adherents.com/largecom/com_romcath.html accessed 01/06/2011

Wooden, C. (2011). Vatican did not tell bishops to cover up abuse cases, spokesman says. *Catholic News Service,* Jan. 19. Available at http://www.catholicnews.com/searchresults.htm?cx=0084 02456443019734212%3Ac_emx4vppak&cof=FORID%3A11&q=Vatican+did+not+tell+bi shops+to+cover+up+abuse+cases%2C+spokesman+says&sa=Search#1110 accessed Jan. 21, 2011.

Woods, J. (1907). *Annals of Westmeath: Ancient and Modern.* Dublin: Sealy.

Would You Believe (2011). Documentary, RTE Television. Screened Jan. 17, 2011.

Yip, A. K. T. (2009). Sexuality and the church. *Sexualities, 6*(1), 60–64.

Young, J. L., & Griffith, E. E. H. (1995). Regulating pastoral counselling practice: The problem of sexual misconduct. *Bulletin of the American Academy of Psychiatry and the Law,* 23, 421–432.

Zehr, H. (1985). Retributive justice, restorative justice. Occasional paper no. 4. *New Perspectives on Crime and Justice Series, MCC Office on Crime and Justice.* Reprinted in G. Johnstone (Ed.), *A Restorative Justice Reader* (pp. 69–82). Portland, OR: Willan Publishing.

Zehr, H. (1990). *Changing Lenses: A New Focus for Crime and Justice.* Scottsdale, PA: Herald Press.

INDEX

Page numbers followed by "n" indicate notes.